NARRATIVES of DISSENT

War in Contemporary Israeli Arts and Culture

NARRATIVES of DISSENT

EDITED BY
Rachel S. Harris AND Ranen Omer-Sherman

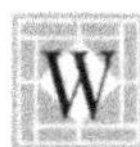

Wayne State University Press
Detroit

17 16 15 14 13 5 4 3 2 1

Library of Congress Cataloging-in-Publication Data
Narratives of Dissent : War in Contemporary Israeli Arts and Culture /
Edited by Rachel S. Harris and Ranen Omer-Sherman.
Pages cm
Includes bibliographical references and index.
ISBN 978-0-8143-3803-2 (pbk. : alk. paper)—ISBN 978-0-8143-3804-9 (ebook) (print)
1. War and literature—Israel. 2. Art and war.
I. Harris, Rachel S. (Rachel Sylvia), 1977– II. Omer-Sherman, Ranen.
PN56.W3N37 2012
700'.458569405—dc23
2012029607

Publication of this book was made possible through the generosity of the Bertha M. and Hyman Herman Endowed Memorial Fund.

Typeset by Keystone Typesetting, Inc.
Composed in Scala and Scala Sans Pro

CONTENTS

Introduction

Zionism and the Culture of Dissent

Ranen Omer-Sherman

> We have to guard ourselves from might and simplistic thinking, from the corruption that is in cynicism, from the pollution of the heart and the ill-treatment of humans, which are the biggest curse of those living in a disastrous region like ours.
>
> —David Grossman, from the eulogy for his son, Uri, who fell in the Second Lebanon War

For younger Israeli men and women, a true sense of national belonging has almost always required a commitment to serving in the Israel Defense Forces (IDF), and many later consider the occasion of their military inductions as a joyous rite of passage. For a representative account, one need only begin with this singular moment in Avraham Burg's gripping memoir, which speaks for many more than those of Burg's own generation, recalling that dream of wearing one of the great icons of national heroism, the coveted beret of the paratroopers:

> The red beret was a legend since the British Mandate. Hannah Czenes and the other World War II paratroopers, the heroes who liberated Jerusalem and the Western Wall in the Six-Day War, all wore a red beret. They were the models of heroism, attracting us like moths to a flame. Every child dreamt of a red beret folded under the shoulder strap, paratrooper wings on the chest, and red boots. Being a paratrooper was pure Israeli-ness at its best, and I wanted to be one. I wanted to run fast, strike, sneak around, and fight.[1]

As a typical youth of the 1960s who came of age between the Six-Day War and the Yom Kippur War, Burg was hyperconscious that the paratroopers embodied the demarcation between the powerless Jew of exile and the confident and empowered Hebrew future. Hence, as a youthful idealist, Burg sought to "be an Israeli hero, different from my father, the Jew in exile. He walked and I ran; he escaped and I jumped from the sky" (116). He recalls his fierce pride leaping in harness from the high training tower that generations of Israeli paratroopers (including this writer) have come to know as "the Eichmann": "I climbed the Eichmann as the son of a Jewish refugee from Germany, jumped and landed as an Israeli that even Eichmann could not scare any more" (116).[2] Yet just as ardent young men like Burg grew up under the influence of both traumatic history and the constant menace of future wars, their earliest understandings were also inevitably densely filtered by *cultural* renderings and interpretations of war's mythic and ideological significance. Indeed, no social phenomenon provides a more urgent sense of collective identity than war. For instance, in Avraham Balaban's elegiac memoir of his kibbutz childhood, he recalls the indelible influences of the songs of the War of Independence and the Suez War, in particular Haim Gouri's lyric "Bab el-Wad" commemorating the siege of Jerusalem:

> The music teacher who came to the kibbutz every Tuesday, taught us this song when we were in fourth grade, and after the first couple of lines the chatting and laughter and throwing of paper planes ceased. The armored convoys to Jerusalem had left from our woods, we saw their burnt-out shells on our annual trip to Jerusalem, and the melody seeped into us like water into the soil and raised delicate flowers of sorrow. This sorrow brought me closer to myself, the way a wound or a pain brings one closer to oneself, and at the same time submerged me entirely in the singing group.[3]

For Balaban the powerful emotive effects of such militaristic songs created a "dual sense of intensified, solemn, burnished selfhood combined with total self-oblivion," suggesting that they dissolved the self into the collective in his childhood imagination.

Considering those lyrics' powerful ideological uses (in a chapter evocatively titled "Singing and Crying: Homeland Songs"), Balaban further examines how the "battles and the fallen . . . in those songs intensified the sorrow, and the more it grew, the greater the joy. The greater the sadness, the more beautiful we became in our own eyes, convinced that people are measured by the degree of sadness they have in them. . . . These songs molded us at will, implanted in us strange longings . . . and attached us to the great family of children returning to their motherland and promising her liberty and eternal loyalty" (101). Even today he wonders at the power "Bab el-Wad" wielded over his childhood—the song was a veritable "Israeli identity card, the identity of everything we dreamed of being" (102).[4] But just what did this renewed Jewish national identity *amount to*, as expressed in the soaring imagery and tropes delineated in this and other period songs of martial sacrifice?[5] Above all, Balaban recalls the stirring resonance for a spartan time, a society of "abbreviated families," pioneers who had left their doomed families in Europe and youngsters who separated themselves at a young age to fight for the State of Israel:

> Native Israeliness absorbed the intensity of a life-and-death struggle. But it was not only the struggle that shaped the particular character of this identity. After all, many other countries achieved independence after a prolonged struggle. We find other reasons in the core of the song: "Here we fought together on the rocks/ Here we were one family, we all." "One family" means companionship and comradeship in arms, and all that they imply.... it was the shortest way to forge a bond between the generations, to create an illusion of family where there was none, an illusion of roots in a place of sand and rocks. And these songs certainly fulfilled their purpose: all the schoolchildren in my native kibbutz, who learned these songs and sang them in youth movement meetings, parties, and holidays, are living in Israel today. Our children, however, are scattered all over the world. I can testify that, as a child growing up in the kibbutz . . . I was a complete outsider. Yet when I sang these songs I was a faithful, enthusiastic kid . . . a total Israeli, confident of his strength and the justice of his cause. In retrospect, I am amazed by what a huge part of me was this Israeli identity—as though I was first of all an Israeli, and only secondly an individual child with his own personality. (103–4)

As Balaban's experience with the constructed nature of identity would suggest, many Israelis were raised with an indelible sense of a national belonging reinforced through songs and other cultural narratives. Beginning in 1948 with the War of Independence, further conflicts followed in 1956 (the Suez Crisis), 1967 (the Six-Day War), 1968–70 (the War of Attrition), 1973 (the Yom Kippur War), 1982 and 2006 (the First and Second Lebanon Wars), as well as 1987–93 and 2000 (the First and Second Intifadas). Furthermore, there were many other military engagements such as Operation Litani (1978 in Lebanon), the Gulf War (1991), and Operation Cast Lead (2008–9 in Gaza). As Harris states, "The centrality of the army, militarization, and the soldier within the nation-building enterprise is evidenced not only within the encounters themselves, or even within the ways in which war shaped Israel's political agendas, but also in the explicit construction of the notion of precisely what it meant to be an Israeli—both at home and abroad."[6] Within Israel this meant that the military often created and disseminated culture, while simultaneously being the subject of culture. Abroad it meant the creation of an identity for Israel focused on depictions of the soldier as a metonym for the state struggling as the weak against the strong, the few against the many. With a few notable exceptions (more on this below), it would be many years before those forms would begin to transmit anguished questioning and contradictions of the official narrative, and this collection was conceived to account for how those changes came to be a dominant narrative in the expression of writers, artists, musicians, and other Israelis.

Although the condition of war is a terribly intimate and familiar realm for Israelis, it is not the editors' claim that Israel's literary, cinematic, or artistic products somehow makes experience of war sensible or enables us to transcend the most horrific endeavor that human beings engage in. And yet as Balaban testifies, somehow they are *essential* nonetheless, bearing witness to a society's fragility and exhaustion as well as its fervent hopes for a better future, for a generation of youth not cynically sacrificed on war's terrible altar. Inevitably, whether overt or otherwise, the mythic permutations of the Akedah—the sacrifice of Isaac—are never distant from the works addressed in this volume.[7] The biblical story of the Akedah has long imbued such works with urgently suggestive, uncomfortable layers of meaning. Just who are the respective killer and martyr, the father and the angel? Who is doing the sacrificing, and where is the divine redeemer who might intervene at the last possible moment to stay the hand with the knife that precipitously hovers over the child? As such tormented questions intimate, the aftermath of every war in Israel created a different generational response, one that, with the notable exception of the euphoria surrounding the 1967 war, sometimes amounted to a weakening of the national narrative. However, on the whole, it wasn't until the advent of Israel's "new historians" that the heavily mythologized War of Independence was portrayed in a far less flattering light.

It has now been over two decades since the appearance of Benny Morris's *Birth of the Palestinian Refugee Problem: 1947–1949* (1987) and Tom Segev's *The Seventh Million: The Israelis and the Holocaust* (1991). In these works, the young historians brought to life important details of the Zionist leadership's actions against the indigenous Arabs of Palestine. Although initially dismissed as radicals, Morris's and Segev's meticulous archival research eventually wielded unprecedented influence over a new generation of scholars. Subsequently, in the summer of 1999 the IDF's History Division cosponsored the publication of *The Struggle for Israel's Security*, which offered an unsparing assessment of Israel's policy toward Arabs throughout the 1950s. According to Daniel Polisar, that same year also saw the appearance of a new curriculum by the Ministry of Education that introduced into ninth-grade classrooms across the country the first three textbooks about Israel aimed at teaching history from an expressly "universal" (as opposed to "nationalist") perspective.

Perhaps the text that departed most radically from earlier pedagogy is *A World of Changes: History for Ninth Grade*, edited by Danny Ya'akobi and published by the Ministry's Curriculum Division, which attributes the victory of Jewish forces over five Arab armies in the War of Independence to the Jews' organizational and logistical edge rather than to the traditional notions of determined leadership, brilliant military tactics, or individual heroism that once held sway, even suggesting that "Israel precipitated the Six Day War by acting aggressively against Syria in the months prior to the outbreak of fighting."[8] Yet it is also important to emphasize that in the immediate aftermath of the War of Independence, there was *already* a literary struggle over representing what transpired, most notably revealed in the urgent voice of S. Yizhar, whose fiction was largely concerned with the nation's conscience.[9] In the short story "The Prisoner" (composed during November 1948), an Arab peasant is seized from the pastoral landscape and abused during his interrogation. Yizhar's protagonist recoils uneasily from the insidious toll that war has taken on his comrades' ostensible decency, as in this passage that scathingly underscores the fate of liberal humanism in wartime:

> And there were some who had steady jobs, some who were on their way up in the world, some who were hopeless cases to begin with, and some who rushed to the movies and all the theater and read the weekend supplements of two newspapers. And there were some who knew long passages by heart from Horace and the Prophet Isaiah and from Chaim Nachman Bialik and even from Shakespeare; some who loved their children and their wives and their slippers and the little gardens at the sides of their houses; some who hated all forms of favoritism, insisted that each man keep his proper place in line, and raised a hue and cry at the slightest suspicion of discrimination; some whose inherent good nature had been permanently soured by the thought of paying rent and taxes; some who were not at all what they seemed and some who were exactly what they seemed. There they all stood, in a happy circle around the blindfolded prisoner.[10]

Repulsed by the rapidly escalating cruelty he witnesses ("kick him—he's an Arab; it means nothing to him" [71]), Yizhar's protagonist struggles mightily, but only within himself. In the end he fails to act, and the mute prisoner is led off, his execution a likely prospect, the text insinuates. Of Yizhar's early stories, Nurith Gertz astutely observes: "He is supposedly dealing with the Israel-Arab conflict but actually his subject is the conflict between Israeli and Israeli; that is, between what is revealed in the Hebrew literature of the War for Independence and what is suppressed in it."[11] More notoriously, Yizhar's 1949 novella *Khirbet Khizeh* (published just months after the war's end) addressed the grim reality of Palestinian dispossession and the flawed behavior of the IDF toward civilians.[12] Inexplicably only very recently translated and published in English (in spite of the fact that it was read and debated by generations of Israelis who first encountered it as part of the standard high school curriculum), it still makes for disturbing reading and is widely considered a masterpiece of wartime testimony that raises uncomfortable questions regarding the mythic stature of the conflict itself.[13]

In his afterword to the new Ibis edition of *Khirbet Khizeh*, cultural historian David Shulman praises the very fact of its publication (and strong public resonance): "here is a case where the Establishment seemed to make room for a dissonant, destabilizing voice, something in the tradition of the Hebrew prophets—the voice of conscience . . . Yizhar wrote about what he himself had seen and felt" (115–16). Shulman, a passionate peace activist who has confronted Jewish settlers vandalizing Palestinians' orchards, claims a direct genealogy between the novella and "today's peace movements, peopled by ordinary human beings who will not, under any circumstances, lend their hands to blatant injustice. None of us could formulate the matter with Yizhar's unflinching forcefulness, but there is not one of us who would fail to recognize the feelings he describes—the outrage, the terrible confusion, the grief, the sense of collective self-betrayal, the isolation from one's friends and fellows, the paralysis and hesitation, the bodily urge to protest" (128). Yizhar's story follows the increasingly alienated protagonist's portrayal of the violent expulsion of Palestinian villagers by Israeli soldiers in the final months of the war. Throughout, the narrator of *Khirbet Khizeh*'s lyrically foreboding language contrasts the landscape's natural beauty with the desolate aftermath of human conflict: "These bare villages, the day was coming when they would begin to cry out. As you went through them, all of a sudden, without knowing where from, you found yourself silently followed by invisible eyes of walls, courtyards, and alleyways. Desolate abandoned silence. Your guts clenched" (26). And in the novella's final pages, this witness stands accused and humbled by the silent dignity of a pair of refugees, mother and daughter: "Then we saw a woman who was walking in a group of three or four other women. She was holding the hand of a child about seven years old. There was something special about her. She seemed stern, self-controlled, austere in her sorrow. Tears, which hardly seemed to be her own, rolled down her cheeks. And the child too was sobbing a kind of stiff-lipped 'what-have-you-done-to-us.' It suddenly seemed as if she were the only one who knew exactly what was happening. So much so that I felt ashamed in her presence and lowered my eyes" (104). Although, as with so many of Yizhar's protagonists, it comes too late, this soldier endures a shattering epiphany: "Something struck me like lightning. All at once everything seemed to mean something different, more precisely: exile. This was exile. This was what exile was like. This was what exile looked like. . . . I had never been in the Diaspora . . . but people had spoken to me . . . taught me, and repeatedly recited to me, from every direction, in books and newspapers, everywhere: exile. They had played on all my nerves. Our nation's protest to the world: exile! It had entered me apparently, with my mother's milk. What, in fact, had we perpetrated here today?" (104–5). This remorseful character's revelation suggests it is as if the very moment one discovers traces of the self in the Other (and vice versa), the ideological fervor and nationalist rationales of wars and occupations that once seemed compelling are lost forever to the disenchanted individual. Israeli artists and writers have been saying much the same ever since, whether through the arts of satire, black humor, stark realism, or myriad other forms of aesthetic engagement, as the essays before you vividly delineate.

However, it is not as if such critical art fully escapes a wary, occasionally censorious impulse by a society that, after all, cherished its heavily idealized origins as much as any other nation. Meron Benvenisti recounts the difficulties that surrounded Ram Loevy's filmed adaptation of Yizhar's work: *The Story of Khirbet Khizeh,* which was scheduled to air on Israeli State Television in the beginning of 1978. In the days just prior to its televising, there was a storm of public controversy over "the damage that was liable to be done to the educational message of the justice of Zionism by portraying it as a movement responsible for dispossession. The screening . . . was perceived by some as an act perpetrated by 'bleeding-heart' supporters of the PLO, intent on besmirching Israel's image in the eyes of the world."[14] The eradication of Palestinian villages was such a contentious issue that it was not substantively addressed again on Israeli television until 1998, which marked the fiftieth anniversary of the founding of the state. At that time, Israel State Television first aired the now iconic documentary series *Tequma* (Revival), which examines the history of the state since 1948 and does not shy away from the Palestinian exodus in 1948.[15] Yet Benvenisti asserts that the public's attention remained focused on "the dilemmas posed by . . . the occupation of the West Bank and Gaza Strip and its injustices" and subsequently the "obliterated landscape" of Khirbet Khizeh and all the other sites of dispossession remained "encased . . . in a sheath of forgetfulness and self-righteousness" (241). In this critique, Yizhar's narrative of conscience was effectively invalidated, as the public's "remorse was directed toward the other side of the 'green line,' to the Occupied Territories; the eradicated Arab landscape inside the sovereign State of Israel had become, perforce, part of 'the mother country,' regarding which there was no place for guilt feelings"(241). The violent dispossession of Israel's Arab population was a story still too uncomfortable for mainstream media to reckon with.

Long before David Grossman's public eulogy for his son Uri (who fell in the Second Lebanon War) struck a powerful chord in the war's aftermath, he had been preoccupied with denouncing the unending entanglement of his society with the seductions of military might.[16] Even in Grossman's biblical exegesis of the story of Samson in the Book of Judges he cannot resist pausing to examine the troubling implications of a Samson-like psychology reverberating throughout his country's tumultuous modern history:

> In Hebrew, he is almost always referred to as "Samson the hero," and elite combat units of the Israeli army have been named after him, from "'Samson's Foxes'" of the 1948 War of Independence to the "'Samson'" unit created during the first Palestinian Intifada in the late 1980s. . . . Yet there is a certain problematic quality to Israeli sovereignty that is also embodied in Samson's relationship to his own power. As in the case of Samson, it sometimes seems that Israel's considerable military might is an asset that becomes a liability. For it would seem, without taking lightly the dangers facing Israel, that the reality of being immensely powerful had not really been internalized in the Israeli consciousness, not assimilated in a natural way, over many generations; and this, perhaps, is why the attitude to this power, whose acquisition has often been regarded as truly miraculous, is prone to distortion.[17]

For Grossman, "Samsonian modes of behavior" are highly visible in the tendencies to "ascrib[e] an exaggerated value to the power that one has attained; to making power an end in itself . . . to using it excessively" and also in resorting "almost automatically to the use of force instead of weighing other means of action." Grossman traces this malady to the near-apocalyptic anxieties of his countrymen:

> The well-known Israeli feeling, in the face of any threat that comes along, that the country's security is crumbling—a feeling that also exists in the case of Samson, who in certain situations seems to shatter into pieces, his strength vanishing in the blink of an eye. This kind of collapse, however, does not reflect one's actual strength, and often carries in its wake *an overblown display of force, further complicating the situation.* All of this attests, it would seem, to a rather feeble sense of ownership of the power that has been attained, and of course, to a deep existential insecurity. This is connected . . . to the very real dangers lying in wait for Israel, but also to the tragic formative experience of being a stranger in the world, the Jewish sense of not being a nation " 'like other nations'," and of the State of Israel as a country whose very existence is conditional, whose future . . . is steeped in jeopardy, feelings that all the nuclear bombs that Israel developed, in a program once known as the " 'Samson Option'," cannot eradicate. (89–90; emphasis added)

It is not a stretch to perceive the applications of this prophetic critique in considering either the Second Lebanon War or "Operation Cast Lead" (the Gaza War). When considering a writer (whether early Yizhar or a contemporary figure like Grossman), it is worth taking note of Gershom Gorenberg's stark observation: "That Israeli writers can more easily reexamine their own side's actions may be one of the fruits of victory."[18] Indeed, that harvest of literary questioning is strongly reflected in the IDF's surprising interest in the moral power of narrative. In 1992 the Israel Ministry of Defense published *Battleground,* an anthology edited by Aharon Amir. In Benvenisti's account of the origins of this project, he explains that Amir sought "to provide young soldiers serving in the Occupied Territories with a compilation that will impart to them 'a sense of the dimensions of time and depth that are often absent from the consciousness of the Israeli who is experiencing the dispute as if it were some sort of puzzling, unanticipated calamity, a product of historical accident or plain arbitrariness.' In this collection, the editor included many authors in whose writings are expressed 'the pressures and the hardships involved in the confrontation with the people of the Land [the Palestinians]. . . . These pressures often produce remorse, impatience, pangs of conscience, and emotional and mental discomfort.' " Amir's language anticipates the censorious responses of the zealous: "these reactions can seem to the reader like revelations of defeatism or of alienation from national interests and values" but he defends their value both for their representative nature and because they reflect "the best of Hebrew writing" (Benvenisti, 242).[19]

In the period addressed in the collection before you, Israeli cultural representations of the trauma of war came to depend even more on the writer or artist's individual experiences than they reflect official histories. By the time of the 1982 invasion of Lebanon, many Israelis were thoroughly alienated from the core principle that their country used force only when there was no alternative.[20] For many observing the past few decades, what has often seemed most reassuring is that, in spite of Israel's pervasive culture of militarism, the IDF was capable of the kind of relentless self-examination that might ensure more humane standards in subsequent conflicts. However, it must be noted that others view Israel's official unqualified rejection of the Goldstone Commission's report on the 2008 Gaza War crimes with some concern.[21] Subsequent media reports suggest that in the aftermath of the Gaza invasion, there indeed seems to have been a surge of censorious defensiveness, a reluctance to even consider the most painfully incriminating aspects of what may have transpired, whatever the source.

Aside from our different genders, as editors Rachel S. Harris and I felt that the disparate political perspectives and backgrounds we bring to bear would constitute an important asset (though both of us have lived extensively in Israel, one of us identifies as left of center, while the other identifies as centrist; one of us served in the IDF, while the other was raised within the Israeli educational system) especially as it now seems more difficult than ever to hold conversations about Israel, even if academic in nature, that are not instantly polarizing. We have even greater confidence in the quality of the scholarship gathered here. The nineteen chapters presented in this anthology represent an exciting diversity of experiences, cultural interests, and disciplinary perspectives. These works address both the incremental and radical changes in individual and collective consciousness that have permeated Israeli culture in response to the ubiquitous affliction of war. From the earliest wartime writings of S. Yizhar until the global phenomenon of films such as *Beaufort, Waltz with Bashir,* and *Lebanon,* the Israeli artist's imaginative and critical engagement with war and occupation has been informed by the catalysts of mourning, pain, loss—often accompanied by a biting sense of irony. In conceiving this project we thought that it was most critical to highlight aesthetic narratives that have wielded a profound impact on Israeli culture.

For readers curious about this volume's emphasis on Israeli cultural texts from the 1980s and beyond, we felt strongly that a dramatic shift occurred, a transformation that can be traced to several factors. The Israel-Egypt peace agreement in 1979 demonstrated that the Arab-Israeli conflict "was no longer a threat to the existence of Israel." In his discussion of late twentieth-century representations of the IDF, Yuval Benziman credits this event with creating "the notion that Israel could defend itself through peace agreements . . . the option of giving peace for land could be implemented." In 1982 the Lebanon War "altered the way the Israeli public viewed relations between Israel and its neighbors, as the war revealed that Israel was not necessarily only a peace-seeking state, but also an initiator of war."[22] In 1987 the First Intifada erupted and the new perception of an oppressed collective struggling for its own independence began to change Jewish-Israelis' understanding of the implications of the wider conflict. These salient changes, along with the growing conflict between Israel's Jewish and Arab citizens, inspired many of the cultural texts discussed here.[23] Inevitably, many of the contributors wrestle with a deeply ingrained two-part narrative of Israeli cultural history. In essence, this paradigm presumes that Israeli history and Israeli cultural works were long distinguished by their ardent faithfulness to a staunchly Zionist, nationalist, and triumphal narrative in which the sacrifice of the young in war was a tragic but absolutely necessary fulfillment of the collective's security needs.[24]

In the antithetical phase of this narrative, resistance, skepticism, and greater focus on individual lives and the role of the individual conscience begins to take over. Yet this narrative, while remarkably pervasive, entails a sort of historical amnesia, forgetting the formidable cries of conscience exhibited by S. Yizhar (discussed above), and those directly inspired by his questioning in the post–War of Independence generation immediately following. Although some have vigorously argued the case for the government failures of the 1973 Yom Kippur War as the traumatic catalyst that first provoked the severe attrition of public confidence and the change in political regime in 1977 which exposed the increasing rejection of the founding generation's ideological positioning, 1982 is most often invoked as distinguishing the period in which unquestioning support for the military and self-sacrifice truly began to wane. As editors, we recognize the multiplicity of factors that led to direct changes in Israeli society during the 1970s, but focus on their effects primarily from the 1980s onwards, for it is this period that also saw the most changes in Hebrew literary representations (as well as other vital cultural fields). As Benziman observes of the 1980s, "a considerably greater number of texts that focused on the conflict were written. The preferred genre was now the novel, instead of the short story, which allowed . . . for a more polyphonic representation of the conflict, in which the Arab voice could be heard. Some novels were written from a dual Jewish-Arab point of view. . . . Arab characters became rounder and more complex and no longer were stereotypes that merely project on the Jewish hero, but were now independent characters who exposed the reader to the Arab perspective" and, perhaps of greatest significance, "a few Arab novels became part of the canon of Hebrew literature" (332).[25] In this same period, as Ella Shohat demonstrates in her landmark study *Israeli Cinema: East/West and the Politics of Representation* (1989), the Arab-Israeli conflict played a far more important role in Israeli cinema than was previously the case. Finally, as Dan Urian ably documents in our own volume, a staggering plethora of Arab characters and the presence of the Palestinian narrative utterly transformed the Israeli stage. Many of Israel's narratives during the 1980s portray war as utterly deranged, hallucinatory realities, notably devoid of any sense or tangible mission, a trend still highly visible in the popular films made about the First Lebanon War in recent years.[26]

Perhaps what has most changed is that, whereas earlier critical voices, such as those of Yizhar, Benjamin Tammuz, and later Amos Oz and A. B. Yehoshua, undeniably ventured strong critiques of aspects of Zionist memory and military ethos, the skeptical cultural productions in the post–Lebanon War period expressed an uneasy consensus within the Israeli polity. Undeniably embittered by the futile deaths of Israel's young soldiers, the dismal lack of resolution and tangible security gains after eighteen long years of occupation of southern Lebanon led to new kinds of protest. There was less disparity between the dissent of artists and that of the larger society, suggesting that works by Ron Leshem, Ari Folman, and other figures discussed in these essays connected at a deeper level with Israel's collective psyche, meeting far less resistance than was felt by artists in earlier periods. Some of the essays affirm this binary structure in their arguments, while others challenge them or otherwise demonstrate ways in which the early paradigm of heroic sacrifice still endures (for example, see Yaron Peleg's discussion of the disparate approaches to how soldiers regard their fates in Ron Leshem's original novel *Beaufort* [*Im yesh gan eden*] and Joseph Cedar's film adaptation). Whether encountered explicitly or more obliquely, it is a sign of this paradigm's profound influence that so many of the essays here are stirred by its implications.

We begin with "'Music of Peace' at a Time of War: Middle Eastern Music Amid the Second Intifada," ethnomusicologist Galeet Dardashti's overview of the fraught relations between Jewish Israeli and Palestinian Israeli musicians against the pressures of violence, politics, and regional instability. Drawing from her remarkable experiences and interviews with acclaimed musicians such as Yair Dalal, Amal Markus, and the Arab Orchestra of Nazareth, Dardashti (herself an accomplished Middle Eastern musician) examines the euphoric days of "coexistence" music and East-West fusion inspired by the Oslo accords up to the current woeful climate of mistrust disenchantment and disengagement between Jewish and Arab artists. Dardashti raises provocative questions about a nexus of issues including conflicts over national and ethnic forms of identity, cultural appropriation, exploitation, and the limitations of peace activism. In "Privatizing Commemoration: The Helicopter Disaster Monument and the Absent State," Michael Feige considers a variety of commemorative expressions of mourning, ranging from a provocative song lyric's post-ideological appeal for young Israelis, to controversies that surrounded the construction of a public monument for the soldiers who fell in Israel's most tragic military accident. Feige's savvy analysis exposes the critical challenges undertaken by what he calls society's "memory entrepreneurs."

As noted above in the discussion of "Bab el-Wad," the popularity of songs shoring up national identity and collective will during, and in the aftermath of, Israel's recurring periods of martial crisis cannot be overestimated. Even in times of peace, it must be stressed, military troupes have long served as dynamic incubators for mainstream developments in Israel's musical culture. Despite a tradition of music that called for peace, even among the military's musical troupes, it was not until the fairly recent emergence of a rock star like Aviv Gefen in the 1990s that a singer enjoying mainstream success would voice lyrics that offered a sharp critique of the country's unflagging militarism.[27] In "'Cyclic Interruptions': Popular Music on Israeli Radio in Times of Emergency," Danny Kaplan traces music broadcasting's role in embodying the country's official "mood" throughout the First Gulf War, Second Intifada, and Second Lebanon War, vividly demonstrating how the trauma of war and terrorism are not allowed to stand as unmanageable shocks to the system but are rather naturalized and assimilated almost seamlessly into the quotidian fabric of the nation's life through lyrical and melodic strategies. Noa Roei explores a far less lachrymose, even triumphal, form of commemoration ("Consuming Nostalgia") illuminating how everyday consumer goods and displays such as New Year greeting cards and advertising exhibited and idealized the military subject to solidify a sense of collective will and determination. Since the founding of the state, the commemoration of dead soldiers has resulted in painful controversies over personal versus official forms of mourning. In "The Photographic Memory of Asad Azi," Tal Ben Zvi examines a haunting series of paintings based on photographs in a family album that constitute the son's artistic struggle with the meaning of his father's legacy as a Druze soldier who served in the IDF. Sayah Azi was the son of a Syrian Druze father who arrived in northern Israel from Syria in 1948 and remained in the Israeli village of Shfar'am to be close to his sisters who had married Druze men from the Israeli side of the border. During the 1950s he joined the border guard where, for ten years, he mainly served in a police unit whose objective was prevention of infiltration along the country's northern border. In 1961 he was killed by fire from a Syrian patrol along that same border. His son was five years old at the time of his father's death and years later struggled to come to terms with his father's complex identity and heritage through the images Ben Zvi illuminates in her unusual discussion. Liav Sade-Beck's ethnographic study, "'We Shall Remember Them All': the Culture of Online Mourning and Commemoration of Fallen Soldiers in Israel," raises pertinent questions concerning the relatively recent role of "virtual" commemoration in online communities. Sade-Beck sensitively deliberates whether the latter has genuinely transformed the culture of mourning and commemoration of Israel Defense Forces soldiers by creating new patterns and narratives, or merely replicated traditional national patterns and narratives that have been largely unchanged since the founding of the state in 1948.

As emphasized earlier, the losses of war have inspired a substantial literature of commemoration. Modern Hebrew poetry, frequently drawing on the prophetic power of biblical verses, proves an especially potent conduit for expressing rage, sorrow, and guilt over the enduring violence and hopelessness. As Tal Nitzan affirms in the powerful anthology of lyrical dissent, *With an Iron Pen:* "poetry becomes a rebellious act that unsettles axioms, generates question marks, and asserts the right of readers and writers as one to doubt, protest, and rise up." For precisely such reasons, we were eager to include essays highlighting the powerful impact of Israeli poetry's voices of conscience. Esther Raizen's "Bereavement and Breakdown: War and Failed Motherhood in Raya Harnik's Work" considers the "poetics of bereavement" through the work of one of the leading voices of the "Family of the Beaufort." This group of parents and other relatives of six fallen soldiers led a significant protest movement in the wake of the 1982 Lebanon War and came to embody new developments in the public behavior of "the bereft"—open criticism of the Israeli government and its policies, occasional refusal to partake in the myth-building narration surrounding the fallen soldiers, and insistence on coming to terms with the fact that the shared experience of bereavement provides little, if any, actual comfort to families. In Raizen's moving account, she examines how Harnik provided the Israeli public with an intimate glimpse into her private grief through three poetry collections, six children's books, and a memoir, published over the span of two decades.

Ably demonstrating the potent and proliferating role of poetry in new public forums of unprecedented access and circulation, Adriana X. Jacobs's "From IDF to .PDF: War Poetry in the Israeli Digital Age" examines the startling immediacy with which Hebrew poetry now responds to suffering on both sides of the Israeli-Palestinian conflict in virtual literary and political communities. Thus, aside from providing a forum for urgent new voices, "the novelty of going online allows these poems to emerge alongside the news of war, to challenge war in its own time." Dahlia Ravikovitch's (1936–2005) poetry, recently made available to English readers through the vibrant translations of Chana Bloch and Chana Kronfeld, has long been celebrated both for the poet's extraordinary artistry and political courage. Recipient of the Israel Prize (1998), Israel's highest cultural honor, Ravikovitch published ten volumes of poetry, as well as short story collections and books for children. Ilana Szobel's penetrating "'Unveiling Injustice': Dahlia Ravikovitch's Poetry of Witness" offers fresh insights into lyrics addressing Palestinian suffering, especially "Hovering at a Low Altitude," one of the poet's most harrowing indictments of atrocity and the indifference on the part of both the Jewish individual and the collective. For Szobel, Ravikovitch's searing language of testimony constitutes a brave counternarrative to myth, "a refusal to believe in the Israeli claim that the Zionist country goes to war only when it has no other choice" and "stand[ing] courageously in the face of the departure from innocence, bring[s] us all closer to the process of awakening."

Turning to the realm of prose fiction, we are pleased to include Shiri Goren's incisive discussion of the Argentine-born writer Gabriela Avigur-Rotem. While not yet well known abroad, in Israel each of Avigur-Rotem's literary works has reaped critical acclaim and important awards, including the President's Prize (2002). In *Heatwave and Crazy Birds,* her heroine, Loya, a middle-aged flight attendant, uncovers dangerous knowledge about her family's history in the Holocaust, a journey that obliquely illuminates the dangers of her present, the mid-1990s, a period in which violence between Israelis and Palestinians escalated, and the political extreme grew more dangerous, culminating in the assassination of Israeli prime minister Yitzhak Rabin. More recently, Avigur-Rotem's *Ancient Red* (Adom atik) (2007) explores pivotal historical figures from the time of the First Aliya (including the poet Rahel and Sarah Aharonson, a member of the Nili spy ring who was captured and tortured by the Turks), skillfully blending factual details with speculative anecdotes. Goren's "War at Home: Literary Engagements with the Israeli Political Crisis in Two Novels by Gabriela Avigur-Rotem" not only situates these novels' powerful portrayals of the individual's suffering and resistance in relationship to national trauma, both Arab and Jewish terror, the surrender of the domestic sphere to the nation's travails, but also reveals the uneasy way these themes reflect critical events in Avigur-Rotem's own life.

For Adam Rovner, Israeli fiction from the early 1970s to the present is troubled by uneasy intimations of apocalypse. In "Forcing the End: Apocalyptic Israeli Fiction (1971–2009)" he reveals how moral and political misgivings in the aftermath of military actions and the ever-present threat of vulnerability play a critical role in the apocalyptic dystopias of novelists, including Orly Castel-Bloom, Amos Kenan, Amos Oz, and Savyon Liebrecht, culminating in the nightmarish rendering of the inner and outer landscapes of war in Ari Folman's *Waltz with Bashir* (2009). In her related discussion, Glenda Abramson highlights the remarkable degree to which the uneasy political currents that inform the Israeli war literature of the 1980s can be traced to the poetry and fiction addressing the War of Independence in 1948. In "Oh, My Land, My Birthplace: Lebanon War and Intifada in Israeli Fiction and Poetry" she observes that "of all Israel's wars, the 1982 Lebanon War . . . aroused the most bitter reaction within the diaspora and Israel itself," provoking demonstrations on the left and counterdemonstrations on the right. These developments were further intensified by Israeli writers' growing attention to the injustices that stoked the first Palestinian Intifada, ultimately inspiring a creative storm of vehement protest narratives by David Grossman, Yitzhak Laor, Natan Zach, and many others for which Abramson identifies crucial iconic antecedents in the moral odysseys of S. Yizhar's (Yizhar Smilansky) 1948 warrior protagonists "which questioned the effects of the war on the soldiers, their treatment of the enemy and the ambiguity of the war for the much-heralded Jewish redemption, the notion of *en brera* ('no choice')."

Philip Metres begins his essay recounting an uncomfortable pedagogical situation familiar to many of us—namely, the biased perceptions and stereotypes American students frequently bring into the classroom when confronting the Middle East, Islam, and the Israeli-Palestinian conflict (all too often exacerbated by the American media). Metres's "Vexing Resistance, Complicating Occupation: A Contrapuntal Reading of Sahar Khalifeh's *Wild Thorns* and David Grossman's *The Smile of the Lamb*" provides the kind of incisive comparative reading of Israeli and Palestinian narratives that would seem essential but is still inexplicably rare. Both Grossman and Khalifeh have been highly praised for imaginatively and morally complex works that have grappled meaningfully with the painful histories of their respective people's struggle with the Other. Inspired by Edward Said's notion of "contrapuntal reading," Metres proposes that in approaching these paradigmatic Israeli and Palestinian literary narratives, "we must account for the particularity of each literary and cultural tradition" but also "consider how this literature gets enacted at the level of praxis, of social and political implications." Such a hermeneutics has profound implications, not merely for future conversations among literary scholars, but indeed for the kinds of truly just and humane considerations of the two people's (inevitably interdependent) narratives that are so essential for future understanding and coexistence.

Esther Fuchs examines a vitally critical cultural paradigm that has taken hold in the past two decades in "Gender, War, and Zionist Mythogynies: Feminist Trends in Israeli Scholarship," which provides an eminently accessible introduction to the vital role of Israeli feminist scholarship. Beginning in the late 1980s and throughout the 1990s, new Israeli feminist voices boldly challenged nationalist ideology, especially the militarization of society, sharply interrogating the gendered nature of discourses of warfare and, more importantly, the fundamental concepts and theories that justify and normalize war as an approach to conflict resolution. Analyzing groundbreaking works by Yael S. Feldman, Hanna Herzog, Orly Lubin, Nira Yuval-Davis, and other influential scholars, Fuchs takes us on a remarkable journey through the critical milestones that distinguish this highly consequential and versatile wave of scholarship.

As Dan Urian notes, since the first war in Lebanon, a staggering number of Israeli plays have highlighted Arab characters or otherwise emphasized the Palestinian side of the conflict, and there have even been a few Palestinian productions about the violent intifadas that managed to cross the Green Line. His truly authoritative "Representations of War in Israeli Drama and Theater," the sole essay to address the far-reaching impact of war on the Israeli stage, grapples with the monumental history of both the theater (as "a vociferous artistic opposition" to failed government policies) as well as audience response. Urian capably traces those developments from the early days of the state, when sentimental dramas about martial sacrifice seized the public's imagination, through the bleak and satirical postmodern productions of recent decades: "From the mid-1970s war began to lose its aura, and its heroes, particularly those generals that had been so admired in the past, were represented as tragic figures or even as 'punished' by means of critical satire, alongside and contrasting with figures of men unable to adapt to the military culture." While especially concerned with controversial dramas that attracted large audiences and often heated debates, Urian also pays close heed to the growing presence of women's voices on the Israeli stage, including especially alternative milieus such as the acclaimed Akko Festival. He provides an essential overview of the productions of salient works by Hanoch Levin, Hillel Mittelpunkt, Yigal Mossinsohn, Yehoshua Sobol, among others examining the cultural impact of national companies as well as experimental fringe productions.

Our collection would be woefully incomplete without substantial discussion of the recent cultural phenomenon of self-interrogative cinema such as *Beaufort, Waltz with Bashir,* and *Lebanon,* Israel's impressive proliferation of personal and historical films about its Lebanon wars, that are in some ways analogous to the roles played by the United States' Vietnam War films (*Full Metal Jacket, Apocalypse Now, Casualties of War,* and others) as catalysts for that country's historical consciousness and conscience. Apropos of that, Rachel S. Harris and I are grateful to Samuel Maoz, the director of *Lebanon* (2009), for his generous permission to include the powerful image of incongruous wartime juxtapositions that graces our cover. As a former soldier who served in Lebanon during the months of Operation Litani (1978), I was frequently struck by the extraordinary beauty of its landscape amid chaos, violence, and my own palpable dread. From the moment I first glimpsed the chilling poetry of this scene, I knew that I would never find a more fitting illustration of the powerful achievements of Israeli cinema's recent reckonings with the violent past. Aside from winning the Golden Lion at the 2009 Venice film festival, *Lebanon* received extraordinary critical praise for its relentless portrayal of an inexperienced Israeli tank crew's claustrophobic and terrifying experiences during the 1982 Lebanon War. Maoz, who was a tank gunner in that conflict, claims that Israel's 2006 invasion jolted him with a renewed sense of responsibility to prevent a younger generation from being used as pawns. Thus, a quarter of a century after his own emotional trauma, he sought to create an empathic portrait of hapless soldiers plunged into absurd and ultimately futile chaos: "I wrote *Lebanon* straight from my gut. No intellectual cognition charted my path. My memory of the events themselves had become dim and blurred. Scripting convention, such as introductions, character backgrounds and dramatic structure did not concern me. What remained fresh and bleeding was the emotional memory. I wrote what I felt."[28]

The first of our cinematic essays, which frequently examine war through the prism of gender, Yael Munk's comprehensive survey, "From National Heroes to Postnational Witnesses: A Reconstruction of Israeli Soldiers' Cinematic Narratives as Witnesses of History," provides essential contexts for understanding the complex politics of representation in the earlier waves of Israeli cinema that preceded Maoz's *Lebanon*, from the mythmaking portrayals of heroic death in films such as *Hill 24 Does Not Answer* and *They Were Ten* to the plight of the individual traumatized by inescapable histories in more recent years, or cinema "as an act of resistance . . . against still dominant national norms." In Rachel S. Harris's "A Woman's War: The Gulf War and Popular Women's Culture in Israel," our sole essay to address the traumatic period following the Iraqi invasion of Kuwait, when the United States pressured Israel to keep a low profile as its civilian population absorbed the impact of numerous Iraqi Scud missiles, she discusses the unprecedented impact of a military emergency on the domestic realm. In films such as *Siren Song* (1994), adapted from the novel by Irit Linor, and Arik Kaplun's *Yana's Friends* (1999), which both feature young female protagonists, Harris uncovers crucial sociological distinctions between that experience and Israel's earlier defensive wars. Individuals and even small families trapped in the sealed rooms specially prepared to shield against chemical attack within private apartments suffered a "heightened sense of isolation" in "psychologically stressful environments." The sense of "communal participation, collective memory, and shared experience that had characterized previous Israeli wars" in the past was severely diminished. As Harris demonstrates, these war narratives are also imbued by gender that reveals a social transformation: "the unique experience of the Gulf War empowered women—who became the caretakers and held centralized positions during the war, without neutralizing their femininity," while men, in "losing their traditional position of military command and heroism" were also forced to meet challenges that complicated their own traditional wartime roles.

Beaufort, a highly praised film based on Ron Leshem's novel *Im yesh gan eden* (If There Is a Heaven) (2005) is addressed by Yaron Peleg in "*Beaufort* the Book, *Beaufort* the Film: Israeli Militarism under Attack," which offers a provocative yet nuanced comparison between the tone and substance of the narrative's translation from page to screen. Peleg argues that in the original, Leshem's IDF soldiers are filled with self-doubt and soul-searching; they ultimately conform to the traditional mold of warrior patriots that forms an important continuum of Hebrew literature. In sharp contrast, Joseph Cedar's film version (2007) veers toward stark nihilism; its misguided war sacrificing young men seemingly without cause or justification. Both works pay heed to the unprecedented degree to which Israeli public opinion had turned against what seemed to be a futile war and were immensely popular in Israel. Peleg speculates that in spite of their disparate approaches to tragic loss, both works succeeded "because they evoked or tapped into two conflicting notions or forces that coexist in Israel today: vestiges of the *ancien* Zionist *regime* that is waging an increasingly losing war against the inexorable forces of history, and a maturation of a culture that is coming to grips with the limitations of its power." Drawing this book to its close, Philip Hollander further discusses the impact of the First Lebanon War on recent developments in Israeli cinema. His "Shifting Manhood: Masculinity and the Lebanon War in *Beaufort* and *Waltz with Bashir*" reveals how this new wave of films endorses "alternative masculine forms grounded in the family's nurturing atmosphere that stress the pain of loss and the sanctity of human life, the lives of citizens and non-citizens alike. Through widespread adoption of such forms, the films gesture towards the possibility for eventual peace between Israel and the Palestinians, and between Israel and its neighbors." That unsentimental but hopeful outlook, affirming the potent (perhaps even transformative) role of cultural narrative in contemporary Israel, provides a worthy foundation to launch this collection's unprecedented examinations of war, society, and artistic conscience.

Notes

We are deeply grateful to Kathryn Wildfong at Wayne State University Press for her warm encouragement throughout this journey. We also wish to thank Todd Hasak-Lowy and Shachar Pinsker whose thoughtful reflections and astute suggestions helped shape and improve this entire collection.

1. Avraham Burg, *The Holocaust Is Over: We Must Rise from Its Ashes* (New York: Palgrave Macmillan, 2008), 116. Subsequent references and quotations cited parenthetically.

2. His was the generation that received the Holocaust refugees with marked ambivalence at best: "We received the emasculated, displaced survivors, but locked our hearts to them. We judged them harshly, too harshly. We maintained the ideological, mental and spiritual disconnect that the Zionist pre-state Israel imposed on its Diaspora origins. We forced ourselves not to understand their experience and its context" (106).

3. Avraham Balaban, *Mourning a Father Lost: A Kibbutz Childhood Remembered* (Lanham, MD: Rowman and Littlefield, 2004). References cited parenthetically. The Arabic Bab el-Wad (*Shaar Hagay* in Hebrew) means "Gate of the Valley," a narrow gorge that was the site of numerous Arab road blockages and ambushes during the siege of Jerusalem. The song "Bab el-Wad" reads:

> Here I am passing, standing by the stone.
> An asphalt road, rocks and ridges.
> Day goes down slowly, sea-wind blows
> Light of a first star, over Beit Maschir.

Bab el-wad,
Do remember our names forever,
Convoys broke through, on the way to the City.
Our deads lay on the road edges.
The iron skeleton is silent like my comrade.

Here pitch and lead fumed under the sun,
Here nights passed with fire and knives.
Here sorrow and glory live together
With a burnt armoured car and the name of an unknown.

Bab el-wad

And I walk, passing here silently,
And I remember them, one by one.
Here we fought together on cliffs and boulders
Here we were one family.

Bab el-wad

A spring day will come, the cyclamens will bloom,
Red of anemone on the mountain and on the slope.
He, who will go on the road we went,
He will not forget us, Bab el-wad.

As a representative song of its day, Balaban says the lines embody the powerful "combination of youth and its yearnings, the terrors of war and the joy of victory, in a struggle for a homeland which is also Mother." At the same time they reveal not a "trace of ambivalence . . . as to the justice of the Israeli cause. The Israeli soldiers are the good and the brave, right is on their side, whereas those who oppose them are the evil ones, threatening the integrity of the family. . . . I can testify that that was how we were brought up. We were convinced that we were wholly justified in our conflict with the Arabs, and that we were special, beautiful, and wonderful." Thus, awakening from youthful idealism was like being "expelled from the womb twice" (104).

4. In *Almost Dead* (New York: Harper Perennial, 2010), Assaf Gavron's intricately plotted black humor novel (Tanin Pigua, Kinneret-Zmora-Bitan, 2006) about a suicide bomber and the strange events that causes his path to cross with Eitan, an Israeli national celebrity, this "old song of mourning" is heard by Eitan everywhere he goes during a time of escalating terrorist incidents: "How many times was I going to hear it in the coming days?" (91). Later, he sits in a café and suddenly notices that everyone seems transfixed or perhaps paralyzed by the song's power and unending resonance: "I hear the music: 'Bab al-Wad.' First star's light above Beit Mahsir. Some people were moving their lips to the lyrics. I turned away and looked outside at the electric pale blue. Jerusalem itself seemed to be sitting under the sky like a growth of mould. It looked coated in fear" (134).

5. One of our essayists, Esther Raizen, further illuminates the period Balaban evokes: "Hebrew war poetry written during World War II and in the early years of the Jewish State was characterized by the need for synthesis of the horror with the message of deliverance. This need gave birth to poems that, although not ignoring the death and the agony, tended to minimize

them by weighing them against national necessities and gains. Statehood and independence were seen as dramatically offered to the nation by those who had died, and accepted with solemn appreciation and promises to cherish their memory. The strong ties between soldiers, expressed as a solid, sublime entity in the term *re'ut* (camaraderie), were second only to the bond with the land." See her *No Rattling of Sabers: An Anthology of Israeli War Poetry* (Austin: Center for Middle Eastern Studies, the University of Texas at Austin, 1995), xix.

6. Rachel S. Harris, "Samson's Suicide: Death and the Israeli Literary Canon," *Israel Studies* 17, no. 3 (Fall 2012).

7. The essential discussion of the Akedah motif and its literary and political permutations in Hebrew literature and beyond can be found in Yael S. Feldman's magisterial *Glory and Agony: Isaac's Sacrifice and National Narrative* (Stanford, CA: Stanford University Press, 2010). As she eloquently delineates the "metaphorical knife in the Israeli psyche," Feldman examines how "the Lebanon War produced [a] boom of Israeli literary and artistic aqedot, intensifying the pacifist features [of earlier periods of artistic engagement]: Isaac as a passive victim rather than an active self-sacrifice; inter-generational cooperation replaced by paternal violence; and no voice (heavenly or earthly) averting the hovering knife" (284).

8. Daniel Polisar, "Making History," *Azure* 9 (2000), http://www.azure.org.il/article.php?id =294, accessed August 16, 2009.

9. S. Yizhar was the pseudonym of Yizhar Smilansky (1916–2006). Born in Palestine, he served as a member of Knesset for many years (including Ben Gurion's government) and is most renowned for his epic 1958 novel *Days of Ziklag,* which follows the struggle of a unit of Israeli soldiers to protect a remote Negev outpost during the 1948 war. He served as an intelligence officer during 1948.

10. S. Yizhar, "The Prisoner," trans. Violet Chulock Rycus, in *Sleepwalkers and Other Stories: The Arab in Hebrew Fiction,* ed. Ehud Ben-Ezer (Boulder, CO: Lynne Rienner, 1999), 57–72. Quotation appears on 61–62. Subsequent quotations cited parenthetically in the text.

11. Nurith Gertz, *Captive of a Dream* (Hebrew) (Tel Aviv: Am Oved, 1988), 56.

12. S. Yizhar, *Khirbet Khizeh,* trans. Nicholas de Lange and Yaacob Dweck (Jerusalem: Ibis Editions, 2008). S. Yizhar and David Shulman quotations cited parenthetically.

13. Aside from the 1948 War of Independence, other conflicts occasionally alluded to in the essays in this collection include 1956 (the Suez Crisis), 1967 (the Six Day War), 1968–70 (the War of Attrition), and 1973 (the Yom Kippur War); however, for reasons addressed here, much greater focus is devoted to the artistic and cultural reverberations of later military engagements such as 1978 (Operation Litani, fought in Lebanon), 1982 and 2006 (the First and Second Lebanon Wars), 1987–93 and 2000 (First and Second Intifadas), as well as and Operation Cast Lead (2008–9 in Gaza).

14. Meron Benvenisti, *Sacred Landscape: The Buried History of the Holy Land since 1948,* trans. Maxine Kaufman-Lacusta (Berkeley: University of California Press, 2000), 240. Subsequent quotations are cited parenthetically in the text. The film version Benvenisti alludes to, featuring the popular singer Gidi Gov, was released on DVD in 2010.

15. In more recent years, especially in the aftermath of the war in Gaza, there has been a steady proliferation of television shows including Danny Siton' and Itzik Lerner's *Yes, Ms. Commander* (which aired on Channel 8), a series that followed the basic training experiences of inductees with "troubled" or criminal backgrounds, and Yaheli Gat' and Yalon Gurevitch's *Reserve Duty Soldiers* (Channel 1), which documented a battalion of reservists. Critic Ruta Kupfer describes the series'

grim ironies: "Ordinary citizens are pulled out of their daily routine—work, earning a living, bank loans, family life—don a uniform and find themselves in the middle of the night in Tulkarm, banging on the doors of wanted persons and arresting them while their mothers wail." Both productions, made with varying degrees of cooperation from military authorities, candidly examined the soldiers' political perspectives and, according to Kupfer, also share the IDF's "holy trinity: rifle, Bible, and tears." See Ruta Kupfer, "In Aftermath of Gaza Drama, New TV Shows Focus on the IDF" (February 12, 2009), http://www.haaretz.com/hasen/spages/1063618.html.

16. Grossman is surely the contemporary writer whose morally anguished work bears perhaps the closest relation to the late Yizhar; his epic *Isha Borachat Mi-Besora* (Hakibbutz Hameuchad, 2008) has been widely hailed by Israeli readers and critics alike as a genuinely transformative novel about the consequences of Israel's militarism, already perceived by many as Israel's definitive "antiwar" novel. Ora, the mother of an Israeli soldier determined to return to the front in the final days of his service, is one of the most memorably complex heroines in Israel's literary history. In an early scene, as she prepares to part from her son she considers her own sense of vulnerability as well as the other families present, imagining them all as witless participants in a tragic, repetitive farce that unites the generations: "It was all a huge irredeemable mistake. It seems to her that as the moment of separation approaches, the families and the soldiers fill with arid merriment, as if they have all inhaled a drug meant to dull their comprehension. The air bustles with the hum of a school trip or a big family excursion. Men her age, exempt from reserve duty, meet their friends from the army, the fathers of the young soldiers, and exchange calls and laughter and backslaps. 'We've done our part,' two stout men tell each other, 'now it's their turn.' Television crews descend on families saying goodbye to their loved ones. Ora is thirsty, parched . . . Every time her gaze falls on the face of a soldier she unwittingly pulls back, afraid she will remember him" (64). Jessica Cohen's extraordinary English translation appeared as *To the End of the Land* (New York: Knopf, 2010). Uri Grossman was killed in Southern Lebanon during the final hours of the war (his tank took a direct hit from a rocket as the crew struggled to rescue soldiers from another destroyed tank) while his father was still completing the novel. In his postscript, Grossman writes that "Uri was very familiar with the plot and the characters. Every time we talked on the phone, and when he came home on leave, he would ask what was new in the book and in the characters' lives. ('What did you do to them this week?' was his regular question.) . . . At the time, I had the feeling—or rather, a wish—that the book I was writing would protect him."

17. David Grossman, *Lion's Honey: The Myth of Samson*, trans. Stuart Schoffman (New York: Canongate, 2006), 88–89. Subsequent quotations cited parenthetically in the text. In Hebrew: *Dvash Arayot* (Tel Aviv: Yediot Ahoronot, 2005).

18. In the same essay, Gorenberg offers a succinct observation on the sheer incommensurability of Palestinian and Israeli narratives. From Gorenberg's perspective, the pre-1948 "Jews were returning to their ancient homeland. . . . But it is also a classic Zionist account, and is just one face of history. Seen from the other direction, foreigners were coming to settle the land, to colonize it. The argument between these accounts is like a debate over whether water is really oxygen or really hydrogen. That both are partly true is the starting point of the tragedy of the Israeli-Palestinian conflict." Gershom Gorenberg, "The War to Begin All Wars," *New York Review of Books*, May 28, 2009, http://www.nybooks.com/articles/22701#fn5.

19. In a related development, the IDF's chief of staff with the participation of other senior officers collaborated with the Israel Democracy Institute to produce *Morality, Ethics, and Law in*

Wartime (Jerusalem: Israel Democracy Institute, 2003) based on proceedings from the Army & Society Forum, resulting in a book that addresses, with great candor, a range of difficult issues including the use of Palestinians as "human shields" during military operations as well as documented atrocities. Most crucially, this publication devotes an entire section to "The Issue of Narrative," which the summary describes as "complex . . . because it touches on the roots of the conflict. There are those who perceive the war as a fight for the very survival and existence of the State of Israel, while others perceive the actions of the Palestinians as a war of independence of a conquered people who are using guerilla warfare as a means of liberating themselves from the yoke of occupation. Others describe the narrative not as a regular warlike struggle for territory, but as a battle of survival between cultures and civilizations. This lack of consensus leads us to an inherent controversy on the question of defining strategic objectives. Why are the soldiers being sent out to fight? What are the objectives that Israel must define for the present conflict and that the army must carry out? . . . Different narratives lead to differing perspectives not only regarding the nature of the conflict itself, but also regarding the manner of its solution: how do we define victory in this war?" Perhaps the most interesting and challenging of the searching questions presented in this document concerns the burden of "articulating the narrative and objectives of the conflict." Does this responsibility ultimately fall on "the intellectuals, the political echelon, or to the army itself?" (20–21).

20. Like many others, Ehud Luz identifies the post–Lebanon War period Israel's moral watershed: "The 1982 Lebanon war and the Palestinian-Arab uprising (in Arabic, 'Intifada') of 1987–93 posed severe moral tests for the Jews of Israel, for they necessitated painful confrontations with noncombatant populations on a scale unknown since the War of Independence. Broad sectors of the Jewish population were shocked into a profound moral reckoning. For the first time, the Zionist consensus, whose slogan had always been 'There is no alternative,' came into question, and society was deeply divided. It was perhaps a sign of the change that later took place in Israeli public opinion over the question of compromise with the Palestinian and recognition of their national rights" (*Wrestling with an Angel: Power, Morality, and Jewish Identity,* trans. Michael Swirsky [New Haven, CT: Yale University Press, 2003], 212).

21. In a later controversy that dominated the Israeli media's attention in April 2010, former IDF soldier Anat Kam was charged with espionage for stealing and leaking military documents to *Haaretz* reporter Uri Blau (while Kam was still a soldier) that demonstrated that high-ranking Israel Defense Forces officers had approved targeted assassinations of wanted Palestinians in the West Bank even when the Palestinians might have been safely apprehended. Such authorization directly violated a High Court (Israel's Supreme Court) ruling. Knowing that she might be severely punished for the theft, Kam asserted that when she "burned the material [onto a CD] I thought that in the test of history, people who warned of war crimes were forgiven." See Ofra Edelman, "Anat Kam: I Stole IDF Documents to Expose West Bank War Crimes," *Haaretz* (April 12, 2010), http://www.haaretz.com/hasen/spages/1162458.html.

22. See Yuval Benziman, "Contradictory Representation of the IDF in Cultural Texts of the 1980s," in *Militarism and Israeli Society,* ed. Gabriel Sheffer and Oren Barak (Bloomington: Indiana University Press, 2010): 329–45, quotation appears on 331. Subsequent quotations are cited parenthetically in the text.

23. Notably, the 1990s were also marked by unprecedented forms of popular protest reflected in dramatically increased numbers of conscientious objectors, or outright refusal to serve in the IDF. A public letter signed by leading Israeli officers, using the familiar language of heroism and

sacrifice, inspired a movement of resistance by soldiers who formed the Yesh Gvul movement, refusing to serve in the West Bank.

24. We are profoundly indebted to an anonymous reader's astute observation about just how pervasive and entrenched this paradigm is, both within the discourse of our contributors and in the history of Israeli cultural production.

25. Benziman singles out the prominent examples of Emile Habiby's *Pessoptimist* (1982) and Anton Shammas's *Arabesques* (1984), both critically acclaimed and widely translated novels, in which: "Arab characters collaborate with the IDF [and] present cases of Arabs who want to be part of the society that rejects them, and who realize that to be accepted they must play a part in the security institutions. Yet since the conflict is between Jews and Arabs, and because the IDF is a tool in the hands of the Jewish people, Arabs will never be equal partners in the security services and therefore will never be part of Israeli society" (341).

26. As an anonymous reader points out, the post-2000 period may yet reveal another shift that reflects the Israeli polity's embrace of the right, which may eventually cause Israeli narratives of dissent to be deemed "out of the mainstream," as in the early years of statehood.

27. See Ilan Pappé, "Post Zionism and Its Popular Cultures," in *Palestine, Israel, and the Politics of Popular Culture,* ed. Rebecca L. Stein and Ted Swedenburg (Durham, NC: Duke University Press, 2005), 77–95. Pappé also identifies Chava Alberstein and Nurit Galron as part of the "decisive minority in the Israeli pop music world" to voice protest songs directed against the behavior of Israeli soldiers during the First Intifada (85–86).

28. Emmanuel Levy, "Lebanon: Interview with Director Samuel Maoz," *Cinema 24/7,* http://www.emanuellevy.com/comment/details.cfm?id=15640.

I

Private and Public Spaces of Commemoration and Mourning

Chapter 1

"Music of Peace" at a Time of War

Middle Eastern Music Amid the Second Intifada

Galeet Dardashti

I boarded an airplane for Israel to conduct the bulk of my dissertation fieldwork in late winter 2003—the height of the Second Intifada—as nearly every day brought new Palestinian suicide bombings in Israel and Israeli targeted killings in the Palestinian-ruled territories. The escalation of seemingly interminable violence and political instability led to the electoral victories of the staunchly right-wing Ariel Sharon as prime minister in both 2001 and 2003, based in large part on the Israeli public's confidence in his ability to fight terrorism. Israeli policy toward Palestinian life under Sharon focused on techniques such as military incursions, curfews, roadblocks, and destruction of public institutions and infrastructure with the full support of US President George W. Bush.[1] Because many Palestinian Israeli citizens of Israel had expressed solidarity with the Palestinian struggle, their loyalty to Israel became highly suspect.[2]

It was during such a political climate that in 2004 Avigdor Lieberman—then minister of transport—proposed a plan known as the "Populated-Area Exchange Plan," under which Palestinian Israeli towns adjacent to areas under Palestinian Authority would be transferred to Palestinian Authority, and only those Palestinian Israelis who agreed to live within Israel's new borders and pledged loyalty to Israel would be allowed to remain Israeli citizens. Although the plan did not ultimately pass, its proposal underscores the ultranationalist fervor that emerged at this time of war. The Israeli political left—in favor of a political nonmilitary solution to the conflict and willing to make territorial and other concessions in exchange for a peace agreement with the Palestinians—was shattered.

The gloominess of the 2000s in Israel stands in sharp contrast to the unfettered hopefulness of the previous decade. I began my research on Middle Eastern music in Israel for my master's thesis, during the euphoric period of the 1990s—amid a very different political climate. At that time, Israeli Jews and Palestinian Israelis were forming a range of Middle Eastern-and Arab-influenced bands. No academic had yet written on the subject of this emergent music scene, and I was excited about it on a number of levels. As a self-professed "liberal" American Jew, the new political developments of the 1990s occurring in Israel inspired me. I spent my junior year of college studying at the Hebrew University of Jerusalem. My Israeli friend, Danit, and I watched the signing of the Oslo Accords on TV in her dorm room in 1993; we felt that we were witnessing a crucial moment in history.

When I started hearing some of the new Middle Eastern and Arab music coming out of Israel a few years later, I was optimistic. I knew from my own grandfather's experience as a renowned Iranian singer who immigrated to Israel in the 1960s that Israel had not always been a hospitable place for Middle Eastern music.[3] In spite of the country's large Mizrahi (Jews of Middle Eastern and North African background) and Arab population, Middle Eastern musical traditions were marginalized and almost entirely excluded from dominant musical media for several decades. This began to change in the 1980s and particularly in the 1990s as hegemonic notions of Israeliness were called into question.

"Post-Zionism" became a pivotal term in the scholarly and public discussions about Israel's possible transition from a colonizing military society into a globalized capitalist society.[4] The post-Zionist model also rejected the nationalist ambition to form a cohesive universal identity, adopting a postcolonial discourse that gave voice to subaltern sectors of the population such as Palestinian Israelis and Mizrahim.[5] The 1990s marked a period when Israelis were highly optimistic about prospects for peace with Palestinians. This, in part, contributed to a flowering of groups performing Middle Eastern and Arab music, many of which emphasized coexistence between Israelis and Palestinians. I was quite excited about studying these political and cultural changes occurring in Israel. By the time I submitted my master's thesis in 2001, however, the Second Intifada was well under way.

In this essay, I examine some of the grassroots Middle Eastern- and Arab-influenced art music that began proliferating in the Israeli public sphere in the 1990s and how these musical practices shifted as the political climate changed drastically with the Second Intifada. I highlight the ways in which Middle Eastern musical practices became coopted by a multitude of local and transnational players amid the increasing deployment of music in Israel during a period of war. As I demonstrate, the Middle Eastern music scene set in motion in the 1990s continued to flourish during the turbulent and violent period of the 2000s.[6] In fact, though the government and local municipalities withdrew much of their support for arts programming due to budget cuts, new financial sponsors entered the Middle Eastern music scene. It became even more important to these sponsors, government representatives, and music producers that these performances—often framed as concerts of collaboration between Palestinian Israelis and Jewish Israelis—continued amid the constant warfare; they represented glimmers of hope for peace to audiences in Israel and abroad.

It became increasingly clear to me, however, that such performances often did not represent what was happening in the music scene. Although there were many Israelis involved in the performance of Middle Eastern and Arab music—both Jewish and Palestinian—few musical collaborations actually happened between Palestinian Israelis and Jewish Israelis. In many cases, this framing of the Middle Eastern and Arab music scene as representative of coexistence was not pernicious, but rather gave those in attendance a hopeful respite from the unrelenting violence. Yet in some instances, it seemed that because the funding for the concert or festival was based on the premise of coexistence, some collaborative projects were specifically created for that purpose.

During Israel's prestate years and the first two decades of the nation's existence, government entities were heavily involved in "inventing" and promulgating Israeli national culture, as they believed it to be a powerful method for instilling national unity among its diverse Jewish population—comprised primarily of new immigrants from all over the world. Although the Israeli state continues to sponsor some cultural activities, both government indifference to the arts and the need to increase government spending on security have gradually led to a dwindling of state-sponsored cultural arts programs within Israel.[7] The state no longer concerns itself with the policing of its national musical culture.

In *The Expediency of Culture: Uses of Culture in the Global Era,* George Yúdice argues that one of the striking effects of globalization is the broad invocation of culture as a resource for social change. Unlike in several decades past when culture was administered and wielded on a national scale, in today's global era, culture is often coordinated on many levels, both locally and supranationally, by corporations, private foundations, and the international nongovernmental sector.[8] Such theoretical musings have relevance to the Israeli case. As violence between Israelis and Palestinians increases, local Israelis and many international parties have deployed Middle Eastern music—seen by many as the ideal bridge-building tool between Palestinians and Jewish Israelis—quite significantly. "Culture has become the slippery terrain on which change is sought."[9] As I demonstrate, Middle Eastern music in Israel has become a resource for the improvement of Israel. I examine some of the implications of this new deployment of music as musicians and their music are used to wage larger political battles to which the artists may not subscribe.

The Making of a National Culture

While the official establishment of Israel as a nation-state occurred in 1948, its national character began to be forged in the 1880s as Jews began arriving from Europe in growing numbers; by 1920 the Jewish population in Palestine had reached approximately 80,000.[10] David Ben Gurion's notion of antisectorialism (*mamlachtiut*) sought to use the biblical legacy of Jewish history in Palestine to establish the universally binding character of the new state. Jewish law (*Halakhah*) became a fundamental component of the Israeli legal system, Jewish holidays became national holidays, and archaeological sites deemed to be those mentioned in the Bible became national sites.[11] This invented national identity became part of government policy once Israel became a state in 1948.

Similarly, the antecedent of an Israeli national musical style was deliberately created beginning in the 1920s. By the time Israel declared independence in 1948, the cultural character of the state had already been "invented," defined, and set by the Israeli establishment, according to a primarily Western aesthetic. With the establishment of the state, government-controlled radio, and later television (established in 1968) played a powerful role in determining what became accepted as Israeli popular music, for up until 1990, Israeli broadcast media was exclusively controlled by the state's Israeli Broadcasting Authority (IBA). As a prerequisite for full social integration, all subsequent immigrants were encouraged to abandon their previous cultural traditions in order to embrace the official national Israeli culture.

The exclusion of Middle Eastern and Arab music during Israel's early years was pervasive because of this state-controlled media. Under IBA control, "Voice of Israel" (Kol Israel) the station responsible for the domestic and international radio service, had only one Arab-language channel that aired Arab music. Its Arabic-language programming was primarily intended as public diplomacy toward Israel's Arab neighbors across the borders. Its secondary target was the Palestinian population of Israel. The Arabic-speaking Mizrahim within Israel was its last priority. The station established its Arabic Orchestra in 1948. Composed of the recent Jewish Iraqi immigrant musicians and—after 1957—some Jewish Egyptian immigrant musicians, the IBA's Arabic Orchestra served a valuable political function for the state by attracting its listeners to the propaganda programming that followed its high-quality Arabic musical interludes.[12] Aside from the Arabic-language radio station, Middle Eastern music was only minimally featured on mainstream Israeli radio when the state-run folklore ensembles were aired; this always occurred during specific unpopular time slots. In the 1970s, however, the second generation of Jewish Middle Eastern Israelis finally grew weary of such second-class treatment.

Embracing Arab Culture

By the late 1980s and early '90s, *musika mizrahit,* a Mediterranean-styled pop music that grew out of the Mizrahi working-class cassette culture in the 1970s, had just begun to pervade the Israeli public sphere after years of exclusion from a Eurocentric Israeli establishment.[13] Israeli ethnic music (*musika etnit yisraelit*) emerged in Israel in the late 1980s—less than fifteen years after *musika mizrahit* entered the scene—but by that time, cultural and national discourse had already shifted to valorize notions of cultural integration;[14] "hybridity" was becoming the new recipe for "authentic" Israeliness and national belonging. In the early years (the late 1980s to themid-1990s), ethnic bands primarily fused traditional Eastern styles with Western classical music and jazz.

Beginning in the early 1990s Israelis witnessed many crucial changes in their daily lives. In addition to the one Israeli national TV channel operating since 1968, in 1993 the commercial Channel 2 finally began broadcasting in Israel. By 1994, with the cable television infrastructure in place, Israelis had the option of choosing between forty television channels in more than a dozen languages. Non-government-regulated commercial radio stations were also introduced only in the early 1990s. As a result of the shift to commercial media, *musika mizrahit* became an instant hit on new television shows and began to pervade the new radio stations ruled by ratings, not the tastes of government officials.[15] The mainstream success of *musika mizrahit* not only made the sounds of Arab music begin to sound less foreign to Israelis but also emboldened Mizrahi and Palestinian Israeli musicians interested in bringing more traditional Arab music to the fore.

With the conclusion of the Second Intifada, the signing of the Oslo Accords became the watershed event for Israelis' openness to Arab culture. Israelis had already earned a reputation as notorious international travelers decades earlier; it became trendy for young Israelis to backpack in the Far East, South America, the Indian Peninsula, or Oceania for several months or up to a year, after their mandatory army service. With the signing of the Oslo Accords in 1993, however, Israeli tourists were ready to traverse a previously forbidden frontier right in their backyard—the Middle East; following new diplomatic agreements with its neighbors, Israelis traveled to Morocco, Jordan, and Egypt in unprecedented numbers.

Historically, Israel's Palestinian citizens have experienced years of state-sanctioned discrimination, underdevelopment, and political disenfranchisement. In the context of this increased exposure to Arab cultures and optimism for peace, however, government policies toward Palestinian Israelis became more inclusive and tolerant. Official Israeli discourse shifted, encouraging Israelis to pursue "coexistence" (*du-kiyum*) with their Palestinian conationals.[16]

Indeed, this period marked the height of musical collaborations of Arab music between Palestinians / Palestinian Israelis and Jewish Israelis such as those of the bands Bustan Abraham, Alei Hazayit, and Yair Dalal's many Palestinian collaborations.[17] These ensembles performed primarily for Jewish Israeli audiences in Israel and diverse audiences abroad. Because of their coexistence messages and mix of Palestinian, Palestinian Israeli, and Jewish Israeli band members, these groups benefited tremendously from this new era.[18] Neither Alei Hazayit nor Bustan Abraham performed songs of a political nature, yet the highly charged and exciting political changes occurring in Israel made their music seem of great political importance.

By the mid-1990s, not only did demand for their performances increase in Israel and Europe, but it even extended to the West Bank and the Arab world. These performances were always of high political import: in 1993 the Israeli government invited Alei Hazayit to perform at a ceremony marking the first implementation of the Oslo Accords; in 1995 the group performed a concert for UNESCO in Ramallah; that same year they became the first Israeli group to perform in Jordan.[19]

Yair Dalal emerged onto the ethnic music scene in Israel in the mid-1990s as the first Mizrahi musician to clearly articulate how his own Iraqi-Jewish identity was part of a cultural heritage Israel's Palestinians shared. In 1994 Dalal, who was barely known in

Israel at the time, was invited to perform in Oslo to mark the one-year anniversary of the Oslo Accords and the awarding of the Nobel Peace Prize to Israeli and Palestinian leaders. He took a choir of Palestinian and Israeli children with him, and they performed a song he composed called "Zaman es-Salaam" (Time of peace) together with another Norwegian children's choir. This launched his career, and today he is Israel's most well known international emissary of Arab music.

Dalal's framing of his own dual Arab Jewish identity was key to his success in the mid-1990s. His biography in his 1996 release, *Samar,* stated:

> Yair Dalal was born in Israel in 1955. His family is originally from Iraq. . . . He is one of the last musicians to represent the Arab Jewish music from Iraq. His background gives him the seeds to develop this rare mix of traditional and modern, Jewish and Arab, Oriental and Western. Yair Dalal is also a strong advocate for peace in Israel and devotes his talent to abolish the ideological barriers between people and in particular between Jews and Arabs. To him, when based on esteem and mutual respect, cultural fusion becomes an essential element to communication between peoples.

While Dalal certainly did his share of East-West musical fusions in the 1990s, it was the East-meets-East concept of shared culture between Jew and Palestinian that made his image so appealing, particularly to audiences abroad.

Music was not the only medium through which Jewish Israelis began forging connections and identifying with Palestinians. In the late 1980s and early 1990s Mizrahi filmmakers, poets, and academics began creating works that reflected new conceptions of an "Arab" identity they shared with Palestinian and Palestinian Israelis. Haim Bouzaglo's film *Fictitious Marriage* (1988), for example, calls fixed notions of Israeli identity into question; when Eldi, an Arab Jew, is mistaken for a Palestinian worker in Tel Aviv he opts to adopt that identity, which takes him as far as Gaza. Similarly, in the poem "Purim Sequence" by the Mizrahit poet Tikva Levi, the narratorial voice describes listening to the Palestinian musical group Sabrin and expresses anxiety that she might be mistaken for a Palestinian:

> I turn down the volume
> so only I can hear
> my paranoia is transmitted to the door or the window
> someone might think that whoever listens
> to Arabic is an Arab
> And come to kill me[20]

It was also in the late 1980s and early 1990s that radical Mizrahi academics such as Ella Shohat and Yehuda Shenhav began underscoring the similar experiences of discrimination and oppression dealt to both Mizrahim and Palestinians at the hands of a

Eurocentric Israeli establishment. Such Mizrahi expressions of identification with Palestinians reflected a "New Levantine discourse," which Israel had not witnessed until this peaceful period.[21]

Musical Infrastructure

While the post-Oslo enthusiasm for Middle Eastern music in Israel was certainly significant, there were still very few Israeli infrastructural institutions for young Israelis interested in studying and performing these musical traditions. This changed quite rapidly, however, with a successive sprouting up of several new music programs and venues, particularly in the Tel Aviv area and Jerusalem. Bar Ilan University became the first school offering formal Middle Eastern musical instruction in 1993. In particular, 1995 was a crucial year with the opening of two schools in Jerusalem. The Department of Oriental Music at the Jerusalem Academy of Music and Dance—a true music conservatory—opened its doors for the first time, and the Center for Classical Oriental Music and Dance, offering courses on a range of Middle Eastern musical traditions (Arab, Persian, Turkish) and certain forms of Middle Eastern dance opened in Jerusalem's Musrara neighborhood as well.[22] The Arab-Jewish Community Center in Jaffa—opened in the early 1990s—began offering private and group lessons on Arab musical instruments, and soon the prestigious Rimon School of Jazz and Contemporary Music began offering a course on Arab music taught by Yair Dalal.[23]

Within a few short years, an ethnic music scene took shape. Many young Israelis of all types—the largest percentage Mizrahim and Palestinian Israelis—became students of Middle Eastern music and formed bands.[24] Reflecting the above developments, in 1996 the Zionist Confederation House in Jerusalem shifted its focus to concerts of ethnic music and became "The Center for Ethnic Music," and the Inbal Dance Theater in Tel Aviv expanded into the Inbal Ethnic Arts Center in order to "showcase the rich heritage and exquisite arts of each ethnic community."[25] Many of the Palestinian Israeli students and graduates of the Jerusalem Academy of Music and Dance became members of the Arab Orchestra of Nazareth, founded in 1990.[26] A few Arab cultural performance locations opened for the first time in the early '90s to specifically serve the Palestinian Israeli community, including Al Midan in Nazareth and both Al Midan and Al Soraya in Haifa; the Israeli government heavily subsidized all of these spaces.[27]

Middle Eastern Music in Israel Amid the Intifada

I conducted most of my dissertation fieldwork between 2003 and 2004—the height of the Second Intifada—during a very different political climate than that of the Oslo euphoria of the 1990s. Not only had all of the collaborative groups mentioned above disbanded, but also physical contact (let alone musical collaboration) between Israelis and Palestinian noncitizens of Israel had become virtually impossible with military closures in effect in response to suicide bombings.

But even many of those collaborations that were not rendered impossible by border closures became difficult as a result of political tensions. Although Yair Dalal had forged an ongoing collaboration of several years with the Bedouin Ensemble, Tarab, their relationship ended in 2003. That year, one of the organizers of WOMAD (the World of Music, Arts, and Dance Festival)—one of the largest world music festivals, where Dalal has performed several times—informed Dalal that members of Tarab had accused him of exploiting them only for his own personal gain. Dalal was heartbroken.[28]

Moreover, Dalal, whose career was built on the success of Oslo, also felt wounded in the aftermath of his 2004 efforts to collaborate with Palestinian Israelis in Israel. The Oud Festival, which he cofounded in 2001, and other Middle Eastern and Arab music projects he and other Jewish Israelis helped to initiate, always made an effort to include Palestinian Israelis, yet he complained that Jewish Israelis were never invited to the Arab music festivals that the Palestinian Israeli community staged, such as the Jabus Festival and the Tarshiha Festival. Dalal found this exclusion both hurtful and "uncourageous."[29]

It was a difficult time for Israeli ethnic musicians like Dalal who relied heavily on earnings from performances in Europe to make a living. During the Second Intifada, however, Israeli musicians were boycotted from almost all European festivals. The economic ramifications of the boycott coupled with increasing tensions between the musicians ultimately led to the disintegration of Bustan Abraham in 2003.[30] According to Dalal, the number of students wanting to study with him and other teachers of Arab music had also decreased slightly.

The Fragility of "Peace"

The 1990s marked a period when many Israelis opened up to Middle Eastern and Arab music, in part because of their optimism toward peace, but when I spoke to Israelis in 2003–4, things had changed for some. Dan Golan, the cultural attaché of the Israeli Ministry of Foreign Affairs, spoke openly to me about this issue. Golan, who had always self-identified as left wing, confessed that the enthusiasm he had felt for Arab music in the 1990s had waned with the shattering of his hopes for peace. He described to me the viscerally negative sensations he experienced when hearing Arab music in recent years. Golan was not proud that he had unwittingly developed such an outlook but attributed the change to feeling betrayed by Palestinians whom, in his view, had rejected peace.[31]

Amal Murkus, a Palestinian Israeli singer/songwriter who sings in Arabic, expressed frustration with the fragility of the Israeli public's openness to Arab music:

> When we are in war Arabs are hated, when we are in peace . . . "Let's bring an Arab singer, let's make peace" . . . And lately the political situation has been so difficult with so many bombings, and when I've been invited to participate in a big festival, a good festival and a bombing happens, suddenly my performance has a different mood or people don't come to my

> performance, you understand? . . . There is a lot of tension all the time and as an Arab singer—people take it out on me, get angry at me if I perform in Tel Aviv.[32]

Many of the Palestinian Israeli musicians who had begun enjoying the fruits of Oslo saw some of the public's enthusiasm for their performances melt away.[33] Although most Israelis I spoke with did not clearly articulate the link between changes in their music preferences and the political situation, as Golan did, the number of former "peacenik" Israelis that I knew personally who had moved significantly to the right in just a few years was staggering.

Mizrahi Pride

The beginning of the Second Intifada occurred at a time when Mizrahim were experiencing the biggest surge of pride in their own Mizrahi identities ever witnessed historically in Israel. Shas, the increasingly powerful Mizrahi religious political party, won ten Knesset seats in 1996, and by 1999 it had won an unprecedented seventeen seats. An additional 200,000 people voted for the party that year. These votes didn't come only from ultra-Orthodox Mizrahi Jews but from Mizrahim (mostly working-class Mizrahim) who were "seeking a new social ideology and a new movement to lead them."[34] The all-Mizrahi movement Hakeshet Hademokratit Hamizrahit (the Mizrahi Democratic Rainbow Coalition), a group that promotes equal rights for Israel's Mizrahi population, was founded in 1997. Most of those active in Hakeshet were radical Mizrahi middle-and upper-class intellectuals. Mizrahim from all social classes were a part of this new surge of pride.

I had already observed Mizrahi pride as palpable in the late 1990s, and by 2003 Mizrahim had embraced their *Mizrahiyut* in even more overt ways. For third-generation Israelis, in particular, one's specific Mizrahi ethnicity became of particular interest during this period as many began constructing their own identities heavily on the cultural legacies from which they had become disconnected. For example, Mizrahim, quickly identifying my physical traits as similar to their own, would often ask me "Mah At?" ("What are you?"), so as to know whether I was Iraqi, Yemenite, Iranian, or Syrian. Mizrahim were interested in both connecting to their roots and forging bonds with others who shared them. In musical terms, by the late 1990s, many had begun to move away from the panethnic and hybrid pop musical styles of the 1980s and '90s, focusing instead on what they viewed as more "pure" musical traditions (i.e., Persian, Iraqi, Moroccan, Turkish), which many Israelis began to view as more "authentic."

Performances of Middle Eastern music set into motion in the 1990s, therefore, did continue during the Second Intifada. During this turbulent and violent period, however, Jewish musicians such as Yair Dalal began focusing more strongly on their own heritages. Dalal's 2002 album, *Asmar,* on the Magda label, was an album mostly focused on Iraqi music. Almost all of the musicians on the album were of Iraqi heritage, such as Avi Agababa and Asaf Zamir, Dalal's regular percussionists. In addition, Dalal featured guest musicians Yossef Shem Tov (oud) and Albert Elias (ney), and recorded a song composed by Salim Al-Nur. Shem Tov and Elias were legendary Iraqi musicians and Al-Nur a famous Iraqi composer and Dalal's private teacher of Arab music; all of them—over the age of seventy—immigrated to Israel from Iraq in the 1950s.[35] The album also contains a poem written by the Iraqi-born Israeli poet, Ronny Someck. Unlike many of his previous albums, there is no mention of Palestinians on this album or of Dalal's activism to bring peace between Arabs and Jews.[36]

The Festivals

One early morning during the summer of 2003 I caught a ride to Nazareth from Tel Aviv with Moti,[37] the producer of the Culture of Peace Festival. Moti was accompanying the Israeli pop singer Sigal,[38] a singer he managed at the time, for an audition with the Arab Orchestra of Nazareth, which he also managed. I had interviewed Moti on his work producing performances of Arab music in Israel, and he invited me to come along for the day trip to Nazareth on condition that I only observe and not ask any questions until after the audition. He didn't want to make Sigal nervous—she was nervous enough. "They know I'm not an Arab, right?" she asked as we drove along the way. "I'm sure that I might make some mistakes on the Arabic or something." "Yes, they know," said Moti. "I told them that you are my friend and that you are a well known singer among Israelis."

The Arab Orchestra of Nazareth is comprised almost exclusively of Palestinian Israeli male musicians from Nazareth.[39] They work with a number of Palestinian Israeli singers depending on the repertoire they are performing in Israel or abroad. Amid the recent popularity of Arab and Middle Eastern–infused music in Israel, Sigal, a Jew of Iraqi and Moroccan background, had become interested in performing classical Arab music with the orchestra, following the path of the more well known Moroccan-descended Jewish Israeli pop sensation Zehava Ben. Like Ben, Sigal had recently started studying Arabic language and singing, wanting to connect more with her Arab roots.

When we arrived at the orchestra's rehearsal space in Nazareth, the musicians wanted Sigal to sing every Arab song in her repertoire. The atmosphere was casual and relaxed, and although Sigal didn't know all of the Arabic lyrics, a few of the musicians would chime in and help her whenever she forgot the words. After the audition was over, Moti talked to the orchestra leader, Suheil, in private. According to Moti, Suheil liked Sigal's voice but was concerned that she didn't sing the songs in an authentically Arab way, as they were "meant to be sung." Suheil wasn't convinced that the audience would respond well to her. Moti, however, conveyed to me that he managed to convince Suheil that having Sigal, a Jewish Israeli, collaborate with the Palestinian Israeli musicians on a few songs at Tel Aviv's Culture of Peace Festival would be a big hit with those in attendance.

All three of the primary Middle Eastern music festivals that still occur annually in Israel were founded during the intifada between 2001 and 2003 despite the difficult economic and political situation. Furthermore, the biggest festival, the Oud Festival, grew steadily each year as it continued gaining global sponsors. Although the Israeli government and Jerusalem Municipality did continue to sponsor the festival, its largest sponsorship came from the Beracha Foundation (a Jewish American–funded philanthropic organization that promotes coexistence in Israel), the Goethe-Institut (a German cultural institution primarily supported by the German government that encourages international cultural exchange), and the Jerusalem Foundation (an Israeli nonprofit that seeks to create a just society for all citizens of Jerusalem, emphasizing coexistence as a primary mission).

The importance of maintaining this musical scene—in spite of budget cuts—with music performed by both Palestinian Israelis and Jewish Israelis in Israel, was underscored in the 2003 Oud Festival brochure with written statements from two government officials. The first, from Uri Lupolianski, Jerusalem's mayor, contained these words:

> The occurrence of the Festival is of great importance, especially in these days of tension. The festival brings together composers, instrumentalists, singers and song writers—Jews and Arabs—who unite to form a joint creation, when these days its meaning is more encouraging than ever. Maybe this way, through respect toward Arab culture, we shall find a new way to express our longing for a life of patience and tolerance. The festival draws music lovers from every spectrum of Israeli society every year, and therefore contributes a great deal to bringing peoples' hearts closer together and bridging gaps and chasms like only music can. (Author's translation)

Micha Yinon, head of administration of culture in the Israeli Ministry of Education, Culture and Sports, expressed similar sentiments:

> The Fourth Oud Festival takes place this year during a difficult period, both in terms of security and financially. In addition, the decreasing number of visitors to the city of Jerusalem makes the occurrence of festivals and cultural events more difficult. However this places even greater importance on the occurrence of this festival, which maintains optimism and faith in coexistence and hope for a culture of peace. The festival is a testament to the power music has for bringing souls together, and allowing creations and dialogues between those close and far, the admirers and the enemies, from every religion, ethnicity, age and gender. (Author's translation)

Although the government officials focus their discourse on the festival's importance as a symbol of hope and "coexistence" between Palestinians (referred to as "Arabs") and Jewish Israelis, in actuality there were conspicuously few musical collaborations between Palestinian and Jewish Israelis that year. The Middle Eastern music schools that opened in the 1990s described above had self-segregated into two camps—those that primarily served Palestinian Israelis and those that served Jewish Israelis, primarily Mizrahim.[40]

Like the Oud Festival, the 2003 Culture of Peace Festival—Tel Aviv's biggest Middle Eastern musical festival—featured many Palestinian and Jewish Israelis performing Arab music, with very few of them performing on stage together. In fact, the only performances featuring both Palestinian Israelis and Israeli Jews collaborating together were those specifically conceived and constructed by the festival producer, Moti, such as the one described above. Moti, the manager of the Arab Orchestra of Nazareth, sees himself as a left-wing activist and began producing concerts of Arab music in the late 1980s as a political statement against racism in Israel. As someone who had already spent years forging connections in the Israeli pop and jazz music industry, he made it his mission to bring Arab music performed by Palestinian Israeli musicians to reputable concert halls for the Jewish public. In 2002, at the beginning of the Second Intifada, Moti founded the Culture of Peace Festival in Tel Aviv and has continued serving as the festival's artistic director and producer.

The Culture of Peace Festival is supported by the Rosa Luxemburg Foundation, an organization that supports initiatives that work toward resolving the Israeli-Palestinian conflict. Although the ethnic music scene was not producing many collaborative projects featuring Jewish and Palestinian Israelis by 2003, it seemed that some were created in order to satisfy the conditions of the funders. In this case, the musicians were not just performing as part of the Culture of Peace Festival, but asked to stand in as actors performing a "culture of peace." As Barbara Kirshenblatt-Gimblett argues, "Exhibitions are fundamentally theatrical, for they are how museums perform the knowledge they create."[41] Like exhibitions, curated performances often involve quite a bit of framing on the part of producers in order to convey the messages they convey; although audiences generally experience the performance as a direct musical expression from those on stage, there are sometimes other forces at play in the musical process.

It seemed that the coexistence ensembles—many of which had formed at the grassroots level in Israel in the 1990s—were being re-created amid this period of warfare to satisfy the agendas of global sponsors. Here, the notion of "production fetishism,"[42] one of the effects of globalized capitalism, is useful:

> Production has itself become a fetish, masking not social relations as such, but the relations of production, which are increasingly transnational. The locality (both in the sense of the local factory or site of production and in the extended sense of the nation-state) becomes a fetish which disguises the globally dispersed forces that actually drive the production process.[43]

While it appeared to audiences that Palestinian and Jewish Israelis were collaborating just as they had a few years before, the actual impetus for many of these performances was concealed.

Sigal, the singer described above, eventually did perform with the Nazareth Orchestra at the 2003 Culture of Peace Festival" in Tel Aviv. As Nezar and Suheil explained to me, Moti insisted that she collaborate with them in order to produce a "coexistence moment." Unfortunately, as Suheil had predicted, Sigal wasn't well received by either the Jews or the Palestinians in the audience. Many audience members felt that Sigal, a musician accustomed to performing in clubs, rather than concert halls, didn't make the transition gracefully. Not only did her overly ornamented vocal rendition of Farid Al-Atrash's "Ya Gamil" fall flat, but also her flirtatious dancing during the instrumental sections seemed quite out of place to many in attendance. Even some of the instrumentalists on stage appeared to be having a difficult time holding back their laughter. Early on in her performance of the piece, members of the audience began talking among themselves fairly loudly—largely ignoring her.

Many of the other performances at Moti's Culture of Peace Festival in 2003 were, however, received very well by audience members. In one such performance, the Palestinian Israeli singer Lubneh Salmah from Nazareth sang some of Oum Kalthoum's songs accompanied by the Nazareth Orchestra. This concert, in particular, attracted Israelis of all types. Like most concerts featuring the music of Oum Kalthoum, audiences evaluated the singer's performance based on her ability to mimic the ornaments that Oum Kalthoum sang and often improvised in her renowned performances of the 1940s, '50s, and '60s. Nearly all in attendance greeted Salmah's performance with an enthusiastic standing ovation. At that point, the mayor of Nazareth came to the stage to thank the audience and the concert's benefactors. He began speaking in English, a more neutral language in Israel, when some members of the crowd yelled "*B'arabee*" ("speak in Arabic"), and after contemplating this for a few seconds, he switched to Arabic and some—in particular Palestinian Israelis and some Mizrahim—cheered, proud to have Arabic spoken and sung at such a prestigious concert hall in Israel. The mayor delivered the entire speech in Arabic. Most Israelis do not speak Arabic, however, and my Israeli friend of Mizrahi background who beamed with glee during the entire concert (which was performed solely in Arabic) was offended when this political figure spoke in a language not spoken by many in attendance, including her. Suddenly, a perfectly enjoyable concert of entertainment and cultural pride seemed to pose a nationalist threat.

Concluding Thoughts

In his book *The Festive State,* David Guss explains that as the festival "is transformed into an icon of 'national tradition,' a borrowed image of difference made to stand for the nation as a whole . . . the subtle ambiguities of local performance, the layerings of history and context, must all but be eliminated."[44] Although in the Arab world Oum Kalthoum was viewed as one of the greatest symbols of a highly anti-Israeli Arab nationalism, here in the Israeli context at the Culture of Peace Festival, the performance of Oum Kalthoum's *Inta Oumri* (a piece performed constantly in Israel) is to serve as a means for bringing the Mizrahim, Ashkenazim, and Palestinian Israelis together, putting differences aside. But when those on stage began speaking Arabic (as opposed to singing it) the moment of cultural harmony melted away, reminding those present of the current political realities dividing them.

As investing in Arab culture in Israel is increasingly viewed as one of the gateways to peace, Palestinian Israeli musicians and their representatives have to navigate diverse interests in order to appeal for funding from the government, international NGOs, and private sponsors in Israel and abroad. My intention is not to implicate culture brokers, especially in a place as fraught with political turmoil and cultural complexity as Israel. For the most part, they have very well meaning intentions. As anthropologist Steven Feld reminds us, however, musical projects "embarked upon with self-consciously progressive political and aesthetic agendas are neither innocent of nor discursively free from postcolonial critiques."[45] In their quest to mainstream Middle Eastern and Arab music in Israel and appeal for available funding, however, culture brokers do sometimes offend and co-opt some of the very Palestinians they are attempting to support.

Having had the opportunity of conducting a brief fieldwork stint on Israeli ethnic music in the sunny days of the 1990s, I wondered how the violence and instability of the Second Intifada would impact Israeli acceptance of Middle Eastern and Arab cultural expression.[46] In 2005 Rebecca Stein and Ted Swedenburg wrote that "the 1990s' popularity of 'Arab' culture, restaurants, and places among Ashkenazi Israelis has now been eclipsed by the rise of anti-Arab phobia and racism and by the nostalgic return to canonical Zionist cultural practices."[47] My own research disputes these claims; Arab cultural expressions in Israel during the Second Intifada remained in demand. As I have demonstrated, however, rather than building bridges with their conationals, Mizrahi and Palestinian Israelis separately began delving more deeply into what they and others viewed as their own historical musical legacies. They could accomplish this now that the musical infrastructure described above had been created. Palestinian Israelis studied largely at the Arab Music Conservatory in Jerusalem, while most Jewish students studied at Bar Ilan, at the Center for Classical Oriental Music and Dance in Jerusalem, or at Yair Dalal's private studio in Jaffa, opened in 2003.

The impetus for collaborations of coexistence between Palestinian and Jewish Israelis during the Second Intifada only rarely came from musicians themselves. Yet as the conflict worsened, Israeli culture brokers and festival organizers were able to garner more global funding sources than ever for Middle Eastern music in Israel, assuring funders that these musical activities had the potential to bridge the divide between Palestinians and Jewish Israelis. In some instances, Israeli Middle Eastern music festivals co-opted these music practices, "thematizing" relations between Jews and Arabs. As Barbara Kirshenblatt-Gimblett notes, "Curatorial interventions may attempt to rectify the errors of history, and make the heritage production a better place than the historical actuality it represents."[48] Such "curatorial interventions" are highly relevant for the Israeli context in understanding the powerful ways in which music curators can frame present-day realities, obscuring any signs of conflict and the issues of power at play during periods of war.

This does not discount the power of music for uniquely bridging cross-cultural divides in Israel and beyond. In fact, some musical collaborations between Israelis and Palestinians can be quite effective for bringing the groups together. For example, the nonprofit Jerusalem Foundation has supported the Arab Jewish Youth Orchestra of the Beit Alpert Music Center in Musrara since its formation in 1986, bringing Jewish and Arab young people together through music.[49] Similarly, the Israeli government established a Middle Eastern music youth camp where eighteen Palestinian Israeli and twelve Jewish Israeli young musicians come together to learn some of the great Arab classical works.[50] These initiatives offer rare opportunities for young Jewish and Palestinian Israelis to form relationships.

Sameer Makhoul, a Palestinian Israeli musician and the conductor of the Arab Jewish Youth Orchestra, believes strongly in the power of such community arts initiatives in bringing Palestinian and Jewish Israelis together:

> There is a conflict here. But I believe that you and I can live together here in peace. We can. And that I want to make music between Arabs and Jews here—I also believe that that also brings our hearts together a bit—allows love. It influences people, all the time—it influences people. I have no doubt. Jews performing Arab music learn something about my culture, the education. It brings people together.[51]

Sameer not only leads the orchestra but also teaches mostly Jewish students in the Center for Classical Oriental Music and Dance. He is probably one of the few Palestinian Israelis his Jewish students know personally. The Palestinian Israeli musician George Samaan, like Makhoul, also sees teaching Arab music to Jewish Israelis as one of the most important things he does. When we spoke in 2004, he had seven private students studying oud with him. All of these students were Jewish, and he refused to charge them any fee for these lessons. "My goal and challenge is to have the oud represent the Jews as well," he explained.

Music does have a unique ability to bring people together, and so it is unfortunate that most of the Middle Eastern music schools have become—for the most part—segregated. Still, I am certain that Jewish Israeli performers of Middle Eastern and Arab music have more opportunities for interaction with Palestinian Israelis than do most of the rest of the Israeli Jewish population. But when a Palestinian Israeli musician's livelihood is dependent on collaborating with Jewish Israelis, I don't believe it can produce lasting results. Since Jewish Israeli producers and culture brokers are usually the ones holding the purse strings, the power dynamics are quite blatant. This comes to the heart of why disingenuous staged performances that reinforce unequal power relations can be damaging.

In this chapter, I illustrated what I argue is an increasingly common phenomenon today: the deployment of music by a multitude of local and transnational players to solve political and social problems. Amid the ultranationalist period of the 2000s, the framing of some of the musical performances as "collaboration" sometimes played a role in obscuring the violence and the ugly reality of the Israeli political scene. Although it is tempting to cite all musical collaborations between Palestinian Israelis and Israeli Jews as evidence of political prophecy or as the transcendence of conflicting ideologies, my analysis underscores the necessity of examining some of the external factors involved in shaping these musical innovations and encounters.

Notes

1. Baruch Kimmerling, *Clash of Identities: Explorations in Palestinian and Israeli Societies* (New York: Columbia University Press, 2008), 293.

2. In 2000, Palestinian citizens of Israel demonstrated their solidarity with this Palestinian struggle—blocking off roads and throwing stones. Responding with massive live fire, the Israeli police killed thirteen Palestinian Israelis and wounded several hundred. This response and the Jewish public's indifference to it shocked Palestinian Israelis deeply and contributed to their decision to boycott the 2001 election, denying Labor their traditional support. Sharon, the Likud candidate, won the election by a large majority but with the lowest historical turnout (Kimmerling, *Clash of Identities*, 283).

3. Despite his acclaimed fame in Iran, when Yona Dardashti and his family immigrated to Rishon le-Ziyon, Israel, in 1967, he found few opportunities for professional performance. The larger Israeli public took no interest in such Eastern-sounding music, and the Iranian community was mostly concerned with its integration and assimilation in Israel. Dardashti traveled back to Iran a few times a year to give performances up until the Islamic Revolution in 1979, after which he could never again.

4. Yoav Peled and Adi Ophir, eds., *Israel: From Mobilization to Civil Society?* (Hebrew) (Tel Aviv: Ha Kibbutz Ha Meuchad and Van Leer, 2001); Yael Yishai, *Between Mobilization and Pacification: Civil Society in Israel* (Hebrew) (Jerusalem: Carmel, 2003).

5. Uri Ram, "Four Perspectives on Civil Society and Post-Zionism in Israel," *Palestine-Israel Journal of Politics, Economics, and Culture* 12, no. 5, issue on Civil Society (2005); Ariella Azoulay and Adi Ophir, "One Hundred Years of Zionism: Fifty Years of a Jewish State," *Tikkun* 13, no. 2 (1998): 68–71.

6. Although this was true in Israel, many opportunities for performance abroad disappeared for Israeli musicians during the Second Intifada, as I explain later in this chapter.

7. Ilan Ben-Ami, "Government Involvement in the Arts in Israel—Some Structural and Policy Characteristics," *Journal of Arts Management, Law, and Society* 26, no. 3 (1996): 195–220.

8. George Yúdice, *The Expediency of Culture: Uses of Culture in the Global Era* (Durham, NC: Duke University Press, 2003).

9. Ibid., 158.

10. This figure includes the native Jewish population already living in Palestine.

11. See Nadia Abu el-Haj's *Facts on the Ground: Archaeological Practice and Territorial Self-Fashioning in Israeli Society* (Chicago: University of Chicago Press, 2001) for a critical assessment of the long-standing relationship between nationalism and archaeology in Israel. See also Mi-

chael Herzfeld, *Ours Once More: Folklore, Ideology, and the Making of Modern Greece* (Austin: University of Texas Press, 1982), who demonstrated the way in which the Greek nationalist project convinced the population that its folklore was continuous with the classical civilization of Hellenic Greece.

12. In the 1970s, the orchestra increased its size and added two Palestinian Israeli violinists from Nazareth. The orchestra also periodically employed Palestinian Israeli singers to perform at festivals. Galeet Dardashti, "The Buena Vista Baghdad Club: Negotiating Local, National, and Global Representations of Jewish Iraqi Musicians in Israel," in *Jewish Topographies: Visions of Space, Traditions of Place*, ed. Julia Brauch, Anna Lipphardt, and Alexandra Nocke (Aldershot, UK: Ashgate, 2008); Inbal Perelson, "Ha-mosdot ha-musikalim shel ha-mehagrim me-arzot ha-islam bashanim ha-rishonot shel medinat israel" (The musical institutions of the emigrants from the Islamic countries during the first years of the state of Israel) (PhD diss., Tel Aviv University, 2000, preface in English); Motti Regev, "Present Absentee: Arab Music in Israeli Culture," *Public Culture* 7, no. 2 (1995): 443–45; Esther Warkov, "Revitalization of Iraqi-Jewish Instrumental Traditions in Israel: The Persistent Centrality of an Outsider Tradition," *Asian Music* 17 (1986): 9–31.

13. For more on the rise of *musika mizrahit* see, for example, Amy Horowitz, "Performance in Disputed Territory: Israeli Mediterranean Music," *Musical Performance* 1, no. 3 (1997): 43–53; Motti Regev and Edwin Seroussi, *Popular Music and National Culture in Israel* (Berkeley: University of California Press, 2004); Motti Regev, "The Musical Soundscape as a Contest Area: 'Oriental Music' and Israeli Popular Music," *Media, Culture, and Society* 8, no. 3 (1986): 343–55.

14. Virginia R. Dominguez, *People as Subject, People as Object: Selfhood and Peoplehood in Contemporary Israel* (Madison: University of Wisconsin Press, 1989), 120.

15. The most noteworthy example on television was *Taverna*, a popular show that aired for years in a prime time spot beginning in the late 1990s. The program was much like a typical talk show, but the guests were predominantly performers of *musika mizrakhit*.

16. Rebecca Stein, *Itineraries in Conflict: Israelis, Palestinians, and the Political Lives of Tourism* (Durham, NC: Duke University Press, 2008); Rebecca Stein and Ted Swedenburg, introduction to *Palestine, Israel, and the Politics of Popular Culture* (Durham, NC: Duke University Press, 2005).

17. See Benjamin Brinner's book *Playing across a Divide: Musical Border Crossings in Israel and the West Bank* (Oxford: Oxford University Press, 2009). Interestingly, Brinner notes that the impetus for these collaborations was the First Intifada in 1987, when the Palestinian leadership declared a ban on live music at weddings and other celebrations and Palestinian musicians needed to seek out other performance opportunities and income.

18. Alei Hazayit had both Palestinians and Palestinian Israelis in their group while Bustan Abraham had only Palestinian citizens of Israel in the group. Performing abroad, therefore, was much easier for the latter group since they all had Israeli passports.

19. Brinner, *Playing across a Divide*.

20. This poem was translated by Ammiel Alcalay in *After Jews and Arabs: Remaking Levantine Culture* (Minneapolis: University of Minnesota Press, 1993).

21. Alcalay, *After Jews and Arabs*.

22. Up until this point, Palestinian Israeli musicians had very few opportunities for public performance and earned their income mainly from performing at weddings and other celebrations.

23. In East Jerusalem, the school for Arab classical music also opened in the late 1990s offering instruction primarily for Palestinian noncitizens of Israel.

24. Dardashti, "The Buena Vista Baghdad Club"; Galeet Dardashti, "The *Piyut* Craze: Popularization of Mizrahi Religious Songs in the Israeli Public Sphere," *Journal of Synagogue Music* 32, no. 1 (2007); idem, "Discourses of the Middle Eastern Musical Aesthetic in Israel" (master's thesis, University of Texas at Austin, 2001).

25. *Inbal Ethnic Arts Center Spring Season Brochure* (Tel-Aviv: Inbal Ethnic Arts Center, 1998).

26. The orchestra receives a large portion of its funding from Israel's Ministry of Science and Art. Before an Arab music infrastructure was set up, a large number of the members of the orchestra were Jewish immigrant musicians from the former Soviet Union.

27. Government subsidies for these performances were heavily cut during the Second Intifada.

28. Dalal related this story in 2004 during a car ride he gave me on the way to the Arab music class he was teaching at the Rimon School of Jazz and Contemporary Music.

29. Interview with author, 2004.

30. Brinner, *Playing across a Divide.*

31. Interview with author, 2003.

32. Interview with author, 2004.

33. The public's loss of appetite for Arab music at times of violence was not unique to the Second Intifada, however. As Brinner (*Playing across a Divide*) recounts, Alei Hazayit had three of their performances canceled after a 1996 deadly bombing in Tel Aviv. Yet usually within a couple of weeks, Israelis—so accustomed to such occurrences—resumed their daily routines.

34. Sami Shalom Chetrit, "Mizrahi Politics in Israel: Between Integration and Alternative," *Journal of Palestine Studies* (Autumn 2000): 51–65, at 59.

35. For more on these elderly Iraqi musicians and how they began garnering Israeli mainstream media attention, see my essay, "The Buena Vista Baghdad Club."

36. There is, however, a "Prayer for Peace" from the Yom Kippur liturgy sung in maqam dashti (a mode, the liner notes explain, that is common to Iranian and Iraqi music) by Maureen Nehedar, a young Israeli singer of Persian background.

37. A pseudonym.

38. A pseudonym.

39. The Arab Orchestra of Nazareth has also been called "Haifa's Arab Orchestra" in earlier periods. All of the Palestinians discussed here are citizens of Israel (not residents of Gaza or the West Bank, Israel's Occupied Territory). For the most part, the Jewish population of Israel and the Israeli mainstream refer to this group as Arab Israelis or simply "Arabs" (*Aravim*). Some Arab citizens of Israel, however, object to being referred to as "Arabs" since it obscures their national aspirations as Palestinians. Therefore, although most of my informants referred to themselves as "Arabs" when speaking with me (an outsider), throughout this article, I refer to this group as Palestinian Israelis.

40. The Arab Music School at the Hebrew University of Jerusalem's Music Conservatory primarily attracts Palestinian Israelis, while all the other schools cater to Jewish Israelis.

41. Barbara Kirshenblatt-Gimblett, *Destination Culture: Tourism, Museums, and Heritage* (Berkeley: University of California Press, 1998), 3.

42. Arjun Appadurai, "Disjuncture and Difference in the Global Economy," *Public Culture* 2, no. 2 (1990).

43. Ibid., 16.

44. David Guss, *The Festive State: Race, Ethnicity, and Nationalism as Cultural Performance* (Berkeley: University of California Press, 2000), 13.

45. Steven Feld, "From Schizophonia to Schismogenesis: On the Discourses and Commodification Practices of 'World Music' and 'World Beat,'" in *Music Grooves,* ed. Steven Feld and Charles Keil (Chicago: University of Chicago Press, 1994), 289.

46. Dardashti, "Discourses of the Middle Eastern Musical Aesthetic in Israel," 92.

47. Stein and Swedenburg, introduction to *Palestine, Israel, and the Politics of Popular Culture,* 13.

48. Kirshenblatt-Gimblett, *Destination Culture,* 8.

49. There is historical significance in Musrara being chosen as the site for this orchestra (as well as for the Center for Classical Oriental Music and Dance). The area was originally developed by Palestinian Arabs in the late nineteenth and early twentieth century. During the war of 1948 the Arab residents fled or were expelled. Until 1967 it marked the border between Jordanian East Jerusalem and Israeli West Jerusalem, and in the early 1950s it became a development town where new immigrants, primarily from Arab countries, were settled; like other Mizrahi development towns, it became a focus of economic distress and poverty. The disenchanted Mizrahi youth of Musrara established the Israeli "Black Panther Movement" in the 1970s. Musrara, therefore, has significance both for Palestinian Israelis and Mizrahim.

50. During Ehud Barak's tenure as prime minister (1999–2001), the camp was created by the Forum for National Consensus, which seeks to bring Palestinian Israelis and Jews closer together.

51. Interview with author, 2004.

Chapter 2

Privatizing Commemoration

The Helicopter Disaster Monument and the Absent State

Michael Feige

Introduction

Nothing will hurt me, nothing
Not a woman not a terrorist bullet, nothing
That is what I promised my brother, sister, parents.
And I cried in the nights and worried in the days
Because I was afraid that something would hurt my parents
And my father's voice echoed for years in my head
"If something happens to you
There is no point in my living
There is no point in tomorrow"
If you are standing there above me
I assume that I did not keep my word
I am truly sorry.

The soldier who wrote these words, Erez Shtark, was killed in a helicopter crash, along with seventy-two of his comrades, on their way to Lebanon on February 4, 1997, adding an eerie prophetic meaning to his lyrics. Set to music and performed by one of Israel's top rock bands, Knesiat Hasechel (the church of the brain), the song is well known and quite popular among Israeli youth.[1] I heard the song repeated time and again when visiting the monument commemorating the soldiers killed in that crash, located on the northern border of Israel near the town of Kiryat Shmona; no other representative of Israel's rich repertoire of bereavement songs was heard at the site.

Sending their sons to battle, Spartan mothers used to demand that their sons return either holding their shield or laying on it, victorious or dead. While Israel has often been referred to as a modern-day Sparta, the song paints a different picture, in which returning alive, victorious or not, is more important for the parents than military glory and honorable service. Heroic death for a worthy cause serves no consolation for a grieving family. While the comparison of Israeli militaristic culture to Sparta was always a gross exaggeration, in later years, especially in and after the First Lebanon War (1982–2000), a strong shift of values, further away from Spartan ones, can be detected, and Shtark's lyrics, along with the monument commemorating the event in which he perished, are such examples.

Songs written on or by fallen soldiers have been quite common in the Israeli bereavement culture repertoire, and Shtark's composition is no exception. It is far from unique in stressing the tragic outcomes of war rather than its purpose or heroics; in that respect the lyrics follow a long line of similar artistic creations going back to Israel's War of Independence in 1948. In Israel, the motif of the living-dead soldier addressing his loved ones—and the nation in general—from his grave is an often-used dramatic ploy. In Natan Alterman's iconic poem "The Silver Platter" of 1947, associated with the War of Independence, commonly read at state ceremonies, the two soldiers, a boy and a girl, are depicted ambiguously, and one cannot tell whether they are alive, or have been shot dead. They approach the perplexed nation declaring that they are the silver platter on which the Jewish state was given. Another famous song of the early 1970s, "The Song of Peace," became an informal hymn for the Israeli peace movement. In that composition, the dead order the living to let go of them in order to fight for peace. The dead often "enjoy" a metaphoric existence in Israeli society and are assumed to have a moral stand and a clear voice, either calling for militaristic toughness or for compromise and peace.

The uniqueness of Shtark's song therefore resides not in genre, but rather in its extreme reflexivity and total lack of regard to national issues. Unlike the two other examples above, the writer of "Nothing Will Hurt Me" expresses a post-ideological era, with staying alive for the sake of his close relatives as the only motivation mentioned. If the soldier's family sent him to the army proud of his patriotic contribution, or expecting military glory and advancement through the ranks, none of this is present in the lyrics. While Alterman's "The Silver Platter" renders national purpose to death in battle, and "The Song of Peace," demands to stop using military death to legitimate further wars and bloodshed, Shtark's song disregards nationalism and heroism altogether, making it a subversive text in the Israeli context, and a surprising choice for educational groups to be listening to at the monument. Reading the words, it seems as if the song was somewhat arbitrarily appropriated into the context of war and remembrance, as the young soldier does not differentiate between the dangers of a woman and terrorists, who in today's world, target civilians no less than soldiers. Without prior knowledge, the reader needs to guess that the song is connected to a military context. In any case, it is not a song that encourages young Israelis to enlist; it is quite easy to deduce the opposite. Why Zionist youth groups sing such anti-militaristic lyrics when visiting a war memorial warrants further clarification.

Placed within a different artistic lineage, this poem sounds quite in tune with the sardonic and morbid culture that developed among Israeli soldiers in Lebanon. In the first weeks of fighting in 1982, television crews brought back to the viewers a whimsical soldier limerick, mimicking a known children's song inviting an airplane to take them to the sky. The soldiers transformed this benign song to: "Come to us airplane /take us to Lebanon / we shall fight for Sharon [Israeli Minister of Defense at the time—M.F.] / and return in a coffin." Soldier subculture is often iconoclastic and critical of the lofty words used to send young men to battle. Apparently, the sense of absurdity and futility that accompanied the seemingly endless bloodshed in Lebanon led to Israeli cultural depictions that were the Israeli equivalent of *Catch-22* or *M.A.S.H.* This was best expressed in soldier literature that came out during the two decades of Israel's presence in Lebanon, culminating with the award-winning book *If There Is a Heaven* by Ron Leshem, turned into the award-winning film *Beaufort.*[2] The senselessness of war and the arbitrary fate of accidental soldiers, as far away as one can get from the Zionist ideology that legitimized sacrifice, were well expressed in these and other artistic expressions.[3] After young soldiers had their pictures taken or were filmed for television, they jested about how the images would look in a memorial book or special documentary made after their deaths. In group photos of units they jokingly stood at some distance to one another, to leave room for the circle that would be drawn around their faces in future newspaper obituaries. "Whatever does not kill you makes you tougher," is a common soldier proverb (unknowingly adopted from Friedrich Nietzsche); "whatever does kill you makes your mother tougher," added the sardonic soldiers in Lebanon, sublimating their fear into black humor.

Not surprisingly, soldiers' mothers were not amused, and many joined the Four Mothers political movement, aimed at withdrawing the IDF from Lebanon, often contrary to the overt wishes of their sons. In Shtark's poem, the soldier is placed in a passive posture, listening to what his family desires, and trying to be "a good boy" in remaining alive. The acting subject in the poem is his father, who unlike fathers before him shamelessly acknowledges the forthcoming grief without demanding his son be a Spartan hero first. Rather than strengthening his son he instills the fear of death in him and reshuffles his priorities by placing family first. To use an analytical term developed in Israel by literary scholar Hanah Naveh, the father in the poem has adopted the maternal discourse on war.[4]

On Internet sites, young Israelis, soldiers or soldiers to be, express their attachment to the song, connecting it to their feelings, fears, and often political beliefs. They mention that the song affects them most while visiting the monument commemorating the disaster, with the writer's name among the list of the dead. Ironically, the army does not allow the rock group Knesiat Hasechel to perform in army camps before soldiers, because the band's leader has not served in the army. Yet in contemporary Israel, one does not have to be a soldier, or even to be accepted by the army as a legitimate representative, in order to voice the deepest anxieties of youth. While the army and its spokespersons stress the importance of military ethos, collectivist values, and general enlistment, they are increasingly faced with subversive undercurrents that are becoming prominent in Israeli public discourse and soldier culture.

This chapter examines crucial changes in Israeli bereavement culture through concentrating on the commemoration of the helicopter disaster, and especially on the monument constructed on the spot where one of the helicopters crashed. Through discussing the process of its creation and its semiotics, I shed light on the ways Israelis make sense of the traumatic Lebanon experience, especially on the profound transformation occurring in the commemoration of dead soldiers in Israel—leading away from the nationalistic ethos of heroism and sacrifice. A further claim I make is that bereavement is undergoing a process of growing privatization.

Following globalization, liberalization, and the growth of consumer culture in Israel, public resources have partially and gradually started accumulating in private hands.[5] While this process is apparent in the economic sphere, it can also be detected in the transformation of Israeli culture, to the point that some critics regard it even as the "privatization of Israeliness."[6] Privatization, I want to claim, has reached the most sacred Israeli values; namely, the commemoration of fallen soldiers, and the memorial of the helicopter disaster is an extreme case for this growing trend.

Changing Bereavement Culture in Israel

The cult of the war dead always had a meaningful presence in Israeli history, society, and politics, even from the prestate era, and especially after the 1948 War of Independence, a war that claimed the lives of 6,000 young Israelis, approximately 1 percent of the population.[7] The necessity of sacrificing young lives in order to survive in a harsh environment and gain independence, coupled with the elaborate militaristic culture that started to emerge from the 1950s, made the army, its generals, soldiers, and especially its dead, the main focus of the emerging Israeli culture.[8] This can be seen through books, theater, poetry, popular songs, and especially commemoration in time and space; namely, in the Memorial Day for the Fallen Soldiers and in the monuments, scattered across Israel in a density found in no other country.[9] An unspoken pact between the state and its citizens determines that death in battle is symbolically worth more than death in a civil context, that the state has a sacred obligation to its soldiers and to the family left behind, and that mythical eternal memory in the pantheon of heroes is a compensation offered for the loss of actual life in battle.[10]

This pact between the state and its citizens was based on mutual understandings and established presuppositions. The three major agreements, as publicist Rubik Rosenthal articulates, are that the war dead are a necessary price that must be rendered for the continuing existence of the nation and the state; that private mourning and national remembrance are complementary, and in no way contradict each other; and that bereavement is sacred and placed beyond political differences.[11] As Rosenthal, along with others, contend, at present all three presuppositions are contested. Parents, along with social movements and political parties, question the sacrifice of soldiers on what they consider to be unjustified wars and unnecessary military blunders. Grieving parents often feel they want to reappropriate their fallen son from the grasp of the army and the national ethos, and contest the representation of fallen soldiers in military cemeteries and state rituals.[12] Various ideological groups, either oriented to the left or to the right, use the names of fallen soldiers to voice their political convictions. The national grief over fallen soldiers has become privatized and politicized, losing its consensual aura and its ability to offer some kind of condolences to grieving parents.[13]

The changing demographics of death within the context of the Israeli-Palestinian conflict have further undermined the hegemonic hold of commonly accepted axioms. As the editors of this volume point out, the 1973 Yom Kippur War was Israel's last "conventional war," in the sense of national armies standing across definable battle lines. The two Lebanon Wars, both intifadas, and the Israeli passive participation in the First Gulf War, have all redefined danger, heroism, and sacrifice, and were all highly contested, either because the Israeli army faced civilians, getting entangled in complex moral issues of military occupation and popular revolt, or because government and military decisions encountered substantial inner-Israeli opposition. With the targeting of the Israeli home front, the number of casualties among the Israeli civilians and residents increased, far outpacing the number of soldiers killed. A bitter struggle ensued, conducted by organizations fighting on behalf of terrorist victims for inclusion in the large family of bereavement. Furthermore, as victimhood within the context of the national conflict is regarded as an entry ticket into Israeli society, Israelis had to contend with the arbitrariness of terrorists' target groups, most not an integral part of the Zionist ethos. Non-or anti-Zionist ultra-Orthodox women, children, and old men; guest workers from Africa; partygoers in Tel Aviv, all targeted by terrorist attacks, openly or tacitly began demanding their place in the Zionist pantheon of dead heroes.

Technology has further transformed Israeli memorial space. The massive entrance of the Internet into the commemorative culture in Israel weakened the hold of the military establishment on the meaning of heroic death and enabled private citizens to both construct their own virtual site and express grief, anger, and political opinions in a less controlled environment and often anonymously. The appearance of "virtual commemoration" stresses the weakening of the state and the growing importance of civil society in the establishment of new modes of national commemoration, more defused and less controlled than before.[14]

The change in the context and practices of commemoration attracted the attention of researchers. Literary scholars, as Dan Miron and Hanah Naveh detected, presented and analyzed a "minor" language of commemoration, coexisting with the major, dominant, national one, strengthening it and subverting it at the same time.[15] The minor language, a more feminine, motherly voice, brings back to the surface the familial everyday life, the uncompromising grief of death, and the inability of the national rituals and clichés to repress the devastating consequences of losing a son at an early age, regardless of cause. While this maternal language was always present, spoken by both genders, it has gained much more prominence with the transformations of Israeli society and the decline of the national bereavement culture.

Sociologist Edna Lomsky-Feder conceptualizes this change in a different manner. In examining school Memorial Day ceremonies, she detected a systematic change from a heroic concept of nationalism and the prominence of the warrior ethos, toward a nationalism based on victimhood and an ethos of suffering. Even state school ceremonies enable divergent, subversive, feminine voices to penetrate through the formal national discourse, challenging the hegemony of the bereavement order, with children and youth facing their recruiting to the army as their primary cliental.[16] Following these changes, Rosenthal made a far-reaching declaration: "The natural interest of Israeli society today is to terminally kill the bereavement ethos, to deconstruct it completely to its two components: private grief will be returned to the families, and become a tragedy like other tragedies; national grief will be totally institutionalized, will stop to bother us, and will be frozen in pantheons, monuments and ceremonies."[17] While Rosenthal's prediction may be somewhat harsh and premature, it does shed light on Erez Shtark's morbid poem. Getting oneself killed by a terrorist bullet, or for that matter getting hurt by a woman, is a private affair, a pact discussed between the young man and his family, outside the scope of the absent state and nation. The fact that such an iconoclastic song is chosen as the authentic pedagogical representation of death within a military context attests to the changes that Israeli culture has undergone. In view of this history of commemoration, the question of how the Lebanon War is commemorated—and within it the disaster where Shtark and his friends have perished—receives special importance.

The Helicopter Disaster in Its Historical Context

On February 4, 1997, on a rainy night, two military helicopters, carrying sixty-five Israeli soldiers and eight crewmen, took to the sky en route to replace troops in Lebanon. The soldiers were heading for a long and dangerous service just across the northern Israeli border, where the IDF was hemorrhaging at a rate of twenty soldiers per year. Traveling by ground convoy, exposed to the fire of the Hezbollah warriors, was considered especially hazardous, which is why flying the few miles into Lebanon was regarded as the safest method for replacing weary troops. On that night, things went terribly wrong: soon after takeoff, as the two helicopters turned off their lights, they collided and crashed, one into a forest, and another near an empty motel room at the *moshav* (agricultural community) Shear Yishuv. All seventy-three soldiers were killed in what turned out to be the worst accident, civil or military, in Israel's history.

The next day, as the scope of the disaster was revealed and the funerals took place, a day of mourning was declared, with flags lowered to half-mast and schools holding commemoration gatherings. One editorial called the event a national trauma, and added: "We thought that we couldn't live with three dead soldiers a week. Now we have lost 73 soldiers in one hasty minute."[18] The media dedicated many pages to describing and trying to cope with the disaster, and the writer Moshe Shamir drew the link between the location of the disaster and Tel Hai, the place where Yosef Trumpeldor, the national hero, died in 1920. In an early attempt to ascribe significance to the incomprehensible, he stated that a clear line leads from the heroes of the past to the dead of today.[19] Renowned novelist A. B. Yehoshua felt that the national mourning was extreme, signaling the peculiarity of the prolonged Lebanon War:

> You can see here some kind of a guilt feeling of a hedonistic society that enjoys the life of peace, a kind of perpetual guilt towards the soldiers, those who are dubbed as sitting ducks. Maybe this feeling led to a decision of a national mourning day. The sense of solidarity was all inclusive because it fell in the stitches between war and accident. The mourning following this accident was much greater than had it been a plane of Israeli tourists on their way to Europe.[20]

Seeking to determine the causes of the crash, Minister of Defense Yitzhak Mordechai commissioned an inquiring committee, headed by former head of the air force, General David Ivri. Some high officers were eventually punished, though the causes of the accident were never fully explained and were attributed mainly to the harsh weather conditions, and the fact that, due to security constraints, the helicopters flew in total darkness. Some of the grieving families contested the conclusions, and fourteen went all the way to the Israeli high court, claiming that the committee report was a whitewash determined by camaraderie within the air force. The high court declined their claims, and the quest for answers on what caused the accident did not become a major issue in the public discourse.

Another argument to reach the Israeli high court was whether to name the event "an accident" or "a disaster." This might seem a trivial semantic quibble, but for the parents it was important to determine that their tragedy was a national disaster, not just a mishap, and is therefore connected to fulfilling a national duty. On the standard military tombstones in the military cemeteries the inscription read: "fell in the line of duty in the helicopter accident." The parents demanded that the inscriptions be changed to "fell on his way to military action in the helicopter disaster." The Ministry of Defense claimed that every accident is a disaster for the families involved, and as commemoration is a unified national endeavor, naming only one event a "disaster" would constitute an unjustified discrimination against other families. In May 2001 the court ruled in the parents' favor. The court ruling was a legal expression of the growing power of parents vis-à-vis the Israeli military establishment, even in matters of framing the nature of military incidents.

The helicopter disaster was probably one of the most urgent motivations for Israel's eventual evacuation of Lebanon on 2000. In the wake of the event, Four Mothers, the most influential social movement opposing Israel's stay in Lebanon, was formed.[21] The accident thus became a singular event that symbolized the war, and therefore its commemoration became the main commemorative effort regarding the way that the war would be understood in future years. In retrospect, eleven years later, the IDF chief of staff Gabi Ashkenazi said: "there are events in the life of a people that are burned in consciousness as a collective moment—you understand the meaning and realize that a substantial thing has happened. Such was the helicopter disaster."[22]

A Disaster in Search for a Commemoration

The large number of dead in the helicopters' disaster, coming from different social groups, brought about a multitude of commemorative practices, some collective and others private. The entire gamut of memorial options in contemporary Israel was represented, in numerous locations and by a variety of entrepreneurs. Before concentrating on the main monument, some attention should be given to other, prior, alternatives, of which the adaptation of Erez Shtark's lyrics is but one example. Due to the number and variety of commemorations, I shall mention just a few, those that exemplify the transformation of commemorative practices in Israel and the richness of the commemorative sphere.

At the spot where one of the helicopters fell in the *moshav* of Shear Yishuv, near an empty guesthouse, various makeshift commemorative elements were placed, created, or declared. At the time it was not at all clear if the main place of remembrance would be at the spot where either of the helicopters crashed, and if so, which of the two. There was a potential tension inherent in each decision, as some of the parents wanted to remember their sons on the exact spot where they died. At the moshav, the object to consume most of the longing was a tall old oak tree that was hit by the crash, yet survived. In Israeli sacred iconography trees symbolize life, and the injured tree appealed to the grieving parents as a memorial site.[23] Eventually the tree had to be cut down, an event that rekindled tragic memories as a symbolic repetition of the initial disaster. The name of Shear Yeshuv became synonymous with the disaster, and the residents of the community chose to commemorate the disaster themselves, planting a forest holding seventy-three trees. Apart from that, the local residents tried to drive out other commemorative tributes as they disrupted local daily life.

Many parents made their private decisions regarding the commemoration of their children. Yoav Keidar cultivated a hill near his home kibbutz, Negba, as a commemorative forest in memory of his son and a friend who also perished in the crash, the hill of Tom and Tomer. Until the inauguration of the official northern monument, this site was the gathering place of the bereaving families on the annual commemoration day. It serves the kibbutz educational activities on a daily basis, and is understood to represent correctly the memory of the fallen soldiers. "This is not the battle heritage. I despise this term. This is a life heritage," claims Tom's father, "my biggest fear is that the hill will become a white elephant [meaning that it will be neglected—M.F.] . . . Eventually I estimated that there will always be Zionist people who would continue to take care of the place." A friend of Tomer added: "For me this is not a memorial garden like other monuments dispersed around the land. Tomer loved nature, and he is present in this place more than any other place."[24]

For their part, Avi Afner's parents organized walks around Israel. Their first was in 2002, when they set out on the famous "Israel Trail," traversing most of Israel's best-known hiking sites; subsequently, they have attempted to carry out this project on an almost yearly basis. Their commemorative journey takes almost two months, starting at the southern tip of Israel, Eilat, concluding at the site of the new monument in the northern tip of the country, where they hold a ceremony on Israel's Independence Day. Portions of the route are dedicated to different fallen soldiers, and those soldiers' family and friends often join the march. Trying to widen the appeal, the journey is dedicated to those who died in the helicopter crash, in Israel's wars in general, and in terrorist attacks. With the hundreds who join the group along the way, there emerges a community of bereavement that walks together while discussing questions of Israeli identity and coping experiences. Every day of the journey starts with an introduction of the participants, a ritual commemorating those to whom the day is dedicated and a short prayer. The name of the fallen soldier, Avi, was turned into an acronym "efshar beyachad"—we can do it together—accentuating the inclusive nature of this commemoration.[25]

Other parents took a much more personal approach to commemoration. Arie Rosenberg, Shahar's father, decided to spend his life doing what his son would have done had he remained alive. He went on tours around the world and shared his experiences on the Internet:

> The idea of a trip to Australia started to flow in my veins while I was fulfilling my son's last request. Shahar fell in the helicopter tragedy above Sha'ar Yeshuv. He left me the job of drinking a large glass of orange juice in Manali, a picturesque town in the north of India just below the range of snow-topped mountains of the Himalaya. There I vowed that as long as I could, as long as I would have the strength, I would fulfill what Shahar was unable to do. I would see with my/his eyes, smell with my/his nose, hear with my/his ears and taste with my/his tongue all the far and distant places that had always been of interest to him, places that he had always intended on visiting and seeing. There and then I decided that my youngest son would from then on become my shadow like the words of Yehuda Poliker's song "My shadow and I set out on the way."[26]

As personal as this type of commemoration may be, the Internet enabled the father to collectivize it in surprising ways, developing an audience for his trips. He went on to publish booklets, dedicated to his son, telling of his travels. At various places the dead were commemorated through monuments, either dedicated to the remembrance of the entire disaster or individual soldiers. At the Beit Lid army camp there stands a monument for the dead from the Nahal Brigade, and in the city of Petah Tikva there are both a general large monument and a synagogue commemorating the event. The various commemorations catered mainly to individual needs of parents and specific requests of institutions or municipalities. While the collective nature of the disaster was invariably mentioned, each of the dead was taken back into his living world and commemorated according to the wishes of his close relatives and friends.

The most collective commemoration the parents held, apart from the monument itself, is a gathering on the annual commemorative day, at a school at kibbutz Dafna. Starting from the third year after the disaster, the parents organized, along with the army, a series of meetings in which issues of military leadership, commitment, and ethics are discussed. High officers attend, along with soldiers stationed nearby and youth groups. The daylong gathering culminates with a ceremonial event, which dignitaries such as Israel's president and prime minister often attend, and the minister of defense and the army chief of staff invariably do. The day is an impressive collaborative tour de force, where the parents declare their trust and faith in the army, while the army declares of its long commitment to the bereaved parents and to its own tragic history. It should be noted that, notwithstanding the participation of a few hundred, the gathering on the northern border of Israel is to a large extent a private one, of those affected by the disaster, not observed in any way by the general Israeli public. The challenge facing the creators of the main monument was how to, at the very least, replicate the coalition created in the memorial days; namely, to articulate the desires of individual parents, create a place that is meaningful within the military ethos, while making the tragedy memorable to the rapidly forgetting Israeli public.

Building the Monument: Power, Finance, and the Changing Place of Memory

Constructing an expensive public monument is invariably a complex and contested procedure, and the helicopter disaster monument was no exception. Still, the unique contours of the power struggle are important in understanding and mapping the changing Israeli commemorative sphere. Throughout the long process, the parents of the dead soldiers were the driving force behind the construction. As a group the parents were relatively young—in their forties and fifties—many of them having the means, energy, and motivation to articulate and collectivize their tragedy. Not all parents joined the group; some had reservations on the forced, arbitrary, collectivity that unified the parents, based solely on common tragedy, and others did not want to have a constant painful reminder of a tragedy they still could not comprehend. A mother stated: "as far as I am concerned, the state ends in the north of the Sea of Galilee."[27]

The Ministry of Defense and the IDF offered their assistance, yet ultimately took a back seat to the families' initiatives. This division of labor was customary in Israel through its history, yet the extent to which it was executed in this case reflected the transformation in Israeli bereavement culture, as the state and its organs receded from enforcing their concepts of heroic death and attendant aesthetic conventions. The dominance of the parents in the process entailed lengthy delays because of their internal dynamics, recurring problems of funding, and relative weakness vis-à-vis various national and municipal agencies, until the privatization of bereavement, reaching new extremes, enabled the monument to be eventually finished.

The concept of collectively commemorating the fallen soldiers sprung up almost instantly after the disaster. The parents organized, held a meeting, and created a committee. The minister of defense, Yitzhak Mordechai, suggested a low-key commemoration whose nature he did not specify, an idea that was declined out of hand by most of the parents. Some of them went to the opposite extreme and suggested a large functional public building, yet their idea was rejected on grounds of high construction and maintenance costs. Famous Israeli sculptor Dani Karavan was consulted. As one of the dead soldiers was his relative, he declined to take a formal active part in the planning and construction, yet, drawing on his vast experience, he pointed out the critical importance of maintenance costs, helping the parents and architects to reach crucial decisions.

The members of kibbutz Dafna were reluctant to relinquish the grounds near their cemetery required for the project, and the project stalled for six years. The Ministry of Defense came to the aid of the parents and arranged for alternative land to be given to the kibbutz in exchange, yet the negotiations went on for years. According to the parents, the kibbutz demanded, apart from land, a license for an illegal restaurant built nearby, and to prevent visitors to the monument from passing through the Kibbutz. "Do you want us to arrive by helicopters?" was the sarcastic response of a bitter mother. "They have forgotten that our soldiers, our sons, fell in defense of their village," added another parent.[28] The kibbutz members claimed that the land was their livelihood and pointed to the nearby graveyard: "anyone who is critical of the people of Dafna should first go to the kibbutz cemetery and check how many of their sons are buried there."[29] Eventually, eleven square kilometers were specified for the monument, and in return the kibbutz received more than double that land size.[30] This lengthy affair is yet another manifestation of the implications of the privatization of bereavement: even the kibbutz members, known champions of national causes, were unwilling to sacrifice resources for such a lofty cause without worthy material compensation.

The complex monument was designed by architect Shlomit Shlomo, garden designers Haim Cohen and Gilead Sharon, and sculptor Rami Feldstein, with Dani Karavan participating in an advisory capacity. The parents were involved in all decisions, yet Feldstein claimed that he enjoyed complete artistic freedom. The parents had final say on the artists that were chosen, while the state had no say in the construction of the main monument commemorating the Lebanon War and soldiers killed in the line of duty.

As a private group effort, the construction's financing was a major burden on the parents. They turned to the Department for Soldier Commemoration at the Ministry of Defense for assistance, yet they encountered a bureaucratic problem: according to the criteria of money allocations, the recipients have to be defined as an army unit, such as infantry, armor, or intelligence. In a similar disaster in 1977, fifty-four soldiers were killed in a helicopter crash in the Jordan Valley, yet most belonged to the paratrooper unit, and therefore their monument could be funded. In the case of the 1997 disaster, the soldiers belonged to numerous different units; no specific unit was willing to take sole representational responsibility, and the parents would not have agreed to have their sons commemorated under the auspice of the "wrong" unit. The parents brought their problem to a special exceptions committee, and in a precedential ruling their group was defined for that matter an army unit, allowing them to receive funds for their monument.

Altogether, the Ministry of Defense financed roughly a third of the monument's cost, which soared to $1.2 million (USD). The rest of the funding came from private or institutional donors, and the burden of securing the money, taken on voluntarily by some parents, was a difficult one indeed. Many took loans to help the project, and some contractors waived their fees. On the tenth anniversary of the disaster one of the leading women of the group was interviewed in the media and voiced her bitterness on the inability to finish the project. At that point Arkadi Gaidamak, one of Israel's richest citizens, a flamboyant and shady oligarch emigrating from the former Soviet Union under the threat of legal prosecution in France, stepped in to add the needed sum of half a million dollars. This was by no means Gaidamak's first offering to replace the state in matters that are considered part of its established role: he offered his help to the residents of Sderot attacked by rocket missiles from the Gaza Strip, and volunteered to buy army gear for Israeli soldiers, all highly controversial acts giving rise to public debates regarding the diminishing role of the state. The fact that a project defined as national and sacred was being financed by a private citizen (who speaks very little Hebrew) reflects on the deep changes within bereavement culture in Israel.

Publicist Avirama Golan discussed the uncomfortable feelings the bereaved parents had about Gaidamak's contribution. Wealthy individuals have always given donations for public causes, and Gaidamak's attempt to use his money to gain acceptance and respectability in his new society was nothing new in Israel or elsewhere. Golan detected the uneasy reception by the public as well as the significance of the event for the changing Israeli socioeconomic order: "The public, seeing how the last threads of government responsibility to its citizens are being torn, how easily wealthy individuals penetrate all systems and gain power and influence that circumvent politics and government, deciphers the story of the helicopter disaster monument in the same fashion. Yes, the commemoration internet site of the Ministry of Security still declares that commemoration is not a private but a public affair, but in this story . . . the sense of abandonment and disintegration have overcome those facts, and the parents have acted according to that spirit. And thus came the only stable factor today in Israeli society—money—and also bought the commemoration."[31]

The parents themselves were frustrated by having to accept Gaidamak's contribution. Bracha, Erez Shtark's mother, said in an interview: "It is disgusting that the state does not finance the construction of the monument and relies on donations of private individuals. Were the children killed in the service of the state or in the service of Gaidamak? . . . In this case, the state does not have to be a *shnorer*."[32] Indeed, the disquiet infiltrated into the Knesset, where MP Ran Cohen proposed a law demanding the state take responsibility for financing commemorations. The monument was finally inaugurated eleven years after the disaster, on February 13, 2008, but that was not the end of the parent's' financial ordeal. The maintenance fee, reaching about US$25,000 annually, became the next problem. Observing similar monuments around the country left the parents worried: apart from the few that are regularly visited, most deteriorate due to lack of constant maintenance. The responsibility lies with the municipal council. In the case of the helicopter disaster monument, the local Higher Galilee municipal council tried to distance itself from the event and the responsibility to commemorate, claiming that the crash actually took place in the sky of the adjacent Mevo't Hermon municipality. As it looks at this moment in time, the emerging compromise is that annually the Ministry of Defense will provide the requisite budget to the Higher Galilee municipal council. However, the ordeal of commemoration does not stop with the completed construction, but is recreated anew at certain intervals and is an ongoing process that has no clear resolution in sight.

Symbolizing Disaster

In their planning, the architects took into account three major factors that influence the building of most monuments: artistic aspirations; the requirements of their clients (the bereaving parents in this case); and traditional motifs seen in other monuments, which they either wanted to emulate or to contrast.[33] Israeli monuments have certain salient characteristics that the helicopter disaster monument has adopted, and in certain places transformed. An examination done by Ester Levinger has shown that 60 percent of the monuments in Israel are walls, pillars, or huge stones, another 30 percent are actual statues, and 10 percent are environmental elements. The names of the fallen soldiers are usually mentioned in a list that does not differentiate according to rank. Often remnants of the war, such as weapon parts, army vehicles, or cement and concrete fortresses, serve to remind the visitor of the context in which the soldiers have served and died. In some cases the monument is part of a larger complex, consisting of a ceremony plaza and lecture rooms. The writing on the monument often borrows biblical themes, connecting the fallen soldiers to heroes from the mythical history of the nation.[34] The expansive and complex helicopter disaster monument used most of the above attributes.

The first ideas were very different from the ones eventually accepted. Architect Yosef Nachmani initially offered a glass cube from which a light beam would illuminate the sky for half an hour daily, starting at 7 p.m., the hour the helicopters crashed: "The glass, in its transparency, comes to describe the purity of the dead, the interior of the children," Nachmani suggested. He also offered a high leaning watchtower that, apart from enabling the visitor to see the view, would instill the fear of falling and insecurity in an attempt to evoke the terror of the soldiers' final moments. The newspaper reporting on this plan assured the readers that there would be railings for safety.[35] The plan that was eventually adopted would follow a different, less dramatic, logic.

The helicopter disaster monument consists of two distinct spaces with different commemorative logic, loosely tied together, sharing an uneasy common existence one next to the other. Ritualistic spaces are often likewise divided, in a way that encapsulates complementing and often contrasting messages. To bring one notable example, in the Vietnam Veterans Memorial, a statue of three soldiers was added near the original granite wall by a different architect, as an attempt to correct what many thought was an infuriating diminishing of the honor of the troops.[36] In the case of the helicopter memorial, the two components fulfill different functions, correcting each other's weak spots and enabling a richness of symbolism and locations that holds a better chance of attracting visitors. In one site, the forest where one of the helicopters fell, there is a secluded spot on a quiet stream, shaded by trees, forming a place for reflection. The second space is a man-made environment, a wide field with a reflecting pool, huge rocks, a water tunnel, lawn, and some other components.

The monument developed around the actual place where one of the helicopters fell. The idea of creating a place of memory on the exact location of the disaster preceded the monument. Soon after the tragedy, members of the nearby kibbutz placed pebbles, each naming one of the fallen soldiers, on the tree. A large board with the engraved names was also added by one of the parents. Soon the makeshift emergent elements started to deteriorate and disappear and were replaced by similar elements—pebbles with names and a plaque—that could better withstand stormy weather. The early commemoration was institutionalized and incorporated into the larger, architecturally designed, commemorative space.

Undoubtedly the most impressive commemorative element within that space was contributed by nature itself: the stream and the tree, creating a shaded spot of reflection, and contrasting dramatically with the horror that occurred years before on exactly the same spot. The tranquil ambiance is accompanied by an uncanny feeling of sitting on the exact location of the crash, where the dead soldiers are substituted by pebbles with their names. The confined space invites visitors to present their own contributions, such as placing candles, pictures and poems next to the names on the stones. One young group that I have seen was excited to find the name of Erez Shtark, the writer of the song they liked, and played his song to him, adding another morbid layer to the evolution of that song. The scope of the disaster means that many cities and towns in Israel have their "private" dead soldier, and different groups concentrate on a specific name they feel especially attached to.

The more expressive and extrovert monument is outside the shade of the tree and consists of a wide field with a reflecting pool and seventy-three massive granite boulders on a grassy lawn. Submerged right at the surface level of the pool are the same number of basalt plaques with the names of the soldiers, and visitors have developed the practice of placing stones on the plaques in accordance with Jewish tradition whereby a visitor leaves a stone at the gravesite. The water from the pool cascades through a narrow stone canal toward another pool, where it swirls and disappears into the ground. Unlike the area under the tree, this field and its elements were meticulously planned, and each component is rich with symbolic meaning, all discussed and described openly by the

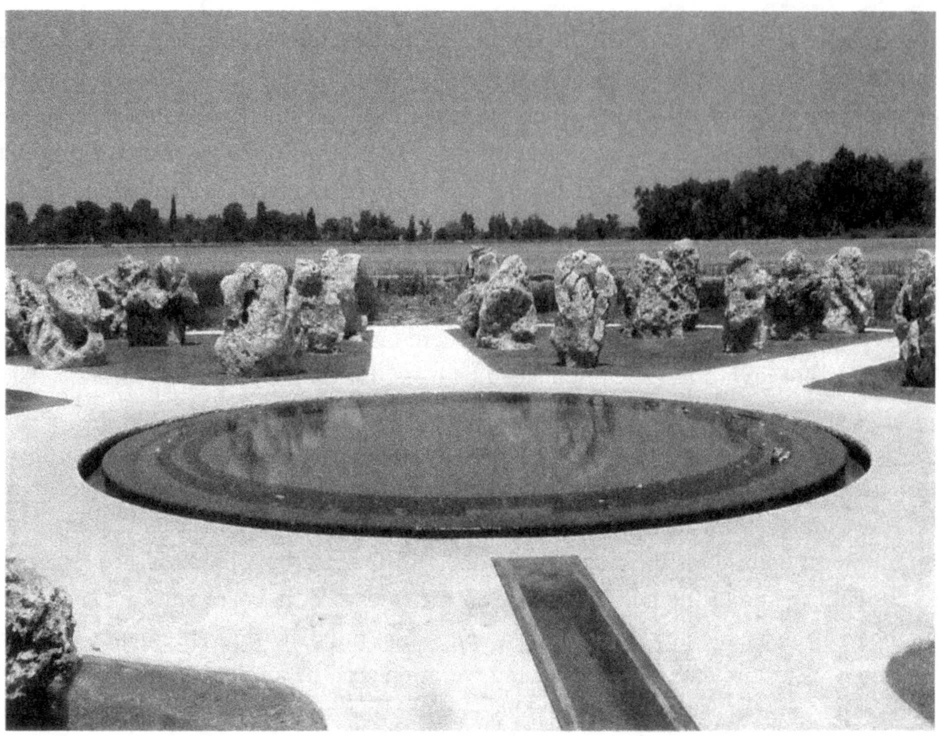

The reflecting pool and stones at the monument.

planners and bereaved parents. The common motif of taking a recognizable part of the army vehicle and using it as a monument was transformed into allegory. Assumingly, seeing an actual part of a helicopter would have been too traumatic for the parents, and instead the helicopters are symbolized in ways that are far from obvious so as not to overburden a grieving visitor. In the pool there are three whirls, the stones are set around the pool in a circle, and the water in the cascading pool whirls around making a loud noise, all meant to allude to the shape and noise of a propeller. It takes some imagination to connect the symbol to the symbolized.

The reflecting pool is an idea that appears in many commemorative sites, in and out of Israel. "Water symbolizes life," said Raya Afner. "You find here a symbolization of death combined with life. . . . We wanted a living site, not a monument, a site that will commemorate the seventy-three fallen soldiers through pleasure and beauty, and not only from the hard place of death."[37] The idea of equality in the face of death was of great importance, and there existed a prerequisite to have the parents of all soldiers agree to participate with their son's name mentioned in the privately built monument. This ideal was shattered as the two Arab names were defiled while the monument was still under construction. Afner was quick to encounter the danger and declare the equality of all commemorated on the monument: "the soldiers fell while they were on their way to defend the very ugly people who defiled the monument. Fadi and Camal, just like my son, went to protect residents, and it does not matter if they are Arabs,

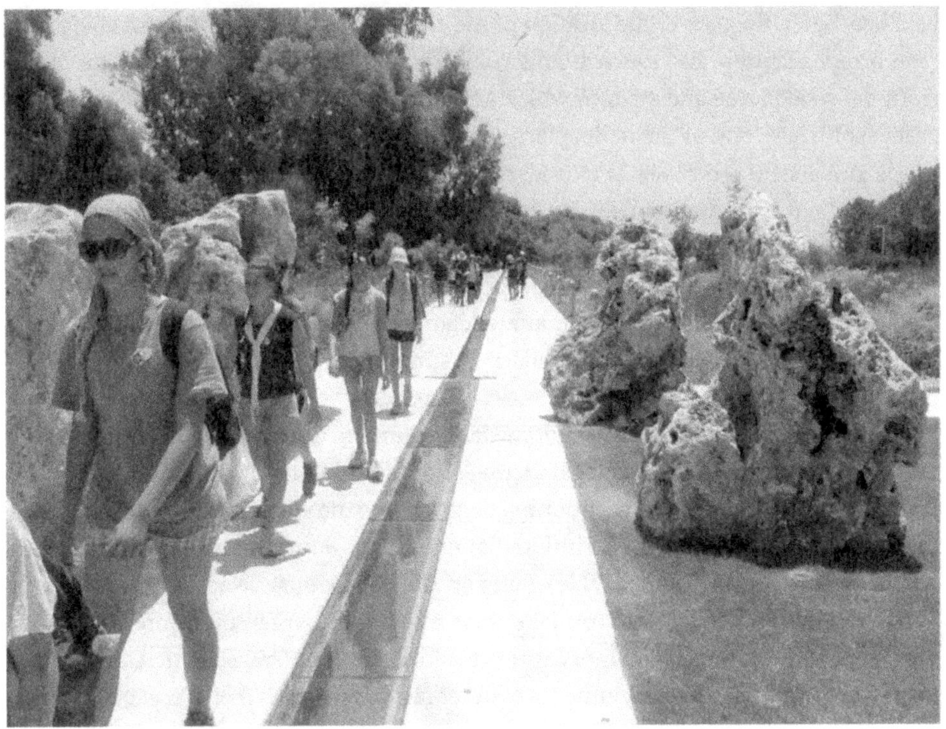

Visiting children walking past the cascading water and the stones at the helicopter disaster monument.

Druze or Jews."[38] The seventy-three huge boulders were an attempt to add objects symbolizing the unmovable and eternal. Unembellished rocks taken from the area were used, each weighing twelve tons. The planners wanted each to have a name, but the parents refused, claiming that they didn't want the place to look like a graveyard.

In the lawn there are red windflowers that blossom only for a short period each winter. The idea the flowers express, like that of water, is of death and rejuvenation. Haim Cohen, the gardener of the project, explained: "windflowers symbolize the cycle of life. They blossom in winter and die in the summer." This is another motif that was important for the architects, creating a monument that changes its appearance through the seasons, and the comforting symbolism of revival was important for the parents. The idea is invisible to the visitor coming out of season, and the symbolism is incomprehensible even to those who see the field when the flowers blossom.

Between the two spaces there is a large, twenty-ton limestone rock that tells the story of the fateful night and lists alphabetically the names of the fallen soldiers. Otherwise, it is difficult to decipher the meaning of the monument by looking at its different components. Looking from above, the assumed place where God, the dead soldiers, or other flyers over the field can see, the monument assumes meaning. The large propeller alluded to in the reflecting pool and the granite stones, with the small one in the draining pool, connected by the cascading water tunnel, together appear from above to be a helicopter, flying over the location of the crash. Again, the visitor is not able to see "the bigger picture," and the symbolism is geared to an invisible outside gaze. Apart from the shaded tree and stream, which are "obvious" in the sense that they mark the exact spot where one of the helicopters crashed, the rest of the commemorative space needs guidance if the visitor is to understand the meaning of the obscure symbolism. For Israelis, this formation does connote commemoration, yet each component begs for a specific explanation.

The monument is thematically conservative, building on such accepted symbolism as rocks, flowers, a reflection pool, and allegories to parts of the vehicle, though the symbolism tends to be obscure and reflect artistic preferences. The spread-out nature of the monument enables it to include most components found in other monuments in Israel, making it, in a sense, a meta-or mega-monument. Common in Israeli commemorative culture is the idea of expressing grief and loss rather than nationalism, heroism, and purposefulness, and not mentioning or specifying the enemy. The very existence of the monument attests to Israel's influential militaristic ethos, yet its components tend not to be militaristic in nature. When going private, the parents saved motifs of previous national monuments yet tried to make their monument larger and more impressive than others. The parents as memory agents could decide for themselves that they wanted to emulate and transcend monuments of other historical events that preceded them.

In Conclusion: The Changing Commemorative Space in Israel

Arriving at the monument on an unusually hot Tuesday morning in July, I was surprised to see how many people visited the site with me. Most of the visitors I saw on that quite ordinary day were members of youth movements, arriving by the hundreds in organized groups. Other hikers stopped at the place, Israeli tourists in buses were taken there by their tour guide, and there were some visitors who came individually. Some hikers emerged from the woods after walking in the stream, using the monument as a stop along the way through the landscape of northern Israel. It was obvious that the monument was on its way toward becoming a focal point for tourists and for secular-national pilgrims wishing to pay their respect and express their condolences.

Israelis take commemoration very seriously. The memorial activity following the helicopter disaster is a case in point, as a multitude of projects—much more than the number of the dead soldiers—have sprung up, some newly invented and very imaginative, others that keep evolving, and many that disappear quickly. Monuments, memorial gardens, memory books, Internet sites, hikes, bicycle rides, songs, and written texts are only a few of the many efforts, most of them with a keen and experienced eye toward their own tragic temporality, and therefore attuned to the costs of maintenance and the power of ritual to keep up the relevance of the horrific events in the mind of Israelis.

The problem encountered by the grieving parents in the wake of the disaster was twofold. On the one hand, under the growing specter of privatization they could not

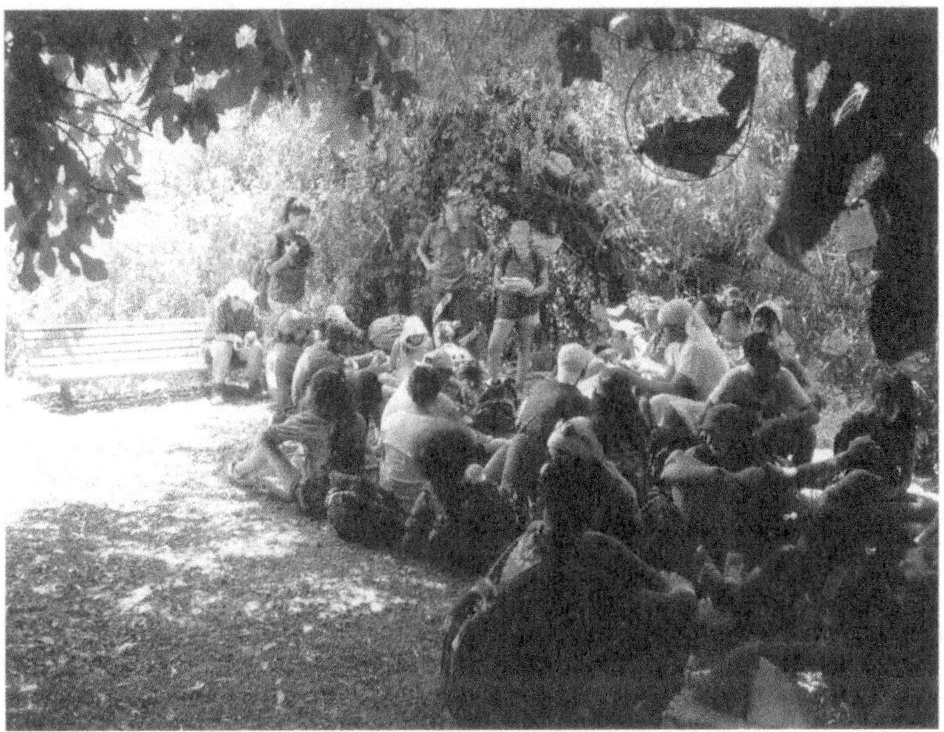

Youth movement children visiting the helicopter disaster memorial site.

whole-heartedly entrust the commemoration to government agencies. On the other hand, the Lebanon War itself, and within it the disaster in which their sons perished, did not fit well with the basic concepts of battle heroism worthy of national remembrance. The soldiers died due to a tragic accident, and apart from demanding more cautiousness in the future, the lessons to be learned from the event were very limited. The dead did not sacrifice themselves for the country, nor did they avert a great danger at the cost of their lives. A hint of the "inconvenience" of the parents coping with the futility of their children's death can be seen in their legal struggle to have the event considered a disaster on the way to engage in battle rather than merely an "accident," thereby salvaging some semblance of heroism.

The helicopter crash symbolizes the Lebanon War in general, a formative experience for a generation of young Israelis, and a bleeding wound accompanying Israeli culture, society, and politics for two decades. With the IDF fighting against an elusive enemy while civilians protest at home, with no end or clear goal in sight, the war became an epitome of futility (overshadowed only by the Second Lebanon War six years later). The relative peace that came to the region after the unilateral withdrawal in 2000 reinforced the sense that the war could either be averted or could have ended sooner, and the heavy casualty toll the Israeli army paid was avoidable. This Lebanese military context defines sacrifice as futile and sets a challenge to memory entrepreneurs who struggle to render meaning to the monuments they conceive.

The context of globalization, neoliberal economy, and the transformation of Israeli society toward capitalism and growing privatization place further obstacles in front of parents wishing to commemorate their children. With the weakening of the state, the families could not turn to a clear authority that would determine the appropriate commemoration, its size and cost, or even ensure the erection of a respectable monument. On the other hand, the families could act relatively free of state supervision, deciding for themselves what their monument would look like, and through guilt, pressure the state to support a private enterprise. The result was that practically all of the commemoration was conceived, produced, and financed by the families and private institutions, land was acquired from a kibbutz only after years of negotiation, and an oligarch such as Gaidamak stepped in to subsidize the finishing of the monument. It should be remembered, however, that constructing a fully private monument was never an option, and not only because the most important resource—land—had to be secured from state agencies; the only belief system that could supply meaning to the grieving parent, whose children perished while in the army, was the national one. While the state representatives found it hard to comply with the demands of the parents, the parents insisted that their efforts are connected to nationalism and heroism.

Returning to Shtark's song, it can now be seen how indicative it is of the context in which it was written and composed. Fighting terrorism, the song contends, is dangerous, yet not that much different from being hurt by a woman. The soldier's father has nothing to say about the national contribution of his son, and all he wishes for is for is his safe return. If there is betrayal and disappointment in the song, it is the soldier hurting his family through his own death, for which he feels obliged to apologize. Israeli dead soldiers are returning to their families, as the nation that sends them to battle lessens its involvement in their commemoration. "If something happens to you / There is no point in my living / There is no point in tomorrow"—isn't this pointlessness exactly what the national bereavement culture was meant to encounter?

Notes

The research for this essay was done with the help of Moran Ben-Shoan, Adi Berko, and Mor Dvorkin.

1. To see a video clip with the song, see http://www.youtube.com/watch?v=IKDWRWqPS3s&feature=related. This clip is critical of war and militarism, transforming the soldiers to children. For a different presentation, stressing war and bereavement, see http://www.youtube.com/watch?v=LmwQBvgVxm8&feature=related.

2. Some of the books reflecting on the soldier experience in Lebanon or in the Occupied Territories, are (all in Hebrew): Barak Hamdani, *Dust* (Jerusalem: Keter, 2006); Shai Lahav, *Go to Gaza* (Tel Aviv: Ma'ariv, 2005); Or Spibak, *Whose Golani* (Jerusalem: Scene, 2001); Boaz Newman, *Good Soldier* (Lod: Zmora-Bitan, 2001); David Bossi, *Mother Misses the Words* (Jerusalem: Keter, 2006); and Ron Leshem, *If There Is a Heaven* (Lod: Zmora-Bitan, 2005).

3. The same holds for two other successful Israeli movies discussing the Lebanon War, *Waltz with Bashir* (directed by Ari Folman, 2008) and *Lebanon* (directed by Shmulik Maoz, 2009).

4. Hanah Naveh, "The Israeli Experience and the Experience of a Female Israeli," in *Will You Hear My Voice: Representations of Women in Israeli Culture,* ed. Yael Atzmon (Tel Aviv and Jerusalem: Van Leer and Hakibutz Hameuhad, 2001), 303–24 (Hebrew); Hanan Hever, "Gender, Body, and the National Subject: Israeli Women's Poetry in the War of Independence," in *The Military and Militarism in Israeli Society,* ed. Edna Lomsky-Feder and Eyal Ben-Ari (Albany: State University of New York Press, 1999), 225–60.

5. Uri Ram, *The Globalization of Israel: McWorld in Tel Aviv, Jihad in Jerusalem* (New York: Routledge, 2007).

6. David Ohana, *The Last Israelis* (Tel Aviv: Hakibutz Hameuhad, 1998) (Hebrew).

7. Emmanuel Sivan, *The 1948 Generation: Myth, Profile, and Memory* (Tel Aviv: Ma'arachot, Ministry of Defense Publishing, 1991) (Hebrew).

8. On Israeli militaristic culture, see Baruch Kimmerling, *The Invention and Decline of Israeliness: State, Society, and the Military* (Berkeley: University of California Press, 2001); Uri Ben-Eliezer, "The Civil Society and the Military Society in Israel," *Palestine-Israel Journal of Politics, Economics, and Culture* 12, no. 1 (2005): 49–55; Yagil Levy, *The Other Army of Israel: Materialistic Militarism in Israel* (Tel Aviv: Yediot Aharonot, 2003) (Hebrew).

9. According to Ilana Shamir, there are more than one thousand monuments in Israel commemorating somewhat more than twenty thousand dead, which is a higher proportion by far than any other state in the world. Ilana Shamir, *Commemoration and Remembrance* (Tel Aviv: Am Oved, 1996) (in Hebrew). For further research on Israeli commemoration, see Avner Ben-Amos and Ilana Bet-El, "Holocaust Day and Memorial Day in Israeli Schools: Ceremony, Education, and History," *Israel Studies* 4, no. 1 (1999): 258–84; Yoram Bilu and Eliezer Witztum, "War-Related Loss and Suffering in Israeli Society: A Historical Perspective," *Israel Studies* 5, no. 2 (2000): 1–32; Maoz Azaryahu, *State Cults: Celebrating Independence and Commemorating the Fallen in Israel, 1948–1956* (Sede Boker Campus: Ben-Gurion Research Center, 1995); Matityahu Mayzel and Ilana Shamir, eds., *Patterns of Commemoration* (Tel Aviv: Ministry of Defense Publishing, 2000) (Hebrew); Udi Lebel and Zeev Drory, "Undecided Past—National Identities and Politics of Diversity: The Mount Eitan Commemoration Site," *International Journal of Euro-Mediterranean Studies* 2 (2008): 215–38.

10. A starting point for this hierarchy of death can be seen in the early years of Zionist settlement in the Land of Israel. Yonatan Frenkel, "The 'Yizkor' Book of 1911: A Remark on National Myths during the Second Aliah," *Contemporary Judaism* 4 (200?): 67–96 (Hebrew).

11. Rubik Rosenthal, *Is Bereavement Dead?* (Jerusalem: Keter, 2001) (Hebrew).

12. A famous example is the bitter legal battle over the inscription on tombs in military cemeteries. See Yossi Katz, *Heart and Stone: The Story of the Military Tombstone in Israel* (Tel Aviv: Ministry of Defense Publishing, 2007) (Hebrew).

13. Udi Lebel has written on this issue in general and especially on the way it manifested itself in the past, as soldiers of right-wing clandestine paramilitary organizations were not incorporated into the national pantheon: Udi Lebel, "Beyond the Pantheon: Bereavement, Memory, and Strategy of De-Legitimation against Herut," *Israel Studies* 10, no. 3 (2005): 104–26.

14. Liav Sade-Beck, "Internet Commemoration in Israel" (PhD diss., Ben-Gurion University of the Negev, 2009 [Hebrew]).

15. Dan Miron, *Facing the Silent Brother: Essays on the Poetry of the War of Independence* (Jerusalem: Keter, 1992); Naveh, "The Israeli Experience and the Experience of Female Israeli."

16. Edna Lomsky-Feder, "The Memorial Ceremony in Israeli Schools: Between the State and Civil Society," *British Journal of Sociology of Education* 25, no. 3 (2004): 291–305; Edna Lomsky-Feder, "The Bounded Female Voice in Memorial Ceremonies," *Qualitative Sociology* 28, no. 3 (2005): 293–94.

17. Rosenthal, *Is Bereavement Dead?*, 10.

18. Yosef Lapid, "National Trauma," *Ma'ariv* 6, no. 2 (1997).

19. Moshe Shamir, "A Shouting Distance from Tel Hai," *Yediot Aharonot* 6, no. 2 (1997).

20. Ruti Sinai, "The Pain Race for Long Distances," *Haaretz* 9, no. 2 (1997).

21. Sara Helman, "From Soldiering and Motherhood to Citizenship: A Study of Four Israeli Peace Protest Movements," *Social Politics* 1, no. 2 (1999): 292–314.

22. Oshrat Nagar Lewit, "Remembering the 73 Soldiers," *Ma'ariv* 13, no. 2 (2008).

23. An interesting comparative example is the tree at Gush Etzion. See David Ohana, "Kfar Etzion: The Community of Memory and the Myth of Return," *Israel Studies* 7, no. 2 (2002): 145–74.

24. http://www.ynet.co.il/articles/0,7340,L-3360326,00.html.

25. http://www.avi-beshvil-israel.org.il/index.html.

26. http://www.shaharozenberg.co.il/letters_to_shahar.htm#3.

27. Sharon Gal, "20 Dunams of Memory," *Haaretz* 23, no. 2 (1999).

28. Eitan Rabin, "Waiting for a Monument," *Ma'ariv* 14, no. 1 (2001).

29. Avi Ashkenazi, "The Pain and the Anger," *Ma'ariv* 31, no. 8 (2000).

30. Appears in the Israel Land Administration website: www.mmi.gov.il.

31. See Avirama Golan, "A Monument Full of Money," *Haaretz* 14, no. 3 (2007).

32. http://www.ynet.co.il/articles/0,7340,L-3373149,00.html.

33. An elaboration of these principles with an interesting comparison can be seen at the Korean War Memorial at the Washington Mall; see Barry Schwartz and Todd Bayma, "Commemoration and the Politics of Recognition: The Korean War Veterans Memorial," *American Behavioral Scientist* 42 (1999): 946–67.

34. Ester Levinger and Ilana Shamir, *Commemoration and Remembrance* (Tel Aviv: Am Oved, 1996) (Hebrew).

35. Gal, "20 Dunams of Memory."

36. Robin Wagner-Pacifici and Barry Schwartz, "The Vietnam Veteran Memorial: Commemorating a Difficult Past," *American Journal of Sociology* 97 (1991): 376–420.

37. This and other interviews were done by Moran Ben-Shuan and Adi Berko.

38. http://www.ynet.co.il/articles/0,7340,L-1941673,00.html.

Chapter 3

"Cyclic Interruptions"

Popular Music on Israeli Radio in Times of Emergency

Danny Kaplan

Radio has become a part of the everyday fabric of life in industrialized societies. Precisely because of that, the effects of its omnipresence remain for the most part understudied.[1] The same holds true for contemporary Israeli radio. Although it often goes unnoticed, Israeli radio plays an important role in engineering the national mood, particularly in times of emergency. Radio has always played a central role in shaping Israel's Jewish-Zionist national culture. Since 1948 the state-owned public radio as well as the military radio enjoyed near-exclusivity in the local media and explicitly socialized listeners to Zionist values. In everyday life the radio specialized in educational programs, in regulating and disseminating spoken Modern Hebrew, and in inculcating Western-oriented music genres.[2] In times of emergency radio news bulletins were the first to report of terrorist attacks, announce the outbreak of war, and officially recruit the reserves by announcing call-up codes for military units. In these moments of crisis the radio's easy accessibility to events on the ground proved valuable for live reportage and provided the public with a sense of control.[3] Over the years the advances in the mobility of television coverage and the increase in televised "disaster marathons" have seemingly diminished the radio's explicit functions in times of emergency.[4] Yet despite this changing mediascape and the growing competition from television and the Internet, I describe in this chapter how contemporary Israeli radio has actually attained a unique positioning in covering national events, not as a bearer of news reports but as an engineer of collective emotions, by way of music broadcasting.

The current analysis draws on an ethnographic study of music programming in national and regional radio stations. Between 2004 and 2009 I conducted in-depth interviews with music programmers, broadcasters, and station directors in most stations and held participant observations in selected stations as well as in public sites of commemoration. I was interested in particular with broadcasting practices during memorial days and in times of emergency, examining how broadcasters and programmers produce musical shifts between everyday life, times of commemoration, and times of emergency.[5] In what follows, I focus on the role that music plays in engineering the national mood through the systematic patterning of music programming in times of emergency.

The Radio Music Revolution

Since the 1980s Israel's socialist political culture has undergone a gradual change toward liberal reforms and a free market economy. Accordingly, the government aspired to promote a policy of "open air" in the field of communications through privatization and decentralization of the electronic media. In 1995 the government established a new authority for commercial broadcasting, which chartered new radio stations on the basis of a regional geographical allocation of radio frequencies. Although the legislators sanctioned the new stations to provide "adequate representation of distinctive topics that would cater for the local residents and their special needs," in practice most regional stations have followed the public networks in presupposing and targeting a relatively homogenous secular or quasi-traditional Jewish audience within their designated region.[6]

The relative uniformity in radio broadcasting is manifest in the choices of music programming. As television and Internet-based communication have gradually come to dominate the verbal domain of mass media, radio stations across the world increasingly concentrate on the music domain.[7] A similar process has taken place in Israel. In 1971 the offshore "pirate" station known as The Voice of Peace began to broadcast Western pop music throughout the day. The military network, Galei Tzahal, developed a new format mixing popular music with talk material that significantly increased its appeal among the youth.[8] Faced with the mounting popularity of both stations, the Kol Israel network established in 1976 a new station, Reshet Gimel ("third station"), devoted solely to pop music and later on exclusively to Israeli pop music. The new music programming signaled a change of guard in Israel's popular genres. The dominant musical genre that crystallized in Zionist culture since the early twentieth century was Shirei Eretz Yisrael (Songs of the Land of Israel). The Hebrew lyrics focused on the national landscape, settlement, and agricultural activity, and the melodies were based on European folk and classical structures, predominantly Russian folk songs that the first waves of Ashkenazi settlers shared. With the spread of pop-rock music from the 1970s and onward, Shirei Eretz Yisrael gradually lost their exclusive hegemony.[9]

Two other nearly concurrent organizational changes contributed to what can be best described as the radio's "music revolution." First, in 1993 the military network established Galgalatz, a substation specializing in nonstop pop music combined with traffic updates. It introduced a successful format of easy listening known in the American radio market as "adult contemporary."[10] This repertoire revolves around soft rock hits spanning two or three decades, aiming for the twenty-five- to forty-nine-year-old age range. Galgalatz adapted its AC repertoire to include a slightly larger portion of contemporary hits to cater for the younger soldier and teenager audience and supplemented the Anglo-American repertoire with a share of Israeli songs with a similar soft rock sound. Second, with the establishment of regional radio many of the new stations tried to imitate and compete with Galgalatz in standardizing their music through AC playlist programming, while still maintaining some sense of distinctiveness to accomplish a strategic market positioning. However, almost none of the new stations adopted the characteristics of a pure "format radio" that airs a distinct and limited playlist targeting a differentiated musical "niche," as is common in the US radio market.[11] Rather, in their attempt to compete with the national networks over the general audiences, the regional stations adopted a combination of talk and music programming colored by mainstream pop music playlists. Eventually, much of the variation in the stations' musical style boils down to the choice of balance between English and Hebrew songs. Another important source of variation across radio stations derives from the adoption of Mizrahi music. Mizrahi ("Oriental") music developed among Jewish musicians of Middle Eastern and North African background influenced by popular Arabic music and had been systematically excluded from mainstream radio programming.[12]In recent years a selected list of Mizrahi artists broke through the playlists of mainstream influential stations such as Galgalatz by developing "light Mizrahi" music based on pop style arrangements.[13]

"Make the People Cry in a Second"

On the face of it, the music revolution on Israeli radio might suggest that much of the radio's earlier role in disseminating national values would diminish. For how can pop-rock music, with its universalistic, at times individualistic ethos, become a vehicle for national indoctrination? Rock in particular is often associated with values of sub-or counterculture and is often a vehicle for rebellious, antiwar sentiments.[14] However, nation-states often "ethnicize" global pop-rock genres and tailor their cosmopolitan appeal to meet local consensual needs.[15] Israeli radio programmers ingeniously link particular pop songs to current events in ways that purposely or inadvertently load them with national identification.

Although it operates in a more subtle way than news and talk programs, music programming can convey and manipulate national identification through the management of collective mood. This was an explicit assumption put forward by music programmers throughout their interviews, as Guy Bazak, the senior music programmer at Radio Haifa, has affirmed. Guy noted that the decision to switch to emergency programming is made by: "The program manager and by myself, according to our gut feeling. We provide the mood and we can change it. I can make a person cry in a second." This recognition of the intense emotional power of music radio is reflected in basic procedures of music programming. In their interviews, programmers have laid out a variety of considerations for selecting and editing songs in ways that combine aesthetics with mood.

Some considerations relate to the *internal* logic of programming, such as choosing the appropriate genre, beat, and groove for the specified time slot or finding the right common theme, whether musical or verbal, that would form a smooth link, or segue between songs. However, another major set of considerations deals with matching the song's content with collective *external* contingencies and events. (The single most common example programmers described is occasions of rainy days, a relatively infrequent occurrence in local Israeli weather that can be feted with innumerable songs rich in rain imagery.) As I elaborate below, the same logic of matching a song with external events has highly significant ramifications for the management of mood in emergency situations.

"On the Rooftops of Tel Aviv": From the First Gulf War to Tel Aviv's Centennial

Look for me tonight in closed spaces
Look for me at home and at strangers' places.
Indeed now is the end of autumn
The timing is right and you're not late
If you don't find me now
You won't get me later.
On the rooftops of Tel Aviv, something is happening tonight
Not from the heat, not from the cold, I've been hiding here
On the rooftops of Tel Aviv, someone is watching tonight
Shadows moving on white curtains.[16]

In 2009, the city of Tel Aviv celebrated its centennial anniversary. The official launching of the festivities took place in Rabin Square in a musical extravaganza roughly 250,000 people attended. Top artists performed popular songs dedicated to Tel Aviv, climaxing with the hit "On the Rooftops of Tel Aviv" performed by the original singer, Alona Daniel, together with three rock bands that were literally staged on high rooftops around the square. The song attained second place in the centennial "Tel Aviv song parade" conducted that year by Reshet Gimel public radio.[17] Daniel's rock song draws on an atmosphere of anticipation and lust. It seems to tap on the self-image of several generations of Tel Avivians, which at one point or another engaged in the city's secular singles scene. However, unlike other Tel Avivian songs recounting a similar lifestyle, Daniel's song has also a war history, which may account for its reclaimed popularity.

During the First Gulf War in the winter of 1991, most Israeli citizens were confined to their homes every night in anticipation of Iraqi missile attacks that were mainly targeting greater Tel Aviv. With the sounding of the alarm siren people were instructed to enter a designated "sealed room" and wear gas masks, fearing a chemical warhead attack. At the time, Israeli radio consisted only of the public networks, which served two main functions during the war. The first was strictly instrumental: both networks unified their news broadcast services and in addition assigned a "quiet channel" that aired only the alarm sirens and the ensuing announcements by military authorities, enabling people to sleep undisturbed at other times. But in their ongoing programming the stations also served a more expressive function, aiming to provide companionship and comfort during the many nights of tension. In this context, music programmers were confronted with the question of how to address the prolonged emergency situation without overburdening and dispiriting the audience. Because that war presented a prolonged period of crisis but with few local casualties and no active Israeli military involvement, programmers may have felt they could replace the solemn songs of Shirei Eretz Yisrael traditionally associated with times of emergency with a more contemporary, seemingly casual sound, as long as the lyrics somehow related to the collective experience of tension.[18]

Daniel's song, which had just come out a few months earlier, was the perfect solution. Its lyrics have no direct bearing on the war, but the imagery of closed spaces, Tel Aviv rooftops, the temporality of autumn's fading days, and the mixed emotions of alienation and anticipation that the song conveys, coincided perfectly with the general mood of a population hiding in sealed rooms, at times standing on rooftops in search of missile strikes. Similar to the mundane logic of matching a rain song to the external occurrence of stormy weather, radio programmers matched the song's imagery with this singular kind of "atmospheric turbulence." Consequently, despite the song's energetic rock mood and erotic undertones (that were far removed from the associations of war or nationalism), "On the Rooftops of Tel Aviv" emerged as one of the local "hymns" of the First Gulf War. As the song's war "heritage" became forever engraved in Israeli collective memory, it could be exalted as one of Tel Aviv's leading songs during its recent centennial anniversary.

Marketing Warfare: Radio Haifa during the Second Lebanon War

An ethnographic study of Radio Haifa during the Second Lebanon War in 2006 offers a closer look at some of the practices of Israeli radio during wartime. Radio Haifa is a regional-commercial radio station established in the privatization reforms of the 1990s, offering a mixture of regional and national news reportage, diverse talk shows, and a musical repertoire of mainstream Western and Hebrew pop songs. In recent years, in the face of the growing media field, Israeli radio stations have experienced a systematic drop in audience ratings. During the war and its aftermath Radio Haifa was one of a few stations that gained in popularity.[19] The port city of Haifa, similar to all communities in northern Israel, came under a continuous rocket strike by Hezbollah for over thirty days. Due to flaws in the conduct of the military Home Front Command and in the supply of public services by government agencies, the community was left to its own devices.[20] This vacuum was taken up by the local radio, which warned of incoming rockets, guided and consoled residents during their stay in shelters, and promoted rehabilitation efforts after the war.

The same logic of mobilizing the people guided the radio in its music programming throughout the war. The station purposely applied music as a means to manage the mood and morale of its audience. As soon as the war began, the radio's programming switched almost exclusively to Hebrew music. It did so not in the spirit of the solemn, downbeat songs associated with heavy casualties but following in the tradition that began in the First Gulf War of airing spirited pop songs with contemporary sound, as in the case of "On the Rooftops of Tel Aviv." In this vein, following every siren alarm (the subsequent news update and the authorization to leave the shelters) Radio Haifa's programmers would make a point of airing upbeat Hebrew songs. Guy Bazak, the senior music programmer, argued: "we didn't air sad songs, because we are not depressed. We wanted to keep the morale high from the moment people left the shelters and returned to ordinary life." Radio Haifa became a daily source of consolation and support for its listeners and a cathartic form of release during the routine hours that people spent outside the shelters.

Listeners wrote personal e-mails to the broadcasters, chatted on the radio's Internet forum, or went on air to publicly share their feelings and experiences. Guy describes how meticulously the radio practically engineered and regulated the mood of its listeners: "In the morning we had this [news and talk] show that screamed about the fact that nothing was being done [by the government] and asking why hadn't they declared the city of Haifa a warzone . . . screaming complaints and interviews [with residents] whose small businesses were collapsing." This was followed at nine in the morning with another talk show whose anchor is the wife of the mayor in the neighboring town of Kiryat Motzkin. Guy recalls that her broadcasting style was much more sensitive and soothing: "she would calm down the people from the area, speak to them from the heart. She communicated more emotionally." And finally, in the subsequent slot: "between 10 to 12 a.m. we broadcasted a retro party, the message being that we will go on dancing alongside the alarm sirens. We would play dance music and the alarm interrupted. So we'd give a fifteen-minute update and then went back to our party, until the next alarm." The war not only exposed the station to new audiences but also helped enhance its appeal in the long run. The station effectively "bought" its reputation by displaying a clear patriotic stance during the war, as Guy recalled: "Listeners who didn't know us and came to stay, stayed because we bought them with reports, with language, with talk, with care—people [from the radio staff] slept here in order to help in case of a siren alarm at night." Similar to the renewed popularity of the hymn from the First Gulf War, as Radio Haifa's "war heritage" became engraved in the local memory, the station gained critical stature in the community.[21]

Furthermore, in order to sustain peak ratings after the war, the station directors struggled to come up with musical solutions that would replace the sound of the sirens and still attract their newly discovered audience from the wartime, which turned out to be older than they assumed. Consequently, the station reformulated its main musical format based on a French model of "Radio Nostalgie," consisting of higher proportions of songs from the 1960s, '70s and '80s. Taken together, the station's commercial success benefited from its display of civic responsibility during wartime, combined with a calculated market positioning in its music programming.

Musical Mood Shifting as Ritual

The preceding examples demonstrate how Israeli radio in both public and commercial stations assumes a self-assigned role as an engineer of the national mood during war and other national emergencies. It does so by applying a basic programming logic of matching a song with external events in ways that correspond to the public mood in that instance. In some circumstances the programming intends to even alter and shift the public mood, as for instance when Radio Haifa aired upbeat Hebrew songs to boost the morale in between siren alarms. This accepted management of collective mood by the radio, and particularly the unique practice of mood shifting, is not limited to times of emergency. In fact, its roots can be traced to a long-standing ritual in Israeli radio that I elsewhere analyzed as the "commemorative mode" in radio programming.[22] This ritual emerges most distinctively in music programming during memorial days, when all radio stations play a restricted repertoire of songs commonly referred to as "memorial day songs," typically borrowed from the genre of Shirei Eretz Yisrael, but with a focus on themes of war and sacrifice. As the old genre faded from everyday music programming, memorial days have become a form of radio-borne museum dedicated to Shirei Eretz Yisrael.[23]

On these days of commemoration the homogeneity of programming schedules across stations is quite striking. Unlike the thematic variety of Shirei Eretz Yisrael, on Memorial Day programmers select a distinctly uniform set of songs from the canon of that day.[24] For instance, on Memorial Day for Fallen Soldiers the typical songs originate from the "heritage" of Israel's wars and center on themes of fallen soldiers, sacrifice, and friendship.[25] The broadcast day formally begins at 8:00 p.m., launched by a nationwide siren. An hour earlier most stations already begin airing calmer songs, still within their particular musical repertoire. But immediately following the siren almost all stations shift to canonic memorial songs and keep up this special programming throughout the next day, accompanying the ceremonial activities across the country. The memorial programming comes to a sudden end at 8:00 p.m. with the beginning of Independence Day celebrations. At this time all radio stations perform an abrupt switch from memorial songs to an upbeat rhythmic programming that prompts the celebrations of Independence Day. The musical movements to and from Memorial Day provide a collective mood shift, from the indeterminate, manifold feelings of everyday life to a synchronized, homogeneous sentiment of solemnity associated with commemoration and culminating with a twist to feelings of elation and jubilation associated with Independence Day.

These and other rituals of commemoration programming broadcasted by both public and regional-commercial stations several times a year is a distinctive feature of Israeli radio, which has critical ramifications for times of emergency.

Songs for Low-Intensity Warfare: Terrorist Attacks during the Second Intifada

Terrorist attacks with heavy casualties present a good example of emergency broadcasting that is closely linked to the practice of commemoration programming. Most Israeli radio stations, including commercial stations, respond to fatal attacks with an immediate shift of music programming to a repertoire of downbeat songs borrowed from the genre of Shirei Eretz Yisrael, as again affirmed by Bazak of Radio Haifa: "In the event of a terrorist attack we immediately report it and then [play] three to five melancholic songs. Then we evaluate what has happened. In the past we would devote the whole day, evening and night, like when there was an attack on bus no. 37 (in Haifa), with 12 people dead, all night long there were quiet songs." The appropriate playlist, often termed "terrorist attack songs," is largely indistinguishable from the canon of memorial songs. Indeed, radio programmers tend to lump the two categories together, as exemplified in the following account by Eran Litbin, a music programmer from Kol Israel:

> We've had these really beautiful songs that were simply appropriated for tragic circumstances, songs that used to be really beautiful and turned into songs of mourning, of traumatic situations in the country. You play them and you immediately make the listener feel that something has happened and he doesn't know what. . . . Everyone says the most beautiful songs are during Memorial Day [for Fallen Soldiers] and the Holocaust [Memorial Day]. People said it was fun to listen to the radio during wartime, because that's when they air the best songs.

Eran's comment illustrates how both broadcasting in memorial days and in emergency situations fall under the logic of the commemorative mode based on memorial songs. He also notes how tragic circumstances have paradoxically become a singular haven for fans of Shirei Eretz Yisrael and vice-versa. Such songs can no longer be aired at other times.

The advent of mass terrorist attacks, especially those led by Hamas suicide bombers, first in 1994 following the Oslo Accords and then from 2000 onward following the outbreak of the Second Intifada (Palestinian uprising) resulted in recurring alternations between everyday life and periods of crisis. This required a transformation in the way the media coped with emergency situations. Following a paradigmatic change in the military's security and combat doctrines from operations involving full-scale warfare to operations of low-intensity warfare, radio programmers were also inclined to readjust their policies. They felt that the public had become saturated by the stark shifts between musical genres after each terror attack and that they should not foster such a strict atmosphere of crisis, where any song of Shirei Eretz Yisrael becomes an instant alert "that something has happened." Instead they adopted a more diffuse practice commonly referred to as "moderating the music," where programmers simply softened the ongoing pop-rock programming or incorporated "light" versions of Mizrahi music with a flavor of Shirei Eretz Yisrael rather than switch entirely to the old genre.[26] The emergency repertoire has changed to a more contemporary sound, incorporating quiet, downbeat songs but with little thematic relevance to themes of tension or mourning.

Conclusion: War and Terrorism as Cyclic Interruptions

It is no coincidence that recent periods of conflict in Israeli history have began to be officially named as a *sequel* to previous conflicts, such as the Second Lebanon War, or the Second Intifada. Israel's repeated involvement with war and terrorism generates a sense of inevitable continuity, an understanding of emergency that differs from the conventional notion of a sudden, unexpected disruption to everyday life. Radio music practices during emergency events can shed some light on this unique understanding, especially when placing them in the broader context of Israeli society as an "interrupted system." Baruch Kimmerling analyzed the ways that the Israeli state over the years developed institutional, organizational, and cultural arrangements that facilitated the mobilization of society back and forth from circumstance of tense routine to a state of active warfare, not only in its efficient recruitment of military reserves but also in its ability to maintain and sustain civic and economic life in times of emergency. The interruptions to the routine have undergone a process of institutionalization that enables the society to persist unremittingly in the face of the prolonged military conflict.[27]

Kimmerling's analysis is based on the social adjustments between routine and total war, following a study of the 1973 Yom Kippur War. The recent changes in military conflict to low-intensity warfare and the increasingly recurring incidents of terror attacks intensified the oscillation between routine and emergency, leading to a state of constant interruptions. A concrete example of how the Second Intifada intensified cultural processes of institutionalization as an interrupted system can be found in some of the organizational arrangements developed in most radio stations during the heyday of mass suicide bombing. In order to be constantly ready for the possibility of broadcasting a long session of "terrorist attack songs," many stations prepared a ready-made file on the computer, a special preprogrammed playlist of songs termed "emergency kit" or "terrorist attack file" to be automatically aired in the uncertain hours following the attack, or during the night when programmers are away from the station.

In real-time circumstances, however, such shifts to a state of emergency require careful deliberation by radio staff. Unlike memorial days, which provide a clear set of guidelines for mood shifting, terror attacks are by their nature chaotic, fluid, and uncertain. As such they raise constant dilemmas concerning the exact circumstances that deserve a change of mood. At stake is the evasive and perplexing morbid task of assessing the number of casualties and deciding what would be the proper "threshold" for a mood shift and for how long. As Guy noted: "If for instance there are three people dead, and, it's not easy to say it, just ten injured, so you know that after an hour or two you can return, maybe not to party music but to songs that aren't too sad." This is where the practice of "moderating" the music to downbeat songs without applying a complete shift between musical genres became useful insofar as it provided broadcasters with a more subtle negotiation of the emergency situation.

Eran Litbin explains how "neutral" songs, songs that are quiet but not too sad, could assist in avoiding an audience overreaction: "I always keep a neutral song on standby in my '[gun] barrel.' If suddenly there's a report on a terror attack I immediately have to find a song. But it shouldn't be too sad because there might not be any fatal injuries and we wouldn't want to cause alarm." Eran employs the common Hebrew idiom "in the [gun] barrel," which means keeping something ready for use. It reveals not only a general attitude toward a state of emergency, but in this case also an association between songs and gun bullets. Really sad songs can be compared to real deadly bullets in that they should only be aired in case of fatal injuries. By using "neutral" songs, however, perhaps the equivalent of a blank cartridge, the public can be kept on alert without becoming too alarmed. The minimal change of tempo from upbeat to downbeat and back in line with the latest news updates has become an efficient solution for the logic of the interrupted system in times of frequent fluctuations: moderation replaced interruption.

Radio programmers not only borrow the practice of mood shifting from commemoration to wartime programming, but also frame the emergency circumstances in terms of the repetitive, *cyclic* quality of the commemorative mode. Indeed, addressing terror attacks within a framework of cyclic rituals reveals the deep-seated implications that the notion of interrupted system has for Israeli understandings of emergency. Public response to the escalating terror in the Second Intifada provides an illuminating case in point. Tamar Liebes and Zohar Kampf documented the media coverage of the escalating terror attacks from 2000 to 2005 and interpret the increasingly mellower coverage over time and fewer public demands for military or political response as an expression of collective "routinization."[28] In contrast, I argue that at least on the radio the distinction between ordinary life and the disruptive events was unequivocally retained, albeit subtly, through mood-shifting techniques such as music moderation. The disruption was not normalized or neutralized but rather incorporated into a culturally available system of cyclic interruptions. A slight public signifier of the emergency situation could suffice to mobilize the people, not into political action, but into the commemorative mode, enhancing national identification through a sense of collective convening and belonging.

In other words, through these patterns of music programming, the erratically recurring terror event is not routinized but rather ritualized so that it can continually arouse public solidarity. Its ritualistic quality facilitates the mobilization of society and enables people to adapt to the shifting back and forth from routine to emergency, experiencing the interrupted system as a steady, stable situation. As Émile Durkheim noted, the recurrent character of ritual activity reinforces individuals' sense of stability, security, and belonging to the community.[29] The threat of terrorism is codified as a periodic interference ad infinitum and thus incorporated into the very fabric of the community: similar to spells of stormy weather, terror becomes naturalized as a cyclic interruption.

Notes

1. Jo Tacchi, "The Need for Radio Theory in the Digital Age," *International Journal of Cultural Studies* 3 (2000): 289–98.

2. Derek Penslar, "Transmitting Jewish Culture: Radio in Israel," *Jewish Social Studies* 10 (2003): 1–29.

3. Tamar Liebes, "Acoustic Space: The Role of Radio in Israeli Collective History," *Jewish History* 20 (2006): 69–90.

4. Menahem Blondheim and Tamar Liebes, "From Disaster Marathon to Media Event: Live Television's Performance on September 11, 2001 and September 11, 2002," in *Crisis Communications: Lessons from September 11*, ed. A. Michael Noll (Lanham, MD: Rowman and Littlefield, 2003), 185–99.

5. Pilot interviews in the public radio networks were conducted with the assistance of Noa Bergman. Subsequent fieldwork in regional stations was conducted in collaboration with Orit Hirsh. The research was supported by the Hammer Scholarship of the Second Authority for Television and Radio. This note serves as the source documentation for in-text quotations from these interviews. For an elaborate analysis of the interactions between radio broadcasting in times of commemoration and in times of emergency, see Danny Kaplan, "The Songs of the Siren: Engineering National Time on Israeli Radio," *Cultural Anthropology* 24 (2009): 313–45.

6. Second Authority for Television and Radio, Law of the Second Authority for Television and Radio—1990, accessed August 14, 2009, http://www.rashut2.org.il/critic_judge.asp?refCatId=115 (Hebrew). By 2010 only five of the seventeen regional stations focused on differentiated audiences, such as the Palestinian community of northern Israel, the Sephardic ultra-Orthodox community, or the Russian immigrant population.

7. Andrew Crisell, ed., *More Than a Music Box: Radio Cultures and Communities in a Multi-Media World* (New York: Berghahn Books, 2004), vii.

8. Penslar, "Transmitting Jewish Culture," 21.

9. Motti Regev and Edwin Seroussi, *Popular Music and National Culture in Israel* (Berkeley: University of California Press, 2004).

10. See Henrich R. Greve, "Patterns of Competition: The Diffusion of a Market Position in Radio Broadcasting," *Administrative Science Quarterly* 41 (1996): 29–60.

11. The US radio field is characterized by strong commercialization and standardization. For critical overviews, see Bob Lochte, "U.S. Public Radio: What Is It—and for Whom?" in *More Than a Music Box: Radio Cultures and Communities in a Multi-Media World*, ed. Andrew Crisell (New York: Berghahn Books, 2004), 39–55; Jarl A. Ahlkvist and Gene Fisher, "And the Hits Just Keep on Coming: Music Programming Standardization in Commercial Radio," *Poetics* 27 (2000): 301–25.

12. See Galit Saada-Ophir, "Borderland Pop: Arab Jewish Musicians and the Politics of Performance," *Cultural Anthropology* 21 (2006): 205–33; Regev and Seroussi, *Popular Music.*

13. For an analysis of recent changes in Mizrahi music following the privatization reforms, see Danny Kaplan, "Neo-Institutional Analysis of the Rise of Light Mizrachi Music on Israeli Radio, 1995–2010," *Sociologya Israelit* (forthcoming) (Hebrew).

14. Paul E. Willis, *Profane Culture* (London: Routledge and Kegan Paul, 1978); for a study of Galei Tzahal's odd combination of rock and militarism, see Menahem Mautner, "Galey Zahal or the Unification of Rock and Death," *Plilim* 9 (2001): 11–51 (Hebrew).

15. Martin Cloonan, "Pop and the Nation-State: Towards a Theorization," *Popular Music* 18 (1999): 193–207.

16. "On the Rooftops of Tel Aviv," song written and performed by Alona Daniel, from the album *Party in the Dungeon* (Tel Aviv: Hed Arzi, 1990) (Hebrew).

17. "The Opening of the Centennial Celebrations in Tel Aviv," *City Mouse Online,* April 4, 2009, accessed August 14, 2009, http://www.mouse.co.il/CM.articles_item,607,209,34774,.aspx, 2009 (Hebrew); Einav Shif, "Who Are the Winners in Tel Aviv Song Parade?" *Walla,* April 29, 2009, accessed August 14, 2009, http://tlv100.walla.co.il/?w=/6/1476702 (Hebrew).

18. Motti Regev, "Organizational Fluency, Organizational Blocks, Cultural Relevance: The Case of the Music Industry in Israel," *Teoria Ve-biqoret* 10 (1997): 123 (Hebrew).

19. Radio Haifa almost doubled its ratings during the year of the war in Lebanon from 9.5 percent to 17 percent (in a survey of regional exposure) and presented in 2007 another increase of around 25 percent (in a survey of national exposure). See Second Authority for Television and Radio, "Audience Survey for 2006," accessed August 14, 2009, http://www.rashut2.org.il/about_survey.asp (Hebrew); Li-Or Averbach, "Gaydamak Presents: Weak Radio," *NRG,* January 23, 2008, accessed August 14, 2009, http://www.nrg.co.il/online/4/ART1/687/578.html (Hebrew).

20. State Comptroller, "The Deployment and Functioning of the Home Front during the Second Lebanon War," *State Comptroller's report,* July 2007, accessed August 14, 2009, http://www.mevaker.gov.il/serve/contentTree.asp?bookid= 494&id=157&contentid=&parentcid=undefined&sw=1024&hw=698 (Hebrew).

21. The radio publicized its intensive involvement in the war. It launched a special day of programming marking the first anniversary of the war, which centered on the deeds of its own reporters and appeared in the radio's website at the time under the title "Our radio is a war hero."

22. Kaplan, "The Songs of the Siren."

23. Ariel Hirschfeld, "The Smile of Elifelet," *Panim* 17 (2001): 70–79 (Hebrew); Talila Eliram, *Bo Shir 'Ivri (Come Thou Hebrew Song)—The Songs of the Land of Israel: Musical and Social Aspects* (Haifa: Haifa University Press, 2006) (Hebrew).

24. The commemorative mode is most prominent and comprehensive on Memorial Day for Fallen Soldiers and on Holocaust Memorial Day. On some stations it is also applied to Memorial Day for Yitzhak Rabin and on Tisha B'Av, a religious fast commemorating the destruction of the Second Temple. Despite the relative uniformity of the commemorative programming, some radio stations present distinct variations based on their musical profile and market positioning. See Danny Kaplan, "National Mood Stations: The 'Commemorative Mode' of Israeli Radio Broadcasting during Memorial Days and Times of Emergency," *Megamot* (forthcoming) (Hebrew); Motti Neiger, Eyal Zandberg, and Oren Meyers, "Localizing Collective Memory: Radio Broadcasts and the Construction of Regional Memory," unpublished manuscript.

25. For a cultural analysis of the interrelations between male friendship, sacrifice, and national

identification in some canonic Israeli songs of commemoration, see Danny Kaplan, *The Men We Loved: Male Friendship and Nationalism in Israeli Culture* (New York: Berghahn Books, 2006).

26. See Kaplan, "The Songs of the Siren."

27. Baruch Kimmerling, *The Interrupted System: Israeli Civilians in War and Routine Times* (New Brunswick, NJ: Transaction Books, 1985).

28. Tamar Liebes and Zohar Kampf, "Routinizing Terror: Media Coverage and Public Practices in Israel, 2000–2005," *Harvard International Journal of Press/Politics* 12 (2007): 108–16.

29. Émile Durkheim, *The Elementary Forms of the Religious Life* (London: Allen and Unwin, 1915).

Chapter 4

Consuming Nostalgia

Greeting Cards and Soldier-Citizens

Noa Roei

June 2007 marked the fortieth anniversary of the 1967 war in which Israel conquered the Golan Heights, the West Bank, the Sinai Peninsula, and the Gaza Strip. Forty years later, competing narratives tell very different stories about that decisive war. On the one hand, the "unification and liberation of the city of Jerusalem" was celebrated, every year, by prayers, parades, and dances as part of the "Jerusalem Day" national holiday. On the other hand, the detrimental effects the annexation of territory had on Israel and its citizens were debated in a daylong event led by various human-rights organizations in Tel Aviv.[1] Several exhibitions at the time were thematically related to the fortieth anniversary of the Six-Day War but were overwhelmingly aligned with critical reevaluations of the conflict and its aftermath. These focused largely on the beginning of the Israeli occupation of the West Bank and the Gaza Strip and the corresponding military rule of some 2 million Palestinian refugees. Cumulatively, these amassed to a multifaceted, critical declaration of the art world against the narrative that portrays the Six-Day War as an unabashed triumph.[2]

In what follows, I examine one such exhibition, *40 Years to Victory*, by Honi Hame'agel, an installation of enlarged and reworked New Year greeting cards from the post-Six-Day-War era on public transport buses in the cities of Jerusalem, Haifa, and Tel Aviv.[3] The exhibition was based on images that display military (even militant) themes, such as parades, portraits of generals, and war scenarios, alongside wishes for a happy New Year. Extremely popular in the years following the Six-Day War, such images disappeared from popular culture around the mid-1970s and became significant nostalgia markers, often found in collections or alluded to by cultural-historical references. Hame'agel's exhibition mobilized nostalgia in order to contend with history, memory, and national identity in Israel today.

In considering *40 Years to Victory* it is important to address the significance of the military postcards in their original context, as New Year greeting cards that circulated just after the Six-Day War. However, my major emphasis examines the significance of the greeting cards in today's culture, especially in light of theoretical approaches to the role of nostalgia in nationalism. My analysis addresses ways that this exhibition's nostalgic insertion of ostensibly dated militaristic imagery into the public sphere challenged the conventional narrative of the transformation of Israeli identity through the years. While the exhibition enabled the Tel Aviv public of 2007 to indulge in nationalist nostalgia, it also confronted the public with the contemporaneity of those seemingly dated images, and thus did not allow the national subject of the third millennium to be easily distinguished from the past propagation of a militaristic national ideology.[4]

Victory Celebrated: Peace, Security, and Sparkles

The custom of sending a greeting card just before the Jewish New Year first originated in Germany during the Middle Ages, eventually spreading to Eastern Europe and later the United States, where it paralleled a custom that appeared in the nineteenth century of sending commercial greeting cards.[5] As the Zionist movement took hold, the cards began to express a Zionist-secular message of pioneering spirit.[6] Thus, a long-established custom of the Diaspora was altered to fit the newly emerging more secular tradition of the State of Israel.[7] The 1960s showed a significant growth in the variety and quality of the New Year cards, pointing to the burgeoning of Israeli society. The most prominent images at the time depicted blooming landscapes, happy family life, and, increasingly, celebratory representations of the Israeli military. Soon after the 1967 war, the popularity and variety of the military greeting cards reached its peak, reinforcing the triumphal militarism of that era.[8]

Greeting cards of that era feature military parades, military arsenal, or portraits of soldiers and generals adjacent to tranquil verbal greetings for "A Happy New Year" in English or "A Year of Peace and Security" in Hebrew. In addition to the pacifying verbal message, the intimidating martial theme is often softened by the small size of the cards, their naive style, and a garlanded or glittering frame. Various symbols of power in the IDF, or alternatively the map of Israel encompassing the annexed territories from the Six-Day War, are transformed into miniature versions that can fit, together with a marching division and a few jets, in the small space of a locket or a greeting card. Indeed, similar themes circulated on other small-sized objects of popular culture from the same period, such as lockets, key chains, and table games. The military greeting cards were part of a material culture that flaunted military power while domesticating it as benign and appealing. They helped to spread the popular adoration of the IDF as the people's army, as well as the idolization of its generals, the celebration of a military glorious past, and the assertion of its promising future.[9]

In a recent study of Israeli and Palestinian picture-postcards, Tim J. Semmerling asserts the postcard's potent role in the cultural politics of national identity discourse. "Postcards," Semmerling writes, "are not merely mundane objects but provocative and

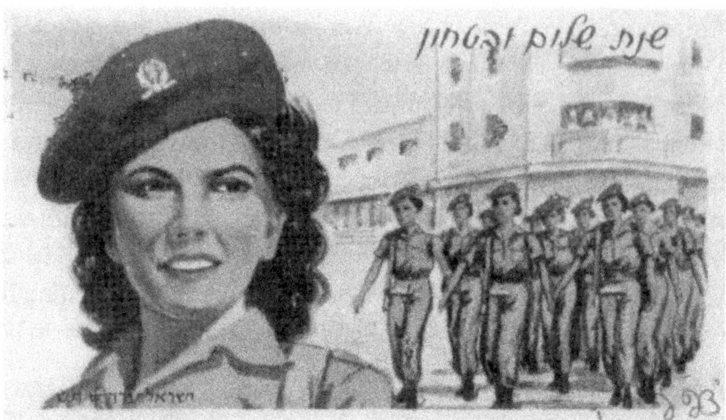

New Year greeting card (military march and woman-soldier portrait), 1950s. Private collection, courtesy of Shalom Sabar.

active presentations of 'national self.' Their makers and sellers consider them expressive declarations and performances of national status."[10]

Semmerling's book includes numerous examples of military imagery on Israeli picture-postcards; this comes as no surprise to anyone familiar with Israeli society and culture. Militarism has always played a key role in Israel's self-perception, and the military apparatus has long been associated with positive values and high principles.[11] Contemporary versions of such "military postcards" vary between portrayals of soldiers as sensible, peaceful bodies to more explicit displays of military vigor.[12] The overt celebration of military strength, however, belongs strictly to the greeting cards of the years just after the Six-Day War. Semmerling does not include the latter in his study, but his research is relevant for our case since the greeting cards used to play a similar role within Israeli cultural politics in earlier periods.[13] Such cards were satiated with semiotic signs related to the construction of Israeli collective identity.[14] They displayed a montage of loved symbols, bringing across a colorful, conventional, and clear message —not unlike an advertisement would for its target audience.[15] Haim Grossman, who has written extensively on the topic of military-inflected material culture in the early days of Israel, notes,

> The military New Year card, one of the more popular types of greeting cards sent in the 1950s and 1960s, is part of a cultural ensemble that belongs to the unofficial texts that make up the communal image. Sometimes these texts, that take part in the historical discourse, disseminate a message more efficiently than the official historiographical ones. The life span of the New Year card is short . . . but its importance as an expression of a visual model that presents the spirit of society is significant.[16]

In one salient example, the textual message on the card (Happy New Year) prepares for a positive, domesticated reinforcement of the military image, and together with the kitsch style and the surrounding decorations, pushes aside the more intimidating as-

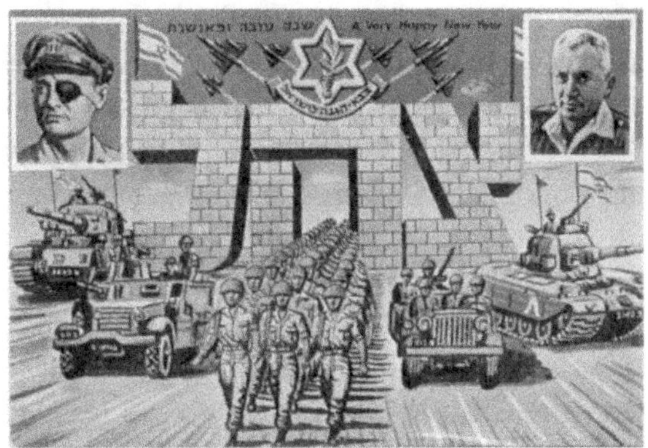

New Year greeting card (military march through victory gate and portraits of generals), 1960s. Private collection, courtesy of Haim Grossman.

pects of this subject matter. Accordingly, the visual image translates the wish for "Peace and Security" to mean that only security in the shape of military power can provide an enduring and authentic peace.[17] Furthermore, the absence of enemy figures or potential harm for the self—juxtaposed with elements such as the selective display of disciplined young bodies in uniform, portraits of respected military figures, and simplified aerial maps that emphasize newly acquired territory—further enhances the notion that military power is naturally beautiful, desirable, and constructive.[18]

But the images on the greeting cards operate well beyond their purely visual frame; they acquire affective significance in their circulation as postcards, being sent from a sender to an addressee anticipating the Jewish New Year. Rosh Hashanah, or the Jewish New Year, often takes place in September, almost half a year apart from the May military parades on Independence Day. The cards that depicted those parades helped to consolidate a narrative of victory throughout the year, connecting that victory with both Jewish and Zionist heritage. If every May citizens gathered in celebratory public spaces, every September right after 1967 they took part in a more passive memorization that brought that event, and their participation in it, back to life.[19]

It is useful to think about this paradigm in relation to Benedict Anderson, who posits that one of the critical elements that made it possible for national communities to "think the nation" was the transformation of temporality involved in historicizing national identities, and the associated surge of interest in the past.[20] Other cultural critics have cited the way that calendars and holidays play a main role in the mapping of the basic temporal structure of societies, "enabling and constraining their abilities to remember different pasts."[21] Communities are to a large extent constituted by their past through collective memories; national identities, specifically, are established and maintained through a variety of mnemonic sites, practices, and forms.[22] Eric Hobsbawm's well-known formulation of "invented tradition" encapsulates the way that the nation—a recent historical phenomenon in itself—consists of a set of symbolic practices and rituals that "seek to inculcate certain values and norms of behaviors by repetition, which automatically implies continuity with the past."[23] In this context it is easy to perceive how Israel's Rosh Hashanah greeting cards provide a rich exemplar of how an invented tradition linked the military, the Jewish culture, and the State of Israel in a tangled narrative of heroism and national redemption. In the late 1960s the experience of the Six-Day War as well as the height of national pride that it engendered was fresh. The greeting cards transfixed that pride into memory in involving citizens on an intimate and domestic realm within the sweeping and impersonal narration of history.

The website "Nostalgia Online" recounts the days when the greeting cards were a substantial industry, especially in the 1960s. A few days before the fall holidays, displays full of cards appeared on every corner, and the amount of cards one received often indicated social status. The relation of consumers to the images depicted on the cards was ostensibly personal, as their choices reflected on how they imagined themselves and their social relationships. Yet recipients too were intrinsically expected to share a similarly nurturing attitude toward the emerging national narrative.[24]

Clearly, the greeting cards of this era should not be read as mere reflections of the Israeli psyche. Rather, in line with Judith Butler's theory of performative reiterations, these served as genuinely active tools for the consolidation of the national self.[25] They allowed their producers, consumers, and recipients to classify the military as an idealized institution intricately interwoven into the fabric of civilian life. Furthermore, the cards enabled the consolidation of an emerging narrative of victory: the construction of a hegemonic (Jewish, militarized) collective identity took place, in part, through a mnemonic practice that narrated a historical moment immediately after its occurrence. In this regard it is worth taking heed of Susan Sontag's argument in *Regarding the Pain of Others,* that "what is called collective memory is not a remembering but a stipulating: that *this* is important, and this is the story about how it happened, with the pictures that lock the story in our minds."[26] The New Year's greeting cards were part of the active creation of collective memory. They reflected an insistent endeavor to secure a specific folksy national narrative that framed the memory of the Six-Day War rigidly as an idealized virtuous moment in Israel's history.

Victory Tamed: From Guns to Cream Cheese

The more militant New Year greeting card disappeared from popular culture quite abruptly during the mid-1970s, together with other applied art objects that featured similar themes. Significantly, the annual Independence Day military parades were also canceled around this time, the last one taking place in May 1973 to commemorate Israel's twenty-fifth anniversary. The change of visual custom—mirroring a cultural mind shift—is commonly associated with the aftereffects of the Yom Kippur War of 1973, which is narrated in Israeli collective memory as the antithesis to the 1967 Six-Day War. Inasmuch as the narrative of 1967 is associated with victory, hope, and national consensus, the memory of 1973 is linked to fear, trauma, and a general decline in the conviction of the strength and ability of the IDF. Processes of individualization during the 1980s further weakened national consensus and contributed to the pluralization of Israeli political and social spheres.[27]

Grossman adheres to this historical narrative by interpreting the disappearance of soldier figures and military themes from applied art objects in the 1970s as a direct consequence of the outcome of the Yom Kippur War, where the cohesiveness and consensus around the military ideal began to waver.[28] Yet it is important to note that related themes have not disappeared altogether from popular culture. The annual military parades themselves may have ceased, yet military exhibitions are presented all over the country on Independence Day, inviting visitors to climb on tanks and play with armory as a family recreational activity fitting the occasion.[29] Correspondingly, while military heroes are no longer depicted next to tanks and missiles on greeting cards, military figures continue to be present in other realms of popular culture. They star in numerous television series and are also found abundantly in commercials and advertisements. Accordingly, a traveling exhibition of the feminist organization New Profile presented a provocative collection of military-inflicted images from entertainment magazines, commercials, and educational material. A quick glance at the online version of this exhibition reveals that later occurrences of consumer-culture-military imagery are stripped of overt signs of power.[30] They mostly employ the unarmed body of the soldier to sell a variety of products, from underwear to mobile phones, cookies, and cream cheese. Signs of potential violence are kept out of the image, and the military uniform serves simply as the generic marker of the body as Israeli. Often figures are not fully dressed, thus hinting at the soft side of the sabra that hides just beneath the toughness of the khaki denim. By and large the military aspect of these commercials remains naturalized and is largely taken for granted as an intrinsic component of Israeliness.[31]

Hence, military imagery still plays a role in the way civil hegemonic society constructs its sense of self through consumerism. But that sense of self has evolved over the years, and now fits a more conscious, wary, and individualized public style. Glittering images of military power that symbolize collective virtue and strength are replaced by intimate renderings of the subjectivity of the Israeli soldier-citizen.

Meanwhile, the military Rosh Hashanah greeting cards have been relocated from consumer culture to private memorabilia collections.[32] These are often alluded to in websites such as "Nostalgia Online," and in sociohistorical reviews. Sometimes, as we shall see in upcoming exemplars, they are used as ready-made material for critical works of art. No longer agents of memory that take part in the dissemination of a national narrative, the greeting cards are now in themselves objects of memory, having become fully integral to that narrative. They conjure recollections of a forsaken tradition and function as signposts of "the way we were." The greeting cards have become, in other words, nostalgic markers, pointing to a past frame of mind that is irretrievable for the present.

"The Way We Were": The Politics of Nostalgia

Nostalgia is generally defined as a longing for a home that no longer exists or has never existed.[33] A medical term in the seventeenth century, nostalgia has evolved to be seen as an incurable condition of yearning for the unattainable, linked to modern conceptions of time, history, and progress.[34] It has frequently been understood in reactionary terms and as a guilt-free homecoming that abdicates one of personal responsibility through the idealization of the past. Among its many detractors is Raymond Williams, who warns us that dwelling on a romanticized past diminishes our capacity to critique or come to terms with the present.[35] Recent studies, however, attempt to demarcate a potentially utopian aspect of nostalgia, based on its resistance to what Walter Benjamin regards as homogenous, empty time.[36] Whether reactionary or utopian, or both, nostalgia is generally understood as an act of memory happening in the present, which allows the past to actively engage with the present and the future.[37]

In *The Future of Nostalgia,* Svetlana Boym distinguishes between two kinds of nostalgia. *Restorative* nostalgia stresses the *nostos,* and attempts a transhistorical reconstruction of the lost home; *reflective* nostalgia stresses the *algia,* and dwells on the irrevocability of the past.[38] Restorative nostalgia is closely related to public memories and manifests itself partly through invented traditions that "offer a comforting collective script for individual longing."[39] Reflective nostalgia, on the other hand, is more closely aligned with personal memories and individual narratives and combines longing with critical thinking that does not attempt to recover a lost identity: the modern (reflective) nostalgic can be homesick and sick of home at once.[40]

If we interpret the New Year greeting cards according to Boym's typology, we see that these were nostalgic objects from their nascence, part of an anxious restorative endeavor to hold on to a specific narrative that was already in the process of disintegration at the time of its creation. In their later incarnation as dated memorabilia, however, the greeting cards fit the notion of reflective nostalgia. They do not attempt to bridge a gap and recreate an unattainable moment (as would a restorative endeavor) but dwell on times gone by. For Boym, reflective nostalgia has a critical potential, as it may mock past national ideals while appealing to shared cultural frameworks of memory. The dated greeting cards indeed point to two separate types of memory, invoking what is now seen as a controversial national ideal, while alluding to a supposedly trouble-free popular tradition. They thus contain a combination of longing (for a dated consensus) and reflection (on what was wrong with that consensus). However, this juxtaposition does not engender critical reflection in and of itself. In this specific context, framed as memorabilia, the greeting cards fit more closely with the detracting view of nostalgia as a guilt-free homecoming that allows one to dwell on lost traditions. For, as memorabilia, the greeting cards stress the notion that they indisputably belong to times past.

As collectors' items, the cards are distinguished from their applied-art counterparts, the TV and billboard advertisements, which play an active role in today's consumer culture as they display toned-down versions of military scenarios. This distinction assumes cultural progress in the shape of a more cautious approach toward military power. It camouflages the continuities between the messages of the present and the past, such as the idealization and beautification of the military subject and the commodified blending of the civilian and military spheres. Nostalgia, like progress, is based on the modern

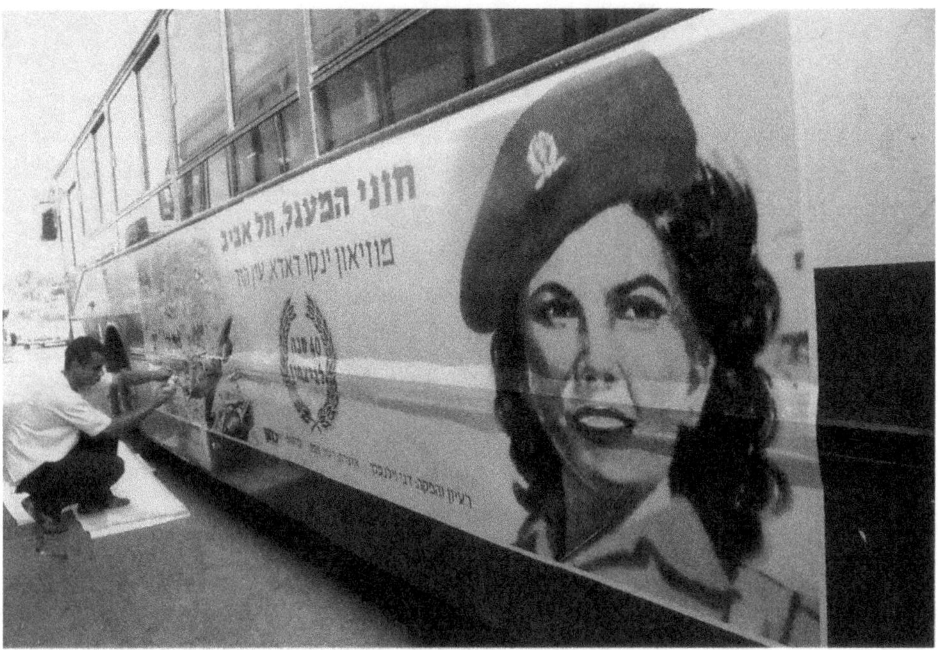

Honi Hame'agel, *40 Years to Victory*. Street view (woman-soldier portrait), June 2007, Tel Aviv. Courtesy of the artist.

conception of unrepeatable and irreversible time:[41] what we long for (the way we *were*) marks the way we *are no longer*. The dwelling over an irretrievable past may thus include a reliance on the modern notion of the irreversibility of time, which helpfully serves to keep at bay those aspects of past narratives that no longer fit the image of the contemporary national self.

Victory Resumed: From Postcards to Billboards and Beyond

In June 2007, the exhibition *40 Years to Victory* presented adaptations of the 1960s greeting cards. These appeared on three hundred public buses in Jerusalem, Haifa, and Tel Aviv in the form of twenty different posters. Each poster was composed of a collage of elements from the militant greeting cards, blown up in size but otherwise untouched: the same smiling woman-soldier was leading her parade around the city street, the same generals presented an overview of military jets or of a map portraying the "greater Israel," the same texts called for a "Happy New Year" of "Peace and Security." In addition, each poster boldly displayed the following information: the name of the artist (Honi Hame'agel, Tel Aviv); the name of the museum (Yanco-Dada Museum, Ein-Hod); a short colophon (mentioning producer Dani Vilensky, curator Raya Zommer-Tal, and sponsor Cnaan Media in Motion Ltd.); and the exhibition title, *40 Years to Victory*, designed as a medal of valor.

Buses in Israel exhibit a variety of advertisements; many are commercial, but it is

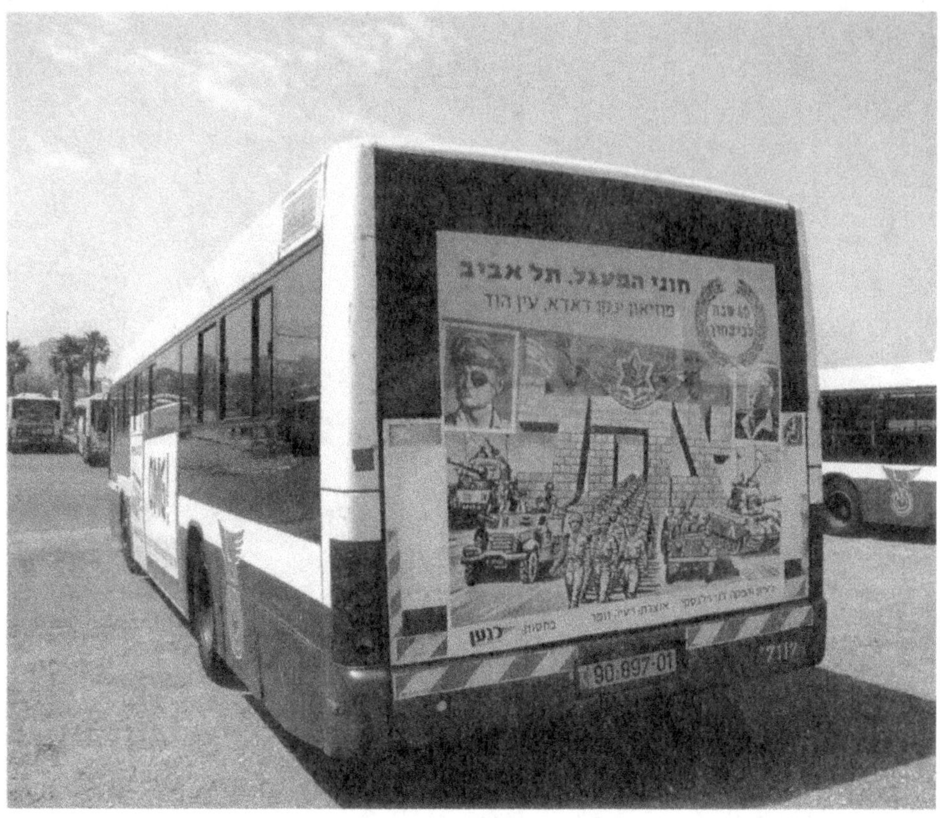

Honi Hame'agel, *40 Years to Victory*. Street view (military march through victory gate and portraits of generals), June 2007, Tel Aviv. Courtesy of the artist.

not uncommon to see also political or civil-society campaigns.[42] The sponsor of *40 Years to Victory*, Cnaan Media in Motion Ltd., holds the tender for advertising on public buses in Israel. On their website, Cnaan outlines the benefits of the media, emphasizing the size of the images, which are hard to ignore; the mobility of the images that therefore reach a large amount of potential clients; and the fact that the target audience is a "captive audience" that has no control over exposure to the material.[43] Thus Israeli city dwellers see a wide variety of messages on buses as an ordinary part of urban life, and *40 Years to Victory* fitted nearly seamlessly into this context. The curatorial information displayed in bold letters over the iconic images accommodated their presentation as contemporary advertisements, perhaps for a faraway exhibition. The evocative images and the memories they engendered were presented in the exhibition as objects for consumption in the present. In so doing, the exhibition succeeded in reproducing the inconspicuous existence of the militant images in the public sphere: bus advertisements today are as routine as were objects of popular culture forty years ago, and so the greeting card images were reinstated into visual culture and took part, again, in the daily customs of their viewers. The differences between past and present became more particular and focused on the changed interaction between consumers and products. If

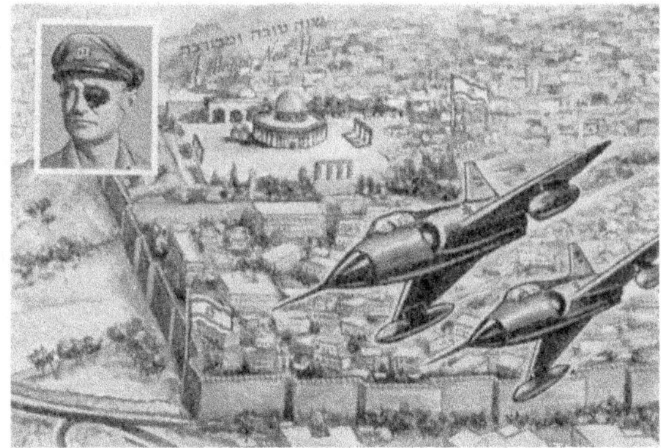

New Year greeting card (Jerusalem, jets, and Moshe Dayan), 1960s. Private collection, courtesy of Haim Grossman.

in the past the act of sending and receiving the greeting cards involved the body of the citizen-consumer on an intimate level, that current relationship is more passive as the images target a "captive audience" that has no control over their exposure. Whereas in the past the greeting cards incorporated the recent memory of war into the September New Year festivities, now the May anniversary of the war cites the wish for a happy New Year and thus includes the Jewish calendar within its frame. If previously the greeting cards were composed of a personal message on the one side and a generic message on the other, now the bus billboards make no distinction between the voice of the artist and that of the curator, sponsor, or producer. These differences, however, only emerge distinctly when we treat the rhetoric of the images on equal grounds, in relation to their varying historical contexts: both then and now, images of idealized and glorified militarism are offered to the receptive citizen-consumer.

40 Years to Victory circulated on streets that previously hosted the May military parades as well as the September Rosh Hashanah card stands. It underscored the fact that both modes of presentation distributed the same images in the same city streets, to a similar public. The exhibition presented the greeting-card images as natural components of contemporary consumer culture and pointed to the fact that ideology and commerce were/are intimately intertwined, both then and now. As a result, what seems at first to mark the difference between old and new—then we had tradition, now we only have commerce—ends up conflating temporalities, alluding both to the calculated commercial aspect of the old greeting cards and to the current affective social bond that the bus advertisements are based on.

This is not to say that the bus advertisements are simple reiterations of their earlier counterparts; in fact, the exhibition's logic is based on an understanding of the New Year greeting cards as something of the past. However, while *40 Years to Victory* refers to a communal frame of mind that no longer exists, it does so by making that past very *present*. What was displayed no longer identified a mainstream spirit, so that the images could only be understood in a nostalgic sense, yet the way in which the images were displayed was adapted for contemporary culture. This combination of a dated message with an up-to-date format created a temporal conundrum, perhaps the most interesting aspect of the entire exhibition. The New Year greeting cards were configured anew as

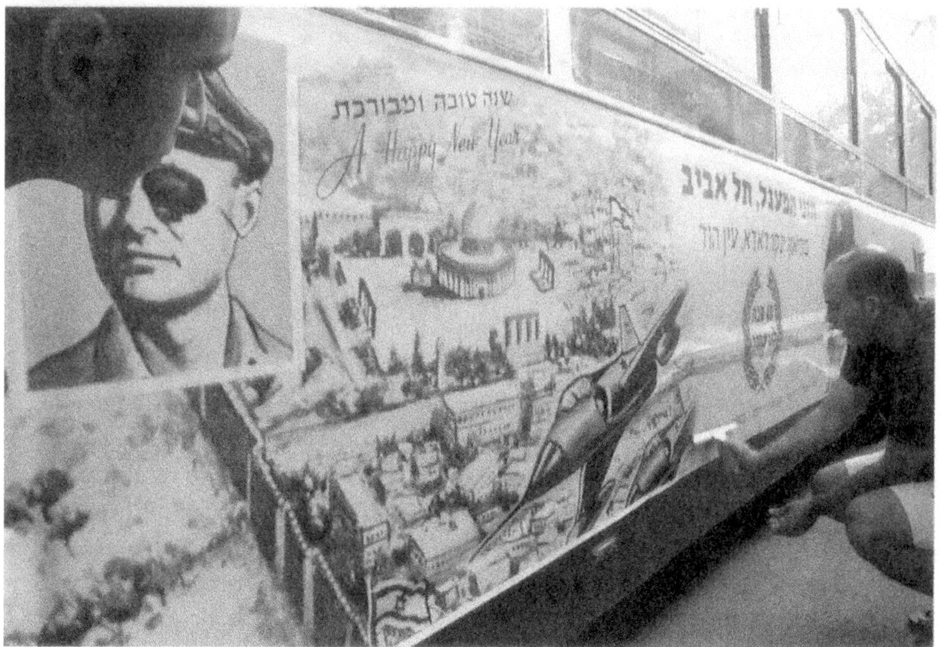

Honi Hame'agel, *40 Years to Victory*. Street view (Jerusalem, jets, and Moshe Dayan), June 2007, Tel Aviv. Courtesy of the artist.

memory agents that function in the visual culture of today. As a result, they did not operate exclusively within the frame of reflective nostalgia, but also performed an act of restorative nostalgia, as they attempted a transhistorical return to their original role as sculptors of national memory.[44] A short detour helps to make this point more clear.

At the same time that *40 Years to Victory* was exhibited on buses, the exhibition *Six Days Plus Forty Years* was on display at the Yad Lebanim section of the Petach-Tikva Museum, not far from Tel Aviv. Curated by Rona Sela, this encompassed a small but striking collection of artworks that amounted to a somber reflection on the militarized consciousness of the 1960s, and on its persistence in the present.[45] Journalistic photographs and propaganda films were displayed on the walls next to the artworks, and the New Year cards were presented with other commercial-art objects (medallions, bubblegum wrappers, and children's games) in a glass box at the center of one of the gallery's rooms. Here the juxtaposition of present contemplative artworks and past pseudo-propagandistic visual images created a thematic distinction between the two periods.[46] The name of the exhibition, too, posed different temporal periods against each other: six days here, and forty years there.

The exhibit *Six Days Plus Forty Years* hardly lacked complexity, since in many ways it presented a more comprehensive critical analysis of the militarized state of affairs in Israel, both in the past and in the present, than did *40 Years to Victory*. Yet it is illuminating to compare *40 Years to Victory* directly to *Six Days Plus Forty Years* to highlight the disparate ways in which each located the greeting cards in the present. In *Six Days Plus*

Forty Years, the cards are crystallized in the past together with other commercial art products and journalistic photographs. They are presented as memory objects that no longer function as creators and propagators of a sociopolitical message. Under the glass frame, the cards become static signs documenting "the way we were," their content critically reflected on by later artworks and theoretical analysis. In contrast, the same cards in *40 Years to Victory* are designed to propagate a restorative nostalgia and to distribute their visual message in the present, for the present. They are configured to function in the culture of today; *40 Years to Victory* proposes that the memory and identity portrayed in the greeting cards may not be as dated as they would seem. In addition, the exhibition highlights the fact that the greeting cards have never stopped playing an active role, that their mnemonic significance as memorabilia is no less pertinent to the present construction of the Israeli psyche than their historical role as carriers of holiday salutations.

Provocations and the Limits of Critical Discourse

Honi Hame'agel's name sounds as if it is merely a suggestive pseudonym (it is the name of a Jewish scholar and miracle worker from the first century BCE), but it is his authentic name, and this obscurity fits the artist's performative handling of his identity, which often leaves interviewers baffled or otherwise skeptical.[47] A professed follower of the Dada movement, Hame'agel is known for exhibitions, installations, movies, and performances that pose absurd and inciting situations and question the standards of art. Many times his work takes a crude, even vulgar form and involves bodies and fluids in ways that both repulse and attract his audience.[48] In their restraint, the bus advertisements of *40 Years to Victory* are distinct from the artist's previous projects. Customary images found in Hame'agel's work, such as naked bodies with hints of sadism or portraits with provocative sensual aesthetics, are missing from the bus billboards. However, the exhibition also included peripheral images that fitted Hame'agel's signature, adding pseudo-pornographic figures to the collage of the New Year greeting cards. Tellingly, these treated images were confined to the space of the Janco-Dada Museum and to the exhibition's opening event on June 1, 2007. Thus the exhibition comprised two separate visual events: one with almost untreated reproductions of the greeting cards on the buses, the other with more provocative images confined to the museum. The catalog of the exhibition offers a synthesis of both treated and untreated images in a way that implies that the provocative collages actually circulated in public space.[49]

In response to queries, both artist and curator explain that the bus operators would not approve of more provocative versions of the postcards, and that the traveling exhibition would not be able to take place otherwise.[50] Working within the public sphere demands conformity to rules and regulations, and this play between the art world and the market, with the question of what can be debated where, runs through most of the artist's oeuvre.[51] Nevertheless, Hame'agel insists that his political critique comes through just as well in the tamer images. The mere act of reinstating dated visions of

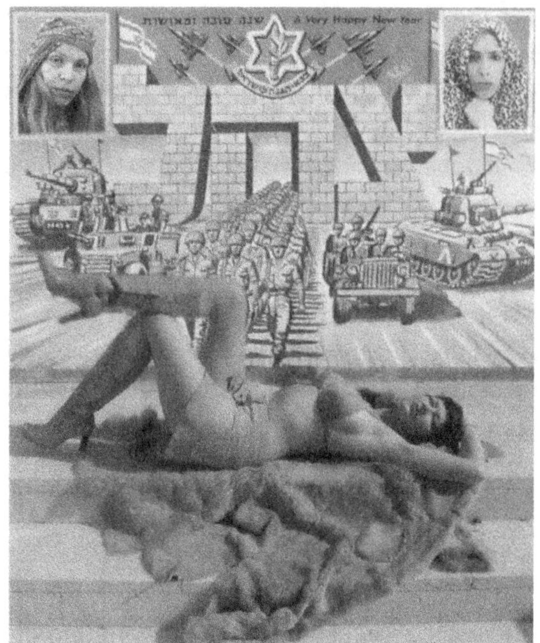

Honi Hame'agel, *40 Years to Victory.* Untitled (military march through victory gate and model on carpet), 2007. Catalog reproduction, courtesy of the artist.

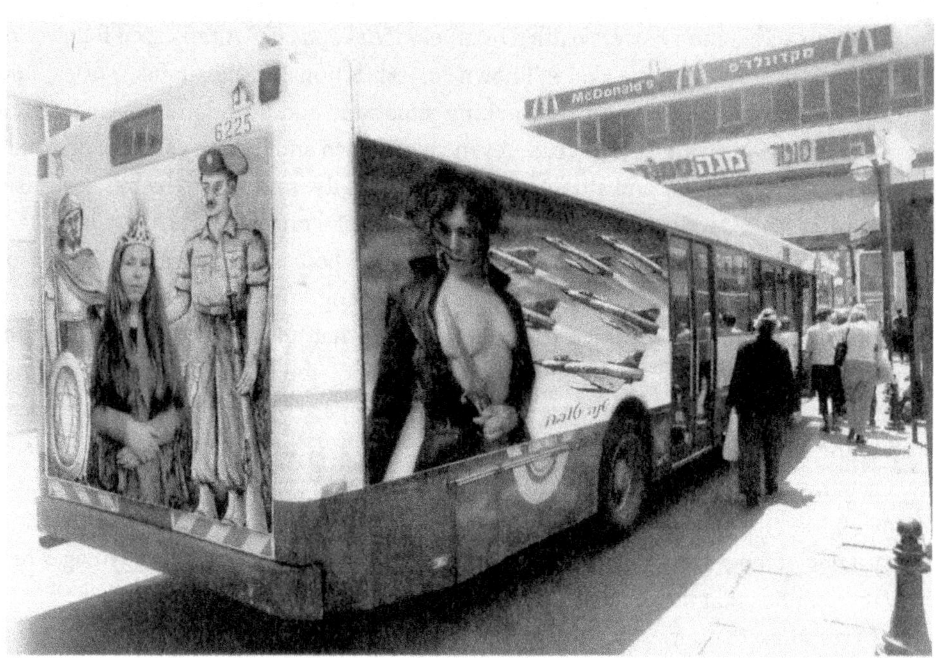

Honi Hame'agel, *40 Years to Victory.* "Tel Aviv under Attack," digitally manipulated street view (model, knife, and jets), 2007. Catalog reproduction, courtesy of the artist.

military grandeur in public should lead, according to his view, to a critical reflection on those days of glory.[52]

The framing texts of the exhibition point to visual clues that emphasize the artist's critical intentions. The catalog text explains how the once-adored generals are degraded as they feature next to daily consumer goods on the buses, and underscores that the promise of peace and security is emptied out as it is presented on the very vehicles that were the main target of suicide bombing attacks in the 1990s.[53] The analysis is made more explicit by the titles that accompany the documentation in the catalog, so that photographs depicting the exhibition as it travels in the city streets are characterized as *Russian Roulette, Area Prone to Suicide Bombings, National Consensus,* and so forth. However, when the exhibition is experienced separately from the catalog's explication, the encounter leaves space for more ambiguous readings than the explanations of its makers would allow. Visually and functionally, the advertisements do not present a thematic reversal in relation to the 1960s greeting cards. After all, one could argue that the generals are no less degraded when their portraits are presented on bus advertisements as when they are on miniature sparkling postcards. That reading depends entirely on the eyes of the beholder. When we take into account that many political campaigns present portraits of their representatives on bus billboard advertisements we see that the location of the *40 Years to Victory* images does not, in and of itself, lead to reflective criticism. Thus it does not necessarily mark the present as more aware or critical of military ideology. Still there is an expectation for the public to receive *40 Years to Victory* as an "impossible" gesture and to come to terms with the exhibition's sardonic undertones.

In his review of *40 Years To Victory,* Haim Grossman questions the intelligibility of that move.[54] While Grossman acknowledges that "positioning material that belongs completely to the past, in an urban setting of the present . . . leads to an uncomfortable dialogue," he argues that the traveling exhibition was generally received as an enjoyable nostalgic reminder during the present hard times.[55] Grossman points to the fact that the exhibition was not vandalized, while other contemporaneous street-art images went through "street censorship" and were torn apart shortly after they were mounted. One example he points to is a poster made by artist David Tartakover, entitled *40 Occupation* and composed of images, statements, and colors that promote the Palestinian narrative.[56]

Grossman explain the difference between how Tartakover's and Hame'agel's works have been accepted—the one destroyed, the other left intact—by pointing to the fact that *40 Years to Victory* fails to present a lucid alternative narrative. He concludes by dismissing Hame'agel's work as a flirtatious dialogue with symbols of Israeli society.[57] To some extent, this critique exists already *within* the exhibition, in its peripheral visual additions, the opening event, and the catalog. For, faced with the artist's confidence in the transparency of his critique, one cannot but wonder why were the more provocative versions of the billboards necessary, if not as a supplement to make sure the bus billboards were not to be misunderstood as sincere gestures of unreflective nostalgia.

Indeed, the exhibition is filled with provocative contradictions. On various levels,

40 Years to Victory calls for a conventional response and negates it at the same time. For one thing, Hame'agel stages a critique of consumer culture and the art market when he conflates the art object with advertising material, but at the same time, he accepts the institutional embrace of the Janco-Dada Museum and the generous patronage of the Cnaan advertising company, a move that leads to confusion regarding the subversive aspect of his endeavor. Furthermore, while *40 Years To Victory* is framed as street art, which leaves the constraints of the museum behind,[58] the self-censorship of the semi-pornographic images counters the claim of the freedom attained by relocation, and suggests that the absurd element of Honi Hame'agel's art operates within restrictive rules and regulations. A similar discomfort arises in relation to the exhibition's assertion of its critical treatment of historical ideals: the smooth glide of the images through the city streets seems conspicuous when taking Hame'agel's signature style into account. Thus, on the one hand, *40 Years to Victory* cries out in the name of artistic critique and sees the artist as a prophet of the apocalypse, and on the other hand, it is after all a tamed aesthetic event, a coproduction of various institutions that were all too happy to participate in an avant-garde event as long as it didn't "create provocation."[59]

However, what makes *40 Years to Victory* pertinent in my view is the fact that it remains ideologically ambivalent. This ambivalence prevents an ethical relief on the part of the art critic or the collector of memorabilia and may lead to an "uncomfortable dialogue," in Grossman's terms, as it restores a past frame of mind. I would argue that *40 Years to Victory* is more relevant in its vague and contradictory version on the buses than in its provocative revisions in the museum and catalog. Precisely because the bus advertisements mimic (rather than comment on) the performance of the greeting cards, they allow for a glimpse into the mechanisms that engender collective memories and identities. *40 Years to Victory* can just as well be interpreted as a celebration of militarism: this weakness is the exhibition's strongest point.

Hame'agel's provocative version of the greeting cards in the Janco-Dada Museum and in the exhibition catalog, Tartakover's poster and the objects on display in the exhibition *Six Days Plus Forty Years*, all maintain a temporal as well as ideological distance in relation to the greeting cards because they frame the memory of the 1960s militant state of mind as naive in comparison to the more self-aware present. Such recontextualizations, critical as they were, do not challenge the way that the greeting cards operate in contemporary culture. In contrast, the revived, but not revised greeting cards on the buses refuse this distinction and conflate present and past. More subtly perhaps, they raise doubts as to whether times have really changed and whether we contemporary viewers can wash ourselves free of the overt militaristic identity and ideology that seem to fit only in historical collections.

Conclusion: Nostalgic Operations

In his book *Twilight Memories*, Andreas Huyssen reminds us that the past is not simply there in memory, but must be articulated to become memory. There is an unavoidable fissure between experiencing an event and remembering it through representation.[60] The trajectory of the Rosh Hashanah greeting card images illustrates that the act of remembering is far from static, and that it has more to say about the culture that performs it than about the event that is brought back to light.

A specific type of memory, nostalgia too negotiates the place of certain histories within contemporary culture. Following Boym's distinction between restorative and reflective nostalgia, we can see that *40 Years to Victory* makes use of *both*, as it refers in different ways to the different pasts of the greeting cards. On the one hand, the visual citation of the greeting cards simply follows their current trajectory as nostalgic markers and conjures (both critical and uncritical) reflections on "the way we were." On the other hand, the relocation of the greeting cards into contemporary consumer culture makes a restorative move, bridges the gap between past and present, and so claims relevance for the cards' message today. Both moves are nostalgic, overlapping in their frame of reference but not in the narratives they construe.[61] The one keeps the past at bay (but dwells on it), while the other makes it preposterously present. The work of the past is repackaged as a contemporary occurrence, and so there are no clear boundaries between what is past and what is present, what is remembered now and what was remembered then, and how those memories shape the bodies to which they belong.

In complex ways, *40 Years to Victory* manages to straddle the seductions of nationalist nostalgia with exposing the mechanisms of nostalgic imagery, which are always inherently ideological.[62] The exhibition's edge, in fact, does not target those who may agree with its overt celebratory message, or those who side with Hame'agel's provocative adaptations in the Janco-Dada Museum. Rather, the truly subversive message of this show is aimed at those who treat the New Year greeting cards as objects of the past. The exhibition creates an impossible mnemonic constellation that goes against the idea of progress, while not resulting in the idolization of dated ideals: if the revolutionary potential of nostalgia lies in what Benjamin terms "blast[ing] open the continuum of history," Hame'agel blasts that continuum open in order to insinuate to the exhibit's Israeli audience that they have not changed as much as they might like to imagine.

Notes

1. For a short introduction to the Jerusalem Day national holiday, see the official Knesset website, http://www.knesset.gov.il/laws/special/eng/jerusalem_day_law.htm. For an overview of the human rights debate and related protests, see Adam Keller's blog, http://zope.gush-shalom.org/home/en/channels/archive/1181638993.

2. Examples include the exhibitions *Desert Generation* at the Jerusalem Artists House (organized by Larry Abramson, David Tartakover, Saliman Mantzur, and David Reeb) and *The Last Forty Years* on the Rothschild Boulevard in Tel Aviv (organized by the NGO Yesh Din), as well as *Acts of State 1967–2007* at the Minshar For Art gallery in Tel Aviv (curated by Ariella Azoulay) and *Six Days Plus Forty Years* at the Petach-Tikva Museum (curated by Rona Sela).

3. The English title of the exhibition appears in the catalog as *The 40th Anniversary of Victory*.

This translation lacks the more assertive quality of the Hebrew title, which literally translates to *40 Years to Victory*. Since the Hebrew title appears on all of the images and affects their legibility, I take the liberty of using my own literal translation of the original Hebrew title throughout this essay.

4. I would like to thank the artist, Honi Hame'agel, and the designer of the *40 Years to Victory* catalog, Shosh Wasserman, for their generous help in obtaining reproductions for this publication.

5. Shalom Sabar, "Hundred Years of 'Good Year' Greetings: To the History of the Custom and Its Artistic Development," in *Next Year: Greeting Cards from the Kibbutz*, ed. Muki Tzur (Givat Haviva: Yad Yaari, 2001), 11–12, 18.

6. Haim Grossman, "Soldier and Army of Peace and Security: Images of the Israeli Soldier and Army in the New Year Greeting Cards," *Zmanim* 81 (2003): 42.

7. Sabar, "Hundred Years," 26–27.

8. Ibid., 33; Grossman, "Soldier and Army of Peace and Security," 51.

9. For a thorough study of the part played by the popular culture of the 1960s in the dissemination of military-inflicted ideology, see Rona Sela, *Six Days Plus Forty Years* (Petach Tikva: Petach Tikva Museum of Art, 2007).

10. Tim J. Semmerling, *Israeli and Palestinian Postcards: Presentations of National Self* (Austin: University of Texas Press, 2004), 1–2. Semmerling's book conducts a close analysis of both Israeli and Palestinian postcards to show how each group advances its national narrative through this medium. The book was praised for its ability to show how "seemingly random scenes of people and places can convey important political meaning" (Stephen Zunes, review of *Israeli and Palestinian Postcards: Presentations of National Self*, by Tim J. Semmerling, *Political Communication* 23, no. 3 [2006]: 368), and criticized for its comparative strategy that obliterates the political inequality between the two national communities (Kamal Boullata, review of *Israeli and Palestinian Postcards: Presentations of National Self*, by Tim J. Semmerling, *Journal of Palestine Studies* 34, no. 4 [2005]: 109–10).

11. The pervasiveness of military themes within Israeli civilian society and culture has been discussed by many. For an introduction into the topic, see Uri Ben Eliezer, *The Making of Israeli Militarism* (Bloomington: Indiana University Press, 1998), and Baruch Kimmerling, *The Invention and Decline of Israeliness: State, Society, and the Military* (Berkeley: University of California Press, 2001).

12. Semmerling, *Israeli and Palestinian Postcards*, 37–41.

13. Sabar, "Hundred Years," 29–35.

14. I refer here to hegemonic Jewish Israeli society, since clearly the tradition of sending a Rosh Hashana greeting card was not a part of the lives of religious and ethnic minorities in Israel. In what follows I focus the analysis on this hegemonic group alone.

15. Grossman, "Soldier and Army of Peace and Security," 46, 53.

16. Ibid., 42.

17. Ibid., 48.

18. In this context, the use of portraits of women-soldiers on the greeting cards can be understood as what Chava Brownfield-Stein termed "erotic militarism." According to Brownfield-Stein's study, figures of women in uniform help to blur the boundaries between the civil and the military spheres, as well as to frame the military apparatus as something to be desired. Chava Brownfield-Stein, "Women Soldiers in the Field of Vision: A Fantasy of the State, a Discussion on the Eroticization of 'Civil-Militarism' in Israel through Visual Representations of Women-Soldiers [1948–1968]" (PhD diss., Bar-Ilan University, 2006).

19. The IDF parades, pictured on many of the greeting cards, recurred every year on Israel's Independence Day, around May, from 1948 until 1968 when they were officially canceled due to financial concerns. After 1968 there was only one more parade in 1973 to celebrate Israel's twenty-fifth anniversary. Since that time there are stationary weapon exhibitions on display around Independence Day, as well as aerobatic spectacles from time to time, but no more parades. For a historical overview of the parades, see Haim Grossman, "The History of IDF Parades on Independence Day," *Ariel: Journal for Yediat Ha-Aretz* 183–84 (2008): 12–35.

20. Benedict Anderson, *Imagined Communities: Reflections on the Origin and Spread of Nationalism* (New York: Verso, 1991).

21. Jeffrey K. Olick and Joyce Robbins, "Social Memory Studies: From 'Collective Memory' to the Historical Sociology of Mnemonic Practices," *Annual Review of Sociology* 24, no. 1 (1998): 116. For an elaboration on this argument, see Eviatar Zerubavel, "The Calendar," in *Hidden Rhythms: Schedules and Calendars in Social Life* (Berkeley: University of California Press, 1981), 70–100.

22. Olick and Robbins, "Mnemonic Practices," 124.

23. Eric J. Hobsbawm and Terence O. Ranger, *The Invention of Tradition* (Cambridge: Cambridge University Press, 1992), 1. On this note, the book *Contested Pasts: The Politics of Memory* by Katharine Hodgkin and Susannah Radstone (New York: Routledge, 2003) offers a large collection of essays that discuss memory in the national context.

24. A thorough analysis of this phenomenon can be found in Sela, *Six Days Plus Forty Years.*

25. Butler argues that repetitions over time normalize societal norms, that the citation of a social imperative fortifies the status of this imperative and at the same time makes the citer into a subject. This argument is clearly outlined in Judith Butler, *Bodies That Matter: On the Discursive Limits of "Sex"* (London: Routledge, 1993).

26. Susan Sontag, *Regarding the Pain of Others* (New York: Farrar, Straus and Giroux, 2003), 76–77.

27. For a critical overview of how the significance of the 1967 war was constructed, see Tom Segev, *1967: Israel, the War, and the Year That Transformed the Middle East,* trans. Jessica Cohen (New York: Metropolitan Books, 2007). Uri Ram offers a succinct account of the trajectories of Israeli collective memory and national identity in "National, Ethnic, or Civic? Contesting Paradigms of Memory, Identity, and Culture in Israel," *Studies in Philosophy and Education* 19, no. 5 (2000): 405–22. Finally, Yoav Gelber provides an illuminating study of the relations between memory, history, and propaganda in the Israeli context in his book *History, Memory, and Propaganda: The Historical Discipline at the Beginning of the 21st Century* (Tel Aviv: Am Oved, 2007).

28. Grossman, "Soldier and Army of Peace and Security," 53.

29. A salient critique of this newer tradition can be found in the work of the comic duo Yossi Atia and Itamar Rose, featured in the film *State of Suspension* by Mieke Bal and Benny Brunner from 2008, where exhibition visitors create on-the-spot *tableaux vivants* to portray the ambiance of a war of their choice.

30. The exhibition *Let Them Study War No More* from 2001 can be visited at the *New Profile* website, http://www.newprofile.org/?p=13#more-13 (in Hebrew).

31. A significant exception is a fairly recent TV commercial by the telecommunication company Cellcom. The commercial featured a group of soldiers playing football with an invisible team that is located on the other side of the Separation Wall. The commercial sparked heated discussions debating its ethics, as well as demands for its removal. It would be interesting, in a further study, to analyze why this commercial hit a nerve while many others pass unnoticed. For

more information regarding the commercial and the social debate around it, see for example Seth Freedman, "Cellcom's Cynical Commercial," *guardian.co.uk*, July 20, 2009, and conversely Yariv Oppenheimer, "Cellcom Ad Brave Display of Reconciliation" on the *Peace Now Israel* blog.

32. While military images from the late 1960s circulate on picture postcards today, and in that sense still take part in contemporary consumer culture, they emphasize the defensive nature of the soldiers rather than the army's strength (Semmerling, *Israeli and Palestinian Postcards*, 49–50), and thus echo the stylistic change that has been described above in relation to contemporary commercials and advertisements.

33. Svetlana Boym, *The Future of Nostalgia* (New York: Basic Books, 2001), xiii.

34. For an overview of the fortunes of "nostalgia," see Fred Davis, *Yearning for Yesterday: A Sociology of Nostalgia* (London: Free Press, 1979); and Marianne Hirsch and Leo Spitzer, "'We Would Not Have Come without You': Generations of Nostalgia," *American Imago* 59, no. 3 (2002): 253–76. For an overview of the various (and sometimes contradictory) understandings of nostalgia, see Suzanne Vromen, "The Ambiguity of Nostalgia," *YIVO Annual* 21 (1993): 69–86, and Michael Pickering and Emily Keightly, "The Modalities of Nostalgia," *Current Sociology* 54, no. 6 (2006): 919.

35. Vromen, *Ambiguity of Nostalgia*, 71.

36. Walter Benjamin contrasts homogenous, empty time with messianic time: the former abides to the modern conception of progress while the latter has a utopian dimension as it can "blast an era out of the homogeneous course of history" and resist its course. Walter Benjamin, "On the Concept of History," trans. Harry Zohn, in *Walter Benjamin: Selected Writings*, ed. Howard Eiland and Michael W. Jennings (1940; Cambridge, MA: Harvard University Press, 2003), 396. More recently, Hirsch and Spitzer discuss the potential of "resistant nostalgia" in the form of a "critical utopianism" that helps to imagine a better future. Hirsch and Spitzer, *Generations of Nostalgia*, 256.

37. Mieke Bal, Jonathan Crewe, and Leo Spitzer, eds., *Acts of Memory: Cultural Recall in the Present* (Hanover, NH: University Press of New England, 1999), xi–xv. A different attitude is presented in Christopher Lasch, "The Politics of Nostalgia," *Harper's Magazine*, November 1984, 65–70. Lasch blames nostalgia for betraying the past by isolating it, and thus denying its influence on the present. His view, however, can be understood as another take on how nostalgia operates as a memory act in the present.

38. Boym, *Future of Nostalgia*, 41–49.

39. Ibid., 42. Boym defines restorative nostalgia in line with Hobsbawm's take on invented traditions, as well as his distinction between habits of the past and habits of restoring the past.

40. Boym, *Future of Nostalgia*, 50.

41. Ibid., 10.

42. In this respect, see Uri Ram, "Citizens, Consumers, and Believers: The Israeli Public Sphere between Capitalism and Fundamentalism," *Israel Studies* 3, no. 1 (1998): 24–44. Ram outlines the relationship between consumerism and localist identity culture in Israel through an analysis of the general elections of 1996, and argues that the methods of the promotion of parties were detrimental for the practice of democracy.

43. "Cnaan Media in Motion: Advantages," Cnaan, accessed December 12, 2010, http://www.cnaanmedia.com/apage/18566.php.

44. Boym, *Future of Nostalgia*, 46.

45. Some of the artworks in the exhibition use the documentary material of the Six-Day War

time frame as their raw material, such as David Reeb's painting *Dayan & Arik* (1999), David Tartakover's collage *Victory* (1989), and Suka Glotman's movie *1968 Reversed Parade* (1999). Other works point to various aspects of militarism in contemporary visual culture, including photographs from Adi Nes's *Soldiers* series (1999), the Limbus Group's *Embroideries of Generals* (1997), and Gilad Ophir's *Shooting Targets* (1997).

46. This is especially true for the visual culture objects presented under a glass window in the center of the room.

47. See for example Lior Perry, "The Legend of Honi Hame'agel," *Koteret*, 1996; and Sarit Fox, "Shit Can Be Aesthetic Too: Conversation with Honi Hame'agel," *Ma'ariv*, March 1, 1996.

48. On one occasion Hame'agel locked his audience inside a cage, and on another he dripped blood on their heads. Performances that are more toned down, such as the recreation of the bathware chain store at the Janco-Dada Museum in 1996, usually include an element of bodily confrontation. It should be mentioned that Hame'agel's work deals predominantly with the place of the Holocaust in contemporary Israeli culture, and that on some occasions he makes (thought-) provoking connections between the memory of the Holocaust and militaristic aspects in contemporary Israeli society. Due to the scope of this text, these issues will not receive further attention. More information on the artist and his oeuvre can be found at http://www.hameagel.co.il.

49. A selection of images from the catalog can be found on the artist's website, http://www.hameagel.co.il (in Hebrew).

50. The rules of censorship that Cnaan Media abides by refer generally to "public sensitivity." While it is hard to pin down exact regulations, there are a few clear cases where advertisements were not mounted on the buses, mostly in relation to the portrayal of women within the Jerusalem district. See, for a case in point, Jonathan Lis, "Advertising Firms Censor Signs for Fear of Vandalism," *Haaretz*, November 27, 2008, accessed December 12, 2010, http://www.haaretz.com/print-edition/features/advertising-firms-censor-signs-for-fear-of-vandalism-1.258363.

51. For example, in March 1996 Hame'agel turned a candy store in the Dizengoff Shopping Center in Tel Aviv into a temporary museum, changing the names of products and conducting the behavior of the salesmen, all with the given consent of the center's director. His exhibition *Baptism*, also from 1996, was sponsored by the Homely chain for bathroom furniture and reconstructed one of the chain's shops, including its workers, at the Janco Dada Museum in the village of Ein-Hod. *40 Years to Victory* thus follows the trail of previous exhibitions in its confusion of art with artifact, as well as of museum-like and commercial space. In this light, the large space that the colophon fills up on the circulating bus billboards becomes clear: since here, the sponsor and the location of the exhibition belong to the advertising world, the work itself turns to be an advertisement, advertising its own existence.

52. Dana Gilerman, "What a Wonderful War," *Haaretz*, May 1, 2007, accessed November 29, 2010, http://www.haaretz.com/hasite/objects/pages/PrintArticle.jhtml?itemNo=854079.

53. Raya Zommer-Tal, *The 40th Anniversary of Victory 1967–2007* (Ein Hod: Janco-Dada Museum, 2007).

54. Haim Grossman, "Flirtatious Dialogue between Billboards and Symbols in Israeli Society," *Ofakim Hadashim* 37 (2007), accessed December 12, 2010, http://ofakim.org.il/zope/home/en/1181463089/1181995193.

55. Grossman, "Flirtatious Dialogue."

56. Tartakover is a well-known artist and graphic designer as well as a dedicated collector of Israeli memorabilia, which he sometimes uses as the base for his work. For Israel's fifty-fourth

Independence Day in 2002, Tartakover designed a provocative cover for *Ha'ir,* a weekly local newspaper, which alluded to the destruction of Palestinian houses. The publication led to reader complaints and a police file and provoked the cabinet's legal advisor to state that the artist is approaching red lines that cannot be crossed. Nevertheless, while Tartakover's combination of the New Year greeting card image with controversial political emblems did not pass without turmoil in the public sphere, the artist received the prestigious Israel Prize for his labor as educator, designer, and documenter within the field of Israeli design a mere two days after the above-mentioned warning. Neri Livneh, "On the State of the Political Artist," *Haaretz,* February 13, 2004, 52–54; Naomi Meiri-Dan, "Art, Architecture, and Politics in Triumphal Arches during the 20th Century," *Protocols: History & Theory* 10 (2008).

57. Grossman, "Flirtatious Dialogue."

58. Zommer-Tal, *40th Anniversary.*

59. Curator Zommer-Tal further delimits the critical aspect of Hame'agel's work when she defines him, in relation to another installation, as someone who turns everything into a celebration (quoted in Perry, "Legend of Honi Hame'agel.")

60. Andreas Huyssen, *Twilight Memories: Marking Time in a Culture of Amnesia* (New York: Routledge, 1995), 3.

61. Boym, *Future of Nostalgia,* 49.

62. Susan Stewart writes that "nostalgia, like any form of narrative is always ideological . . . nostalgia wears a distinctly utopian face, a face that turns toward a future-past, a past which has only ideological reality." Susan Stewart, *On Longing: Narratives of the Miniature, the Gigantic, the Souvenir, the Collection* (Durham, NC: Duke University Press, 1999), 23.

Chapter 5

The Photographic Memory of Asad Azi

Tal Ben Zvi

My Father Is a Soldier is a comprehensive exhibition based on four principle series of paintings—"soldiering," family, the Venus series, and the donkey-messiah series. This ensemble exemplifies how, during the last decade (since 2000) Asad Azi has increasingly drawn upon photographs from his family albums as a key source of his work. Each photograph appears in a number of works of a similar theme, in which the artist employs a variety of painting styles. This serialization exposes both Azi's unique artistic language and changing attitude in the face of the personal memory triggered by the photograph.

This essay focuses on only three photographs from the family album, to which Azi returns repeatedly in his works. These are three black-and-white images associated with everyday, private family life, not with historic public events. These photos constitute the core of the "soldiering" that features in his works, as they connect the father's death, the eldest son's orphanhood, and the image of the youngest son and namesake in a continuum depicting the biographical and symbolic fate of a single nuclear family.

Three Photographs: Father, Eldest Son, Son and Namesake

In the first photograph, from 1956, the soldier father appears dressed in uniform, lined up for military roll call of the border guard. The origin of the photograph remains unknown; the photographer was probably one of the soldiers, who must have given this picture to Azi's family. Sayah Azi is not holding a weapon in the photo. He stands at attention with his chest thrust forward. His shadow is clearly visible on the photograph's bright, glossy surface. An empty space spans before him, and behind him what seems to be a military base—a few trees, a barracks, and another soldier who holds a weapon while standing at attention next to a flagpole, on which an unidentifiable flag flies.

This is one of the few photographs that Azi possesses of his father, Sayah Azi, a

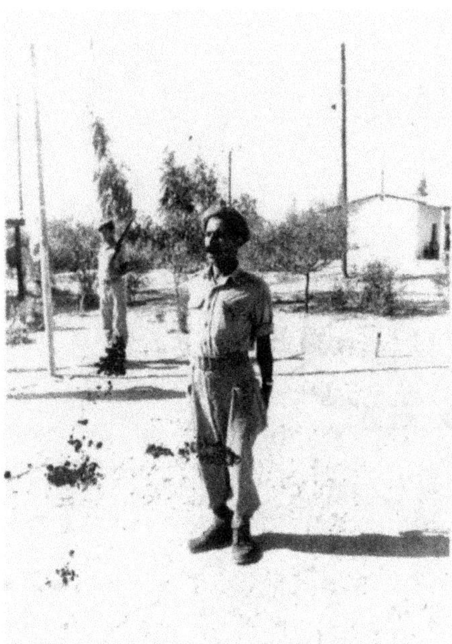

Sayah Azi, 1956.

Druze of Syrian origin. His father arrived in northern Israel from Syria in 1948. At the end of the war he remained in Shfar'am because he wanted to be near his sisters, who had married Druze men from the Israeli side of the border.[1] During the 1950's Sayah joined the border guard in the Israeli army in which, for ten years, he mainly served in a police unit whose objective was the prevention of infiltration through the country's northern border.[2] On May 30, 1961, he was killed by a Syrian patrol in one of the skirmishes that erupted frequently along the Israeli-Syrian border.[3]

Azi was five years old at the time of his father's death, the oldest of four children (Asad, Ibrahim, Faris, and Hayel). The youngest brother, Sayah, born after his father's death, was named after him. His mother, Akaber, was thus left with five orphans. In the second photograph, from 1962, about a year after his father's death, Azi, aged seven, is pictured on a bicycle between his two younger brothers, Ibrahim and Faris, aged six and five, respectively. The boys are wearing matching plaid shirts. Visible behind the boys in this indoor photo is a pile of mattresses. There are two disturbing elements in this family photograph: the first is that Azi looks like a girl in this picture, with long hair pinned with a lace bow; the second is that young Azi holds his father's military pistol in his hand. The photographer was a young Iraqi Jew named Habib, who, during those years, traveled among Shfar'am residents, taking family photos.

Until he was seven years old, Azi's hair had never been cut, a consequence of the intimate circumstances of his birth: before he was born, his mother suffered the miscarriages of two baby boys, after which she gave birth to a girl who died because of medical complications at the age of four months. Three years later, his mother became pregnant again and in order to protect the unborn child she vowed to Jethro, the Druze prophet, that if she was to give birth to a son, she would not cut his hair until he would

Asad, Ibrahim, and Faris, 1962.

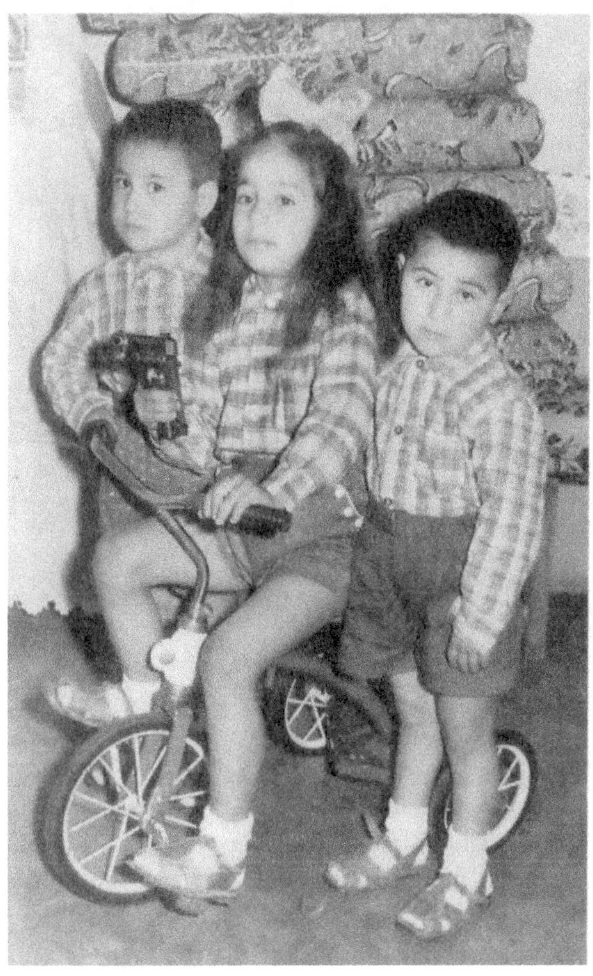

become six years old, at which time she would cut his hair at Jethro's gravesite and sacrifice a sheep as an offering of thanks. When Azi reached the age of six the women in the family began preparations for the feast, but about a week before the event his father was killed. His mother canceled the ceremony and did not cut his hair, despite pleas from family members. Azi relates how his mother had waited for some sign from the prophet. One evening Azi was standing on the porch of his house, gazing at a white towel, which suddenly transformed before his eyes into a white billy goat. The following day, his mother visited Jethro's grave, sacrificed the goat, and cut her son's hair.

The third photograph was taken on November 19, 1985, at the graduation ceremony of the youngest brother's officer training. In this photo the mother appears in the center wearing a long white head covering and a long dress. This is an important family moment for her: the youngest son, Sayah, is following in his father's footsteps. The son, not holding a weapon, stands with his arm around his mother's shoulder, while she embraces him around his waist. Six young men stand behind them: the two brothers, Ibrahim and Faris, a cousin, and two other friends who accompanied the mother to the

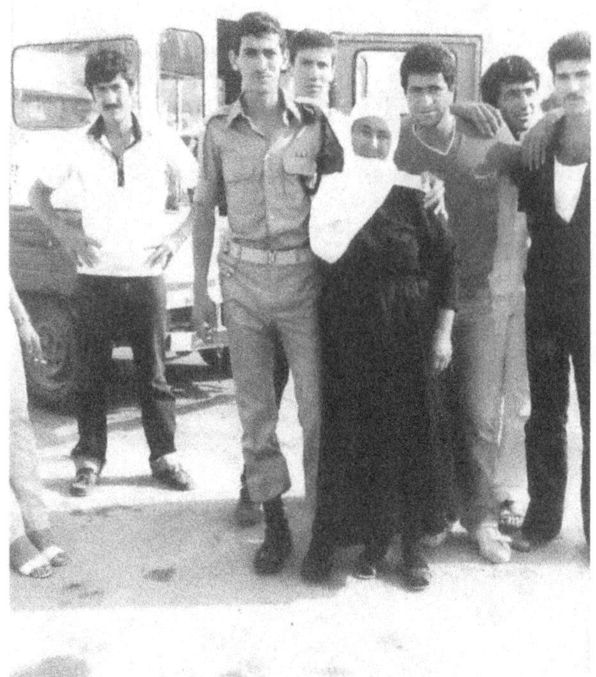

Sayah Azi, November 19, 1985.

ceremony. Faris, in a gesture of intimacy, places his hands on the shoulders of the two men standing to his right and left.

Sayah Azi the son served in the border guard for many years, until his retirement from service at the rank of commander, in 2005. The photograph may have been taken before or perhaps after the ceremony, and there is no visible clue as to the location or character of the event. The identification of soldiering in the photograph is based on Sayah's uniformed figure, military-issue boots, beret tucked into the shoulder board, and *Shalom Hagalil* war insignia pin, awarded to soldiers who served during the 1982 war, affixed to his shirt pocket. Family and friends, touching and hugging, appear like a single unit in this photograph. The photographer remains unknown, but was most probably a family member or friend.

The choice of photographs creates a closed circle of masculinity, beginning with the image of the father, the soldier, continuing with the image of the eldest son holding a pistol in the company of his younger brothers, and ending with the image of the youngest son and the father's namesake standing proudly next to his mother and surrounded by his family, whose presence forms a wall of intimacy and security.

Soldiering

The father's enlisting in the border guard after 1948 was to be a defining moment in the futures of his five orphaned sons, and especially in Azi's life, because it placed "soldiering" at the heart of the family, thereby establishing a link between identity, masculinity, and soldiering. I would like to examine the father's fateful decision, and moreover the historical circumstances surrounding this particular period in Shfar'am, where many of the residents became refugees after 1948.

After 1948 Shfar'am remained an integrated town of Christians, Druze, and Muslims.[4] Some of the area's Palestinian residents who had become "absentee landlords"[5] in their destroyed villages relocated to town. Others, the refugees, returned even during the war, only to wait in vain for reunification with refugee families in Lebanon and Syria. It is possible to assume that Sayah Azi, of Syrian origin, was not indifferent to their fate. Azi the father remained in Shfar'am. As a foreign resident without farmland or extended family he was obliged to support himself and make do in the complex reality following the *nakba* (lit. catastrophe, Arabic term used to describe the events of 1948) under martial law that was lifted only in 1965. Sabri Jiryis notes that the military administration ruled vast areas of the country (in the Galilee, the *meshulash* [lit. the triangle, the northern Sharon area comprising the villages of Um al Fahm and Kfar Kasem, among others] and the Negev) wielding very broad administrative authorities and operating a special network of military courts, but it was all aimed at the Arab citizens living in these areas. The military police regularly boarded buses and other vehicles in the area of Nazareth and Shfar'am, instructing the Arabs to disembark and then thoroughly checked their identities. Those without travel permits issued by the military governor of their residential area were jailed and tried in military courts. Some Druze were permitted to travel freely within and beyond the areas controlled by the martial law, as part of a policy intended to present the Druze as a separate people, thereby casting doubt on their belonging to the Arab nation. Following this same policy, in 1957, the Druze were decreed a "recognized religious sect," and thereafter it was decided that the word *Druze* be entered in identity cards and other official documents in the space designated for nationality, in order to differentiate them from "Arab."[6] The Druze population's attitude toward the compulsory enlistment law, which was applied to it in 1956, was not homogeneous. Many families were divided between supporters of and those who opposed the enlistment. Figures from the IDF's enlistment department, part of the army's manpower branch, show that out of 197 Galilean Druze men who were called up at the beginning of 1956, only fifty-one reported voluntarily for service. Of the 117 eligible young men from the Druze villages on Mt. Carmel, only thirty-two reported.[7]

In contrast to common wisdom and in partial contradiction to Israel's claim that the Druze asked to be conscripted, they were, to put it mildly, unenthusiastic about serving in the IDF. Their willingness to make a "blood covenant" with the IDF was, so it turns out, restricted and conditional. There were a number of reasons for the opposition to serve in the army, some of them personal (the natural reluctance and apprehension that people usually have with regard to army service), some connected to internal Druze politics (the community's division into factions that had different viewpoints of the issue), some relating to larger political influences (Druze identification with Arab nationalism or concern that service in the IDF would adversely affect their ties with Druze living in Arab countries).[8] In order to overcome the resistance, the police started arresting army refuseniks and, at the beginning of 1957, a special operation was conducted to locate refuseniks in Druze villages.

Against a background of steep unemployment in Shfar'am and the Galilee region, pressure was put on Druze youth to enlist in the Israeli army. Under the recruitment agenda, it was decided that the police were to use force in the form of arrests and the opening of criminal proceedings against draft evaders. As a means of persuasion, Druze youth were promised many significant benefits during the time of martial law, as opposed to the threats that were made according to which travel permits would be revoked from those who did not serve in the IDF, as well as the imposition of additional sanctions.[9] Under these circumstances, Sayah Azi, who enlisted in the IDF border guard and served near the northern border, was killed in 1961, facing the Syrian landscape—his birthplace.

The compulsory enlistment created a division between the Druze and other Arabs in Israel. Soldiering, therefore, then as now, marked a central conflict for many in the Druze society, heightening the tension between belonging to Israeli society on the one hand and to Arab society on the other. However, already in the 1960s it could be said that the identification of some Druze intellectuals with the Arab national movements was clear evidence that the question of whether the Druze should be part of the Arab national movement was still an open one and that it aroused tension within the community.[10]

The issue of Druze army service was a continuous source of concern for Arab society in Israel throughout all of the country's wars, especially with regard to the fighting along the northern borders between Syria and Lebanon. There, extraordinary encounters would take place between Druze family members who would often meet on two opposing sides of the battlefield. Salman Natour, a Druze poet and author from Daliyat al Carmel, writes about the First Lebanon War:

> Summer 1982. June was hot as usual . . . the planes flying over our village were loaded with ammunition and napalm, to be emptied over Lebanon's green fields. The fire began on June 4 and has not stopped since. When the fire of sadness burned in the skies of Daliyat al Carmel, and the choking feeling of grief and fear would spread throughout the village, the army trucks began to load up the enlisted young men transporting them to the battlefield, leaving the mothers with tears in their eyes. Why are they taking them to war?
>
> . . . We have a neighbor who was born in Lebanon and she gave birth there to three sons. She fell in love with another man and ran away with him to Palestine in 1948. They married and lived in our village and had three sons. The sons she left behind in Lebanon grew up and became fighters in the progressive Socialist Party, the party of Walid Jumblatt, while her children in Daliyat al Carmel were compulsorily enlisted. The truck loaded

> them up on the morning of June 5. I went over to her and found her sitting alone in her house; she sat, bent over, on the floor, holding a handkerchief soaked from the unending stream of tears that poured from her eyes, and she didn't say a word. "For whom do you cry, our neighbor?" I asked her. She raised her head and dabbed at the tears on her face and said, "the children!" I needed to gather extraordinary strength to ask her: For which of your sons do you weep? For those you left behind there [in Lebanon], or those just taken away on the truck, to there, to Lebanon? I didn't dare ask. As did she, so did I await her sons' return, in order to ask one question: Did you kill anyone there?"[11]

Many references to the emotionally charged subject of military service appear in Arabic literary texts, and in a number of artistic projects.[12] One such example is a collection of stories titled *Soldiers of Water,* by Naim Araidi, a Druze poet and writer from Maghar, a village in northern Israel. This volume presents a description of soldiers enveloped in white water that rises up from the sea. An abstract vision far removed from the image of aggressive militarism, it thus emphasizes all the more forcefully the passivity of the storyteller, until his return to the village.[13]

Shunning militarism and emphasizing the personal toll of service in the Israeli army are the themes of two plays in Arabic that were performed at the Al-Niqab Theater in Isfiya in 2002–3. The play *The Command,* written by Dr. Masoud Hamdan and directed by Salah Azzam, deals with the confrontation between a Druze soldier whose brother's house is demolished and representatives of the military police who arrive in the village with a police force, a court injunction for house demolition, and a bulldozer. The play *Salah Returns from the Army* is an adaptation of Dalton Trumbo's 1939 antiwar novel *Johnny Got His Gun.* The play tells the story of Salah, a young Druze who enlists in the army and returns gravely wounded, both physically and emotionally. Salah exposes the tragedy of war, its horrors and the price paid by the simple man when he it is trapped in it.[14]

Neither of these plays is unusual. Similar discussions have been taking place regularly in the Arabic-language newspapers, where the image of the soldier is expropriated from the nationalist-militarist discussion; on the other hand emphasis is given to the toll of soldiering as a sacrifice and the image of the soldier as a victim of historical, social, and political circumstances that began in 1948 and whose end is not in sight.

Paintings of the Soldier Father

Soldiering is a recurrent motif in the three separate family photographs that Azi chose as a basis for his paintings, although it appears that the word *soldier* that accompanies the works is detached from the semantic structure that is associated with militarism. Images of the father and the son appear alone, cut off from the background of the military units in which each of them served, and neither one holds a weapon. The only

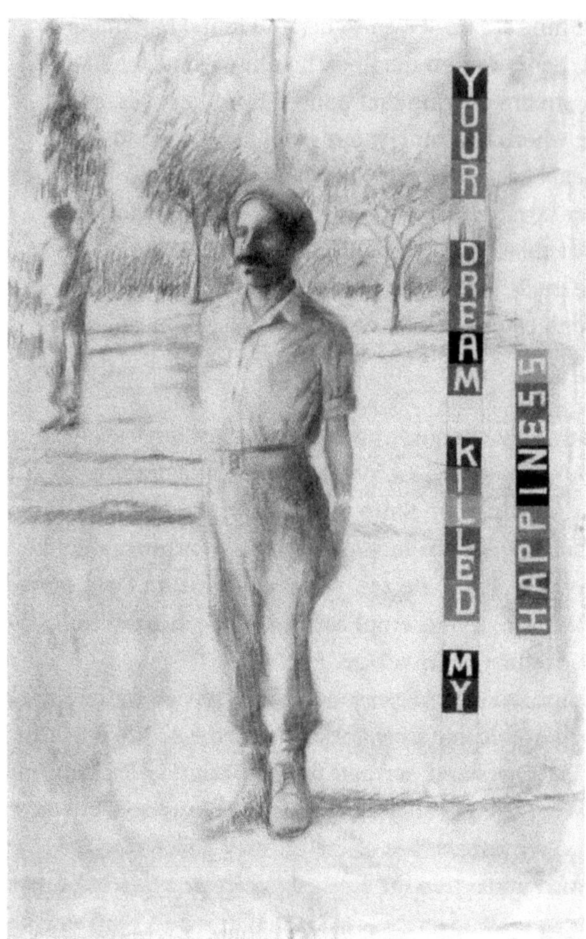

Father 2, 2004, 169 x 100 cm, mixed media.

weapon that appears in the photographs is in the hands of the boy, the eldest son, and it is merely a signifier rather than a deadly weapon.

In the series of paintings in which the image of the father-soldier appears, it seems that Azi is juxtaposing internal artistic themes such as composition, color, form, and text with the very real presence of his father. Azi is careful to preserve the format of the original photograph, its monochromatic palette, and, in a number of works, the sense of the figure's scale in relation to the viewer's gaze. This visual practice preserves the status of the original photograph as a witness to the father's presence in the artist's life, though in opposition to this image, Azi presents uncompromising colorfulness in the series *Signs of War.* In this painting, the father's image, executed as well in the technique of drawing, fills the entire canvas, which is washed in brown. On the right are the uncompromisingly colorful "military ribbons," which bear the English inscription: YOUR DREAM KILLED MY HAPPINESS.

The military ribbons appear in another work in which the image of the father

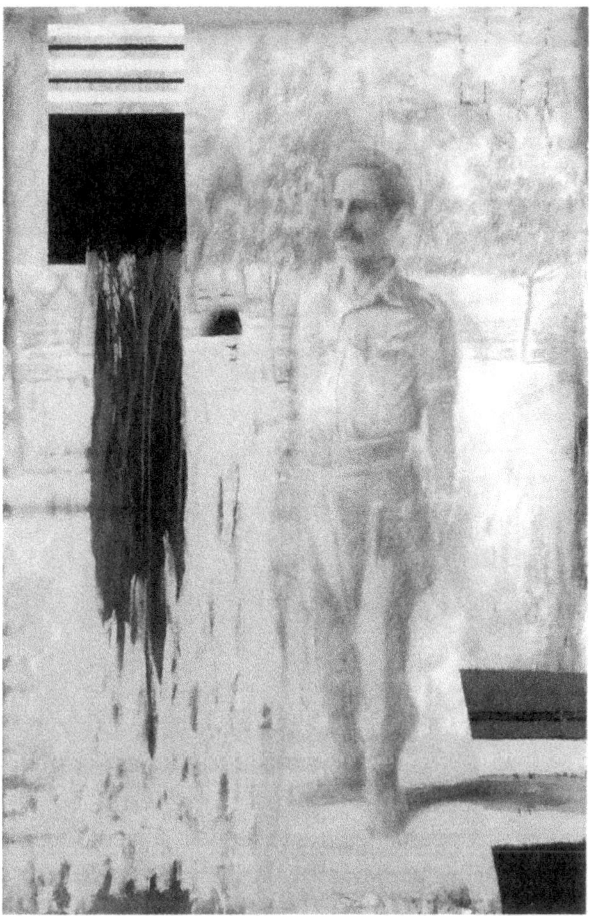

Father 7, 2004, 160 x 105 cm, oil and pencil on canvas.

appears in brown uniform. The tree behind is covered in green foliage. Black-and-white stripes with a black square appear in the upper part of the painting—a kind of military badge—and below there is an expressive patch of red fluid that drips to the bottom edge of the painting. Stripes appear again on the right side, here in black and green, and the father's shadow is cast on them. Azi marks the military ribbons in his works as a "surface that is divided into color sections." These color sections are not an improvisation on the original; there is no rationale in the choice of colors, and they are, therefore, a sign of war's irrationality and meaninglessness.

The symbolism of Israel's wars encoded in the military ribbons, as signifying the difference between those who were killed in battle, those who were killed in the course of a military drill, and those who died in traffic accidents, is not given expression here. "Your dream of becoming a soldier," argues the orphaned son before his father, "killed my happiness." But the father-soldier stands before the text with empty arms, without a flag, without a weapon. He kills no one and does not take part in any act of heroism.

In several paintings, Azi deviates from the format of the original photo. Here, he rather copies only the image of the father, placing it in an especially colorful setting of a

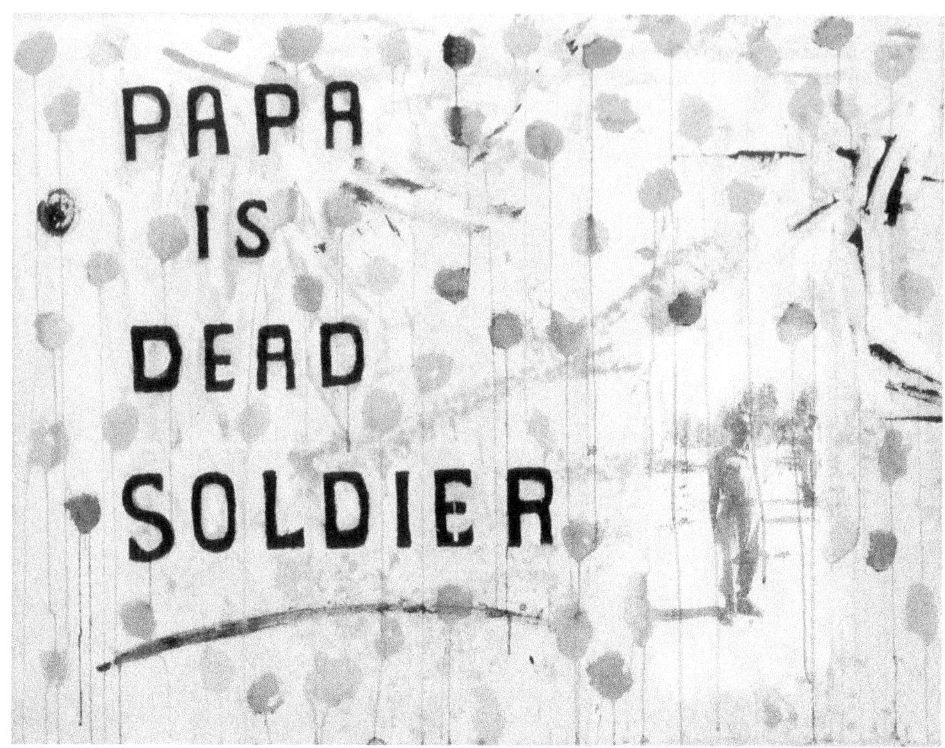

Father 8, 2004, 165 x 105 cm, oil on canvas.

painting. Opposite the image he adds texts in English that say that his father is a dead soldier. In one particularly colorful work, the father's image appears on a surface that is filled with colorful dots on which is written in black, in English: PAPA IS [A] DEAD SOLDIER. Another work from the same series is divided into a number of colorful squares that create a picture of a grid, in which multiple, relatively small images of the father from the photograph may be seen. Expressive brush strokes are visible in this painting, as well as the words: MY DADDY IS A DEAD SOLDIER, in colorful lettering. In another painting, the surface of the canvas is divided in two, with one part divided into a grid made up of many squares, some bordered in color, and others empty. A bold brush stroke draws the eye to the other half of the painting where the isolated image of the father is set against a uniform mustard color surface. Above is a black sky and dark red sun. The following words appear on the painting: MY DADDY IS [A] DEAD SOLDIER.

These English sentences that denote the father's death establish a connection to the main characteristic of the photograph in the modern age, as based on the theoretical writings of Roland Barthes—that is, the process of connotation that builds the photographic message. In his writings, Barthes emphasizes the process of the connoted message of the photograph, in other words the subjugation of the secondary meaning of the photographic message that is executed in the various levels of the photographic process. These processes of connotation are based among other things on positioning, in other words, the positions of the figures seen in the photograph, the objects that appear in the image, and the text that appears in or accompanies the image in the form of a caption. As a result of these connoted codes, the reading of a photograph is always historical and dependent upon language and culture. Stressing this, Barthes notes: "Thanks to its code of connotation the reading of the photograph is thus always historical; it depends on the reader's 'knowledge' just as though it were a matter of a real language [*langue*], intelligible only if one has learned the signs."[15] Thus Azi's image of the father-soldier appears in the original photograph and subsequently in the form of drawing in the works of art, and thus undergoes immediate categorization and is understood literally and in truth as such. Even before we read the written text, we read as a matter of fact the word *soldier* in the photo/drawing, while this reading divides the viewers of the painting or the readers of the text into separate linguistic communities, communities of language, society, and culture.

Shfar'am, the city where Asad Azi was born, has a complicated identity. Residents are Christian, Druze, and Muslim, living in an Arabic-speaking environment, where Arab Palestinian culture and identity have existed for generations. Azi is a graduate of Haifa University as well as of Tel Aviv University; he teaches at Beit Berl Academic College, School of Art, and lives and works in Jaffa. For the past thirty years he has been actively engaged in Israeli culture and in the Hebrew language. Much has been written about Azi's identity as an Arab Druze artist working in Israel,[16] but in the context of this exhibition, it is important to emphasize the semantic dimension of the Hebrew and Arabic languages in general and their presence in the contemporary art scene. Azi writes, "My father is [a] dead soldier" in English, not in Arabic or Hebrew, as a signifier that is outside of the linguistic system in which he functions. On the levels of plain language and written text, the word *jundi* (جُنْدِيّ), which means soldier in Arabic, is not present in his works, just as the Hebrew word for soldier, *hayal* (חייל), is also missing. However, on this primary level, once the image is visually grasped and literally actuated, the presence of both of these words is forcefully felt.

The semantic space of the image of "soldiering" is a prominent characteristic of Israeli art. From 1948 until today, the image of "soldiering" has reflected myths, values, and notions connected to Israeli national culture, the military history of Israel's wars, the recruitment of its youth, and the idea that "it is good to die for our country," the feelings of victimhood and grief, the world criticism of the ongoing Israeli occupation of the West Bank and Gaza, the Palestinian intifada, the Lebanon War, the settlements, and more. These criticisms are part of the historical narrative of Israeli art, and these images have quickly become its canon. Throughout the continuum of these images of "soldiering," the men and women soldiers in the works are almost always either Jews or enemy soldiers. The depiction of Arab, Druze, or Bedouin soldiers—all citizens of Israel—has been almost nonexistent in Israeli art, from its inception until today. Thus Israeli art creates and reflects a closed system of imagery that strengthens the national ethos that is based on Jewish-Hebrew identity. Unusual in this respect is a single photograph that appears in the book *The Israelis* by Micha Kirshner. The photograph, *The Grave of Colonel Nabiha Mer'i* in Hurfeish, was published in the newspaper *Ma'ariv* in 1996 (Nabiha Mer'i, born in the Druze village of Hurfeish, a colonel in the Israeli army, was killed by Palestinian fire in the Gaza Strip during confrontations connected to the riots that followed the opening of the tunnel under the Western Wall.) In the photo, flower wreaths surround the base of the grave marker. The sign bears the IDF symbol, Mer'i's personal number, rank, date of burial, 27.9.1996, and the text (in Hebrew) "Soldier Memorial Unit, Department of Rehabilitation—Ministry of Defense." The photo is a bit burned, yellowed, a kind of orange-gold. Kirshner treated the photo: between the wreaths he scattered green patches of color, like camouflage, and on the golden tear he created two gray patches and between them glued ripped pieces of newspaper that spell out the sentence, in Hebrew, "Son of the country."[17]

Azi is aware of the literal meaning of the word for soldier in Hebrew and in Arabic, just as he is aware of its cultural and political meanings in these languages, yet, opposite them, he places the English language as an interim space, a kind of momentary delay. In this context, English is not just a foreign, nonindigenous language, seemingly neutral and universal, the international language of the art world, but rather an especially charged language, which in the historical circumstances of the British Mandate, is identified with 1948 and the traumatic division of the Arabic and Israeli space.

The English word *soldier* that appears in the works is used as a kind of interruption, block, and border against the immediate categorization of the word *jundi* in Arabic and *hayal* in Hebrew. This interruption briefly delays the cultural and political appropriation of the situation by these languages, and all that that implies. This interruption creates an interim period that allows for various readings while studying the painting. This suspension marks a linguistic, cultural, and political division and conjures questions about appropriation, belonging, identity, and the meaning of identifying with someone or something.

Paintings of the Eldest Son and the Pistol

The second family photograph, in which the artist figures as a child with long hair, holding a pistol, appears in another series of works. In this series Azi not only preserves the format of the original photograph but also brings it to life, and turns it according to his memory from black and white into color. The colorfulness is not expressive but more realistic in its character, and its purpose is to make the original photographed scene more approachable and to create the possibility of returning there.

Making the original scene approachable becomes the visual subject, which Azi enables through his use of an authentic object that features in the original photograph—namely, the shirts worn by each of the boys when the photograph was taken. Azi returns to his house in Shfar'am, to the closets inside, and finds the shirts that he and his brothers had worn when they were children. He cuts out a square from each shirt, and creates in each work a double layout, in which on one side of the canvas is the painted scene of Azi and his younger brothers dressed in these plaid shirts, and on the other side is a square piece of fabric, in a pattern that is identical to one of the shirts worn by

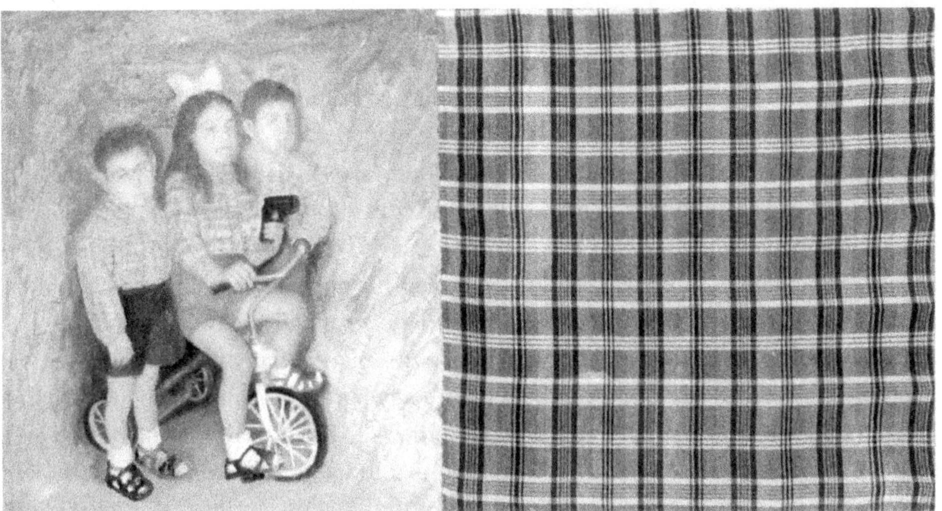

Three brothers and a gray shirt, 2005, 85 x 45 cm, oil on canvas.

one of the children in the painting. The actual piece of fabric appears sometimes like a curtain that covers something and at other times as an abstract geometric space. The background of the children's images changes from painting to painting: in one of them, the painted mattresses are visible behind the boys, in another the background is made of monochromatic brush strokes, and in the third a mirror leaning against the wall is seen next to the boys, on which the image of the mother holding a baby is reflected. As opposed to the strict adherence to the photographic format in the works that are based on the photo of the father, is seems that here there is a quest for and meditation on the actual scene in the photograph. Azi remembers quite clearly the circumstances under which this photograph was taken, and the fact that the photographer, Habib, the Jew of Iraqi origin, asked that the pistol not be pointed in his direction, but rather to the side. However, it appears that despite this recollection, he does not rely on it entirely and therefore offers a number of settings for this scene that are removed from the original photograph.

Benedict Anderson points to the role of the photograph in the construction of biographic memory "backwards in time." According to Anderson, the photograph is the most conclusive type in the huge modern accumulation of documentary evidence that records apparent continuity and emphasizes its loss from memory. "Out of this estrangement," writes Anderson, "comes a conception of personhood, identity . . . which, because it cannot be 'remembered,' must be narrated."[18] The biographic story therefore rests on a sequence of photos from an album, which creates a seeming series and wholeness. Azi, however, is aware of the impossibility of finding comfort in the imagined awareness of childhood, and in his painting he builds a semantic sketch in Arabic that is made up of pieces of the whole.

The word *yatom* in Hebrew (lit. orphan) is *yatim* (يـتـيـم) in Arabic, meaning singular and unique. The orphan symbolizes the part that is missing from something that is more whole, and orphanhood is also an expression of the part that is missing from the intimate relationship of the parents. The word in Arabic for gun is *fard* (فَـرْد), which can mean private (as in a soldier's rank), singular, alone, unique, and one of a pair. The pistol is thus single—a weapon that fires in single rounds, one bullet at a time, as opposed to a rifle that fires in multiple rounds. But it also signals the missing part—one of a pair. Indeed, traditionally in Arab culture the gun was always positioned next to the sword. Analogously, the artist's girl-like appearance with a lace bow in his hair is a unique presentation, one that is indeed singular; his appearance might be said to be *inferadi* (إِنْـفِـرَادِيّ) in other words, individualistic, singular, and unique.

Azi creates a complete composition out of parts, pieces of identity that do not make a complete whole, but are unique in both their being partial and their dialogue with the imagined whole. Azi returns to this photograph as a foundational image, but also as a sore that refuses to heal. As against this imagined unity of the three orphans in their identical shirts and poses, in the framework of the nuclear family, the artist pits the taking apart, the partialness that can never create a single imaginary whole.

Paintings of the Son and Namesake

In the series of paintings that portray Sayah the son and his mother standing together, Azi's painterly attitude comes to the fore; it is characterized by the disconnection of the paintings in the series from the original photograph on which they are based. This painterly viewpoint has three main characteristics: Firstly, Azi cuts off completely the image of the mother and son from the context of family and friends and places them in a separate scenic space; secondly, after separating the image of the mother and son from the original photo, he turns them into images of a man and a woman of nonspecific age; thirdly, the painterly act points to the breaking free from the photographic image, and to the focus on the physical, expressive act of painting that is executed partly with fingers rather than with a brush.

Only one work features a full-size black-and-white drawing of the original. This drawing, however, becomes the background for the foreground images of the mother and son, which are reproduced in color. The coloring here is dramatic: the sky is colored a pale blue as is the mother's dress, the uniform is brown and the boots and beret are red. The colors seep beyond the borders of the figures, and drip from them toward the bottom of the canvas.

Images of the mother and son with blurred faces also appear in works done on paper printouts from AutoCAD, a graphics computer program architects use. In one such painting, images of the mother and son appear at their most expressive. The upper part of the work is a sort of sky painted in stormy splashes of light blue. The mother's face looks like a blotch of color, and her body and her son's face appear as a single patch of color. Printed on the background are sentences in Hebrew, among them, "Tel Aviv University," "Department of Engineering," "European system," and such. As the only presence of the Hebrew language in this exhibition, these phrases offer an alienated

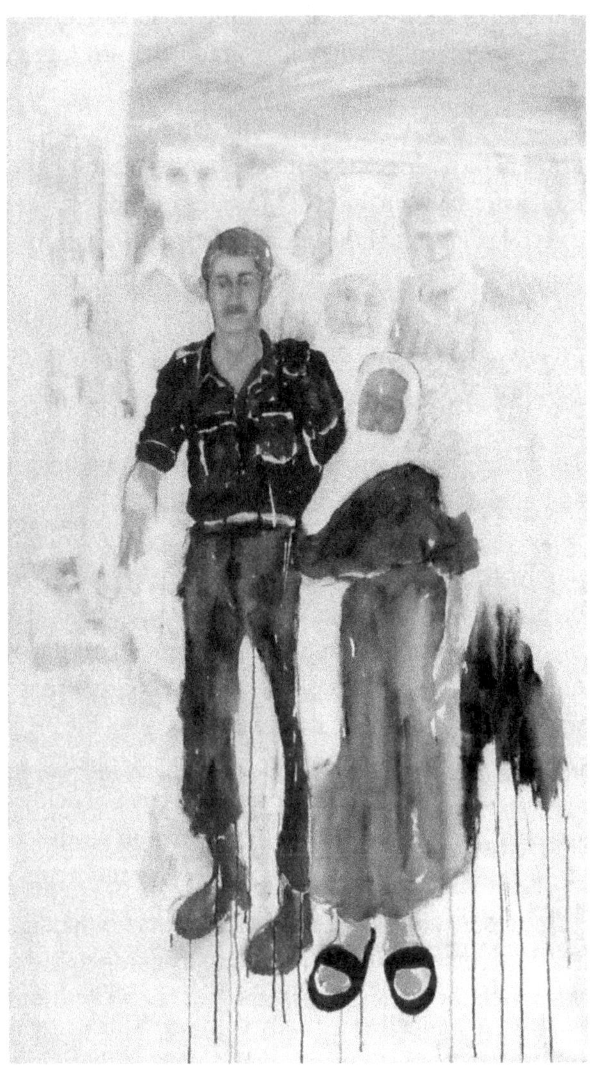

Mother and son, 2008, 175 x 105 cm, oil and pencil on canvas.

and technical space that is far removed from the personal sentences in English that tell about the father and his death, or the letter in Arabic, addressed to the father, that tells of the son's loneliness and fragile emotional state.

The soldier's pose as he stands next to the woman is self-conscious, as if aware of its being a conventional sign of manliness, stability, and authority. The soldier stands at attention; he is tall and looks directly at the viewer. Azi compromises this pose by emphasizing the soldier's skinny legs, which, in something of a caricature, make him look a bit like a scarecrow. The painterly treatment also draws attention to the scarecrow-like quality, as for example in the soldier's arm, which is not painted in its entirety, and thus appears fragmented and detached. Color drips from the soldier's body, draining out of him, and he seems to be transparent, permeable, vulnerable, and exposed. The blurred face and watery color destabilize the female figure, and thus the two figures seem to move apart from each other; the emotional connection between mother and soldier wanes to the point where they gradually turn into symbols without the physical substance or realistic presence that exists in the original photograph.

There is a fundamental difference between the expressive painterly quality, with drops of color dripping from the figures, in this series of works, and the photographic monochromatic qualities of the painting in the soldier-father series and the realistically colorful paintings of the boy with the pistol. It seems that in the mother-son series, Azi subverts two systems of authority that are inherent to the original photographs: the first is "soldiering" as a source of the father's authority, and the second is the authority of the mother, who guides her son to continue in his father's footsteps, notwithstanding her widowhood.

The images of the father-soldier, the eldest son holding the pistol and the youngest son and namesake in the original photographs, create a continuity of soldiering, a closed circle of masculinity that outwardly appears to be the cohesive force of the nuclear family. The original photos show us the power of certainty, a sense of security that is based on the feeling that "he was there," which accompanies the photographed moment. Vis-à-vis this moment of certainty, Barthes maintains, one must assess the relationship of the photograph to death: "It's true that a photograph is a witness, but a witness of something that is no more. Even if the person in the picture is still alive, it's a moment of this subject's existence that was photographed, and this moment is gone . . . each perception and reading of a photo is implicitly, in a repressed manner, a contact with what has ceased to exist, a contact with death."[19]

Azi's painterly attitude wrestles with moments of parting—from what no longer exists, from personal memory that yearns for the moment of truth, and from certainty. The constant returning to the original photographs in these works expresses an unending search for a grieving process that is ongoing, and in which there is neither acceptance of the situation nor any comfort. This brave and profound search exposes the intimate space of the private home, with all the subtleties of feelings that flow between the father, the orphaned sons, the youngest son and namesake, and the mother, thus exposing the heavy price that is paid by each family member and by the entire family for "soldiering," which looms over the family photographs like a dark shadow, like a vow that cannot be absolved.

Notes

A previous version of this essay was published in the exhibition catalog *Asad Azi, My Father Is a Soldier,* exhibition curated by Meir Ahronson, Ramat-Gan Museum (Tal Ben Zvi, "The Photographic Memory of Asad Azi," 2009).

1. At the time of the British Mandate, some Druze men regarded themselves as part of the national Arab (Palestinian) movement, while others supported the uniqueness of the Druze and even called for ties with the Zionist movement. Thus in the 1948 war, there were Druze who sided

with the Jewish forces, Druze who joined the Arab forces, and many others who maintained their neutrality. From the beginning of 1948, attempts were made by the headquarters of the Arab Rescue forces, led by Fausi El Kaukaji, to enlist Druze mercenaries in Syria. Four hundred Druze soldiers enlisted because of the hunger and unemployment that prevailed in Jabel Eldruz at the time. This regiment arrived in March 1948, and settled in the Shfar'am area. The Druze who assisted the Haganah and the IDF provided a liaison between the Haganah commanders and those of the Druze regiment who had arrived from Syria to fight alongside the Arab forces. They succeeded in pushing some of this regiment's fighters to defect. See Benny Morris, *The Birth of the Palestinian Refugee Problem, 1947–1940* (Cambridge: Cambridge University Press, 1989), 33; and M. Kais Firro, *The Druze in the Jewish State* (Leiden: Brill, 1999), 43.

2. Since 1956 the compulsory enlistment law has been applied to the Druze population in Israel.

3. On the official Druze memorial site "Yad le-Banim ha-Druzim," the following inscription appears: "Sayah Azi, son of Ibrahim, born in 1923, in the Druze Mountains, Syria. Immigrated to Israel in 1948 and settled in Shfar'am. In 1956 enlisted in the Border Guard and joined the company stationed in the north. On May 30, 1961, while at the *Mishmar ha-Yarden* base near the Syrian border, shots were fired toward the observation station. Upon hearing the shots Azi went down toward the station with a fellow military policeman, in order to investigate and offer assistance. When he returned, Azi was shot in the head by a Syrian sniper. He was killed instantly. Sayah's funeral took place in Shfar'am, and according to the wishes of the family his body was interred in the military cemetery in Osafia. He is survived by his widow, Akaber, who is three months pregnant, and their four sons." See http://www.druzim.co.il.

4. Benny Morris notes that on July 14, 1948, after heavy shelling of the Muslim quarter in Shfar'am, soldiers of the seventh brigade entered the city to find it almost empty of Muslim residents. Thousands had fled east to Sepphoria. On the next day, IDF planes bombed Sepphoria, killing a few residents. Panic broke out in the village and most of the inhabitants were driven north to Lebanon. The village was destroyed later and the Zippori (Sepphoris) National Park was built on the ruins. See Morris, *The Birth of the Palestinian Refugee Problem*, 268–69.

5. The term *absentee landlord* in Israeli law is applied to any property owner who left Israel and moved to an enemy country between November 29, 1947, and September 1, 1948.

6. Throughout their history, the Druze never enjoyed the status of a separate religious group. The Ottoman authorities did not award them this right, nor did the British Mandate change their legal status. They were subject to the Muslim juridical system. On the other hand, the Druze population in Israel was awarded an independent religious status in a three-stage process: The first stage was in 1957, when the minister of religions recognized the separate status of the Druze as an independent religious group, within the capacity of his authority according to the Religious Groups Act of 1926; the second stage took place in October 1961, when the Druze principal spiritual authority was recognized as a three-member "religious committee," headed by Sheik Amin Tarif, one of the notables of the village of Julis in the western Galilee; and the third stage was on December 25, 1962, when the Knesset completed this process by passing the law of the Druze Courts. Since then, members of the Druze population have been judged in these courts in matters that are within the authority of the religious judiciary institutes. See Sabri Jiryis, *The Arabs in Israel* (Beirut: Al Atiahad Press, 1966), 24; and Firro, *The Druze*, 168.

7. Hillel Cohen, *Good Arabs* (Berkeley: University of California Press, 2009), 160.

8. Hillel Cohen describes in detail the Druze resistance to enlistment in the IDF, noting that

the reasons for this resistance were enumerated by dozens of sheikhs from Shfar'am and its surroundings, in a letter that they sent to the prime minister and the minister of defense (February 18, 1957): "In light of the difficult and delicate conditions in which we find ourselves, we reject finally and absolutely the demand to perform mandatory labor in the Israel Defense Forces. We are Arabs in Israel and we have a duty to perform all the obligations that civil law imposes on us, such as paying taxes. But it is extremely important to know that we are first of all Arabs, and no Arab fights against his brothers under any circumstances and in any place." These were weighty reasons, and hundreds of Druze signed a petition to this effect. The opposers also expressed their fear that mandatory army service would not only harm the community in Israel but also create hardships for the Druze in nearby countries. For a few months, it seemed that this mass resistance would require the Ministry of Defense to reconsider its position. But this was not the case. The draft resistance movement did not long withstand the arrests and efforts at persuasion. The support it received from the community leadership dissipated, and the protests slowly died out. See Cohen, *Good Arabs*, 161–62.

9. Ibid., 189–99; Maria Rabinowitz, "Incorporation of Members of the Druze Sect into the IDF and the Workforce," in *Proceedings of the Knesset* (Jerusalem: Knesset, 2008), 226–27 (Hebrew).

10. Cohen, *Good Arabs*, 168.

11. Salman Natour, "Remembering the Place, Place of Memory," *Gag* (1998): 90–91.

12. One of the few artistic projects that address the complexity of the army service in Israeli-Arab society is the 2005 series *Ha-Gashashim* (the trackers) by the photographer Ahlam Shibli. The series is made up of eighty-five photographs that document the Bedouin soldiers who volunteer in the IDF. With her camera, Shibli follows the Bedouin privates in the army, at their homes, and in surrounding public spaces. In the exhibition text, Shibli notes that the series studies the price that a minority is forced to pay the ruling majority, perhaps in order to be accepted, to change its identity, to survive, or for all these reasons and more. See Ahlam Shibli, *Trackers* (Koln: Verlag, 2007), and John Berger, *Hold Everything Dear* (London: Verso, 2007). See further, http://www.ahlamshibli.com/Works/Trackers.htm.

13. Naim Araidi, *Soldiers of Water* (Tel Aviv: Ha-Sidrah Ha-Petuha, 1988), 114.

14. The play, *Salah Returns from the Army*, an adaptation of Trumbo's novel *Johnny Got His Gun*, was translated and directed by Salah Azzam, performed by Moujib Mansour. The play was performed at the Masrahid festival in Acre in 2003, where it won the prize for Boldest Script, awarded by the weekly *Terfiizion*. See further, http://alniqabtheatre.com.

15. Roland Barthes, "The Photographic Message," in *Image, Music, Text*, trans. Stephen Heath (New York: Hill and Wang, 1977), 28.

16. See Gal Ventura, "Identity Problems in the Work of Asad Azi" (master's thesis, University of Jerusalem, 1998 [Hebrew]); Meir Ahronson, *Asad Azi, Journey to the Chronicles* (Ramat Gan: Ramat Gan Museum, 1999); Neta Gal-Azmon, *Foreign Language: Asad Azi and Meir Pichhadza* (Um al Fahem: Um al Fahem Gallery, 2005); Ganit Ankori, *Palestinian Art* (London: Reaktion Books, 2006).

17. See Micha Kirshner, *The Israelis* (Or Yehuda: Hed Artzi, exhibition catalog, 1997) (Hebrew).

18. See Benedict Anderson, *Imagined Communities: Reflections on the Origin and Spread of Nationalism* (London: Verso, 1991), 204.

19. See Roland Barthes, "On Photography," in *The Grain of the Voice: Interviews, 1962–1980*, trans. Linda Coverdale (New York: Hill and Wang, 1985), 356.

Chapter 6

"We Shall Remember Them All"

The Culture of Online Mourning and Commemoration of Fallen Soldiers in Israel

Liav Sade-Beck

Introduction

Israeli society has long devoted a central position to the commemoration of soldiers who lost their lives during their national service. Along with the rituals of Remembrance Day and Independence Day, an entire culture of commemoration of soldiers has also developed. This memorial culture is implemented through statues, booklets, assemblies, events, ceremonies, and more. Some commemorative activities are accomplished through the private initiative of the bereaved families and friends, while others are arranged by public and national agencies, such as government institutions, municipal bodies, and various organizations established for that purpose. Since the turn of the twenty-first century, virtual commemorative websites in memory of fallen soldiers have proliferated. The flourishing of these sites, particularly the constant increase in the number of private websites giving voice to different styles of commemoration, are closely associated with two parallel processes that have taken place in Israeli society over the past two decades: First, the separation from the ethos of "just war," which led to a crumbling of the standing and image of the IDF (Israel Defense Forces), and the development of a civilian culture as a substitute for the necessary militaristic culture of the early years of statehood; second, the computer revolution and the massive, rapid penetration of digital media, foremost among them the Internet, into Israeli households. The merging of these two processes led to a rise in the participation of civilians in the public political discourse in Israel, narrowing the distinction between private and public space and adding to the ever-increasing democratization of society, including the "privatization" of mourning.

This chapter examines the question of whether virtual commemoration has remade the culture of mourning and commemoration of fallen soldiers in Israel by creating new patterns and narratives, or whether it merely replicates the traditional patterns and narratives of commemoration that have long characterized the culture of bereavement in Israel.

A paradox lies in parents' opposition to the IDF, the government, and "unjust war." In an important sense, bereaved families' attempts to challenge the hegemonic memory have also undermined their own exclusive position in the "circle of the bereaved" in Israel. To restore their lost position in this "hierarchy of bereavement" and its accompanying social privileges, bereaved families once again sought to include the death of their loved ones under the rubric of a "beautiful death" in the service of nation and homeland. Thus they once again replicate the Zionist-nationalist rhetoric of the state, which they themselves have been working to deconstruct.

Even websites that protest actions or errors by the IDF and the Israeli government, criticize their conduct, or demand improvement (any of which actions deemed unacceptable until about two decades ago, and would never have been publicized) do not contradict the hegemonic message dictated by the Zionist tradition and militarist culture that developed in Israel since the founding of the state. On the contrary, not only do the commemorative online memorials present the fallen soldiers as heroes, but alongside their criticism, they also call for a reinforcement of traditional norms, such as military heroism, comradeship in arms, and self-sacrifice for the homeland. As additional groups enter the arena of commemoration, their representation of self and their agenda seems to preserve and even reinforce the metanarrative of Zionism, which maintains its dominant position in the culture of bereavement in Israel.

Background

The official government commemorative website, Izkor (Jewish liturgical prayer for the departed, lit. May He remember), presents a worthy case study for examining the expression of patriotism and heroic death in official commemorative websites. Here I describe processes that led to the breakdown of hegemonic memory and old patterns of commemoration, the roles of the nationwide "family of bereavement," and of the media in this process. Between 2001 and 2003 I conducted anthropological fieldwork, concentrating on Israeli memorial and commemorative websites and virtual bereavement and loss support communities. My research was conducted both online and offline, using three integrated, complementary, methods of data gathering: online observations, interviews, and analysis of documents and articles from the electronic press and Internet databases. In-depth interviews were conducted with people who initiated, established, and manage the websites. Simultaneously, nonparticipatory online observations were carried out, and I analyzed documents and other varied materials associated with online commemoration and mourning.[1]

The beginning of the twenty-first century witnessed a clear and constant rise in the number of home computers in Israel, users, frequency of Internet use, and variety of services. Israel's Central Bureau of Statistics (CBS) reported that by 2004, 83 percent of all Jewish households in Israel had a high-speed Internet connection.[2] The rapid and widespread proliferation of the use of the Internet in Israel lies at the heart of the technological impact on online memorial processes. Between 2001 and 2003, the number of online memorial websites (especially personal sites) grew from 130 to 300.[3] Official websites commemorating the fallen located at the heart of the national consensus, such as those who fell in Israel's wars and terrorist attacks, or devoted to political figures such as assassinated Prime Minister Yitzhak Rabin, feature much more inclusive and uniform content, leaving less room for individual bereavement, as they attempt to avoid issues of social conflicts in Israeli collective memory. For example, the official Izkor site presents a uniform format: a single portrait photograph of the soldier, date of birth and date of death, short biography (from the Izkor booklet published by the Ministry of Defense), and location of the burial site. By way of contrast, individual memorial websites are much more detailed, featuring extensive space for expressions of personal bereavement and integrating multiple practices of commemoration, for example, an informal picture on the opening page; birth and death dates; photo gallery; detailed biography; eulogies and condolences; letters; poems; and links for contacting the family, members of the community, or website managers. Visitors may write in a visitors' book or light a virtual memorial candle. More complex private websites often add audio/video clips, background music, artwork, activities for commemorating the deceased, and links to existing physical memorial monuments. Examples are memorial sites for famous public figures, for individuals killed in accidents or who died from illnesses, and private memorials for fallen soldiers or victims of terrorist attacks. Although the latter two categories are already featured on official websites, families and friends want a more individual interpretation of their death, from glorification of the departed through protest against the "Establishment." The majority of these websites commemorate "acceptable" deaths, but maintains tacit silence over deaths from less politic causes such as suicide, murder, drugs, or family violence. The few websites devoted to such deceased are usually for famous figures such as Israeli singer Ofra Haza, who died of AIDS, or model Anat Elimelech, murdered by her life partner. Between the official and private websites are the community websites for entire towns wiped out in the Holocaust or groups of soldiers and victims of terrorist attacks killed together. Such websites include formal official characteristics along with spaces for more personal expression, similar to private websites.[4]

Society's Commemoration of National Bereavement in Israel

It was during Israel's early years that the culture of commemoration took form, inspired by two traditions: the Jewish religion which had developed a mourning culture while in the Diaspora, taking the biblical precept "Zakor" (Remember) and applying it to the individual as well as to the collective, and the national-secular tradition emphasizing

Zionist ideology and practice. Zionism considers the establishment of the State of Israel part of the continuum of Jewish history, comprising the Return to the Homeland, Redemption of the Land by the *halutzim* (agricultural pioneers), and the nurturing of the "New Jew," the fighting "sabra" (native-born Israeli) with plow in one hand and gun in the other, willing to sacrifice himself (or herself) for the Land and the Jewish People. Zionism emphasized the role of the collective and marginalized the individual, which impacted the patterns of commemoration. Official agencies commemorated soldiers and reinforced the relationship between the individual and the nation, thereby informing and shaping the nations' collective memory.

The War of Independence (1948) set the initial tone, with the establishment of special cemeteries and national memorial days. The massive toll of human life in the battle for nationhood was invariably prefigured in foundational heroism myths that imbued the fallen with an existential significance on a national level as willing sacrifices to win independence for the state and realize the vision of Zionism. This myth of heroism reached its peak following the Six-Day War of June 1967. The great number of fallen, the operational achievements in battle, and the military ascendance led to euphoria among the Israeli public, and even some stirrings of messianic expectation. Against the backdrop of continued conflict with the Palestinians and the neighboring Arab countries, military service in Israel became, in time, both the index of civic feeling and patriotism and the basis for the differential distribution of social benefits, for example, status and political power. Loyalty to the state was perceived as a function of willingness to sacrifice oneself, placing the combat fighter at the top of the civilian hierarchy, posing the soldier/civilian as the quintessential model of the good citizen. In turn, the rites of bereavement were intertwined with the formation of civilian militarism and imbued with elements of the sacrosanct.

The culture of commemoration is extensively reflected in the numerous memorial monuments built over the years for those fallen in Israel's wars. Scholars have noted two major characteristics: there are more memorial statues in Israel than other types of sculpture, and they are considered educational art embodying a system of symbols to represent national ideals. Israeli society's intensive cultural engagement with memorials intensifies their cultural uniqueness. The memorials concentrate on the model aspect of the fallen soldiers and emphasize the intimate connection between the entire nation and its heroes. These ideals began to break down at the end of the twentieth century. In his critique of nationalism, post-Zionist sociologist Uri Ram considers the nation-state's practices to be a discourse of repression reflected in Zionism and neo-Zionism. Based on this approach, Ram describes nationalism as "a structured identity which is coerced and limited," melting down various identities into a single identity.[5] Like others, Ram describes post-Zionism as a phenomenon that began in the 1990s and "exposes the contradiction in defining the State of Israel as Jewish and democratic." He pointed out the twin forces of liberalization and individualization as the main factors.[6] The canonical depictions of commemoration of heroic death prevented articulation of personal stories, unless they, too, could be shown to reinforce national values.

Websites could now offer the opportunity to join in private and collective bereavement by posting links on online commemorative sites to lead surfers to other sources of memory and real-life memorial events. These links essentially extend the bereavement processes, such as links to the physical gravesite, monuments, and ceremonies, thus helping to create and replicate collective bereavement through private bereavement.

Patriotism and Reflections of Heroic Death in Virtual Institutional Commemoration

Governmental memorial websites maintain the ethos of formal national commemoration, with narratives of "beautiful," heroic death, essentially seeking to include the dead within the framework of the country's collective memory. Among the most important site is the official government website Izkor,[7] built by the Ministry of Defense Department of Families and Commemoration, the Computer and Information Systems, and the Division for Organization and Administration. The website, constantly updated, displays stories of the fallen in all of Israel's wars, members of Israel's security forces, including underground fighters (since 1860, the year of the first settlement outside Jerusalem's Old City walls), and Jewish Brigade fighters with the British forces in World War II. Soldiers who died of illness or in accidents while on active military service are also included, as are soldiers who died years after demobilization from injuries sustained during their service.

The site welcomes visitors with the statement, "You are about to enter a unique memorial website, established to honor of each of the fallen in Israel's battles, from the beginning of the Zionist struggle in the Land, through the founding of the state and to this very day. This website is a cairn for each of the warriors.[8] The text shows the intention to bond the government's canonical commemorative style to private bereavement and the collective and its historical tradition. Shimon Laor, one of the builders of www.izkor.gov.il (in Hebrew), described the design approach, realizing that the public would see it as "representing the government. Let's call it a memorial monument . . . as such, it operates as a kind of uniform public element at the expense of the private element and the place of the individual." The style is similar to most of the virtual memorials; each departed individual has a separate page, with photograph, name, rank, birth date and place, and the circumstances and time of death. The background usually contains motifs identified with the culture of commemoration, such as the flag, torches, trees, candles, symbols of the military unit, high school, municipality, and the like. Israeli monuments to the fallen also have a didactic goal, which is why they emphasize clear symbols linked to the collective's core values. Similarly, institutional websites use familiar images from other arenas of memory, such as school curricula or official memorial ceremonies. Dominant colors give a feeling of officialdom, or the IDF dress uniform palette of blue, white, gray, and black, and sometimes greens and browns reminiscent of fatigues and weapons.

Uniformity of design and integration of symbolic and near-monochromatic color elements reflect a desire to preserve similarity among the fallen, similar to public commemoration in the military cemeteries, collective monuments, and official ceremonies, which help to transform the space from a private entity to part of a whole, making an individual's story a piece of the mosaic that is the nation's central narrative. A sample textual analysis of the Izkor individual display pages shows rhetoric seeking to appropriate death in battle to emphasize the collective struggle of nation building. The majority of the texts emphasize courage and patriotism, often associating death in battle with recent or distant historical events. Content mostly emphasizes good soldiering, operational professionalism, love of humanity and the land, and basic values of the IDF ethical code.[9] Comments that do not fit these general guidelines are barely mentioned or are marginalized. One example is on the page on the late Elad Shiloh, killed with four other soldiers in "the Tze'elim Disaster II."[10] The eulogy begins with Elad's army career and ends being about his character: "He was everything that his parents, this home [the kibbutz], this country, and this earth could have asked for." The military accident that led to Elad's death drew wide media coverage and commissions of inquiry, but receives only one isolated line on the memorial page, with no mention of the public arguments: "Elad was killed in a training accident at Tze'elim in southern Israel, during a drill for military operations." By omitting the details, the death of Elad, member of an elite unit, can be included as a "beautiful death" in the service of the state, without damaging the IDF's image.

In contrast, the commemoration of a soldier's death under heroic circumstances perpetuates the ethos of comradeship-in-arms. The circumstances are set forth in bold details on the memorial page. An example is the page devoted to Yotam Gilboa, killed in the Second Lebanon War,[11] describing how he was shot while trying to extract a fellow soldier from a "vicious exchange of fire." His commander added, "Yotam's courage is part of Jewish heroism from Biblical times to the present . . . a peerless fighter." The collective memory of the Jewish people is familiar with the motif of self-sacrifice, from the biblical figure of Samson, to martyrdom at Masada, through modern secular Zionism with the myth of Joseph (Yosef) Trumpeldor. The Israeli soldier is associated with a long history of fighting for the land of Israel. The Izkor website represents a genre of official government memorials preserving the familiar narrative framework of formal commemoration constructed during the early days of the new state, which was dominant for decades. Ceremonial, hierarchic language conveys a uniform, clear, and unambiguous message, deliberately ignoring information that would weaken the hegemonic position of the Israeli soldier. However, it is crucial to remember that cyberspace has fluid boundaries. Recently constructed official websites demonstrate the trend of integrating collective commemoration "from the top down," with the multiple voices of individual commemoration "from the bottom up," reflected in the emphasis on the military persona of each soldier as a common theme in the memorial sites. Personal content reflecting individual identity, such as photographs, biographical details, and even critical statements, are also posted, but these expressions of the increasing individualization in Israeli society fail to create the impact intended. The new details are also recruited in the service of the national collective, as the soldiers in the majority of the web pages create a uniform message, blurring the individual differences.

Even the recent option to add direct links from the personal pages of the fallen soldier to private memorial websites set up by civilians, such as relatives and friends, only partly helps deconstruct the traditional "top down" hierarchy, though it does recognize private agents' rights to personal memory.[12] At the same time, many private commemorative websites have links to the Izkor site and memorial pages of others killed in the same incident or sharing a background (such as high school, youth movement, or kibbutz). These bidirectional links enable contemporary consumers of memory to experience a continuum of the general narrative told by the nation about its fallen, together with individual memorial expressions. Links to military cemeteries provide data on the physical location of the gravestone while enabling a virtual gravesite visit to create a topographical "metamap" of Israel's national bereavement through which visitors can roam, testing its boundaries. The virtual topography creates a mental representation of the physical reality, blurring boundaries as the visitor flows from the familiar to unfamiliar, from broad ethos to narrow case, and from one narrative to another.

During periods of tension in Israel's security situation and frequent suicide bomber attacks, the frequency of site visits rises, as does visitors' willingness to leave comments. Surfers thus take an active part in the creation of national memory, perhaps because the public's sense of personal security is shaken, intensifying awareness of the fragility of existence with an increase in interactive participation in acts of memory. The major differences between the pattern of commemoration characterizing official virtual sites of memory and private memorial websites stand out when comparing texts by the soldier's family and the official display page. One such example is Refanael "Fani" Muskal's page, where the traditional commemorative themes on the official Izkor site reflect the society's core values linking the individual soldier's death to the nation's history,[13] but whose private website contains harsh criticism of the government by the bereaved parents who perceive the government as holding human lives cheaply.[14] His father described "standing above Refanael's grave, after we found out about the errors in the war . . . we called upon the Prime Minister to take responsibility and step down." A comparison between the two versions shows that the arena of virtual commemoration enables a parallel display of several narratives, each one enlisting the death of the soldier to emphasize its desired message. Thus the virtual commemorative space becomes a stage of struggle between various memory agents attempting to restructure memory, each for its own needs.

The Politics of Memory: The National "Family of Bereavement" and the Media in the Deconstruction of Collective Memory

Among the most important changes in Israeli society since the Six-Day War of June 1967 is new understanding of the behavior of Jews in the Diaspora and during the

Holocaust, greater pluralism in Judaism, a rise in nationalistic sentiment, and a debate on the IDF and the concept of "just" war. These processes intensified after the outbreak of the First Intifada in 1987 and a rising Palestinian national movement, growing stronger since 1976 as Israel coped with terror attacks. Civilians began to question the necessity of deploying the military to solve political problems because of the huge sacrifices, and led to a severe drop in public trust of the government and the military. Although the protest groups were small, they accumulated significant social visibility, which led to additional groups becoming highly critical.

These developments began to deconstruct the hegemonic Zionist narrative that had shaped the commemorative practices during Israel's first few decades of independence. It now became an arena of struggles between various groups wishing to shape memory and identity in Israel. The collapse of the ethos of bereavement was one symptom of this breakdown. The overall social consensus that loss of life is the unavoidable price of the continued existence of the nation and the country and that it is above political differences, all collapsed one after another to undermine the status of the ethos of bereavement as a foundational element in the society's cohesiveness. Journalist Rubik Rosenthal associated this collapse with the end of the "great wars," and stated in 2001 that "civic society expects the soldier to remain alive."[15]

Another example of this mood can be found in an interview by bereaved mother Nava Doron, calling her soldier son's Zohar's death in Lebanon "a senseless and illogical thing." Zohar's parents, Nava and Tommy Doron, opened their son's commemorative website with the words "Our Zuzi," his nickname.[16] Ilan Itzhayek, Ynet Internet news editor, compared private websites adhering to the hegemonic narrative and others that were more individualistic. Although one website was "very moving [on Brigadier General Erez Gerstein], because each loss is moving" he felt that it is "an industrial site, it's synthetic, almost propagandistic. The difference between him and Zuzi is that Zuzi takes your guts and tears them apart."[17] The weakening of the bereavement ethos encouraged the "privatization of grief" in other areas, such as a legal battle in the early 1990s that gave parents the option to personalize headstones in military cemeteries, which up to then were uniform. Sociologist Edna Lomsky-Feder observed that changes in Israel's culture of commemoration stand out primarily in the annual Remembrance Day ceremonies held in the schools.[18] The heroic, restrained aspect has now been replaced by ceremonies emphasizing emotion, personal pain, and loss of life, based on personal texts. Furthermore, the borders between civilians who died in terror attacks and soldiers fallen in battle are blurred, nullifying the commonly accepted hierarchy of bereavement in Israel. Lomsky-Feder asserts that "instead of memorial ceremonies, mourning ceremonies are being conducted. People are . . . establishing new ceremonial practices."[19] Bereaved parents are spearheading changes in mourning practices. Whereas previously the family "mourned their fallen soldier secretly, while the state transforms him into a national asset through monuments, remembrance days, cemeteries, and utilizes him as a vital element in the national rhetoric," parents began to compete with military and government institutions to shape the collective memory and culture of commemoration, a trend also reflected in parents' legal battles to produce full disclosure from the IDF on the circumstances of their sons' death; parents' presence at trials following military accidents; and petitions to personalize their children's military gravestones. Furthermore, whereas parents were considered heroes for sacrificing their children on the altar of the state and integrated into the "family of bereavement," (through which they passively accepted the death of the soldier and received social honors through military funerals) while faced with the social demand to serve as "living monuments," private commemoration challenges these actions. Families began to eschew this obligation of acceptance and inclusion, thereby opening up their right to criticize the establishment.

Despite attempts by political and military powers to prevent bereaved parents from entering the arena of commemoration, in time parents' organizations and movements were founded, seeking to change the status quo and take the sphere of security out of the hands of the hegemony, so impermeable to public criticism. Rosenthal stated that protest by bereaved parents whose sons were killed at the Beaufort was what led to the legitimization of bereaved parents' involvement in cases of soldiers' deaths and helped break down the consensus that bereavement is above politics and needs no civilian involvement or supervision. One of the most outstanding reflections of this involvement was the social protest movement Four Mothers. Founded in 1997 by mothers of soldiers in elite units who lived in the north, the mothers demanded that the IDF get out of Lebanon. Their long-felt frustration was translated into political action following the 1997 helicopter disaster in which seventy-three IDF soldiers lost their lives.

Anthropologist Dan Rabinowitz observed as early as 1998 that the success of the Four Mothers arose from the fact that immediately after they joined the public discourse in Israel from a clearly feminine position of "wife and mother," they couched their statements in a new language, talking "IDF-ese" and "security speak." Anthropologist Tamar El Or stated in this context that one does not have to be a mother, or even a woman, to speak from the position of a "soldier's mother," since it is a metaphorical stance open to all members of the society—men and women alike.[20]

A large part of the bereaved parents' struggle found its expression in close, intensive contact with the media and their adoption of public relations methods.[21] The families' relationship with the media began in the 1980s, but the worsening situation in Lebanon and the new tabloid *Hadashot,* which began to compete with the veteran daily *Yedioth Ahronoth,* helped disrupt the delicate balance between private and public spaces, preparing the ground for interviews with bereaved parents even before the traditional seven-day mourning period was over. During this period, new media coverage norms were created, which integrated the civilian voices of the bereaved parents. These norms were reinforced during the 1990s with the creation of Israel's Second Channel, followed by cable television and satellite channels.

The objective of the civilian pressure groups was to influence the public agenda, supplement or contradict official spokespersons' reports, and encourage features on relevant topics. They publicly responded to IDF statements with their own allegations, sometimes with explicit demands to representatives of the establishment. Sharon Attias's film *The Hillers* also known as *Kaddish Pa'am Shniya* (Memorial prayers a second time) (2005), centers on a bereaved couple's struggle to discover the circumstances of the death of their soldier son, Daniel Hiller, portraying the complex relations between the Hillers and the IDF on one hand and the media on the other.[22] Parents' organizations overcame army censorship and reticence and exposed the system to public scrutiny. Their subversion of the military hegemony founded a new relationship between the civilian public and the military establishment and subjected the political-military hegemony to competition. Parents succeeded in penetrating the public discourse, reshaped systems of public memory, and informed the political agenda and its attitudes toward security issues.

Shaking up the IDF's hegemonic hold over national memory and commemoration practices, and forcing the nation's institutions into greater transparency, proved a double-edged sword for the parents, whose stance now undermined their exclusive status at the forefront of Israel's "circle of bereavement." In addition, by challenging the IDF, emphasizing the operational failures, and claiming excessive use of military force, certain sectors of the public increasingly distrusted the IDF. This then led to a lessening of the willingness to consider the death of soldiers as a necessity in safeguarding the country's security, and of the willingness of soldiers to serve. The heroic aura that surrounded death in battle gradually dissipated. Fallen soldiers were no longer perceived as warriors setting out on vital missions to protect the homeland, and death was no longer described as the inevitable result. The bereaved families were no longer a cohesive group and began to raise contradictory demands. Under these new circumstances, the families found it increasingly difficult to maintain their position as a "living monument" to "sublime death." Devaluing soldiers' deaths in battle and the persistent struggle waged by the families of those murdered in terrorist attacks to equalize their status and join the "family of bereavement" further challenged official commemoration. Blurred boundaries and the loss of status for the families of fallen soldiers then inspired new moves to return to the top of the "hierarchy of bereavement." Parents once again wished to include their soldier sons' death in the framework of "beautiful death" in the service of the nation, which provides social status and extra civic rights. Thus, paradoxically, they began to replicate the Zionist national rhetoric of the state that they themselves helped to deconstruct. Messages that formerly penetrated Israel's national culture of mourning "from the top down" through institutional and governmental agencies, were now being formed "from the bottom up." Among the means bereaved families employed to restructure the national-Zionist rhetoric is the establishment of private virtual memorial sites, which redraw and strengthen the borderline between national and other types of bereavement, restoring it to the supreme status such death enjoyed in the past.[23] Indeed, the many memorial websites to fallen soldiers built over recent years emphasize heroic soldiering, love of homeland, and the willingness to sacrifice. Photographs of the soldier-son in uniform, symbols of his military unit, information about his activities as a soldier, and eulogies by commanders have taken central stage in a great majority of these virtual memorials.

One outstanding example of this tendency is the memorial website for Tzachi Itach.[24] Most of its pages emphasize his being the last Israeli soldier killed on Lebanese soil prior to the IDF withdrawal, clearly reflecting the designers' desire to provide Tzachi with national status, backed up by the text. Private websites exhibit greater artistic freedom in design and content than official websites, with more complex layers. For example, webmaster Nikola described his objective for the commemorative website for his comrade-in-arms, Eitan Belachsan,[25] officer in an elite paratroop unit, cut down on a mission in Lebanon in 1999: "The message . . . is the value of giving of yourself to others and to the state." The webmaster considers the website not only as a private site of memory for friends and family, but also as a straightforward educational tool, whose success in inculcating values can be seen from visitors' reactions.

Widowed Na'ama Gavish also expressed a similar viewpoint for her website in memory of her husband, Avraham, murdered by a terrorist who infiltrated their home. Her objective was less to preserve her husband's memory as a unique entity than to inculcate ideals such as excellence, love of the army, and religious Jewish principles, such as the ideal of the "Book and the Sword," that is, Torah study combined with self-defense.[26] We can see how online memorials demonstrate a clearly controlled and shaped message engaging traditional narratives of military heroism, self-sacrifice, and patriotism, emphasizing the image of the "New Jew" in contrast to the passive Diaspora Jew, returning to the mythological sabra figure. The commemorative website serves as a dynamic backdrop for the presentation of the fallen soldier who becomes an ideal model, representing values considered by the proponents of his memory to be ideal, whose loss is indeed a loss for the nation. The impressive presentation (graphics, pictures, and text) enhances both emotive and ideological responses, as a result of which, families convey their ideological messages and leverage their individual bereavement to win social recognition. Virtual commemoration thus allows families to create associative discourse on a personal level, to demand their place in the hierarchy of bereavement through the use of narratives of soldierly heroism and self-sacrifice on behalf of the collective, while simultaneously holding a deconstructive critical discourse on the public level.

National Bereavement in Institutional Media

In Israel the mass media serve as a space for the presentation of mourning and play a role in the restructuring of patterns of commemoration. Several scholars have described the far-reaching changes in media coverage of national disasters and bereavement in Israel. During the 1950s and '60s, media coverage of national bereavement maintained a restrained and discreet character, recognizing the clear limit between families' private loss and between the entire nation's public mourning. The press dared not interview relatives of the fallen at the funeral, but made do with listing biographical data without extensive emotional descriptions. However, in the 1970s, the border between private and public spheres began to show cracks as the media gradually began to push its way into the homes of the mourners. One example was the 1979 television interview with Smadar Haran of Nahariya, whose entire family was murdered by a terrorist. In contrast to what was acceptable practice at the time, Haran granted interviews shortly after the attack.

The trend became more widespread during the 1980s, creating norms of news coverage that allowed reporters to interview newly bereaved parents, forming a platform for their overt protest even during the initial seven-day mourning period prescribed by Jewish tradition. Oren Meyers, who has written extensively on collective memory, described the change in Israeli newspapers' imagery of soldiers. Weekend editions in the 1960s published many photographs of active, victorious soldiers. In 1988 a weekend supplement in *Maariv* published the first newspaper photograph of an Israeli soldier confronting a woman. In 1998 the same newspaper published a photograph of a group of Israeli POWs. Voices of parents, friends, and siblings were heard much louder than in the past, even when striking at the national cohesiveness or criticizing the government and the IDF. Encouraged by the media, bereaved families began to unhesitatingly reveal personal details, photo albums, letters, and diaries of their dear ones. This trend concretizes the transition from the perception of bereavement as a national motif and of the dead as the "property" of the army to seeing the soldiers as individual entities—fathers, brothers, husbands, or sons whose loss shattered lives.

By 1993, when Israel's Second Channel began commercial broadcasting, the Israeli media began to use bereavement to raise their ratings. This trend became stronger with the new century, with more literary descriptions of disasters, emotional outbursts, and heartbreaking monologues by bereaved families, and less mention of "the dry facts." Visual content became more extreme, with on-site filming and set phrases full of pathos to describe the dead. At the same time, military disasters began to receive wider coverage in contrast to other news, and soon wide coverage of all funerals and military mishaps were given prominent space in the newspapers. Israeli news coverage stepped up the drama of each event. Shelly Geffen Kushlevitz described the change as a "transition to feminine discourse," reflected, for example, in showing soldiers crying openly, after years of avoiding any weeping soldiers on film.[27] Geffen Kushlevitz observed that the media ceased using great myths for conveying messages, and instead began presenting the stories of private heroes to idealize the fallen. However, this led to a banalization of violent death, whether in battle or terrorist attack. Journalist Rogel Alpher defined the tendency of the "TV eulogy formula" as showing people killed in terror attacks not as "multifaceted personalities, but pure beings, one-dimensional and flat."[28] Virtual communication enabled bereaved parents to overcome the homogenization of bereavement portrayed in the traditional media. The Internet offers an alternate space, where new content and meaning can be poured into narratives and make their lasting presence known in the public space.

Nikolai Yaniv, who created the website to commemorate fallen soldier Yochai Porat, wrote about the unlimited aspect of cyberspace, with its unlimited capacity for data.

"People read newspapers then throw them in the garbage. . . . But on the internet, the story exists all the time."[29] In contrast to the pattern that developed in the "old-time media," virtual commemorative sites by private memory agents do not present biography and character description as a set piece, but broaden the picture of the fallen from several different and unique angles. Webmasters try to integrate original material created by the deceased themselves, such as letters, stories, paintings, or poems.[30] For example, the website in memory of Omer Shalit, one of the seventy-three soldiers killed in the helicopter disaster,[31] features Omer's poetry and writings.

Omer's website is part of a commemorative trend that makes no attempt to adopt rhetoric justifying soldiers' death (such as, "They fell for the sake of life," or "They died to enable us to live"). Neither does the site criticize the reality of the security situation that led to his death, but instead strives to create deeply expressive intimate, personal, and unique aspects to distinguish Omer from the collective. The site launches him back into the public space not as a national asset but as a unique individual. The masculine-military elements on the site, such as symbols of his IDF unit, are marginal in amount and importance as compared to the personal contents, such as Omer's mother's intimate eulogy ten years later, or memories from his best friend, Ron. His speech expresses unwillingness to accept his friend's death, which seems to him unnecessary and unjustified. His statements also demonstrate the deep bonds of male friendship between Israeli men that psychologist Danny Kaplan calls *homosocial ties*. These fraternal bonds, although usually not translated into close day-to-day relationships in civilian life, are still perceived as deep and ideal bonds based on mutual commitment to eternal friendship. Feelings toward the missing comrade are expressed with great intensity. Kaplan considers the military comradeship bonds as a hegemonic model for intimate relationships between men, even for those who have not experienced heroic battles or have served together.[32]

The fraternal friendships formed during army service are also reflected in chains of commemorative sites linking fallen soldiers who share a common denominator.[33] For the most part, linked sites are individual memorial sites for soldiers killed in the same military operation. The unique nature of the online medium facilitates a display of multiple uncensored narratives to give personal bereavement a strong presence with great depth and many details. The web provides a broad platform for personal messages and content on various issues, but primarily prevents memory from becoming momentary and transitory. Online commemorative sites easily integrate into the broader trend of bringing in different voices of commemoration to represent the fallen in a more complex light. As a public space of national bereavement, the Internet is an ideal place not only for private memory agents to preserve and reinforce hegemonic memory but also to display alternatives unable to find an outlet outside of cyberspace because of tight supervision and control wielded by institutional memory agents, including the media.

The low level of control characterizing online activities facilitates criticism and protest of the military-political establishment. And, indeed, in recent years, private memory agents have begun to include in their commemorative websites stories of failure and betrayal. As far back as the early years following independence, the Jewish collective in Israel defined its identity, among other means, through nurturing "rites of bereavement" and glorification of its dead fallen in battle. According to modern codes, a clear, coherent narrative of uniformity was structured, designed in accordance with the core values of the Zionist movement, including military heroism, and values of patriotism and love of the land of Israel. In Israel, civic spirit may be measured first and foremost by the extent to which an individual is willing to be sacrificed for the nation. Over the past few decades, an "economy of bereavement" grew up around this canonical heritage of memory, reflected in the drive by various civilian groups to be counted among the traditional "family of bereavement" and to receive the social, cultural, and financial benefits hitherto reserved for this unique group. This process, which began in the 1970s, intersected with the new Internet technology adopted by various players in the space of commemoration in Israel. The Israeli public, which had been methodically excluded from memory-shaping activities reserved for government and institutional agencies, now adopted the virtual medium as a tool for appropriating private bereavement from the public plane and making social demands.

Against the backdrop of these opposing processes, and following the assassination of Prime Minister Yitzhak Rabin in late 1995 that aroused very painful emotions of personal and collective loss, the Jewish public in Israel grasped the Internet as a legitimate space for creating a memorial "from the bottom up," to express feelings and be active partners in creating private and national memory simultaneously. Along with the numerous private memorial websites for soldiers, specific virtual support communities arose directed toward parents, siblings, and partners of fallen soldiers. The rapid expansion of these communities shows the goal of these groups to develop an awareness of bereavement and demonstrates their attempts to recruit the virtual medium for processing mourning and formulating collective memory. These bereavement groups charged the new virtual commemorative space with the potential of deconstructing the patriarchal Zionist metanarrative, which had dictated the guidelines for the culture of bereavement in Israel for decades, in favor of other narratives. Paradoxically, despite multiple voices arising from the various bereavement communities within the space of virtual communication, and despite the fact that the websites facilitate arguments, challenge, expressions of hostility, ambivalence, and other emotions, the message that runs through all of the commemorative websites established over recent years is uniform.

The activities of the civilian bereavement groups do not arise from a strong desire to promote other narratives, but rather from a common striving to gain entry to the "bereavement elite" in Israel. Because of this, many of the private virtual websites being set up in memory of civilian dead are characterized by enlisting the hegemonic Zionist metanarrative, and emphasize aspects of courage, heroism, and love of nation and homeland. Through association with the national-military discourse, the civilian bereavement groups attempt to bypass the mechanisms of silencing used by the hegemonic discourse, and make their presence known on the map of collective bereavement using the new medium of the Internet.

Notes

1. "Observation" is not used here in its traditional meaning of physically observing interactions. The present research literally "domesticates" anthropological research methods by taking the researcher out of the field of society to place her in the virtual field of research through the home or office computer. I surveyed material using search engines and indexes of leading Israeli portals to locate commemorative websites and online loss and bereavement communities in Israel, then mapped and classified them. Using the online dimension at this point allowed me to use the relative advantages of Internet research to the fullest by enabling geographical expansion and greater accessibility to the research population. During the course of the surveys and observations, many memorial and commemorative websites were identified then classified on an axis from private sites through community sites to official government websites. Among the official websites are sites that are "virtual twins" (an Internet website with a parallel physical site in the world) of existing memorial statues.

2. Data from Teleseker survey. Entire report available at http://www.ontop.co.il/marketing-TIM-stats.htm. The number of Internet users in Israel continued to rise through 2006, according to data from Internet World Stats, when Israel boasted approximately 3.7 million Internet users, which was about 51 percent of the population. (This figure comprised the total number of people of all ages, with access to the Internet and basic user skills.) For complete data, see http://www.internetworldstats.com/middle.htm#il.

3. It should be noted that during this period there was a dramatic increase in Internet users in Israel and modes of use of the net. The sharp rise in the number of online memorial sites therefore is part of this trend. The trend continues even now, especially the large number of websites built after the Second Lebanon War. For further details, see http://www.nrg.co.il/online/1/ART1/497/478.html

4. The second stage of the research followed the initial location, classification, and mapping of the Israeli commemorative websites and online bereavement communities. I monitored a representative sample of about thirty websites across the spectrum of public and private initiatives.

5. See http://ofakim.org.il/zope/home/he/1124479600/1124971296.

6. Ibid.

7. See http://www.izkor.gov.il

8. Ibid.

9. See http://www.idf.il/1497-en/Dover.aspx

10. See http://www.izkor.gov.il/HalalKorot.aspx?id=513542

11. See http://www.izkor.gov.il/HalalKorot.aspx?id=517360

12. Such a link, for example, can be found on the memorial pages for Yaeir Nissim Turjeman, killed by Palestinian fire on the Dotan IDF base in 2004. See http://www.izkor.gov.il/HalalKorot.aspx?id=517115.

13. See Refanael's private page at http://www.refanael.co.il as compared to his page on the Izkor site: http://www.izkor.gov.il/HalalKorot.aspx?id=517362.

14. See http://www.refanael.co.il.

15. Rubik Rosenthal, *Is Bereavement Dead?* (Jerusalem: Keter, 2001) (Hebrew).

16. See http://www.zohardoron.net/tmunot.html.

17. Ilan Itzhayek, interview.

18. Edna Lomsky-Feder, "From National Memory Agent to Local Mourning Community:

Remembrance Day Ceremonies in Israeli Elementary Schools," *Megamot* 42, no. 3 (2003): 333–87 (Hebrew).

19. From the article, "Remembrance Day Ceremonies Change Character." See http://news.walla.co.il/?w=/9/713979/@@/item/printer.

20. Tamar El Or, Soldier's Mother. The Four Mothers movement conference in Rosh Pina, 1992 (Hebrew).

21. From the article, "The Politicization of Bereavement." See http://www.itu.org.il/Index.asp?ArticleID=1743&CategoryID=548&Page=1.

22. See http://movies.yahoo.com/movie/1809424061/details for preproduction synopsis in English, and online reviews in Hebrew at http://www.nrg.co.il/online/5/ART1/070/095.html.

23. In this context, Arie Kizel, who writes on issues of education, history, and the media, has noted that at the top of the bereavement hierarchy in Israel are soldiers who fell in wars, military operations, or accidents. In next place are the victims of terrorist attacks, followed by infants and children killed in civilian accidents. In recent years, women murdered by their partners have penetrated the national consciousness. At the lowest rung of the ladder of bereavement are foreign workers, Bedouin, Arabs, and Druze.

24. See http://www.tzachi.netvision.net.il.

25. See http://www.eitan.org.il.

26. See http://www.gal-ed.co.il/gavish.

27. Shelly Geffen Kushlevitz, "From Self-Sacrifice to Victim: The Role of the Media in Covering Bereavement in Military Accidents," in *Security and Media: The Dynamics of a Relationship* (Bitahon vetikshoret: Dynamica shel yehassim), ed. Udi. Lebel (Sde Boker: Ben-Gurion University of the Negev Press, 2005), 284–310 (Hebrew).

28. Alpher Rogel, "In This Way My Death in Terrorist Attack Will Be Covered," Haaretz, December 5, 2011, http://www.haaretz.co.il/misc/1.754096 (Hebrew).

29. See http://www.yochai.com.

30. The practice of displaying poems by the subject of the commemoration not only adds the personal angle to the narrative of memory, but also forms continuity with the national tradition of the culture of bereavement represented in poetry and song, among other forms. This tradition, which began with Haim Hefer and others, continues to serve to this day as a tool for conveying messages about the personality of the dead soldier, which is why it constitutes part of the contemporary way in which the culture of memory is shaped. An excellent example is Haim Hefer's poem, "Dudu."

31. See http://www.omershalit.com.

32. Danny Kaplan, *The Men We Loved: Male Friendship and Nationalism in Israeli Culture* (New York: Berghan, 2006).

33. One example of such a linked chain of sites are those in memory of Daniel Shiran, Dr. Igor Rotstein, and Omri Haim Almakayes-Yaakobowitz, killed in the same tank in the Second Lebanon War. Each site is linked to the others. See http://omri-haim.com; www.danielshiran.co.il; http://sites.google.com/site/igormem.

II

Poetry and Prose

Chapter 7

Bereavement and Breakdown

War and Failed Motherhood in Raya Harnik's Work

Esther Raizen

Raya Harnik (b. 1933), whose son, Guni, the commander of the Golani Brigade commando unit, fell in the battle of the Beaufort (June 6, 1982) together with five of his soldiers, has been the most vocal member of what is known as the Family of the Beaufort. This group of parents and other family members of the six fallen soldiers, led the protest movement in the wake of the 1982 Lebanon War and came to represent a new direction in the public behavior of "the bereft"—open criticism of the Israeli government and its policies, occasional refusal to partake in the myth-building narration surrounding the fallen soldiers, and insistence on the notion that the shared experience of bereavement provides little, if any, comfort to families. Harnik afforded the Israeli public an intimate glimpse into her world with three poetry collections, six children's books, and one memoir, published over the span of twenty-three years. This chapter discusses Harnik's poetics of bereavement, examines the dialogue between her works in poetry and prose, and illustrates what emerges as an overarching theme in her literary expression—motherhood as a casualty of war, destined for breakdown and exposed in its weakness and loneliness. Harnik's mother character is acutely aware of her failure to protect her sons and of her complicity in their demise. This awareness combines with stubborn adherence to the Zionist dream to produce a sense of paralysis and great sadness, out of which emerges the terse and honest written idiom as a powerful reminder of vitality and youth.

So I am disqualified twice
Once as a woman
And once
As a flier of doves.[1]

In 1993, Raya Harnik, a writer, activist, and bereaved mother, was awarded the Ze'ev Prize for Children's Literature for her second children's book *Oh, My Brother.*[2] The judges, noting that this was an important work "not only because of its subject matter, but also because of its immense artistic value," praised *Oh, My Brother* for its tenderness, clean style, reliable and nonornate language, sharp perspective, and narration that is "entirely clean of mendacity, dependable, and sensitive."[3] When invited to the podium, Harnik spoke briefly of a chance meeting with Ze'ev in 1951, saying nothing at all about the book itself or her work as a writer. This episode encapsulates the artistry of Harnik as a tightrope walker, suspended up high in the limelight, negotiating the delicate balance of expectations between what her work could have been yet is not, should have been and is, and claiming the prerogative of silence. Her poems, published through the early 1990s, combined with her political activism to suggest perhaps that "behind the aggressive fighter, known for her struggle for full and just judgment of those responsible for the Lebanon War, hides a sensitive poetess."[4] Her children's books represent a singular attempt to address war and bereavement through the eyes of a child: Harnik uses the somewhat naive, often confused, and brutally honest voice of a young narrator to reflect on the experience of the Israeli family. She focuses on the bereaved family as a vulnerable unit, condemned to a schizophrenic existence that is fueled by the need to keep up appearances of strength as it crumbles in pain, sending individual members into loneliness. Central to the predicament of the family is the collapse of the mother who, unable to cope with the challenges that life throws at her, sinks into anger and depression, threatening to drag the whole family down with her. Harnik's narration highlights the conflict between the desire to immortalize and idealize the fallen as a means of attaining some form of consolation, and the recognition that this very desire serves to strengthen a social norm that insists on denying the finality, violence, and ultimate senselessness of dying in a war, and nurtures the seeds of future disasters. Drawing on the dialogue between Harnik's poems, memoir, and children's books, in this essay I outline what I see as a component of the Israeli war experience that Harnik captures with the utmost clarity; namely, the perils of motherhood trapped in an endless cycle of violence, bereavement, and great sorrow, in a world marked by frailty, disillusionment, and power—the frailty of a society threatened by external enemies and internal deterioration; the disillusionment with the Zionist dream that presents itself in its full vitality and resilience in the very challenge to its realization; and the power of small words to document it all.

Harnik's son, Guni, was born in 1956 and grew up in Jerusalem. He enlisted in 1974, came up through the IDF ranks, and was eventually assigned command over the Golani Brigade's elite commando unit, *sayeret golani.* On June 6, 1982, he was killed in the battle of the Beaufort with five of his soldiers.

In *Bereavement and the Living Legend,* Mordechai Rotenberg, himself a bereaved father, defines and ranks three classes of fallen soldiers in terms of their myth-producing powers. At the bottom of the ranking lie the soldiers who committed suicide, above them those killed by friendly fire, and above them the ultimate heroes—those who fell in the line of duty. Guni Harnik is Rotenberg's first illustration for the latter category, followed by Yoni Netanyahu, commander of the Entebbe Raid (1976).[5] The circumstances of Guni's last days are, indeed, prime myth material: A day after celebrating his reentry into civilian life, Guni heard about the green light given to the attack on the Beaufort and rushed to join his former unit. The incoming unit commander was wounded, leaving the position to Guni. Guni's vehicle overturned on the way to the Beaufort, and he continued on foot, uniting with his soldiers and leading a battle that should not have taken place the way it did: The IDF's invasion routes into Lebanon were changed; the immediate capture of the Beaufort, which had been meticulously rehearsed for months, was deemed unnecessary; and the Northern Command issued a directive to postpone the attack, which failed to reach the unit. Because of various delays and mishaps, what was planned as a daytime battle turned into a night attack, with the column of soldiers proceeding, on foot, under the lights of the unit's armored personnel carriers, and suffering immediate casualties, among them Guni. Israeli control over the fort was secured early in the morning of June 7, and later that day, Prime Minister Menachem Begin and Defense Minister Ariel Sharon were brought to the top of the Beaufort together with a group of reporters. Begin, unaware of the soldiers' death, announced to the nation that the Beaufort was captured without casualties on the Israeli side, an episode that became a powerful symbol of the impotence and callousness of the Israeli leadership.[6] According to Ze'ev Schiff and Ehud Ya'ari, who documented the battle, Guni, "known for unabashedly dovish views . . . made no secret of the fact that he opposed a deliberately instigated war. Yet now the soldier in Guni Harnik came to the fore. His comrades were going out to battle, and he just couldn't bear to be left behind."[7] The loyalty of the peace-loving soldier who opposed the war yet joined his comrades and eventually lost his life became one of the central motifs in the Guni Harnik myth and a point of conflict for Raya Harnik. While she insisted on the importance of nurturing the myth ("it is very difficult when your son is a myth . . . but it is important to me that he turns into a myth. I very much care that people talk about him and that he has become a part of the IDF's battle heritage"),[8] she also adamantly refused to portray him, or herself, as a pacifist.[9] Harnik's first children's book, *Guni* (1990), reflects the difficulty inherent in the attempt to cultivate a myth while insisting on its realistic dimensions: Harnik speaks very openly of Guni's upbringing and personal tendencies that combined to produce a child, and later a man, unusually preoccupied with war, fighting, the military, and the responsibilities of a commander. The myth is given the upper hand: "Why was Guni, my beautiful child, killed?!" she asks at the end of the book, and responds:

> because he loved his homeland
> and he loved his friends
> and thought that he was responsible for those under his command.
> He was not killed because he hated Arabs,
> and he was not killed because he wanted to be a hero

> He was killed because of the love for this beautiful land which he roamed in his childhood and youth.
> And for the army which he thought was the best of them all. And for the *sayeret* and its soldiers in whom he believed.[10]

The myth-producing narration in *Guni* culminates with the predictable statement on the hope for peace—Guni wants the child-reader to live in peace and grow up happy, like he did:

> And if there is peace, and no more wars,
> Then the story about Guni will be like a legend.
> Something that you remember—like a dream, like a poem.
> Which begins like all stories:
>
> Once upon a time there was . . .
> Once upon a time there was my son, whose name was Guni.[11]

The young reader is fully immersed in the tragedy that befell both the hero and his mother, and can easily recognize the foreboding hints that Harnik weaves into the otherwise quiet, almost matter-of-fact narration as she builds up Guni's life story toward his inevitable death. The mix of pride and sorrow that permeates the story reveals Harnik's trust in the ability of children to absorb the complexity of the mother-narrator's position, albeit up to a point. Missing from *Guni* is the recognition of the mother's complicity in her son's death, which emerges as one of the most prominent themes in Harnik's work as a whole. In an interview with Rubik Rosenthal in the course of his work on *The Family of the Beaufort,* Harnik recalls Guni's determination, since his early childhood, to become a soldier and commander, and focuses on an episode during the 1967 war when eleven-year-old Guni, hearing about the capture of the Etzion Block, burst into tears, exclaiming: "They have now captured all the places. What is there left for me to capture?"[12] "Guni," suggests Harnik,

> felt in 1967 what I felt in 1948—that he had missed his chance to conquer something. I suddenly realized that my talking all of these years about the heroism of the Maccabees and Trumpeldor was not just talking. He internalized it, very deeply. . . . I feel responsible . . . Immediately after the [1982] war I felt that the responsibility was fully mine, that I was solely and directly responsible for Guni's death. A child like this, a fertile ground for my heroic fantasies, if you don't want anything to happen to him, you must educate him in the opposite way. . . . It was absolutely prohibitive to tell a child like Guni about Trumpeldor. And we went ahead and added visuals to the stories. We took him to Tel Hai and dragged him to Nabi Yusha and climbed to Tel Fahr with him. There is no site in the country that has anything to do with a story of heroism that we did not get to with Guni.[13]

In the April 3, 2002, entry of her memoir *One Year,* Harnik, reacting to a mother who proclaimed on the radio, "I will not send my son to this war," records a suppressed memory from the fateful week in June 1982, which struck her twenty years after the fact: She was the one who actually made the contact between Guni and his unit. She received a phone call from the brigade office asking for Guni's number, and either gave it to the caller or contacted Guni herself. Harnik concludes: "not only did I send him to war, I sent him to his death."[14] Her struggle with guilt is not limited to Guni—it extends to her other three children and grandchildren, and comes up time and again in her memoir and interviews when she discusses emigration. While she wavers between wishing it for her grandchildren and dismissing the possibility for them and for any further generation, she knows exactly where she herself stands: She would never be able to leave Israel, because her principles would stand in the way, and she would be back and involved, instantaneously, especially when the first bombs hit Tel Aviv. "And, of course, the children, and the screwy education which I gave them, and my commitment to them because of this education . . . how is this possible?" she asks (122). Recognizing her culpability and holding on to the very principles that are at the base of that culpability is a trap with only one solution: "My only consolation is that I am almost seventy years old, and perhaps I will not live to see what happens . . . and really, nobody will miss me. Perhaps I will be successful in that" (122). Indeed, Harnik refers numerous times to her desire to disappear and die, and openly admits having contemplated suicide. Her memoir gives clear indications of deep depression, loneliness, bitterness over her children's lack of empathy and appreciation, her sense of being a burden, which becomes increasingly acute over the years, and their sense that "they came out well in spite of their mother, not because of her" (144). Harnik is convinced that her failure as a mother is her own fault, and is a trait she inherited from her mother and is likely to bequeath to her daughters.[15] "I do not like to talk about mother," she writes, "neither with psychologists nor with others. I cannot escape the common knowledge that she had, or should have had, an impact on my life, but if there was such an impact, I try to erase it" (20). Harnik suggests that she did not love her mother, and doubts that her mother loved her—the mother would have given her life for her daughter, but had nothing to offer her by way of comfort or love. Harnik mentions occasional arguments and anger with Guni, and continues to argue with him after his death ("why did you hurry, what was so urgent again?"),[16] but finds a measure of love for him in the effort to keep him alive after his death. Her unwavering dedication to her other children comes through very clearly in her memoir, only to be undermined by Harnik's own admission that it is futile, ineffective, at times harmful, not reciprocated, and, mostly, useless as a means of protecting them.

A determination to protect that is mocked by fate features prominently in Harnik's early poetry.[17] One of her most quoted poems is the first in a set called "Poems of Attrition," written in 1970, at the height of the War of Attrition following the 1967 war:[18]

I will not sacrifice
My first born as burnt offering.
Not me.

Night after night God and I
Barter
Who ought to have what.

I know and am
Grateful.
But not my son
And not
As burnt offering.[19]

Poems for Guni, Harnik's first poetry collection, builds up chronologically from 1960 to 1982. The early poems project an unmistakable certainty about an imminent disaster, which gives them a tragic aura:

All nights are a battle
With the truth that is more horrid than any dream
I cry. But remember
To be thankful for the day.
Counting moments with compassion.
Gathering hours. Days.
Hoping.
But knowing with awful certainty
Where all the years are rushing
And waiting. (1962)[20]

Harnik's early poems are short, her lines condensed, the language simple and direct, and the punctuation sparse, consisting primarily of periods. This directness, which defies any expectation that a reader may have about poetry as a work of concealment fraught with hidden intentions, invites the reader to engage immediately and honestly with an unmitigated set of messages, which, with little effort, can be distilled into a life story of a mother who has lost her son and endeavors to tell what bereavement is like. Harnik's poetics of bereavement are based on the stunning effect of the simple word that does not allow the reader to escape the message while contemplating the form. Her great anxiety, projected in terms of prophetic powers, ties the poems together and draws the reader to a woman who lives with the certainty of death while both her husband and son are still alive. From her characters' names to the episodes relayed in her poetry and prose and their striking parallels in her memoir and interviews, Harnik's work openly invites involvement in her real-life experience, thwarting any attempt to separate the narrative voice from the writer herself. Occasional symbolism, allusions to biblical motifs, and the somewhat more elaborate nature of her third collection, *Poems* (1992), detract very little from these dynamics.

While Harnik's poetic voice projects the severe anxiety of motherhood, and her memoir and interviews are marked by anger, loneliness, and despair, her children's books occasionally allow an unmistakable humorous outlook. Nevertheless, they too focus mostly on perils, specifically those of a family that is exposed to a war situation and wrestles both with the situation itself and with the mother's response to it.

Summer Time (1999) is told from the perspective of a boy who is about to go on summer vacation when his father is called up for reserve duty. The mother has plans of her own for the summer, and the boy ends up spending the long vacation with his great-grandfather, bonding with a colt and learning responsibility and the value of hard work in the process. The first chapter introduces the reader to a boy who is not too fond of school and struggles with quizzes, too much pressure, and grades that are not always satisfactory. His mother, a teacher by profession, pushes him to invest more in his studies and excel in his work, while his father is more forgiving and sensitive to his needs.[21] He comes home from school one day and senses that the mother is unusually tense. His first reaction is to assume that he is the cause of her grief: "What happened? Did I do something wrong? Nothing comes to mind. Even my room is not unusually messy."[22] The reason becomes clear when he notices on the dining table a brown envelope with a "military post" stamp. The father's looming reserve duty very quickly turns into a family crisis. The mother blames the father for remaining active in a combat unit while he could, at his age, do something less onerous and leave for a shorter time period. "He simply loves the army. For him it is vacation time," she exclaims (10). Her teacher development plans for the summer are thrown off by the need to take care of the children now that the father will be gone, and her frustration is directed at the father and his male friends who seemingly delight in the opportunity to shed off their home responsibilities. Her angst worsens when she realizes that the father is going to serve in Lebanon, where he was wounded in 1982 (another reason why he could, in principle, request a different form of service). The tension between the parents turns into concern for the father's safety, which engulfs the family as a whole. A conversation between the father and his son brings up the loyalty ethos and the family as its price:

> Father spoke of the "fighters' camaraderie." How all the guys from the battalion are like a family. How unpleasant it would be to disappoint them. And someone has to do guard duty in the north . . .
> But why Lebanon?
> Father was quiet. Then he said that this was not up to him to decide. A soldier follows orders. Especially when he is an officer.
> "We," said father, "do not refuse orders."
> And I do not know if "we" means our family, or his battalion. (22)

The military unit as a family substitute and pretext for escape from responsibilities is similarly developed in *A Diary from the Sealed Room* (1991). The book describes the experience of a family in "Zone A" (metropolitan Tel Aviv) during the 1991 Gulf War from the perspective of Ronen, a nine-year-old boy, encouraged to record his experiences in a journal.[23] The tensions within the family, which includes four generations and goes in and out of the sealed room, gas masks, and a plastic-covered crib, rise to the surface in what can be described as a bittersweet comedy in which a child grows to understand that "war is not a good thing for children. It is not good for other things either."[24] The father becomes increasingly excited as he imagines himself leaving for service, to the dismay of the mother (in this story the call never arrives, and the father is stuck with the family, trying to feel useful by talking to his "sources" in the military and his army friends, and exhibiting great relief when he can finally go back to work). The mother tries to go back to her high school teaching job, only to be called back home immediately by the great-grandmother after a screaming match between her and the children left under her supervision, and the episode develops into a family fight. While at the end life goes back to normal, and the parents seem to be in peace, the potential for tension remains hanging over the family that is portrayed with a clear division of roles: Men do their job but wish to escape, women exhibit neurotic behaviors under the relentless pressure to provide solutions for whatever happens within the family and the broader community, and children crave support that the family fails to provide and are by and large left to fend for themselves.[25]

In *Oh, My Brother* (1993) Harnik assumes the perspective of a ten-year-old boy, Ronen, whose brother, Giora, fell in battle. Ronen is keenly aware of the hardships with which the individual members of the family and the family as a whole struggle, but at the same time decries his own neglect by the family and the added uncertainties that he, young and forgotten in all discussions that matter, is left to experience. Ronen is afforded a very broad perspective on the family situation and other situations interwoven into it: a future son-in-law of whom the parents disapprove; the fundamental disconnect between the secular and the religious; the obsession with "who is to blame" for a soldier's death; the dilemma of a bereaved brother who has always prepared himself to join a combat unit and is pressured to give up this dream; the constant pretending for the sake of someone—the children, the neighbors, the soldiers who are still on the front lines, the nation; and so on. One of the themes that string the plot elements together is the collapse of the mother. Following her son's death, she goes into a prolonged depression and is not capable of caring for her other children. The relationships between her and her husband are constantly strained: At some point the mother blames the father for the son's death: "had he thought about security in this way a year ago, perhaps Giora would not have been killed . . . his positions had 'pushed' Giora to his death."[26] In a typical fashion, the father resorts to avoidance: "Father leaves for work every morning earlier and earlier. After work he is busy with all kinds of Ministry of Defense matters, and in the evening he speaks for hours with the father of that Yehiel who was killed with Giora" (13). He leaves the house and eventually goes to the United

States for a period that may or may not conclude with reconciliation—the fear of divorce hangs over the children all the way to the end of the story. The mother tries everything, from hospitalization to putting on a "normal" appearance and returning to her work as a teacher, but the reader is fully aware of her continuous crisis and reaches the end of the story with severe doubts about her ability to overcome the tragedy. Ronen is dismissive of common clichés like "I have no choice, it is for the children" (13) or "continue her life as usual" (12), and suggests that his mother actually does not care about her remaining children except, perhaps, for her older daughter, Hila, "because only to her she can tell the horrid dreams about Giora" (13). Hila, who is twelve years older than Ronen, and is likely the one who actually raised him (39), calls every day and works hard with the social worker to keep the family together.[27] At some point she has to give up her studies in order to take care of the family. In one conversation with Ronen, Hila, who managed to find a supportive future husband (Gabbi) and build some sort of a normal life, and who "always tells the truth" and treats Ronen as a grownup, suggests:[28]

> I cannot help you much, because I am not home but also because I can barely help myself. I am fortunate to have met Gabbi, otherwise I do not know what would have happened to me. But you cannot help me, neither do you need to.
>
> But mother? Mother should have carried on her roles as usual. On whose shoulder would the children cry if not their mother's? And what happens instead? Every morning she calls me and cries for half an hour on the phone, and I need to comfort her. I cannot help her, and she not only does not help me, she burdens me. (90)

The same helplessness of the female character is ascribed to the social worker who does her best for the family yet often fails to help, and, by extension, to the national effort she represents.[29] The reader, aware of the sincerity of her labor on behalf of the family, is invited to listen in on a phone conversation between her and the father, where only the father is given a voice: During a snowstorm he calls the social worker at home and reports to her that the mother "says that she is not able to lie in bed under a blanket when the child lies in the snow . . . she almost went out to the mountain to cover him!" (34). He is not very happy with the response on the other end of the line, blurting: "it does not help me that this is a known phenomenon" (34). This episode encapsulates Harnik's dismissal of psychological clichés that are often used in the treatment of bereaved families as ineffective in battling the loneliness in which the family inevitably finds itself. Describing what is, indeed, a known phenomenon, this scene also provides a powerful link to a main theme in Harnik's poetry—the graveyard as it evolves into a family space in which mother and son can, to some degree, unite.[30]

Harnik's poems occupy two very distinct spaces and movement patterns: one is a mountain toward which a man rushes, and the other is an enclosure defined by a folding inward movement:

Once I was the Land of Israel
I was the State of Israel
Today I am Jerusalem
Soon
Mount Herzl
Soon
You.[31]

The preferred space for the mother narrator is small and enclosed, shifting between the home and the grave, both of which combine to define the domestic realm:

My house is full of
Photos of
People.
Dead and also alive
At the moment.
Sometimes it is hard for me
To distinguish
Between the two.
The transition is not
So sharp—
The dead touch me
At time with their gaze
And the living turn away
From me.
And it happens that I too
Am vexed.
Whether I belong
To these—
Or to the others.[32]

Darkness dominates both spaces, threatening any glimpse of light that may appear:

Child you went too far
You really overdid it now.
Let's stop this game
Utter a sound—utter a sound
In the dark. To indicate place and direction
I will turn on the lights
Come back home. Come back to sleep.

Child, if you do not come back now
You will not come back. And no light

Will turn on in the dark. And your home
Will collapse next to you and me with you—

And the stars over your grave. (30)

The small, enclosed space at times offers momentary comfort not only to the mother but also to the dead son himself ("My son my son, I hear how this torrent / approaches. Don't be afraid / like Moses in his basket you are safe")[33]—the son, in fact, is afforded in death a measure of solace his mother can only wish for:

Now you are finally resting
My tired, restless son.
Your broad shoulders are increasingly narrowing
To fit the measurements of the coffin and the dirt.

Now you are finally safe
My beautiful son, pursued by danger.
Your legs gradually stretch out
Your body is protected inside the lands
Whose borders you had marked in running . . .[34]

As her own death wish remains unfulfilled, Harnik's mother imposes upon those among whom she lives the apparition of a prelife state, describing her existence in terms of a breathless old woman who carries a dead fetus. In three poems titled "Pregnancy Poems for a Dead Child"[35] the mother illustrates her struggle with the enormous weight and pressure of a fetus who is twenty-five years old ("a fetus who is twenty-five years old is too much / for one women who is not particularly strong" [43]), equating her inability to envision his deterioration in the grave with the inability to imagine his development as a fetus. Unlike a fetus, she suggests, the dead child has no book nor a picture, as "ultrasound does not penetrate / the grasses nor the dirt" (44). Unable to see the dead child, she offers a strategy of remembrance based on his life—looking at a photo album backward, from the end to the beginning, so that

He remains forever a baby
One week old. Covered in a blanket
And the light of love.
And so a memory will always remain
Of a past. Something infinite
That will never end. (45)

This strategy of memorializing through photographs is exhibited in *Guni,* which is a photo album as much as it is a book.[36] *Guni* begins in the traditional way, with baby pictures, and progresses through Guni's youth to a photo of his grave.[37] The flipping backward effect is created by the certainty of Guni's death, which is present from the early pages of the book, and the deceitfulness of memories is represented by the two photographs that close the book—one of two happy boys at the seaside, and another of Guni with his mother, his arm wrapped around her shoulders. The adult reader is not fooled by the smiling faces of mother and son, knowing full well how fragile and unfulfilling this closeness is:

> Someone will always be at my side
> When I call someone will answer.
> Not softly will he carry my pain
> But his arm will support my shoulder
> And on his shoulders my head will lean
> With a cold, distant and cruel gaze
> He will carry me with him
> To a world of men and war
> And occasionally a little bit of love.[38]

This "little bit of love" is denied, year after year, during memorial services, where mothers experience the greatest loneliness among family and friends. Friends are scattered, writes Harnik. "The children stand next to me, but not close. Nobody holds my hand, let alone puts an arm around my shoulder. I am always trapped in the feeling that because there is no real religious ceremony, that is, we don't read all the psalms but only a psalm of David 'whence will my help come . . .' my help will come from no one."[39]

Unmitigated loneliness permeates Harnik's work, emerging as one of the most powerful overarching themes in her literary corpus. I would like to suggest that this theme demands primacy in defining the essence of Harnik as a political activist and writer who is one and the same: Harnik is not the sensitive poetess who hides behind the aggressive fighter, but rather the aggressive fighter who relies on the delicate sensitivities of literary expression to place her exactly where she wants to be: a sore finger pointing at those responsible for the national decline—herself, at times, among them; a wounded mother committed to constantly disturbing and stirring Israel's culture of commemoration that has become too comfortable with itself. This deliberately uncomfortable posture keeps alive Harnik's call for the recognition of motherhood as a casualty of war, one that often remains forgotten in the very stratified commemoration culture in which Harnik's own son and his comrades are bound to occupy a prime position.[40] This posture is also her antiaging potion, so to speak, a powerful response not to physical aging, to which she is bound to succumb, but rather to the aging of her grief, which threatens to bring with it an increase in *internalized* involvement with her long-lost child.[41] Harnik does not wish to subscribe to internalization—she insists on affecting the external and social, and hence must distance herself from anything that might signal, even if to the slightest degree, conformity or comfort. Hence the detachment, when it comes to grief, from the Family of the Bereft, the Family of the Beaufort, or, for that matter, her very own family.

And yet loneliness is not given the final say in Harnik's work. Her latest book, *Boots for Nadav* (2005), allows for an unexpected measure of happiness, fulfillment, and gratefulness for the simple pleasures that make life worthwhile. This colorful children's book, which holds not the slightest hint to war or conflict, allows the mother character, now a grandmother, to bond with a grandson over a toy mouse and a small pair of blue boots that she had promised to buy him come the fall. The illustrations very clearly suggest Harnik's likeness, but more importantly, her familiar character is fully present, telling of an unmistakable respect for children and an unwavering commitment to their happiness: "I made a promise, and promises are something that one must keep."[42] Knowing where to go to find exactly the pair that the grandson desires when it looks like no such boots can be found is, finally, a victory for the grandmother character—the woman who in *One Year* speaks about the deep depression that sends her to bed where her greatest desire is not to wake up, is ready here to take an afternoon nap, and wake up with a smile.

Notes

I am grateful to Raya Harnik for permitting me to use her work in this essay, and for her comments on the translations.

1. Yehudit Kafri, *Iniquity of Summer* (Tel Aviv: Sifriyat Poalim, 1988), 23, a reference to: "These are the ones disqualified [for testimony]: A dice player, a usurer, pigeon fliers, traffickers in seventh year produce, and slaves. This is the rule: Any testimony that a woman is disqualified to give, so are they" (*Mishna Rosh Hashanah* 1:8, and elsewhere). Like Harnik, Kafri, a poet and activist, has been centrally involved in the Israeli protest movement. Her short poem is a powerful testimony to the predicament of a woman "peacenik" who tries to raise her voice in favor of peace and is immediately and very predictably judged for overstepping her bounds.

2. Raya Harnick, *Oh, My Brother* (Tel Aviv: Am Oved, 1993) (Hebrew: Achi, achi). The prize is named after the writer Aharon Ze'ev (1900–1968) and is awarded yearly to authors who write for children and youth.

3. Zohar Shavit, Menuha Gilboa, and Gershon Bergson, "Reasons for Awarding the Prize to Raya Harnik for Her Book: Oh, My Brother," *Sifrut Yeladim Venoar* 20, no. 2 (1993): 10–11.

4. Tamar Meroz, "I Carry with Me," *Haaretz Supplement*, June 12, 1987, 17, 19. While Harnik is one of many Israeli mothers who have written and spoken against the war in Lebanon and subsequent operations, her persistence and often cantankerous statements brought her to the forefront as a constant nuisance to the political establishment, which was captured by Yehudit Winkler in "Pain with a Political Message," *Haaretz*, May 14, 1992, B1: "Political and military establishments are highly tolerant of a mother's tears, anxiety, and fears that strengthen and nourish, after all, the currently fashionable myth. They are not particularly tolerant, to say the least, when [mothers] also express political thinking and threaten to undermine what is considered a national consensus."

5. Mordechai Rotenberg, *Bereavement and the Living Legend* (Tel Aviv: Miskal-Yediot Aharonot, 2005). (Hebrew: Shchol veha'agada hachaya.)

6. On the battle, see Ze'ev Schiff and Ehud Ya'ari, *Israel's Lebanon War* (New York: Simon and Schuster, 1984), 124–31.

7. Ibid., 126–27.

8. Raya Harnik, quoted in Rubik Rosenthal, *The Family of the Beaufort* (Tel Aviv: Sifriyat Poalim, 1989), 112. (Hebrew: mishpachat habofor.)

9. Jacobo Timerman, who wrote a book about the Lebanon War (*Diario de la guerra más larga,* translated as *The Longest War: Israel in Lebanon* [New York: Knopf, 1982]) and dedicated it to Guni, noted that Guni was a member of the political group Peace Now and a pacifist. Harnik responded with an open letter to Timerman, insisting that neither was the case. "I know," she wrote, "that there are people who think that I have tarnished Guni's image. I cannot even turn him into a 'hero' of the Left, because of the doubts—his and mine" (quoted in Rosenthal, *Family of the Beaufort,* 113).

10. Raya Harnick, *Guni* (Jerusalem: Carmel, 1990), 68.

11. Ibid., 69.

12. Rosenthal, *Family of the Beaufort,* 106. *The Family of the Beaufort* captures the battle story through the individual stories of each one of the fallen soldiers and weaves it together with the story of the families as they grapple with the deaths and come together as a group. While this 1989 document mentions occasional conflicts between the members of the family, the overarching theme is that of closeness, mutual responsibility, and comfort in the shared experience. In a 1992 interview with Rosenthal, following Begin's death, Harnik still claims that family is alive and well (Rubik Rosenthal, "He Has Again Disappeared from the Battle," *Hadashot Supplement,* March 20, 1992, 11, 13, 50). Ten years later, commenting on the death of Yehoshua Zamir, whose son, Yaron, fell in the Battle of the Beaufort, Harnik explicitly states that she dislikes the epithet "The Family of the Beaufort" and detests the term "The Family of the Bereft," attributing the persistence of these terms to Rosenthal's writings (Raya Harnik, *One Year: A Personal Journal* [Jerusalem: Keter, 2004], 203. [Hebrew: Shana achat: Yoman ishi.]). Rosenthal himself was instrumental in challenging the epithet "The Family of the Bereft," suggesting that bereavement is a very lonely experience and dispelling the notion that private bereavement and bereavement at the national level complement each other and that "The Bereft" are united by their common experience into one big family, supported by the national "bereavement ethos." For the shifts in the Israeli "bereavement ethos," see Rubik Rosenthal, *Is Bereavement Dead?* (Jerusalem: Keter, 2001) (Hebrew: Ha'im hashchol met?); and Oz Almog, *Farewell to "Srulik"* (Or Yehuda: Zmora-Bitan, 2004). The Etzion Block, located between Jerusalem and Hebron, was captured by the Arab Legion in May of 1948, and the inhabitants of three of its four settlements were taken captive. The Bloc, which came to represent a major trauma in Israeli history, was captured by the Israelis during the 1967 war and resettled. The same episode is recounted in *Guni,* but in a much more balanced way—there Guni is "a little sad and a little happy" (Harnik, *Guni,* 32)—happy "for obvious reasons," and sad because there is no place left for him to conquer when he becomes a soldier.

13. Rosenthal, *Family of the Beaufort,* 107. See similarly in Meroz's "I Carry with Me": "The expectations were mine, and he paid the price. The terrible thing about it is that I still think that the qualities which I instilled in him are correct. Things like love for the Land, bravery, camaraderie.

But they used these boys and their qualities for other things which were totally wrong." See also "Guni is dead, and I feel guilty for his death because of the nationalistic upbringing that I gave him from the time he was a baby. His blood is on my hands!"—this statement was made a week after the battle in an interview with Bruria Avidan-Barir (*Laisha,* June 14, 1982, quoted in *Lilith* 11 [Fall–Winter 1993], 17, http://www.lilith.org/shop/download/v11100_Fall_Winter_1983–05.pdf, accessed August 29, 2009).

The Maccabees were the second-century BCE Jewish fighters who freed Judea from the rule of the Seleucids and eventually established the Hasmonean dynasty. Joseph Trumpeldor was the leader of the group that defended the northern settlement of Tel Hai. He fell in the battle over the settlement (March 1, 1920), leaving the legacy of "it is good to die for our county," which has become a staple of the Zionist narrative. The police fortress of Nabi Yusha controlled the road to the northern Galilee and to the settlements of Ramot Naftali and Manarah. It was captured in May of 1948 after three battles that left twenty-eight soldiers dead and a legacy of commanders who do not abandon their wounded troops. The battle of Tel Fahr, an outpost in the Golan Heights (June 9, 1967), left the Golani Brigade with thirty-four dead and established it as the major infantry unit within the IDF. Nabi Yusha and Tel Fahr were obviously mentioned by Harnik because of the symbolic similarities between them and the Beaufort.

14. Harnik, *One Year: A Personal Journal,* 14. *One Year* is a series of short commentaries written between March of 2002 and April of 2003 and combined into a memoir. In her commentaries Harnik reacts to events during the most difficult year of the Second Intifada and the months leading to the second Gulf War, and reflects on her own life, on Guni's, on the future of her children and grandchildren, and on the Zionist dream. "This war" in the mother's comment, is a reference to a large-scale IDF operation in the West Bank (March 29–May 10).

15. A typical example of her self-criticism is the episode in which she recalls her husband's death. When she returned from identifying his body Guni was standing at the door and tried to hug her, but "instead of allowing him and crying with him, I hurried in to talk to the children" (Harnik, *One Year: A Personal Journal,* 182). Meir Harnik, Raya's husband, was killed in a motorcycle accident in 1972. Rubin and Katz-Richterman, in their study of bereavement patterns among parents of fallen soldiers, suggest that the nature of the relationship with the bereaved parent's mother was particularly predictive of anxiety. They refer to the role of mothering in building a secure and integrative self and suggest a strong correlation between positive sentiment regarding the maternal introject and functionality and security. See Simon Shimshon Rubin and Dvorah Katz-Dichterman, "The Contribution of Relational History and Attachment Patterns to Long-Term Outcome to Bereavement," in *Loss and Bereavement in Jewish Society in Israel,* ed. Ruth Malkinson, Simon Shimshon Rubin, and Eliezer Witztum (Tel Aviv: Misrad Habitachon, 1993), 51–70.

16. Raya Harnik, *Cemetery in Jerusalem* (Tel Aviv: Sifriyat Poalim, 1987), 8. (Hebrew: Mishirey har hertzel, yerushalayim.)

17. "Guni was destined to die in this war, and the Beaufort was the best place one could find for him. Our leaders waited for him around the corner, and would have caught him one way or another. This is an irrational thought, but I believe in it with all my heart" (Harnik in a 1986 interview with Rosenthal [Rosenthal, *Family of the Beaufort,* 118]).

18. "During the war of attrition," Harnik recalls, "it became clear to me, finally, that there is no end to our wars. You may escape one, but the one after it will catch you" (Harnik in an interview with Rosenthal, ibid., 107).

19. Raya Harnik, *Poems for Guni* (Tel Aviv: Hakibbutz Hameuchad, 1983), 9. (Hebrew: Shirim leguni.)

20. Ibid., 7.

21. This division of roles is very common in Harnik's work, mirroring her own family dynamics. From the perspective of a mother-narrator, the "understanding" father figure represents a mixed message—on the one hand he is criticized for ignoring the everyday challenges of real life, leaving them to the mother, and on the other he allows a nagging question to permeate the narrative; namely, whether it is possible that the mother has been wrong all along in pushing her standards too hard on the children and the family as a whole. The young boy who is not particularly fond of school is also a common theme in Harnik's work—see, for example, the description of Guni: "More than anything, and all the time, Guni did not want to go to school. For school is for girls, he said. . . . Guni wanted to play soccer, swim in the pool, and most of all he wanted to be the commander of the neighborhood army" (Harnik, *Guni,* 27). Or "Q. What was Guni like? A. Intelligent but not an intellectual" (interview with Bruria Avidan-Barir, see note 13 above). A child-reader is likely to identify with a boy who is not necessarily stellar in everything he does, while the trained adult reader immediately recognizes one of the mythical-sabra characteristics, the boy who has his mind set on a role that is greater than his own personal or intellectual development, who prefers physical work to school, and the outdoors to the domestic space, much like Moshe Shamir's quintessential Sabra Elik in *With His Own Hands* (Tel Aviv: Sifriyat Poalim, 1951).

22. Raya Harnik, *Summer Time* (Tel Aviv: Sifriyat Poalim, 1999), 8. (Hebrew: Hasyach shehitsil et hachofesh hagadol.) Subsequent quotations are cited parenthetically in the text.

23. Like the hero-narrator of *Summer Time,* Ronen is not excited about schoolwork. While he is not, by his own admission, that terrible a student, he is "a bit lazy, failing to concentrate in class" (Raya Harnik, *A Diary from the Sealed Room,* [Tel Aviv: Sifriyat Poalim, 1991], 28 [Hebrew: Yoman min hacheder ha'atum]), and "would not write anything unless they really force [him] to do so" (7). Engaged in occasional mischief, he is ready to disobey his parents, and his journal clearly reflects an expectation that as a boy and Israeli he overcome all fears and certainly not reveal that he is actually scared at times.

24. Harnik, *Diary from the Sealed Room,* 61.

25. Zvia Ben Shalom, who reviewed the book for the daily *Al Hamishmar,* noted that the journal, whose entries were written by Harnik in real time and broadcasted on Kol Yisrael's youth magazine program "berosh tsair," shows "much empathy to the problems of the young reader/listener" (Zvia Ben Shalom, "Nine-Years-Old Ronen from 'Zone A.'" *Al Hamishmar,* May 10, 1991, 21). Indeed, while writing is portrayed in the book as an activity that offers therapeutic benefits, the fact that Harnik assumed the character of a child and awarded him the power of description and growth through observation, betrays a conviction that permeates her work: Children are keen observers and have great capacity for understanding complex circumstances. The tendency to dismiss them as "too young to understand," or, worse, ignore them completely, is a form of victimization that is common within Israeli society. This theme is similarly developed in *No Noise between Two and Four* (Tel Aviv: Sifriyat Poalim/Miskal, 1993 [Hebrew: Beyn shtayim le'arba tsarich lihyot sheket]), in which Harnik describes the childhood of a German-born girl experiencing the tensions in Europe of the late 1930s from the relative safety of Tel Aviv.

26. Harnik, *Oh, My Brother,* 24. Subsequent quotations are cited parenthetically in the text.

27. In her May 23, 2002, entry of *One Year,* Harnik recalls the dynamics within her own family during the war of independence—when the sirens would sound in Tel Aviv, her younger brother

would run into her bed. "It did not occur to him, as it did not occur to me or to my mother, that he could sleep in her bed. It so happened that even when the bombing of Tel Aviv was over, he would run to me whenever he heard an airplane and beg to sleep with me. Why not with mother?" (Harnik, *One Year: A Personal Journal,* 67).

28. Gabbi, as it turns out, is also a member of a fighting unit, which implies that he, too, may die in battle, leaving Hila herself in the position of a widow. The normality, then, is at best presented as temporary.

29. On the predicament of both the families and the state, see Gilam Tamir, "Long-Term Adjustment among War Bereaved Israeli Parents," in Malkinson, Shimshon Rubin, and Witztum, eds., *Loss and Bereavement in Jewish Society in Israel,* 213–30. Tamir suggests that "in the State of Israel, bereavement is not an individual process only, but rather a collective experience" (224), nurtured by the daily struggle with war and death, and by the strong feeling of continuity of fate, as many of the parents who participated in his study were directly or indirectly affected by World War II, some of them were children during the war, members of families that perished, or a second generation of Holocaust survivors. According to Tamir, both the collective and the parents live with clear ambivalence: The Israeli collective expects them to overcome their pain and be strong so that they can represent the society that overcomes its pain and becomes stronger, but they are expected not to do it too fast and ignore their national role as "the bereaved," as symbols. The parents themselves are also stuck with ambivalence—on the one hand they expect social and emotional support, and in parallel find it difficult to accept the support that is offered to them and conclude that the society shows lack of compassion and consideration.

30. The concern with the weather and the physical conditions at the grave appears in *Oh, My Brother* in a scene where Ronen's older brother, Eitan, disappears during the same snowstorm and returns with hypothermia, having spent the night at the grave site. Ronen himself contemplates presence at the grave site: "If I were dead, perhaps it would have been more pleasant to lie under a white blanket of snow than under the rain and mud" (Harnik, *Oh, My Brother,* 13). Harnik's *Cemetery in Jerusalem* and *Poems* (Seasons of the year) powerfully project a mother's struggle with the weather—see, for example, a poem that opens with the recurring dread of "Winter has come again": "Rain rain not this time. Not to him / Let the fields be scorched. Let the flocks die of thirst / But you, rain, do not touch him" (Harnik, *Cemetery in Jerusalem,* 18), or the set "Seasons of the Year," where rain is dreaded ("My own son in the deep darkness in the rain. / I know that you are cold / you are totally wet") (Harnik, *Poems* [Tel Aviv: Yaron Golan, 1992], 9 [Hebrew: Onot hashana]), and summer is described as "the season that consoles" ("I know that you are not cold / and you are not wet / the earth clods are warm / and good to you") 7.

31. Harnik, *Cemetery in Jerusalem,* 19. Herzl Mount in Jerusalem is Israel's national cemetery.

32. Harnik, *Poems for Guni,* 24. Judging by its position in the book, this poem was written around 1980. The poems are cited parenthetically in text.

33. Harnik, *Poems,* 10.

34. Harnik, *Poems for Guni,* 29.

35. Harnik, *Cemetery in Jerusalem,* 43–45. Subsequent passages cited parenthetically in the text.

36. A similar technique is used in *No Noise between Two and Four,* which combines Harnik family photos and drawings by Christina Kadmon. The last of the illustrations portrays Harnik as a smiling young girl on her way to school, with German soldiers marching over her head.

37. This photograph still has the gravestone with the standard statement "fell in Operation Peace for the Galilee." Harnik, like other bereaved parents who decried the notion of a premedi-

tated war fought in the pretext of peace, called upon the Ministry of Defense to replace the gravestone, and in 1991 won her battle—the gravestone was replaced with one that said, "fell in battle in Lebanon." See Aviva Lori, "Raya Harnik Erased the 'Peace for the Galilee' from Guni's Gravestone," *Ma'ariv Saturday Supplement*, January 3, 1992, 7. See also letters from Yehoshua Zamir, whose son, Yaron, fell in the Battle of the Beaufort, to Ariel Sharon and Menachem Begin (February 6 and April 23, 1983, http://books.eserver.org/nonfiction/survival/documents.html, accessed August 29, 2009).

38. Harnik, *Poems for Guni*, 23.

39. Harnik, *One Year: A Personal Journal*, 72.

40. For the stratification of the commemoration process, see Rotenberg, *Bereavement and the Living Legend*, and also Emmanuel Sivan, "To Remember Is to Forget: Israel's 1948 War," *Journal of Contemporary History* 28, no. 2 (1993): 341–59. Sivan argues that trends in the "organization of memory" have given a distinct advantage to certain social groups in the process of commemoration, a position of power, that I argue here, Harnik wishes to claim.

41. For the concept of "aging of grief," see Ruth Malkinson and Liora Bar-tur, "The Aging of Grief: Parents' Grieving of Israeli Soldiers," *Journal of Personal and Interpersonal Loss* 5 (2000): 247–61.

42. Raya Harnik, *Boots for Nadav* (Bney Brak: Sifriyat Poalim/Harkibbutz Hameuchad, 2005), 9. (Hebrew: Magafayim lenadav.)

Chapter 8

From IDF to .PDF

War Poetry in the Israeli Digital Age

Adriana X. Jacobs

On December 27, 2008, the Israel Defense Forces (IDF) entered the Gaza Strip under the code name Operation Cast Lead (*Mivtsa 'oferet yetsuka*). The military operation was provoked, ostensibly, by a series of rocket attacks orchestrated by Hamas paramilitary groups that were directed at Israeli towns. Over the course of three weeks, the IDF attacked areas of Hamas support: training camps, arms smuggling tunnels, weapons caches, police stations, and other areas from which Hamas forces were presumably planning and arming for future attacks against Israeli citizens.[1]

On January 1, two days before the ground invasion and five days after the outbreak of war in Gaza, a group of contemporary Israeli poets, writers, translators, and visual artists published a joint literary response to the war. *Latset! Asufa neged ha-milchamah ba-'aza* (Get Out!: An Anthology against the War in Gaza) represents a collaboration of the journals *Etgar, Ma'arav, Sedek, Dakah, Ma'ayan,* and *Gerila Tarbut.*[2] It features a number of young contemporary poets—Mati Shmuelof, Eran Tzelgov, Roni Hirsch, Merhav Yeshurun, for example—as well as veterans like Rami Saari, Aharon Shabtai, Tal Nitzan, and Salman Masalha. It also includes translations into Hebrew of poems by the Israeli Arab poet Tawfik Ziad and the English playwright Harold Pinter, as well as song lyrics by Phil Ochs, a US protest singer who was active in the anti-Vietnam movement.

Quoting from a brief, uncredited article that appeared on Ynet, the online arm of the print daily *Yediot Achronot,* "the decision to put together the anthology was made during a rally against the military campaign in Gaza, which was held [on January 1, 2009] outside of Defense Minister Ehud Barak's house . . . and attended by most of the writers and artists."[3] A run of one thousand copies of the anthology was printed in Kfar Qassim, an Israeli Arab town near Tel Aviv. On January 3, the editors created a website for the anthology at asufa.blogspot.com, which they updated over the next couple of months with links to articles and reviews, in effect, creating their own archive of the press and online reception of the anthology (see the appendix).[4] On January 8, I received an e-mail from Jo Ellen Green Kaiser, editor-in-chief of *Zeek: A Jewish Journal of Thought and Culture,* inquiring if I would be interested in providing translations for a possible English publication of the anthology. It was a rush job. "I need the translation today if possible," she wrote, "as I am trying to do all this before the Gaza incursion ends (and the best pundits think it will end on January 20, not coincidentally when Obama is inaugurated)."[5] I sent her two translations that night. As she predicted, the war ended soon after and, in a subsequent e-mail, she reported that funding for the project did not materialize.[6]

As a scholar of Israeli literature, particularly poetry, this entire episode challenged, in various respects, the mode in which I typically approach and research a literary text. In the process, it raised a number of issues and questions, which I probe in this chapter, with regard to literature in the digital age. In particular, through the close reading of select poems from the anthology, I focus on the relation between immediacy and aesthetic value, considering the extent to which the quick digital publication of *Latset!* potentially compromised its quality, all the while constituting a value in its own right. Indeed, the editors of *Latset!* seem to anticipate a negative correlation between immediacy and quality when they remark in their introduction that "some of the advantages and disadvantages of the collection before you are on account of the speed and urgency with which it was edited."[7] But Israeli journalist Doron Koren was nonetheless scathing in his critique of the anthology: "There are authentic and touching lines here and there, but most of the anti-war anthology *Latset,* which came out with great speed owing to the war in Gaza, suffers from a clear anti-poetic flaw: banality."[8] Ultimately, he argued, the ability of the anthology to influence an Israeli readership relied on the aesthetic value of the works themselves, rather than their topical nature, a long-standing concern in critical assessments of antiwar and protest poetry. The appearance of the anthology was timely and newsworthy; indeed, its very title—"get out!" in Hebrew—positioned it as an event in real time.

The Ynet article was one of the first media outlets to call attention to the anthology. An English version of the same article appeared two days later with an entirely different set of comments (*tokbakim* in Hebrew, from the English "talkback"), most from the United States and abroad.[9] The Hebrew version, on the other hand, reached a more Israeli, Hebrew-speaking audience and also garnered twice as many comments as the English version (forty-three and twenty, respectively).[10] There were a few, seemingly minor, differences between both articles: the English version shortened quotes from the editors and did not include the list of participating journals and editors. Did these differences potentially shape the reactions and observations that readers submitted over the next two weeks? The Hebrew article, arguably, contextualized more thoroughly the anthology in contemporary Israeli literary culture and politics. It also quoted directly from the anthology, stating clearly how the anthology aligned itself with antiwar protest activity around the country. By and large the readers of the English-language article were responding to the *idea* of the anthology, whereas the Hebrew-language readers had access to the anthology itself and could make their own evaluation of its content, should they choose to do so. Nevertheless, for a literary scholar, these comment threads provide an unclear picture of the reception of the anthology. For one, the comments on Ynet are moderated according to editorial policies that vary from publication to publication. Also, online identities are easily fabricated and frequently anonymous, making any demographic evaluation of the anthology's reception a bit difficult. At the same time, these comment threads introduce voices that traditionally have been left out of the official reception of literary texts. They offer an alternative to the academic book review or carefully selected "Letter to the Editor."

In the case of *Latset!*, once traditional forms of production and distribution were unavailable, the Internet came to occupy multiple roles simultaneously: hosting the anthology, facilitating its dissemination, tracking and archiving the flow of its reception, to name a few. In this sense, the very fact of being online seems to challenge more authoritative channels of literary consumption and control—namely, print. To some degree, the final destination(s) and reception of the anthology were unregulated, thereby allowing it to simultaneously inhabit and construct an expanding cyberspace that challenged the politics and regulation of Israeli print culture. (Local printers, for instance, refused to print the journal.) In her study *Control and Freedom: Power and Paranoia in the Age of Fiber Optics*, new media scholar Wendy Hui Kyong Chun argues that the perception of the Internet as a "free" space is partly an illusion:

> The current configuration of fiber-optic networks challenges disciplinary and regulatory power. Telecommunications monopolies, rules and regulations have been and continue to be revised, many regulatory techniques have been rendered ineffectual, and many new, more invasive techniques are being introduced. The sheer number of Web sites, the multiple paths, and rapidity with which sites are altered, built, destroyed, and mirrored makes regulation of this new mass medium far more difficult than any other. . . . However . . . it does make prosecution easier.[11]

On the one hand, publishing online bypasses, or seems to bypass entirely, authoritarian or state-controlled media, in that sense offering to the independent publisher the freedom to publish on his or her own terms. Nevertheless, the idea of a free Internet or the Internet as a democratic, let alone anarchic, space is also a deception. As Chun points out, web activity is not invisible—the location and consumption of information is regularly archived, mapped, and observed. The flow of information that users often take for granted is constantly regulated. The freedom of movement and range of access that the Internet allows is an advantage of going online, but it is also an illusion. What if the Israeli government were to decide tomorrow to block sites like blogger.com, which hosts the *Asufa* site? Or a hacker erased the content of the website for kicks? Where would this information go, how would the average public user be able to retrieve it?[12] As quickly as information emerges online it also disappears, thereby imparting greater urgency to the task of archiving and evaluating these materials, an area where the contribution and participation of scholars could prove to be vital.

The upside of digital publishing is that it capitalizes on immediacy, a quality that continues to elude print culture. War and protest poetry anthologies in print traditionally have relied on wider temporal and cultural frames to address the effects and aftereffects of war. The Israeli anthologies *No End to Battles and Killing* (Eyn tikhlah le-kravot u-le-hereg) and *Border Crossing* (Chatsiyat gvul) were notable for how rapidly they were produced and disseminated as a response to the 1982 Lebanon war, and particularly to the Sabra and Shatila massacre.[13] This is particularly true of English translations of Israeli war and protest poetry. One example that comes to mind is the 1998 collection *No Rattling of Sabers: An Anthology of Israeli War Poetry*, edited by Esther Raizen, which belatedly responds to the 1991 Gulf War but also addresses the place of war in Israeli culture in much broader terms.[14] Simply put, it takes time to collect, edit, and publish a print anthology. Nevertheless, this temporal lag is significant and, arguably, necessary. In order to keep the content of the anthologies current and relevant, editors and publishers often must frame these collections through a much wider lens, one that shapes directly the kinds of poems that these collections include. In her essay "What's the Use? Writing Poetry in Wartime," Alice Templeton argues this distance is necessary; it imparts "clarity" to a situation where "immediate involvement," that is, standing too close to the situation, "tends to reduce poetic singularity to a monotonous flatness, exhausting language itself."[15] The poet and translator Tal Nitzan touches on the tension between perspective and immediacy in her introduction to the print anthology *With an Iron Pen: Hebrew Protest Poetry, 1984–2004*, when she observes that "the Israeli occupation of the West Bank is a multifaceted, multifront phenomenon that has spanned four decades, wherein trauma follows trauma with relentless speed, horror and frequency."[16] For Nitzan, the twenty-year time frame ("trajectory," in her words) allows the poet, editor, and reader to stand back and detain the language and images of war in order to evaluate them from all sides. On the one hand, the prolongation of the Israeli-Palestinian conflict has allowed time to process and evaluate the situation from multiple perspectives, but at the same time, there is a sense that the printed poetic text always lags a few feet behind the real-time horrors of war.

This poetry protests the long duration of the Israeli-Palestinian conflict, but it is not an act of protest in *real time*. *Latset!*, however, responded to the events that unfolded at the outbreak of Operation Cast Lead alongside protest activity (i.e., rallies, demonstrations, editorials) with the kind of immediacy that the Internet facilitates and encourages. In fact, in addition to the numerous news outlets both in Israel and abroad reporting on the developments in Gaza, one also could receive daily updates on IDF activity via the website of the IDF Spokesperson's Unit, "the Israel Defense Forces' professional body responsible for media and public relations in Israel and around the world.[17] Although the editors of *Latset!* were the first to address the potential disadvantages of producing the volume so quickly, the novelty of going online allowed these poems to emerge alongside the news of war, and thus challenge war events in their own time, a detail that was not overlooked in the reactions and reviews that the anthology garnered.[18]

Latset! became a "poem event" in the words of literary critic N. Katherine Hayles. Whereas the printed literary text is unchangeable, the digital text is best described as "a *process* rather than an object."[19] "Electronic literature reveals the text as a performance riddled with time even as it also extends in space," Hayles argues in her essay "The Time of Digital Poetry: From Object to Event."[20] In other words, the electronic text occupies simultaneously a continuous past, present, and future as it travels unfettered through cyberspace. Although asufa.blogspot.com arguably constitutes a "permanent address" for the anthology, the actual .pdf file can be—and has been—hosted in numerous other sites as well, and each time a user visits the website, he or she experiences the text in their own real time. The idea that the electronic text occupies, on the Internet, a continuous present and presence is complicated in the case of *Latset!*, which also positioned itself as an act of real-time protest. About a week after the collection appeared online, I received the .pdf attachment of the anthology in an e-mail message from my colleague Eran Tzelgov, an editor of the journal *Dakah* and a participant in the project. By then, it was old news, and a few weeks later the war was over. What were the poems "protesting" now? Could they continue to stand up on their own without the urgency of the original context?

Interestingly, in a blog post on *Latset!*, editor Mati Shmuelof remarks that *Latset!* is a direct descendant of *Adumah*, a collection published in 2007 that confronted and challenged Israel's "class struggles" through poetry, music, and prose.[21] Indeed, there is a significant overlap between the authors and editors of both collections. The inclusion of previously published works represents a conscious move to link *Latset!* to a history and movement of Israeli protest poetry, to bring a "multifaceted" and historically wide lens to a relatively brief military operation that is also part of an ongoing conflict, not only in terms of war but also in terms of the very values that prevail in Israel's contemporary, "free market" society. The presence of Pinter and Ochs in *Latset!* also opens provocative ways for reading the anthology as a collective statement against the perils of imperialism in a global and technological age. The translation of Ochs' "Draft Dodger Song," for example, replaces Vietnam-era cultural references with contemporary Israeli ones (e.g., the US draft dodger becomes the Israeli "refusenik").[22] The participation of the organization "Gerila tarbut," guerrilla culture, also suggests a way of framing the online distribution of the anthology as an anarchic form of protest.[23] Indeed, the anthology contains two prose testimonies by antiwar protestors in Israel.[24] These testimonies recount protest activity in various Israeli cities, some taking place within a day of the anthology's appearance, further underscoring *Latset!*'s self-characterization as a form of "social action."

In its role as an expression of protest and social action, *Latset!* is an obvious counterpart to the 2003 online anthology *100 Poets Against the War*, a groundbreaking collaboration of Anglophone poets in response to the escalating war in Iraq.[25] As with *Latset!*, the works gathered included texts written specifically for the collection as well as previously written, and published, poems. In the editor's introduction to the first edition, the Canadian poet Todd Swift writes:

> This chapbook anthology, *100 Poets Against The War,* has been timed to appear on January 27, 2003, the date on which Hans Blix delivers his weapons inspections report to the United Nations. It is widely expected that this report will either act as a trigger for war, or begin the process whereby the United States of America in fact disregards the will of the UN, and makes a unilateral . . . preemptive strike upon Iraq.[26]

With this date looming, the anthology emerged as its own strike against war. The introduction, like the one in *Latset!,* also pointedly remarks on the swiftness of the project:

> It may hold the record for being the fastest assembled global anthology; it was first conceived and announced on January 20, 2003, a mere week before its first appearance. *Only the speed of the Internet,* and the overwhelmingly positive support of so many poets, who shared the project with their colleagues and personal networks, could have made it happen. (My emphasis)[27]

Abiding by the ethos of do-it-yourself (DIY), Swift restricted the anthology to fifty pages (compare with *Latset!*'s seventy-six), making it relatively easy and affordable to print and distribute. Two new editions emerged during the course of the next two weeks, appropriately called *100 Poets Against the War Redux* and *100 Poets Against the War 3.0*.[28] To give visibility to new voices, Swift replaced some poets and added new ones. He also corrected typos in the first edition that were the inevitable result of putting the anthology together under such time constraints. By March, an expanded print edition was available through Salt Publishing, and Swift and his collaborators continue to update their website with new content and news.[29]

A comparison of the two projects raises the question of the potential aesthetic limitations of "speed and urgency," which also touches on the debate between protest and aesthetics that has preoccupied US literary discourse for decades.[30] Templeton argues that protest poetry that abandons a "lyric aesthetic" gives in to "war's depleting effects."[31] "The question of protest literature is imbedded in the ambiguity of both of those terms," observes Paul Later, a professor of English at Trinity College, " 'Protest' is not, after all, a conventional literary term like 'iambic pentameter,' 'sonnet,' or 'fiction.' It is a social dynamic, and the relationship of art—largely produced by individuals—to such social movements is always, at best, ambiguous and conflicted."[32] The editors of *Latset!,* on the other hand, consciously sacrifice a polished lyric aesthetic for the sake of protest. They are far more invested in the collection as a form of direct action. In 2005 Nitzan wrote "of course the poets who wrote against the war in Lebanon did not believe their words would end the war or cause the army to retreat; however, since then, the very concept of 'protest poetry' in Israel has been seen more and more as an isolated and useless cry in the dark."[33] Four years later, *Latset!* challenges this lament. Ido Bar-El's contribution to the anthology is succinct: "hafsakat esh." Cease-fire. The words hover on the page, surrounded by white space, arresting the reader's gaze and breath. These words, on the contrary, have the power to provoke a physical response, to make the reader pause.

Latset! includes "Khan Younis," a poem by Nitzan that made an earlier appearance in the collection *With an Iron Pen* (*Be-'et ha-barzel*), which she also edited.[34] The speaker of Nitzan's poem is a parent preparing to kiss a scratch on a child's hand. The cat responsible for the wound has been "banished to the balcony." Although the cultural and national identities of the speaker and addressee are never stated explicitly, they can be inferred by the title of the poem, which refers to a city and refugee camp in southern Gaza. The city has been a launching pad for Qassam rockets into Sderot and other nearby Israeli towns and settlements, and as a result has been a target of frequent IDF raids over the years. In Nitzan's poem, the relatively innocuous, quotidian scenario that opens the poem becomes the pivot for an opposition between the wounds of Israeli children and their Palestinian counterparts. "But your little boy knows terrors / no kiss can wipe away," the speaker remarks to the father of the other child. Only two years old, the Palestinian child lacks innocence, "already knows / how to warn his mother / to crouch down / when the shots fly into the house." The succinct phrase "our efficient bullets" establishes a relation between the speaker and those responsible for the crossfire. Although the fate of the family inside the house is not revealed, the image of the "bullet-riddled sign" that states "Attention! Families live here!" in English, Hebrew, and Arabic makes it clear to the reader that danger has not been averted. Nitzan closes her poem with provocative personification of the Palestinian home in a state of mourning, "from perforated boilers, water / runs down the house's cheeks." The damage inflicted on the sign underscores a failure of language, any language, to offer protection, also true for the lullaby that the father sings as bullets rain on the house ("The window through which the wind creeps— / close it now and lie down to sleep").

Nitzan's poem offers a self-critique of the protest poem and the incapacity of poetic language, in general, to catalyze action. Poetic language, like the sign, can call attention but it cannot stop the storm of bullets.[35] The words on the sign can't *do* anything, but in writing the poem, and calling attention to its language, Nitzan's poem opens a space of consciousness with the potential to persuade, disturb, and energize the reader. At the same time Nitzan articulates the limits of the protest poem. The poem's inclusion in *Latset!* testifies to the (unfortunate) continued relevance of the poem and the place and wounds it is describing. Nevertheless, by avoiding references to specific events and dates, Nitzan's poem succeeds in articulating the wounds of the Israel-Palestine conflict on language, homes, and relationships through a wide historical lens situated in a continuous present.

Templeton's argument that poets who offer a journalistic testimony of their "direct involvement" with war "most often sustain the war-dominated imagination that they claim to write against" proves relevant for several poems in *Latset!*.[36] An example of the kind of poetry that Templeton critiques is Shira Stav's "Voice of Israel from Jerusalem" (*Kol yisrael mirushalayim*), which opens with the news that the National Security cabinet has declared "Operation Cast Lead will continue."[37] The language of the poem is standard Israeli journalese—even its very title borrows from the standard opening for Kol Israel's hourly news reports—and includes references to a number of well-known Israeli political figures: then Prime Minister Ehud Olmert, Minister of Defense Ehud Barak, then Minister of Foreign Affairs Tzipi Livni, and Benjamin Netanyahu (who at this writing is prime minister of Israel). The juxtaposition of war news with comments on the rate of the dollar and weather reports is an attempt to parody objectivity and the attitude that "life goes on," but in the process, Stav's poem reproduces the very detachment it seems to try to critique.[38] On the one hand, Stav's attempt to create a poem within the restrictions of the news broadcast demonstrates the fundamental differences between journalese and poetic language, the latter assuming a testimonial—and almost prophetic—role. When poetic language successfully illuminates events in the here and now it does so through the perspective of time and experience, which Stav's poem marks by its use of the future mode. The poem ends in the closed, insular space of the news studio with the disquieting lines: "The rockets will rust / the missiles will cease to be useful / the rain will rinse the faces / and no one will see the tears / Back to the studio." Ultimately, however, this space fails to provoke. Despite its attempt to challenge the "war imagination," the poem, ultimately, is restricted by it, in large part because its cultural references are too local and specific. The poem makes its (political) connections and relations so direct and obvious that the reader is unable to introduce other "linkages," to use Muriel Rukeyser's term. Such connections are vital, following Rukeyser, because they allow readers to participate in the creation of the poem as a larger unity, a unity that war aspires to undermine and enclose in its own restrictive, contained space. On the one hand, the "speed and urgency" of *Latset!*'s publication works in favor of Stav's poem; at the time of publication, many of the details her poem contains were current and relevant. On the other hand, these same details date the poem far too restrictively, something that Nitzan's poem, for instance, avoids. As a result, "Khan Younis" continues to speak to and of the "matsav" (the situation) years later, in present time.

Although Merhav Yeshurun's three-part poem "Three Poems for Children" addresses local and topical politics, it also contextualizes the events of his poem in a more expansive historical framework through a clever and poignant revision of Dan Pagis's iconic Holocaust poem "Written in Pencil in the Sealed Railway Car":[39]

here in this carload
I am eve
with Abel my son
if you see my other son
Cain son of man
tell him that I am

In his poem, Yeshurun transports Pagis's text to an Israeli checkpoint, casting a pregnant Palestinian woman as the poem's "Eve":

here at this checkpoint
I am giving birth
to my son
if you see Fat Ehud
with a son in his belly
tell him
mine is no longer

Yeshurun's poem not only positions itself in the "you are here" that poet and minister Arnold Kenseth asserts is the site of protest poetry, but gestures in its very tone, language, and form to Pagis's poem.[40] The checkpoint, like Pagis's "carload," is a loaded signifier, "minimalist lines drawn on a canvas thick with public knowledge," to quote Sidra Ezrahi's reading of Pagis's poem.[41] Stories of pregnant Palestinian women giving birth or suffering miscarriages at Israeli checkpoints have become international news, and were the subject of a 2009 report of the United Nations High Commissioner for Human Rights.[42] In Israel, the group Machsom (in English, MachsomWatch) emerged precisely to challenge these kinds of scenarios. Yet by adopting the form and language of an iconic Israeli Holocaust poem, Yeshurun provocatively constructs a much more complex, contentious historical framework. As in Nitzan's "Khan Younis," Yeshurun's poem attempts to forge a relation between Jewish Israeli and Palestinian suffering, and does so by forcing the Hebrew reader of the poem to adopt the voice of the other. Nevertheless, whereas Nitzan juxtaposes Israeli and Palestinian suffering to highlight their differences, Yeshurun engages a more problematic relation (at least within Israel's cultural discourse) by conflating the Jewish Holocaust with Palestinian suffering, and does so by appropriating one of the most well known Holocaust poems in Israeli literature. Additionally, the poem's "Ehud Hashamen"—ostensibly a reference to Ehud Barak—alludes to Yigal Mossinsohn's children's adventure series *Hasamba,* which was set during the British Mandate and related the exploits of a secret society of children (including the character Ehud Hashamen) who worked clandestinely for the Haganah (a Jewish paramilitary group that predated the IDF) on behalf of Jewish statehood.[43] Yeshurun strips this allusion of its characteristic nostalgia. For the Palestinian mother at the checkpoint, "Ehud Hashamen" and the "son" in his belly embody an ongoing, hegemonic national narrative—passed down through generations—that has cast her as an enemy of the state, leaving her bereft of her own legacy.

Latset! marks an important intersection between traditional forms and new media in contemporary Israeli literature, but its flaws can't be overlooked.[44] Aside from significant typos, which can be attributed to the editors' rush to get the anthology out, it is not incidental that the more complex, evocative, and aesthetically interesting poems in *Latset!* were, more often than not, texts written and published well before the events of Operation Cast Lead (e.g., poems by Saari and Nitzan).[45] Additionally, the inclusion of

Pinter and Ochs hints at correlations with American and Western warmongering that, on the whole, remain too subtle and undeveloped.[46] The anthology begs for revision, for its own redux or 2.0 version, but that hasn't materialized. Nevertheless, although asufa .blogspot.com hasn't been updated in months, this doesn't mean that *Latset!* has ceased to be active. The Egyptian poet Nael Eltoukhy has translated several poems into Arabic, which were published in Lebanon in the journal *Alghaoon*.[47] A print version of selected poems from the anthology has appeared in Egypt as well, to wide acclaim, but the future of the *Latset!* anthology remains uncertain.[48]

"The impression that this poetry imprints in the minds and hearts of the public can be seen mostly only from the distance of time," Nitzan writes in her introduction to *With an Iron Pen*, but her observation could apply just as well to *Latset!* The translocation of the poems and images in *Latset!* from the printed page to the digital frame (including Nitzan's "Khan Younis") enacts processes of engagement and distribution that turn these texts and images into "poem-events," potentially narrowing that gap between protest and clarity. In other words, when a reader stumbles upon a webpage, whether or not it has been updated or changed in a day or in years, the reader experiences the material in the digital frame as a real-time event. In this respect, the digital poem is always already immediate, the impression it makes a matter of bandwidth and not (just) years.

Appendix

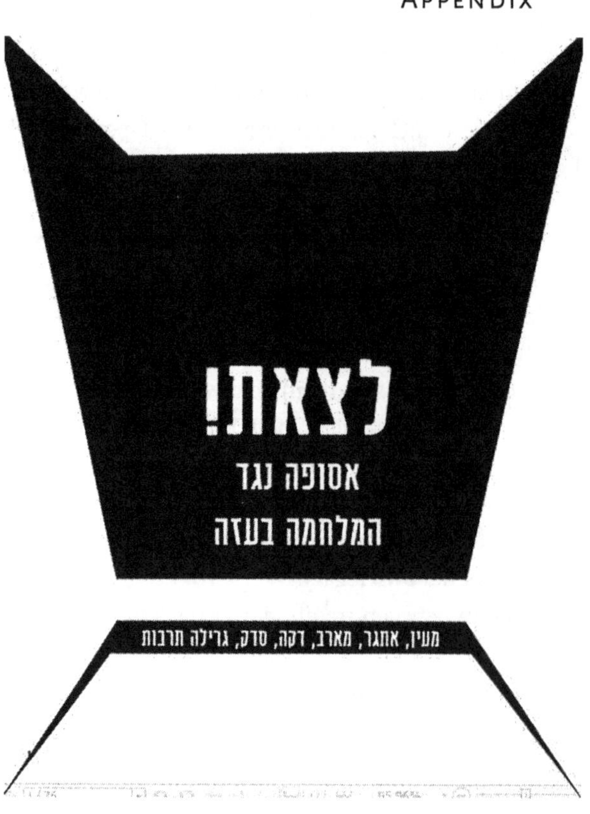

Latset! Asufat shirah neged ha-milchamah be-'aza (Get Out! A Poetry Anthology against the War in Gaza). Kfar Qassim: anonymous publisher, 2009. Available at http://asufa .blogspot.com.

Notes

1. A ground invasion followed on January 3, 2009, and by January 18, Israel declared a unilateral ceasefire. Complete withdrawal took place on January 21.

2. Boaz Yaniv, ed., et al, *Latset! Asufat shirah neged ha-milchamah be-'aza* (Get Out! A Poetry Anthology against the War in Gaza) (Kfar Qassim: anonymous publisher, 2009). Available online at http://asufa.blogspot.com. All translations from the Hebrew are mine unless otherwise noted.

3. Ynetnews.com, "Israeli Anthology against Gaza War Published," January 5, 2009. http://www.ynetnews.com/articles/0,7340,L-3649731,00.html, last accessed January 12, 2010.

4. http://asufa.blogspot.com/, last accessed January 12, 2010.

5. Jo Ellen Green Kaiser, e-mail to author, January 8, 2009.

6. Jo Ellen Green Kaiser, e-mail to author, January 18, 2010.

7. Yaniv, *Latset!*, 2.

8. Doron Koren, "They Rushed Too Quickly to Get Out" (Mihru miday latset), Ynet.co.il, January 14, 2009. http://www.ynet.co.il/articles/0,7340,L-3655316,00.html, last accessed January 14, 2010.

9. "Israeli Anthology against Gaza War Published," *Ynetnews.com.*

10. Ynet.co.il. "No Time to Save" (Lo choskhim zman), January 3, 2009, http://www.ynet.co.il/articles/0,7340,L-3649420,00.html, last accessed January 12, 2010.

11. Wendy Hui Kyong Chun, *Control and Freedom: Power and Paranoia in the Age of Fiber Optics* (Cambridge, MA: MIT Press, 2006): 15. Emphasis in original.

12. China is a frequent subject in discussion on state control of the Internet and new media technologies. In response to a recent flare-up with Google over restrictions on e-mail access of Chinese dissidents, the Chinese Foreign Ministry succinctly but pointedly declared that foreign Internet companies must comply "in accordance with [Chinese] law." Andrew Jacobs, "Follow the Law, China Tells Internet Companies," *New York Times*, January 14, 2010, http://www.nytimes.com/2010/01/15/world/asia/15beijing.html, last accessed January 15, 2010. See also Wikipedia, "Internet Censorship in the People's Republic of China," http://en.wikipedia.org/wiki/Internet_censorship_in_the_People%27s_Republic_of_China, last accessed January 15, 2010. Social networking sites on the Internet, particularly Twitter, Facebook, and blogs, were credited with helping to mobilize and sustain protest activity in the aftermath of the 2009 Iranian elections. Wikipedia, "Role of the Internet during 2009 Iranian Election Protests," http://en.wikipedia.org/wiki/Role_of_the_Internet_during_2009_Iranian_election_protests, last accessed on January 15, 2010. See also "The Internet and Politics: Revolution.com," Guardian.co.uk, January 4, 2009, http://www.guardian.co.uk/world/2010/jan/04/iran-politics-blogging-internet, last accessed January 15, 2010.

13. Hanan Hever and Moshe Ron, eds., *No End to Battles and Killing: Political Poetry from the Lebanon War* (Eyn tikhlah le-kravot u-le-hereg: shirah politit be-milchemet Lebanon) (Tel Aviv: Ha-kibbuts ha-meuchad, 1983); Yehudit Kafri, ed., *Border Crossing: Poems from the Lebanon War* (Chatsiyat gvul: Shirim mi-milchemet Lebanon) (Bnei Barak: Sifriat po'alim, 1983).

14. Esther Raizen, ed., *No Rattling of Sabers: An Anthology of Israeli War Poetry* (Austin: Center for Middle Eastern Studies at the University of Texas at Austin, 1995). See also the anthology *After the First Rain: Israeli Poems on War and Peace*, edited by Moshe Dor and Barbara Goldberg, which includes a foreword by Shimon Peres (Syracuse, NY: Syracuse University Press, 1998).

15. Alice Templeton, "What's the Use? Writing Poetry in Wartime," *College Literature* 34, no. 4

(2007): 44. Templeton's distinction between a "poetics of clarity" and a "poetics of protest" owes much to Muriel Rukeyser. See note 22.

16. Tal Nitzan, introduction to *With an Iron Pen: Twenty Years of Protest Poetry*, trans. Rachel Tzvia Back (Albany: State University of New York Press, 2009), 1.

17. http://idfspokesperson.com, last accessed January 12, 2010.

18. *Latset!*'s website, asufa.blogspot.com, includes a list—with links—to reviews, news items, and blog entries related to the anthology. As a disclaimer, I must mention that my own website, www.stingykids.net, is cited in this list. On January 7, I published a brief blog entry on the anthology and included a translation of Roni Hirsch's poem "She Was Killed in Gaza" ("Ne'hergah be-'aza," in *Latset!*, 63). Adriana X. Jacobs, "Latset," Stingy Kids, posted on January 7, 2009, http://www.stingykids.net/2009/01/latset.html, last accessed January 12, 2010.

19. N. Katherine Hayles, "The Time of Digital Poetry: From Object to Event," in *New Media Poetics: Contexts, Technotexts and Theories*, ed. Adalaide Morris and Thomas Swiss (Cambridge, MA: MIT Press, 2006), 185.

20. Ibid., 206.

21. Mati Shmuelof, May 2, 2007, "Adumah-asufat shirah ma'amadit," http://www.notes.co.il/mati/31540.asp.

22. In contemporary Israeli Hebrew, the term "refusenik" refers to individuals who refuse to comply with their obligatory military service.

23. Gerila Tarbut (Guerilla Culture) represents a diverse group of artist-activists (particularly poets) in Israel who have mobilized in recent years on behalf of various social justice issues: racial and gender inequality, economic disparity, the unionization of workers, and the end of the Occupation, to name a few. See http://www.gerila.co.il for more information about the group and its current activities.

24. Yonatan Pollack, "Untitled," in *Latset!*, 20–21; Ran Tsoref, "An Account of a Small, Quiet and Contained Demonstration 29.12.08" (Kronika shel hafganah ketanah, shketah u-metsumtse-met), ibid., 37–38.

25. The anthology is available online as a downloadable .pdf file at http://www.nthposition.com/100poets.php, last accessed January 12, 2010.

26. Todd Swift, "Editor's Introduction," in *100 Poets Against the War*, i. See above note.

27. Ibid., i.

28. Both of these versions are also available at http://www.nthposition.com/100poets.php as .pdf downloads.

29. Todd Swift, ed., *100 Poets Against the War* (London: Salt Publishing, 2003).

30. Cf. Muriel Rukeyser, *The Life of Poetry* (1949; Ashfield, MA: Paris Press, 1996). Rukeyser's groundbreaking exploration of the importance of poetry in wartime concludes with the conviction that "to be against war is not enough . . . there is another way of being against war and for poetry" (213). Rukeyser's comments on poetry in wartime recall those of the Hebrew poet Leah Goldberg. In her pivotal essay "'Al oto noseh 'atsmo," "On the Very Space Subject," which appeared in 1939 in *Ha-shomer ha-tsair*, Goldberg argued that poems that allowed readers to dream, imagine, and explore realms beyond their immediate reality were vital in times of war. Love poems, she claimed, reminded readers of what made them human, a reminder that was always in greatest need in wartime, when human values and humanity itself were most under threat. It was Goldberg's position that during times of war poets should create a conscious poetry without sacrificing aesthetic values.

31. Templeton, "What's the Use? Writing Poetry in Wartime," 44, 46.

32. Paul Lauter, "Teaching Protest Literature," *The Free Library* (June 22, 2007), http://www.thefreelibrary.com/Teaching protest literature.-a0168432826, accessed January 15, 2010.

33. Nitzan, introduction to *With an Iron Pen,* 2.

34. Tal Nitzan, "Khan Younis," in *Latset!,* 71. For Rachel Tzvia Back's English translation, see Tal Nitzan and Rachel Tzvia Back, eds., *With an Iron Pen: Twenty Years of Protest Poetry* (Albany: State University of New York Press, 2009), 33.

35. This is also the central dilemma for readers of Dahlia Ravikovitch's well-known poem "Hovering at a Low Altitude," whose Hebrew speaker witnesses the violation and murder of an Arab girl from "a low altitude" but does not intervene.

36. Templeton, "What's the Use? Writing Poetry in Wartime," 44.

37. Shira Stav, "Voice of Israel from Jerusalem" (Kol yisrael mirushalayim), in *Latset!,* 48–49. Kol Yisrael is the national radio station, which has a number of channels.

38. For a more detailed analysis of the politics of the "life goes on" mentality in Israeli culture, see Shiri Goren's contribution to this volume, "War at Home: Literary Engagements with the Israeli Political Crisis in Two Novels by Gabriela Avigur-Rotem."

39. Merhav Yeshurun, "Three Children's Poems" (Shloshah shirey yeladim), in *Latset!,* 54–55. Yeshurun has published poems in various journals, including *Etgar.* He is also the author of the collection *Yeshurun on the Pole of Inheritance* (Yeshurun 'al kotev ha-'izavon) (Tel Aviv: Plonit, 2007). Dan Pagis, "Written in Pencil in the Sealed Railway-Car," in *Variable Directions,* trans. Stephen Mitchell (San Francisco: North Point Press, 1989), 29. For the Hebrew original, see "Katuv be-'iparon ba-karon he-chatum," in *Kol ha-shirim* (Tel Aviv: Ha-kibbuts ha-meuchad and Bialik Institute, 1991), 135.

40. "The strength of poetry as a vehicle of protest is that a well wrought poem involves us, blood and bone, heart and mind, in the experience providing and provoking the protest. A poem is that use of language and measure which reenacts in the reader what has already happened to the poet. . . . It is this capacity to embody (incarnate) protest that gives the poet the advantage over others who decry the times in editorials, letters, placards, the brightest satirical prose. . . . The poem does not simply urge; 'Think on these things.' It pushes us into the fray, into an active 'You are here!'" Arnold Kenseth, *Poems of Protest Old and New* (New York: Macmillan, 1968).

41. Sidra Ezrahi, "Reclaiming a Plot in Radautz: Dan Pagis and the Prosaics of Memory," in *Booking Passage: Exile and Homecoming in the Modern Jewish Imagination* (Berkeley: University of California Press, 2000), 161.

42. Human Rights Council, Tenth Session, "The Issue of Palestinian Pregnant Women Giving Birth at Israeli Checkpoints: Report of the High Commissioner for Human Rights," February 26, 2009, http://unispal.un.org/UNISPAL.NSF/0/C7067BCF833833DE85257571006853D3, last accessed January 14, 2010. The 2006 Israeli film *The Bubble* (Ha-bu'ah), directed by Eytan Fox, dramatizes this scenario in its opening scene. An Israeli soldier (played by actor Ohad Knoller) patrolling a checkpoint attempts to deliver the baby, who is stillborn.

43. Born in Mandatory Palestine, Mossinsohn (1917–1994) was an author and playwright best known for his *Hasamba* series, which he first published in 1950. The name *Hasamba* is an acronym for *Havurat sod muchletet behechlet* (The Absolutely Secret Society). I want to thank Shiri Goren for alerting me to this crucial allusion.

44. It is important to note here that the editors and participants of *Latset!* are not promoting radical new forms of writing, but rather using the Internet to offer alternatives to traditional

means of distribution. The .pdf file produces a kind of snapshot of the text and minimizes the risk of changes to text formatting and to the resolution and alignment images as documents move across cyberspace and through word processing clients. This is a particularly urgent consideration for poetry where line arrangements and spacing are often critical to meaning. Nevertheless, though the .pdf evokes the two-dimensionality of the printed page (and can easily become the printed page), the ability to read these files on a web browser, as an embedded text (for example, via Scribd) or with a .pdf reader like Preview or Adobe Reader opens the possibility of different kinds of reading experiences.

45. Rami Saari, "A Developed Mind" (Moach mefutach), in *Latset!*, 59; Tal Nitzan, "Khan Younis," in *Latset!*, 71.

46. Harold Pinter, "Ha-mavet ulay mizdaken" (Death May Be Aging), in *Latset!*, trans. Yeara Shechori and Daria Kasovsky, 10; Phil Ochs, "Dibur shel mishtamet" (Draft Dodger Rag), in *Latset!*, trans. Yehoshua Simon, 34. Pinter published several antiwar poems throughout his career, most notably following the 1991 Gulf War and the 2003 invasion of Iraq. His 2003 collection *War* (London: Faber and Faber) gathers eight poems and a speech written in the aftermath of the Iraq war invasion. In 2004 Pinter was awarded the Wilfred Owen award for poetry, which recognizes major contributions to genre of war poetry. The poem "Death May Be Aging" is dated April 2005.

47. Nael Eltoukhy, trans., "Selected Translations from *Latset!*," *Alghaoon* 12 (February 2009): 8–9. A pdf file of this issue is available at http://alghaoon.com/alghaoon/files/gawoon12.pdf, last accessed January 12, 2010.

48. Nthposition.com, on the other hand, not only continues to host the files for all three versions of *100 Poets Against the War* but also is continuously updated with news, literature, translations, and reviews.

Chapter 9

"Unveiling Injustice"

Dahlia Ravikovitch's Poetry of Witness

Ilana Szobel

> I think that the role of poetry is, somehow, to fortify human strength; to stand against all the inhumanity surrounding us. . . . Eventually I try, maybe, to unveil injustice or ugliness. I think that the role of all art is to offer human strength . . . I am taken by literature or deterred by it according to the writer's capacity to observe; according to his ability to unveil injustice where it exists.
>
> —Dahlia Ravikovitch[1]

Introduction: "She Had a Lookout"[2]

Dahlia Ravikovitch (1936–2005), the 1998 Israel Prize laureate, is one of the most revered and adored writers among both readers and scholars of modern Hebrew literature, and one of the most influential figures in the Israeli canon. Between 1959 and 2005 she published eight books of poetry, three collections of short stories, eight books of children's verse, and various translations of children's classics and English poetry. Ravikovitch had a major role in the establishment of the "Statehood Generation," a group of writers that included Yehuda Amichai, Natan Zach, David Avidan, Yona Wallach, and Dalia Hertz, and that came of age in the years following the establishment of the State of Israel in 1948.[3] By celebrating the personal and placing it at the very center of their poetry, they challenged the state-building, collectivist ethos and rebelled against the collectivist national agenda of the former generation of Hebrew Zionist poets.

In the years following the First Lebanon War in 1982, Ravikovitch was dedicated to writing protest poetry, focusing primarily on the suffering of Palestinian Arabs. Most of these poems are collected in the books *True Love* (1987) and *Mother with a Child* (1992).[4] Her poetry is characterized by the solidarity of the speaker with the victims. While referring to the political aspects of the war and of the First Intifada (1987), and to the suffering she witnesses, Ravikovitch also defines her own way of seeing, raising acute questions about the actual position of witnessing and testimony, its significance and its implications. For Ravikovitch, from the moment of being exposed to Wrong, the option of silence and evasion cannot exist.[5] Her political writings frequently invoke the act of witnessing as an act of criticism and protest that contains power and responsibility. Ignoring this aspect means cooperation and complicity. In this chapter I focus on Ravikovitch's poetic and moral position of witnessing; the indelible connections made among responsibility, guilt, immorality, and national identity.

Ravikovitch's protest, her subversive voice, politically and poetically, surfaces through questions of national identity, testimony, and complicity. Her protestation does not settle merely for emotional solidarity, but it also provides intellectual criticism in regard to the Israeli political mechanism responsible for the creation of evil. In other words, the exposure of suffering that characterizes this poetry is not a result of a mimetic representation of suffering, but rather stems from a process that unveils the existence of evil in its political and social contexts. Evil in this context is understood not as immanent in the world, but rather as a product of human acts, and therefore it is examined, explored, and analyzed in its political and private contexts, and not in theological or metaphysical terms. The speaker's relation to suffering and victimhood is inextricable from her gaze, which identifies with the suffering and experiences it as if it were her own. Traditionally the witness position inherently creates some kind of distance between the witness and the subject being witnessed. What is unique about the witness position in Ravikovitch's writing is that despite the distance the witness identifies with her subject. This unique perspective enables the speaker to be at the same time both an essential critic and a local viewer. This combination between distance and identification—the position of the essential critic and that of the local viewer—enables the speaker in Ravikovitch's political writing "to tell in details all about the Wrong, misery, oppression and insecurity."[6] In other words, Ravikovitch's writing exposes the mechanism of evil, both through the private suffering of individuals and also through its global and universal aspects.[7]

Witnessing and Responsibility: "All This Trouble / Upon Me and My Head"[8]

> [While I am writing a poem] I feel more relaxed, as always happens when somebody expresses something that bothers him. It can be that nothing has changed, but he has said it, and I have also said it, and this is my status: status of a watchman and of a witness.
>
> —Dahlia Ravikovitch[9]

The poem "The Window" positions both the speaker and the reader inside the house, and it presents Ravikovitch's particular perspective: "Whatever a person needs / I saw in that window."[10] As with most of the poems in the book *True Love,* which indicates the beginning of Ravikovitch's political writing,[11] here the looking is not general, overhead, and sketchy, but rather stems from a personal and private "window." It is not an all-encompassing view that sees the totality of the outside world, but rather, it creates a perspective that sees things through a window. Ravikovitch experiences the world through a partial and limited vision; as the speaker of "Freezing in the North" declares, "Most of the act / I didn't know and I haven't seen."[12] It is a fairly protective position, intermittently touching and pulling away, and witnesses (to some extent) without intervening. This position places a transparent but concrete limit on the artistic act; the window is the frame for Ravikovitch's work, and, crucially, it serves as an aperture for her gaze, and not as a representation of enclosure in a room. The window does not block the gaze, but rather enables a personal perspective for observation. In her words: "I wrote only about my personal perspective, as I always write. It was much easier for me to write poems about the Lebanon War. I wrote out of a sense of guilt; a sense that I am part of making the iniquity."[13] This condition combines distance and caution in an extreme way throughout the poem "Hovering at a Low Altitude," thus presenting the speaker's approach toward severe wrongdoing.[14] The poem does not define "*what is* the reality that the artist ought to see—a brutal act that has been done to an innocent young girl" (emphasis added), but rather defines *the way of seeing* that same reality.[15] Most significantly, the poem raises questions about the very meaning of testimony and its implications.

The poem's position merges two contradictory aspects: an aesthetic distance from the discussed object/subject, and a commitment to representing it. This approach is similar to the distance characterized in Alberto Giacometti's art. (For Giacometti, as Jean Paul Sartre describes, "distance is not a willing isolation, not even a movement of retrogression. It is a requirement, a rite, a sense of difficulty, the product . . . of attraction and repulsion."[16]) Barbara Mann astutely considers how the poem "has been admired as a great philosophical achievement because it simultaneously embraces both the distance of aesthetics and the passion of engagement."[17] The "hovering at a low altitude" position expresses a central element in the relationship between an event and the testimony about it. Ana Douglass suggests that the connection between trauma and testimony is not a relationship between the source and its observer—namely, the trauma is not the "original" that the witness watches—but the testimony is simultaneously external to and inherent in the trauma. A sign and a symptom of the event thus lingers, a traumatic trace that challenges the standard assumption in which testimony can be *about* an original event. Following Jacques Derrida's "logic of supplement," Douglass proposes that we consider the relationship between a testimony and an event as something that is at the same time foreign or supplemental to the event and a necessary essence of it.[18]

Thus, since the testimony is both external and essential to the trauma, we might understand the moment of being exposed to the Wrong as a moment of collaboration with the establishment of the trauma. Therefore, the testimony in the spirit of "Hovering at a Low Altitude" is not a concrete presence but an awareness of the events and is related in Ravikovitch's writing to taking responsibility for what is being seen. From the moment of exposure to the locus of the trauma, which is also the incident in which the trauma is created, ignoring Wrong is not an option.[19] A similar paradigm is expressed in the poem "Freezing in the North": "What do I need with all these, / to think about all these / to remember all these / . . . / all this trouble / upon me and upon my head."[20]

Nevertheless, in "Hovering at a Low Altitude," the poem's voice is also aware of the difficulty of being in such a position, and of the emotional mechanism that enables the witness to pay no attention to injustice:

She still has a few hours left.
But that's not what I'm thinking about.
My thoughts cushion me gently, comfortably.
I've found a very simple method,
Not with my feet on the ground, and not flying—
Hovering
at a low altitude.[21]

This is neither a total avoidance ("flying") nor an absolute identification; the speaker does not place herself in the victim's position and does not interfere for her sake ("feet on the ground"), rather she is in an in-between state: hovering at a low altitude. This hovering actually embodies recognition of the status of witnessing, in other words it is a refusal of the option of escape:

With one strong push I can hover and whirl around
with the speed of the wind.
I can get away and say to myself:
I haven't seen a thing.[22]

One might argue that this refusal is well aware of its limits, and it does not develop to become rebellion. The separation between *a refusal* and *a rebellion* is very significant according to Adi Ophir: a rebellion has to offer a political alternative and to give reasons for its preferences, where a refusal can settle with a general moral sensitivity.[23] We must not conclude from this separation that the refusal is a minor or inferior act; the refusal stands at the center of any change in general, and of political writing in particular.[24] Throughout the collection *True Love,* Ravikovitch moves between a refusal to outright rebellion, but she only reaches the latter in her book *Mother with a Child.*

Even if it seems that the poem enables, allegedly, a choice between "feet on the ground," "flying," and "hovering at a low altitude," in fact the shaping of the seeing (the witnessing) as the "Archimedes's point" of the different possibilities (given that even the flying does not cancel the looking) does not enable the speaker to ignore the *awareness* of the Wrong. The position of witnessing—with its limitations on the one hand, and the responsibility it carries on the other hand—does not enable a renouncement of the awareness. Furthermore, it does not enable erasure or ignorance of the event and does not allow for the denial of complicity (which is inherent to the testimony) in its creation.

In an earlier poem, "All Thy Breakers and Waves," Ravikovitch comments on the nature of her witness position that will characterize most of her writing: "and I saw the tears of the oppressed / fade away on their cheeks."[25] But what does it mean to see the tears fade away? Why does the speaker focus on the moment of fading away? Yochai Oppenheimer reads this as a statement about the role of the political poet, about the poet's obligation to the victim's tears, about his duty to speak on behalf of their tears.[26] I would add, however, that by focusing on the tears fading away, Ravikovitch distinguishes between the people who experience the horror and the people who witness it. Ravikovitch's speaker does not look directly at the horror but at its victims. Lot's wife looked at the horror directly and became a pillar of salt (Genesis 19). In other words, she internalized the tears and became an ultimate representation of pain: crying. Ravikovitch does not look at Sodom, but at Lot's wife. She witnesses the iniquities, although her poems do not deal with them, or with the crying eye as a result of the iniquities. Rather, her poems focus on the very act of looking at the iniquities. To put it differently, Ravikovitch's political writing centers on the eye that sees the tears of the oppressed, in its responsibility toward this tear, and in the guilt that stems from that same witnessing.

Despite the distinction between the one who experiences the suffering and the witness to that suffering, Ravikovitch's observation does not create a buffer between her world and the victim's world. The eyes that are directed inside, the eyes that are directed outside, the eyes that bring her literature into being—are all the same organs of perception. It is as though Ravikovitch observes through the eyes of Narcissus, and it is this observation that serves as the basis for her writing, just as she writes in her poem "True Love Isn't What It Seems": "Ourselves we love with great devotion, / attuned to ourselves with rapt attentiveness."[27] I suggest we read Ravikovitch's political writing in light of this poetic declaration, since it does not allow for a separation between the personal layers and the external ones or between her private life and political events. This is not just because "the personal is political," but mainly because the way Ravikovitch deals with the external/public stems from this same absolute self-attentiveness. The attentiveness to another's suffering is not disconnected from her personal suffering; the public problem is also a personal problem, and another's problem is also her own problem. Ravikovitch once said: "when the housing minister decided to confiscate lands from Arabs in Beith Zaphapha, I felt as if somebody had come to my place in order to confiscate part of my apartment."[28] In this description she expresses the intrinsic structure of her entire oeuvre, and of her political writing in particular. Even though she is neither among the decision makers nor among the people who are affected by these decisions, she experiences the events from a position of almost total identification with the victims.

According to Emmanuel Levinas, it is possible to defend against evil only when each and every one of us accepts responsibility for others, and this is achievable by recognizing the fact that "I" can be responsible for something "I" have not done, and by adopting a misery that is not "mine."[29] We find a similar attitude in Ravikovitch 's witness who identifies with the subject being witnessed (her "identifying witnessing" position). This is related to the "transparent skin"—"a skin that does not protect the flesh / at all," as she writes in her poem "We Had an Understanding"—and that creates a subject that functions simultaneously as a victim and as the one who unveils the other's victimhood; a subject that exposes the suffering and experiences it at the same time.[30]

This orientation is the basis for the protest in Ravikovitch's work. Seeing the suffering and being ceaselessly aware of it—in fact, being unable *not* to be aware of it—is what enables her to articulate the Wrong. Thus Ravikovitch's protest develops from within the suffering. It is the protest of the sufferer, protest most genuinely expressed from the "identifying-witness" position. Ravikovitch is aware of the ambivalence expressed in her work. The reader, the same as the speaker, finds himself in the situation described in the poem "Hovering at a Low Altitude": he can "get away and say to [himself]: I haven't seen a thing," but even so he will always be aware of the events, a witness to the Wrong. Again, even if Ravikovitch's poems allegedly enable her readers to choose between "feet on the ground," flying, and "hovering at a low altitude," the poems do not allow the readers to be silent or to hide their awareness of the Wrongs by avoiding the very act of seeing.

The biblical references in the poem "Hovering at a Low Altitude" extend the discussion and relate testimony and responsibility to questions of power, guilt, and complicity:

The girl is right there,
no one else around.
And if she runs for cover, or cries out—
there's no place to hide in the mountains.[31]

The last two lines contain references both to biblical rape laws (Deuteronomy 22:23–29) and to one of Jeremiah's destruction prophecies (Jeremiah 23:24). Biblical law imposes some of the responsibility of a rape onto the victim: it finds her guilty if she does not cry out and innocent if she does. In Ravikovitch's poem, the responsibility is upon the witness, the person who hears the scream, and not upon the afflicted. Ravikovitch exposes the blindness to the Wrong; for her, a horror that occurs in the "field," among "craggy eastern hills"—not "here" but "over there"—does not remain unheard and unseen. The very act of witnessing negates the possibility of avoidance of knowledge. Therefore, inaction or the lack of reaction make the witness complicit and elicit guilt.

The allusion to Jeremiah's prophecy links this guilt with a position of power. This position of power is expressed both in the direct reference to God's strength and in the specific content of the prophecy that deals with the punishment that will befall both the leaders and false prophets, who incite their people to diverge from the path of righteousness. The prophecy emphasizes that the leaders and the prophets—and not the people—will suffer most of the punishment. In other words, the blame lies mainly with those who have the power to influence the people. The power Ravikovitch's poem refers to is, thus, not just that of the man who hurts the girl, but also the power of the witness, a power that is embodied in her awareness of the event. Hence, in Ravikovitch's oeuvre, the witness occupies a position of power that demands responsibility and that contains guilt.

The connection between testimony, power, and guilt is expressed also in the poem "On the Attitude toward Children in Times of War."[32] The poem was written—as is mentioned at the end—as "another variation of Zach's poem that deals with the question of whether there were exaggerations in the reports about the number of children that were killed during the [First] Lebanon War."[33] Allegedly, both Natan Zach's poem "On the Desire to Be Precise"[34] and Ravikovitch's reaction to it, deal with the role of language in shaping the political reality:

> And then there was a major exaggeration in the body count:
> There were some who counted about a hundred, and some counted several
> hundreds
> And this one said, I counted thirty-six burnt women
> And his friend said, You are wrong, because it was only eleven
> And the error is deliberate and political, not accidental[35]

A closer look at the poem, however, reveals that Zach's irony does not refer to the sources that use language and the linguistic mechanism in order to create and justify evil. Rather, his irony refers to the engagement in everything that surrounds the suffering but not in the suffering itself. With his signature irony, Zach describes the extreme indifference to and disaffection toward the horrible events and their victims: the exaggeration is in counting the corpses, not in the killing itself. The poem presents a very long list of killing techniques (slaughtering, shooting, crucifixion, burning, and such) as a supposed distraction, and the doubt that people should feel is in regard to the reports, not in regard to the events themselves.

According to Oppenheimer, "the indirect way in which Zach chooses to refer to the theme of war and death is expressed by his parodic style."[36] Unlike Oppenheimer, I believe that it is not an indirect way but rather that it is the most direct way for Zach; it is a precise description of his (and Ravikovitch's) position: he is witnessing the events, even if he does not see them directly. He knows about them and is aware of their existence, and therefore, even though he was not directly present when they occurred, he has become a witness who cannot choose silence. In my opinion, Zach quotes the discourse about the war not simply in order to decipher and better understand the reality he refers to in his poem, but mainly in order to examine both his own position as a writer toward the events and the reality of other Israelis on the home front—a reality that just seems detached from the "close north" (meaning Lebanon). Zach stresses how seemingly easy it is to disconnect from the events of the First Lebanon War, but at the same time it is very clear that this indifference and disconnection contains a moral dissatisfaction and a significant danger.

Ravikovitch's identification with the suffering and misery of the refugees enables her to see and to express directly the guilt that Zach can only hint at. She describes the refugee's conditions as miserable and hopeless, and also as a mortal threat, which "our own [Israeli] troops" are responsible for:

Benighted children,
At their age
they don't have a real worldview.
And their future is shrouded too:
refugee shacks, unwashed faces,
sewage flowing in the streets,
infected eyes,
a negative outlook on life.

And thus began the flight from city to village,
from village to burrows in the hills.
As when a man did flee from a lion,
as when he did flee from a bear,
as when he did flee from a cannon,
from an airplane, from our own troops.

"On the Attitude toward Children in Times of War"[37]

The refugees' escape and their wanderings are described as attempts to escape an enormous force, just like man's attempt to escape God on Judgment Day: "And men shall go into the caves of the rocks, and into the holes of the earth, from before the terror of the Lord, and from the glory of His majesty, when He arises to shake mightily the earth" (Isaiah 2:19). Despite the intensity of these efforts to run away, the refugees are forlorn; similar to the man who cannot escape God's power on Judgment Day, the refugee will not be able to escape his conquerors: "It will be as though a man fled from a lion, only to meet a bear, as though he entered his house and rested his hand on the wall, only to have a snake bite him" (Amos 5:19). The uneven power relation between the refugees and "our own troops" does not enable the refugees any chance of survival, which is why this pursuit is so immoral, and which is why the victimizer should not be able to return to his everyday life and routine after participating in such events. The moral severity of these actions will prevent any peacefulness:

He who destroys thirty babies,
it is as if he'd destroyed one thousand and thirty,
or one thousand and seventy,
thousand upon thousand.
And for that alone shall he find
no peace.[38]

It doesn't matter how "precise" the language or the counting is; in fact, the wider and more organized the language becomes in the poem "On the Attitude toward Children in Times of War," the more specific and increased the sense of guilt in the reader. Thus Ravikovitch joins Zach's position of testimony, but adds to it the significant aspect of responsibility and guilt.[39]

"Guilt-Ridden Poems": The Contaminating of Language and the Departure from Innocence

> The poems that were written during the Lebanon War were guilt-ridden poems. This is the uniqueness of the current political poetry: the poets' collective recognition of guilt
>
> —Dahlia Ravikovitch[40]

> When I hear that a child was killed, or even two students, not exactly kids, I feel that I share the blame
>
> —Dahlia Ravikovitch[41]

Presenting suffering from the position of the witness enables Ravikovitch to understand, interpret, and depict the existence of evil in its political and social contexts. This perspective exposes the social mechanisms and arrangements that cause misery that could be avoided, and challenges the witness to depart from his/her imaginary innocence. By spreading the guilt among varied centers of power and by applying the idea of permanent guilt, Ravikovitch's political writing does not allow anyone in Israeli society to elude the presence of guilt and responsibility.[42]

The political mechanism uses power and violence, which are not conceptualized and presented as such. In other words, one of the main aspects of a violent regime is that its violence is represented by and to itself as nonviolence, as justified punishment, or as a neutral necessary evil. To enable this, the violence must be blurred and neutralized, because without this action, the violence would require punishment. Furthermore, it is necessary for such an established violence to have an invisible mechanism that will facilitate its fulfillment and "normal" management, because, as Michel Foucault notes, "power is tolerable only on condition that it mask a substantial part of itself. Its success is proportional to its ability to hide its own mechanism."[43] In order to do so and to facilitate its standard conduct, the political mechanism of the hegemonic law uses several central ploys: a strict binary way of thinking (us-them, Jewish-Arabic, right-wrong, and such), euphemisms, a self-serving definition of the victim (turning him into an object), and the denial of the material body of the casualties.

At the same time, while the hegemony constructs all these narratives in order to justify its violence, the victims and those who identify with the victims strive to deconstruct these narratives and to unveil the hidden interests they contain.[44] As part of this social and cultural arena, Ravikovitch's poetry exposes these hegemonic ploys in Israeli behavior by insisting upon the blurring of binary boundaries, by focusing on the unique suffering of the victims, and by positioning the body as an autonomous subject. These poetic devices rail against the politics that enable the simultaneous creation and denial of violence. Ravikovitch's poetry, thus, shifts the focus from the consolatory political narrative to its very own existence and internal mechanism. Protest poems such as "Blood Heifer," "Freezing in the North," "Mother Is Walking," "The Story about the Arab Who Died in a Fire," and "Associations" are well aware of that hidden political mechanism and oppose it by refusing to participate in the political procedure responsible for the concealment of victims. The contemplation of the individual, the unique, and the body does not allow for the continuance of the consolatory political narrative.

In the poem "Blood Heifer" (see appendix 1), the blurring of the identity of the poetic subject is the main device that designs the poetic situation.[45] The poem keeps from its readers two pieces of information that are usually crucial in political poetry: national identity and historical background. The poem refuses to provide information about the nationality of either the victim or the aggressor; further, there are no details concerning the concrete historical situation. Therefore, the moral position depicted in the poem is not concerned with issues of nationality; rather, it demands that the readers examine the situation as is, without the normative evasion that the national context may provide. The blurring of the concrete national identity does not blur the power relationship and does not hide the iniquity, but rather exposes them.

The character in the poem is described in language that symbolizes a type and not a subject. The stereotypically Jewish symbols of glasses and a skullcap characterize him; yet from the moment of his injury, through his dying and until his death, his religion and nationality are obscured: "and he's not a Jew anymore, / not an Arab— / in limbo." In the light of the ambiguity concerning the private and national identity of the injured subject, the acuteness of the description of the suffering body and his demise is glaring. From the moment the injury is inflicted upon the body, the person who could be characterized according to his religion and national identity becomes both "anyone," a human being, and "someone" who deserves a name, a unique identity: "man like dust in the wind, / but who was that man / lying there lonely in his blood?" Beyond every sophisticated social mechanism and political decision lies the wounded person steeped in his isolation, with no other recourse but to consume his own blood.

The poem reminds us that the tormented body should not be left unseen. Fittingly, the poem exposes the physical aspects of the victim: the asphyxia, the torn body, and the blood that runs from the body. These details point to the mechanism that disavows the material body of the subject and thereby enables the routine of violence and evil to exist in the guise of necessary politics.

The obscurity at the beginning of the first stanza continues in the second one:

> Havoc in the marketplace; people shouting, Why
> are you murdering us?

Others rushing
to take revenge.

It is not clear here who is the killer and who is the murdered, who is the avenger and who is the shouter. The circular nature of murder and revenge contains the reality that the murderer might also be murdered one day; the victim can also be the victimizer in the future—and so on, in an endless cycle of violence. The blurring of nationality and the shift in focus from the national to the human demands an acknowledgment of the victims' suffering and of the necessary action, as relevant to both sides of the dispute. It is a situation of horrible suffering and difficult violence, but nevertheless, there is no way to identify the guilty party. Such a situation demands the ritualistic fulfillment of the biblical Blood Heifer law.[46]

Amid the hate and the violence, Ravikovitch reminds the reader of two moral codes: one from Exodus 23:5: "Whenever you see that the ass of someone who hates you has collapsed under its load, do not leave it there. Be sure to help him with his animal." Meaning, there are situations in which people are obligated to help even their enemies. And the second, the Blood Heifer law (Deuteronomy 21:1–9), which claims that bloodshed in and of itself is not atonement. According to this biblical law, a ritual of absolution must be carried out (after any violent act) even if it is impossible to determine who is to blame, or if the real culprit cannot be found.

One should note that only two of the duties in the biblical Blood Heifer law are mentioned in the poem: slaughter a heifer and scatter its ashes to the river.[47] The main act of the ritual, however, is missing. In the biblical ritual the leaders of the city are commanded to wash their hands in the river and declare that they did not commit the crime or see it happen. It seems that the omission of such a crucial detail in the poem insinuates the modern Israeli leaders' guilt; in relation to the First Lebanon War they can carry out the violent part of the ritual, but they cannot cleanse themselves of the blame. This is because they actually do have a role in the violence, and, unquestionably, they see it happen. The participation of the leaders in the ritual, therefore, is a demagogic utilization of the innocent party's position that invalidates any claim to innocence. Similarly, to create a situation that explains war as a mere military operation or as an obligatory war, which is intended only to defend citizens, is a way to associate the consolatory political narrative that presents the evil as necessary.[48] By creating a radically vague situation and ostensibly accepting the consolatory narrative, Ravikovitch exposes its falsification, the danger buried within it. Indeed, the situation is complex, and it is impossible to simply define who is "the good" and who is "the bad"; the two sides both produce violence and are victims. But one should not conclude from this any kind of justification for the continuation of violence from a defensive position. On the contrary: the necessary conclusion is that no one is entirely guiltless.

Interestingly, the blurring that characterizes the poem allows for the simultaneous existence of various types of guilt: the guilt of the leadership, for example, does not cancel out the guilt of the public. The presentation of various types of guilt in the poem is brought about by the poetic organization, which uses biblical intertextuality that presents many options as to the sources of evil. The expression "disturbance" (אלוהים מהומת) in the second stanza, for example, offers nationalism as one possible source of evil. This unique biblical expression appears in a very violent description of Judgment Day in Zechariah 14: 13. This description of Judgment Day focuses on the establishment of a Hebrew national identity (mainly by excluding all other nations), and on the centrality of Jerusalem to the same. In the fifth stanza, the root ע.ל.ע ("but who was that man / lying there lonely in his blood?") implies another cause of evil. It is a unique root in the bible, which appears in Job's answer to God (Job 39:27–30). This intertextuality reminds the reader of the existence of unpreventable violence, for which only God/nature is responsible. Presenting multiple sources of evil and violence perhaps blurs the source of guilt, the ultimate responsibility for the crime. But it is important to notice that it is not a blurring that enables evasion of responsibility; rather, it is a blurring that implements the inclusion of many types of guilt. Furthermore, it is a vagueness that makes it impossible to be innocent. Ravikovitch's political poetry presents the unavoidable culpability of all human beings who live in a historic period and space in which an iniquity is committed.

Her lyrics uncover the mechanism that makes the illusion of innocence possible. The multiplicity of guilt that appears in the poem "Blood Heifer" deconstructs the political mechanism, which is based on the binary separation between guilt and blamelessness. Ravikovitch refuses to take part in the political narrative, which forms the victimized Israeli, and which only tries to defend its existence. It is a refusal to believe in the Israeli claim that the country goes to war only when it has no other choice, or in a much more specific argument, that the First Lebanon War was not a war, but rather "a military operation to protect the northern settlements."

The issue of guilt in Ravikovitch's political poetry, then, is inseparable from the crucial protest, which exposes the political mechanism that enables the existence of evil. The poem "Get Out of Beirut"[49] (see appendix 2) serves as another apt example for the way in which Ravikovitch's poetry does not simply settle for the expression of a moral position toward what occurred. Rather, the poem indirectly accuses the guilty party and unveils the linguistic mechanism that enables the immoral act.

As Ofra Yeglin has demonstrated, the role of language in blurring brutality is a recurring issue in Ravikovitch's poetry. The linguistic mechanism that is adapted to justify evil supplies arguments of legitimization and rationalization that help to maintain situations of suffering while simultaneously denying their existence.[50] When Ilan Lotenberg asked Ravikovitch about her public role, she replied:

> My role is to protest against the cheapening of terms. . . . If someone is claiming that Jews do not run wild, mistreat and murder, that is an inverse anti-Semitism. It is a contamination of the thought, and one who knows some history, also knows it led to very distorted acts. That is why, if I ask myself what I have been doing here—and for many years I have done several

> things in this country—I think that in total I was trying to contribute my part to keeping the clarity of thought and to being cautious about contaminating terms.[51]

This is exactly what the speaker in the poem "Get Out of Beirut" does: she protests against the cheapening of terms and keeps clarity of thought by exposing the historical points at which language was used to create iniquities.

The poem infuses the suffering of refugees with the blame of those responsible. It also exposes the linguistic manipulation that justifies that suffering. The poem is a kind of fugue, or, to adopt a term from the poetics of prose, the poem is based on free indirect speech, that is to say, on an integration of several voices in the text. This device enables multiple voices to be spoken in the poem by activating many speakers, positions, and attitudes. However, most relevant to our discussion is that this particular technique centers on blurring. The blurring in the poem—both of the victim and the victimizer's identities, and that of the free indirect speech—is the central poetic device that exposes suffering, injustice, and the mechanism that creates them. The description of the refugee's suffering is combined with blaming; the poem presents both the misery of the individuals (babies with purulence on their eyes, the RPG children, and being "unaccounted for people") and the political, linguistic, and logical mechanism that caused this misery, and enabled it. The last stanza of the poem carries an extreme description of the refugees:

> You won't be welcome anywhere.
> You're human beings who were thrown out the door,
> you're people who don't count anymore.
> You're human beings that nobody needs.
> You're a bunch of lice
> crawling about
> that pester and bite
> till we all go nuts.[52]

This strident representation demands a critical reading. The language of genocide penetrates the speech of the expellers, creating a dissonance that requires one to read the stanza as combined discourse, and not as evidence of the speaker's position. The combined discourse reflects attitudes common during the First Lebanon War, and was formed with the help of conscious and subconscious linguistic mechanisms that dehumanized the enemy and created a convenient distraction from the mainly moral, problematic aspects of the war. Referring to the refugees as "a bunch of lice" recalls the media's common use of the expression "purification of terrorists' nests" (a pun that is based on the Hebrew homonym of *Kinim,* which with a different spelling means both lice and nest). The metaphoric use of "nests" as a synonym of terror organizations creates the dehumanization of the enemy and the so-called necessary need of calamitous actions. The poem unveils the mechanism that "purifies the terrorists' nests" for the "protection of the northern settlements." This mechanism creates the illusion that it is not killing human beings, but rather, exterminating vermin. In this sense the refugees are no longer people who were ejected from their homes, but instead just "a bunch of lice."

Furthermore, the poem actually exposes another aspect of the sociopolitical mechanism that enables suffering: the mistaken order of cause and effect. The speaker's description of the refugees' suffering and their tough conditions does not mean to be disrespectful or offensive, but rather, it attempts to express and reflect *the consequences* of the act of occupation, the experience of being a refugee. Ugliness, poverty, and helplessness are not the characteristics of the enemy but the results of the military domination and the ejection of people from their homes. One does not expel the "repulsive" enemy; rather, expulsion creates another individual's repulsive situation.

By suffusing this poem—and many other political poems such as "Blood Heifer," "Jewish Portrait," "You Can't Kill a Baby Twice," "Laying Upon the Waters,"[53] and "Mother Is Walking"—with poetic ambiguity and the free indirect speech technique, Ravikovitch seemingly "quotes" the language that is used in order to cover brutality and to maintain and justify standing social order. But by so doing, Ravikovitch actually explores the manipulative and destructive power of language and subverts the political mechanism, which is supported by the same language. She exposes the order of gratuitous evil in society through searing poetry that emphasizes the responsibility of the witness for the establishment of the historical narrative, and stands courageously in the face of the departure from innocence, bringing us all closer to the process of awakening.

Appendix 1

Blood Heifer
He took one step,
Then a few steps more.
His glasses fell to the ground,
His skullcap.
Managed another step,
bloody, dragging his feet.
Ten steps
and he's not a Jew anymore,
not an Arab—
in limbo.

Havoc in the marketplace; people shouting, Why
are you murdering us?
Others rushing
to take revenge.

And he lies on the ground: a death rattle,
A body torn open,
blood streaming out of the flesh,
streaming
out of the flesh.

He died here, or there—
no one knows for sure.
What do we know?
A dead body lying in the field.

Suffering cleanseth from sin, it is said,
man like dust in the wind,
but who was that man
lying there lonely in his blood?
What did he see,
what did he hear
with all that commotion around him?
If thou seest even thine enemy's ass
lying under its burden,
it is said, thou shalt surely help.

If a dead body is found lying in the field
if a body is found in the open,
let your elders go out and slaughter a heifer
and sacrifice its ashes in the river.[54]

Appendix 2

Get Out of Beirut
Take the knapsacks,
The clay jugs, the washtubs,
the Korans,
the battle fatigues,
the bravado, the broken soul,
and what's left in the street, a little bread or meat,
and kids running around like chickens in the heat.
How many children do you have?
How many children did you have?
It's hard to keep the children safe in times like these.

Not the way it used to be in the old country,
in the shade of the mosque, under the fig tree,

where you'd get the kids out of the house in the morning
and tuck them into bed at night.

Whatever's not fragile, gather up in those sacks:
clothing, bedding, blankets, diapers,
some memento, perhaps,
a shiny artillery shell,
or a tool that has practical value,
and that babies with pus in their eyes
and the RPG kids.
We'd love to see you afloat in the water with no place to go
no port and no shore.
You won't be welcome anywhere.
You're human beings who were thrown out the door,
you're people who don't count anymore.
You're human beings that nobody needs.
You're a bunch of lice
crawling about
that pester and bite
till we all go nuts.[55]

Notes

This work is a revised translation of my article "'Hovering at a Low Altitude': Testimony and Complicity in the Political Writing of Dahlia Ravikovitch," in *Sparks of Light: A Selection of Critical Essays on the Work of Dahlia Ravikovitch*, ed. Hamutal Tsamir and Tamar Hess (Tel Aviv: Hakibbutz Hameuchad, 2010), 444–69. Many thanks to my friend Taly Ravid for her help in translation-related matters (and much more).

1. Quoted in Idith Zertal, "Poetry—A Soul without a Body," *Davar*, July 8, 1966. All translations are mine unless otherwise noted.

2. Dahlia Ravikovitch, "Cinderella in the Kitchen," in *True Love* (Tel Aviv: Hakibbutz Hameuchad, 1987), 39.

3. According to Michael Gluzman, Ravikovitch was never seen as a leading figure in the poetry of the Statehood Generation. See Michael Gluzman, "'To Endow Suffering with Elegance': Dahlia Ravikovitch and the Poetry of the Statehood Generation," *Prooftexts* 28 (2008): 282–309.

4. Ravikovitch, *True Love;* Dahlia Ravikovitch, *Mother with a Child* (Tel Aviv: Hakibbutz Hameuchad, 1992).

5. I am capitalizing the word "wrong" here and throughout the essay because I am using it as a concept, to connote the Hebrew word *A'vel*, which encapsulates evil, wrongdoing, and injustice.

6. Shulamit Levo-Vardinon, "A Fall before the Lift-Off: Horrible Life in 'Death in the Family,'" *Davar*, March 16, 1979, 20.

7. Hamutal Tsamir's reading of the poem "The Messiah's Arrival" exposes political, national, and public involvement in Ravikovitch's early writing that was usually considered to be personal.

By exposing political aspects in so-called personal poems, Tsamir challenges the strict distinction between "political poems" and "personal lyric poems," and shows that Ravikovitch's poetry combines between the two supposedly separate categories. Hamutal Tsamir, "The Dead and the Living, the Believers and the Uprooted: Dahlia Ravikovitch, Mourner and Prophet," *Mikan: Journal for Hebrew Literary Studies* 1 (2000): 44–63; Hamutal Tsamir, *In the Name of the Land: Nationalism, Subjectivity, and Gender in the Israeli Poetry of the Statehood Generation* (Jerusalem: Keter Books; Beer-Sheva: Heksherim Center, 2006).

In the light of this claim, I wish to emphasize that my use of the terms "political writing" or "protest poetry" throughout this essay refer mainly to poems that deal directly with national-political issues, such as the First Lebanon War (1982) or the First Intifada (1987). This methodic choice does not duplicate the dichotomy between Ravikovitch's personal writing and her political one, but rather emphasizes the impossibility of separating the two. This is not just because "everything is political," but mainly because Ravikovitch's political understanding stems from the same emotional mechanism that establishes her personal writing. Thus by focusing on the "identifying-witnessing" position I wish to claim that Ravikovitch's sensitivity to the suffering of others is not detached from her own suffering. Ravikovitch's writing exposes the victimhood of others and interprets the political through a prism of a sufferer and of being a victim herself. Her speaker experiences suffering and exposes the suffering of others simultaneously, and by so doing does not enable a separation between the personal and the political.

8. Ravikovitch, "Freezing in the North," *True Love*, 62.

9. Quoted in Ilana Zukerman, ed., "True Love: Printed Excerpts from a Radio Broadcast," *Proza* 100 (1988): 108–11, 109.

10. Ravikovitch, *True Love*, 27–28.

11. For Ravikovitch's reference to the difference between her early political writing and that of the books *True Love* and *Mother with a Child*, see Zukerman, "True Love: Printed Excerpts From a Radio Broadcast," 109. For a discussion of her earlier political writing, especially in regard to the poem "What's Happening," see Yochai Oppenheimer, *Political Poetry in Israel* (Jerusalem: Magnes Press, 2003), 334–40.

12. Ravikovitch, *True Love*, 60.

13. Quoted in Sima Kadmon, "I Am Always the Defeated Side," *Ma'ariv*, February 8, 1991, 22.

14. Ravikovitch, *True Love*, 31–33. Nissim Calderon describes the different stages in publishing the poem "Hovering at a Low Altitude." Ravikovitch submitted it to the periodical *Hadarim* before the First Lebanon War. After the war she gave her permission to include it in the collection *There's No End to the Battles and Slaughter: Political Poetry of the Lebanon War*, edited by Hannan Hever and Moshe Ron (Tel Aviv: Hakibbutz Hameuchad, 1983), but in her book *True Love* she chose to locate it in the section "The Window," and not in the section "Issues in Contemporary Judaism" that is dedicated to her political writing. See Nissim Calderon, *A Sense of Place* (Tel Aviv: Hakibbutz Hameuchad, 1988), 12.

Accordingly, Nili R. Gold Scharf reads this poem not merely as a political poem but rather as a response to a personal psychological trauma. See Nili R. Gold Scharf, "Hovering at a Low Altitude," in *Reading Hebrew Literature: Critical Discussions of Six Modern Texts*, ed. Alan Mintz (Hanover, NH: Brandeis University Press, 2003), 221–31.

15. Ariel Hirschfeld, "Ravikovitch after a Decade," *Yediot Aharonot*, January 9, 1987, 21.

16. Jean-Paul Sartre, "The Search for the Absolute," in *Giacometti: A Catalogue* (Tel Aviv: Tel Aviv University Art Gallery, 1984), 8.

17. Barbara Mann, "Hovering at a Low Altitude," in *Reading Hebrew Literature: Critical Discussions of Six Modern Texts,* ed. Alan Mintz (Hanover, NH: Brandeis University Press, 2003), 218, 220.

18. Ana Douglass and Thomas A. Vogler, eds., *Witness and Memory: The Discourse of Trauma* (New York: Routledge, 2003).

19. For the difference between women's low gaze and men's high gaze, and especially for the feminist-political potential within this low gaze, see Orly Lubin, "Low Gaze, Freed Gaze," in *Igael Shemtov: Low Landscape Low Reality* (Tel Aviv: Loushy Art and Editions, 2004).

20. Ravikovitch, *True Love,* 62.

21. Chana Bloch and Ariel Bloch, eds. and trans., *The Window: Poems by Dahlia Ravikovitch* (New York: Sheep Meadow Press, 1989), 104.

22. Ibid.

23. Adi Ophir, "Beyond Good: Evil—An Outline for a Political Theory of Evils," *Theory and Criticism* 1 (1991): 63.

24. See Derrida's discussion about Melville's story "Bartleby the Scrivener," mainly about Bartleby's "I would prefer not to." Jacques Derrida, *The Gift of Death,* trans. David Wills (Chicago: University of Chicago Press, 1995), 74–77.

25. Dahlia Ravikovitch, *Deep Calleth unto Deep* (Tel Aviv: Hakibbutz Hameuchad, 1976), 13. Chana Bloch and Chana Kronfeld's translation captures the beauty and the unique poetics of these lines: "And I beheld the tear of the oppressed / turning to naught on their cheeks" (147). In Chana Bloch and Chana Kronfeld, eds. and trans., *Hovering at a Low Altitude: The Collected Poetry of Dahlia Ravikovitch* (New York: W. W. Norton, 2009), 147.

26. Oppenheimer, *Political Poetry,* 340.

27. Bloch and Kronfeld, *Hovering at a Low Altitude,* 188.

28. Quoted in Ayelet Negev, "Dahlia Ravikovitch Speaks about It All," *Yediot Ahronot,* February 23, 1996, 22, 26–28.

29. Emmanuel Levinas, *Otherwise Than Being; or, Beyond Essence,* trans. Alphonso Lingis (The Hague: Springer, 1981).

30. Ravikovitch, *True Love,* 42.

31. Bloch and Bloch, *The Window,* 104.

32. Ravikovitch, *True Love,* 69–70.

33. Ibid, 70.

34. Nathan Zach, *Hard to Remember* (Tel Aviv: Hakibbutz Hameuchad, 1984), 60.

35. Ibid.; Esther Raizen, ed. and trans., *No Rattling of Sabers: An Anthology of Israeli War Poetry* (Austin: Center for Middle Eastern Studies at the University of Texas, 1995), 138.

36. Yochai Oppenheimer, "The Right to Say No: Auden, Zach, and Laor in a Political Contex," *Alpayim* 10 (1994): 241.

37. Bloch and Kronfeld, *Hovering at a Low Altitude,* 197.

38. Ibid., 197–98. The line "He who destroys thirty babies" opens the first and the last stanzas of the poem. The allusion to Sanhedrin 4:5—"whoever destroys a single life in Israel, it is as though he has destroyed an entire universe, and whoever saves a single life in Israel, it is as if he has saved an entire universe"—makes clear that hurting even one child is like hurting the world. Additionally, it reminds the reader of the huge importance of human life in the Jewish culture and hints at the double standard in regard to the Palestinian people. But even more significantly, Ravikovitch's use of this well-known Talmudic reference activates in the reader a sophisticated emotional mechanism: the Hebrew reader, who is familiar with the phrase "whoever saves a

single life *in Israel,* it is as if he has saved an entire universe" instinctually assumes that the hurt babies in the poem are Jewish victims (from "Israel"), and therefore feels identification and sorrow for them. Only at the end of the first stanza is the real national identity of these victims exposed: "in a year, God willing, they'd be soldiers / in the Palestine Liberation Army." Now the reader has to modify his mercy, which was directed at his own people, to victims of a different nationality. A similar literary device occurs in the poem "Hovering at a Low Altitude" (*True Love*). According to Chana Kronfeld, Ravikovitch has the girl in the poem constituted as Arab and as Other "only after the reader has found it difficult to ignore her humanity—in other words, can no longer emotionally accept her as other" (Chana Kronfeld, "A Lebanon War Poem?" in *Reading Hebrew Literature: Critical Discussions of Six Modern Texts,* ed. Alan Mintz [Hanover, NH: Brandeis University Press, 2003], 241.)

39. As I have shown in a different essay, the poem "You Can't Kill a Baby Twice" discusses the implications of complicity not just on the victims but also on "our sweet soldiers." See Szobel, "Hovering at a Low Altitude."

40. Quoted in Dalia Karpel, "Another Book, True Love," *Ha'ir,* November 28, 1986.

41. Quoted in Zukerman, "True Love," 109.

42. According to Shoshana Felman, anyone who exists in an iniquitous historic space is necessarily involved in the blame. Further, according to Felman, this is a permanent involvement, an existential state in which the innocence can come to mean a mere lack of awareness of one's own participation in the crime. Since innocence is an illusion, guilt and innocence no longer stand in contradiction to each other, but rather represent different levels of awareness. From this perspective, "one can only be, thus, paradoxically enough, *guilty* of one's very *innocence*" (Shoshana Felman and Dori Laub, *Testimony: Crises of Witnessing in Literature, Psychoanalysis, and History* [New York: Routledge, 1992], 196, emphasis in the original). What Felman actually suggests is a process of coming to awareness, a process of awakening and relinquishing one's innocence.

43. Michel Foucault, *The History of Sexuality,* trans. Robert Hurley (New York: Pantheon Books, 1978), 86.

44. Ophir, "Beyond Good," 67.

45. Ravikovitch, *True Love,* 67. See appendix 1.

46. "If a slain person is found lying in the open country in the land which the Lord your God gives you to possess, and it is not known who has struck him, then your elders and your judges shall go out and measure the distance to the cities which are around the slain one. It shall be that the city which is nearest to the slain man, that is, the elders of that city, shall take a heifer of the herd, which has not been worked and which has not pulled in a yoke; and the elders of that city shall bring the heifer down to a valley with running water, which has not been plowed or sown, and shall break the heifer's neck there in the valley. Then the priests, the sons of Levi, shall come near, for the Lord your God has chosen them to serve Him and to bless in the name of the Lord; and every dispute and every assault shall be settled by them. All the elders of that city which is nearest to the slain man shall wash their hands over the heifer whose neck was broken in the valley; and they shall answer and say, Our hands did not shed this blood, nor did our eyes see it. Forgive Your people Israel whom You have redeemed, O Lord, and do not place the guilt of innocent blood in the midst of Your people Israel. And the blood guiltiness shall be forgiven them. So you shall remove the guilt of innocent blood from your midst, when you do what is right in the eyes of the Lord" (Deuteronomy 21:1–9).

47. The scattering of the heifer's ashes to the river is Ravikovitch's addition to the original biblical ritual. See Juliette Hassin, *Poetry and Myth in Ravikovitch's Work* (Tel Aviv: Eked, 1989), 166.

48. Adi Ophir, *Speaking Evil: Towards an Ontology of Morals* (Tel Aviv: Am Oved, 2000); Ophir, "Beyond Good," 62, 72.

49. Ravikovitch, *True Love*, 65. See appendix 2.

50. Ofra Yeglin, "Did I Forget? Well, Who Cares? On Three Poems by Dahlia Ravikovitch," *Rehov* 2 (1995): 71–81.

51. Ilan Lotenberg, "Half a Poet," *Hadashot*, June 4, 1993, 58.

52. Bloch and Kronfeld, *Hovering at a Low Altitude*, 195.

53. Ravikovitch, *Mother with a Child*, 20–21.

54. Bloch and Bloch, *The Window*, 98–99.

55. Bloch and Kronfeld, *Hovering at a Low Altitude*, 194–95.

Chapter 10

War at Home

Literary Engagements with the Israeli Political Crisis in Two Novels by Gabriela Avigur-Rotem

Shiri Goren

Gabriela Avigur-Rotem's novel *Ancient Red* (*Adom Atik,* 2007) opens with the rapid disintegration of an Israeli home: the father's sudden and fatal stroke; the mother's subsequent soul searching in a remote rural settlement in northern Israel; and the daughter's involvement in an unhealthy romantic relationship, which ultimately pushes her to attempt suicide. It is hardly a coincidence that the last evening the three characters sit together, watching television in their homey living room, is November 4, 1995, the night of the assassination of Prime Minister Yitzhak Rabin. Rabin's death marks a symbolic moment of rupture between the political right and left wings of the "national Jewish home," but for Ra'anana, the heroine of *Ancient Red,* it also signals the breakdown of her family and household. Her narrative ends with another symbolic moment in Israel's recent history: the riots of October 2000, a dramatic internal clash between Palestinian Arab citizens of Israel and law enforcement authorities.[1]

These metaphorical private and collective broken homes echo the very literal destruction of a house in another novel by Avigur-Rotem, *Heat Wave and Crazy Birds* (*Hamsin Ve'tziporim Meshuga'ot,* 2001). Set in 1994, the novel focuses on a forty-eight-year-old flight attendant who returns to her hometown in order to take over a house that she has inherited. Here, too, the house stands at the center of the narrative: the story starts with the heroine entering it and ends, completely against her will, with its literal destruction.

The continuity between the novels is striking, especially when one considers the thematic gap between the two narratives. While *Heat Wave and Crazy Birds* concerns itself with children of the second generation of the Holocaust and what it means to be an Israeli in the 1990s, *Ancient Red* focuses, at least on the surface, on questions of gender inequality and relations between men and women. Nevertheless, as I show, the domestic sphere occupies a central place in both novels and critically examines the personal consequences of Israel's political turmoil. Informed by scholarly literature on domestic space and critical discussions of the separate spheres paradigm, this article offers a reading of the two novels as reflecting the harsh consequences that *past* and *present* brutality in the public sphere inflicts upon personal realms: from the home to the family to the language of intimacy.

Life Must Go On

Gabriela Avigur-Rotem was born in 1946 in Buenos Aires, Argentina. Her parents, passionate Zionists, immigrated to Israel in 1950, when she was almost four. Avigur-Rotem began to write poetry in Hebrew when she was only eight years old, but did not publish until 1980 when her first collection, *Dulcinea*, appeared. Her first novel, *Mozart Was Not a Jew* (*Mozart lo haya yehudi*), came out in 1992. Already in this novel Avigur-Rotem demonstrates her preoccupation with the relations between public and private spaces as she looks into the daily lives of diasporic Jewish homes in South America. In her second and third novels, which I discuss here, the matter of the imagined separation between the private sphere and the collective public space becomes a major theme.[2] Both *Ancient Red* and *Heat Wave and Crazy Birds* go far beyond the binary of the separate spheres without dismissing the model altogether. Rather than celebrating the domestic sphere as removed from the politics of the day, Avigur-Rotem is interested in understanding the interplay of public and private in the Israeli sociopolitical arena.

An apt case study for a contemporary application of the separate sphere model is the perception of public and private in Israel's political situation, which Israelis term *Hamatzav*. Between 1993 and 2006, Israeli society experienced close to five hundred terror incidents, which resulted in numerous injuries and casualties on both the Israeli and the Palestinian sides.[3] In general, the Israeli public viewed this violence that Israeli officials sometimes termed "Low-Intensity Conflict" as random or sudden and did not immediately connect it to the occupation of the West Bank and Gaza.[4] In fact, on many occasions the Israeli leadership and public opinion makers complimented the public for its "firm stand" and "heroic perseverance" in the face of Palestinian terror.[5]

An essential quality of this Israeli "perseverance" amid political crisis was maintaining a sense of normalcy in daily life. The Israeli version of stoicism did not derive from impassiveness but rather from a strong sense that there were no other available alternatives. The common perception in Israel was that the political crisis barely influenced life in the private sphere. This notion manifested itself in the popular saying that life must go on(*ha-hayim hayavim lehimashekh*), which articulated the desire, or need, of mainstream Israeli society to maintain stability.

Israelis, therefore, viewed the private home as a shelter that protected its residents from everything that went on outside. It seems that they needed the illusion of the separate spheres in order to believe that they were always capable of closing the door and being safe. This exercise, however, as Avigur-Rotem's protagonist in *Heatwave and*

Crazy Birds soon discovers, fails completely. The house standing at the center of the narrative is riddled with both physical and metaphorical cracks and is doomed for destruction.

Heatwave and Crazy Birds: A Belated Return to the Old House

This novel's main protagonist, the stewardess Loya Kaplan, returns to Israel after a twenty-five-year absence. She arrives in her hometown in order to take over a house that she has inherited. The house, however, is not yet hers and, as a matter of fact, never will be. The very moment in which Loya finally embraces the house as her home—in the last scene of the novel—constitutes its ultimate destruction. Upon returning to the *shikkun* (the old neighborhood), Loya, who also narrates the novel, defiantly refuses to buy any newspapers, listen to the news on the radio, or watch TV. Instead, she entrenches herself in the house, which soon becomes the arena of an intimate investigation of her family's past, especially the unspoken occurrences of the Holocaust.

According to the terms that Loya's surrogate father, Barak Davidi, specified in his will, the house, yard, and orchard would become hers only after she found an adequate location to scatter his ashes. The novel follows Loya's inability to decide what to do with the ashes and whether or not to sell the land. The narrative also depicts her belated mourning over the loss of three close family members: her biological father, Professor Ota Kaplan; his best friend, Davidi; and Nahum, Davidi's son, Loya's soul mate and de facto brother throughout their childhood. Toward the end of the narrative Loya discovers that Nahum (Yan) was her real sibling and that they shared a mother who left them when Loya was five. The abandonment of the mother occurred in the pre-oedipal stage, that is, in the early period of Loya's childhood, from which she only carries fragmentary recollections.[6] One salient example: Loya has a talent for languages and speaks all the European languages except for German and Czech. The latter, literally and figuratively is her mother tongue. Nevertheless, since Loya unconsciously associates Czech with a nonverbal emotional trauma, the language is "forgotten" and Loya never manages to relearn it, or even remember that she used to speak it.

The clash between the individual present and the collective past, so central to Avigur-Rotem's novels, is intensified by Loya's prolonged absence from the Israeli territory. The figure of the flight attendant, who presumably lives in a secluded capsule detached from time and place, forms an ideal candidate through which to develop the character's alienation from or deautomatization toward Israeli society. It is not by chance, then, that Loya, constantly being in-between geographical places, has no home of her own. Loya is convinced that this is the best possible way to live, and constantly reiterates the virtues of flying: "What do I lack for up there [. . .] protected from cold, from heat, from big spaces, from bad surprises" (18).[7] Since the death of her father, she has lived as a constant transient removed from life and incessantly moving from one place to another. Leaving her childhood neighborhood behind, Loya becomes an immigrant by choice, reminiscent of the figure of the wandering Jew and a symbol of the modern individual whose path of life is determined primarily by temporal fluidity and lack of stability.

Professor Kaplan's sudden passing in 1967, before the Six-Day War, kept Loya away from her hometown and childhood memories until 1994, when the storyline takes place. The year 1967 symbolically signifies in the novel the starting point for the decline of the idea of "good old Eretz Israel" (*Eretz Israel ha-yeshana ve-hatova*). As a matter of fact, according to the novel, this historical year marks the transposition of the *idea* of "good old Eretz Israel" into an *ideal* of something that no longer exists in reality. The novel thus presents 1967 as a moment of innocence lost not only for the heroine but also for the Israeli nation as a whole. In addition to the obvious political connotation of the occupation and the militarization of Israeli society, 1967 functions here as a threshold for a nostalgic perception of how Israel used to be.

In her influential study *The Future of Nostalgia,* Svetlana Boym explains that although at first glance nostalgia is longing for a place, it actually is a yearning for a different time. Boym further observes that nostalgia is not always about the past: "It can be retrospective but also prospective. Fantasies of the past determined by needs of the present have a direct impact on realities of the future. Consideration of the future makes us take responsibility for our nostalgic tales."[8] Following Boym's formulation, I argue that nostalgia in the novel becomes an ambivalent sentiment that reflects Loya's complicated relationship with her past, as well as Avigur-Rotem's critique of the present. During the twenty-seven years that span the time between 1967 and Loya's homecoming, the heroine remains in a metaphorical comatose state. Her return to the old neighborhood signifies for her, and perhaps for an entire generation of Israelis, that the time is ripe not only for awakening and sobering up from this presumed coma but also for an in-depth personal and collective soul searching.

Indeed, Avigur-Rotem's narrative portrays the evolution of Israeli identity over time. As Risa Domb suggests, "the temporal dimension operates from the opening pages, establishing a style in which several time-scales run in parallel. [. . .] The emotional baggage Loya brings with her is continually colliding with the reality of the present, and the more she encounters the present, the greater her nostalgia for the past."[9] A sense of nostalgia is further informed by a series, or perhaps a catalog, of Israeli cultural artifacts that come into play through the protagonist's imagination. The titles of the chapters, for example, all starting with the local, guttural Hebrew letter *ḥet:* Heatwave (*ḥamsin*), "the old gang" (*ḥevre*), *Ḥummus,* "The month of *Ḥeshvan,*" "blooming squills" (*ḥatzavim*). For the Israeli reader, these words convey a specific set of cultural associations, and some of them (*ḥevre, Ḥummus, Ḥatzavim*) easily provoke nostalgia. Moreover, Iris Milner maintains that Avigur-Rotem's text enlists various artifacts and posits them as background scenery for the narrative's occurrences in order to signify typical Israeli nativeness.[10] Thus, probing what it means to be an Israeli in the 1990s, Avigur-Rotem's writing—through Loya's recollections of the old neighborhood —"pushes all the right buttons" for an Israeli audience, particularly readers of the

Statehood generation who came of age in the 1950s and the 1960s. Children's games, common folk songs and old slang, infiltrate the novel creating a local, homey feeling and produce a constant sense of nostalgia. Later on, however, Avigur-Rotem purposely undermines this sentiment while placing it in conjunction with poignant criticism of fashions that are customary in contemporary Israeli society.

The Domestic Territory and the Jewish Past

Despite producing this nostalgia in the reader, the character of Loya always fears what delving into the past might uncover. This fear suggests a possible reason for Loya's refusal to settle down in Davidi's house. She *resides* in the house but does not *live* in it. The internal space of the house equally attracts and repulses her. In the first months Loya sleeps in the living room across from the pyxis, a heavy lidded clay pot, where Davidi's ashes await her decision. For a long time she does not enter any of the other rooms, making sure to keep them locked: "every keyhole like a little girl cut out of darkness; a giant head attached without a neck to a widening dress, without arms, without legs, signaling cold-cold-cold" (12). The darkness Loya glimpses through the keyholes relates to the dark secrets the house conceals. Indeed, Davidi's house literally hides the intimate knowledge of Loya's father's experiences in the Holocaust. Like the wild roots of the ficus in the yard that creep beneath the building threatening to destroy it, so does the imminent knowledge of Loya's family story.

Despite the protagonist's best efforts to contain and control this unveiling of the family's history, once she starts opening the rooms of the house, she can restrain neither the pace nor the content of what she exposes. Loya conducts a metaphorically Freudian archaeological dig through repressed childhood memories through a physical exploration of the geography of the house, beginning in the main floor and ending deep in the semihidden basement. She progresses slowly from one room to another, revealing layers of secrets pertaining to her own past and present.

When she finally enters the main bedroom she discovers a double bottom drawer with an envelope addressed to her. Here the narrative offers a realization of the famous metaphor of the "inner crypt," coined by the psychoanalytic theorists Nicolas Abraham and Maria Torok to describe a metaphorical space that hides repressed content.[11] Likewise, Loya's envelope contains her father's journal from the years of his imprisonment in the Terezin Ghetto. The diary reveals not only suppressed information about Loya's mother but also the core and essence of the powerful bond between Ota Kaplan and Barak Davidi. According to the journal, in October 1942 Kaplan managed to escape a death transport but later discovered that Davidi, his student and friend, took his place in that transport. Consumed with guilt and regret, Kaplan married Davidi's pregnant wife, Milna, in order to save her from being deported. Milna then gave birth in secret to a healthy boy and succeeded in smuggling the baby, Yan (later Nachum), out of the ghetto. Reading the journal, Loya finally realizes the origin of the intricate relationship in her nontraditional family. If this revelation was not enough, reading further in the journal she discovers that she was born to Kaplan and Milna in Italy en route to Israel under the name Lea. The name change symbolizes a shift in Loya's entire self-perception, one caused by unearthing startling facts about her family.

In an old suitcase in the basement Loya also discovers two letters in Czech and learns that her mother, Milna, who could not choose between her two husbands, decided to migrate from Israel back to Eastern Europe, leaving her two children and husbands behind. This revelation sends Loya on a journey to the Czech Republic in an attempt to find the mother whom she always thought was dead. While meeting Milna allows Loya to gain a better understanding of her father as well as herself, the process does not lead to the desired *tikkun,* or restoration, of the self, nor does it repair the broken relationship with the mother. Like Tirza, the protagonist of Ruth Agnon's novella *In the Prime of Her Life* (*Bidmi yameiha*), Loya's exposure of her repressed childhood trauma does not set her free from her past and present demons.[12]

The family's suppressed past, uncovered in Israel of 1994, parallels another, very much present "return of the repressed. "During her stay in Davidi's house, Loya finds out that an illegal Palestinian worker has been hiding in her basement. With this discovery, Avigur-Rotem's novel exposes the violent consequences of the Israeli-Palestinian dispute precisely by disrupting the common dichotomy of public and private, dramatizing the imaginary nature of the separation between them.

The Political Crisis Enters the Private House

Despite Loya's attempt to focus on her personal matters, she cannot escape the reality of the public sphere in 1994, a deadly year in the political conflict between Israelis and Palestinians. Events in the Israeli political arena constantly disrupt Loya's domestic, personal account, just as Davidi's house is literally invaded by a Palestinian murder suspect lurking in the basement. The eleven chapters of the book, aligned according to the Jewish calendar—from Rosh Hashanah to the end of the summer—follow specific terror events: the Cave of the Patriarchs massacre (199–200), the suicide bombings in Afula on Holocaust Memorial Day (246), and Hadera on Israeli Fallen Soldiers and Victims of Terrorism Remembrance Day (326–28), as well as the political rift in Israeli society that directly relates to the assassination of Rabin (72, 336).

By incorporating real events in her fictional plot, Avigur-Rotem produces a space in which traumatic moments in the public sphere are played and replayed in different forms and variations. Unlike the media, which relates public information only in the moment and then moves on, Avigur-Rotem's novels offer the reader an opportunity to reconsider the consequences of each individual trauma, its collective impact on daily life. For Avigur-Rotem, to paraphrase Marianne Hirsch, writing serves as a proclamation of needs, desires, and expectations that defiantly articulate and justify the deep fears that terror as an instance of the security and political crisis creates. Her novels provide a space in which these fears can be experienced and expressed, and in which the repression of these fears can be undone.[13]

The novel's' heroine, preoccupied by the search for her personal history, does not notice that another person resides in the house. When security personnel arrive and arrest the Palestinian worker, Loya hides in a closet holding a knife in self-defense. Although there is no proof that the worker is a terrorist, her sense of persecution connects in her mind the events of the Holocaust with the terrorist act of the murder of the Haran family in Nahariya in 1979: "behind a double door, in a room opening from the depths of the wardrobe, families hid, strangled crying babies so they wouldn't betray them, something like that happened in Nahariya too, when we handed out the paper in the plane a few of the passengers burst out crying" (93).[14] Interestingly, this literary depiction relates to a real experience of the author. In 1993, a Palestinian terrorist managed to drive a suicide car into Avigur-Rotem's peaceful neighborhood in Ramat Efal.

As in the fictional scene, the man was caught before harming anyone, and security forces safely neutralized the car. Nevertheless, they arrested the Palestinian terrorist much too close to home, only three meters away from the bedroom of Avigur-Rotem's elder son.[15] At this very moment the political conflict entered the private home, and for the author the domestic space ceased to be safe and protective. The author relates a similar sense of insecurity when depicting the events of October 2000, which appear in *Ancient Red*. Then, Palestinians from the western Galilee villages Arabe and Sakhnin surrounded the Jewish settlement of Avtalyon, where she currently lives, and Israeli authorities bound residents to their home for two days.[16]

Henri Lefebvre argues that space is a product of social experience and that a perception of space can be constituted by an event. If literary depictions of homes function as "representational spaces"—to borrow Lefebvre's conceptual category from his seminal work *The Production of Space*—these real-life incidents form remarkable examples of the ways in which an anxiety of terror, or fear for personal safety, seep into fictional narratives and influence the geography of an imaginary space.[17] Indeed, the unhomely, broken, private houses in both of Avigur-Rotem's novels echo the crises of the Israeli present as well as those of the Jewish past. In *Heatwave and Crazy Birds* the house itself—its structure, rooms, basement, and yard—becomes essential for the progression of the plot. No wonder then that the book ends with the complete destruction of this very house.

In the first page of the novel the narrator describes the ficus in the yard as follows: "nothing grows below it and behind it and its roots run into the house" (7). Elsewhere she compares the house to "a child's building-block between the jaws of the ficus tree" (164). While these descriptions serve as warning signs for a possible destruction of the home, Loya's attentions are occupied with discovering her family's past. Paralleling the exposure of the past, the roots of the tree keep growing and subsequently render the house less and less inhabitable. Paradoxically, the more Loya comes to terms with her family history and with the contemporary Israeli political state, the more unstable the house becomes.

Upon returning to the old neighborhood, following the journey to find her mother, Loya finally knows what to do with the pyxis. On the way back from the airport, she scatters Davidi's ashes in the ruined city of Caesarea, by the Mediterranean Sea. Now that she has fulfilled the last term of Davidi's will she is ready to go home:

> So, I've arrived, the suitcase is a lot lighter, but it's pitch dark, why aren't the street lamps on, and what's this, what's this here in the garden, on the scar in the ground a huge tractor, with a giant shovel sticking out in front of it, yes, it's a tractor [. . .] who the hell put a tractor in my garden, I hurry to the house, but it's boarded up with criss-crossed planks, there's a note or letter nailed to them with a big nail, a notice from the council, but how can I read it in the dark, maybe if I stand under the street lamp, but first to drink, first of all to drink, I hurry to the garden faucet [. . .] but its mouth isn't even damp, not even a single drop is hiding in its throat, it's absolutely dry, [. . .] turns on empty until it sticks and I hear the sound the pipes make at the end of the water khkhkhrrrrrrrrr. (373)

The lack of water, intensified by the guttural, discordant *ḥet* creates a sense of loss. Water symbolizes life, promise, and a new creation. Without it, the house becomes a dead place. In the reality of the narrative, it appears that the domestic space can no longer sustain the tensions between the anxiety of the present and the secrets of the past. The foundation of the house is full of cracks and thus, upon exposing all of its secrets, it collapses.

If we choose to contextualize the trope of the private house through the allegorical lens of the national Jewish house, the novel bleakly concludes that the present composition and structure of the house compromises its longevity.[18] Indeed, Avigur-Rotem encourages such an interpretation:

> The Zionist base we tried to build is riddled with cracks and is doomed to destruction. The materials beneath the roots of the tree, [the parts] below the house, will destroy it. In the fifty-four years of Israel's existence more Jews have been killed here than anywhere else in the world. So what did we accomplish? Did we discover a wise solution? In this book I scrutinize that question.[19]

Heatwave and Crazy Birds offers an incisive insider's perspective on Israel of the 1990s. The application of the private territory, as an inevitable extension of the Israeli sociopolitical sphere, assists in stressing the complex relationships between the past and the present. For Avigur-Rotem the interrelations between the private and the public are a crucial key for understanding contemporary Israeli society. She further develops these ideas in her subsequent novel, *Ancient Red*.

Ancient Red: Past and Present Brutalities

One of the final scenes of *Ancient Red* (2007) portrays the centennial of Tzofia (Tzofkeh) Pedhazur, the great matriarch of the heroine's family.[20] This highly symbolic scene takes place on the first day of the October 2000 riots in the apocryphal Galilee village Kfar Zunz, named after Leopold Zunz (1794–1886), the founder of the Wissenschaft des Judentums. Grandmother Tzofia, whose name invokes the Israeli national anthem, as well as Proverbs 31:27, returns home after spending the morning in the hospital.[21] She is pale, tired, and disoriented; her white and blue dress (pointedly similar to the Israeli flag), which she digs out from the back of her closet, reeks of mothballs. The gift she receives for the occasion, a book of artwork by her late youngest daughter (who committed suicide a few years before) is handed to her on a silver tray, reminiscent of Natan Alterman's influential poem "The Silver Platter."[22] Her granddaughter, Ra'anana, a clothing designer in her thirties and also the novel's main protagonist, holds her hand, constantly checking Tzofkeh's faint pulse, making sure that she is not dying.[23] One cannot disregard the numerous Zionist emblems that fill this scene, through which the author reflects upon the state of Zionism in the new millennium. The portrayal is far from kind. Indeed, *Ancient Red* provides a thought-provoking perspective to critically examine the metanarrative of the Jewish state.[24]

The novel offers an intriguing way of looking at the Zionist continuum, as it intersperses throughout the present-day narrative ten historical chapters. Spanning the years 1913–21, the historical chapters recreate the voices and depict the stories of a number of mythological and lesser-known Zionist figures. By focusing on individuals, their personal relationship, indecisiveness, confusion, fears, and desires, Avigur-Rotem establishes a kinship between figures of the past and the mundane characters of the "here and now." She productively applies catastrophic events and past and present brutalities in order to rethink the relation between Zionist history and present-day Israel. The connections between the past and the present are many: some are rhetorical or associative, others geographic-territorial. Photographs appearing at the end of the historical chapters connect the reader back to the present-day narrative; yet, in other cases, personal objects serve as transitions for the fictional narrative interchange of past and present.

The contemporary story, which examines the years of 1995–2000, begins and ends with symbolic moments of rupture in Israeli society. The first scene the novel portrays takes place in Tel Aviv on the evening of November 4, 1995, less than two hours before the assassination of Prime Minister Rabin, near the site of the murder. The novel ends on the second day of the dramatic internal clash between Palestinian Arabs, citizens of Israel, and law enforcement authorities, which was later termed the October 2000 Riots. Here, too, the location of the scene in the Galilee village is physically close to the disastrous events that resulted in the deaths of twelve Palestinian Israelis, one Palestinian, and one Jew.[25] The novel, however, does not directly relate to any event of national magnitude, aiming instead to keep the narration within the private sphere. For example, the narrative does not dwell on Rabin's murder, only mentioning it twice throughout 567 pages. One of those references occurs during a phone conversation between Grandmother Tzofia and Ra'anana:

> "Hi Grandma, how's it going?"
> "What do you mean how's it going!" she cried out, almost bursting my eardrum: "Don't you listen to the radio? Turn it on right now. Rosa's son[26]—they killed him! They just announced it."[27]

This scene reconceptualizes the national trauma of the assassination, morphing into an intimate, familial statement regarding the death of a friend's son. This treatment renders the public murder as a personal event with no explicit political content. Likewise, the novel mentions the event of October 2000 as causing a major traffic jam that threatens to cancel Tzofia's celebration.

In addition to Ra'anana, Be'eri Slonim, an architect in his fifties, is another protagonist in the novel. Despite their evident age difference, both Be'eri and Ra'anana belong to a middle generation of Israelis whose parents founded the Israeli state, and their children—at least in Be'eri's case—constantly question its legitimacy. The narrative consists of Ra'anana's and Be'eri's shifting perspectives, which also complement each other. Nevertheless, the gaps between their worldviews are fundamental, and it often appears that they tell two completely different stories. The conservative, hesitant man and the assertive (though lost) young woman share a recent painful and traumatic separation from the loves of their lives. These wounds, yet to be healed, shape their indecisive advances toward each other. As a result, the actual relationship between Ra'anana and Be'eri is full of impediments and miscommunications and offers only few redeeming qualities. The unflattering portrayal of the present-day protagonists depicts them as solipsistic and self-centered, incapable of seeing anything beyond themselves. Their prolonged, ambivalent relation continues to deteriorate as Ra'anana considers revealing to her former partner that she is pregnant from the one disappointing sexual encounter they shared. The novel ends when Ra'anana faces an opportunity to miscarry by drinking a poisonous herbal tea that a close family friend offers her.

In a striking departure from the rest of the novel, the closing scene, narrated in the third person, is stylistically reminiscent of Yosef Haim Brenner's 1911 novel *From Here and There* (*Mi-kan u-mi-kan*).[28] This literary affinity strengthens the novel's assertion of the inseparability of past and present narratives. Almost one hundred years apart, both novels ultimately offer a metaphysical quest for truth and the essence of existence:[29] Brenner's *From Here and There* raises questions with regard to the fate of the Jewish nation, whereas Avigur-Rotem's *Ancient Red* aspires to answer what it means to live in a place that constantly evokes history, to exist in a present so tied to an unresolved past. As in her former novel, *Heatwave and Crazy Birds, Ancient Red* reflects upon the current state of Israelis and harshly criticizes a number of aspects of present-day Israel.

Interestingly, the closing scene of *Ancient Red* is not the only one in which the novel alludes to Brenner's work. Readers can glimpse the ascetic author himself through the bitter and indignant perspective of Yosef Luidor, who was murdered alongside Brenner in Jaffa in May 1921.[30] Luidor's account accompanies nine other unique historical narratives comprised of numerous voices that creating a sort of Bakhtinian polyphony, that is, a narration in which the characters' voices take preference over the narrator's voice.[31] The historical characters that speak or are spoken about in the novel are Sarah Aharonson, Yosef Lishanski, and Avshalom Feinberg of the NILI Spy Ring; authors Dvora Baron and Yosef Luidor; poet Rachel Bluwstein; Dvora Drekhler of the Tel Hai defenders; Dr. Weitz of the Alexandria exiles; Rivka Aharonson, the sister of Sarah Aharonson, and Shoshana-Haya Bogen, a second Aliya Pioneer who committed suicide.

Of the impressive list of figures whose stories the novel recounts, only two escaped an unnatural, violent death at a young age.[32] The lives of all the others ended abruptly before their time by suicide, lynching, murder, or terminal illness. This is particularly significant for it is those catastrophes that situate the characters within the Zionist narrative in the first place. Many of the figures the historical chapters discuss would have remained unknown had it not been for their disastrous, abrupt deaths. In fact, stories such as the battle on Tel Hai, the rise and fall of the NILI underground, or the riots in Jaffa became formative and even sanctified as mythological narratives in the process of constructing Israel's national memory. As Benedict Anderson stresses in his seminal monograph *Imagined Communities,* it is those stories that help sustain a deep horizontal comradeship within the imagined community, regardless of the actual inequality and exploitation that may prevail in the nation.[33]

The Zionist narrative, a story of struggle and response, builds upon such collective memories. Historian Billie Melman explains that the Israeli discourse, both in the historiography of *Eretz Yisrael* before and after the establishment of the state and in the broader public debates, "is marked by an intense interest in collective memory, in methods of commemoration, and in the preservation of certain narratives of the past and the forgetting of others. This interest is also a re-examination of national identity: of its boundaries and of what it includes and excludes."[34] Psychologists Daniel Bar-Tal and Gavriel Salomon argue that collective narratives do not have to reflect truth. Instead, they portray a functional truth that is necessary for the group's ongoing existence.[35] Political scientist Robert Rotberg likewise claims that collective narrative exists as a coping mechanism in a situation of interminable conflict. Such narratives encapsulate both the legitimacy of the cause and the nature of the sacrifices that support coping under stress.[36]

In dealing with such charged, mythological moments in Zionist-Israeli history, Avigur-Rotem's narrative focuses on their subjective quality, thereby stressing the personal angle of the formative myth. She is less interested in the disaster itself and more so in the circumstances that led the characters to act as they did. Indeed, as with the contemporary events, the novel leaves the actual catastrophes outside of the narration, beyond the pale of the text. Moreover, the selection of lesser-known, or perhaps even secondary figures (Luidor instead of Brenner, Dvora Drekhler and not Trumpeldor,

Rivka Aharonson instead of Sarah) to recount these events sheds new light and offers a fresh perspective on otherwise exhaustively familiar narratives.

Ancient Red's focus on the most mundane matters and the finest details of the historical characters' private lives despite the impending dramatic events opens a window to the domestic lives of the characters. I offer to term this quality of Avigur-Rotem's narration "the private face of Zionism," that is, the ability to view occurrences and encounters in the private sphere, as equal agents in the chain of events that led to the catastrophe in the first place and later, to the creation of the myth and the formation of the national story. It is precisely through the lesser-known characters that this quality is revealed.

Much like the contemporary protagonists Be'eri and Ra'anana, the historical characters are obsessed with personal relationships, romantic quests, and how others perceive them. An essential theme in the novel, which characterizes the contemporary as well as the historical narratives, is the difference between men and women and their inability to find common ground. This lack of communication between the genders serves as a broader metaphor and a key to understanding the novel in its entirety. This idea is reminiscent of Amalia Kahana-Carmon's powerful metaphor from her 1984 novella *The Bridge of the Green Duck,* where she compares the relationship between non-Jews (*Goyim*) and Jews (*Yehudim*) to the relationship between men and women.[37] All of Avigur-Rotem's characters, present day and historical alike, fail to truly see the other, whether it is a family member, potential romantic partner, or the Arab neighbor. Nation and race, the novel suggests, function in a manner similar to gender divisions.[38] When it comes to collective memories, Jews and Arabs speak different languages and adhere to different narratives. The novel's assumption is that the small space of the Israeli state is saturated with competing narratives. The abundance of voices and perspectives in the novel stresses not only the temporality of the various stories but also the instability of historical memory in general. The lack of a coherent narrative therefore suggests that one account cannot adequately describe the elastic nature of reality, and Israeli reality in particular.

The author creates a convincing, at times, heartbreaking portrayal of these historical figures. She does that, in part, through comprehensive and exhaustive research of primary and secondary material.[39] Avigur-Rotem generates empathy for her characters, despite and perhaps specifically due to the way she lingers on their many flaws and inconsistencies. Each chapter presents a different writing style, colored with the unique speech of the historical figures as well as expressions and transcription of the Hebrew (and sometimes other languages) common for the time period.

The effect of Avigur-Rotem's narration is a productive demythification of iconic figures and events in the Zionist national narrative. It is productive in that the author does not wipe out the national story but rather dwells inside it. She then centers her account on the specific individuals who stood in the midst of these events, rather than on the events themselves. By appropriating the unique voice and speech of each of the historical characters, Avigur-Rotem constructs a narration "from within." The author then goes beyond the myth to show the human element, that is, to demonstrate how the Zionist heroes, who created the myth, were, after all, regular, average people. Furthermore, the historical chapters demonstrate how in many of these catastrophic incidents, people were not led by strong ideology but rather found themselves in devastating situations that became mythic as a result of personal distress, sometimes even by mere chance. As Avigur-Rotem observes: "The heroic characters were in fact like everyone else, but they managed to find strength in crisis situations. It's quite possible that each and every one of us would have acted in the same way."[40]

Life Goes On?

Thematically, geographically, and metaphorically, the novel realizes the interconnection between past and present. For example, Ra'anana participates in a tour at the Aharonson's house in Zikhron-Ya'akov, and later visits the cemetery near Tel Hai. On another occasion both protagonists go on a romantic hike in Hirbat mantzur al-akev where Avshalom Feinberg used to ride his horse. Such creative acts project the "here and now" on the mythological history of Zionism (and vice versa) and parallel two other projects in the novel: the first is the art of Hayale, Ra'anana's aunt who committed suicide, and the second is Ra'anana's task of compiling a memory book with works by her late aunt. Ra'anana is entrusted with going over Hayale's property in order to compile a selection of her pieces for a book to be published by the family. This is the first time she views the works from a critical perspective, and the reader knows that they must resonate with her, for they keep reappearing in her narration.

Hayale created innovative collages out of family and self-portraits, newspaper clippings, and symbolic "Zionist posters," such as the lion sculpture in the Tel Hai monument, a female Yemenite immigrant, and young lovers next to a military tank. She used to put her own face in the pictures, sometimes in lieu of a participant or an object, other times as an additional character. She then gave a provocative title to the new creation. In one piece, Hayale pasted a photo of herself as a small child patting the sculpture of the Lion in the Kfar Giladi cemetery and gave it the title "Good Dog" (74). Her artistic sensibility reflects a dark, provocative humor that entertains the imaginary viewers but also disturbs and alienates them. As a grand metaphor for the novel itself, Hayale's works approximate the past and the present, the collective and the private, in order to call into question national narratives and symbols and their function in the life of contemporary Israelis.

While the novel starts and ends with significant moments in the Israeli public sphere, it also depicts crucial personal encounters. The first scene, along with the assassination of Rabin, portrays Ra'anana's initial meeting with Hayale's former romantic partner, Nehoshtan (Nah'tche) Reudor. The married middle-aged man fascinates her, and Ra'anana falls in love despite her best judgment. The narrative presents this moment as the starting point of her downfall, resulting in a complete breakdown two years later, following their separation. The end of the relationship turns out to be so traumatic that Ra'anana attempts suicide. In the same manner, the riots of October 2000 lurk in the background of the final scene of the novel when Ra'anana contemplates her possible future as a mother. The juxtaposition of Ra'anana's personal narrative with national traumas exposes the private face of the national narrative and collapses the categories of the private and public spheres. Avigur-Rotem further demonstrates this complete and utter interdependence through Ra'anana's retrospective description of the creation of the long-lasting wound Reudor caused. Associating the affair with the death of her father and the breakdown of her family, of all the metaphors Ra'anana could have used to describe their first meeting, she chooses the aftermath of a terror attack:

> I had to take the material and disappear from there. But I just didn't. I was drawn to stay there like one is drawn to a site of a terror attack; precisely to watch what they [the authorities] try to conceal, the wreckage and the blood and sometimes, if you arrive immediately after, some body parts as well. Before they clean and collect and put everything back in place so they can take photos and prove that everything went back to normal, life goes on. Look: the bus stop stands intact, including the ad with that swim-suit model, the shop windows are whole and through them one can see shoes, dresses, cookies, a packed coffee shop. *Life goes on, life is stronger than everything else.* It's a fact.[41] (Emphasis mine)

It is the personal trauma then, not the collective one, that haunts Ra'anana's present. Nevertheless, the trauma is consistently referred to in the language of the public sphere. Ra'anana applies the terror metaphor to suggest that her life has not returned to normal. As a matter of fact, the entire narrative attests to that. While family members, friends, and even the media constantly reiterate the "life goes on" mantra, for Ra'anana, reality shattered on November 4, 1995, and the life that followed would never be the same.

Notes

I am especially grateful for the helpful suggestions and astute comments of my mentor, Yael S. Feldman. I also wish to thank Adriana X. Jacobs and Ziv Eisenberg for their incisive critiques and suggestions.

1. I use the term *internal* to differentiate between the events of October 2000, which occurred within the borders of Israel, and those of the Second Intifada, which relate to the continual dispute with the Palestinians of the West Bank and Gaza. While both affected the Israeli public space, the narrative of *Ancient Red* is more concerned with the violence within, created by the events of October 2000.

2. The metaphor of the separate spheres has served as a literary model and analytical tool since the late 1960s. Concocted in the nineteenth century by Alexis de Tocqueville and later adopted by second-wave feminist historians and literary scholars, the trope aimed to describe a social structure in which the division of *public* and *private* reflected the binary of gender. See, for

example, Cathy N. Davidson, "No More Separate Spheres!" *American Literature* 70, no. 3 (1998): 443–63; Lora Romero, *Home Fronts: Domesticity and Its Critics in the Antebellum United States* (Durham, NC: Duke University Press, 1997).

3. Historically, it is convenient to mark the boundaries of the period under consideration here by two significant moments: The Declaration of Principles (September 1993), and the Second Lebanon War (July–August 2006). Both events signify political controversies that in turn represent major crises in Israeli identity. The number of terror incidents mentioned in the text is based on data collected from the Israeli Foreign Ministry, Magen David Adom in Israel (Red Cross), and the Palestinian Red Crescent Society (PRCS). As with other issues in the Israeli-Palestinian dispute, the numbers are highly contested. It is important to note, however, that this number covers only incidents with injuries and/or casualties. For a comprehensive list of terror incidents on the Israeli side, see "Fatal Terrorist Attacks in Israel since the Declaration of Principles," http://www.jewishvirtuallibrary.org/jsource/Terrorism/ victims.html. For data on Palestinian casualties, see, for example, http://www.palestinercs.org/.

4. Tamar Liebes and Yoram Peri, "Electronic Journalism in Segmented Societies: Lessons from the 1996 Israeli Elections," *Political Communication* 15 (1998): 27–43; See also Tamar Liebes and Zohar Kampf, "The P.R. of Terror: How New-Style Wars Give Voice to Terrorists," in *Reporting War: Journalism in Wartime,* ed. Stuart Allan and Barbie Zelizer (New York: Routledge, 2004), 77–95.

5. See, for example, Stevan E. Hobfoll and Daphna Canetti-Nisim, "Exposure to Terrorism, Stress-Related Mental Health Symptoms, and Defensive Coping among Jews and Arabs in Israel," *Journal of Consulting and Clinical Psychology*74, no. 2 (2006): 207–18. See also working papers prepared for the Hertzliya Conference summarizing yearly "Indices for National Resilience," http://www.herzliyaconference.org/_Articles/Article.asp?ArticleID=2554&CategoryID=310.

6. For an extensive discussion of the implication of the pre-oedipal stage on the development of women, in particular, mother-daughter bond during the pre-oedipal stage, see Freud's essays "Female Sexuality" and "Femininity" in Elisabeth Young-Bruehl, ed., *Freud on Women* (New York: W. W. Norton, 1990), 321–62.

7. Gabriela Avigur-Rotem, *Heatwave and Crazy Birds* (Tel Aviv: Keshet, 2001). Translated from the Hebrew by Dalya Bilu. Unless otherwise noted, quotes from the novel are taken from this translation. I wish to thank Dr. Deborah Guth, editorial director of the Institute for the Translation of Hebrew Literature, for allowing me to use Bilu's unpublished translation for this article. The marking of page numbers that appears following this quote and henceforth in the body of the text is based on the Hebrew. This translation has been subsequently published: Gabriela Avigur-Rotem, *Heatwave and Crazy Birds* (Urbana-Champaign: Dalkey Archive Press, 2011)

8. Svetlana Boym, *The Future of Nostalgia* (New York: Basic Books, 2002), xv–xvi.

9. Risa Domb, "Nothing Is as It Was: Time and Change in *Heatwave and Crazy Birds* by Gabriela Avigur-Rotem," *Identity and Modern Israeli Literature* (London: Vallentine Mitchell, 2006), 90–103.

10. Iris Milner, *Past Present: Biography, Identity, and Memory in Second Generation Literature* (Tel Aviv: Am Oved, 2003), 44–45.

11. See Nicolas Abraham and Maria Torok, *The Wolf Man's Magic Word: A Cryptonymy,* trans. Nicholas Rand (Minneapolis: University of Minnesota Press, 1986).

12. Loya's character also echoes Mira, Ruth Almog's protagonist in the novel *Roots of Air* (*Shorshei 'Avir*). However, unlike Tirza and Mira, whose mothers form a significant (real or imagined) presence in their lives, Loya's mother is absent and never spoken about throughout her childhood. Loya's *tikkun*, therefore, is aimed mostly at her father, and the novel indeed offers his journal as a way for her to reconnect with him posthumously. For a comprehensive reading of Ruth Almog's *Roots of Air* and a comparison with Agnon's novella, see Yael Feldman, *No Room of Their Own: Gender and Nation in Israeli Women's Fiction* (New York: Columbia University Press, 1999), 208–20.

13. Marianne Hirsch, "'What We Need Right Now Is to Imagine the Real': Grace Paley Writing against War," *PMLA* 124, no. 5 (2009): 1768–77.

14. In April 1979 four Palestine Liberation Front (PLF) militants landed on the shore of Nahariya, Israel, where they traveled by boat from the Lebanese town of Tyre. The raid resulted in the deaths of four Israelis—including a father, Danny Haran, and his two daughters—and two of the perpetrators. One of the children, a two year old, was smothered by her mother, Smadar Haran, while hiding with a neighbor in a crawl space above their bedroom. Two of the perpetrators, Samir Kuntar and Ahmed al-Abras, were captured, convicted of murder by an Israeli court, and sentenced to several life sentences. Both were later exchanged in prisoner swap deals, al-Abras in 1985 and Kuntar in 2008.

15. Gabriela Avigur-Rotem, interview by Shiri Goren, Avtalyon, Israel, July 11, 2007, my translation. Gabriela Avigur-Rotem, "How Dreadful Is This Place: Thoughts about the Local," *Mikarov* 8 (Spring 2002): 139–43.

16. Ibid.

17. Henri Lefebvre, *The Production of Space* (Oxford and Cambridge, MA: Blackwell, 1991), 33, 39.

18. For a discussion of national allegory, see Fredric Jameson, "Third World Literature in the Era of Multinational Capitalism," *Social Text* 15 (1986): 65–88; and "A Brief Response," *Social Text* 17 (1987): 26–28. For an application of Jameson's theory to Israeli literature, see Hannan Hever, "From Hebrew Literature to Israeli Literature," in *Coloniality and the Postcolonial Condition: Implication for Israeli Society*, ed. Yehuda Shenhav (Tel Aviv: Van Leer Institute and Hakibbutz Hameuchad, 2004), 414–37.

19. Gabriela Avigur-Rotem, address, Beit Ariela, Tel Aviv, December 2001. Translated and quoted by Risa Domb, *Identity and Modern Israeli Literature*, 91.

20. Gabriela Avigur-Rotem, *Ancient Red* (Or Yehuda: Kinneret, Zmora-Bitan, Dvir, 2007). Henceforward references to the novel will appear with page numbers in the body of the text.

21. The Israeli national anthem, *Hatikva* (The Hope), by Naftali Hertz Imber reads: "Ayin le'Zion Tzofia." Proverbs 31:23, "Tzofia halikhot beyta ve'lehem atzlut lo tokhel."

22. "Magash hakesef" by Alterman first appeared in *Davar*, December 19, 1947.

23. This scene invokes the fourth conversation of A. B. Yehoshua's *Mr. Mani*, in which Efrayim Shapiro cannot find Hertzl's pulse during the second Zionist conference in Basel (1899). Shapiro in this scene perceives Hertzl as a dreamer or a delirious person whose days are numbered. The missing pulse reflects the young doctor's skeptical view of Zionism, as well as Yehoshua's implied notions of the Jews of the Diaspora. See *Mr. Mani*, trans. Hillel Halkin (New York: Doubleday, 1992), 221–28.

24. *Ancient Red* is dedicated to Gershon Shaked, the scholar who coined the term "The Zionist metaplot" (*Alilat ha'al ha'zionit*). Shaked's conceptualization applies the Zionist metaplot as the primary thematic focus through which to classify the entire corpus of modern Hebrew literature

(1880–1990). While this theoretical structure has been contested in recent years by younger generations of literary scholars, there is no doubt about the extensive influence of this model on the scholarly field of modern Hebrew literature.

25. "The October 2000 Events" is a term used to describe the week-long riots, which swept through the Arab sector in Israel. Several days of protests and civil disobedience in northern Israel in solidarity with the Palestinians escalated into violent clashes between Arab citizens of Israel and the Israeli police. As mentioned earlier, the October 2000 Riots were conducted by Israeli Palestinians (citizens of Israel) in support of the Second Intifada, which erupted in September 28, 2000. The narrative of *Ancient Red* is concerned with the violent events within Israel and the Galilee in particular.

26. Tzofia refers here to Rabin's mother, Rosa Cohen.

27. Translated by Adriana X. Jacobs.

28. Esti Adivi-Shoshan stresses the gender reversal in her comparison of the last lines of Brenner's narrative and those of Avigur-Rotem. She observes: "The endings describe a drop of water about to fall, an old woman lighting a fire in the stove while baking pita bread, and the presence of thorns crowning the characters. In Brenner's novel, the thorns crown the men, the heroes of the Second Aliyah, while in Avigur-Rotem's work the crown of thorns is transferred to the female dynasty. [. . .] The story of the Second Aliyah ends with Brenner's famous line, 'The existence was an existence of thorns. The account has yet to be settled.' And Avigur-Rotem answers him, speaking to the female characters: 'Did you hear the news? It is not over, this whole business it seems to be only beginning.'" *Haaretz Online*, July 27, 2007, http://www.haaretz.com/hasen/spages/886691.html.

29. For a detailed reading of this aspect in Brenner's novel, see Boaz Arphali, *The Negative Principle—Ideology and Poetics in Two Stories by Y. H. Brenner* (Tel Aviv: Hakibbutz Hameuhad, 1992), 36–52.

30. The murder of Yosef Haim Brenner, along with four other Jews, occurred on May 2, 1921, during the second day of the Jaffa riots. Together with the previous year's Nebi Musa riots, the Jaffa riots are commonly considered to be the first violent confrontation in what would later become the Israeli-Palestinian conflict.

31. According to Mikhail Bakhtin, "a character's word about himself and his world is just as fully weighted as the author's word usually is; it is not subordinated to the character's objectified image as merely one of his characteristics, nor does it serve as a mouthpiece for the author's voice. It possesses extraordinary independence in the structure of the work; it sounds, as it were, alongside the author's word and in a special way combines both with it and with the full and equally valid voices of other characters." Mikhail M. Bakhtin, *Problems of Dostoevsky's Poetics* (Minneapolis: University of Minnesota Press, 1984), 7.

32. Those are Rivka Aharonson and Dvora Baron. Dr. Weitz, of the Palestinian exiles in Alexandria, is excluded from this list as his voice serves in the novel as a mediator to convey an imagined fascinating conversation between Sarah Aharonson (Madam Avraham), Dvora Baron, Ira Yan, and their host in Alexandria, Maruska Aboulafia.

33. Benedict Anderson, *Imagined Communities: Reflections on the Origin and Spread of Nationalism*, rev. ed. (London: Verso, 1991), 6–7.

34. Billie Melman, "The Legend of Sarah: Gender, Memory, and National Identities (Eretz Yisrael/Israel, 1917–90)," in *Gender and Israeli Society: Women's Time*, ed. Hannah Naveh (London and Portland, OR: Vallentine Mitchell, 2003), 55–92.

35. Daniel Bar-Tal and Gavriel Salomon, "Israeli-Jewish Narratives of the Israeli Palestinian Conflict: Evolution, Contents, Functions, and Consequences," in *Israeli and Palestinian Narratives of Conflict: History's Double Helix,* ed. Robert Rotberg (Bloomington: Indiana University Press, 2006), 19–46.

36. Robert Rotberg, "Building Legitimacy through Narrative," in *Israeli and Palestinian Narratives of Conflict: History's Double Helix,* ed. Robert Rotberg (Bloomington: Indiana University Press, 2006), 1–18.

37. Clara, the protagonist, recounts a conversation with her father: "non-Jews and Jews are like men and women, my father would always say. Why, I once asked. For the determined opinions of each side, regarding itself. And regarding the other." Amalia Kahana-Carmon, *Up in Montifer* (Tel Aviv: Hakibbutz Hameuhad / Siman Kri'ah, 1984), 116.

38. Yet the novel's overall feminist approach appears derivative and somewhat old-fashioned. This is particularly evident in the presentation of the views of Be'eri's left-wing, feminist daughter only through his traditional nonemphatic eyes. Through the gaze of Be'eri, his daughter appears as an irrational extremist and at times almost as a caricature.

39. The novel's bibliographical list consists of an astonishing nineteen pages. The compilation was not printed in the novel itself but was available for readers online.

40. Gabriela Avigur-Rotem, interview by Shiri Goren, Avtalyon, Israel, July 11, 2007.

41. Translated by Adriana X. Jacobs and Shiri Goren.

Chapter 11

Forcing the End

Apocalyptic Israeli Fiction, 1971–2009

Adam Rovner

Nostalgia for Nightmare

Israelis know the world will end not with a whimper but a bang: a boom followed by shrill silence. Since the early 1990s, suicide bombers have detonated their explosive belts in public spaces, sidewalk cafes, and buses throughout the country. These visions of apocalypse are familiar from the nightly news—tattered, blood-streaked clothing hanging from tree branches, a thunderhead of diesel smoke rolling over a bus's blackened shell. Recent Hebrew literature depicts such images, of course, though cataclysmic scenarios appear as early as the 1970s. Hebrew literature's imaginings of future apocalypse have always been refracted through the prism of contemporary Israeli experience. My purpose in this essay is to provide an overview of how apocalypse has been figured in Hebrew letters of the last four decades. What follows is not a close reading of texts or a survey of theoretical literature on trauma and catastrophe. Instead, this essay offers a brief history of the end of time, as recorded in Israeli fiction from 1971 to 2009. I focus particularly on Hebrew literature that has found an audience among Anglophone readers in order to suggest the psychosocial significance these translated representations of The End have for readers in the Diaspora.

In the introduction to his valuable, albeit unfortunately named book, *The Boom in Contemporary Israeli Fiction*, scholar Alan Mintz laments that more Hebrew literature is not read and published in the United States. The reason for this oversight, he suggests, is that Hebrew literature provides "the kind of demystifying knowledge that many American Jews would sooner not have," since "the construction of American Jewishness is often dependent upon an idealization of Israel."[1] Mintz is surely correct in noting that American Jewry prefers a milk-and-honey-coated version of modern Israel. Nonetheless, he does not explain why nearly forty years worth of apocalyptic Hebrew fiction has in fact been translated into English worldwide, and is thus readily available to American readers.[2] I would argue that the central reason these literary works were selected for translation is precisely *because* they acknowledge that Israeli reality falls short of the Zionist ideals of cultural rebirth and national security. To clarify further: what explains the existence of these works in translation is that readers in the Diaspora seek to reinforce the mythology of Israel's heroism and military prowess, while at the same time they seek to retain a martyrology of Jewish victimization.

Mintz alludes to a similar animating impulse within Hebrew literature itself in a 1978 essay, "New Israeli Writing," later reprinted in *Translating Israel* (2001).[3] Mintz's essay notes that Israelis live in tension between a promise and a threat; they are caught between the secular messianism of Israel's founders and the exterminationist rhetoric of its neighbors. And so, he maintains, Hebrew literature reveals a twofold escape attempt from the anxieties of the present either by (1) seeking refuge in comforting visions of the past or (2) imagining a dissolution of uncertainty in a future end of history. Mintz emphasizes further that "one of the chief functions of Israel's literature, especially its prose literature, has been to represent and also to criticize [the] dual urge toward nostalgia and apocalypse in Israeli consciousness."[4] The tensions Israelis live under have not significantly diminished in the more than thirty years since Mintz first published his trenchant remarks, and neither has this tension in Hebrew literature been attenuated.

Oddly, in his essay Mintz does not actually focus on apocalyptic literature as critics tend to understand the genre and as I am using the term.[5] To most critics, apocalypse involves images of collective devastation, "a disaster . . . of overwhelming, disorienting magnitude," as critic James Berger succinctly defines it in *After the End*.[6] Nonetheless, Mintz's observation about the "dual urge" in Israeli consciousness remains valuable, and an exploration of explicitly apocalyptic Hebrew literature does indeed reveal an affinity between nostalgic and cataclysmic thinking. We might further say that some Israeli fictions imagine a kind of future Holocaust, going so far as to reveal, *pace* Arnold Band, a nostalgia *for* nightmare.

The phenomenon of apocalyptic Israeli literature participates in the wider Western trend toward literary and cinematic representations of disaster and its aftermath that has proliferated since the mid-twentieth century. The "myth of decadence"—images of an inevitable, fatal decline and fall—have existed since ancient times, of course.[7] But fiction and film visions of apocalypse flourished after revelations of the Holocaust in Europe, the atomic bombing of Hiroshima and Nagasaki, and of mass atrocities committed during the Vietnam War.[8] So although apocalyptic fiction is strictly speaking about the end of history, it is most assuredly a historically grounded genre. Israeli literary development over the last several decades suggests that misgivings about recent military actions in Lebanon and in the Occupied Territories, continued civilian vulnerability in the wake of terrorism, and the ever-present memories of the Holocaust have brought apocalyptic thinking to the fore. Yet the process of the literary reterritorialization of Israel from eternal holy land to land of eternal holy war remains uncharted.

Dream into Nightmare

From Isaiah's sublime vision of swords beaten into plowshares (2:4), to Zionist patriarch Theodor Herzl's prophesied Jewish state, the Jewish literary imagination has recorded the many promises of the promised land. Contemporary theory has exposed the instrumentality of literature and its spread through "print-capitalism" to the project of nationbuilding.[9] Yet perhaps only Herzl's vision of a reborn Jewish state in *Altneuland* (1902) may be said to have directly contributed to the emergence of a wholly new political and social order: the State of Israel. In *Altneuland,* Herzl imagined the creation of a Europeanized, modern, technocratic Jewish state in the Middle East. Herzl was influenced by other utopian visions of his era, most notably American Edward Bellamy's *Looking Backward* (1888), which appeared in an authorized German translation by radical American rabbi Solomon Schindler in 1890.[10] At one point in Herzl's novel, a character even discusses favorably the "noble communistic society" Bellamy's novel constructed.[11] The tree of literary filiation thus reveals how the chronotopic perspective of Bellamy's utopian novel was successfully disseminated through translation, then adopted and transformed by Herzl to suit his own literary and political commitments.

Herzl's *Altneuland* was published nearly simultaneously in 1902 in Nahum Sokolov's Hebrew translation as *Tel Aviv.* Sokolov attempted to capture the spirit in Modern Hebrew of the German (and Yiddish) title of Herzl's novel, which means "old-new land." Notably, the translator was forced to resort to a neologism that combines a term signifying an archaeological mound, "tel," with the word for "spring," the season of rebirth. The book appeared within a cultural context in which language and literature were important means for disseminating Zionist principles. The existence, diffusion, and influence of Herzl's prophetic work thus owes a particular debt to the cosmopolitan art of literary translation, which promoted the spread of fin de siècle reformist discourse. Indeed, this era witnessed a particular obsession with constructing an Edenic "universal language" to aid in international communication and thereby speed establishment of the brotherhood of man. The most famous effort to craft a universal language remains one-time Zionist Eliezer Zamenhof's Esperanto. In some ways, Modern Hebrew might even be considered a "constructed language"[12] aimed at cementing a common bond between members of far-flung Jewish communities, and thereby obviating the need for translators.

The very fact of a translated book's appearance in Hebrew in that era was evidence of Zionism's qualified successes. Tel Aviv, Israel's vibrant cultural capital, which celebrated its centennial in 2009, derives its name from Sokolov's Hebrew translation of Herzl's fantasy. I know of no other city whose name derives not only from fiction but also from translated fiction. Tel Aviv, in name and character, is forever marked by fin de siècle trends of cosmopolitan intellectualism. Few countries demonstrate as strong a link between nation and narration as modern-day Israel. Broad boulevards lined with once-refined Bauhaus buildings, their stucco facades now chipped from the bite of salt air, testify to Tel Aviv's past as a European vision of the Jewish future. Tel Aviv, you might say, is a faded New Jerusalem. Streets bearing the names of writers like George Eliot and Émile Zola make the city's roadmap read like a philosemitic college syllabus. As with so many borders in Israel, the ones between literature and life are blurry.

Utopian literature is notable as a genre for revealing many cross-border incursions between the domains of the fictive and the real. Indeed, utopian literature's story worlds have historically been viewed as instruments in the struggle to transform the real world. The philosophical and sociological "foundational principles" of utopias explicitly aim to reform society; fundamentally, utopias seek to call into being a new world and sweep the old one away.[13] From its inception, Zionism revealed itself as a utopian nationalist project in its efforts to create a Jewish state, a reborn people, and an alternative Jewish ("Hebrew") culture. And while utopian writers and thinkers as diverse as H. G. Wells and V. I. Lenin imagined that a new breed of human must first come into being in order to institute and perpetuate paradise, Herzlian Zionism imagines that the territorial paradise of Israel will call forth a new breed of Jew.[14] According to normative Zionist thinking, the establishment of an independent Israel promised to put an end to centuries of homelessness, and would, following World War II, provide a measure of consolation for the destruction of European Jewry in the Shoah. To once again cite Isaiah, such territorial utopianism gestures toward the redemptive and "making the crooked straight" (40:4). The fundamental "religious nature of utopianism" has long been recognized, and Herzlian Zionism is no exception.[15] However, the eschatological strivings of Zionist thinking pose a central challenge to rabbinic prohibitions against hastening the messianic era—against "forcing the end" [Dehikat Haketz]. Many ultra-Orthodox Jews reject Zionism because it contravenes this injunction. Thus utopian thinking both undergirds the Jewish imagination and is anathema to it.

Zionism, considered as a messianic project, endorses the essential axiom of utopian thinking; that is, that "utopia presumes that something (the rotten state of society, human corruption, gender difference, or life on earth) must first come to an end."[16] Utopian thinking always contains within it the seeds of apocalyptic thinking about the "End." Naturally, Zionism too has always been pregnant with apocalypse. Many canonical Hebrew writers reveal themselves to be both prophets of consolation, forecasting a Jewish renaissance, and prophets of rage, predicting Jewish decline if their calls for reform go unheeded. Since Israel's establishment, Hebrew literature has inscribed in its pages this thematic of redemption and destruction, which makes its presence felt in everyday idiomatic Hebrew. To cite one well-known example, the Shoah, the systematic murder of two-thirds of European Jewry, is linked in the same breath with *Tequma,* the heroic struggle for Jewish national revival in a prelapsarian Israel. Those generations who did not witness or participate in the dyad of catastrophe (Shoah) and rebirth (Tequma) have come both after the *end,* and after the *beginning*. Consequently, a sense of belatedness is common in Israeli arts and culture.

This sense of belatedness, which has appeared at least since the 1970s, has become less wistful in the intervening decades and more sharply critical of contemporary Israeli society. Some literary representations of Israel, generally termed post-Zionist, elaborate on the failings of Zionism and question Israel's contribution to Jewish continuity. Today, literary scholars in both America and Israel tend to construe apocalyptic Hebrew literature as post-Zionist, and hence subversive. Yet these scholars are unable to account for the fact that significant authors and central texts of this so-called post-Zionist wave of fiction are somehow both radical *and* representative of Hebrew literature.[17] The resolution to this paradox is straightforward: post-Zionist writers are not in fact radical. Their works are representative because they respond directly to the messianic foundation of the Zionist project, and in many cases to Herzl's central utopian text, *Altneuland.* Like utopian literature, dystopian literature and apocalyptic literature serve as reformist discourse. Passages that scholars often identify as "post-Zionist" protest within contemporary Hebrew letters are in fact reifications of the system post-Zionism supposedly seeks to dismantle.

"Post-Zionist" writers present dystopian and apocalyptic scenarios as deviations from the ideal, that is, the utopian Zionism of fin de siècle progressivism. The utopianism of Herzl and other late nineteenth-and early twentieth-century writers is undone in apocalyptic Israeli literature of the late twentieth and early twenty-first centuries—undone to be made anew. Hebrew literature's utopic and dystopic fictions endorse a vision of Zionism whose decadence and perversion they decry. In so doing, these texts treat Zionism as transhistorical; indeed, they fundamentally promote Zionism as Jewish telos. The so-called post-Zionist texts tend to treat the Jewish national project as a crooked thing to be made straight, not as something whose time has passed. Contemporary Israeli literature might then more rightly be considered postapocalyptic rather than post-Zionist. And given Israeli fiction's longing backward glance toward a utopian—that is, emphatically *modernist*—conception of Israel, can much of contemporary Hebrew literature even be considered "postmodern" at all?

There is nothing new in Jewish literature about predicting the end as a means to forestall it. In its search for spiritual perfection, the Jewish imagination has seen apocalypse augured in Israel's landscape for millennia. From its first chapters, the Hebrew Bible records the devolution of God's handiwork: sinful Adam and Eve are expelled from Eden, the rape-ocracies of Sodom and Gomorrah are destroyed by sulfurous rain, and the Israelites witness their territory become "a land that eateth up its inhabitants" (Numbers 13:32). Only a few short passages after Isaiah's promise of ultimate peace, he foresees a day of judgment in which "every tall tower" will be brought low (2:15). These words echo uncannily today after the terrorist attacks in the US on 9/11. Later, Ezekiel's manic visions of the wars of Gog and Magog set new standards for destruction: convulsive earthquakes, doomsday battles, plagues of pestilence and blood, and terrifying storms that ravage the land (chapters 38–39). Under the blazing Mediterranean sun, a people less persecuted than the Jews would have had to blind themselves to conjure such dark futures.

Today Ezekiel's nightmares are embraced as a playbook by everyone from evangelical Christians, who rapturously read the *Left Behind* series, to Jewish messianic nationalists, whose faith in God does not preclude their packing Uzis.[18] Small wonder, then, that the name of a peak on Israel's topographic map, Har Megiddo, was slurred into the everyday English synonym for the end of days: *Armageddon*. Even Arab nations seem to read Ezekiel for inspiration, threatening to "throw the Jews into the sea," turn Tel Aviv into a "crematorium," or "wipe Israel off the map" entirely.[19] Given these hostile pronouncements, it comes as little surprise that Israelis are entrenched in a siege mentality.

Herzl's epilogue to *Altneuland* challenges readers to create a Jewish homeland, stating that "if you will it, it is no dream."[20] The modern Israeli nation-state has thus been summoned from the language of fiction, from the world of dreams. Speech *acts* and words *write* the Jewish future. So Israelis naturally fear their enemies' genocidal sentences will build toward the exclamation mark of oblivion. Arab exterminationist dreams become Israeli nightmares. And though the world may think Israel a military Goliath armed to the teeth, Israelis see themselves as a beleaguered remnant of a persecuted people, chastened by the history of anti-Semitism and haunted by the Holocaust. The understandable paranoia of Jews in the twentieth century has given rise both to Israel's militaristic culture and to a profound discomfort with its newfound power. The results of this ambivalence are literary works that tend toward the apocalyptic. In some cases, this literature is a conscious or unconscious revision (or subversion) of Herzl's *Altneuland,* as Yigal Schwartz has demonstrated in *Do You Know Where the Lemon Blooms* (2007).[21] Sir Isaiah Berlin, suggested that the decline of utopian thinking in the west is due to twentieth-century acknowledgment of the incommensurability of subjective experience and personal values.[22] In Israel the replacement of literary utopia by its secret-sharer, dystopia, suggests that others' subjectivities and values—and others' grievances—may have broken through the scrim of ideology to achieve recognition.

Imagining the End: 1971–2009

Many in Israel's peace camp recognize that the ongoing flares of war and spasms of terror in the region may be blamed on the country's occupation of the Palestinian people. Just after the nation's swift victory in 1967's Six-Day War, a paradoxical fascination with Israel's destruction appeared in Hebrew literature and has continued apace for the last four decades. Celebrated author and peace activist Amos Oz channeled these anxieties early on in his novella *Late Love* [Ahavah Meuheret] (trans. 1975 [1971]). The aging narrator, Shraga Unger, is a chain-smoking, sour-smelling grotesque person who travels the length and breadth of Israel to warn of impending disaster at the hands of the Soviet-supported Arab nations who aim to "kill the whole Jewish people with a single blow."[23] Shraga views apocalypse as inevitable, and Israel merely an "unstable, impermanent, almost pathetic" sliver of land "stretching between the arching sea and the vast deserts."[24] He imagines Soviet saboteurs walking about undetected, and Siberian snowstorms that will sweep in to wipe "Tel Aviv completely off the face of the earth."[25] In these passages and others, the age-old anti-Semitism of Russia follows Jews from the motherland to their new homeland, arms their enemies, and remains as implacable a foe as the weather.

The more immediate threat, however, is the internal corruption of the Zionist ideal symbolized by environmental degradation. His old friend Liuba insists that "acids, filth, [and] gas" choke the food and water, turning Tel Aviv, once "a bright town, caressed by the breeze" and "the tang of the sea," into a wasteland.[26] The city and the ideals upon which it was founded have been "trampled . . . underfoot."[27] In the face of such deterioration, Shraga is forced to agree that "time is running out, running out."[28] Tel Aviv's degeneration and the threat of Israel's destruction that Shraga imagines parallel his own physical ruin. As in many subsequent Israeli works of fiction, the human body and the body politic are inseparable.

The misery of Shraga's present makes him despair of the future, and so he impotently longs to rectify the sorrowful recent past of Jewish victimization. Shraga conjures a revenge fantasy wherein "an armored Jewish maelstrom . . . inscribing a savage Hebrew message" spreads across Europe as they defeat the Nazis and other "butchers of the Jews."[29] Ultimately, Shraga's imagination blasts into outer space, envisioning spaceships that transport the Jewish people "to some faraway planet in another galaxy . . . beyond the reach of any power" where they can "rebuild a kind of heavenly Jerusalem."[30] In Oz's novella, the promised land is forever deferred, Jerusalem remains a spiritual ideal suspended beyond reach, and the end is always nigh.

The late Amos Kenan, a harsh critic of Israeli policies, crafted Hebrew literature's most famous apocalyptic novel, *The Road to Ein Harod* [Haderekh el Ein Harod] (trans. 1988 [1984]), just three years before the first Palestinian intifada erupted in 1987.[31] The book takes its name from an early kibbutz that became a powerful symbol of Israel's utopian aspirations. As a closed collectivist structure of enforced conformity, the intentional community of the kibbutz conceals the dystopian within its utopian foundation. Perhaps it is in the kibbutz, also the topography of much of Oz's early fiction, that one can most clearly see in microcosm how a utopian civilization breeds dystopian discontent. Political Zionism aimed to end Jewish homelessness by restoring Jews to their ancestral land and having them work the land, which pioneers did on kibbutzim throughout Israel. But to accomplish this, the movement's leaders jettisoned thousands of years of Jewish culture in favor of creating a "New Hebrew" who would plow the fields and bear arms to defend them. Kenan's novel notes the link between this rhetoric of rebirth and the dangers of such a rupture: "[They] conceived of a new world, a different one, but what finally came to pass was that even the old world was obliterated."[32] What remains, the book implies, is a long road going nowhere.

In Kenan's depraved new world, the protagonist rebels against a military junta that seizes power and proceeds to "cleanse" the country through the murder of liberal dissidents and Arabs. The sardonic hero, a former soldier who once drove Palestinians from their villages, must now team with an Arab insurgent to guide him across hostile territory. Echoes of the Holocaust appear when they witness mass killings and bodies tumbling into an open pit: "One of the military men, an officer it seems, orders the others to line up. [. . .] Fire. The people fall down. A small bulldozer drives up and quickly digs a ditch. The soldiers roll the bodies in, and the dozer covers them up."[33] Here, as in Oz's novel, the memory of the Nazi war against the Jews is projected onto a cataclysmic future confrontation with Arabs and internal enemies. The doomsday motif becomes explicit when the mismatched pair makes their way to the sanctuary of "Free Ein Harod" and pass through Har Megiddo. "Armageddon is always waiting for you"; the hero reminds himself—and the reader—of the term's derivation.[34] Later, he is taken prisoner by a revenge-obsessed general who launches "circumtemporal" missiles back through time to obliterate historical enemies of the Jews: Nebuchadnezzar, Titus, and Cossack hetman Khmelnitsky to name but a few.[35] Here, as in Oz's novella, the past of Jewish victimization must be mastered in order to forestall Israeli vulnerability. When the protagonist does finally emerge from an underground bunker, he sees that Israel has returned to a pastoral, biblical landscape, "a blossoming meadow of green."[36] Apocalyptic futures compel writers to seek utopia in the past. And Kenan, like others, suggests the world must be destroyed in order to be saved.[37]

Two acclaimed novels by Orly Castel-Bloom are more playful, but no less dark than Kenan's. The perverse *Dolly City* (trans. 1997 [1992]) appeared during the First Intifada when Palestinians armed with slingshots battled Israeli soldiers in the streets of Gaza and throughout the West Bank. The novel offers a hallucinatory trip through a hellish version of Tel Aviv called Dolly City, "the most demented city in the world."[38] There everyone is on the run, and "since they're always running, there's always someone chasing them, and since there's someone chasing them, they catch them, execute them and throw them in the river."[39] Our tour guide on this lunatic safari is Dolly, who lends her name to the surreal city whose contours shift and melt like a Dalí landscape. The city's architecture and external geography are mapped to Dolly's own warped internal psychology.[40] The novel suggests that reality is constructed by perception and incommensurable values, and that the real world stubbornly remains a function of radical subjectivity.

Dolly herself is a failed doctor who kills and tortures without provocation or conscience. She defends her violence, noting that if "the State of Israel can't control the Arabs in the territories, how can anybody expect me, a private individual, to control the occupied territory inside me?"[41] Throughout the novel, the heroine uses her scalpel to carve a border-shifting "map of the Land of Israel"[42] into her adopted son's back, brutalizing him in an attempt to bind him to her and to the state: *l'etat, c'est elle*. The world of Dolly City, with its lunatic cast of magicians, doctors, rabbis, politicians, and pseudo-Zionist ideologues, turns the Jewish state into a phantasmagoric house of horrors where children are sacrificed in the name of expanding borders, and where the memory of the Holocaust underlies self-destructive neuroses.

Massive four-hundred-story apartment towers thrust skyward from Dolly City's filthy streets, suicides plummet to their deaths, imaginary cancers riddle the cityscape, and all trains run to Dachau. Dolly's actions clearly invoke the Holocaust when she travels to Germany to kidnap a baby in order to "remove his kidney, and transplant it in to the body of my only son."[43] She chooses Germany because "of all the people that ever lived, [the Germans] were the most swinish."[44] Ultimately, she makes her way to an orphanage, which for Dolly becomes a site for cruel experimentation that resonates with memories of sadistic Nazi doctors. At one point, Dolly leaves the orphaned babies "lying there with their guts spilling out" while she takes a coffee break.[45] Nonetheless, the woman who runs the orphanage, and who identifies herself as the granddaughter of an SS officer, tells her there is "no need . . . to feel any guilt whatsoever" for the cruelty she provokes.[46] Dolly's apocalyptic world reveals morality as a luxury, and her resultant worldview substitutes the Jew as victimizer for the Jew as victim.[47] The explicit evocation of Nazi crimes and German guilt in the novel does not function to create a moral equivalency with Dolly City's fugue-state of Israel. On the contrary, the logic of Dolly's mad discourse is exculpatory. Dolly's promiscuous violence stands in for an Israeli paranoia that sees every threat as existential, and hence all actions as justifiable, based on the long history of Jewish suffering and vulnerability. Susan Sontag noted in her discussion of "the imagination of disaster" that doomsday scenarios frequently provide an "extreme moral simplification" in which "one can give outlet to cruel or at least amoral feelings."[48] In confirmation of Sontag's observation, the Israeli imagination of disaster frequently discloses amoral fantasies of extreme violence, nowhere more so than in Castel-Bloom's work.

The author's febrile and yet more somber depiction of a doomsday Israel, *Human-Parts* [Halakim Enoshi'im] (trans. 2004 [2002]), appeared a decade later during the Second Intifada. The Palestinian weapon of choice by that time had evolved into the explosive belt packed with shrapnel. In an era that had increasingly embraced the irrational, Castel-Bloom was forced to write in a hyperrealistic mode. Palestinians appear in the novel almost exclusively as terrorists who turn human lives into "human parts" with the push of a button. Here, unlike in *Dolly City*, Jews are cast as victims. And while explicit references to the Holocaust are absent in the book, the visions of burned bodies incinerated in suicide bombings evoke the ever-present European trauma as well as Israel's reality. The book opens with a journalistic account of people "blown to pieces . . . on the bus, at the railway station, at the café . . . and just crossing a busy street."[49] Afterward, survivors recall their terror with the same formula—"Suddenly I heard a boom"—a phrase all too often repeated on Israeli TV and radio by witnesses to carnage.[50]

Such journalistic banalities are central to Castel-Bloom's novel and aesthetic, as scholar Todd Hasak-Lowy has noted.[51] Celebrity reporters in the novel channel the disembodied voices of average Israelis who fear their cross-town trip will end with their bodies on a slab at the forensic pathology institute of Abu Kabir. There, corpses are identified by "teeth, hands, shoes, rings," but sometimes there's just "nothing left to bury and they put in stones, or pieces of wood, so that the family will think they're burying something."[52] The government is unable to deal with the emergency. The exhausted president collapses under the strain, and his cabinet can only pursue a policy of restraint despite the "scores of deaths" caused by mounting terrorist attacks.[53] The flip side to this image of Israel's living hell is the virginal heaven promised to the Islamist *shaheed,* or martyr, who detonates himself in the name of jihad. Dystopia and utopia, those estranged blood brothers, pitch their tents close by.

Despite its obvious grimness, *Human Parts* swings into gallows humor with descriptions of a "Saudi flu" epidemic and violent weather "straight from the North Pole" that dumps eight feet of snow on Israel, while hailstones clobber pedestrians, and sailboats float through the flooded streets of Tel Aviv's exurbs.[54] No clear answer for the climatic aberrations are forthcoming, though a "geologist and expert on environmental studies" suggests that an undersea volcano erupted, thereby causing the disruptions and spewing sulfur dioxide into the nation's water.[55] As for the influenza outbreak, some speculate that it is part of an Arab program of "biological warfare."[56] Israel's doctors and hospitals are overwhelmed: "whoever didn't die by suicide bombs or car bombs died of the Saudi flu."[57] The body count mounts to such an extent that "in the cemeteries they began to bury the corpses one on top of the other."[58] As in Oz's *Late Love,* recurrent images of the frailty of bodies and the degradations of the environment expose an imaginary Israel on the verge of collapse in *Human Parts.*

The natural world flung into chaos is also the setting for Nava Semel's *And the Rat Laughs* [Tzhok Shel Achbarosh] (trans. 2008 [2001]), a novel that focuses specifically on Holocaust history and memory. In the penultimate section of the novel, Semel imagines a "Great Ecological Disaster" in the year 2025, which gives rise to a cybernetic society on the cusp of the twenty-second century.[59] The Shoah has been forgotten as a moral imperative in this storyworld: "When we're in the grip of the past," one character admonishes, "we relive all of the scourges [of] . . . violence, brutality, fear, and rage."[60] The memory of Jewish suffering in the Shoah therefore persists only as a dimly recollected myth distorted beyond recognition, popularized and commodified through anime, video games, and pop songs. Even the past itself has been overcome—that is, excised—thanks to "memory bypass" surgery.[61] Despite the powerful taboos against uncovering Holocaust history, an anthropologist's clandestine research takes her to the sovereign micronation of TheIsrael in a quest to retrieve something of the suppressed past.

TheIsrael is described as "a society addicted to the present . . . and determined to focus exclusively on whatever will serve to justify its future existence."[62] This fascination with the present has even led TheIsrael to abandon its "Zionist ideology and [the] Jewish religion."[63] Much like Israel in 2009, Semel's fictional state in 2099 views its survival only in the "short-term."[64] Such anxieties endure despite TheIsrael's territorial divorce from its enemy, ThePalestine. In Semel's novel, TheIsrael's concern over its future is not remediated by a two-state solution. Instead, TheIsrael's "obliteration of the past has led to a pathological distortion in the way they perceive the future"—a future that always "includes a cataclysm."[65] Semel's twin specters of amnesia and paranoia provide a snapshot of a contemporary Israeli society scarred by yesterday and fearful of tomorrow. As is no doubt clear by now, early Zionism's rhapsodies over Israel's pastoral terrain give way in the literature of the new millennium to panoramas of catastrophe. Hebrew apocalyptic fiction focuses obsessively on geography and environment because in contemporary

Israeli society, it is land—territory, homeland, place—that is valued at the expense of the individual. In these narratives, place has power, individuals lack power.[66]

One of Israel's brightest talents, author and playwright Savyon Liebrecht, crafts an even bleaker future than does Semel in the title story of her collection, *A Good Place for the Night* [Makom Tov LaLeilah] (trans. 2005 [2002]). Gila, an Israeli traveling through Europe by train, survives an unidentified catastrophe "much worse than Chernobyl," thanks to her nicotine habit.[67] The walls of the smoking car wherein she indulges her addiction somehow shield her and an American man from a deadly force that lays waste to the world. In the aftermath, only a grisly tableau of corpses frozen in lust and grimace remains. Gila and the American become a kind of postapocalyptic Adam and Eve who wander the ruins of Poland, set up house on the edge of a contaminated zone, and struggle to avoid a mysterious funnel that threatens to swallow up everything in its path. As in other apocalyptic texts, a hostile and arbitrary environment—funnel clouds and dead zones—limit the abilities of characters to express their autonomy. Landscape becomes destiny.

The night after the blast, Gila thinks of how her mother in Israel will receive news of the disaster, and likens her own fate to that of her brother, a casualty of war: "Her mother would get into bed like she had when told of the death of her son in Lebanon and refuse to eat or drink."[68] Three years later, with no sign of rescue from her stark nightmare world, Gila's pessimism has grown to the point that she recognizes that Israel too may have been destroyed: "Who knows what she would find at home [in Jerusalem] . . . Maybe the Arabs, the former owners, had come back to reclaim the house . . . Maybe the house was deserted and the turquoise shutters had rotted and her beloved family was sitting motionless" like those who had been killed in the catastrophe on the train.[69] In Gila's imagination, Arab return to Israel is equated with total catastrophe.

Like Semel, Liebrecht is well known in Israel as a writer preoccupied with Holocaust memory and the second-generation's relationship to the past. This paratextual knowledge helps position her tale as a kind of Holocaust survival narrative. Indeed, early on Gila imagines the joy that will greet news of her miraculous escape in precisely these terms: "How happy they'll be when they find out she was one of the survivors!"[70] The fact that Gila endures on the funereal ground of Poland further reveals Liebrecht's story to be a kind of futurist Holocaust fiction. Several references to the memory of the Shoah are even more unmistakable. The invocation of a train journey through Poland involving "smoking cars" that *allow* for Jewish survival serves as a clear indication of the bitter ironies that structure the thematics of trauma in Liebrecht's tale. The transposition of survival from the national homeland to a temporary "good place for the night" on foreign soil intimately connects twenty-first-century Israeli vulnerability with Jewish decimation in mid-twentieth-century Europe.[71]

Traumatic memory is also at the heart of Ari Folman's graphic novelization of *Waltz with Bashir* (trans. 2009 [2008]), based on his Academy Award–nominated film of the same name. In Israel, the film is often referred to as a homegrown *Apocalypse Now,* highlighting the parallels the Vietnam War has to the Lebanon War within Israeli culture, and by analogy, to apocalyptic thinking. Folman has noted that his familiarity with graphic novels originally influenced his animated documentary and led to its book adaptation, which features illustrations by animator-artist David Polonsky, who also collaborated with Folman on the film.[72]

The story follows Folman's efforts to regain repressed memories of his military service during Israel's invasion of Lebanon. To fill in the holes of his past, he interviews other veterans tortured by flashbacks and night terrors, which are rendered by Polonsky in vivid, chromatic tones. Snarling dogs charge through the streets of Tel Aviv. A naked giantess emerges from the Mediterranean. Dead soldiers come to life in a zombie-like marine landing along a beachfront promenade. And then, Folman's illustrated stand-in recalls, "suddenly—boom! . . . My memory blew wide open."[73] Images of Tel Aviv's prosperity dissolve into a bullet-riddled and cratered Beirut. The text (and film) not only suggest these two cities are apocalyptic mirror images but also firmly link Jewish vulnerability in Israel to Palestinian misery. The vision of Tel Aviv degenerating into an apocalyptic Lebanon warns readers that Israeli achievements can collapse in the blink of an eye. One possible reading of these scenes suggests that Israeli society must remember the recent Jewish past of victimization in the Holocaust and in warfare with Arab enemies in order to do justice to the Palestinians in their midst today. A second possible reading suggests that Israeli society must be on constant alert, opting for aggressive action rather than risk becoming vulnerable.

Following the assassination of Lebanese president-elect Bashir Gemayel, his Christian supporters sought revenge against their Muslim countrymen, leading to the slaughter of hundreds, if not thousands, of Palestinians in the Sabra and Shatila refugee camps in 1982. The term *camps* is doubly resonant in the graphic novel and film. Folman witnessed the attack's aftermath as a teenage recruit. And while the Israeli military did not take part in the massacre, they allowed Christian militia to enter the camps and were slow to stop the bloodshed. Both of Folman's parents were Auschwitz survivors, and much like Art Spiegelman does in *Maus* (1986, 1991), the author-narrator struggles with the unspoken terrors that haunt him and his family. Folman finally comes to the realization that his blindness to the atrocities he witnessed are a cipher for his family's—and his society's—inability to come to terms both with the Holocaust and with Israel's oppression of the Palestinians. Still, despite the underlying indictment of Israeli disregard of Palestinian suffering, the invocation of Holocaust memory serves to justify Jewish national aims. The novel and film preserve the oscillation between images of the Israeli as victim—or potential victim—and images of the Israeli as victimizer. Here, as in the other works discussed, nostalgia for nightmare ultimately reaffirms the Zionist metanarrative and provides a critique of social reality's deviation from the ideal.

The End

Historian Yosef Hayim Yerushalmi contended that fiction, in particular the novel, "provides at least a temporary modern surrogate" for the "metahistorical myth[s]" that allow Jews to confront their past and their future.[74] The metahistorical myths found in apocalyptic Hebrew literature allow readers to confront the catastrophe of the European Jewish past and the terrors of the Israeli present, even as they imagine a cataclysmic future. Israeli fiction of The End may be seen as a kind of Holocaust literature that exposes the recent trauma of the Jews as victims, while at the same time hinting that the role of Jews as victimizers may too bring about catastrophe. In a kind of return of the repressed, apocalyptic Hebrew literature connects the fate of dispossessed Palestinians to Jewish vulnerability during the Shoah. Taboos against linking together Jewish and non-Jewish suffering are more powerful in the Diaspora than in Israel. To paraphrase and quote Ludwig Wittgenstein, the translation of Hebrew texts into English may thus be a way of allowing non-Israeli readers of English to "speak about what must otherwise be passed over in silence" within their Diasporic communities.[75]

Knowledge of Jewish vulnerability during the Shoah, marginalized by the Zionist metanarrative that rejects victimhood, and knowledge of Palestinian persecution, suppressed by the Zionist metanarrative that insists upon a purity of arms, each attempt to displace the other in a battle for psychic terrain in these works. Yet Hebrew writers, their Israeli audience, and an elite of Anglophone readers have edged ever closer to acknowledging Arab Israeli writer Emile Habiby's still controversial assertion that "your Holocaust [was] our disaster."[76] As Habiby implies, and as Walter Benjamin's angel of history observes, in the end we can see only "one single catastrophe which keeps piling wreckage upon wreckage."[77] And from this perspective we learn that history has neither angels nor devils, just men and women who are products of their times.

Notes

1. Alan Mintz, *The Boom in Contemporary Israeli Fiction* (Hanover, NH: Brandeis University Press, 1997), 6.

2. There are, of course, a number of apocalyptic works since the 1970s, some significant, that have not been translated into English, including Yitzhak Ben-Ner's *Angels Are Coming* ([Malachim Ba'im] 1987); Hagai Dagan's *The Land Is Sailing* ([Ha'aretz Shatah] 2007); Boaz Izraeli's *Where Is Everyone* ([Eyfoh Kulam] 1997); Amos Kenan's *Shoah II* (1975); and Benjamin Tammuz's *Jeremiah's Inn* ([Pundako Shel Yeremiyahu] 1984).

3. Alan Mintz, *Translating Israel: Contemporary Hebrew Literature and Its Reception in America* (Syracuse, NY: Syracuse University Press, 2001).

4. Alan Mintz, "New Israeli Writing," *Commentary* 65, no. 1 (1978): 64.

5. For example, the works Mintz considers by authors such as Shulamith Hareven, Aharon Appelfeld, and A. B. Yehoshua do not present images of collective devastation, which I take to be essential to be considered apocalyptic. The texts Mintz examines are about the personal experience of catastrophe, not about impersonal destruction. Aharon Appelfeld's *Badenheim,* while it treats the Holocaust, does so only in an allegorical manner and presents no truly apocalyptic scenarios. One could claim that the city of Badenheim does become a kind of dystopia, however.

6. James Berger, *After the End: Representations of Post-Apocalypse* (Minneapolis: University of Minnesota Press, 1999), 6.

7. Matei Calinescu, *Five Faces of Modernity* (Durham, NC: Duke University Press, 2006), 151.

8. See Berger's identification of some of these same events as animating postapocalyptic American literature in *After the End*, xii. See also Susan Sontag's discussion of nuclear war and the historicity of apocalypse in "The Imagination of Disaster," in *Against Interpretation and Other Essays* (New York: Farrar, Straus and Giroux, 1966), 218, 224.

9. Benedict Anderson, *Imagined Communities* (New York: Verso, 2003), 36.

10. See Arthur Mann, "Solomon Schindler: Boston Radical," *New England Quarterly* 23, no. 4 (1950): 468. Schindler later penned his own sequel to Bellamy's book, *Young West* (1894).

11. Theodor Herzl, *Old-New Land (Altneuland)*, trans. Lotta Levenson (New York: Bloch Publishing, 1960), 145.

12. In this vein, see Benjamin Harshav, *Language in Time of Revolution* (Berkeley: University of California Press, 1993), and Itamar Even-Zohar, "The Emergence of a Native Hebrew Culture in Palestine, 1882–1948," *Poetics Today* 11, no. 1 (1990): 175–91.

13. Leona Toker, "*Hard Times* and a Critique of Utopia: A Typological Study," *Narrative* 4, no. 3 (1996): 219.

14. John Carey, introduction to *The Faber Book of Utopias*, ed. John Carey (London: Faber and Faber, 1999), xiii–xiv.

15. Calinescu, *Five Faces of Modernity*, 63.

16. Natalia Skradol and Ephraim Sicher, "A World Neither Brave Nor New: Reading Dystopian Fiction after 9/11," *Partial Answers* 4, no. 1 (2006): 154.

17. Sacvan Bercovitch notes this paradox in American literary studies and relates it to the utopian imagination in "The Problem of Ideology in American Literary History," *Critical Inquiry* 12, no. 4 (1986): 644.

18. This series of remarkably popular books by Tim LaHaye and Jerry B. Jenkins dramatizes the end of days and the rapture according to fundamentalist Protestant theology.

19. This much-quoted threat has been distorted over time, but finds its source in claims made in 1967 by Ahmad al-Shuqayri, one of the founders of the PLO. For a history of this infamous threat, see Moshe Shemesh, "Did Shuqayri Call for 'Throwing the Jews into the Sea?'" *Israel Studies* 8, no. 2 (2003): 70–81. The Iraqi military claimed in fact it had done so during the First Gulf War. See *Human Rights Watch World Report 1992* (New York: Human Rights Watch, 1991): 687. The Iranian president, Mahmoud Ahmadinejad, stated this in 2006. See Ethan Bronner, "Just How Far Did They Go, Those Words against Israel?" *New York Times*, June 11, 2006, 4.

20. This version of Herzl's injunction is most commonly cited both in idiomatic Hebrew and in its English translation. The rendering of the German original provided by the English translator is, "if you do not wish it, all this . . . will remain a fable." See Herzl, *Old-New Land (Altneuland)*, 296.

21. Schwartz discusses this point explicitly in *Do You Know the Land Where the Lemon Blooms: Human Engineering and Landscape Conceptualization in Hebrew Literature* (Hebrew) (Or Yehuda: Kinneret, Zmora-Bitan, Dvir, 2007), 89. He addresses Herzl's *Old-New Land (Altneuland)* in general on pp. 83–159 (Hebrew).

22. Isaiah Berlin, "The Decline of Utopian Thinking in the West," in *The Crooked Timber of Humanity: Chapters in the History of Ideas*, ed. Henry Hardy (New York: Knopf, 1991), 20–48.

23. Amos Oz, "Late Love," in *Unto Death*, trans. Nicholas de Lange (New York: Harcourt Brace Jovanovich, 1975), 99.

24. Ibid., 162.

25. Ibid., 102, 119.

26. Ibid., 141, 147–48.

27. Ibid., 149.

28. Ibid., 150.

29. Ibid., 154, 156.

30. Ibid., 163.

31. The novel has an interesting history in English and was translated twice, once from the original Hebrew in 1986 by a pseudonymous translator for a London-based specialty publisher, and again in 1988 from the French translation for Grove Press. It appears that the pseudonymous translator, M. Hutzpit, is actually Dina Hecht. The name "Hutzpit" likely derives from the martyred rabbinic sage, Rabbi Hutzpit, known as "the interpreter." I have learned from personal correspondence with the Institute for the Translation of Hebrew Literature (Hilla Megged, e-mail message to the author, October 15, 2008) and with Grove-Atlantic (Meredith Kessler, e-mail message to the author, October 7, 2008) that the Saqi Books edition is unauthorized, despite its reprint in 2001. My suspicion is that Saqi, a specialty house devoted to Arab-and Islamic-interest works, published Kenan's text because of its indictment of the Israeli military and political establishment. Kenan's wife is also unaware of the Saqi book's version according to Megged. Given the questionable legal status of the Hutzpit/Hecht translation and its relative unavailability, I have elected to quote from the authorized Hollo translation.

32. Amos Kenan, *The Road to Ein Harod,* trans. Anselm Hollo (New York: Grove Press, 1988), 30.

33. Ibid., 29.

34. Ibid., 30.

35. Ibid., 99–101.

36. Ibid., 104.

37. This logic of the End is reminiscent of American apocalyptic thinking following the Vietnam War. Such logic reached its apotheosis in the infamous quote (1968), variously attributed, regarding the Tet Offensive: "we had to destroy the village in order to save it."

38. Orly Castel-Bloom, *Dolly City,* trans. Dalya Bilu (London: Loki Books, 1997), 88.

39. Ibid.

40. Cf. Todd Hasak-Lowy, "Postzionism and Its Aftermath: The Case of Orly Castel-Bloom," *Jewish Social Studies: History, Culture, Society* 14, no. 2 (2008): 93.

41. Castel-Bloom, *Dolly City,* 110.

42. Ibid., 132.

43. Ibid., 51.

44. Ibid.

45. Ibid., 54.

46. Ibid., 55.

47. See Berger on the jettisoning of morality in postapocalyptic worlds in *After the End,* 8.

48. Sontag, "The Imagination of Disaster," 215.

49. Orly Castel-Bloom, *Human Parts,* trans. Dalya Bilu (Boston: David R. Godine, 2004), 6.

50. Ibid., 7.

51. Hasak-Lowy, "Postzionism and Its Aftermath," 97.

52. Ibid., 101.

53. Ibid., 100–101.

54. Ibid., 3–4.

55. Ibid., 15–16.

56. Ibid., 23.

57. Ibid.

58. Ibid., 24.

59. Nava Semel, *And the Rat Laughed,* trans. Miriam Shlesinger (Melbourne, Australia: Hybrid Publishers, 2008), 130.

60. Ibid., 126–27.

61. Ibid., 149.

62. Ibid., 142.

63. Ibid., 143.

64. Ibid.

65. Ibid.

66. Compare Sontag on science fiction disaster films in "The Imagination of Disaster," 216.

67. Savyon Liebrecht, *A Good Place for the Night* (New York: Persea Books, 2005), 224.

68. Ibid., 226.

69. Ibid., 228.

70. Ibid., 226.

71. Perhaps the title of Liebrecht's tale recalls Max Nordau's support of the British government's offer to the Zionist movement of territory within the East African Protectorate, a proposal Nordau termed a *nachtasyl,* or "night shelter."

72. See Liel Liebovitz, "This Animated Life: An Interview with David Polonsky," *Words without Borders: The Online Magazine for International Literature,* http://wordswithoutborders.org/article/this-animated-life-an-interview-with-david-polonsky/, February 3, 2009.

73. Ari Folman, *Waltz with Bashir: A Lebanon War Story,* trans. Riva Hocherman, art by David Polonsky (New York: Metropolitan Books, 2009), 28.

74. Yosef Hayim Yerushalmi, *Zakhor: Jewish History and Jewish Memory* (Seattle: University of Washington Press, 1982), 98.

75. Cf. Ludwig Wittgenstein, *Tractatus Logico-Philosophicus,* trans. D. F. Pears and B. F. McGuinness (New York: Routledge, 1974), 89.

76. Emile Habiby, "Your Holocaust—Our Disaster," *Politika* 8 (1986): 26–27 (Hebrew).

77. Walter Benjamin, "Theses on the Philosophy of History," in *Illuminations,* trans. Harry Zohn (New York: Schocken, 1969), 257.

Chapter 12

Oh, My Land, My Birthplace

Lebanon War and Intifada in Israeli Fiction and Poetry

Glenda Abramson

The period between the Lebanon War in 1982 and the First Intifada in 1987–93 brought about a critical political change in Israel. The Yom Kippur War, which had profoundly shocked the nation, altered Israel's perception of war, stripping it of the last vestiges of romantic determinism and destroying Israel's belief in its own invincibility. Some sense of national optimism was restored by the Camp David peace accord between Israel and Egypt in 1977. With the new desire for reconciliation, Israeli liberals felt a sense of anxiety about the Israeli army's treatment of the Palestinians on the West Bank. The Lebanon War, the intifada, and the growing power of right-wing militancy and religious Zionism solidified the long-standing artistic opposition to the official right and ultranationalist factions.

Of all Israel's wars, the 1982 Lebanon War (Operation Peace for Galilee, *Mivtsa shalom hagalil, "Sheleg"*), which began on June 6, 1982, aroused the bitterest reaction in Israel. It instigated an unprecedented political crisis in Israel that also severely damaged Israel-Diaspora relations. The reaction among Jewish left-wing intellectuals over the Sabra and Shatila massacre was predictably furious.[1] Throughout the 1980s and 1990s, people in theater, cinema, literature, art, and popular culture demonstrated their objection to Israel's policy of war and occupation. The theater in particular focused its repertoire on the "Palestine Question." Dan Urian reports that almost a hundred plays relating directly or indirectly to the Lebanon War and the intifada were staged between 1982 and 1993, most of them in fringe theaters but an appreciable number in mainstream venues.[2] Amos Oz and David Grossman published a series of interviews with Israelis—Jews and Arabs—and Palestinians.[3] The question of the artist's role, which had been abstract and almost academic, suddenly attained far greater relevance for the Israeli reading public in the face of the revival of political art following the Lebanon War. The literature in particular reiterated some of the disquiet that had been so prominent in war writing in the 1950s, and it revealed an authentic protest against a new kind of war whose dimensions were wholly unfamiliar in the Israeli context.

To define protest or dissident literature is difficult in any circumstances, but much more so in Israel, given the relationship of consensus between the liberal intellectuals and the Labor government until 1977 when the path to protest was simplified by the advent of Likud. "Dissidence" is generally taken to be active opposition to authority, especially to an established religious or political system or belief. To this day dissident writers are punished or imprisoned, or they are driven to circulating their work as samizdat. This is not the case among Jewish writers in Israel. Literature of *dissent* from the ideology of the Israeli establishment had been produced from the earliest days of the state, from the time of S. Yizhar's iconic story "Hashavui" ("The Prisoner," 1949) and Yoram Matmor's little-known play, *Mahazeh ragil* (An ordinary play) of the same year. This and other literature highlighted some of the anomalies in Israeli politico-cultural thinking. The question to be asked now is whether this dissent held a specific political aim, a striving toward social change, rather than consciousness raising, which appeared to be its central function. After 1967 a more pointed opposition became prevalent, particularly in Hebrew drama where Hebrew playwrights were punished by banning and censorship, but not imprisoned, for what they wrote. After the Yom Kippur War in 1973 the subtext of suppressed anxiety continued to linger beneath the surface as long as a Labor government was in power, even if it was corrupt and even after the failure of the war and its attendant recriminations. Actual social protest (as opposed to literary protest) was as yet unknown in Israel, protest that signifies a broad opposition to official policies and that is realized in action rather than by words alone.

In this chapter I examine examples of fiction and poetry of dissent and literary protest relating to the Lebanon War, the First and Second Intifadas, and the policy of occupation, all of which stunned the Israeli liberal camp and turned world opinion against Israel's government. There is no antiestablishment posturing in these works, as we find in some of the literature of an earlier period, rather a shocked awareness that Israel could behave as "a nation like all the other nations" in the most damaging sense.

Fiction

Post-Lebanon writing was rhetorical and unrestrained in its rage at the first Israeli military action in which civilians were involved. The works crystallized the Manichaean perception of Arab and Jew, which had already informed the earliest literature of the state. One dystopian work actually questions the future of post-Lebanon Israel as a moral entity. *Haderekh el Ein Harod* (*The Road to Ein Harod*, 1984),[4] by the novelist and dramatist Amos Kenan, ran to five editions in 1984 and one in 1985 but did not achieve lasting popular success. Kenan, one of the outspoken left-wing political writers of the 1970s, had already offended the critics and the public with a post-Six-Day-War play titled *Haverim mesaprim al Yeshu* (Comrades tell stories about Jesus, 1972), which the censorship board banned. The play excoriated all the hallowed institutions of Israeli society, including the army, parents, and patriotic sacrifice. While *The Road to Ein Harod* does not mention the Lebanon War, one can assume that its tone of violence and apocalyptic fury is a response to it. *The Road,* a subversive, if not dissident, work, reduces the Arab-Israeli conflict to a single relationship, that of a Palestinian, Mahmoud, an escaped prisoner, and an Israeli narrator, Rafi (the generic name for all the Israeli soldiers in the tale), both fleeing from a repressive and brutal Israeli military dictatorship. Although Rafi's name aligns him with the army and all the other military Rafis, he has assumed a subjectivity that neutralizes it. From the start Rafi stresses that the Israeli and the Arab are indistinguishable in appearance and that they both originate from "the orchard."[5] Now they are seeking the sanctuary of Ein Harod although the novel does not clarify the nature of the place, where or what it is.

The novel's subtext is a celebration of the Israeli landscape and of biblical history, although the reality of modern Israel punctures the biblical ideal. References to the biblical texts that are often ecstatic, including the *akedah,* line the novel as an affirmation of the Jews' historical possession of the land, a land that has now been corrupted by realpolitik. Nevertheless, the question the novel ultimately asks is precisely that of possession or the possibility of the land being shared. The argument proceeds throughout the length of the book and the two fugitives' flight. It is encapsulated in a short exchange:

> We deserve a place [says Mahmoud]
> In our place [replies Rafi].
> Beside you.
> There's no such thing in the world. There's only either or.
> There is such a thing in the world. It's not only either or. (55)

An uneasy cooperation, based solely on their need to survive, develops between the two men as they make their way to the fantasized haven of Ein Harod, in a journey whose pictorial violence has scarcely been equaled in Hebrew literature. At the same time, both protagonists share the novel's paean to the land and landscape. At one point Mahmoud falls to his knees and puts his forehead to the earth.

> There was a moment of silence.
> Mahmoud rose.
> Oh, my land, my birthplace, he sang.
> Oh land, my land.
> A sad, melodious song, a shiver ran through me.
> Land, my land, sang Mahmoud. I knew that when he sang about his land which is my land, he sang about his land which isn't my land. . . . I had no part in Mahmoud's land, I had no inheritance. (94)

The irony of this passage is that the song Mahmoud sings is by the Hebrew poet, Saul Tchernichowsky, who, like Mahmoud and Rafi, extolled the landscape of Eretz Israel, in his case with a subtext of Jewish nationalism. Kenan's choice of this poem for the Palestinian to sing is the most powerful symbol of the indivisibility of the land and the crucial but unattainable unity of its inhabitants.

Rafi notices during their long odyssey that the Arab villages, so rich in history, are empty, and that apart from Mahmoud he has not seen any of their inhabitants. His musings offer a subversion of the ideology of conquest, rejecting the idea of patriotic dying: "What is Zion and what is Jerusalem in the face of life and what is more exalted than life and what is lower than Zion Jerusalem if it means to die and conquer the mountain" (93). He disassociates himself from the Jewish history of conquest, from 1948 all the way back to ancient Israel, while celebrating the intrinsic relationship of modern Israel to the Bible. Kenan writes scenes of elegiac memory: Rafi glorifies the landscape of his forefathers, the prophets, and the man sitting under his vine, all the while mourning its loss. The wealth of biblical allusions throughout the novel is not unusual for writers of Kenan's generation, that of Amos Oz and A. B. Yehoshua, despite their proclaiming themselves to be divorced from tradition and the Jewish past. From the time of the Second Aliyah (1904–14), land and God were interwoven in literature, and neither the *dor ba'aretz* generation nor its successor, *dor hamedina,* the state generation, were to separate them. There is also something of the 1950s Israeli Canaanite philosophy that argued for a unified ancient East stretching over much of the Fertile Crescent, in Rafi's emphasis on the Bible as the only authentic pre-exilic Jewish history.

The identity of Ein Harod is left undefined. It could signify Rafi's death; at the end of the narrative he achieves a kind of peace: "I don't hear voices any longer and I don't know if I'm deaf. . . . Now, at last, I feel good. I'm in Ein Harod" (120). It could be a pocket of resistance, sending out clandestine radio broadcasts to which Rafi listens before fleeing the military police. Ein Harod could also represent the possibility of starting afresh, of reaching a kind of political nirvana, or of Rafi singing Mahmoud's song, which is a Hebrew song. However, Mahmoud is executed by the military commander, together with other victims of the regime. Rafi realizes that he will be unable to reach Ein Harod without him.

> His death is pointless and I won't forgive them. If the last thing I ever do will be to avenge his death, I'll do it . . . not because of friendship or love, we were not friends or companions, we were brothers, but brothers of something that we couldn't understand and now how will we understand. If I have to avenge his death, it will be for one reason, because otherwise I will never be able to reach Ein Harod. (104–5)

Kenan's post-Lebanon vision of military dictatorship serves as a grave warning to Israel at the time, with Mahmoud both a reproach and the focus for the horror of the envisioned state. He is also an image for the individual writer's self-reflexive political or moral argument. The entire novel is a lament for the wasted possibilities of peace and unity, its major protagonists ultimately neither the Jew nor the Arab but two nations, a shared history, and the land itself, beloved by both.

The political and psychological watershed of the Six-Day War (1967) induced awareness among the Israelis of the Palestinians as a potential nation. Their problem became central to the Israeli intellectuals' altered perception created by the war. Up to that point the Palestinians as a people, rather than the Arab as victim stereotype or Orientalist exotic, had scarcely been mentioned in the literature. The Lebanon War crystallized the awareness of the enemy as a suffering human being at the same time as Menachem Begin exploited the wars as manifestations of another potential Holocaust against the Jews. It was impossible for this attitude not to permeate into society as a whole, to become an unwanted subtext to the protest.

Yet while the major change of the 1980s lies in the modified perception of the Arabs and Palestinians in many of the works, from stereotyped characters to a realistic portrayal of them, the drama manifested an increasingly hostile attitude toward them, despite the playwrights' liberal credentials. Also, the rather abstract self-definition of the writers as moral victims of their own newly assumed guise of oppressor and conqueror was extended, in the 1980s, to a view of themselves as casualties of a political situation out of control. In many of the works Israeli characters lament the fact that brutalization of the other has, in turn, brutalized them. Another factor that gained prominence in the literature of the 1980s is the acknowledgment of a three-pronged battle between Israeli liberals (and the army), settlers in the Occupied Territories, and the Palestinians, factions that are clearly demarcated in the novels and plays. Characteristic of all these works, both pre-and post-intifada is their dialecticism, many of them incorporating an open political debate. Ultimately, the many problems devolve upon the one that had been argued since the Six-Day War: the morality of adherence to the covenant, that is, the occupation of the land, at the cost not only of its indigenous inhabitants but also of the Israeli soul.

Generally, the political dialectic in Israeli literature was, therefore, not simply a matter of protesting against an unpopular government, since it spanned the entire history of the State of Israel from 1948. It cannot be compared, for example, with the upsurge of artistic protest from the left in the United Kingdom during the Thatcher period. In Israel, dissent had been a constant feature of literature regardless of which side held power in government. The liberal intellectuals, those who constituted the mainstream group of Israeli writers from the start, exhibited subversive tendencies even when nominally supporting and traditionally identified with Labor. There is, therefore, an added quality to the political literature of Israel, one that more specifically defines its dissent and places it on an ideological plane above that of simple objection and perhaps justifies its solipsism. This is a *moral* argument arising from the Israelis' inherited ideologies. Political writing in any case should provide an ethical basis for judgment. According to Robert Boyars, ethical thought typically projects an ideal vision of the way people ought to behave, and this is generally a feature of political fiction.

"Political novels have an ethical foundation . . . the wisdom they project will reflect their sense of what ought to be permanent features of human experience."[6]

All of this, protest and ethical debate, appears in the writing around or incorporating the First Intifada, the Palestinian uprising that began in 1987. Generally, in fiction and poetry the response to this phenomenon, only five years after the end of the Lebanon War, was comparatively muted and limited to a few examples. There was no sustained reference to it or anything that can be called a corpus of writing about it. Ami Elad-Bouskila deems the Hebrew literature written about the intifada to be marginal, an opinion with which Tal Nitzan, editor of a volume of Israeli protest poetry, agrees.[7] What Nitzan describes as "protest poetry" might not have outlasted the Lebanon War, returning to its customary, and much criticized, state of personal introspection, but, together with fiction and drama, it did, to a certain extent, reflect the attitudes to this latest crisis. Altogether, journalism rather than belles lettres had the monopoly over reaction and discussion, and for the first time Israeli fiction relaxed its self-imposed duty of confrontation. The reason for this is probably that, as we have seen, the political views of novelists, dramatists, and poets had been expressed before the uprising began; the intifada itself was the outcome of a situation that had prevailed on the West Bank and in Gaza since the late 1970s, and writers had consequently concerned themselves with settlement and occupation since that time and with Palestinian rights even before that.[8]

Yitzhak Ben-Ner's novel of the First Intifada, *Ta'atu'on* (1990), dramatized in the same year, delineates the next stage in the process: the threats, the hatred, the stoning of soldiers, the tire-burning that explodes into open warfare. Ben-Ner portrays the arena itself, in addition to its human population. Tzevi Barel, writing in *Haaretz,* designates the street (*rehov*) as the "true ruler":

> An order and a real hierarchy characterize the dunghill which is Gaza. Next to the trash cans which are never emptied the overfed cats know that they have to wait until the giant rats finish their evening meal. When the assembly of rats leaves the stinking crates that fill the street, the cats approach. After them come the mice, grab something and disappear into the houses' yards. "This is the only place in the world," says the commanding officer, "where cats are frightened of mice." This is perhaps the only place where it is difficult to say who is a cat, who a mouse, who is the conquered and who the conqueror and who controls whom.[9]

Ben-Ner takes up this nightmarish landscape of the streets in an effort to portray the intifada authentically in fiction, in the tradition of Holocaust literature that attempts to convey the horror through evocation, image, and response. Since the Hebrew language struggles to sustain the reality of the uprising, Ben-Ner leaves it to the soldiers themselves, through faithful representations of their speech-slang, curses, and tormented Hebrew, and their inarticulately truncated vignettes of the place, to provide an insight into their experience and flesh out the newspaper reports. In the novel the world has degenerated into chaos, panic, and filth. Tzevi Barel describes a patrol in Gaza, "on one of those nights when it is possible to touch the stench," treading through the sewage that inundates the streets, and Ben-Ner places a deadly, ineradicable stink at the core of his narrative.[10]

In her survey of the soldiers' responses to all this in Israeli fiction, including Ben-Ner's novel, Adi Mendelsohn-Maoz comments, "The military world is defined as a different universe with its own rules and norms. It is a world governed by the military masculine peer group that encourages violent action as part of boys' attempts to adhere to manly norms of roughness and aggressiveness. In this world, gentle and hesitant behavior is classified as feminine and weak."[11] In one of the novels a soldier fears "being branded with a humiliating 'leftist' label."[12]

Ta'atu'on, the novel's untranslatable title, is a coinage, indicating illusion or delusion, a fate suffered by each of the novel's main characters, and it also has the undertone of trickery or deceit, as in the Spanish verb *burlar.* The story is told by four men whose lives intersect: Holi, a young Israeli soldier arrested and imprisoned for an act of brutality against a Palestinian during a sortie in one of the territories, never named but always referred to as "the violated town"; his father, Oded, a doctor who attempts a form of reconciliation with Palestinian intellectuals; Harul ("thorn," "nettle"), a member of the security forces, who hunts down a Palestinian terrorist; and Michel, a comrade of Holi's who is suffering catatonic shock as a result of his experiences in the territories. This outline gives little idea of the novel's complexity. Without revealing much of the author's ideological position (unusual in Israeli fiction) it explores every variation of political opinion throughout Israeli and Palestinian society by means of a powerful, shocking, eloquent, and often harsh narrative. Physical and psychological brutalization is its paramount theme. The novel begins with Holi's mindless act of violence, a vicious attack after hours of taunting hatred between the Israelis and the Palestinians across the barriers. Physical action is preceded by the violation of language as the two groups deride each other with obscenities and threats, a mixture of Arabic curses and gutter Hebrew that appears to constitute the only means of communication even among the Israeli soldiers themselves. As a result of the press publicity following his assault, Holi develops a strange psychosis: he refuses to wash and smells so dreadfully that he is removed to the army's psychiatric hospital where no amount of washing or disinfection is able to remove his ever-increasing stink. The symbolism of his biological smell is obvious. The narrative gives Ben-Ner an opportunity to air every political stand expressed behind and beyond the Green Line in Israel, certainly in Israeli literature: party-political views, those of the established "right" and "left"; the "them or us" philosophy; guilt; the messianism of settlement and the settlers' biblical validation; the Diaspora mentality: Palestinian attitudes communicating pain, frustration, and intransigence. With all this, Ben-Ner avoids partisanship. Any possibility of his alignment in the novel with any of his left-wing spokesmen is in any case subverted by the novel's ironic ending in a kind of epiphany in which two of the lost and hopeless characters are saved by the bright hearts-and-flowers world of ultra-Orthodoxy.

It is the Harul section that most closely approaches allegory. Like Ephraim, Harul cynically excuses his cruelty with the slogan, "it's all for the homeland." Like Ephraim, Harul is created against the *Palmach* stereotype, even to the blond hair, which is now white not from age but from a sudden shock. He is ruled by an obsession: to catch and destroy a Palestinian, Fawzi, who may or may not be a terrorist but who, according to Harul's delusion, is the leader of the insurrection in the "battered town."

Other than in Holi's narrative, the Palestinians in this novel sometimes come close to the guilt stereotype of previous Israeli fiction despite the fact that after three years of intifada the attitude toward the Palestinians was becoming increasingly negative and accusatory. Yet in Ben-Ner's portrait of the conflict through Holi's monologue, expressing the hatred between Arab and Jew, the Palestinians are portrayed with realism for the first time in Israeli fiction. This does not prevent the continuation of the moral debate that has distinguished Israeli war literature from the start. Oded says, "It seems I have become one of those who have the ability to distinguish clearly the dangers threatening the nation's soul no less than the dangers threatening its body." Since the Arab is no longer a metaphorical formulation of moral angst, the questions about ethical ideology are put directly and become part of the novel's dialectical flow.

Poetry

Post-Lebanon

The literary phenomenon of the immediate post-Lebanon years was the emergence of the Israeli poet into the public arena of protest, stirred into action by the war. Unlike fiction and drama, in previous decades the poetry had resisted commenting on Israeli politics and tended to focus on the personal world of the poet. After the Lebanon War, poetry joined the other genres in protest rather than dissidence, objection rather than disagreement. The change in the verse was, therefore, qualitatively remarkable, although the "protest" poems were still outnumbered by more personal poetry. The advent of Likud and Begin, however, had brought many of the poets, including the respected veterans of the so-called *dor hapalmaḥ*, out of their seclusion. The Lebanon War released their inhibitions. Two anthologies, *Ḥatzayat gevul*[13] (Crossing the Borders) and *Ve'en tikhlah lekravot ulehereg*[14] (No End to Battles and Killing), both published in 1983, were openly critical of every aspect of the war—from the government to the behavior of the Israeli soldiers to the perceived indifference of the Israeli public, due, primarily, to its need for disconnection from political events. This changed after Sabra and Shatila when leading writers and intellectuals, together with bereaved families and friends, came out in public denunciations of the government. Also, for the first time, there was a sense that Israel might not have always been in the right, that it did not always wish for peace, that many of its external and internal policies were faulty, "that it was not always the victim, and that there are other, legitimate sides to the Middle East story [that] slowly encroached on Zionist dogma."[15] Yitzhak Laor offers a poignant reason for the change in the tenor of the poetry:

My young brother Elijah,
before you go to the next war think
about the previous war or should I tell you
how Grandpa on Mom's side
pulled out all his teeth not to go to their war. My young brother Elijah
don't go to their war.
Ve'en tikhlah, 10

This brings Yehuda Amichai's lines to mind:

My father was in their war for four years
Neither loving nor hating his enemy.[16]

"Their" war, the First World War, was a foreign war in which Jewish soldiers gave their lives. "Our" war is now foreign to the Jewish soul. Laor's ironic subversion is in his urging the young soldier not to fight in a war that no longer enjoys the consolations of *ein brera*, "no choice," as previous Israeli wars had done.

The canon of protest poetry is often constructed not from responses to any single event, either the Lebanon War or the intifada, but to the aftermath of both. It demonstrates a powerful sense of dismay, and sometimes fury, at Israel's posture in relation to the Palestinians. This dismay was frequently to be found in the language as much as the content of the literature of this type. It was often intemperate and rhetorical, graphic and unpoetically explicit. Eitan Kalinski (1936–1986), a poet and Hebrew teacher, provided an angry statement about the destruction of the Hebrew language as a consequence of occupation. His poem begins with an encomium to the Hebrew language, a "pendant / As in silver ornaments / when their words are spoken well." Rabbis and sages have graced the language with nobility and beauty, with their poetry "the quill pen of the soul." Yet in Jenin and Shechem, with the language eternally debased by its surroundings, the quill pens of the soul can no longer function. "I am a defeated teacher / of a defeated Hebrew language." The failure of language brings to mind resonances to German after the Second World War, a language equally debased by its usage and users, and it also implies the failure of Zionism for which the Hebrew language remained the metonym. The "cracked, shrill melody"—contrasting with the earlier image of golden apples adorning the Hebrew of the speaker's students—leads the reader to the filthy and perforated streets of West Bank towns. Hebrew is a broken language used to express the broken promise of Zionism:

Stinking Arab
face the wall
shut the fuck up
you piece of shit
you animal[17]

As a continuation of the angry outbursts of *Hatsayat gevul* and *Ve'en tikhlah lekravot ulehereg,* Kalinski's authentic utterance expresses the despair of loss without any recourse to the excuse of his speaker's own victimhood. Yet like some of the Lebanon poetry, he refers to an idealized past through mention of sacred sources as a contrast to the egregiousness of the present.

Earlier war poetry, unlike fiction, had rarely presented the viewpoint or conditions of the enemy except by showing him as a prisoner, or by the general statement that there are no victors in any war. In the poetry about Lebanon, poems were written about Palestinians, Lebanese families, children, expressing the guilt that, according to the poets, all Israelis share: Dahlia Ravikovitch writes: "What do I need all this for, / to think about, / to remember, / children freezing / in lashing angled rain. / Mothers burn / tatters of tents / to make a nice fire in winter. / He arises, stands, dies and he is free. / All this distress / is mine and on my head" (*Ḥatsayat gevul,* 31). Arieh Sivan describes the scene of destruction seen indistinctly through smoke and fog and ends:

For a certain time the sun will stay
In the middle of the sky-
In which there is not a single cloud
In this season of light
And no man will be able to hide away
Not even in his own shadow.
Ve'en tikhlah, 95

Sivan, who had been writing protest poetry long before the Lebanon War without arousing much attention, displayed one of the most powerful reactions to the war in a selection of poems often consisting of uncompromisingly emotive language, even rhetoric. Phrases like "the tightness of my throat," "cities . . . that will soon reveal their wounds to the world," "fourth-time refugees," "shredded people" with "pierced eyes" set the tone for other verse that, if generally more restrained, is still ideologically consistent. Similar reactions of horror and outrage had been exhibited in the 1948 war poetry as well, but the torn bodies referred to were always Israel's own.

Natan Zach, whose poetry cannot ever be said to be objective, examines the political atmosphere that made possible the incursion into Lebanon in twelve short and bitter stanzas that chronicle the havoc created by Israel's opposing political groups:

Not far from here Rolf was killed in an ambushed car
By the British, the Arabs or Begin—
Who cares. Whoever will be, will be—
The rest will be bombed or blown up, to ensure
No more casualties.
In the shelters of the Likkud, the Ma'arakh, the Agudah.
Ve'en tikhlah, 20

The people in the shelters listen to a special news transmission but the old words—Zach coins "olds" (*yeshanot*) as an antonym to "news" (*hadashot*)—are specially transmitted as well, the Herzlian slogans and other inspiring nationalistic sayings that contradict Israel's destiny as represented by the war: "If you will it, it is no dream"—Herzl's famous promise; "Israel's eternity will not lie," the Hebrew words forming the acronym of NILI, the Zionist underground network.[18] Zach ends his poem with a blunt statement that while it will not be defeated, Israel cannot endure: he is referring to the threat not of the war itself but moral uncertainty, contradiction, and guilt.

The statements in the poetry about Lebanon are not always this explicit. Poets draw allegorical ideas from Greek mythological literature and also from the Bible and Jewish liturgy. As always in Israeli poetry, these form the basis for ironic commentary, as in Mordechai Geldman's poem about a Palestinian who regards Ishmael as the victim of the *akedah*. Sivan writes about the prophet Jonah who exemplifies God's cruelty and the dove (*yonah* in Hebrew, the prophet's name), which cannot prevent the drowning of children. The sense of continuity created by the borrowed words and phrases that in the new contexts assume a significant contemporary meaning is an indictment rather than a consolation: in the endless continuity of Jewish history the promise of peace and salvation has yet to be fulfilled.

The most unequivocal political statements occur in poetry describing the plight of civilians in Lebanon, which gave rise to Meir Wieseltier's observation that "beside Beirut, Prague is a child," comparing the incomparable similarities. In a frequently quoted poem called "Al haratson ledayek" (About the desire to be accurate), Natan Zach speaks bitterly of the pointlessness of those who escape into preoccupation with detail, the exact number of men, women, and children killed, while the implications of the tragedy as a whole are disregarded. Dahlia Ravikovitch writes a gloss on this poem, with an angry, ironic beginning:[19] "He who destroys thirty babies / it is as if he'd destroyed three hundred babies / and toddlers too, / and even eight-and-a half-year-olds"[20] Zach sees mankind's lack of moral discrimination, the human need to be accurate in all circumstances, as a symptom of its ability to kill. Another veteran poet, Avner Treinin, states with heavy irony that the land received from the British in good order is still in good order: "they" have thousands of wounded, "we" have hundreds. Eli demonstrates his awareness of the losses the Lebanese have sustained when he describes a Palestinian returning to his village, now destroyed and deserted, and remembering the past. Then,

I saw my son
coming here, in thirty years' time
a refugee, in exile, muttering:
"here stood the nursery . . . here
the dining room . . . hand in hand with Daddy
on the sidewalk . . . and here was the big lawn
where we used to play until
darkness enclosed us.
Where did it all go?
Where has everyone gone?"
Ḥatsayat gevul, 24–25

The writers who did use the pen to condemn the sword were almost exclusively nominal, if not actual, supporters of the Israeli liberal left. Even moderates like Yehuda Amichai permitted poems to be included in these volumes, while not protesting directly against the specific event. The viewpoint is that of the outraged moral Israeli: most often the outrage is for the dead and wounded soldiers, the fate of Palestinian civilians, and sometimes for the Israelis themselves whose moral integrity had been severely compromised by these wars: "All this distress / is mine and on my head." An unstated but implied comparison or analogy with Jewish fate under generations of oppressive rulers is the underlying sense of this poetry. For example, Zvi Atzmon chronicles the Jewish history of wandering, suffering, "oppressed and beaten, burnt at the stake, drowned, martyred. / Murdered at daylight in the crusades, in the Black Death, in the Cossack revolution and during the Inquisition," and so on. While the conclusion is signaled early, it is nevertheless a scorching indictment both of Zionism and of self:

Every small boy's vengeance will cry out
Suddenly
He gets up in the morning, sees
Children shot at break of day,
Real blood, this week, it's not a story,
Arab children, without a jot of mercy.
In Israel the Jewish nation has arisen
With its two-thousand-year history
As long as within the heart a soul:[21] I am the accused!
Ve'en tikhlah, 12

Similarly, Dahlia Ravikovitch provides a sinister parody of Nazi orders in a poem that was to become the primary statement of the war, "Tinok lo horgim pa'amayim" (You Can't Kill a Baby Twice), referring to the Sabra and Shatila massacre: "'Get back to the camp, march!' ordered the soldier / to the screaming women of Sabra and Shatila. /

He had his orders to obey" (*Ve'en tikhlah,* 55). Underlying and relating to these ideas, therefore, is one with dreadful implications, both backward to Nazism and forward to Israel's military endeavors, that of acting without will, of obeying orders. The indictment is not only of this particular war but also of a more general attenuation of moral authority, yet reference to the Holocaust in some of the poems will always bring Jewish suffering to mind, unconsciously blurring the lines between victim and victimizer even in this poetry of moral outrage.

Intifada and After

Protest poetry takes many forms; as we have seen, Israeli protest poetry, particularly that relating to the intifada and occupation, aims to shock its readers into an awareness of injustice. Much of it is unsubtle condemnation that often strays beyond the borders of poetry into invective, or it is the factual reiteration of events, as if attempting to reinscribe a true record of the events into history. It includes place names, personal names, particularly of Palestinians. It sometimes exhibits self-righteous outrage, a solipsistic self-indictment.

> From the hill
> where we stood you can still see
> the secrets of destruction, sometimes
> we still wonder why we insisted on keeping
> the human image we've lost.
>
> Rami Saari, "Soldiers," 55

The most effective of these poems are less specific, their protest embodied in atmosphere and suggestion rather than event. An example is Yitzhak Laor's "Seder Hayom" ("Order of the Day"), published in 1990. Laor is one of the writers most victimized by his political activities, which, in the Israeli context, become part of the writer's persona. Laor was, at the time, one of Israel's first true dissidents, involved in active protest, his work censored. "I have no choice / but to resist," he writes.[22] Although he won the 1990 Prime Minister's Prize for literature, Prime Minister Yitzhak Shamir refused to sign the certificate awarding the prize. This is certainly not a mark of the political establishment's aesthetic competence, but their response, in this case, to a writer's career of radical activism, quite unique in Jewish Israeli letters. One would expect Laor's work to be heavy with shocking images, condemnation, and so on, but even in his angriest poetry he is able to retain artistic subtlety: his much-quoted poem exemplifies the most evocative of the responses to the intifada.

> Remember
> What Amalek
> did to you

of course,
Over.
Do unto Amalek
what Amalek did to you
of course,
Over.

If you can't
find Amalek,
call Amalek whom you want
to do to him what Amalek did to you
of course,
Over.

Don't compare
anything to what
Amalek did to you
of course,
Over.
Not when you want to do what
Amalek did to you
of course,
Over and out,
Remember.[23]

The poem is based on Deuteronomy 25:17:

> Remember what the Amalekites did to you along the way when you came out of Egypt. When you were weary and worn out, they met you on your journey and cut off all who were lagging behind; they had no fear of God. When the Lord your God gives you rest from all the enemies around you in the land he is giving you to possess as an inheritance, you shall blot out the memory of Amalek from under heaven. Do not forget!

In Hebrew the injunction "zakhor" (remember/do not forget) is the most evocative call for Holocaust remembrance, and in this political poem Laor deliberately brings the Holocaust to mind; it becomes the bar that no other oppression can reach. The battlefield setting reinforces the idea of an army in search of an enemy and of the invalid excuse the state used both to identify and to attack any entity deemed to be the enemy. The poem's final stanza prefigures the international determination of a "disproportionate" response used later to condemn Operation Cast Lead.

A similarly effective poem, also using the biblical text as a reproach, is Zvi Atzmon's poem "Batsiporen Shamir" (With the steel point of a thorn). This is a tapestry of biblical phrases from the books of Isaiah and Jeremiah juxtaposed to provide a recapitulation of the present situation, based on the biblical principles of sin and punishment.[24]

> And thorns and thistles shall grow
> and the land shall be thorn and thistle
> Thorn and thistle will devour
> the land of my people,
> briar and thistle will rise.
> The sin of Judah is written with an iron pen
> engraved with the steel point of a thorn.[25]

The prophets chastise Judah for the sin of idolatry and warn that as a punishment the land will grow only thorn and thistle, that it will become a dry wasteland. In the final line of the poem, taken from Jeremiah 17:1, Atzmon stops the verse in the middle of the biblical line, even though the continuation would strengthen his rebuke, as it did Jeremiah's. Jeremiah continues: "The sin of Judah [is] written with a pen of iron, [and] with the point of a thorn [it is] graven upon the table of their heart, and upon the horns of your altars." In Atzmon's version the line ends with "with the point of a thorn." He is, then, not only indicting the Israelis for their sins, claiming that these are engraved in their hearts, but also indicating the eternal power of writing, confirming that the iron pen and point of the thorn are weapons of protest. In fact the title of the original anthology in which this poem appears is *Ba'et barzel* (2005), published in English as *With an Iron Pen.*

In an interview the poet called this poem "ready-made" and declared that there was not one word or letter that was his own.[26] Nevertheless, the message is profound due to the poem's new order of the well-known phrases. Some of the most provocative poems throughout this particular canon use the Bible either as validation of their viewpoint or as subversion of the Bible's viewpoint. In this case, it is neither: the speaker repeats God's warning as it was given to the prophet and implicitly exhorts the writers to set it down, to be engraved with a steel point, never to be erased. This unmistakable protest poem is more effective for being inexplicit yet in a sense defining the nature of literary protest itself.

As we have seen in many examples, biblical intertextuality is a strong feature of this protest poetry, perhaps because it is safer for poets to use already established responses to perceived wrongdoing, or to indicate that the wrongdoing is entrenched in the people, despite prophetic rebuke or, in Tal Nitzan's words, to "expose also the gap between the divine promise regarding the Promised Land, and the defective reality, proving the falseness of the promise itself."[27] Israeli authors are writing for readers who, whether religiously or secularly educated, are familiar with religious texts and recognize radical distortions of them. Much has been written about the function of the often-disruptive "strong misreadings" of these intertexts, and also their provision of metaphors and archetypes.[28] By manipulating, even subverting, them the authors are able to make political and existential statements.

The intertexts are not limited only to sacred writings. In Shai Dotan's poem, "Rega ehad" (One moment) refers directly to Natan Zach's celebrated poem of 1974, with the same title. Zach's elegiac poem, which has presented interpretive difficulties from the start, relates to a figure, presumably dead, thought by readers to be either Moses, Elijah, Jesus, God, or the speaker's father. The poem is infused with spirituality and regret: the speaker has failed to recognize the figure as a beloved father, mentor, or spiritual leader, until it is too late. Dotan's poem, on the other hand, is a self-berating cry that the speaker was unable to recognize his victim as innocent.

> One moment. I want
> to shout. I shot him. He came towards me
> with a suspicious face. Who knew that his pockets
> were empty, that his bag was filled with clothes.
>
> Maybe he didn't have a work permit,
> or once stole across the border. Perhaps he didn't hear
> the hands yelling, the blood
> pounding in the chest, beating on the temples.
>
> Sometimes he wakes up in my sleep
> hard as lead, empty as the wind,
> telling me: My killer
> I didn't know you were
> so much[29]

The final stanza of Zach's poem reads:

> I couldn't know. I don't blame him.
> Sometimes I feel him getting up
> In his sleep, moonstruck like the sea, passing by me, saying
> My son. My son. I didn't know
> You were, so much, with me.

In Dotan's poem there are echoes of Wilfred Owen's "Strange Meeting," in the enemy's reproachful visitation. His "One moment" is loud and agonized, while Zach's is quiet and contemplative, yet at the core of both is an agonized remorse, and a reproachful haunting. Rather than a subversion of the original text, Dotan's poem provides a commentary to it.

Conclusion

These and other works, however disparate their styles and genres, have a number of features in common. First, the characters in the fiction, as in other Israeli political literature, are inseparable from their political convictions. There is no interrelationship other than with the political natures of each of them. Father-child, husband-wife, lovers, friends, enemies, engage in political discourse, and it is this and nothing else that determines their relationships. Second, also in common with earlier political works, there is in this fiction and poetry a projection of the past onto the present: for example, the biblical promise of settlement in Kenan and the prophetic disappointment in the poetry.

These works protest against a series of events and circumstances, war and occupation, that has led to suffering and tragedy on both sides of the conflict. Yet apart from the implicit Israeli government in *The Road to Ein Harod,* the works of the 1980s and 1990s do not constitute a protest against the actions of a single system, government, political party, or the army. The works are, rather, a protest against the events *themselves,* without consideration, in the literature at least, of cause and effect. It is a *moral* warning about the consequences of these events and actions for the nation's soul. Rami Saari:

> Close to the breast, the soul sits
> Curled up like a boy in a sleeping bag,
> Dry as a flower bulb buried in the middle of the throat.[30]

In a series of agonized quatrains Tuvia Rübner, now in his eighties, questions Israeli moral decency and asks, "Where can we still run from ourselves?"[31]

> This is not what we wanted, no, no, not this.
> Without them who are we and for what?
> We didn't want this, no, not this, we didn't think it would be like this[32]

Dvora Amir:

> I told myself
> Whoever scars a person's home—in the end his eyes will be scarred,
> Whoever demolishes a person's home—in the end his soul will be demolished.[33]

What, if anything, do these works propose? Ultimately all of Israel's war and protest literature offers few solutions. Common to all of it is the sense of ethical disorder, of an existing system in combat with moral imperatives. There is no attempt at political solutions. Kenan's Rafi never finds his own Ein Harod. Ben-Ner's character, Oded, advises dialogue with the Palestinians but is proved to be fatally misguided and goes mad as a result. While most of the fiction on this topic appears to wish for a solution to the conflict, it fails to suggest one, and the texts, almost without fail, reach a pessimistic conclusion, a sense of helplessness, even inertia. Only the playwright Motti Lerner, in a play about settlers on the West Bank titled *Hevle mashiah* (The Pangs of the Messiah, 1988), takes a stand by having his central character, a religious settler, insist on leaving the territories. It was still possible at the time for a left-wing writer to imply, without irony, the moral character of settlers who would not countenance violence:

> Shmuel: We have all been wrong. We have been blind. We've closed our eyes. We didn't want to see the other nation living here. We were blind to its fate from the start. . . . We have brought upon ourselves a corruption of our values . . . we must get up and leave. All of us must leave.[34]

Unfortunately, Israeli writing of protest and dissent of the 1980s and 1990s remains as relevant today as it was then. However, the general literary preoccupations of the present moment have changed, and the poetry and fiction, with some notable exceptions, no longer concern themselves with war and settlement even as the effects of the Second Intifada are still being felt, and a third intifada threatened. Even though—or perhaps because—the poetry's power of utterance has grown even more explicit, violent and strident, also weary and sad, according to Tal Nitzan, "the cultural stand taken by the poets and poems of this anthology represents today a minority position—a minority that is seen by the majority of the Jewish Israeli public as 'self-hating' and as desecrators of sacred ideals."[35] This, as we have seen, was true as well of the earlier war literature and literature of protest even before the 1980s. Yet while some of the oppositional, rather than radical, fiction of Amos Oz, A. B. Yehoshua, and S. Yizhar became canonical and therefore lost its sting, the protest literature of the 1980s and 1990s still has the ability to shock despite its instances of solipsistic self-indulgence.

In a survey of Israeli literature of the last decades of the twentieth century, Rochelle Furstenberg writes, "One might easily surmise that without these writers' [Amos Oz, A. B. Yehoshua, David Grossman, and Yitzhak Laor] consciousness-raising to the plight of the Arabs, there would be no peace process today."[36] This is an optimistic and desirable, if unrealistic, view, and it remains unlikely that any art brings about social or political change, however much it tries to, however loudly it shouts. Yet although the literature of the Lebanon War and during and after the First Intifada did not alter any political or military processes, it certainly drew the readers' attention to them, in this way defining the purpose of literary protest.

Notes

1. The Israeli army invaded southern Lebanon as a response to terrorist activities. Having been driven from Jordan and Syria in 1976, hundreds of Palestinians were housed in refugee camps on the outskirts of Beirut. A Christian right-wing group, the Phalange, was the most

powerful group in Lebanon, and in September 1982, a Falangist, Bashir Gemayel, was elected as head of state. After his murder the Falangists, believing, like the IDF, that PLO fighters were hiding out in the Sabra and Shatila camps, entered the camps and massacred a large number of Palestinians. The IDF did not carry out this massacre, but they did not prevent the Falangists from doing so and, it is claimed, even assisted them.

2. See Dan Urian, "Theatre and the Intifada," *Contemporary Theatre Review* 3, no. 2 (1995): 208. In fact, not only left-wing playwrights used the theater to present their points of view but also those from three other groups with contrasting political ideologies: the settlers, the Palestinians, and the Israeli Arabs (218).

3. Amos Oz, *Po vesham be'eretz yisra'elbastav* (Tel Aviv: Am Oved, 1982), translated by Maurice Goldberg-Bartura as *In the Land of Israel* (London: Hogarth Press, 1983); David Grossman, *Zeman hatsahov* (*The Yellow Wind* [New York: Farrar, Straus and Giroux, 1988]).

4. Amos Kenan, *Haderekh el Ein Harod*, 6th ed. (Tel Aviv: Am Oved, 1985). There is a translation into English: D. Hecht, trans., *The Road to Ein Harod* (London: Saqi Books, 2001). Page numbers for quoted passages appear in parentheses in the text. Page numbers refer to the Am Oved edition.

5. This may be a reference to *Hapardes* (The Orchard), 1972, by Benjamin Tammuz, a symbolic novel about two half-brothers, a Jew and an Arab, fighting over possession of an orchard.

6. Robert Boyars, *Atrocity and Amnesia* (Oxford: Oxford University Press, 1985), 27.

7. Ami Elad-Bouskila, *Modern Palestinian Literature and Culture* (Oxford: Routledge, 1999), 85; Tal Nitzan and Rachel Tzvia Back, eds., *With an Iron Pen: Twenty Years of Hebrew Protest Poetry* (Albany: Excelsior Editions/State University of New York Press, 2009), 2. (English version of the original *Be'et barzel: Shirat meha'ah ivrit, 1984–2004* [Tel Aviv: Hargol, 2005]). Unfortunately the poems in the collection are undated.

8. Probably the best-known example of this is A. B. Yehoshua's 1962 novella *Mul haye'arot* (Facing the forests), in which a forest planted with the proceeds of the Jewish National Fund grows over and thus conceals an Arab village.

9. Tzevi Barel. "Bamamlekhet haholadot" (In the kingdom of the rats). *Haaretz*, n.d.

10. Ibid.

11. Adia Mendelson-Maoz, "Violence, Morality, and Tragedy: The Israeli Soldier in the Hebrew Literature of the Intifada," http://www.inter-disciplinary.net/wp-content/uploads/2010/02/adiapaper.pdf.

12. Ibid.

13. *Ḥatzayat gevul* (Tel Aviv: Sifriyat Po'alim, 1983). Page numbers for quoted passages are found parenthetically in the text.

14. *Ve'en tikhlah lekravot ulehereg*(Tel Aviv: Hakibbutz Hameuhad, 1983). Page numbers for quoted passages are found parenthetically in the text.

15. Yaron Peleg, *Israeli Culture between the Two Intifadas: A Brief Romance* (Austin: University of Texas Press, 2008), 10.

16. Yehuda Amichai, *Shirim,1948–1962* (Jerusalem: Schocken, 1967), 42.

17. Eitan Kalinski, "Moreh lelashon ivrit muveset" ("Teacher of a Defeated Hebrew Language"), in *No Rattling of Sabers: An Anthology of Israeli War Poetry*, ed. Esther Raizen (Austin: Center for Middle Eastern Studies, the University of Texas at Austin, 1995), 148. My translation.

18. Compare with "Your Attention Please" by the Australian poet Peter Porter, which describes

civil preparations for an imminent nuclear attack. The poem ends: "All flags are flying fully dressed / On Government buildings—the sun is shining, / Death is the least we have to fear. / We area all in the hands of God, / Whatever happens happens by His Will. / Now go quickly to your shelters." In *Penguin Modern Poets* 2 (Harmondsworth, UK: Penguin Books, 1962), 108–9.

19. Based on Babylonian Talmud Sanhedrin 4:5: "he who destroys a human soul . . . it is as if he had destroyed an entire world."

20. Dahlia Ravikovitch, *Hovering at a Low Altitude: The Collected Poetry of Dahlia Ravikovitch,* trans. Chana Bloch and Chana Kronfeld (New York: W. W. Norton, 2009), 197.

21. A phrase from the Zionist song later to become the Israeli national anthem: "Kol od belevav pnima nefesh yehudi homiyah" ("As long as within the heart / A Jewish soul still yearns").

22. Nitzan and Back, *With an Iron Pen,* 60.

23. Yitzhak Laor, *Shirim ba'emek habarzel* (Poems in the Iron Valley) (Tel Aviv: Am Oved, 1990), 81–82.

24. Isaiah 5:6, 7:24, 9:17, 32:13; Jeremiah 17:1.

25. Nitzan and Back, *With an Iron Pen,* 117. The translation of this poem from Hebrew is my own.

26. Interview on YouTube. צבי עצמון על פוליטיקה 20.10.09 בשירה-מקום לשירה 14 min. January 31, 2011.

27. Nitzan and Back, *With an Iron Pen,* 7.

28. David Jacobson, *Does David Still Play before You?* (Detroit: Wayne State University Press, 1997); Karton-Blum Ruth, *Profane Scriptures: Reflections on the Dialogue with the Bible in Modern Hebrew Literature* (Cincinnati, OH: Hebrew Union College Press, 1999).

29. Nitzan and Back, *With an Iron Pen,* 65. I have retranslated it from Hebrew.

30. Ibid., 105

31. Ibid., 116.

32. Ibid., 43.

33. Ibid., 87.

34. Motti Lerner, *Hevle mashieḥ* (The pangs of the Messiah) (Tel Aviv: Or Am, 1988), 103.

35. Nitzan and Back, *With an Iron Pen,* 9. It is notable that the majority of the poets appearing in this anthology are born in the early to mid-twentieth century.

36. www.mfa.gov.il/MFA/MFAArchive/2000_2009/2000/2/Israeli%20Literature%201995–1998.

Chapter 13

Vexing Resistance, Complicating Occupation

A Contrapuntal Reading of Sahar Khalifeh's *Wild Thorns* and David Grossman's *The Smile of the Lamb*

Philip Metres

> The main battle in imperialism is over land, of course; but when it came to who owned the land, who had the right to settle and work on it, who kept it going, who won it back, and who now plans its future—these issues were reflected, contested, and even for a time decided in narrative. As one critic has suggested, nations themselves *are* narrations. The power to narrate, or to block other narratives from forming and emerging, is very important to culture and imperialism, and constitutes one of the main connections between them.
>
> —Edward Said, *Culture and Imperialism,* xiii

> Two children of the same cruel parent do not necessarily love each other. They often see in each other the image of the past oppressor. So it is, to some extent, between Israelis and Arabs: the Arabs fail to see us as a bunch of survivors. They see in us a nightmarish extension of the oppressing colonizing Europeans. We Israelis often look at Arabs not as fellow victims but as an incarnation of our own past oppressors: Cossacks, pogrom-makers, Nazis who have grown mustaches and wrapped themselves in keffiyehs, but who still are in the usual business of cutting Jewish throats.
>
> —Amos Oz, *Under This Blazing Light,* 8–9

> *Sumūd*is watching your home turned into a prison. You, *Sāmid,* choose to stay in that prison, because it is your home, and because you fear that if you leave, your jailer will not allow you to return. Living like this, you must constantly resist the twin temptations of either acquiescing in the jailer's plan in numb despair, or becoming crazed by consuming hatred for your jailer and yourself, the prisoner.
>
> —Raja Shehadeh, *The Third Way,* viii

Religious War. Suicide Bombers. Unwanted. PLO. Arafat. Aggressive. These were among the initial (and anonymous) free associations for the word "Palestinian" that my students wrote down and shared during the first day of my course on Palestinian and Israeli literatures.[1] How do earnest and often-thoughtful midwestern college students at a fine liberal arts university come to such reflex impressions? We need look no further than our mass media. Take, for example, a recent issue of *Newsweek* magazine, during the recent battles for control over Gaza between Palestinian factions Hamas and Fatah. The cover photo shows a Hamas fighter, dressed in black and face hooded except for his eyes, straddling atop a tank and holding an AK-47 aloft in the air (pointed, ironically, right to "JOLIE," whose name and story graces the header title: "ANGELINA JOLIE TAKES ON THE WORLD."[2] The main title—"Why Gaza Matters: NEW VIOLENCE, OLD HATREDS AND A GROWING RADICAL THREAT TO AMERICA'S HOPE FOR THE MIDEAST"—attempts to situate the conflict in Gaza as part of *our* concern, *our* hopes for the Middle East (for democracy, ironically, given our complete embargo of the democratically elected Hamas government). The image is menacing, phallic, and almost faceless.

Inside the magazine, the panoply of photos that illustrate the story falls into all-too-familiar categories of Orientalist images of Middle Eastern life: (1) masked fighters, (2) the dead, (3) mourning *hijab*-wearing women, and (4) swarming crowds. All these images, save one, are images of people without faces, whose faces are occluded, shut off, or lost in crowds. If the face-to-face encounter is, to paraphrase philosopher Emmanuel Levinas, the ethical moment, the moment in which we encounter the radical and irreducible otherness of another person, we can say without hesitation that the images displayed in these photographs render such an encounter almost impossible.

There is one exception to this Orientalist cast of images, however. It appears in the blurred face of a Palestinian youth turned toward the camera as he helps others lay a bleeding Palestinian man onto a gurney in an emergency room. He is overcome with terror, and his face is almost pleading. In this moment, we as viewers are interpellated into the scene, and find ourselves in the moment that Levinas describes as when "the face is the other who asks me not to let him die alone, as if to do so were to become an accomplice in his death."[3] For all the possibilities that this photograph invites, it also invites the uneasily imperial response—*we must save these people from themselves*—rather than ask, "How has it come to this?"

Forty years after the Six-Day War, the Israeli military occupation of the West Bank and Gaza Strip (now under nominal Palestinian control), continues unabated. Yet the costs of that occupation—economic, cultural, political, and moral—to both Palestinian and Israeli societies have not gone unnoticed. In marked contrast to the American media's often-depthless, distanced, or worriedly "balanced" stories, Palestinian and Israeli writers have courageously scrutinized and exposed their own nation's myths about occupation and resistance in the post-1967 situation, and have invited readers into the complex lives that confront and are confronted by such political turmoil. Two novels, *Wild Thorns* (1976) by Sahar Khalifeh, and *The Smile of the Lamb* (1982) by David

Grossman, both set in 1972, five years after the Six-Day War, dramatize the social and personal crises that the occupation (and the violent resistance to it) has fomented in uncannily (Freud's *unheimlichkeit*) similar ways; for the Palestinian Khalifeh and the Israeli Grossman—both of whom came of age in the post-1967 landscape—the very possibilities of a home/land as a site of peace and security have fractured.[4] For both Israelis and Palestinians, in Khalifeh's and Grossman's telling, the old ways—the traditional social structures of gender and class, the old stories and myths that have constructed the present—no longer suffice. Yet these novels, addressing primarily their national audience, also differ in some critical ways: (1) how the story is told—that is, their generic choices of narrative style; (2) how the occupation registers existential crises for Israelis and Palestinians; (3) how each represents "the other";(4) how each demonstrates the possibilities and perils of identifying with "the other"; and (5) what possible new formation(s) might result of this slow-burning catastrophe.

Contrapuntal Reading and the Novel: Strategies of Reconciliation or Resistance?

In order to avoid the tendency to privilege one nation's narration over the other—which, arguably, has led to the ongoing violence in the first place—I wish to employ a *contrapuntal* reading strategy. To provide an antidote to the pervasive and damaging Western system of representations of the Orient (i.e., the Middle East) known as Orientalism—and to address the relative absence in his early theorization of non-Western resistance to Orientalism—Edward Said proposes in *Culture and Imperialism* that scholars actively engage both Western canonical literature tradition and the Orient's self-representations through a method called "contrapuntal reading." Employing a musical term that denotes the interplay between two "independent but harmonically related melodic parts sounding together" (dictionary.com), Said's notion of contrapuntalism—read against his notion of imperialism and resistance—rides the tension between being a totalizing theory of global cultural harmonic interdependence and one that emphasizes disjunction and polyphony. At first, Said's usage of the term appears to emphasize and even embrace a vision of a kind of total culture, by:

> reread[ing] [the cultural archive] not univocally but contrapuntally, with a simultaneous awareness both of the metropolitan history that is narrated and of those other histories against which (and together with which) the dominating discourse acts. In the counterpoint of Western classical music, various themes play off one another; yet in the resulting polyphony there is concert and order, and organized interplay that derives from the themes, not from a rigorous melodic or formal principle outside the work. . . . It should be evident that no one overarching theoretical principle governs the whole imperialist ensemble.[5]

Here, Said's notion of contrapuntal reading affirms a fundamentally "organized interplay" between imperial narratives and other narratives (resistant or collaborative), even if such interplay is marked by the kind of multiplicity and ambivalence of Homi Bhabha's revision of Saidian postcolonial theory. In this rendering, Said balances his own double investment and dual identity as philologist and global scholar invested in both Western and non-Western culture alongside his long-standing partisan investments as a Palestinian Arab, exiled from a country that does not formally exist.[6]

Israelis, as both victims of the West and beneficiaries of Western guilt, inhabit a liminal space between West and the non-West. Palestinians, as victims of the West (the Balfour Declaration, US unconditional support of Israel, and such) and the beneficiaries of Arab and Muslim outrage, would seem a simpler case, yet the years of exile have created a substantial polyphony of Palestinian voices, inflected as much by Western discourses of human rights and international law as by more homegrown articulations of resistance. Reading Palestinian and Israeli literature contrapuntally requires acknowledging, first and foremost, the fundamentally asymmetrical power relationship at the heart of the conflict—that the State of Israel (despite its obvious security concerns) wields a military might that makes it virtually impervious to the destructions that its enemies might slaver on about. The cultural work, therefore, in which each novel attempts to engage, will be different.

In the contrapuntal reading of Israeli and Palestinian literature, we must account for the particularity of each literary and cultural tradition, but refuse to leave it at that, and consider how this literature gets enacted at the level of praxis, of social and political implications. In her foundational *Resistance Literature,* Barbara Harlow makes the case for the novel as one of many narrative sites of resistance:

> Narrative . . . provides a more developed historical analysis of the circumstances of economic, political, and cultural domination and repression [than poetry] and through that analysis raises a systematic and concerted challenge to the imposed chronology of what Fredric Jameson has called "master narratives," ideological paradigms which contain within their plots a predetermined ending. The use by Third World resistance writers of the novel form as it has developed within the western literary tradition both appropriates and challenges the historical and historicizing presuppositions, the narrative conclusions, implicated within the western tradition and its development.[7]

In other words, resistance writers have adapted the novel form as a way of telling other stories, not only by sapping its former hold over their own destinies, but also by changing the way the stories are told, and what possible endings might emerge from them. This final point is one I will return to at the end of this essay, when I consider what these two narratives, *Wild Thorns* and *The Smile of the Lamb,* might offer us in terms of imagining the occupation and bringing to light the ways in which each citizenry might resist the logics of unending conflict and move into mutual futures.

Resistance and Its Discontents: *Wild Thorns* and the Struggle of Sumūd

Despite the fact that Palestinian writing has frequently appeared in the vanguard of resistance literature and its theorizations—Ghassan Kanafani coined the name "resistance literature" in the 1960s—Palestinian literature has questioned, complicated, and sometimes rejected romanticized representations of the resistance fighter. In poems such as Harun Hashim Rashid's "Against," Palestinian writing often demonstrates the struggle within Palestinians between an abhorrence of violence and war and the necessity to defend one's rights and one's homeland. Khalifeh's novel *Wild Thorns* compellingly dramatizes the struggle within Palestinian society, within families, and within individual characters, to articulate and participate in a meaningful and productive resistance to occupation. Telling the story of a West Bank Palestinian, Usama, who has returned after five years to engage in violent resistance against the occupation, Khalifeh shows how Usama must confront the ways in which life under occupation differs from his imaginings, but is not the simple defeat and humiliation he perceived it to be. Khalifeh's novel offers a range of responses to military occupation—all of which suggest the need to complicate our notion of resistance, seeing it not only as armed resistance: from Usama's guerrilla tactics, to Abu Adil's courting of journalists, from Basil's youthful radicalism to Zuhdi's emotional reactivism, to Adil's resistance through steadfastly refusing to leave Palestine. Khalifeh dispels Orientalist and monochromatic views of Palestinian society while dramatizing the struggles for individual Palestinians to come to terms with their own existential and personal location vis-à-vis the larger Arab-Israeli conflict. Khalifeh's novel proposes no easy answers about the question of resistance but suggests that the old ways (represented by the downfall of the house of Karmi) no longer suffice.

But what do we mean by resistance? As Diane Elam has noted, though "the concept of resistance enjoys a privileged status in contemporary criticism," *resistance* as a term is both ubiquitous and theoretically uninterrogated. Even the use of a term like *interrogated* in the context of Palestinian or Arab experience more generally demonstrates the abyssal distance between contemporary theoretical discourse and what is going on in prisons around the world, often in our name. *Resistance* as a critical term crystallized in 1966, when Palestinian writer and secular revolutionary Ghassan Kanafani theorized "resistance literature" as literature that was part of the "arena of struggle."[8] The struggle for Palestinians has been various and multiform—but the national struggle has been one for the recovery of land lost in the 1948 war (what Palestinians call the *nakhba*, the catastrophe) and the 1967 Six-Day War, and for the creation of a modern and dynamic Palestinian state. Since Palestinian literature has emerged in the wake of suffering, exile, and occupation, one of its cultural projects has been to recover (and in some sense, articulate for the first time) the repressed or lost facts of Palestinian life. What Edward Said has called the "permission to narrate"—what has been most denied to the Palestinians by the international media—was simply the power to communicate their own histories both to themselves (a people displaced, exiled, or occupied), and to the world outside hypnotized by the Zionist narrative of "a land without a people for a people without a land." Seizing this "permission to narrate" itself has been an act of resistance and an act of cultural survival.

Harlow's *Resistance Literature* expanded Kanafani's term into a theorization of the literature of national liberation movements, from El Salvador to South Africa, and invited us to see these struggles as parallel revolutionary movements, in solidarity ideologically and imaginatively. Yet Harlow's suggestive argument also implicitly and explicitly links resistance literature as an arm of armed struggle. After all, Kanafani's term "muqāwama" implied nothing less than armed struggle. For Harlow, the "resistance writer, like the guerrilla of the armed liberation struggle, is actively engaged in an urgent historical confrontation" (100). At times, Harlow's empowering and celebratory tone belies the bloody contradictions at the heart of national liberation struggles based on armed revolution and the tensions played out for writers between their imaginative labors and their intellectual and political investments.

Khalifeh's *Wild Thorns* (*Al Subar*), published in Arabic in 1976, is a novel that, in its heterogeneous representation of Palestinian life under Israeli occupation, enables a revaluation of resistance as a critical term, inviting a broader conception of resistance that may include armed struggle but also a host of other, less bloody and absolute responses to occupation. For Harlow, this novel "both vestiges the scenario of liberation and armed struggle scripted by the resistance movement's leadership in exile and critiques the atavistic structures of traditionalism that continue to resist social changes from within."[9] While Harlow captures the novel's double-movement, the novel does more than trace and critique the poles of revolutionism and traditionalism; through its employment of the novelistic form, *Wild Thorns* dramatizes the damage that each polarity wreaks upon the present and future. Yet the novel offers no easy solutions. *Wild Thorns* tracks a number of Palestinians whose lives are intertwined, and whose fates are ultimately inextricable from one another.[10] *Wild Thorns* is a remarkably self-conscious novel, embodying the "permission to narrate" as both a creative act of literary imagination and a representation of the nation to itself and to the outside world.[11] Because it begins in the point of view of Usama, a Palestinian romantic turned revolutionary who has been living abroad and is unused to life under military occupation, the novel invites and interpelates the reader—regardless of national origin —into the subject position of the exile.[12]

We see this new reality through Usama's eyes, heightened by his (and, arguably, "our") relative innocence regarding the mechanisms of occupation. Chapter two introduces Usama (and the novel's readers) to the humiliations of checkpoints—confiscations of banned goods, strip searches, and verbally abusive interrogations, as in: "Who's Usama al-Karmi?" "I am." "You are, huh? Why didn't you answer? You were in the toilet. How was it, filthy dirty as usual? Dirty Arabs! We build spotless sweet-smelling toilets and you fill them with shit!"[13] As Usama is interrogated about his reasons for returning, he can hear the screams of a young Palestinian woman who is being slapped around and probed between her legs for smuggled contraband. Anyone who has gone through Usama's experience more than once probably wants to forget and repress it, yet Khalifeh's narration of it—as if for the first time—summoning the sounds, sights, and smells of border control and checkpoints, must be seen as an act of testimony, of imaginative witness, and itself a resistance to the numbingly daily act of border crossings for Palestinian workers and travelers. As such, it brings us—those of us who are not privy to this reality (or even only glancingly)—into imaginative confrontation with the implications of occupation.

Yet Khalifeh's novel is not a mere protest against Israeli abuses but a dramatization of how Palestinians themselves attempt to survive the depredations of occupation. Usama's first act of resistance is a nonviolent one—a struggle of naming. During the border interrogation, Usama informs the soldier that his mother moved to Nablus:

> "My mother moved to Nablus."
> "Why did your mother move to Shekem?"
> "She likes Nablus."
> "Why does she like Shekem?"
> "She's got lots of relatives in Nablus."
> "And why have you left the oil countries to return to Shekem?"
> "I'm returning to Nablus because my father died."

Usama steadfastly holds to the Palestinian name, Nablus, despite the soldier's attempt to erase that name and its reality by calling it Shekem, the Israeli name for Nablus. Usama refuses to cede the name, even though it might mean his interrogation lasts longer, because he refuses to cede Palestinian reality. His version of reality may be misunderstood, misnamed, but it is his and he won't let go of it.

Khalifeh's novel suggests that we need to see such daily acts of resistance as courageous—perhaps even more courageous than acts of armed insurrection. In this way, the novel becomes a dramatization of the trials of *sumūd*, the steadfastness demonstrated by Palestinians who refuse to give up their cultural identity or leave their homeland. Yes, the novel begins with Usama's return to the West Bank and follows him as he plots an act of violent resistance. Yet rather than romanticizing Usama and his mission (which is to blow up buses of Palestinian workers heading for work in Israel to stop their complicity with the occupation), Khalifeh paints him as a vexed, naive, and deeply dangerous romantic who feels he must eviscerate himself of his own dreaminess and, in his thoughts, "become a rocket, a guided missile" (6). Usama's reckless acts (stabbing an Israeli soldier, then bombing a busload of Palestinians heading to Israel) cause reverberations that lead, in the end, to the destruction of the house of his uncle, Abu Adil Karmi, by Israeli soldiers—and, in some sense, to the death of his uncle as well.

Thus Khalifeh weaves Usama's return into the stories of the formerly aristocratic Karmi family, who are the center of this novel, in their various struggles to survive amid the new realities of occupation. Abu Adil, the family patriarch, can resist only through words, yet his daily sessions with journalists seem to lead nowhere, and they dramatize the seeming futility of language and narration. To make matters worse, Abu Adil requires the services of a costly kidney dialysis machine; his body is sucking the family dry. His aged and infirm body—like the infirmities of the patriarchal culture that Khalifeh increasingly addresses in later novels—becomes a figure for a language without vitality, a system whose inequities have become exposed by occupation as empty. Although Zuhdi, like Adil, will say, "words are our only weapon" (79), in an echo of Kanafani's famous novella, *Men in the Sun,* Zuhdi also laments: "we speak, but they don't hear us. Who can we speak to? For God's sake, who can we speak to?" (85). Khalifeh, like Kanafani, sees the older generation's reliance upon words alone to be insufficient; in this metafictional moment, Khalifeh articulates the fundamentally interpellative longings of Palestinian narrative—that it cease being merely an aesthetic object, but a hailing of those others who might make its language into reality.[14]

Wild Thorns thus depicts the traumatic changes to Palestinian life as a result of occupation, and the difficulties of Palestinians to make their way in the new landscape—both political and geographical. *Wild Thorns* is a thick description of place—not of a romanticized land about which the exiles like Usama have fantasized, but of a human geography. Yet at least at one point the translation saps the thickness of description. In an intriguing endnote, Nejd Yaziji remarks that "this passage [describing the now-desolate land of the abandoned Karmi farm], which goes on for a whole page in the Arabic original, is reduced in the English version to a four-line paragraph" (104). What interests me more than a critique of the novel as *genre* is how this particular novel—and its translation into English—creates new ways of seeing the occupation, and what such elisions might tell us about the distance between Palestinian realities and our own. This translatorly elision of description of the land might have been due to excessive particularity, with a host of native terms that seemed unnecessarily detailed for the English reader; it may have been deemed a distraction from the plot. And yet, we might also ask, does not the thick description of the land render more poignantly the heart of the Israeli-Palestinian conflict—who gets to own the land, to be stewards of the land? That the Karmi farm is in desolation suggests that the very "land rhetoric" that underlies Palestinian resistance ideology could not compete with Israeli economic opportunities for the attention of the Palestinian peasant.

Adil, the eldest son and cousin of Usama, has given up working the ancestral farm and is secretly working in Israel to feed his family and his father's dialysis machine.[15] Thus on the surface, Adil is a collaborator, a cynic who sacrifices his dignity and will—simply to keep up appearances for his father. In Usama's eyes, Adil and the rest of Palestinian society "inside" the occupied territories have disintegrated and have lost the will to resist. In a conversation between Usama and Adil, Usama vents his anger at the filthiness and lassitude of Palestinian life: "is this an occupation or a disintegration?"

(28), and asks Adil what he's doing "to oppose what goes on inside" (28). Adil responds, "the same as what you've done to oppose what's outside" (28). Usama, ever the Manichaean thinker, who believes you're either with us or against us, replies: "the picture's perfectly clear, can't you see that?" (29). Khalifeh counterposes Adil's more authorial point of view: "Flicking the flies from his face, Adil replied, 'There's more than one dimension to the picture'" (29).[16]

In this utterance, in this refusal of the absolutism of Usama's view, Adil embodies Khalifeh's novelistic embrace of the multiple yet bound fates of Palestinians; in her imagined world, all characters have human contours—Usama's tragic idealism, Adil's heartbreaking weariness, Basil's youthful radical fervor, Zuhdi's reactive passion, and so on—and each attempts to survive as they can. Yet even Zuhdi, a friend of Adil's, who is distrustful of revolutionaries while in prison and resists the resistance, gets sucked into battle when he finds himself blown off the bus and next to Usama as he fends off Israeli soldiers. Zuhdi's sudden transformation from a *sāmid*(one who practices *sumūd*) into a "wild thorn," one who resists, demonstrates how the occupation draws normally nonrevolutionary people into violent acts. By contrast, Adil's resistance is *sumūd*—survival, staying put, simply not giving up and leaving, is his resistance to occupation, his final stand.[17]

Yet for Khalifeh, Palestinian life is full of contradictions, of "impossible choices," between family and nation, between individual and family, between self and self. And this is precisely why a progressive reading of the novel misses the novel's traumatic kernel. The ultimate brutality of the occupation is that no one is spared from ethical taint; for Usama's act, and for the complicity of Adil's sister holding weapons in the house, the house of Karmi is demolished by the Israeli military. In the waning moments before the destruction, Adil attempts to take out some personal belongings of the family and ends up consciously leaving behind the dialysis machine. He does it, even though he knows his father will die:

> Would you kill a man, then? Kill your own father? But men are always being killed. And if my father goes on living, we'll all die. . . . Me, Nuwar, the children. Haven't we lost enough already? Usama, Basil, the family estate. And all in self-defence. In defence of a dignified, honourable life. Let my father die! No let him live! If you save him, you'll save your own soul from the damnation of a terrible crime. (204)

Although Adil is, finally, the main character of this novel, he is a troubling hero; his refusal of armed resistance does not leave him with any greater moral clarity or authority, and leaves more questions than answers. Adil's complicity in the eventual death of his father suggests that the occupation leaves no hands unbloodied, and that the old order of Palestinian society that Abu Adil represents cannot survive. But what will be there to replace it? Will it be born in the youthful radicalism of Basil, who escapes into the city—a cipher for the increasingly radical generations that have succeeded this novel's historical moment?[18] Will it emerge from those moments of cross-national identification, when Adil carries off the Israeli child who has witnessed the murder of her soldier-father by Usama (160), or the weeping of Israeli prison guards over the tearful reunion of an imprisoned father and his son? (147–48).[19] Or will it be more mundane than that, in the daily persistence of survival that the novel ends with, as "people [go] about their business, buying vegetables, fruit and bread" (207)?[20] Thus Khalifeh's novel functions as both resistance literature and a literature resistant to singular and fundamentalist notions of resistance. Khalifeh helps us see how radicalism is bred out of conditions of extreme privation and humiliation, and the multiplicity of Palestinian responses to those conditions. Finally, Khalifeh confronts the ways in which Palestinians struggle to fill their personal or familial needs against the national needs—and how sometimes the claims of human relations move us beyond the bounds of national allegiance.

Adil's example shows how Palestinians see the humanity of Israelis, even though they often see their worst sides in the context of military occupation. Yet, arguably, the novel ultimately points to the impossibility of any permanent solidarity, at least under the present conditions of occupation. Adil might see the Israeli soldier about to demolish his house as his father, but in the end the soldier will destroy the house anyway. One can critique Khalifeh's novel for what might be seen as stock Israeli characters, and yet she offers an imaginative portrait of how the fates of Israelis and Palestinians are bound. Whether they are bound to end with the bullet or by mutual recognition remains to be seen.

The Israeli Dilemma: Jewish Conscience and the Arab

If the struggle for Palestinian writers has been to gain the "permission to narrate"—to articulate their personal and national stories in ways that will function as both cultural repositories for the dispossessed and interpellative acts to hail the international community to intercede on the behalf of Palestinians—for Israeli writers, the struggle has been to tell the story of this nascent nation-state in ways that might suture the gap between the diasporic religious, literary, and cultural traditions and the new realities of Israeli life. Even in works where the Arab was little more than a stock figure, stories such as S. Yizhar's "The Prisoner"—written and published in the middle of Israel's War of Independence—demonstrate how Israeli writers have engaged in unsparing moral questioning and critique of the abuses of power by an occupying army.[21] Thus Israeli writers have functioned vitally as bearers of conscience and prophets for social justice, even during the moments when the nation-state's very existence seemed in question. Yet according to critics Menakhem Perry and Barbara McKean Parmenter, the early Zionist imagination and its representation in Hebrew literature at least until the 1960s, was suffused with the representational repertoire that Said termed Orientalism.[22] Israeli representations of Palestinian Arabs (whether fellahin or Bedouin) tended, ambivalently, either to idealize them as closer to the land with what Parmenter calls "a clear and condescending paternalism"[23] or to demonize them as threatening forces ready to destroy Jews.

Given the ongoing dynamics of Israeli literature's ambivalent relationship to its Arab coinhabitants, David Grossman's novel *The Smile of the Lamb* (1982)[24] (and subsequent nonfiction *The Yellow Wind*) marked a pivotal moment, where the primal encounter of Jews and Arabs, Israelis and Palestinians, seemed to release its reader from yet another traumatic repetition of inexorable and unending conflict.[25] Part of a vanguard of Israeli writers who emerged after the Six-Day War, Grossman demonstrates an unsparingly honest and self-critical examination of the psychological and moral damage of occupation on Israelis and Palestinians.[26] Grossman illuminates a complex and painful portrait of how a homeland for the Jewish nation, and a triumphant victory for its vulnerable state, have meant suffering for a dispossessed people. Rather than glossing over that pain, Grossman's conscience-rich narrative harkens back to the Hebrew prophetic tradition and extends the vein of Israeli literature of conscience manifested in the works of Yizhar, Amos Oz, and A. B. Yehoshua into a fuller representation of the Arab. By giving voice both to an Israeli soldier in moral crisis (Uri) and an Arab outcast outraged by the death of his son (Khilmi), Grossman's novel opens up the possibility of cross-national identification in ways that echo and extend Khalifeh's novel. In some sense, *The Smile of the Lamb* reads like a response to *Wild Thorns,* insofar as it, six years later, engages in the parallel cultural work of imagining the lives of the Israeli soldiers on the other side of the occupation—but with a similar degree of sympathy and heartbreak. In the following analysis, then, by focusing on narrative technique, character, representations of the occupation and the other, and identification, I explore Grossman's achievement and test its limits against Khalifeh's version of the occupation.

The Smile of the Lamb: Extending *Al-Subar* to Sabras

In contrast to Khalifeh's poetics of everyday life under occupation, *The Smile of the Lamb* is a fractured, self-conscious protomodernist tour de force told from four different narrative points of view in alternating chapters, four monologues of characters undergoing existential crises in the two days covered in the story. *The Smile of the Lamb*'s central drama—at least for the concerns of this essay—concerns the interweaving of the voices and fates of two Israeli soldiers (Uri and Katzman), a child psychologist (Shosh), and an old Arab man (Khilmi).[27] These four narratives encapsulate four ways of telling a story—Uri's stream of consciousness, Khilmi's fabular magical realism, Katzman's third person noir, and Shosh's confessionalism—and dramatize, as Faulkner's multiple points of view do, a world in which unitary, stable meanings have broken down. In each narration, tellingly, the characters have both lost faith in the fictions of their fathers, and have betrayed (or will) their own adoptive sons.[28]

Uri begins the narrative, in medias res, at the point when Uri has finally left the Israeli Defense Forces for good and rushed to Khilmi's side, to share with him the news of the death of his son, Yazdi, and, we learn, to offer himself up as a sacrifice for his loss.

The youthful Uri (whose name means "light" in Hebrew) comes from a Sephardic background and has a kind of open-heartedness and idealism that startles and attracts the more defensive characters around him, especially the cynical Katzman. Uri's longing for a enlightened occupation, for one that helps the Palestinians, flounders when he finds himself unable to counteract the bruising inhumanity of collective punishment that occupation requires; the final straw—the murder of the son of his friend and adoptive father-figure Khilmi—causes him to rush to Khilmi's side and to offer himself as a hostage to end the occupation. Uri embodies the idealism and longing for social justice that Israeli writers have promulgated; his leap, however, from longing to crossing over, might suggest Grossman's own desire to overcome the impasse between Israelis and Palestinians.

Katzman, Uri's friend, by contrast, is thirty-nine and transformed himself from a Polish immigrant to a sabra through sheer force of his own will. His belligerent and self-protective cynicism, he acknowledges, crystallized during his traumatic experience as a young boy hiding in what he calls "the pit" with his father and mother during the Holocaust (174–79). For Katzman, despite his questions about the morality of the occupation, there is no safety in the world (146–50). Still, he marvels at Uri's astonishing openness to the world, and is drawn to his love (18–22). Dramatizing Katzman's own notion of selfhood as opaque, Grossman tells Katzman's story from the distance of the third person, a story that embodies Israel's post-Holocaust trauma, which inflects its fierce warrior ethos and occasionally defiant Nietzschean antagonism with world opinion.[29]

Khilmi (Arabic for "gentle"), an aged Palestinian man who is an outcast in his own society, is a dreamer and storyteller who weaves fabulous tales in order to fend off the brutalities of life—whether from a humiliating social culture or from military occupation (68–72). Like a male Scheherazade, Khilmi tells his stories as an act of survival, a defense against a murderous world where powerful people threaten without remorse. He tried to teach his bastard son, Yazdi (whom he has adopted), a private language that only they would share, to protect him, but Yazdi ultimately rejects his father's fantasies as helpless dodderings of an old fool and joins the resistance forces:

> Father, he says, you dream. We have important things to do. We have to fight.
>
> They are very powerful, I answer, and cannot be beaten by force.
>
> By what, then? By silence? By dreams in a barrel?
>
> How he spoke. How ugly the word "barrel" sounded coming from his lips.
>
> No, not by silence; but by being softer than a feather. More fragile than an egg.
>
> It won't do any good, *Ya ba*. They understand only the language of power.
>
> This will be a different kind of war. Long and arduous. And for weapons we will use stubborn patience and infinite weakness. They will not be able to bear it. (36)

Yet this method of "stubborn patience" (Khilmi's articulation of his own kind of *sumūd*), cannot withstand the crushing force of betrayal. With the death of Yazdi, Khilmi threatens to give up storytelling and to take up violence as the only remaining means of response.

Through the character of Khilmi, Grossman richly explores "concrete details of everyday life in the West Bank and has a variety of Palestinian characters, folkloristic anecdotes, and even a detailed "semiotics" of plants that are unknown to the Israeli reader and called by their Arab names."[30] Khilmi's presence, for Perry, "is exciting and exceptional among Arab characters in Hebrew literature. Nevertheless, it seems impossible to avoid stereotypes in describing the other. In Grossman, too, Hilmi [*sic*] the Arab is close to nature, speechless, occupied with fantasies and day-dreams, passive and insane" (618). Given the critiques of representations of Arabs in Israeli literature, Grossman takes a risk by representing the only Palestinian character as a half-mad, half-blind holy fool who eats soil and rubs himself with lemons to reduce his stink. There is something so excessively Orientalist about the brute facts of the character, stated in this way, and yet Grossman fully imbues Khilmi with a kind of humanity that is undeniable.[31] By making Khilmi an outsider to his own culture, and by making his novel about fictionality itself, Grossman's portrayal inoculates against the criticism of representation that a more realist novel would fall prey to.

For Rachel Feldhay Brenner, *The Smile of the Lamb* is partly a story of how children reject the stories of love and social harmony that their fathers instilled in them, in favor of the intoxicating brew of militaristic domination and social cohesion offered by tribe and state. For Brenner, the fathers' stories attempt to

> rewrite the traumatic effects of defeat and dispossession . . . mental and physical abuse (Khilmi), and the Nazi decree of annihilation (Katzman's father) into stories aimed at forging relationships of love and trust. These tales teach neither submission nor violent opposition to oppression . . . [they instead confront] the dominating system with a story of love and poetic imagination. It is this message of love that the heirs to the stories are meant to communicate to the victorious mainstream, nurtured by stories of militancy, war, and domination.[32]

Read back from her accounts of social justice by other Jewish and Israeli writers, this reading caps her compelling account of a tradition of writers whose works points toward coexistence. In a sense, however, *The Smile of the Lamb* both contains this reading and its opposite. Particularly in the case of Katzman—but arguably in each case—these stories function doubly. On the one hand, as Brenner rightly suggests, they provide a way for the father to protect the son from the depredations of the war and its ways of domination; on the other hand, they also insulate and sometimes even traumatize the child with the single-mindedness of their visions, visions that are incommensurable with the realities the children face later. Thus Katzman feels as if his father betrayed him. In other words, the trauma experienced by the fathers is thus communicated through the stories, the stories become a kind of reaction-formation to the world. Yes, it is true that the sons reject these stories—but they do so because they find them insufficient to the world that they face. In other words, they refuse to be sacrificed upon the altars of their father's imaginations. *The Smile of the Lamb,* in a central sense, is a novel about the rejection of the child to the father's sacrifice, to the father's attempts to placate an implacable God, and a profound fiction at war with fictionality.

Here I have restaged the critical debate, then, between Brenner's notion of fiction as a liberating site of possibility and Perry's notion of the character's fiction as ultimately being lies: "The fact that several characters are involved in weaving a network of lies—including lying to themselves—or a network of fantasies, adds to the difficulty [of this Faulknerian novel]."[33] Grossman's novel, as stated earlier, holds both of these points of view. Fiction clearly has aided and informed the Zionist project of statehood, for example, even as it has turned one eye away from its effects on its Arab coinhabitants. As Perry notes, "personal life and West Bank problems are inseparable. There is an integral Israeli-Palestinian totality reflecting a single set of tendencies,"[34] though those tendencies are about how characters lie to themselves and others in ways that will end up destroying them. In the end, though, these lies do not destroy the state, but actually seem to underwrite it. The state reasserts itself in the end, in part because the lies are fantasies that have no power beyond the few that they have entranced. Still, for Perry, "the fabricated stories are something positive, a journey several people take together, of their own free will, to a 'better world.' But Hilmi's [*sic*] last deed resembles the lies of others. In a desperate attempt to preserve his own world he must act according to the rule opposed to his world" (619).

Grossman stages debates within Israeli society about the occupation through the conflict between Katzman and Uri. During the Six-Day War, Katzman protests the absurd violence of warfare represented by shelling Kalkilya too much; Katzman, like Grossman's portrait of Moshe Dayan, intimates the critique of the warrior trapped in his own cage of paranoia: "Dayan was like a trapped wolf scurrying around his cage. His whole life had been a nervous repetition of this behavior. In his youth, defying death or the battlefield, he had never known what was impelling him . . . the cage that held Dayan was infinitely elastic" (258). The cage, in a sense, is a figure for the inner oppression that the occupation creates for the occupier.

Neither Katzman nor Uri believes in the occupation—in contrast to the messianic Israeli settlers who believe the West Bank is their birthright. Katzman, toward the end of the novel, says that the occupation turns everyone "into hostages" (189), but he rejects Uri's acting through the radical notion of "absolute justice": "[Khilmi and Uri are] talking about absolute values. Either the army withdraws from all the territories or else—Uri dies" (190). For Katzman, absolute justice is a "cowardly evasion of commitment . . . an invention of weaklings . . . a "hormone secreted from my brain" (224). Katzman believes that absolute justice paralyzes people from what needs to be done to secure oneself against the world. At this moment, Katzman—oddly enough—begins to look more like Adil of *Wild Thorns,* and Uri more like Usama. While Uri clearly is a character with whom it may be easier to identify (after all, he is the peace activist of the work), his passionate, naive idealism causes danger for others as perilous as Usama's. What I am suggesting here is that Grossman's novel complicates our own (at least my own) longing for the heroic, conscience-muscled Jew who will follow universal values against the will of the state; the ending solidifies that perhaps those willing to break the impasse may not be the ones whom we expect.

Although Katzman believes Uri is after absolute justice, the novel suggests Uri's outrage against the occupation comes from his own profound experience of helplessness at the collective punishment leveled against ordinary people. When youth in Andal, the town where Uri works, throw a stone and strike an Israeli soldier, Katzman orders that the donkey the soldiers kill in the ensuing "battle" should remain in the center of the town. The decaying donkey becomes, in Uri's eyes, the stinking embodiment of the occupation, whose stench is a kind of undeniable truth. The dead animal, the mute creature unable to speak through its pain—like the Palestinians themselves—becomes too much for Uri to bear: "I could forgive [Katzman] everything except the donkey" (274). Yet arguably what drives Uri equally crazy is how the Palestinians seem to put up with this festering presence:

> Once, just before sunset, a man in an undershirt walked over with a sack and began to winnow flour right in front of the donkey, flour for baking pita bread. Then an old woman led her husband out to sit beside the man, and a few minutes later they were joined by three old men. One was smoking a hookah, and I could almost hear the water bubble in the pipe. Fine white flour flew in the evening breeze and landed gently on the donkey carcass. Another old man rolled himself a cigarette. He sealed it with the slow movement of his tongue. Two little schoolgirls wearing uniforms skipped gaily past the donkey. I started the jeep and took off, oblivious to everything. (277)

The scene of everyday life continuing, despite the donkey corpse at the center of everything, disturbs Uri to the point of deserting the army and giving himself up to Khilmi. Rather than seeing the Palestinians' actions as a profound act of survival, of maintaining daily activity despite the butchery at the center of life—another articulation of *sumūd*—Uri (like Usama in *Wild Thorns*) appears to interpret it as a kind of submission and defeat.

While for Uri the donkey becomes the traumatic embodiment of the occupation, and motivates his rebellion, for Khilmi, the death of his son, Yazdi, brings him to reject his formerly "passive resistance" (242) and remove himself from the legal web of occupation—"those poisoned webs they weave around us, more deadly than naked hatred" (237)—and burn his *huwiya,* the identity card that grants him legal status under military law. Like Antigone mourning her brother, Khilmi removes himself from the web of symbolic order to weave his own web of narrative and, now, agency through violence. Although Khilmi has threatened, since the beginning of the novel, to cease his storytelling, his incantatory narrative persists—though now it is filled with a catalog of humiliations that life under occupation entails. In this contradiction, again, Grossman dramatizes fiction's power and danger—that, in becoming an organizing principle of understanding the world, fictions can exclude that which runs counter to itself. In this heteroglossic novel, Grossman attempts to forge a fiction that can contain, but not domesticate or destroy, the multiple truths interwoven at the heart of the conflict between Israelis and Palestinians.

Khilmi's penultimate story—in which he reveals his story of flying (a dynamite truck of oil speculators blows up and kills all the men of the town)—contains the image of a map that covers everything in his town and world. This map, an image of Cartesian notions of spatial control, industrial capitalism's thirst for oil, and Zionist desire for the land, and of fictionality itself, captures the novel's ambivalence about its own claims for truth:

> a kind of silken map, which the four white youths unfurled . . . the map spread endlessly . . . the map continued to unfurl in their soft hands, and a shadow fell across the crowd as the map flew above them, and the four youths separated farther and farther, climbing over hill and dale, and through the silken map with its red arrows and shining stars . . . I realized I, too, was under the sheer silk, yet I could see above it and watch the youths vanish to the four winds of heaven, and like mildew spreading, there appeared on it a silhouette of the iron monster [the train]. (296)

Thus like fiction itself, like all grand narratives, the map both locates and threatens to suffocate Khilmi in his town. Yet the map, and the whole town, explodes when a bystander lights a match. In Khilmi's story, Grossman attempts to give voice to the subaltern, to the one who is being mapped, whose stories cannot be heard.

The Smile of the Lamb, in this way, advances further than *Wild Thorns* in its exploration and imagination of characters from both nationalities. Yet Grossman's authorial identification with these characters does not preclude his powerful dramatization of the dangers of identification. Identification, as a psychological process of imagining oneself in the life of another, has powerful political possibilities, yet, as the criticisms of identification have shown, identification can be a powerful way of erasing the other.[35] In Uri's powerful identification with Khilmi, Grossman dramatizes how such identification can lead to powerful cross-national acts of solidarity, or—more menacingly—to one's own death (as Khilmi has resolved to kill "adoptive" son Uri rather than let him go, as he let his own son go). Similarly, in *Wild Thorns,* when Adil suddenly recognizes his father's face in the Israeli soldier about to demolish his house, he decides to leave his father's kidney machine behind, leading to his death. Identification's peril—like fiction's peril—is that in imagining the other we risk erasing the other though we also risk erasing ourselves.

For all of Grossman's labors on behalf of protesting the occupation and imagining the possibilities of cross-national identification, *The Smile of the Lamb*'s conclusion courts a return to the same problematic dynamic inherent in Israeli literature. Katzman, in what can only be described as an act of sacrificial love—an act of the father sacrificing himself for *his* symbolic son, Uri—storms Khilmi's cave alone to save Uri, and is shot dead by Khilmi. Yet just prior to the shooting, Uri does not look any longer like a lamb: "it isn't the smile of the lamb anymore, it's a grimacing mask of evil" (323). Brenner argues that "Uri ultimately fails to transform the legacy of love into a stepping stone enabling a dialogue between the warring parties . . . [and] "though the two characters have exchanged positions, the positions themselves have not changed" (267). Whether we read the ending as Katzman's successful transformation into a loving being or Uri's regression to monstrosity, we must also consider Khilmi's fate; as in the ending of Yehoshua's "Facing the Forests," the Palestinian is dragged away by law enforcement, while the symbolic exchange between Uri and Katzman remains central. Thus the Palestinian becomes simply the obstacle that an Israeli character requires to find redemption.

The final sentences of the novel return to the oppressive image of spatial control. In analyzing the land-rhetoric of Israelis and Palestinian, Parmenter argues that "the idea of land transformed into a topographic map constitutes a profound negation of rootedness."[36] Grossman pursues and develops that image to one not simply of topography, but one of the complex distancing apparatus of military surveillance, of land as a set of squared coordinates: "as they make their way down the path, someone runs up carrying a folded stretcher, and far away, in the city of Jerusalem, a helicopter takes off and the pilot traces the little squares on a military map with his finger, searching for Andal" (325). At the novel's end, then, we have the inexorable reassertion of military distantiation, of a seemingly impossible gap between Israeli and Palestinian realities. The city of Jerusalem—the spiritual heart of both Israeli and Palestinian life—here signifies the center of state power, from which the apparatus of control extends. The pilot's finger may be able to locate Andal, the small Palestinian town, on his map, but Andal will not be found.

Endings (as) Beginnings

Ironically, then, while *The Smile of the Lamb* arguably extends the possibilities of cross-national identification and solidarity implicit in *Wild Thorns*, Grossman's novel does not offer any imagination of what coexistence might look like. In both *Wild Thorns* and *The Smile of the Lamb*, the final scenes leave us with a powerful sense that nothing has changed. While *The Smile of the Lamb* represents the reassertion of military order and domination, *Wild Thorns* ends with a scene of life in the marketplace that is a precise repetition of one that occurs toward the beginning of the novel. However, what has changed as a result of each novel is, perhaps, the reader's understanding of the situation —by imaginative identification, by the virtual *living-through* that novels enable. As Brenner has shown, "these literatures [dissent] from the widely accepted ideological propagation of the irreparable antagonism between Palestinian and Jewish national groups . . . [and] shows that the two literatures affirm a complex yet indissoluble affinity between the two communities."[37] The very fact of the numerous parallels in these novels—their careful and critical dramatization of life under occupation, their imaginative attempts to leap into understanding the heterogeneous subjectivities who must cope with the effects of occupation, their longing for images of coexistence—suggests a solidarity between (at least some) Israelis and Palestinians that most media narratives obfuscate.

Further, these novels speak not only to Israelis and Palestinians, to readers of Hebrew and Arabic, but also to all of us who read the works in translation. Implicitly, each of these novels bridles against the limited way that these national readers might conceive of their nation's dilemmas, and imagines and appeals to an international audience as well. Although the cultural work that each novel engages is slightly different, when we read contrapuntally, we can see how *Wild Thorns* represents Palestinian life not only to Palestinians, but to Israelis or Americans as well—showing the pain of occupation but also the complexity of Palestinian responses to it, and posing multiple modes of resistance against each other. Khalifeh herself once remarked that "you cannot liberate the Arabs without liberating the Israelis; you cannot liberate the Israelis without liberating the Americans."[38] Ultimately, while Khalifeh "does not present a viable alternative to the nationalist vision,"[39] she does dramatize the irreconcilable elements of the nationalist rhetoric with the experience of those whom that rhetoric seeks to employ as victims for the patrimony of the generation of 1948. We can see how *The Smile of the Lamb* presents a dramatic argument for the way in which the traumatic past of Jewish suffering and the reactions to those traumas has led to an occupation has made Israelis prisoners to their own military victory.

Perhaps Emile Habiby is correct when he says that "the literary portrayal of Jews and Arabs, each in the works of the other, will not change even when we know one another better and write about each other as individuals—the change will occur only after a political solution is found, which will bring normalization and peace between the two nations."[40] At the same time, these novels have acted as a kind of vanguard for peaceful coexistence, insofar as they not only dramatize the hectic present but also humanize the people that it represents. Sadly, some thirty years after the publication of *Wild Thorns*, and twenty-five after the publication of *The Smile of the Lamb*, the novels continue to speak to the ongoing conflict grinding on in Israel and Palestine, and to the largely absent coverage of the human tragedy that falls beneath the politically charged narrations and mappings of the conflict in the United States.

What Khalifeh's novel offers us today, in its recognition of the economic interdependence of Israel and Palestine, is perhaps a rejection of the short-sightedness of the two-state solution, or at least a rejection of the idea that Palestinian sovereignty is the ultimate positive goal for Palestinians. What we need to see is not the inextricability of the Palestinian state from the Israeli occupation of the West Bank and Gaza, but the inextricability of Palestinian and Israeli futures. Although there are many reasons to reject a single democratic state, the notion of a single democratic state option that once was "formally introduced by al-Fatah . . . in 1968,"[41] is again being proposed by such intellectuals as Ali Abunimah. In the two-state solution, a traditional (in both senses of the term) nationalism suggests no transformation of society, but a retrenchment of old values; it fails to recognize what has been called "the facts on the ground": that 20 percent of the Israeli population is Arab, and that a sizeable portion of the West Bank has been annexed through an aggressive policy of settlement by Israelis. Much work remains to be done—work that necessarily requires the United States, given its historic role in complicating the peace process by abetting the military occupation and settlement of the West Bank simply to initiate the first steps toward mutual recognition. Mutual recognition would move beyond a grudging delivery of land or peace. It must include and become a postnationalist articulation of the common goals of cultural survival. In the end it may be that the walls of nationalism need to be erected, in order that, at some future date, they will be seen as no longer necessary—and will fall almost of their own accord. Yet the probings of the common life done by Khalifeh and Grossman are suggestive of the initial imaginings of two nations in search of a common future.

Notes

Thanks to Jonathan LaGuardia for his research assistance and conversations about this essay. Thanks to my students who have contributed to my thinking about Israeli and Palestinian literature. Thanks as well to John Carroll University's Graduate School, for a research fellowship that supported the writing of this essay, and to the Sustenance Group (Jeanne Colleran, Brenda Wirkus, Diana Taylor, Steven Hayward, John Spencer, Joe Kelly, Jay Newhard, and Derek Cohen) for our talks about Judith Butler.

1. For Israelis, the associations included, in order of frequency: *Victim, Palestinian Conflict, War, Ariel Sharon, Wailing Wall, Mossad, Dangerous, and Government killing innocents.*

2. One of the subtexts of so many Orientalist images is that Arab men are after our women; the placement of "JOLIE" above the gun barrel of the straddling fighter amply satiates that fear.

3. Quoted in Judith Butler, *Precarious Life: The Powers of Mourning and Violence* (New York: Verso, 2004), 131.

4. Khalifeh began writing in earnest after the Six-Day War: "The year 1967 became a watershed year for me in a political and a personal sense. I felt that I could no longer remain an alienated housewife. I had to participate in the predicament of my people and contribute though my writings" (Khalifeh quoted in Suha Sabbagh, ed., *Palestinian Women of Gaza and the West Bank* [Bloomington: Indiana University Press, 1998], 137). Similarly, Grossman once enlisted himself in "the generation that celebrated its bar mitzvah during the Six-Day War" (David Grossman, *The Yellow Wind,* trans. Haim Watzman [New York: Farrar, Straus and Giroux, 1988], 211).

5. Edward Said, *Culture and Imperialism* (New York: Vintage, 1993), 51.

6. In some sense, Said's greatest autobiography has been his criticism, which always keeps in the background the loss of Palestine as its motivating raison d'être.

7. Barbara Harlow, *Resistance Literature* (New York: Methuen, 1987), 78.

8. Ibid., 2, italics hers. Subsequent quotations are cited parenthetically in the text.

9. Barbara Harlow, "Partitions and Precedents: Sahar Khalifeh and Palestinian Political Geography," in *Intersections: Gender, Nation, and Community in Arab Women's Novels,* ed. Suhair Majaj, Lisa, Paula W. Sunderman, and Therese Saliba (Syracuse, NY: Syracuse University Press, 2002), 113–31, at 116.

10. Despite the ways in which life under occupation, and life as an occupier might resemble war, it is important to say that the Israeli/Palestinian conflict is not war in the international legal sense, as a contest between nation-states, since there is no recognized Palestinian state; while for Israel, war has never ended with its Arab neighbors, calling the ongoing situation with the West Bank and Gaza a "war" is inappropriate, and would justify certain state actions as defensive and abnegate the occupying power from its responsibilities under international law, to provide for the needs of the occupied.

11. Khalifeh's novel, which she produced for her senior thesis at Bir Zeit University, was nearly refused; only the advocacy of Hanan Ashrawi led to its acceptance. Khalifeh's use of street vernacular caused some critical consternation, yet it is demonstrative of her questioning of received literary tradition and her desire to confront the status quo by describing life as she witnesses it; in other words, to do the work that novels have done in the past, regardless of the form's political unconscious—to describe and thus to change the present. Moreover, perhaps the very non-national aspect of Palestinian life—marked as it is by exile and occupation—compels its writers and artists to address not only Palestinians, but also the world outside.

12. Intriguingly, the character Usama was drawn from a radical Palestinian whom Khalifeh met. In her recollection, "during my work on [*Wild Thorns*], I met a leftist young man. He was intelligent, ambitious, and a bundle of nerves. He wanted to change the world, and that is exactly what I too dreamed of. But where would be begin? He said confidently: 'We start by changing the system, by breaking the rules, and by setting examples for others.' But I thought to myself: 'I have already broken the rules, but nothing has changed; the law of people has not changed, the family system has not changed, and I have not changed either. So what will it be like for a woman in a society against which she rebels? Can she effect any change if she is outside the system" (Khalifeh, "My Life, Myself, and the World," trans. Musa al-Halool and Katia Sakka, *Aljadid: A Review and Record of Arab Culture and Arts* 8, no. 39 [2002]: 10–11, 26, http://www.aljadid.com/features/0839khalifeh.html).

13. Sahar Khalifeh, *Wild Thorns,* trans. Trevor LeGassick and Elizabeth Fernea (1976 [1985] [2002]; New York: Interlink, 2000), 11; subsequent in-text page numbers refer to the 2000 Interlink edition.

14. In that striking passage, Zuhdi is seen "banging the cane chair with his hand" (85), an indirect reference to the horrifying conclusion of *Men in the Sun,* in which the impotent driver Khaizuran (whose name means "cane"), asks why the three Palestinians who suffocated in his empty water tank did not bang on the sides of the tank. Indeed, in some respects, Khalifeh's *Wild Thorns* functions as a kind of sequel or supplement to *Men in the Sun,* albeit from the post-1967 point of view of those "inside."

15. At the time, about "120,000 laborers were bussed daily to work in Israel, 55% of whom work in construction, the rest in agriculture and industry. Unskilled day labor from the West Bank and Gaza represents 6.5% of the total Israeli work force [taken from 1989 figures]" (Sabbagh, *Palestinian Women of Gaza and the West Bank,* 71).

16. Elizabeth McKee calls this relationship between Usama and Adil an "antagonism, based on the essential conflict between militant resistance and peaceful compromise" ("The Political Agendas and Textual Strategies of Levantine Women Writers," in *Feminism and Islam: Legal and Literary Perspectives*, ed. Mai Yamani [London: Ithaca Press, 1996], 121); yet social change often has required both militant resistance and peaceful compromise, both a Malcolm X and a Martin Luther King—so that the King approach can be seen as the better option. Further, to eliminate the possibility of a third way (as in Raja Shehadeh's approach)—that is, a steadfast resistance that does not resort to violence—is to miss how Palestinian *sumūd* is already a kind of everyday militancy, a nonviolent struggle for dignity.

17. I am indebted to Harlow's reference to Adil as an example of Raja Shehadeh and his articulation of the "third way" (Harlow, "Partitions and Precedents," 118). In fact, Shehadeh's own experiences told in *The Third Way* (1982), a diaristic account by a Palestinian lawyer living in the West Bank, strongly corroborate *Wild Thorns*. One anecdote that echoes the conversation between Adil and Usama occurs between Shehadeh and his cousin, in which his cousin castigates him for refusing to act against yet another Israeli settlement built in the West Bank. Like Usama, the cousin taunts the wearied Shehadeh: "don't you have any pride?" (Raja Shehadeh, *The Third Way: A Journal of Life in the West Bank* [New York: Quartet, 1982], 9). The notion of the *sāmid* apparently received an official designation in the 1978 Baghdad Conference (vii), but Shehadeh notes that it was recognizing a reality already long in existence. It is time that we see the notion of *sumūd* as a Palestinian articulation of nonviolent resistance; such a recognition enables both an understanding of and appreciation for the nonviolence of the vast majority of Palestinians living under occupation, as well as a useful critique of overly naive celebrations of nonviolence as a simple and effective act, without tremendous personal consequences.

18. Khalifeh's novel startlingly anticipates the intifada, that Palestinian popular uprising against Israeli occupation that began in the late 1980s, which included boycotts, demonstrations, and teach-ins; as important as the intifada was, it also failed to shake off the societal relations that Khalifeh and others hoped: "the intifada is a process of reorganizing those internal relationships as much as it is a form of resistance to occupation. If no new social relations emerge, then, unfortunately, we will have fought in vain. After all, the future homeland that we seek is not an abstract idea. It is a concept based on the relations that we aspire to have with one another" (Khalifeh quoted in Sabbagh, *Palestinian Women of Gaza and the West Bank*, 142).

19. Joseph Zeidan argues that Khalifeh does not reduce "Israelis to unfeeling monsters . . . [and that] many scenes humanize the 'enemy'" (*Arab Women Novelists: The Formative Years and Beyond* [Albany: State University of New York Press, 1995], 179), but rather shows how Palestinians experience Israelis in their life under occupation. In this way, the novel is a powerful mirror for both Palestinian and Israeli readers. However, at the same time, since the novel has no real Israeli characters who are imbued with life, it does not offer much in the way of imagining coexistence. Perhaps the occupation itself renders such scenarios almost impossible; perhaps Khalifeh's relentless realism precludes such fantasized relationships. Still, when Um Sabir's anger at Israelis (for the treatment of her husband, who lost his hand in an industrial accident working in Israel) and exultation at the stabbing of an Israeli officer melts into concern for his Israeli daughter, Khalifeh shows both how injustice creates demonization and how a sense of common humanity might trump that feeling of rage (158–59).

20. The novel closes with Adil returning to the marketplace, where life goes on (like in

Auden's famous poem, "Musee des Beaux Arts"); the cycle continues—but we sense the weightedness as we end on "fruit" and "bread"—fruit where the general was killed and bread that represents the tensions of everyday life for Palestinians, whose economy is crushed.

21. See David C. Jacobson, "Patriotic Rhetoric and Personal Conscience in Israeli Fiction of the 1948 and 1956 Wars," in *Israeli and Palestinian Identities in History and Literature*, ed. Kamal Abdel-Malek and David C. Jacobson (New York: St. Martin's Press, 1999), 111–22.

22. Rachel Feldhay Brenner's important intervention, *Inextricably Bonded*, itself a comparative study of Arab and Jewish Israeli fiction, establishes how early figures, such as Yosef Eliahu Chelouche, Ahad Ha'Am, and Martin Buber articulated a post-Zionist critique of mainstream Zionism's approach to Arab Palestinians, from the very beginning of the Zionist project. Further, she notes how the canonization of dissenting Israeli literature has been self-congratulatory and focused on its European liberal affinities as existentialist (Rachel Feldhay Brenner, *Inextricably Bonded: Israeli Arab and Jewish Writers Re-Visioning Culture* [Madison: University of Wisconsin Press, 2003], 10) rather than on the outcomes for Palestinians. Brenner sees in this dissenting literature possibilities for reworking the current conflict, insofar as it excavates the Palestinian Arab past that continues to haunt Israel (142).

23. Barbara McKean Parmenter, *Giving Voice to Stones: Place and Identity in Palestinian Literature* (Austin: University of Texas Press, 1994), 19.

24. David Grossman, *The Smile of the Lamb*, trans. Betsy Rosenberg (1982; New York: Picador, 1990). Quotations are cited parenthetically in the text.

25. Grossman's interest in both the Israeli-Palestinian conflict and the Holocaust suggests a "new position of empathy toward the victim . . . an empathy that was made possible only belatedly, as a deferred action (*nachträglich*, in Freud's terminology), enhanced by the new political and psychological constellation in which Israelis have found themselves [in the post-1967 landscape]" (Yael S. Feldman, "'Identification with the Aggressor' or the 'Victim Complex'? Holocaust and Ideology in Israeli Theater: 'Ghetto' by Joshua Sobol," *Modern Judaism* 9, no. 2 [1989]: 165–78, at 175).

26. A few years later, Grossman's *The Yellow Wind*, a journalistic account of life in the West Bank that became a best seller in Israel, according to Bushnaq, "[brought] news from unknown territory. The people he writes about may pass his readers on the street, but their lives are as remote as those of another planet" (Inea Bushnaq, "Review: West Bank Impressions," *Journal of Palestine Studies* 18, no. 2 [1989]: 138–41, at 139). Despite his "fatalism" about the conflict, Bushnaq sees *The Yellow Wind* as a critical and even unparalleled intervention into understanding the history of Palestine for an Israeli audience (140–41).

27. The fourth narrator, Shosh, a child psychologist married to Uri and carrying on an affair with Katzman, is undergoing a more personal crisis as a result of her sexual involvement with a young patient, who has committed suicide. Most discussions of the novel leave out discussion of Shosh's part, but her presence is suggestive of how parts of Israeli life also have absolutely nothing to do with the Palestinian conflict. At the same time, even this assertion belies the crucial importance that her father, Abner, plays in her life and in the life of a young soldier, Chagai Strutzer, who dies in battle. In Abner's words, "what right did I have to poison him with ideas like 'purity of weapons' or 'combat morality'" (211). Abner's remorse over the effects of his idealization of warriorhood—one of the many fictions (lies) that come back to haunt their tellers—contributes crucially to Shosh's own story and crisis.

28. The list of father/son betrayals is formidable: Uri's grandfather and father; Katzman and

his scholar father; Khilmi and his father; Khilmi and Yazdi; Shosh and Abner; Abner and Chagai Strutzer; Uri and Khilmi; and even, tellingly, Uri and Katzman.

29. An even more extreme version of the Sabra tough is Katzman's fellow soldier, Sheffer. Sheffer is an eminently flat character, but he speaks to a certain point of view that the novel doesn't have; he is a true believer who isn't undergoing a crisis of faith, and he believes Uri is dangerous because of his idealism. Sheffer is more than willing to "play the enemy" (286).

30. Menakhem Perry, "The Israeli-Palestinian Conflict as a Metaphor in Recent Israeli Fiction," *Poetics Today* (Literature in Society) 7, no. 4 (1986): 603–19, at 616. Subsequent quotations are cited parenthetically in the text.

31. During the Israeli war with Hezbollah in the summer of 2006, David Grossman's son, Uri Grossman, was killed. In a story in the *Guardian,* Hillel Schenker quoted his own words: "I once thought of teaching my son a private language, isolating him from the speaking world on purpose, lying to him from the moment of his birth so he would believe only in the language I gave him. And it would be a compassionate language. What I mean is, I wanted to take him by the hand and name everything he saw with words that would save him from the inevitable heartaches so that he wouldn't be able to comprehend the existence of, for instance, war" (Hillel Schenker, "Israel Mourns the Son of David Grossman," *Guardian,* August 16, 2006. Online at http://www.guardian.co.uk/israel/Story/0,,1851043,00.html, accessed June 21, 2007). Grossman imbued this desire to protect his son in Khilmi.

32. Brenner, *Inextricably Bonded,* 252–53.

33. Perry, "The Israeli-Palestinian Conflict as a Metaphor in Recent Israeli Fiction," 617.

34. Ibid., 616. Hereafter cited parenthetically in the text.

35. See Philip Metres, *Behind the Lines: War Resistance Poetry on the American Homefront since 1941* (Iowa City: University of Iowa Press, 2007), 131–34.

36. Parmenter, *Giving Voice to Stones,* 33.

37. Brenner, *Inextricably Bonded,* 3.

38. Peter Nazareth, "An Interview with Sahar Khalifeh," *Iowa Review* 11, no. 1 (1980): 67–86, at 82.

39. Nejd Yaziji, "Exile and Politics of (Self-) Representation: The Narrative of Bounded Space and Action in Sahar Khalifeh's *Wild Thorns,*" in *Cross-Addressing: Resistance Literature and Cultural Borders,* ed. and intro. John C. Hawley (Albany: State University of New York Press, 1996), 87–105, at 100.

40. Quoted in Ehud Ben-Ezer, ed., *Sleepwalkers and Other Stories: The Arab in Hebrew Fiction* (Boulder, CO: Three Continents/Lynne Rienner Publishers, 1999), 17.

41. Harlow, *Resistance Literature,* 176.

Chapter 14

Gender, War, and Zionist Mythogynies

Feminist Trends in Israeli Scholarship

Esther Fuchs

Introduction

Israeli feminist scholarship on war, much like Israeli feminist scholarship in general, has generated a stinging critique of broadly shared interpretations of national priorities and values. In the late 1980s and throughout the 1990s Israeli military institutions and national culture in general were criticized as gendered, exclusionary, and hierarchical. Zionism as such was critiqued as overly militarized and masculinized, and Zionist binary "mythogynies" representing women as homebound breeders and men as protective fighters were deconstructed by literary critics and sociologists alike.[1] The false dichotomization of both gender (man versus woman) and war us versus them) was questioned as a narrative misrepresentation that forced the exclusion of both the national "other" and the sexual "other." Israeli feminist critique of nationalist ideology in general and of militarization in particular questions both the gendered discourses of warfare and the fundamental concepts and theories that justify and normalize war as an approach to conflict resolution. This body of scholarship is critical of the Israeli military establishment and the militarization of Israeli culture. In this sense it partakes in what Joan Wallach Scott defines as the broader orientation of contemporary feminist scholarship. "Critique makes supporters of any system uncomfortable because of its relentless effort to destabilize orthodoxies and its refusal to accept the comforts (and discomforts) of the status quo. The point of critique is not to tear down and destroy but, by bringing to light the limits and inconsistencies that have been studiously avoided, to open up new possibilities, new ways of thinking about what might be done to make things better."[2]

Despite its critical edge, Israeli feminist scholarship is driven by two apparently irreconcilable theories on gender and war.[3] The egalitarian theory is critical of the gendered discourse on war.[4] In its early phases it questioned the traditional exclusion of women from full participation in the military, notably in its elite institutions and crucial decision-making processes. It often points to the actual and crucial historical contribution of women to the army and dismisses social stereotyping and cultural representations to the contrary.[5] The acceptance of women as full participants in the defense and security mechanisms of the nation-state is understood here as a sine qua non of their equal material and symbolic access to the rights, privileges, authority, and power accorded to men. Feminist critics who follow what I propose to define as the "egalitarian" approach tend to focus on the social, economic, and cultural implications of women's unequal level of participation in war. In the Israeli context they call attention to the superficial belief in the actual implementation of full equality in both the Israel Defense Forces (IDF) and in Israeli society, camouflaging the deep divisions between the sexes both on and off the battlefield. Such scholars highlight the stereotypes, stigmatic associations, and derogatory representations of women in dominant cultural representations of war. What I define here as the "pacifist" theory on the other hand is critical of the military as an institution and of war as a fundamentally sexist system.[6] Some theorize war as a quintessentially masculine cultural response to conflict, which is less effective than the feminine traditional strategy of negotiating differences.[7] Some analyze war as an unnecessary, wasteful, and avoidable confrontation manufactured by nationalist fabrications of concepts of masculine honor and heroism that inevitably reinforces male hegemony. Some discuss nationalism as a collective legitimization of the use of force and collective violence in the name of an imaginary community.[8] The appropriate feminist response to war is not to give up national identity altogether but to seek dialogical connection across national divides.[9] It is not to work for greater inclusion, but to engage in resistance against war and the discourse of militarism.

The Egalitarian Theory

Feminist egalitarian critiques of Israel identify and condemn the social and discursive exclusions of women from significant military contexts and texts.[10] The high national priority war and security discourse enjoy in Israel's militarized society and culture is perceived as the main reason for this exclusion. While women are permitted to act in supportive roles, they are not given an opportunity to prove their individual abilities nor to participate meaningfully in the nation's collective effort to survive and thrive. While egalitarian critical analyses of social institutions question this division of labor, critiques of literary canons and representations expose the cultural mythogynies such divisions legitimize and reproduce. My selection here draws on work by Nira Yuval-Davis, Esther Fuchs, Dafna N. Izraeli, Hannah Herzog, and Yael S. Feldman.

One of the earliest publications on inequality in the Israeli Defense Forces was Nira Yuval-Davis's "The Israeli Example." Yuval-Davis argues in this pioneering article that women's equality in Tzahal (IDF) is a myth.[11] The myth derives from the fact that Israel was the first state in the world that issued a mandatory conscription for women. "The belief concerning women's equality in the Israeli army leans heavily on women's military activities during the pre-state period, and even then it was largely a myth."[12] In the prestate era there were no separate women's units, and the division between "front" and "rear" was not yet instituted. Yuval-Davis argues that women were barred from the front and relegated to the rear, fulfilling auxiliary, professional, administrative, clerical, and educational roles, and charged with maintaining morale. Women's military training was focused on limited defensive roles, such as defending their homes and communities in case of attack. Women in combat units were restricted to teaching and training and sophisticated technological roles. Yuval-Davis also notes in this pathbreaking article that despite the universal conscription law women were recruited far more selectively. Release from military service is easily granted on the grounds of religious or conscientious objection, as well as readily available to married or pregnant women. Women's reproductive role seems to displace their military role through the expectation that they produce future male soldiers. Yuval-Davis is careful to emphasize that this disparity is not unique to the IDF and that it constitutes a characteristic feature in all national, professional, or voluntary armies.[13]

Yuval-Davis develops this argument in her more detailed article on this subject titled "Front and Rear: The Sexual Division of Labour in the Israeli Army."[14] Not only does the military participation of Israeli women soldiers not guarantee equality, it can hardly be shown to eliminate women's traditional social subordination. The article's main argument is that "the extremely hierarchical and bureaucratic nature of the modern army can contribute to a gender differentiation and gender inequality even more institutionalized and extreme than in the civilian labour market."[15] In a subsequent essay Yuval-Davis develops her important insight into women's reproductive function.[16]

This function is analyzed within the framework of the ongoing war with the Arab states, or as part of what Yuval-Davis defines as the "demographic race" between Jewish Israelis and Arab citizens of the state (as well as beyond state borders). The number of births has become a political weapon among Palestinian nationalists as well, who claimed the higher birthrate as a demographic victory over the Jews who beat them militarily. The article suggests that "issues of marriage and divorce, birth control and child benefits are intimately linked with claims over territories and citizenship rights, class divisions and plans of mass transfer."[17] In this way Yuval-Davis places the role of women and the issue of gender inequality at the very heart of a political analysis of the Arab-Israeli conflict and the construction of national priorities. The identification of women's roles as reproductive agents, boundary markers, reproducers of national ideology, and participants in economic and military struggles will eventually provide a foundation for a comprehensive theory of gender and nationalism.[18]

In 1986 I published an article titled "Images of Love and War in Contemporary Israeli Fiction: A Feminist Re-Vision."[19] The feminist "re-vision" was meant to reassess and critically examine highly valued and broadly admired war narratives that interpreted Israel's military conflicts in gendered terms. I called for a critical interrogation of the conventional Israeli war text and its essentialist mythical assumptions. As the editors of *Arms and the Woman: War, Gender, and Literary Representation* put it: "all [contributors to the volume] regard literature as implicated in both the war system and the gender system and as instrumental in perpetuating the ancient essentialist war myth."[20] My article questions not the myth of gender equality, but the cultural production, legitimization, valorization, and dissemination of Israeli "mythogynies" or literary representations of women.[21] Israeli war narratives tend to dichotomize gender and war between a masculinized front and feminized rear; most traces of women's participation in or contribution to the war effort are erased. This erasure feminizes the private domain and masculinizes the public domain. The first generation of writers, the Palmach authors of the 1940s and 1950s tended to romanticize this dichotomy, presenting the warriors as the objects of admiration and feminine love. In this phase women are constructed as passive and irrelevant to the war effort. The second more disillusioned literature of the 1960s and '70s, known as the Generation of the State, tends to represent both traditional domestic women and women soldiers as castrating bitches and lethal femmes fatales. "Heterosexual love is exposed as a power struggle, a relentless war leading to atrophy, to psychical and even physical death; whereas military confrontation emerges as a kind of refuge."[22] The narratives thus displace the focus from the violence wrought on the battlefield to erotic struggles, thus normalizing the attenuating moral issue of killing. While men represent war, self-sacrifice, and loyalty to the national cause, women are derogated in this literature as disloyal wives, neglectful mothers, and treacherous lovers. Most spectacularly, women's ultimate sacrifice, their wounding through violence on the battlefield, or their pain of loss at home, is erased. Women are rarely represented as victims of military violence. They are instead portrayed as the tormentors of husbands and symbols of the family and the nation as such. Mainstream Israeli literature reflects an ideological shift from nationalist certainties to critical interrogations of nationalism and its military agendas. The critique of the nation was mediated through a critique of its symbolic representatives: women. Israeli war narratives tend to represent the male protagonist as both the ultimate hero in the nationalist phase and as the ultimate victim in the later critical phase. Women on the other hand, serving mostly as secondary characters, help construct both male heroism and victimization. The personal and erotic victimization of men by women is ultimately symbolic of the destructive function women play collectively as national subject. At best the Israeli woman embodies a threat to national survival; at worst she is entirely edged out of the national narrative.

In an article titled "Gendering Military Service in the Israel Defense Forces," Dafna N. Izraeli argues that the IDF does not merely reflect a social division of labor, but that it rather produces and reproduces the conventional role of women as helpmates to men.[23] "As a structure of power, and as one of the important agencies that organizes the power relations of gender, the military intensifies gender distinctions and then uses them as justifications for both their construction and for sustaining gender inequality."[24] The legalized gender differences in the scope of military service, the level of training, and the institutional frameworks legitimize the notion that national security should not be governed by the nation's theoretical commitment to gender equality. Women's shorter service and their exemption from combat and reserve duties are constantly invoked as the touchstone for their differential treatment. This treatment in turn prevents women from being promoted to military ranks equal to those reserved to men. No woman is of high enough rank to participate in the meetings of the general staff on a regular basis. The closure of senior positions to women also excludes their participation in making the policies that institutionalize their secondary status in the military. Izraeli exposes the ways in which this cyclical reasoning constructs women's military work as fundamentally supportive and auxiliary, releasing men to perform "real" defense duties even in their roles as combat instructors and intelligence officers. Women serve the military as women. They perform stereotypically feminine nurturing and caring work. They are seen as civilizing influences, as symbolic extensions of the home, as the prize of heroes. Women's presence is an incentive for male achievement, while females are careful not to outdo their male soldier counterparts' endurance, stamina, and resilience.

This gendered hierarchy is reproduced outside the IDF as men convert the social and symbolic capital they earned during their military service into economic opportunities in the marketplace. In some occupational fields a specific type of military experience is a condition for entry. Combat experience is also a requirement for a wide variety of security-related jobs. "The interests of the dominant groups—whether in the professional army or the reserves—to preserve their privileged position in the structure of power are experienced as general interests and are, therefore, freely accepted by subordinate groups, such as (Jewish) women."[25] The social prestige the army enjoyed was dealt a blow after the initial defeat the IDF suffered in the Yom Kippur War of 1973 and subsequently in the Lebanon War of 1982, which was broadly perceived as a war of choice and not a war of necessity (*ain brera*). Calls for replacing compulsory service with voluntary and professional service indicate the beginning of a social process of demilitarization. Where the law permits differential treatment, the army tends to increase the gaps. In 1994 Alice Miller brought a lawsuit against the minister of defense, who argued against her admission to a training course based on women's shorter service span. The Supreme Court ordered that Alice Miller be admitted to the training course and judged on her qualifications. In the same year a law was introduced in the Knesset requiring that all military jobs, including combat jobs, be equally available to women. Izraeli concludes her article on a cautionary note, warning that occasional symbolic victories like Miller's should not be misinterpreted as fundamental shifts in military policies: "Ironically then, women's tactical gains, such as opening a crack in the wall that blocks their access to pilot training, may only serve to legitimate and stabilize the gender practices of an organization premised on women's subordination, and thus may be of questionable strategic advantage."[26]

The dichotomization of front and rear as gendered social spaces is identified by Hanna Herzog as the single most important cause of continued inequality between men and women in Israel despite progressive legislation that was passed in the 1980s and '90s.[27] In an article titled "Homefront and Battlefront: The Status of Jewish and Palestinian Women in Israel," Herzog argues that the traditional definition of war as a masculine activity is responsible for the continued exclusion of women from powerful political positions of leadership and influence: "Life in the shadow of a protracted Arab-Israeli conflict and constant threat has become a powerful mechanism that reproduces a gendered binary world."[28] National security issues enjoy an unquestioned status of priority and are materially and discursively controlled by men due to their greater military experience.

This experience is often converted into economic benefits and professional opportunities in civilian life, as well as to managerial and political careers. "Military service as the essence of the Israeli experience goes a long way toward conferring social prestige and determining the hierarchy between servers and non-servers, women and men, Israeli Jews and Diaspora Jews, and more acutely, between Jews and Palestinians."[29] Although Palestinian citizens are excluded from military service, Palestinian society too shows a similar gendered polarization between public and private domains. The Arab-Israeli conflict solidified the traditional Arab family, which has become the locus of social solidarity and nationalism. The price is often paid by Palestinian women who are expected to preserve traditions that keep them in a subordinate status. Herzog argues that the emphasis on family life as women's proper domain is not in and of itself the cause of continued social inequality. It is rather the hierarchical relationship between the public and private that perpetuates women's subordination. Just as it entrenches male symbolic prestige and power, war entrenches the family as women's responsibility. Identified with the family, women are expected to give support and care for the well-being of the men who are called up for military duty. Mothers are expected to extend their maternal duties until the official release of their sons from military service. Wives are expected to be supportive of their husbands who are called up for reserve duty annually. Women's inclusion in the nation's collective coping with security threats is thus confined mainly to traditional feminine behaviors. Women's familial roles also prevent them from investing the time and effort men often invest in their professional careers. Not only are women barred from managerial positions that often require extensive military experience, but also they often forego professional opportunities that could provide them with economic independence. As wives and mothers women cannot compete for the salaries of their husbands, nor can they compete with their militarily better-experienced male counterparts. The feminization of the private sphere creates psychological and social obstacles for women who seek careers in the public sphere, especially in politics. In her book *Gendering Politics: Women in Israel,* Herzog documents in great detail the paradoxical choices and trajectories of women in politics.[30] Women who opt for political careers often hedge their bets, are less assertive and more tentative than men. They report a sense of intrusion into forbidden territory, knowing that they are often perceived as insufficiently qualified to make decisions on behalf of the public. In a field that requires self-confidence and the projection of certainty, such behavior undermines their credibility and blunts their competitive edge.

In an article titled "Hebrew Gender and Zionist Ideology: The Palmach Trilogy of Netiva Ben Yehuda," Yael S. Feldman focuses on the literary representation of the 1948 War of Independence by a woman veteran of that war and member of the crack fighting units of the Palmach.[31] While the Palmach consisted of numerous women who fought in the war alongside the men, few were the women who were acknowledged for their martial courage and prowess, and until recently only one, Netiva Ben Yehuda, chose to write about her war experience. Feldman argues that Ben Yehuda kept silent because she was torn by conflicting loyalties: "It was this conflict—between her Zionist ideological commitment and her sexual equality disillusionment—that had silenced her for three decades."[32] Ben Yehuda's war narrative challenges the gender equality myth much in line with other feminist critiques that emerged in the early 1980s. While the "suffragist" myth of egalitarianism was a much-vaunted value in the Palmach, in reality women were subordinate to male commanders. Ben Yehuda abstained from questioning the authority of her male commander, in one case, with dire consequences, for fear of being perceived as overly cautious, or "weak." On the other hand, her writing demonstrates that women were just as able as their male counterparts to undertake leadership positions. It is also possible to speculate that Ben Yehuda abstained from writing about her war experience because war as such was identified as a male preserve, and a woman's attempt to write about it was widely considered to be inauthentic or overreaching. The discursive entry into the public/national discourse challenged canonic conventions, much as the use of colloquial, macho "speakature" was subversive on several levels. Ben Yehuda's writing subverts the social and military definitions of gendered spaces, much as it subverts rigid definitions of bipolar gender systems. Masculinity and femininity are destabilized in such a way as to challenge the stereotypical gendering of fighting as such. Feldman argues that the Zionist identification of Jewish diasporic experience with femininity and dependence prevented Ben Yehuda from openly expressing her concerns about military decisions by her superiors. Nor was she willing to admit that as a woman in a male-dominated collective, she was miserable. Ben Yehuda's belated publications set the record straight both in terms of the glorification of male prowess and the erasure of female contributions to national victory. Ben Yehuda's reluctance to share publicly her memories and assessments of the war sheds light on other women novelists who also preferred to suppress women's public, national, and collective contributions. Feldman suggests that the reluctance shown by women novelists to represent the "New Hebrew Woman" derives from the conflict of loyalties to Zionist ideology on the one hand and to the personal authentic experience on the other. The personal or private narrative was often at odds with collective expectations. Some women novelists preferred to write "masked" autobiographies, projecting their life stories on distant places and other periods.[33] By displacing their personal retrospections in other contexts these writers seem to be better able to examine the conflict between urgent national priorities and marginalized gendered interests. The vicarious "selves" women writers construct reflect feminist desires that Israeli contemporary reality cannot accommodate. Until recently, this self-limitation has deprived women novelists from claiming their own literary history, or a "room of their own" within the Hebrew literary canon. Contemporary post-Zionist and postfeminist fiction by women seems to have outgrown the gender/nation conflict as their work destabilizes in a postmodern vein all coherent and totalizing identities.[34]

The Pacifist Theory

Israeli pacifist feminists reject the premise that a greater participation of women in the war system will challenge their social subordination or subvert misogyny. Pacifist analyses focus on the fundamental interdependence of violence and definitions of manhood.[35] Their critique focuses on the ways in which militarized constructions of the nation depend on traditional definitions of femininity and masculine aggression.[36]

Pacifist theory perceives the war system as such as serving antifeminist interests. "Military activity is seen as a destructive and primitive expression of masculine competitiveness."[37] It condemns the use of women in the army as a means of domesticating the military and enforcing the vulnerability of women's bodies to sexual assault. Feminist politics according to this theory ought to reject the rationalization and justification of war as a means of resolving national conflict. Rather than a greater inclusion in the nation, the nation itself is understood as gendered, and nationalism as such is perceived as an ideology that is premised on the production of collective conflict. In the following selection I draw on work by Simona Sharoni, Tamar Mayer, Orna Sasson-Levy, and Orly Lubin.

Simona Sharoni's "Homefront as Battlefield: Gender, Military Occupation, and Violence against Women," rejects the use of military force in principle.[38] Although the essay focuses on the use of force against the Palestinian population in the occupied territories during the intifada of 1987–92, it links the war against the Arabs in general to a militarized cultivation of masculine heroism rather than to serious existential security threats. The construction of militarized masculinity hinges on the image of the Israeli sabra as a tough though sweet prickly pear, thorny outside and sweet inside. The new Jew's toughness was required to ward off imaginary offenses by the native Arab population, whose right to inhabit the land was questioned by foundational myths associated with the establishment of the state. Sharoni questions the notion that Israel's successive wars against the Arabs, including the wars of 1948, 1956, 1967, and 1973 were necessary as self-defensive measures and condemns them as displays of aggression and repression. Sharoni juxtaposes the construction of an aggressive masculinity with the discursive and cultural construction of women's bodies as "occupied territories" available for sexual purposes. The militaristic metaphor is sexist to the extent that it justifies military aggression against the enemy on the battlefield and sexist aggression against women on the homefront. The nexus between Israeli militarism and sexism is further developed as a theoretical foundation for feminist alliances between Israeli and Palestinian peace activists in her book.[39] Palestinian women are especially vulnerable as resisters of the occupation, and Sharoni documents instances of sexual abuse and violence Israeli male soldiers committed. Sharoni argues, however, that even Jewish women whose protection from enemy aggression serves as justification for war and occupation are frequent victims of sexist aggression on the homefront. Her central argument in this essay is that the rise in domestic violence, especially in the wake of the intifada and following the Gulf War in 1991, is intimately linked to the war. Jewish feminists who have begun to critically examine the causes of domestic and sexual violence link the rise in reported incidents to the rise in violent tactics against Palestinian resistance. Peace activists in antioccupation vigils by Women in Black in the late 1980s have begun to report verbal and physical assaults against them linking sexual obscenities with political putdowns. But the linkage of militarism and sexism is not only displayed in public. Most disturbingly, and this is the core of Sharoni's argument, the justification of physical violence on the battlefront leads to the normalization of the use of force at home. The binary dichotomy between these contexts is often transgressed as practices learned in one arena are used in another. The sexual justification of masculine control over women's bodies, leads to a political justification of state control over women's bodies, notably in the area of reproduction and abortion. Domestic violence then should be perceived as one form of criminal abuse on a continuum of legal and authorized practices. Sharoni notes that the crucial insight into the ideological nexus between militarism and sexism deserves broad recognition in critical discourses on Israel: "What remains particularly concealed in most existing critiques of Israeli national security is the fact that the rhetoric of national security depends on the preservation of the status quo not only with respect to Israeli-Palestinian / Arab-Israeli conflicts but also with respect to the social construction of gender identities and roles."[40] Scholars committed to social change must continue to critically explore "the relationship between militarism, violence, and the social construction of gender in Israel and elsewhere."[41]

The construction of militarized masculinity is further explored by Tamar Mayer in her essay "From Zero to Hero: Masculinity in Jewish Nationalism."[42] Mayer locates the nexus between the invisibility of women and militarized constructions of masculinity in early Zionist texts. Mayer notes that Theodor Herzl, the "father" of the Jewish state, focused in his writings on reinventing the Jewish man, leaving Jewish women at the margins of the national enterprise. The main reason for this focus was the anti-Semitic charge against the alleged effeminacy of Jewish men in the European Diaspora, where they cultivated servility, subordination, and passivity and other feminine traits as forms of dependent survival. "The New Jew was to be the antithesis of the ghetto Jew whom Herzl and other Zionist thinkers saw as helpless, passive, and feminine and thus in need of major transformation."[43] The early Zionists of the 1890s dreamed of a national liberation that would bring both "freedom and manliness," in Max Nordau's words, to the downtrodden masses. Nordau insisted on modeling the traditional European Jew along the lines of a modern "Muscle Jew." One educational strategy on the road to national liberation was to reclaim an ancient Hebraic past, notably military heroes like the biblical Samson or the legendary Judah Maccabee who led the revolt against the Greeks and Bar Kochba who led a military resistance against the Romans. Another strategy was the cultivation of gymnastics and sports in the early paramilitary Zionist youth movements. The cult of manliness and nationalist revival was ironically inspired by German practices of a return to nature and the land. Eventually, a Jewish return to the ancestral land became inevitable in the process of reclaiming Jewish national roots. To counter anti-Semitic taunts regarding intellectualism and economic dependency, Zionist dreams of a return to the homeland developed the notion of an economic revolution as well. Strenuous agricultural work was to return the new Jew to productive labor and self-sufficiency. The new pioneer settler (*Halutz*) was charged with agricultural labor, while accompanying women (*Halutzot*) were to engage in less manly tasks. The new colonizers were also charged with defense duties to protect the women and children against marauding Arab attacks. Yet Mayer suggests that the Arab attacks on Jewish settlements were not the primary cause for the militarization of cultural life in the early *yishuv*. The educational curriculum in schools included paramilitary training as well as Hebrew, the ancestral biblical language. Schools and youth movements often redesigned religious holidays to fit the new Zionist message of national bravery and self-redemption. Emphasis shifted from spiritual to national leadership. These nationalistic celebrations emphasized nature and homeland. "Because all these heroes were men, the new focus of these holidays contributed greatly to the cult of masculinity that became integral to the emerging Jewish culture in Palestine."[44] Mayer suggests that paramilitary educational projects and the cultivation of a cult of toughness inspired the early emergence of national security as a priority. The Arab attacks that were organized as resistance to encroaching Jewish colonization were misinterpreted as a dangerous existential threat to Jewish survival equal to anti-Semitic hostility. Under the British Mandate several paramilitary and military units operated underground, making membership selective and dependent on absolute commitment to a nationalist cause and male bonding in elite formations. Early on, mythmaking processes of commemoration of fallen heroes and the creation of a nationalist pantheon was reproduced in successive ceremonies and publications: "When national survival is attributed almost exclusively to the heroism of warriors, nationalism and masculinity become inseparable."[45] Yet because this inseparability has been shaped by historical and cultural forces, it can also be subject to change as the nation evolves, matures, and sheds configurations that no longer serve its interests and as more than one privileged group begins to define these interests.

In an article titled "Gender Performance in a Changing Military: Women Soldiers in Masculine Roles," Orna Sasson-Levy questions the premise that greater participation by women in combat duty will transform the gendered regime of the IDF.[46] Since the mid-1990s, numerous combat jobs were opened to women in the air force, army, and navy. In 2000 the Knesset passed a law that opened up to women soldiers all military jobs contingent on individual qualification and need. In the same year, the women's corps (CHEN) was dismantled and several high-rank positions were made available for the first time. Sasson-Levy argues that despite these significant efforts at egalitarian inclusiveness, fundamental attitudes to women and femininity may not be affected as much as first expected. "Women's integration into combat roles thus neither challenges the male hegemony in the military nor threatens the ideology that links masculinity and combat and thereby contributes to the legitimization of Israeli militarism and its gender regime without altering women's lower civil status."[47] Sasson-Levy's study of female recruits in combat units reveals that they adopt discursive and physical identity practices characteristic of male combat soldiers. The women soldiers believe that by adopting such practices they subvert traditional definitions of femininity and masculinity as dichotomous identities, thus naturalizing and legitimizing their participation in traditionally male-dominated units. Sasson-Levy cautions, however, that by adopting masculine identity practices these women reinforce both traditional masculine norms and the military's misogynous culture. At times the mimicry of male voices, vulgar talk, gait, and oversize uniform is a response to mockery from male soldiers. This mockery implies that traditional feminine appearance and behavior is out of bounds in a combat unit. The identity performance female combat soldiers undertake is shed after their release from military service. On some level then the women's performance can be interpreted as a sort of a drag show that held a mirror to the men in the unit, dramatizing their sometimes-abusive behavior and challenging essentialist ideas about gender identity. Yet the identification with the military's gender regime leads women soldiers to distance themselves from female company and traditionally feminine practices. "In their words, these women soldiers articulate a misogynist viewpoint, characteristic of the hegemonic ideology of patriarchal societies."[48] Thus the women themselves comply with and reproduce antifeminine attitudes that define femininity as weak, submissive, and inferior. Sasson-Levy interprets this behavior in postcolonial terms, likening these women soldiers to colonized subjects who seek to distance themselves from their own community in order to gain a sense of self-worth. Traditional women thus become the "other" against whom the female soldiers seek to define themselves. Female combat soldiers tend to also ignore insulting jokes and sexual harassment that are intended to undermine their precarious status as one of the guys. By ignoring sexual offenses the women fend off the intended exclusionary power of the offense. They believe that in this way they prove that they are as tough as the guys. Yet ignoring sexual harassment only legitimizes it as acceptable behavior and may perpetuate rather than put an end to it. On some level then women's mimicry of masculine practices empowers them, but the power these women acquire is temporary and localized as they are seldom promoted or compensated for their military service after their release from military duty. "Ironically, then, women's achievements in the Israeli army might work to legitimize the military gender regime which is based on the subjugation of women."[49]

In an article titled "Gone to Soldiers: Feminism and the Military in Israel," Orly Lubin argues that the participation of women in the IDF serves the interests of the military rather than the interests of Israeli women.[50] Women serve as symbolic extensions of normalcy, family, love, and life, a narrative of desire that contrasts with the threat of death that defines the male military experience. The narrative of female desire displaces and depoliticizes the narrative of violence promising a future of romance and heterosexual happiness. "The woman needs to be constantly there, ready in the background, visually and mentally forming a space and design with her female body, into which the narrative of military violence will dissolve at its critical moment."[51] As the representation of desire and intimacy the woman is both comforting and threatening, as desire is a force that may exceed proper boundaries. Naked or raw sexuality are therefore not included in the photographic economy. Rather, femininity takes on marital, domestic, and familial meaning. The woman's body is also evocative of sexual vulnerability, which on one level distinguishes it from the male body, and on another evokes the male body's vulnerability to sexual violence. This body therefore must be both exposed and hidden. The woman must be both present and invisible, she is paradoxically both of and not of the military, she is a soldier who is also a mother/lover, she is the home on the army base. Only this dual function creates a natural link between the two domains. Lubin focuses in this essay on the double position of the female body in photographic representations of women in the Palmach. These women are framed by domestic spaces, they evoke erotic and intimate postures, though not limited to them, they are photographed along with male soldiers, but evoke singularity and difference, they are shown to handle arms without controlling them. "Such are also all the other photographs: the women are always both part of the military sphere, but never entirely, both representing home, desire and family, but at the site of male fraternity.[52] Pregnant and wounded female bodies are not part of this representation. Lubin includes a photo of a Palestinian woman's body framed within a domestic space displaying a scar. She includes as well a photo of an immigrant woman who stands pregnant at an entrance to a tent. Both identities mark "otherness," women who are categorized as outside the collective military female body. The complex apparatuses of displacement that construct the representation of the female military body demonstrate that it fulfills a destructive role to the extent that they reinforce and legitimize military violence. "Active refusal to fulfill this role, or an active exposure of its performativity and thus its imaginary inventiveness, through cutting the Gordian knot of the dual function of the female body, are the only modes of relieving the woman's body from the cycle of affirmation, enforcement and maintenance of male military rule and violence."[53]

Conclusion

The theoretical divide between egalitarianism and pacifism ought not to create the impression that the above survey can be simplistically reduced to neat categories. A close reading of the texts mentioned here reveals the complexity of the arguments, density of evidence, and diversity of angles introduced in each piece. Some "egalitarian" scholars share much in common with "pacifist" scholars and vice versa. Rather than an absolute contrast, these approaches should be seen as different in emphasis. Scholars who used egalitarian perspectives in the 1980s may identify today as pacifist in theory. The more general critique of militarism in Israeli society and culture suggests that future analyses of gendered aspects will emphasize the pacifist rather than egalitarian perspective.

On the other hand the apparent transformation of the concept of war from military confrontation to the quasi-civilian terrorist organizations that Israel and other Western countries confront may require a new response that destabilizes the gendered definitions of men and women, masculinity and femininity. The rejection of war as a performance of national masculinity may consequently be understood as a specifically Western feminist response that has not sufficiently theorized the position of non-Western postcolonial women who insist on joining nationalist resistance movements around the globe.[54]

Notes

1. Esther Fuchs, introduction to *Israeli Women's Studies: A Reader* (New Brunswick, NJ: Rutgers University Press, 2005), 1–30. See also Esther Fuchs, "The Evolution of Critical Paradigms in Israeli Feminist Scholarship: A Theoretical Model," *Israel Studies* 14, no. 2 (2009): 198–221. "Mythogyny" refers to a cultural mythic construction of women's lives in general and to a literary genre in Hebrew literary fiction in particular. See my book *Israeli Mythogynies: Women in Contemporary Hebrew Fiction* (Albany: State University of New York Press, 1987).

2. Joan Wallach Scott, "Introduction: Feminism's Critical Edge," in *Women's Studies on the Edge*, ed. Joan Wallach Scott (Durham, NC: Duke University Press, 2008), 1–13.

3. Similar theoretical bifurcation is noticeable in other contexts as well. See for example Jean B. Elshtain, *Women and War* (New York: Basic Books, 1987); Lois Ann Lorentzen and Jennifer Turpin, eds., *The Women and War Reader* (New York: New York University Press, 1998); Dubravka Zarkov, "Towards a New Theorizing of Women, Gender, and War," in *Handbook of Gender and Women's Studies*, ed. Kathy Davis, Mary Evans, and Judith Lorber (London: Sage, 2006), 214–33.

4. Judith H. Stiehm, *Arms and the Enlisted Woman* (Philadelphia: Temple University Press, 1989); Cynthia Enloe, *Bananas, Beaches, and Bases* (London: Pandora, 1989); Miriam Cooke and Angela Woollacott, eds., *Gendering War Talk* (Princeton, NJ: Princeton University Press, 1993).

5. Julie M. Peteet, *Gender in Crisis: Women and the Palestinian Resistance Movement* (New York: Columbia University Press, 1991).

6. Betty Reardon, *Sexism and the War System* (New York: Teachers College Press, 1985).

7. Sara Ruddick, *Maternal Thinking: Toward a Politics of Peace* (Boston: Beacon Press, 1989); Sara Ruddick, "Notes Toward a Peace Politics," in *Gendering War Talk*, 109–27.

8. Cynthia Cockburn, *The Space between Us: Negotiating Gender and National Identities in Conflict* (London: Zed Books, 1998).

9. Nira Yuval-Davis, *Gender and Nation* (London: Sage, 1997); Nahla Abdo and Ronit Lentin, eds., *Women and the Politics of Military Confrontation: Palestinian and Israeli Gendered Narratives of Dislocation* (New York: Berghahn Books, 2002).

10. Anne Bloom, "Women in the Defense Forces," in *Calling the Equality Bluff: Women in Israel*, ed. Barbara Swirski and Marilyn P. Safir (New York: Pergamon Press, 1991), 1128–38; Uta Klein, "Our Best Boys: The Gendered Nature of Civil-Military Relations in Israel," *Men and Masculinities* 2, no. 1 (1999): 47–65.

11. Nira Yuval-Davis, "The Israeli Example," in *Loaded Questions: Women in the Military*, ed. W. Chapkis (Amsterdam and Washington, DC: Transnational Institute, 1981), 73–78.

12. Ibid., 74.

13. Nira Yuval-Davis, "Sexual Division of Labour," in *Loaded Questions*, 31–35.

14. Nira Yuval-Davis, "Front and Rear: The Sexual Division of Labour in the Israeli Army," *Feminist Studies* 11, no. 3 (1985): 649–75.

15. Ibid., 649.

16. Nira Yuval-Davis, "National Reproduction and 'the Demographic Race' in Israel," in *Woman—Nation—State*, ed. Nira Yuval-Davis and Floya Anthias (London: Macmillan, 1989), 92–109.

17. Ibid., 105–6.

18. Nira Yuval-Davis, *Gender and Nation* (London: Sage, 1997).

19. Esther Fuchs, "Images of Love and War in Contemporary Israeli Fiction: A Feminist Revision," *Modern Judaism* 6 (1986): 189–96. The article was reprinted in Helen M. Cooper, Adrienne A. Munich, and Susan M. Squier, eds., *Arms and the Woman: War, Gender, and Literary Representation* (Chapel Hill: University of North Carolina Press, 1989), 268–82.

20. Cooper, Munich, and Squier, *Arms and the Woman*, xv.

21. See note 1 above.

22. Fuchs, "Images of Love and War," 269.

23. Dafna N. Izraeli, "Gendering Military Service in the Israel Defense Forces," *Israel Social Science Research* 12, no. 1 (1997): 129–66.

24. Ibid., 131.

25. Ibid., 157.

26. Ibid., 158.

27. Hanna Herzog, "Homefront and Battlefront: The Status of Jewish and Palestinian Women in Israel," in Fuchs, *Israeli Women's Studies*, 208–28. The article appeared originally in *Israel Studies* 3, no. 1 (1998): 61–84.

28. Ibid., 208.

29. Ibid., 214.

30. Hanna Herzog, *Gendering Politics: Women in Israel* (Ann Arbor: University of Michigan Press, 1999).

31. Yael S. Feldman, "Hebrew Gender and Zionist Ideology: The Palmach Trilogy of Netiva Ben Yehuda," *Prooftexts* 20, no. 1–2 (2000): 139–57. See also Yael S. Feldman, *No Room of Their Own: Gender and Nation in Israeli Women's Fiction* (New York: Columbia University Press, 1999), 177–92.

32. Feldman, "Hebrew Gender and Zionist Ideology," 144.

33. Yael S. Feldman, "Feminism under Siege: The Vicarious Selves of Israeli Women Writers," in Fuchs, *Israeli Women's Studies*, 317–30. The article appeared first in *Women of the Word: Jewish Women and Jewish Writing*, ed. Judith Baskin (Detroit: Wayne State University Press, 1994), 323–42.

34. Feldman, *No Room of Their Own*, 225–31.

35. Susan Sered, *What Makes Women Sick? Maternity, Modesty, and Militarism in Israeli Society* (Hanover, NH: Brandeis University Press / University Press of New England, 2003), 104–21.

36. Sheila H. Katz, *Women and Gender in Early Jewish and Palestinian Nationalism* (Gainesville: University Press of Florida, 2003); Meira Weiss, "Engendering the Gulf War: Israeli Nurses and

the Discourses of Soldiering," in *The Military and Militarism in Israeli Society*, ed. Edna Lomsky-Feder and Eyal Ben Ari (New York: New York University Press, 1999), 281–300.

37. Fuchs, introduction to *Israeli Women's Studies*, 17.

38. Simona Sharoni, "Homefront as Battlefield: Gender, Military Occupation, and Violence against Women," in Fuchs, *Israeli Women's Studies*, 231–46. The article appeared originally in Tamar Mayer, ed., *Women and the Israeli Occupation* (New York: Routledge, 1994), 121–37.

39. Simona Sharoni, *Gender and the Israeli-Palestinian Conflict: the Politics of Women's Resistance* (Syracuse, NY: Syracuse University Press, 1994).

40. Sharoni, "Homefront as Battlefield," 241.

41. Ibid., 244.

42. Tamar Mayer, "From Zero to Hero: Masculinity in Jewish Nationalism," in Fuchs, *Israeli Women's Studies*, 97–117. The article appeared first in Tamar Mayer, ed., *Gender Ironies of Nationalism: Sexing the Nation* (New York: Routledge, 2000), 283–308.

43. Ibid., 100.

44. Ibid., 105.

45. Ibid., 112.

46. Orna Sasson-Levy, "Gender Performance in a Changing Military: Women Soldiers in Masculine Roles," in Fuchs, *Israeli Women's Studies*, 265–78. The article appeared first in *Israel Studies Forum* 17, no. 1 (2001): 7–22.

47. Ibid., 267.

48. Ibid., 271.

49. Ibid., 274.

50. Orly Lubin, "Gone to Soldiers: Feminism and the Military in Israel," in *Israeli Family and Community: Women's Time*, ed. Nannah Naveh (London: Vallentine Mitchell, 2003), 164–194.

51. Ibid., 168.

52. Ibid., 176.

53. Ibid., 191.

54. "As some of the old political and theoretical certainties of feminism crumbled, at least two things seem to have become evident: first, women's agency, emancipation and empowerment are not necessarily linked only to liberating and progressive movements. Second, agency, emancipation, and empowerment may not be the best framework at all for studying women's diverse positioning within violent conflict, including women's participation in violence." Dubravka Zarkov, "Towards a New Theorizing of Women, Gender, and War," in *Handbook of Gender and Women's Studies*, ed. Kathy Davis, Mary Evans, and Judith Lorber (London: Sage, 2006), 214–33, at 225.

III

Cinema and Stage

Chapter 15

Representations of War in Israeli Drama and Theater

Dan Urian

Differing from other literary arts (literature, film, and television), the theatrical stage is too narrow to incorporate military battles. The history of drama is nonetheless influenced by war plays. The majority of these engage with the processes surrounding the war, with the changes undergone by those who participated in it, and with its consequences. The presence of war can be felt in particular in the Israeli theater repertoire, which serves to reflect the social and political reality of the violent and continuing disputes. I begin this discussion with a description of the unique characteristics of the Israeli theater, followed by the circumstances of its birth with the 1948 War of Independence, glance briefly at the Yom Kippur War as expressed in the theater, and from there proceed to the many theatrical roles of the two wars in Lebanon and the intifadas.

Theater does not reflect reality as is, but fashions it to fit the particular needs of social groups. Despite this, or possibly because of this, the connection existing between theater and social reality enables both the exposure of repressed conflicts and the manifestation of overt schisms. The concept of theater as an important public stage that both represents reality and participates in designing it arose in the period of the *yishuv* (Settlement), before the establishment of the State of Israel, and it has accompanied the history of the Hebrew theater for the last 60 years.[1] The ideological component has an important historical role in this theater's repertoire (and in the Palestinian theater). Zionist ideology influenced many Israeli playwrights, as well as the translations of foreign plays and the ways of suiting them to the needs of present-day society. Consequently, Israeli theater offers a suitable research field for the examination of representative images among the group of theater-makers and their audiences.

Research has revealed that a great part of the Israeli theater audience is, on average, of Ashkenazi origin, holds an academic degree, and works in the "middle" professions: teacher, nurse, social worker, and such.[2] In a 1990 study it was found that "the most active [theater-goers] in frequency of attendance are educated, religiously traditional [not Orthodox] or secular, native-born Israelis of western origin."[3] "Theatre attendance is strongly linked," according to a survey on leisure and culture in Israel (1998), "to higher education and western origin."[4] Today, theater as an institution—a meeting place and a place in which plays are staged, still serves that group of spectators as a place in which to clarify problems of self, the changes they have undergone, the conflicts they have with other groups, and their attitudes to war as a strategy for determining or solving disputes with the Arabs.

Political and social problems were staged and "solved" in Hebrew drama of the *yishuv* period and in the early decades following the establishment of the state. From the 1980s on, Hebrew culture and theater saw more explicit exposure of conflicts, of disagreements and of contradictions, and of their representation as insoluble—including theatrical debates on the damage caused by the conflict with the Arabs, the prominent characteristics of which are violent clashes and continuous war.

Many Israeli playwrights, following Lucien Goldmann's concept, are *transindividuals*—representing the beliefs and opinions of a particular group in Israeli society. Their *vision du monde* negotiates between the social reality and its portrayal in the theater. *Vision du monde,* according to Goldmann, is that same "principle concrete aspect of the phenomenon that sociologists have been attempting to describe for many years as collective consciousness."[5] Nonetheless, the playwright is not merely a representative of his group or his era, but also has the role of critic (occasionally "prophet"), who can expose, via his work, the motives behind aberrant group consensus, such as the glorification of war during certain periods. The Israeli playwrights belong to an influential group. They write for the stages and actors that in the main identify with their opinions and for a very familiar audience, with which they investigate problems and also shape viewpoints, some specific and others deduced from the text. Sometimes they criticize the prejudices of their audience and its political behavior. Nonetheless, the criticism of most of the playwrights is suited to what can be achieved and to the audience's receptive readiness, a reception that would be impossible without such agreement and cooperation.

One of the prominent playwrights of recent decades is Motti Lerner (b. 1949), a fertile writer with political leanings, who has described his worldview, which is that of many of his group, and declared his obligation as a playwright to prevent war:

> The playwright examining the environment in which he lives can suggest... alternatives to war.... Playwriting in Israel has had a significant influence on the attitude of Israeli society towards the idea of a Palestinian state, the majority of which currently supports the idea thanks also to the works of Hanoch Levin, Joshua Sobol, Joseph Mundi, Hillel Mittelpunkt and others.[6]

Lerner also proffers advice to the playwright wishing to engage with the issue of war; part of which advice relates to his own experience and, as we shall see, the experience of other Israeli playwrights:

> How can the playwright expose the causal infrastructure—social, psychological, mythical and political—that is likely to lead to war? By creating characters that contend with the reasons for war. . . . Empathy is really a key word in this process of reconciliation. How do we create this Empathy? By placing the other onstage. (Ibid.)

Condemnation of war, attempts to prevent it or mitigate its damage, only began to be attempted by Israeli playwrights in the 1970s. In the 1940s and '50s war was at the center of the world of the second generation, the "sabra" generation, the sons of those Jews who had immigrated to Palestine before the establishment of the state, the families of Holocaust refugees and Hebrew-speaking youth who had been educated upon the ethos of pioneering and love for the motherland. The majority was Ashkenazi, members of youth movements who volunteered to make settlement a reality and who fought in the War of Independence. The "second generation" plays (particularly those by Moshe Shamir, Nathan Shacham, Aharon Megged, and Yigal Mossinsohn), emphasize the strong bond existing between these young sabras with their group and the land—as characterizing the culture of "innate patriotism." The writings of this generation reveal a high frequency of expressions of love of the land—they unite individual and nation with love of the land and with the willingness to volunteer, to fight and to sacrifice their lives for this land.

The first play in the Israeli theater, *On the Plains of the Negev,* by Yigal Mossinsohn (1917–1994), was staged at the end of the War of Independence (1949), and saw a run of thirteen years, 227 performances, in front of almost a quarter of a million spectators. A quarter to a third of the Jewish population of Israel saw the play, in particular the majority of the veteran population.[7] The play presents the story of the founding of a kibbutz in the face of Arab attacks during the War of Independence and the death of a kibbutz son while carrying out his mission to evacuate the wounded. The dramatis personae include figures from the second generation, native born, and fighters. In *On the Plains of the Negev* the love for the motherland encompasses two generations: the father, Abraham, objects to evacuating the besieged kibbutz, declaring: "I want to look into the eyes of my Danny as a fighting man and not as a miserable refugee who fled from his land . . . this is the only land that does not turn us into refugees and beggars."[8] The kibbutz is saved, but Danny, the sabra son, is killed in battle. The audience that watched the play at the Habima Theatre in Tel Aviv shared with the actors the same spirit of sacrifice and patriotism.

On the Plains of the Negev is one of the few literary and theater works that responded, during the war, according to Emmanuel Sivan, to "the pressing need among the broad public . . . to confront the materials of reality and knead them into an artistic expression."[9] The writers "painted a picture, whose protagonists were from their same close age group, immigration, origin and education" (121–22), and therefore, "without any intended malice or distortion" (121) provided nourishing myths that glorified the actions of these groups in the war, and played down the roles of other groups (119–21).

One can assume that the spectators attending *On the Plains of the Negev* outnumbered those who had read books of and about the War of Independence. "Masses will run to celebrate an emotional encounter with themselves, with their sorrow," wrote Baruch Kurzweill about the play.[10] The play, which was written in only a few weeks, is, according to Israel Gur, "sloppy and one-dimensional."[11] Despite this, Gur himself admits that he arrived at the play dusty and sweating after a long journey through the Negev, to: "An unforgettable experience . . . I remember well the great excitement that gripped the audience; many wept or cried out loud; for a long time after the play had ended many of the spectators were still wandering the theatre corridors, extolling the play and heaping praise on the actors. Indeed, an atmosphere of sanctity and tragic greatness accompanied one that evening" (ibid.). One of the critics added: "Bereaved parents who had lost their sons acknowledged the remembrance of souls."[12]

The sociorituaI power of the play, and the fierce sense of mourning the spectators shared, particularly among those belonging to the groups represented in the play, sabras and their parents, is revealed in Haim Gamzu's critique: "This simple play affects the spectator like an operation without an anesthetic; an operation on the living flesh of the present. The pain is piercing. At moments the agonizingly ill are drawn to the very limits of suffering. In a short while it will cease. But no! After we have looked into our own deepest depths, we return to ourselves immunized, strengthened."[13]

From the War of Independence (1948) until 1973 there were very few plays on the Israeli stage whose subject was war. It is possible that the swift and expansive victories of the Sinai Campaign (1956) and the Six-Day War (1967) were more suited to literature and to documentaries and film. The Yom Kippur War was different, rocking the foundations of Israeli society and its institutions, being a dramatic political event whose extent affected the national consensus, and also an experience that returned its soldiers to the foxholes, trenches, and bunkers. This was expressed in the theater in *The Joker* by Yehoshua Sobol (b. 1939), directed by Nola Chilton, and performed by the Haifa Municipal Theatre, Stage 2, in 1975. The play features a group of reserve soldiers at an outpost in the north, on the eve of the ceasefire of the Yom Kippur War. They are supposed to set out on a dangerous mission. The veteran soldiers don't want to endanger themselves; they send a young soldier off on the mission in which he will probably die. Sobol wrote *The Joker* following his personal experience during his reserve duty service after the Yom Kippur War, expanding the pool of dramatis personae: "The figures represented a typical cross-section of the population: 'the other Israel,' the educated, the intellectual, and cleaning workers. For me, this was a poignant encounter with the problems of the frustrated sectors of society."[14] *The Joker* was an innovation and turning point regarding the war from the aspect of Israeli playwrights of the period. The positive reception of the play (about 150 performances), as one critic contended, was influenced by the Yom Kippur War: "The audience prior to Yom Kippur would have thrown tomatoes at Sobol. The audience prior to Yom Kippur had grown up on glossy albums with warrior heroes . . . with Sobol these heroes are of an entirely different stuff, one [of them] returns from absence without leave bringing with him hashish from home . . . these are very small heroes but nonetheless are living people."[15]

The comparison with *On the Plains of the Negev* reveals the innovation of *The Joker* and the change in perception of war. Nonetheless, war in Sobol's play, as in those by Shacham, Shamir, and Mossinsohn, still takes place at a geographical distance from the Tel Aviv audience. The sacrifice in Mossinsohn's play, however, that almost reaches sacrifice of the son on the altar of the young nation, disappeared in 1975 to make way for a description of compulsory army service during war, and the figures once again no longer belong only to that one social group that is loyal to the Zionist ethos. *The Joker,* however, has no doubts regarding justification of the war, and the policy that had led to it, but rather expresses anomia, fear, and even a desire to get out of it.

After the 1973 war a process of questioning the Jewish-Israeli-Ashkenazi monolith began to develop in the public sphere, and criticism increased regarding justification of the violent disputes with the Palestinians.[16] The national consensus too, in regard to the justification of war as a means to solving the dispute, began to be increasingly questioned, particularly from 1982.

Expressions of opposition to the policy of force would begin to appear on stage during the first half of the 1980s, with the First Lebanon War. This war disrupted the national consensus and created an oppositional movement that throughout the years witnessed ever-greater entanglement and an increasing number of victims among both Israeli soldiers and Palestinians. Among some of the Jewish public, particularly theater-makers and their audiences, recognition was growing that there was no solution to the problem, other than reaching an agreement with the Palestinians. The Lebanon War and the intifada brought together in the 1980s a vociferous artistic opposition to the policies of the right wing and the national unity governments. The Palestinians became part of the daily reality of violent conflict and peace talks, which brought them closer to the world of the Israeli Jews. In a theater that finds itself representing a group belonging to the opposition, "the Arab question" that had become "the Palestinian question" sparked among Israeli Jews a desire for conciliation, but also a sense of ethnocentric frustration. The Palestinians were perceived not only as those who are subjected to national and economic injustice, but sometimes also as those who "force" upon the young Israeli, missions that contradict his conscience and education; while, in contrast, the growth in hostile actions between Palestinians and Jews reinforced among a great part of the Jewish population the already-existing sense of hostility, hatred, and fear regarding the Palestinians.

In the years following the outbreak of the Lebanon War, over one hundred plays featuring an Arab character were staged in Israeli theaters, in most of which, this figure represented the side of the Palestinian in the dispute. Does this increase in what might be called "the Arab motif" indicate an attempt at dialogue between the two nations, at least from the Jewish side? Research and surveys that examined the attitude of the Jewish majority to the Arab minority in Israel and to the Palestinians in the occupied territories reveal alienation and, in the last decades of the twentieth century, a growth in hostility and in negative stereotypes.[17] Such background information does not invite closeness; quite the contrary—it reinforces the high walls that separate Arabs and Jews.

The process of change that began in perception of the Jewish-Arab conflict in Israeli theater of the 1980s is exemplified in several plays: *Them* (1982), *Mammy* (1986), and *The Jerusalem Syndrome* (1987)—works ranging from the visionary (or delusional) of coexistence and the status quo, to stark description of the conflict, and, toward the First Intifada, the conflict represented as a nightmare of war—as dystopia.

Them was a work of coexistence, a collaborative performance by Jewish and Arab actors, graduates of Israeli drama schools, and staged close to the outbreak of the Lebanon War. Sinai Peter (b. 1954), who played in the show, relates to it as "the key play":

> *Them* ran for about six months and shared with audiences throughout the country a rare agreement regarding Jewish and Arab cooperation. *Them* constituted a significant milestone in the history of political theatre, in presenting a statement and language opposing the culture of war. It was also a comfort to many like me, who felt helpless in the face of the madness of the political systems.[18]

The texts, written and edited by Miriam Kaney and Riad Masarwi (1982), and directed by Josep Chaikin, created a collage of scenes on the dispute between Jews and Arabs. Collage is a genre that links together individual scenes but without creating a "story"; it is a genre that attests to the embarrassment that arises when two "truths" come into conflict. The mutual fears of Arabs and Jews and the history of the dispute, from its inception and up to the First Lebanon War, were staged as a "competition of suffering" between two of the actors—Jewish and Arab, Sinai Peter and Ghassan Abbas:

> **Sinai**: We came home, they didn't tell us that there are Arabs here. When they told us, there was already nowhere else to flee and then they fell upon us, the massacre of Jews in Hebron, the murder in Zefat, you remember that they murdered Brenner . . . [Arabs murdered the writer Joseph Haim Brenner, among others, during riots in Jaffa, 1921].
> **Ghassan**: On the one hand the Jews frightened us. They did Der Yassin to us [During the War of Independence in 1948, members of the Jewish underground movements "Etzel" and "Lehi" killed over one hundred inhabitants of the Arab village Der Yassin, including women and children]. On the other hand, our leaders told us to run away because we'd shortly be returning. We too had our exile . . . refugee camps. The Arabs gave us nothing. . . . They called us traitors, leaving Palestine for the Jews. Return to where you'd been born! To where should we return? The Jews didn't want me and the Arabs didn't want me . . .

Sinai: The entire world is anti-Semitic.
Ghassan: Who is Semitic? I'm Semitic!
Sinai: I'm Semitic.
Both: Anti-Semite!
Sinai: Ma'ale Akrabim [Eleven Jewish passengers murdered by Arabs on a bus, 1954], the coast road [PLO members attack a bus killing thirty-five Jews and wounding dozens more, 1978]. We, whose hands were held out in peace, were forced into six wars.
Ghassan: My house was in the Der Yassin massacre. Kfar Kassem [Following a curfew, the Israeli Border Police killed fifty-one inhabitants of an Arab village, 1956]. They blew up all the inhabitants in Kalkiliya. The military government. Expropriation of lands. Third-class citizenship.
Sinai: Prisoners of Zion.
Ghassan: Administrative detentions.
Sinai: Okay, now listen to me well! One-third of my people were destroyed in the Holocaust.
Ghassan: What's true is true. Mine still haven't been.

Several of the plays staged prior to outbreak of the First Intifada predict its occurrence, including the rock play *Mammy* by Hillel Mittelpunkt (1986), characterized by its author as "a rock fantasy," a new genre in Israeli theater, a sort of theatrical comic in which every single detail relates to the political reality of the time of its initial performance, and of the time of its reprise (during the intifada, 2002).[19] Mammy, the female protagonist of the "fantasy," works in a diner in a distant southern town. Her husband, Nissim, was wounded in the war and is now a "vegetable." Mammy does not give in and, taking her wheelchair-bound husband with her, sets off for the distant city of Tel Aviv. In the big city she works as a waitress in an exclusive pub, where she falls victim to attempted rape by seven disgruntled Palestinian workers. She is saved by a group of right-wing extremists (racist "worms"), and finds herself with her husband in a brothel of the settlement's founding fathers. An encounter with Professor Kopmachine, the eccentric inventor, who gives her a new head, changes Mammy's life. Within a few months she becomes a media and television star. Overcome by her success, Mammy founds a new political movement and preaches a last and final war that will free the nation from the plague of loving life. The committee established to investigate the events of the war finds Mammy responsible for its failure and sentences her and her husband to return to the town in the south and never leave it again. "*Mammy,*" contends Hamutal Tsamir, "succeeds in telling the story of Jewish-Israeli nationalism after 1967 . . . in a radical and profound manner."[20]

For the audience of spectators, particularly those attending performances at the Tsavta Theatre in Tel Aviv, the center of the intelligentsia, and of "leftist" tendencies, *Mammy* was "a political [bad] dream"—controlled by aggressive and vulgar media, represented by "the narrator," a gutter press journalist, "sole" owner of the tale of the rise and fall of Mammy, as representative of the political upheaval that brought the right wing to power in 1977.

Mittelpunkt returned to *Mammy* in his rock opera *Samara,* staged under his direction at Tsavta in 1992, in the continuing life of a Mizrahi couple from a development town, this time during the intifada. Like *Mammy,* the background is that of a "small town in the south." The media are looking for the killer of an Arab girl called Samara Ashrawi. Samocha, a soldier on reserve duty, unemployed, from a development town and whose wife is pregnant, is ready to accept responsibility for Samara's death and go to prison. In return, his friends, members of his patrol, will give him an apartment and a job. Upon his release from prison, however, he discovers that this had been a bad deal. Samara's ghost returns each night to haunt him. "*Samara* is a story of the *intifada* in every way," says Mittelpunkt, "a modern and renewed version of the mythological *Dybbuk* [a renowned play staged by Habima, adapted from the play *The Dybbuk* by S. Ansky, 1922]."[21] Samocha's wife suspects him of having an affair with an Arab girl. She sends him to the Institute for Personality Implants. There he succeeds in ridding himself of the memory of Samara, but, like other Israeli Jews whose emotions have been deeply affected by the dispute whose values and principles have become confused, Samocha's personality too is erased and his thoughts emasculated.

Intensification in representing the conflict culminated in the 1980s, with *The Jerusalem Syndrome* by Yehoshua Sobol, directed by Gedalia Besser, one of the first postmodern (or postdramatic) plays in the Israeli theater. The First Intifada broke out on December 9, 1987, only days after the first performances of *The Jerusalem Syndrome.* The closeness between this apocalyptic vision of the destruction of the Second Temple (and the Third) and the events taking place in the occupied territories, were perhaps among the factors that most affected the audience's reception of the play. Sobol had not anticipated the Arab rebellion that broke out during the period of rehearsals, but he could imagine a similar reality: "While writing *The Jerusalem Syndrome* I experienced the land awash in images arousing fear and hatred ('the two-legged animals,' the 'drugged cockroaches,' the 'terrorists'), addicted to its fears and swept by violent and destructive urges."[22]

The destruction of the Second Temple plays an important role in Sobol's works, especially in the plays *The Jewish Wars* (1981) and *The Jerusalem Syndrome* (1987). A comparison between the plays reveals that during the 1980s a change had taken place in the playwright's approach to the lessons of the destruction of the Second Temple. In *The Jewish Wars* Sobol wished to create a sort of *Lehrstuck* ("study play"), preaching a possible peace, which in the course of watching the spectators would experience a process of awareness of certain facts that had been concealed from them or not sufficiently emphasized during their studies of the history of the period of the Second Temple. Consequently, the play was fashioned as a journey in which the audience began its way with an archaeological excavation of the Citadel (Tower of David), from which it would learn about the past through scientific discoveries. The spectators were supposed to discover that Jerusalem, on the eve of the rebellion, was one of the treasures of the ancient world, in which a multifaceted pluralistic culture had developed, in which Christianity was part of Judaism, and Judaism could have become the culture of the entire ancient world. Those same spectators were then expected to descend into the bowels of the earth, and from within a subterranean burrow to learn through awareness and their senses of the self-destructive powers that emanated from the Jewish Orthodoxy, religious Puritanism, and xenophobia that had taken over the masses and led them to national destruction. In *The Jerusalem Syndrome* the analogy between past, present, and near future are more explicit, and the ubiquitous war distances any chance of peace. In the play, Jerusalem is a city under siege, surrounded by a contemporary army, tired and hungry. The soldiers encounter a group of eccentric madmen, who, under the direction of the professor, their mad leader, stage a play about the great revolt against the Romans and the destruction of the Second Temple. The near future is a desolation with which the playwright threatens his audience, while beyond the theater the Palestinian revolt has only just begun. *The Jerusalem Syndrome* was a dystopic vision in content as well as in its theatrical realization. Sobol chose to write a postmodern work featuring abrupt transitions between different levels of reality: between scenes from the professor's play, set in the time of the Second Temple, and scenes from the near future—within a mad world of insane people, and the "sane" world of other characters. This was a theater that Sobol called "a theatre of awareness" encountering scenes of Jerusalem during the destruction of the Second Temple with Jerusalem of the present day, which, according to the playwright, is "Jerusalem at the end of the Third Temple" (96).

From the beginning of the First Intifada Israeli playwrights began to bring to the stage the difficulties of the divided reality and the need for a critical reexamination of the ideology that had created the State of Israel. The contradictions were particularly sharp between the humanistic and universal components in the Zionist ideology and the brutal reality that had led to "the Palestinian question." The stories and plays by Orly Castel-Bloom (b. 1960) and other artists and writers of her generation, reveal the difficulties in confronting the internal contradiction in the Zionist ethos. "I arrived from a place of Zionism," stated Castel-Bloom, "from a place of accomplishment that was supposed to be full of content, a place devoid of emptiness, a place replete with myths, purpose, mission. But there is something entirely paradoxical here. Fifty years have passed, and this country still has no borders. They haven't been delineated. No-one knows how far one is permitted to go, where the danger lies, and afterwards they wonder that people go off in strange directions."[23] One example among many of the moral failures derived from the violent disputes and wars, as reflected by the "fourth generation" of Israeli playwrights, was the one-man performance *Catch 82* by Roi Reshkess (1992), a play about the war in Lebanon staged against the background of the First Intifada, in which Ziv, a kibbutz son, and a soldier during the battle in Beirut, encounters a group of several "of our mates from the Phalanges," who rape an Arab woman:

> Maybe 60 years old . . . hard to tell the age among these Arab women . . . something between my mother and my grandmother . . . she lay on her back on the ground . . . and a fat fellow fucked her like an animal . . . the one who had just begun to screw her got mad when she fainted just as his turn came . . . he took his "klatch" [a machine gun] from the fellow who had just fucked her and let fly a stream of bullets into her mouth, blowing off her head . . . and I'd just finished my sandwich and got off the crate. The guys asked me what was going on and I said they were fucking the hell out of an old Arab woman . . . I thought that's how it was there, and that's it. Like us on the kibbutz going barefoot to the dining hall and always on bicycles, so they rape old women and then blow her head off!

The war leads to deep changes in Ziv, he is discharged from the army, parts from his friends, and finds himself almost ostracized by his family and the kibbutz. The close contact and friction with the hostile and rebellious Arab civilian population forced upon Ziv and many other Israelis during the war in Lebanon and the intifada turned the Arab into a more realistic figure as well as increasing the fear of him.

The intifada blurred the borders between the Israeli, the Arab Israeli, and the Palestinian theaters. In the early 1980s the Jewish audience encountered the Palestinian theater mainly through productions by the Al-Hakawati Theatre, which predicted the revolt in several of its plays. The colorful theatrical language of the Al-Hakawati plays, drawn from the Palestinian folk theater, such as the character of the storyteller (al-Hakawati), and influenced by the French theater (mainly Jerome Savari and Ariane Mnouchkine), helped the Palestine "narrative" to cross the borders of the Green Line. *Makhjoub and Makhjoub* was the first play by François Abu Salem and his players to be performed on an Israeli stage (1983). Makhjoub, the living-dead, asks the audience during the performance to join him: "Before the coffin will seal you in."

From the very first the intifada constituted a totality of events with a theatrical flavor, given broad coverage by the media while also directing themselves at the media. The popular nature of the rebellion and the closure of the theaters by the military government almost silenced the theater-makers in the occupied territories and in Israel. In 1990, Riad Masarwi (b. 1948) chose to stage *The Ninth Wave,* in Nazareth, featuring giant slides of Palestinian women and children confronting Israeli soldiers, with no text. The intifada encouraged the spread of a verbal folk culture, mostly through nationalist poetry, alongside the development of oral storytelling, graffiti that creates "wall journalism," CDs of songs set to nationalist tunes, and even nationalist elements in the colors of the clothing worn, and in which scarecrows were dressed in the fields.

Among Israeli Arabs the intifada intensified the conflict of identity between their Israeli citizenship and their process of Palestinization, in which they had found themselves since the 1980s. This uncertainty found many expressions in the theater. Actors, directors, and playwrights were forced, due to increasing censorship restrictions during the intifada, to seek other stages within the Green Line. The intifada accompanied them as part of the repertoire of the Arab Israeli theater. The works included the play *Al-Okesh* by Adnan Tarabshe (b. 1958), first staged at the Festival for One-Man Shows at the Bet HaGeffen Theatre (1992). This is a text of an Israeli Arab consumed by a sense of guilt over the passivity of some Israeli Arabs in the presence of the intifada. He volunteers to help but is not warmly received by the Palestinians, who have not forgiven the Israeli Arabs for not fleeing with them in 1948. Al-Okesh wanders from job to job, unable to integrate into Palestinian society, until finally becoming a gravedigger, a profession that was financially highly rewarding during the period of the rebellion. He founds his own independent country in the cemetery and talks to the deceased buried there. These include a stone-throwing hero of the intifada, a collaborator, his beloved who had been killed, and an old Palestinian woman who had witnessed many generations of conqueror and conquered. At the end of the play the Israeli loudspeakers announce a curfew and everybody is asked to return to their homes. Al-Okesh has no home or shelter and is hit by a bullet and dies. This solo performance, set in a small cemetery, is poor in theatrical means. It is the text and the actor's work that constitute its strength. Adnan Tarabshe plays all the parts himself, thereby representing the Israeli Arab, whose "personality" encompasses several identities. *Al-Okesh* also directs criticism against the intifada and its leadership, and the Israeli component of Tarabshe's identity seems particularly dominant when he refers to the masked men and the PLO leadership. In the play a masked man uses Shylock's famous monologue from *The Merchant of Venice* in order to justify his brutal revenge, but Al-Okesh is reluctant to pursue this path, for "in times of struggle, blind hatred does not help" the situation in which the Israeli Arabs find themselves. Another character, of an Arab collaborator with Israel, is not presented only as a negative figure, perhaps because of his "closeness" to the situation in which the Israeli Arabs find themselves, perceived by some Palestinian groups as collaborators with the Israeli Jews.

The 1990s saw a change in the concept of war. Palestinian terror attacks inside Israeli cities intensified—from knife stabbings to the blowing up of buses. War was no longer only in the bunkers on the northern border or a story of the experiences of young men called up to army reserve duty in Lebanon or the occupied territories; it was everywhere, even in Israel's main theater arena—Tel Aviv. The dispute had reached a stage in which "every individual of both communities potentially bore the dispute with him in whatever direction he turned, whether as the injurer or the injured."[24]

Theater-makers introduced a new version of the war, a version with more sober vision and criticism than those that had come before. One interesting example of a critical look backward—to the Six-Day War as a great military achievement, and mainly an expensive political failure, as well as the Yom Kippur War and the lessons learned from it—can be seen in *Gorodish—The Seventh Day* by Hillel Mittelpunkt, directed by the playwright at the Cameri Theatre in 1993. At the heart of the play is the figure of the general who in the 1970s won a hero's glory.

Gorodish is a tragic "biographical" story of the rise and fall of General Shmuel Gonen. Gonen (Gorodish) had fought in the ranks of the Haganah as a youth, advanced in the Armored Corps, and reached the rank of divisional commander. Following the end of the Six-Day War he made a speech calling upon "My heroic brothers in glory," containing the notorious statement manifesting the hubris of several military personnel of the winning army: "We have stared death in the face, and it lowered its eyes." Gorodish's speech had "won" the theatrical criticism of Hanoch Levin already in 1968, in the satire *You and I and the Next War,* in which the general makes his victory speech to an empty parade ground, and finally, after he has unsuccessfully sought a reaction from his soldiers, he raises his eyes to the heavens and salutes. In the Yom Kippur War in 1973 Gorodish failed in his task as commander of the southern front. The Agranat Committee found him among those responsible for many of the failures of the war. He retired from the army and entered into business in Africa, not returning to Israel until 1991.

Mittelpunkt, in his play, settled accounts with the cult of the generals, which had particularly intensified after the Six-Day War, accompanied by victory albums, belligerent speeches, ostentatious parades, performances by military entertainment troupes, and the anthems of the various army units. The play opens with a visit by the journalist Adam Baruch to Gorodish in Africa, and, while "looking back," a series of photographs from his life are shown—from the highest point, fed by the sense of a powerful army, and up to his exit and exile to Africa. The play "integrated" songs and radio broadcasts from the period. *Gorodish* presents the "semiotics of war," particularly focusing on a "reproduction" of the speech Gorodish made to his soldiers at the end of the Six-Day War ("Jabel Livni, July 67. Victory parade. Clear blue skies. Shadows of tanks. Pennant of the 7th brigade. Gorodish makes his speech on an elevated platform . . . the brigade anthem is heard loudly"; the speech is a compilation of flowery biblical passages: "We have not turned our heads towards our beloved ones, who with their iron carriages went up in flames, we did not stand on their blood, and with our wrath we brought in the thunder of our armored death to the heart of the enemy").[25] Alongside Gorodish throughout the play, as well as during the victory parade, stands a soldier by the name of Freedman, representing "a new masculinity" of the antihero warrior, who fails to fit into the army and fulfill his duties, is punished, commits suicide, and his image as a ghost accompanies the general through every stage of the rest of his life.

Gorodish is not only "a theatrical biography" with such historical figures as Golda Meir and Moshe Dayan. The play includes imaginary scenes in which the suicide soldier's ghost wanders about, or head-butts "the mother of all wars," Um Naji, a Palestinian Mother Courage, who, like Bertholt Brecht's character, has lost her three children, and is the playwright's voice and that of the spectators in 1993:

> **Um Naji**: (sorrowfully), Ai, ai, general, general . . . you still don't see. People loved you, because they saw in you what they wanted to see in themselves, and they hate you today, because they see in you everything that they hate to see in themselves. (82)

Gorodish was highly successful in the 1990s (about 240 performances). Most of the spectators were familiar with the characters and some of the events. The younger members of the audience were less familiar with the context, but "translated" the play into their own experiences in the First Lebanon War.[26]

Sociopsychology discerns two main processes of identity construction: constructing one's identity by means of the "Other" or by means of establishing an internal dialogue among the various identity components. The first process demands little energy, particularly when the "Other" supplies the necessary characterization for a definition of the monolithic "I." It is known that in the face of the enemy it is easy for the collective to unite in defining the collective identity. With time, however, greater energy is required in order to maintain this monolithic identity.[27] The process of weakening the monolithic character of the Ashkenazi-Jewish-Israeli identity intensified in particular after the assassination of Prime Minister Rabin (1995). Dan Bar-On contends that "the murder of Yitzhak Rabin by Yigal Amir was a sort of final melt-down, after which it was no longer possible to continue the monolithic 'I' " (80).

Murder, by Hanoch Levin (1943–1999), directed by Omri Nitzan at the Cameri Theatre (1997), was a forceful theatrical expression following the assassination of Rabin. *Murder* is similar to other plays written or staged in the past in the Hebrew theater that focus on the Jewish-Palestinian dispute, but it also differs from them. The similarity lies in the pessimistic attitude of the majority of these plays. Almost all of them express a longing for a peaceful solution, but in most of them such a solution does not lie within the bounds of possibility, and the range of options presented at the end of the play moves between the "open" and the blocked, to the pessimistic. Even though it sometimes seems that the Israeli theater tends toward a "naïve optimism" that contrasts the standpoint of the majority of Israeli Jews regarding the Arabs and the "Palestinian problem," on the subtextual level one can find many expressions of anxiety regarding the "Other," and of rejecting him, that "complement," the represented "accord," with how the dispute is managed in the extratheatrical reality.[28] The innovations in *Murder* lie in the infiltration of the dispute into the homes of the spectators, in exposing the pessimistic perception of the dispute from the very start, and in its intensification by the end.

From start to end, the play is a series of violent acts. It begins with the intifada, in which Israeli soldiers torture a Palestinian youth and murder him. It continues with revenge when the murdered youth's father murders one of the figures who may have been his son's killer, then rapes the murderer's wife and kills her too. The climax of this murderous journey is reached when Jews publicly murder a wretched Arab laborer who is frustrated financially, nationally, and sexually. *Murder* ends in an error of identity, when a blinded soldier mistakes the identity of an old man and identifies him as the bereaved Palestinian father. This error, against the background of the assassination of Rabin, can be perceived as a metonym of the disappearance of the father figure and the fading of any binding authority.

Hanoch Levin was and still is (even after his death) a faithful spokesman of the political subconscious of a particular group among his audiences, including in everything related to the dispute with the Palestinians. In his early satirical works he began to expose the supremacist approach and corruption of politicians and the military and the economic exploitation of the Arabs. It was only later that Levin, together with his faithful audiences, began to recognize that the dispute is not only concerned with two national entities, and that it had become an individual dispute, a war between every Israeli Jew and every Palestinian. Levin and his audience, who had believed in the hope for peace engendered by the Oslo Accords, following the assassination of Rabin realized that the dispute had no solution. *Murder* is a play about disappointed hopes, and these disappointments dictate the central pattern of the play. Levin may have borrowed the mechanism of disappointed hopes from that most shrewd of plays—*Waiting for Godot* by Samuel Beckett. Just as Godot never arrives and will never arrive, so too is peace, according to Levin, long in coming and may never come. The spectators at the two appearances of the boy in *Waiting for Godot,* like the spectators at the two appearances of the messenger in *Murder,* cannot but discern the pointlessness of their hopes. Levin, familiar with his audience and their mechanisms of repression and denial, adds an epilogue without a messenger, which puts an end to any hopes for peace and perpetuates the state of war.

War is men's business. Women theater-makers in Israeli theater deal very little with the subject. Their later engagement with war, from the 1990s, is a critical one, as is their deconstructionist approach to masculinity. In a short article, "Going to the Sea/ Mother" (*Aller a la mer/mere*), the French playwright Hélène Cixous relates to the problematic connection that women have with the theater, which serves the "male fantasy," in which famous female characters (e.g., Electra, Ophelia, and Cordelia) are always the victim, always exploited, accessorized, and, notably, serve to reflect male heroism.[29] A similar "subversive" thinking characterizes women's theater in Israel, possibly nourished by the consistent failure of the wars in Lebanon and the occupied territories.[30]

In the past there were few women Israeli playwrights, and their plays were seldom staged. At the end of the twentieth century a real change occurred in the ways of representation and the place of women in the Hebrew theater. The number of active women playwrights and their plays performed on both mainstream and fringe stages greatly increased, sometimes equaling those of male playwrights. This change led to a growth in the number of female characters on stage, to their focal roles in the plot and to "allocation" of the dialogue, sometimes to the extent of these characters being allotted more dialogue than their male counterparts. The woman director Ophira Hennig describes this stage as "a true revolution," in which "women have something to say, and not only about the classic conflict between career and family. We don't speak from the womb, but from the head."[31] One example of this "revolution" can be found in the adaptation of Aristophanes's *Lysistrata* by Anat Gov (b. 1953) as *Lysistrata 2000*. This is a play in which women speak on a "male" subject, condemning the war. The adaptation transfers the dispute between Sparta and Athens to the Middle East and exposes the stupidity of men, all of whom are represented as ridiculed and childish figures, contrasted with the great political wisdom of the women who attempt by every possible means, even employing the withholding of sex, to bring about peace:

> **Lysistrata**: I might be a woman, but I do have an opinion
> What I shall say, I shall say to the two camps of this war.
> War is the business of barbarians . . .
> Why is there a need to constantly increase territory?
> Didn't your wives tell you that size doesn't matter?
> How can one murder turn a man into a murderer, while a thousand murderers are given a medal?
> Why do we need to control somebody in order to feel important? Why do we need to hate someone else in order to love ourselves?[32]

The place of women's theater on the fringes of the field is structurally recognizable. The "masculine" repertory theater has a tendency toward coherency, a narrative of beginning-middle-end, and a visually spectacular direction: high-tech stages, sophisticated scenery, varied lighting, and an abundance of costumes and props. Women's theater fashions its identity from a position of objection to the mainstream and consequently chooses different characteristics: both the theatrical fringes and women's theater tend toward fragmentation and "poor" theater. These characteristics are fitting due to their very strangeness, which helps to emphasize the worldview of their creators, which deviates from the "norm." One example of such a "female" play was *Medea-Ex,* an interactive performance by Naora Berger, at the Akko Festival (2003),[33] which combined work by the actress with a presentation that employed a new technology in collaboration with the audience, as well as the participation of a virtual audience, and manifested to the actual audience, and the website surfers, the catch in which they find themselves. Rachel Gordin wrote a "thick description" of this female antiwar play:

> The interactive performance *Medea-Ex,* staged at the Akko Theatre Festival, touches upon the difficulty in incorporating a multidimensional reality as a fable of the times in which we live. The Palestinian Medea, who married the Israeli officer Jason, who betrays her—takes her bitter revenge by sending their two children on a murderous mission. She spits out portions of the text of the Classical *Medea* in front of a computer-generated world, screened on the four walls surrounding the audience of spectators. The words that Euripides assigned to Jason: "You live here. Not among barbarians. You learned in our land what justice is and how to abide by the law instead of violence," have not lost their authoritative relevance . . . the flesh-and-blood actress (Khawla al-Haj) is joined by computerized characters on the screens (Jason, Creon, the Nurse, a storyteller called Zara, and a virtual chorus devised as young female cheerleaders), as well as the figures who visit the

> internet site of the performance during the show itself . . . the audience can choose the sequence of the events, but already at the beginning a news flash announces a murderous attack in the capital: "dozens injured, thirteen dead, and two suicide youths from a refugee camp, where their mother lives, Medea" . . . the spectators' situation while watching *Medea-Ex,* resembles more the standpoint of the actress sitting like an invalid in a wheelchair. They are surrounded by different points of view, all of which represent Medea's consciousness. They are only apparently free to choose.[34]

A prominent characteristic of the Israeli war plays of the new millennium (2000 onward) is their "homeliness," as can be learned from the title of the play *War over the Home,* a satirical comedy in the style of *Aristophanes,* by Ilan Hatzor (2002), set in Jerusalem "in about ten years time." The play depicts an endless war, hunger, lack, and destruction throughout the land. The government brings in mercenaries to fill the ranks of the army, and in this play too a group of women determine to put an end to the war by withholding sex from the fighting men. "And within the chaos, a couple, Malachi and Ziona, dwelling on the border and living in recent years on their floor (for fear of snipers) go out to seek a private peace with the enemy."[35]

The ways of representing war in the Israeli theater of the last decade are not only postmodern or satirical; realism and even naturalism serve the theater-makers manifesting the absurd cruelty inherent in solving the dispute by means of war. The very title of the play *War* by the Swedish playwright Lars Noren directs the spectator to the subject of the play—to war, or, more accurately, to the damages of war "at home." *War,* directed by Ilan Ronen (2005), was set on a stage piled with swords, a few dusty pieces of furniture, and characters made up with dirt that also covered the rags they wore. The play hints at the location of the war that had ended in the former Yugoslavia, and at its being an ethnic war, between Christians and Muslims. However, these indications simply anchor the play in a particular context in order to direct the spectators to their own familiar civil-cruel-latest war. These few hints do not enable the Israeli spectators to escape from understanding nonetheless that the intention is to show the damage caused by all wars everywhere, particularly in those places that are close to them personally. Noren expanded upon this: "The play does not deal with war heroes, but with simple people who are trying to survive in the aftermath. . . . I don't know anything about wars, but this very distance enables me to see the big picture, which is sometimes hidden from the eyes of those who live too close to this reality . . . the play focuses on a subject that is very familiar to me: the nuclear family that is trying to survive."[36] The director, Ilan Ronen, indeed avoided setting the play in the Israeli reality and adopted the playwright's stage directions, distancing the testimony whose sole purpose was to bring the spectators closer to awareness of the harm caused by all wars everywhere.

In what way does Lars Noren differ from his predecessors? Mainly in writing a flowing and naturalistic "family" war play that examines how war changes the family. In *War* the playwright and the characters "relinquish" the themes of heroism and fatherhood. The father, a war hero who returns from captivity blind, attempts to continue to live reality as it had once been, but he is abandoned and finds himself without a family.

For the playwright writing in the third millennium and wishing to raise social or political issues, the choice would appear to be between detailed realism and deliberate and even didactic alienation, and perhaps the comic strategy suggested by *Aristophanes* is an additional option or accompanying choice.[37] In *War* Noren does not choose the alienation of a play assisted by the deliberate fragmentation that Walter Benjamin found in the theater of Bertolt Brecht (150–51). Noren is cautious too about overidentification. *War* features "humorous" scenes that do more than break the tension, instead the laughing audience is encouraged to rethink the costs of war and its damage. Noren chooses a theatrical style sometimes called "ultra-hyper-naturalism"—a style in which human reality is compressed into one brief place and time, thereby creating a sociopolitical image.[38] The characters in *War* speak a language "paralleled" in reality, but Noren's dialogue is a "distillation" of his characters' words. Noran fuses together the horrors (small and large), the laughable attempts to create a normal framework for life (e.g., the "rituals" of washing in a bucket and changing clothes before eating the meager meal), and, mainly, the confrontation of the characters with the terrible reality. For these characters the war and struggle to survive have obliterated any ties with moral restraint: the war hero who sexually attacks his daughter; the woman who has given up on her husband and prefers that he die; the father who beats his son to death; the young girl who is ready to seduce her uncle in order to escape from the distress; unusually perhaps, she is a twelve-year-old who has been sexually exploited, but has also preserved some last remnants of love for her entire family, and she too, at the end, abandons her blind father.

From the generic aspect, *War* is a naturalist play about the disintegration of a family following the war. It is impossible, however, to confine it solely to naturalism, for the play has the essence of a new genre derived from the tragic, melodrama, and even the comic. Several spectators attest to this in describing the reception of *War* as a synecdoche that condenses and represents, despite the naturalism, a familiar and harsh reality.[39] One of them noted that this is a "different play without any indication of place or time and despite its reflection of our daily reality in Israel and presentation of the consequences of war, for a change it presents the lives not of heroes, but of ordinary people."[40]

The Israeli theater repertoire has come a long way from its representation of war in *On the Plains of the Negev* to the Israeli production of *War,* more than fifty years later. "War" alters structure and characteristics, and "peace," which in Israel constitutes low-intensity war, is on the ever more distant horizon. From the mid-1970s war began to lose its aura, and its heroes, particularly those generals who had been so admired in the past, were represented as tragic figures or even as "punished" by means of critical satire, alongside and contrasting with figures of men unable to adapt to the military culture. In the 1980s a new perception of war emerged, no longer war on the front and in the distant bunkers but in the next street to the theater and the home. The Israeli theater repertoire of the new millennium includes plays that express opposition to war throughout the entire theatrical field, the mainstream theaters, the experimental fringe theaters, and the theater created by women—war is represented as a failed strategy in attempting to solve the disputes that bring misery to all those involved.

Notes

1. Dan Urian, "Sixty Years of Israeli Theatre: The Social Aspects," *Scene and Screen* 1 (2009): 7–28.

2. Elihu Katz and Michael Gurevitch, *Leisure Culture in Israel: Patterns of Entertainment and Cultural Need* (Tel Aviv: Am Oved, 1973), 102, 117, 12; Urian, "Sixty Years of Israeli Theatre"; Giora Rahav and Shosh Weiss, *Habima Subscribers Survey*, 1985 season.

3. Hadassah Haas et al., "The Cultural Needs," in *Leisure Culture in Israel: Patterns of Cultural Activity, 1970–1990*, ed. Elihu Katz et al. (Tel Aviv: Guttman Institute for Applied Social Research, 1992), 4, 2, 10.

4 *Bracha Report: Cultural Policy in Israel*, 1998, from a summary by Hadassah Haas, *Panim* 10 (Summer 1999): 109.

5. Lucien Goldmann, *Le dieu caché* (Paris, Gallimard, 1959), 25.

6. A http://www.jewish-theatre.com/visitor/article_display.aspx?articleID=3329. Further quotations are cited parenthetically in the text.

7. During the first run of the play *On the Plains of the Negev*, the Jewish settlement population in Israel amounted to about 650,000.

8. Yigal Mossinsohn, *On the Plains of the Negev* (Tel Aviv: Or-Am, 1989), 42.

9. Emmanuel Sivan, *The 1948 Generation: Myth, Accuracy, and Memory* (Tel Aviv: "Systems"—ZAHAL Publishing House, 1991), 121. Further quotations are cited parenthetically in the text.

10. Baruch Kurzweiller, "In the Plains of the Negev," in *A Survey of Israeli Literature: Mass and Articles*, ed. Zvi Luze and Yedidiya Yizhaki (Tel Aviv: Bar-Ilan University, 1982), 168.

11. Israel Gur, "A Poster Play That Made History," *Stage* 91–92 (1982): 21.

12. Y. M. Neimann, "'On the Plains of the Negev' at Habima," *This Week*, February 17, 1949.

13. Dr. Haim Gamzu, *Theatre Critiques*, ed. Michael Handelsaltz (Tel Aviv: Tel Aviv Museum of Art, 1999), 82.

14. Yehudit Livneh, "The Joker Must Go . . ." *Davar*, April 25, 1975.

15. Yaeli, "Degree of Courage," *Al Hamishmar*, June 11, 1975.

16. Dan Bar-On, "The Assassination of Rabin as a Final Step in Breaking the Monolithic Israeli Identity," in *Memory in Dispute: Myth, Nationalism, and Democracy, Studies Following the Assassination of Rabin*, ed. Lev Greenberg (Beer Sheba: Humphrey Institute for Social Research, Ben-Gurion University of the Negev, 2000), 79.

17. Kalman Binyamini, "The Arab Image among Israeli Youth—What Has Changed in the Last 15 Years," *Studies in Education*, October 27, 1980, 65–94; Kalman Binyamini, Political and Civil Standpoints of Jewish Youth in Israel, Research Report, the Hebrew University of Jerusalem, Faculty of the Humanities, Psychology Department, 1990; Ofra Meisels and Reuven Gal, *Hatred of Arabs among Jewish High-School Pupils* (Zichron Yaakov: Israeli Institute for Military Research, 1989); Haviva Bar and David Bar-Gil, *Living with the Conflict* (Jerusalem: Jerusalem Institute for

Israeli Research, 1995); Daniel Bar-Tal and Yona Teichman, *Stereotypes and Prejudice in Conflict: Representations of Arabs in Israeli Jewish Society* (Cambridge: Cambridge University Press, 2005).

18. Sinai Peter, correspondence, November 2009.

19. Nurit Nethanel, "It Is Never about Them, It Is Always about You," *Bamot Ve'Masach* 1 (2009): 66.

20. Hamutal Tsamir, "'Mammy'—After 16 Years of Predicted Chronic War, or, To the Red Fields," Program from *Mammy*, Habima Theatre, 2002.

21. Interview with Aviv Luze, August 11, 1996.

22. Dan Urian, interview with Yehoshua Sobol, "On 'The Jerusalem Syndrome,'" *Chetz*, 1, 96. Further quotations are cited parenthetically in the text.

23. Gadi Taub, "Seeking Another Language: The Cultural Face of Protest," "The Israelis of Tomorrow," *Ha'Ir*, December 11, 1998.

24. Baruch Kimmerling, "Less Politics More Primitivism," *Haaretz*, April 2, 1993.

25. Hillel Mittelpunkt, *Gorodish* (*The Seventh Day*) (Tel Aviv: Or-Am,1993), 37–38. Further quotations are cited parenthetically in the text.

26. Conversation with Hillel Mittelpunkt, July 31, 2007.

27. Bar-On, "The Assassination of Rabin as a Final Step in Breaking the Monolithic Construction of Israeli Identity,"200, 68. Further quotations are cited parenthetically in the text.

28. Dan Urian, *The Arab in Israeli Drama and Theatre* (London and New York: Routledge Harwood, 1997), 130.

29. Hélène Cixous, "Aller à la mer," *Le Monde*, April 28, 1977.

30. Dan Urian, "Representation of Women in Hebrew Drama," in *Jewish Women: A Comprehensive Historical Encyclopedia*, ed. Paula E. Hyman and Dalia Ofer (2006), http://jwa.org/encyclopedia/author/urian-dan.

31. Tsippi Shochat, "Who's Still Afraid of Virginia Woolf?" *Haaretz*, April 13, 2001.

32. Anat Gov, *Lysistrata 2000* (Tel Aviv: HaKibbutz HaMeuchad, 2001), 62–63.

33. Script and sound at www.medeaex.org.

34. Rachel Gordin, "Immigrants in the Land of Internet," *Haaretz*, October 24, 2003.

35. Program for *War over the Home*, Khan Theatre, 2002.

36. Tal Perry, "What Does a Swede Understand?" *nrg*, June 26, 2005.

37. Walter Benjamin, "What Is Epic Theater," in *Illuminations*, ed., Hannah Arendt, trans. Harry Zohn (New York: Schocken, 1969), 147–54. Further quotations are cited parenthetically in the text.

38. Michael Handelsaltz, "No Getting Used to It, Just Surviving," *Haaretz*, May 10, 2005.

39. Keir Elam, *The Semiotics of Theatre and Drama* (London and New York: Methuen, 1980), 28–29.

40. http://www.habama.co.il/show.asp?ShowNo=10130.

Chapter 16

From National Heroes to Postnational Witnesses

A Reconstruction of Israeli Soldiers' Cinematic Narratives as Witnesses of History

Yael Munk

"By your sword you shall live." This was God's ambivalent blessing to the biblical figure of Esau. And though the Jewish people should primarily be the descendants of Jacob, they still live by the sword, and not only metaphorically. In the history of the Jewish people this specific prophecy was unfortunately realized all too soon, becoming further manifested following the renewal of the Jewish people on their land at the beginning of the twentieth century. Not only did wars become an inherent part of Israel's history, but also the involvement of its citizens in the military became a critical turning point in the nation's mentality and behavior, as if the military had overwhelmed society and contaminated even the tiniest of Israel's citizens' practices. During the state's early days it was customary to contend that "all the country is [made up] of soldiers," as if to point at the nation's highest strength—its solidarity. But as time went by solidarity weakened and the concept of blind patriotism was revised, leaving the individual soldier alone on the nation's symbolic and concrete battlefield.

This essay describes the evolution of the Israeli soldier's cinematic representation from early Israeli cinema, known as "national cinema,"[1] to the present, and indicates the shift that has recently occurred in the image of the IDF (Israel Defense Forces) soldier, from that of the righteous, flawless hero to that of victim, bystander, and witness. I note specific turning points in the politics of representation, with particular emphasis on those recent, internationally successful films known as the "Lebanon films": *Beaufort* (Joseph Cedar, 2007), *Waltz with Bashir* (Ari Folman, 2008), and *Levanon* (Shmulik (Samuel) Maoz, 2009). I contend that in order to read these new representations properly, particular attention must be paid to the enormous gap that lies between cinematic military representations from the very first days of the State of Israel, when the image of the soldier served as an extension of the national discourse, to the present day, when images of soldiers not only stand for themselves but also introduce a counternational discourse in which subjectivity rules. Thus the theoretical framework of this essay, although engaging with the war film genre, is more concerned with the fading of nationalism and its substitution by life-saving issues, particularly the soldier-narrator's life. These recent films challenge the issue of national historiography and raise the ethical issue of the soldier's responsibility and/or complicity in the "spectacle" of war, an issue that in recent Israeli war films tends to be partly solved through powerful aesthetic choices that seem to question the "spectacular" nature of war.

Soldiers in Early Israeli Cinema

Wars have haunted Israeli cinema since its inception. As such they always received a privileged place in the films' narratives. Throughout the years, the Israeli screen has helped in turning the war into an unquestionable fact of life, so much so that even "innocent" narratives that at first sight deal with everyday life can reveal, on close reading, war's imminent threat to the protagonists or the effect of its consequences on their lives.[2] Israeli cinema invested much effort in the reconstruction of a national narrative, supported by those who had sacrificed their lives for the birth of the Jewish state. As Ella Shohat wrote: "the death of the protagonists [. . .] is allegorically compensated by the rebirth of the country—the ultimate protagonist of the film[s]."[3] One such example is Thorold Dickinson's *Hill 24 Does Not Answer* (Giv'a 24 Eina Ona) (1955), which remains to this day the cinematic epitome of the national myth and of the role of the Israeli soldier in it. In this film a group of four young soldiers of different national origins—one Irish, the second American, the third a native Israeli, and the fourth a Yemenite girl—are assigned to guard "Hill 24" on the eve of the Declaration of Independence. When all four are found dead at their outpost, the film retraces their story in flashbacks, in which we learn about their deep conviction in the need to protect the Jewish state and their willingness to die for it. Their deaths are thus made less tragic because of the great national cause that they had served. In *Hill 24 Does Not Answer* the four are symbols of the incontestable price to be paid for the state's independence, and their becoming national heroes is seen as worthy compensation for the loss of their lives. A similar approach can be found in the historical narrative of *They Were Ten* (Baruch Dinar, 1960), in which a group of ten settlers confronts the hardships of the barren land, a situation that leads to the death of the only female protagonist. Once again the film presents the death as a painful but worthy cause, that of having contributed to the Jewish nation's settlement on its land.

However, a few years later the general atmosphere changed and Israelis began to feel that they no longer had to justify their right to exist on their land, except, of course, in times of war. Two major war films were made in the late 1960s, demonstrating this new Israeli approach. The first one is Yosef Miloh's 1967 cinematic adaptation of Moshe

Shamir's canonic novel *He Walked in the Fields* (Hu Halach BaSadot) (1947). Set on the eve of the War of Independence (1948), the film follows its literary source and tells the story of Uri (symbolically played by Assi Dayan, son of the most famous Israeli general of all time), the first son born to his kibbutz and educated to unconditional patriotism.[4] After falling in love with one of the kibbutz's newcomers, he suddenly hesitates in the face of his patriotic duty. These hesitations that, according to Nurith Gertz, marked the first break in the national consensus, are solved in the film's narrative when the protagonist puts an end to his hesitation by sacrificing himself in the service of the nation. In other words, the military is no longer seen only as a contribution to the nation's existential needs but also as a way to escape conflicted situations. This approach is repeated in Uri Zohar's *Every Bastard a King* (Kol Mamzer Melech) (1968), whose plot takes place on the eve of the Six-Day War, as two Israeli friends who accompany an American journalist around the country discover the emptiness of their existence. Only when war is declared do the two finally find their true calling: one of them happily goes to the battlefront, where he meets with his friends and fights for victory; the other flies to Cyprus with the purpose of promoting peace talks with the Arab countries. When the latter comes back with no real achievements, he realizes that the war is already over and he has "missed" it, which means that he did not have the chance to participate in the most glorious event of the country. As opposed to the early nationalist films, these two latter narratives present the participation in war as a choice that needs to be made if one wants to give meaning to one's life.

A Dramatic Turnover: Witnesses and Bystanders in *Paratroopers* and *Khirbet Khizeh*

With the emergence of the New Sensibility cinema in the late 1960s, the "national cinema" genre faded and the question of heroism became irrelevant.[5] When it reappeared on the Israeli screen, it was after the trauma of the Yom Kippur War and the right-wing government's first rise to power in 1977. The general feeling of the 1948 Generation was one of failure, not only failure to perpetuate the values inherited from the founding fathers but mostly failure to react to the Six-Day War and its political consequences. Suddenly Israeli cinema turned back to politics, and more particularly to the IDF as one of the main sites where the Israeli politics of occupation is pursued. War was no longer accepted as a fait accompli, and war-associated issues became a predominant theme, but this time the cinematic point of view was overtly antiheroic. The war films produced from the late 1970s and during the 1980s spoke in a provocative, postnational way, deconstructing the dichotomy between us and them, between the nation and the enemy, and replacing it with a transnational humanistic approach.[6]

Two major films focusing on soldiers and their role in supporting the military system were released in the late 1970s, introducing this new era of war films in Israeli cinema: Judd Ne'eman's *Paratroopers* (Masa Alunkot) (1977) and Ram Loevy's *Khirbet Khizeh* (1978). Although both films were conceived long before the political upheaval, their release at this historical moment revealed their creators' sense of guilt vis-à-vis the new political situation that they had failed to prevent. Ne'eman's *Paratroopers* was the first film to deal with the way in which the IDF molds its soldiers. Tracing a parallelism between military training and blind ideological indoctrination, the formalistic plot's first part follows the attempts of Weizman (Moni Moshonov), an unfit soldier, to integrate into a prestigious paratrooper boot camp, and his failure to do so, ending in his suicide. The second part deals with the way his commander, Yoni, whose brutal acts directly led to Weizman's suicide, copes with the tragic events or, rather, refuses to assume any responsibility. A similar iconographic framing showing a large group of soldiers singing "dirty" military songs on their way to a training day opens and closes the film text. The viewer, who has followed Weizman's tragedy and his officer's inability to assume responsibility, understands that the IDF is no more than a blind machine whose functioning will not stop because of one single soldier's death. The repetition of the group shot at the end of the film reinforces in the viewer's mind Weizman's absence and, by extrapolation, the unspoken inhuman aspects of the military system.

Paratroopers was a novel event in Israeli cinema. Not only has military training per se never been at the center of a film narrative but also the depiction of its officers, and particularly of Yoni, revealed the unspoken sadistic sides of the military, whether the IDF or another army. Military training was depicted not as a rigorous process, intended to create the team-building ethos that would eventually turn youth into men, but rather as a system sometimes more brutalizing than combat itself. In an interview with Janet Burstein,[7] Ne'eman admits that what had motivated his writing of the *Paratroopers* script was not his experience during the Yom Kippur War (1973) but rather his witnessing during the Six-Day War of the physical and spiritual tortures implied by military pedagogy.

Basic training in the military teaches a soldier two things: (1) how to injure and kill the enemy and (2) how to endure being injured and being ready and willing to suffer and die. In basic training soldiers learn much about weapons, tactics, and ways to protect themselves and hurt the enemy. But the military does not teach the soldiers anything about the other art to which they are initiated: how to get hurt and how to get used to suffering, and to the idea that they will die soon. All the military tells the soldiers is how to apply dressings to wounds.

Contrary to Nitzan Ben-Shaul's contention, according to which "*Paratroopers* is a film based both formally and rhythmically upon American films protesting the Vietnam War [though] unlike theirs, however, its protest is hopeless, and therefore pointless, and is confined to the military establishment without reference to the public sphere,"[8] *Paratroopers* was a direct criticism of the military ethos that had been so central to Israeli existence, and though it did not offer any viable solution[9] it pointed at a major political issue: the revelation that during basic training young soldiers could be abandoned to the indifferent and often sadistic whims of their officers. This terrible ideological iconoclasm led to the film's ambivalent reception in real time, reflecting Israeli society's inability to cope with the shattering of such a consensus of belief. Only years later was

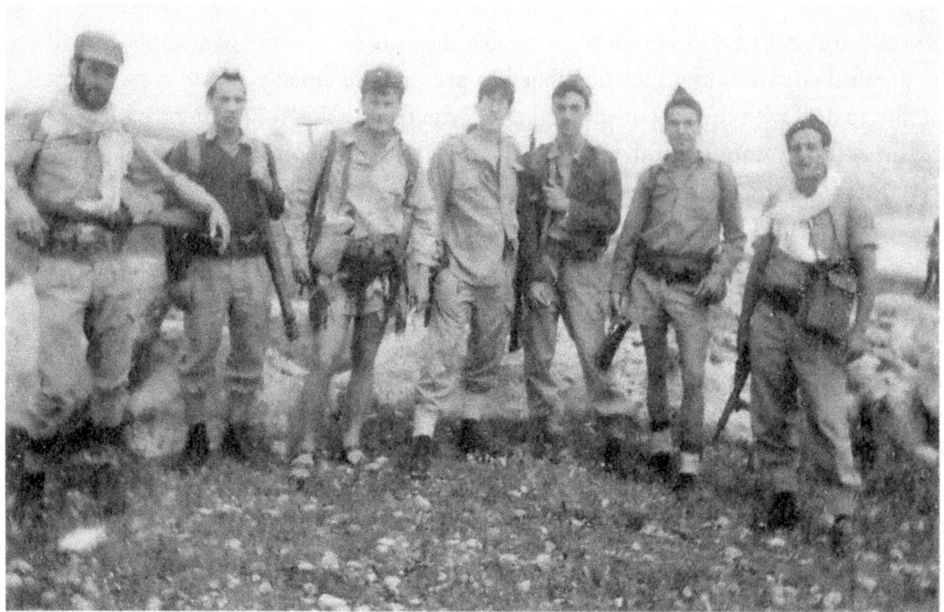

Khirbet Khizeh (1978) from filming.

Paratroopers recognized as one of the major film texts foreshadowing the paradigmatic political turn in Israeli cinema. *Paratroopers* was in fact a testimony from inside the IDF. The invisible witness (who is no other than the filmmaker himself) structured the soldier's destiny into a dialectic plot in which the thesis (unfit soldier is pushed to suicide) and antithesis (this soldier's officer is unable to assume responsibility toward the soldier's family and peers), leads to a synthesis regarding the military's indifference to the individual's life. Weizman's tragic story and the absence of response to it reflected the break in the basic trust between the individual soldier and the military system, a theme that, as this article sets out to demonstrate, has become central to recent Israeli war films.

The other film that predicted this paradigmatic shift in the Israeli consensus was Ram Loevy's *Khirbet Khizeh* (1978), an adaptation of S. Yizhar's eponymous novel based on his own memories of his part in Israel's War of Independence and published immediately after it (1949).[10] *Khirbet Khizeh* narrates in first person singular the story of what seems to be a minor event during the 1948 war. Just like many other Israeli soldiers, a small group of young soldiers was ordered to take the Palestinian village of Khirbet Khizeh,[11] to blow up its houses and expel all the Palestinian women, children, and elderly men remaining there. Following the novel's narration, Loevy's film chooses to keep the voice-over for the description of the events. The narrator is Micha, the handsome fair-haired and blue-eyed sabra (native Israeli). Conforming to the image of the New Jew, Micha is mostly invested in describing the beautiful landscape and at first seems to ignore the moral implications of his deeds. The opening sequence shows the soldiers playing childish games, waiting for orders. When Micha is declared the winner

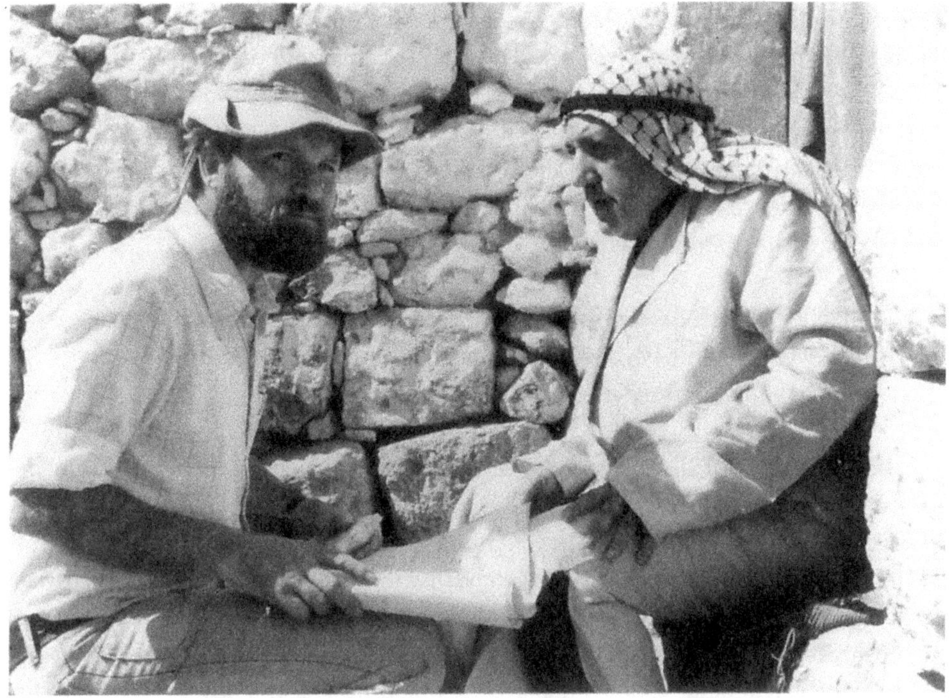

Khirbet Khizeh (1978) from filming; director Ram Loevy on left.

of the competition, the camera freezes his face on the screen in a low-angle shot, in order to create identification between the voice-over and the face of the narrator.[12] Micha's confession progresses, and in spite of his very little involvement in the mission it is carried out and his moral conflict grows. The camera shows him standing aside from the invasion of the village; he silently follows his friends, at most trying to show some human compassion, particularly in the final sequence when he decides to bring water to the evicted Palestinians being loaded onto the truck. But even this purely humanistic act fails to attain its goal, and when he runs back to the truck with the jerry cans of water he finds that it has already departed.

Micha's description should be understood as the confession of the bystander who could not prevent the cruel acts in real time. His stream-of-consciousness narration, interweaving descriptions of the beautiful landscape with his mixed feelings vis-à-vis the mission, forms the basis of the moral conflict of the hero. In his analysis of Yizhar's novel, Hannan Hever contends that just like in the novels of Israel's first generation the national war in *Khirbet Khizeh* obeys the national consensus, according to which the end justifies the means, and the narrator, Micha, understands that the destruction of the village is necessary since the land will serve for the settlement of new Jewish immigrants, those same Jews with whom the new country will be built.[13] In these literary oeuvres, Hever contends, the Palestinian's Otherness remains outside the main narrative and accordingly outside the hero's hesitations and thoughts. Micha's stream of consciousness hints at an analogy between the expelled Palestinians and the expelled

Jews of Europe, as both have become refugees as a result of historical circumstances. The parallelism that is drawn between the two populations attenuates the suffering of the expelled Palestinian villagers as well as the moral dilemmas of the narrator. However, the fact that he reconstructs the "simple operation" he had witnessed and only partly participated in, is to be interpreted as a certain form of remorse, as can be read in the closing sentence of the novel, which is repeated in Loevy's adaptation, against the background of the pastoral landscape:

> And when a hush descends and envelops all, and none disturbs the quiet, which will cry softly beyond all sound—then God will come forth and descend to the valley to see whether the outcry was justified.[14]

Loevy's adaptation, directed almost thirty years after the novel's publication, can be seen as influenced by the political events of the time; namely, the Six-Day War and the ensuing moral deterioration of the Israeli people,[15] and the Khirbet Khizeh mission—as the memory of a primal sin. This may explain why this film adaptation, which was produced for Israel's first and only television channel at the time, was not then released for broadcast and instead elicited a national polemic that ended in the film's censorship for ten years.[16] It should be noted that at the same time Yizhar's novel was part of the high school curriculum, where it was not censored. Perhaps, therefore, there was something in the filmic visualization of the novel that illuminated another layer of the literary text, with the consequent furor. This layer would seem to be the visualization of the bystander's position, a visualization that undermines the traditional representations of the New Jew's heroic deeds.[17] Moreover, Loevy's *Khirbet Khizeh* parallels Micha's inability to prevent the expulsion with his inability to approach the woman soldier with whom he is secretly in love, leveling individualistic concerns with national concerns.

In retrospect, it seems that it was not the human aspect of the mission that was unbearable for Israeli society of the late 1970s, but rather the visual reduction of the Israeli soldier to a bystander. Just like *Paratroopers, Khirbet Khizeh* too succeeded in questioning the Israeli soldier's morality as an individual, a question that at the time could not be asked. This question was to be at the center of the Israeli war films of the 1980s and, in a different configuration, also of those of the 1990s.

As opposed to the 1970s, Israeli cinema of the 1980s deliberately addressed the war issue. One main reason for this thematic shift was the First Lebanon War, the first war to be pronounced a "war of choice." In an interview at the Montpellier Film Festival (France), director Rafi Bukaee, introducing his first film, *Avanti Popolo* (1985), gives an accurate account of the general feeling in Israel at the time:

> In the history of the State of Israel, the Lebanon war was the first time we entered [into war] without a real reason. The very existence of Israel was not threatened. During this war I saw for the first time Israeli planes bombing civilian populations. I saw Palestinians and Israelis suffering in the same

> way from this war and I realized that the only strength necessary for Israel to continue to exist rests in its humanity and its justice. [. . .] During the Lebanon war we were the bad guys, the stupid, the ugly, and the muscled nation that uses its power without thinking, without humanism. (My translation—Y.M.)[18]

Bukaee's words could certainly explain the predominance of the Lebanon War in recent Israeli war films, but, moreover, they also explain the ambivalent moral position of Israeli filmmakers in the 1980s.[19] Opposing Israeli violence and occupation, they could not find a better way to react politically to the actual events than that of adopting the victim's point of view, thus transforming the IDF soldier into the perpetrator, independent of the chain of command to which he responds. Films such as *Avanti Popolo, The Smile of the Lamb* (Hiuch HaGdi) (Shimon Dotan, 1986), or even *Cup Final* (Gmar Gavi'a) (Eran Riklis, 1991) all adopted in a certain way the enemy's point of view in order to reveal the harsh role of the Israeli soldier in the prolonged conflict.

The Lebanon War Films after the Year 2000

The innovative approach discussed above, although widely criticized by those who after the First Lebanon War mistook it for left-wing propaganda, was to disappear in the 1990s as if the time of war was over. In practice, in spite of the signing of the Oslo Accords, the number of bomb attacks on Israeli civilian society grew, accompanied by a growing tension between right-wing and left-wing Israeli politics, which reached a peak with the assassination of Prime Minister Yitzhak Rabin by a right-wing Israeli Jew, Yigal Amir. At the time, however, Israeli cinema was deep into the reconsideration of its roots and origins and did not wish, or according to some could not afford, to deviate from this paradigm.[20]

One exception should be mentioned here: Dina Zvi-Riklis's formalistic film *Lookout* (Nekudat Tatspit) (1991). *Lookout* tells the story of an Israeli soldier posted on a roof in a refugee camp in the occupied territories. Days go by and nothing seems to change in his field of vision except for the presence of a young Palestinian woman and her family. He watches her being married against her will, becoming pregnant, and then becoming a mother. In the background he hardly notices the dreadful consequences of the occupation—her father being jailed by the IDF, and her husband using her young brother to carry a bomb in a shoebox. It is only when the child drops the bomb by mistake and is blown up that the soldier decides to act: he shoots and kills the husband. Using the shot/reverse shot editing technique, Zvi-Riklis limits the spectator's point of view to that of the soldier. In a similar way, the soundtrack is limited to the Israeli radio broadcasts to which the soldier listens, broadcasts that surprisingly do not correspond in any way to the events being watched by the soldier, as if the occupation is not part of Israeli daily life. As a result, the soldier is alienated to the destiny of the Palestinian family and becomes a bystander, watching the events from the outside without intervening (except for the final shooting, which, just like Micha's act in *Khirbet Khizeh,* comes too late and cannot undo the harm already done):

> The soldier, who apparently occupies an Olympian position of power, seeing and controlling everything, is ultimately revealed as someone who knows nothing and does nothing. [When the Israeli troops break into the apartment] he neither takes part in the break-in nor is able to prevent it, although it appears that he would have liked to. [. . .] The only power he has is the power to react after the fact.[21]

As Orly Lubin contends, the positioning of the native-born Israeli in this ambiguous situation precludes any direct criticism of the occupation. However, by revealing the limitations of the power mechanism, *Lookout* points at its critique as such.

Lookout introduces a new kind of bystander, limited in his fields of vision and hearing. But Zvi-Riklis, the only woman director to engage to date with a war feature film, uses this limitation in order to question the soldier's responsibility, as if asking whether a witness can bear any responsibility. This issue would become crucial in the Lebanon films, as Israeli filmmakers turned to their personal experience and retrospectively questioned their part in times of war, particularly in that specific war.

As mentioned above, except for *Lookout,* Israeli cinema in the 1990s expressed no interest in wars and the military in general. Two events, however, abruptly ended this trend—one of a political nature and the second of a cinematic nature. In September 2000, the Second Intifada, known as *Intifadat Al Aqsa,* broke out, bringing back all the repressed memories of a too-violent past, presenting visions of fear and wounded or dead bodies. During this same period, director Amos Gitai, who had returned to Israel in the early 1990s after a decade of exile in France, decided to direct a film about his traumatic memories of an unspoken war, the Yom Kippur War.[22] Gitai's highly personal film, *Kippur,* was released in October 2000, upon that war's twenty-seventh anniversary. What could have been an important cinematic event was, however, overshadowed by the actual events of the Second Intifada. Looking back at the last decade, one can say that *Kippur* reopened the war trope in Israeli cinema and was to mark the first international cinematic success in a series of world recognitions that were to follow.

Gitai decided to frame his film with an intimate situation in which the hero, Weinraub (named after the director's father), is seen making love to his girlfriend in both the opening sequence and in its final one. The extradiegetic saxophone music that accompanies these scenes, which are shot from various angles (as opposed to the war that is almost entirely shot from direct angles), accompanies the lovers' bodies painted in primary colors on a white sheet, until these colors blur and turn into khaki, hinting at the future military scenes. This pastoral intimacy stops abruptly when the hero is called up to reserve service and begins to walk through the empty streets of Tel Aviv on Yom Kippur day. This lovers' scene is repeated at the end of the film. Again the same primary colors on the lovers' bodies, again the saxophone music, except that this time it suggests sadness and melancholy. The film ends on the white sheet as the camera leaves the lovers, revealing a red spot on the white sheet, a symbol of the persisting trauma. The war itself, which occupies the main part of the film, takes place between these two scenes of normal life. Set in the morass of the northern Golan Heights, with very little dialogue, the hero and his two friends perform various Sisyphean attempts to save lives. The climax of these attempts is reached after one injured soldier dies on a stretcher and the three envisage the possibility of not evacuating him on the helicopter. After this dilemma, the three enter the helicopter with the intention of returning to Israel. But as Weinraub looks at the landscape through the helicopter window and sees the places where he used to walk during the last days of the war, a missile hits the plane. The three passengers, all injured to various degrees, are evacuated to the hospital. Ostensibly, Weinraub's war ends here. But the lovemaking scene that closes the film hints that his war does not end upon his return from the front. Like the red stain on the white sheet, it will persist and haunt him in his life's most intimate corners. "War is a chaotic event," says Gitai, "an event that tears one from life's continuity. It pulls people out of their everyday, normal life and ejects them into another existence, under other conditions, in other places. The war, in itself and inside it, is also a chaotic event, and Yom Kippur was even more so, since it was not planned but rather imposed on us, as we know, by surprise. Chaos was the starting notion . . . and the question was how to translate it into cinematic terms.[23]

In order to translate the trauma onto the screen, Gitai recreates his own experience of the war in the most subjective way. The absence of the enemy, as well as the monotonous, repetitive shots, indicate to the viewer that this is not a historical account but rather the reconstruction of the hero's traumatic memory of his attempts to survive, at a moment when survival could no longer be ensured. The landscape, empty of all architectural or aesthetic values, expresses the inner void into which the three men are plunged, as if Gitai were saying that when viewed from the inner self, all war experiences resemble one another.

Like *Lookout, Kippur* too differs from most previous Israeli war films in imposing the viewer's complete identification with the individual soldier's point of view. There is no war outside the limited field of view of its hero. The shooting that tracks Weinraub's acts subjectively reconstructs the war. This narrative technique enables the Israeli soldier's detachment from the IDF's chain of command, and can be considered as the most subversive feature of recent Israeli war films. Moreover, being a testimony in nature, it demonstrates what could not have been told in a national context: the soldier's experience of war.

This may explain the most interesting characteristic of the film: the fact that not a single Israeli soldier shoots even one bullet. Mostly invested in rescuing injured Israeli soldiers, the three men are confronted with death on the battlefield in a completely different way: although death is all around, they are engaged in saving human lives. This is why *Kippur* should be read first and foremost as a testimony, a nonsentimental account of the soldier's most repressed existential fears: losing life, home, and love.

Another subjective account of the war can be found in Eytan Fox's *Yossi and Jagger* (2002). Although not based on the filmmaker's autobiographical experience (the script is credited to Avner Berheimer) the film bears many of the characteristics of the new Israeli war films; namely, the invisibility of the enemy; the constant concern for survival; and, mostly, the need of the soldiers (and officers) to come to terms with their identity, in this case, the homosexual one.

Set in an outpost on the Israeli-Lebanese border, the film tells the story of two officers involved in a secret gay love affair against the background of the snowy Golan Heights. While the bored supporting characters are all solely concerned with survival, the introverted platoon commander, Yossi, and his partner, the extroverted handsome Jagger, dream about the day they will complete their military service and be able to live their relationship openly. The unit is put on alert for terrorist activity, and in the ensuing incident Jagger is fatally injured and dies in the arms of his lover. The film ends with Yossi visiting Jagger's mourning parents, a visit in which his relationship remains disavowed on screen, but for the viewer becomes a confession of his love for his dead partner. The narrative thereby seeks to incorporate the IDF taboo in regard to homosexuality into the national discourse. It does so by ignoring the political context in which the gay love story takes place, avoiding any criticism of the military situation in which they are positioned and restricting the dialogue mostly to the two men's love experience. In this sense *Yossi and Jagger* joins Israeli cinema's contemporary common thread, which is the favoring of the subjective over the national.[24]

In a similar way, Vardit Bilu and Dalia Hager's *Close to Home* (Karov LaBeit) (2006) introduced an unexpected view of women in the IDF, in which two young Israeli women soldiers are posted to patrol in the streets of Jerusalem, controlling the movements of Palestinian pedestrians in the city.[25] The two women, Mirit and Smadar, are contrasting characters, and their efforts are mainly invested in building a friendship around what is considered the main concern of young women: talking, shopping, and falling in love. The two, who seem to be oblivious to the violent atmosphere in which they patrol, are returned to reality after a bomb attack takes place in the city, and they are forced to confront the political impact of their military service. *Close to Home* is remarkable in this sense in that it brings to the screen the IDF experience from the point of view of young women soldiers. In doing so it reveals the everyday violence that has become an inseparable part of Israeli life, not only on the battlefield but also even in the tiniest corner of quotidian existence.

A few years later another Israeli war film appeared: Joseph Cedar's *Beaufort* (2007).[26] It tells the story of Israel's last days on Lebanese soil through the eyes of the soldiers who are left to man the fort until the official withdrawal order arrives. The plot focuses in particular on two contrasting main characters: the combat medic, Koris, who, coming from a well-off family, is not ashamed to toy with the idea of disobeying orders or to cry under pressure, and Liraz, the post's commander, who comes from a peripheral dysfunctional family and who blindly believes in the IDF's ability to provide him with a substitute father figure. Even though the film has no combat scenes (although the outpost is bombarded) and Liraz is never called to actual action, his dedication and his eagerness paint him as an ideal soldier. Yet his time at the Beaufort outpost undermines his firm belief in his mission and in the IDF as a whole. In one of the film's dramatic climaxes he dares to question his admired commander, Kimchi, about his part in the mythological battle over the fortress, and learns, to his great surprise, that the latter had not taken part in the battle since he had been injured just before it began. This revelation is followed by one of the film's central scenes. Set in the bunker's dark control room, Liraz watches an interview with the father of Ziv, the sapper who is killed in the exposition scene. Symbolically, the interview is shown on one-half of the frame, while the other half is filled with official state regalia—the Israeli flag and portraits of the then policy makers, Chief of Staff Shaul Mofaz and Prime Minister Ehud Barak. At first the television screen seems to amplify the state's official voice, echoing the hegemonic voices of the pictured politicians on the right, but then the image of the father gradually fills the entire frame as if the speaker was addressing Liraz (as well as the viewers). The shot/reverse shot editing technique of the scene, which includes cross-gazes between the bereaved father on the screen and Liraz watching him in the bunker, creates the impression that the father's words about the hollowness of the heroic national narrative upon which he had educated his son are in fact addressed to Liraz. "One can blame the army, the generals," says the father, "but these generals are really not responsible for my son. They don't even know him. I'm responsible for him. [. . .] Perhaps I didn't make him understand how precious his life is, that if something bad happens to him the whole world would collapse." By these words the father calls for a privatization of Israeli identity, far from the accepted national ethos and the human sacrifices it requires, and admits on television that the IDF cannot substitute for a father's care and guidance for his son, implying that those who, like Liraz, had believed that the IDF could provide them with a father figure will eventually be disillusioned. This is exactly what happens to Liraz in the film's last sequence: following the explosion of the fortress, the soldiers cross the border back into Israel. After hearing Koris cheerfully announcing to his mother that he is home, Liraz continues to walk toward the camera and, as if realizing the emptiness of the vain rhetoric of a soldier's complete devotion to the military, he falls to his knees and bursts into tears.

A year later, another Israeli war film was again to become a cinematic event: Ari Folman's animated documentary, *Waltz with Bashir.* Based on the director's personal memories as a nineteen-year-old soldier during the First Lebanon War, Folman's animation depicts in a highly subjective way his recovery from this war's traumatic memory. *Waltz with Bashir* opens with a dramatic scene that turns out to be a recurrent nightmare, though not that of the director, but rather of his friend, Boaz. In this nightmare a pack of fiercely barking gray dogs run freely in the streets of Tel Aviv, violently knocking over everything in their way, until they reach an apartment building, Boaz's. At this point the nightmare ends and the director realizes that, as opposed to his friend who is continually haunted by his memories from the Lebanon War, he has repressed these years from his memory. This understanding leads him to investigate the events in which he had been involved twenty-five years ago, through a series of meetings with other friends from his military service at that time, in an effort to reconstruct his forgotten memories from that war. These will appear only at the end of his metaphorical journey into the past, in the vision of a traumatic documentary image of the corpses of the victims of the Sabra and Shatila massacre.

Folman's reconstruction process as presented on screen is unprecedented in Israeli cinema, in designating the individual's wish to come to terms with a terrible, repressed traumatic past that was subtly hidden by a grandiose spectacle in his friends' testimonies. The flashbacks reconstructed thanks to these friends, finally lead the protagonist to his repressed memories, which illuminate the reason for his amnesia: the nineteen-year-old soldier could not come to terms with his passive complicity in this carnage. *Waltz with Bashir* has, consequently, to be read as an ex-soldier's testimony of his complicity in the atrocities carried out in the name of his country, the country that he, as a soldier, represented.

In 2009, Shmulik Maoz's film *Lebanon* (Levanon) was released. Like *Beaufort* and *Waltz with Bashir* it too takes place during the First Lebanon War and bears an autobiographical narrative supported by a powerful iconography that emphasizes its subjective message. Mostly shot from the interior of an Israeli tank, *Lebanon* turns again to the issue of chaos and abandonment of the Israeli soldier on the battlefield. More than once the camera relates to the patriotic scripture on the tank's wall, "The man in the tank will win," which attains an ironic dimension in the film's situation as the four young Israeli soldiers are shown trapped in the tank, fighting for survival. None of the soldiers is concerned with victory; all they care about is staying alive. As the combat situation progresses, the terror on their faces will soon turn into horror that, shot in chiaroscuro, echoes another canonical horror: that expressed by Marlon Brando in Francis Coppola's *Apocalypse Now* (1979). This horror is a reminder for all spectators that war, regardless of its justification, leads the worthiest to the worst.

The camera adopts the point of view of the tank scope, revealing the perspective of the soldier who was supposed to be protected from the violence outside. But violence is all around: whether in the old man begging the invisible tank crew for mercy or in the face of the almost naked woman holding her dead child in her arms. The blind Israeli tank that was shown crushing buildings in its way in *Waltz with Bashir* has now turned into a monster with a human gaze. When seen from the inside of the tank the film reveals this human gaze to be created by fear and madness, anxiety and death. The fact that the protagonist cannot shoot those standing in front of the tank is not a declaration of the IDF's humanism, but rather a revelation of the cost to life of being a soldier. The framing of the film's narrative by two still sequences showing a sunflower field on a bright day in long shot, recalling the lovemaking scenes framing *Kippur,* thus tells the whole story: though nothing seems to have changed after the war, the gaze is different and the simplest actions (making love in the case of *Kippur* or just looking at a sunflower field in *Lebanon*) will never be the same.

Like *Beaufort* and *Waltz with Bashir, Lebanon* won one of the highest awards ever received for an Israeli film: the Venice Film Festival's Golden Lion. One could of course ask what is so interesting about the Lebanon War (1982) that its representation on screen became so sensational. Whereas most critics in Israel (including President Shimon Peres himself at the opening of the 2009 Haifa Film Festival) claimed that in these films the soldier's personal story obtains a universal hue because of its universal representation of human fear and struggle for survival, Israeli film critic Shmulik Duvdevani pointed at the fact that by depicting these soldiers' fight for survival, these films show an ambiguous ideological position, as they detach the IDF soldier from his initial military mission.[27] Accusing *Lebanon*'s director of using "pornographic aesthetics," that is, revealing body parts in extreme close-ups, Duvdevani condemns the film for not bearing a responsible gaze at the war, but rather using the gaze as a manipulative device that according to him turns the Israeli combatant into a victim. However, considering that all personal war films directed recently in Israel have to be read against the traumatic biography of their directors, one should conclude that witnessing, by definition, puts the narrator into the victim's position. In the case of the above-mentioned films, the perpetrator has to be found in Israel's military approach, which believes that any young man is a potential soldier, that is, a potential killer. Thus these recent cinematic testimonies have to be read in a political way, as an act of resistance, or even contestation, against the still dominant national norms. Israeli soldiers are not born killers but, rather, young men seeking to live ordinary lives like their peers in the west. The inability to negotiate a political peace solution in the Middle East, by either Israel or its neighboring countries, condemns these young men to fight, not necessarily those defined as enemies, but for their natural instinct for life.

The Traumatic Experience as Counterhistory

The glorious days of heroic cinema in which a soldier's death for the sake of the state's security was the worthiest experience, are long gone, and in their personal accounts (mostly but not only of the controversial First Lebanon War), Israeli soldiers are tending to realize that they have been the victims of history's blindness. Their positioning on the battlefield as pawns on a chess board has caused their involvement in terrible acts, in which not only others, often defined as enemies, have been injured, but also that they themselves have experienced a life trauma from which they may never recover. This may explain the fact that hegemonic history per se does not exist in these films.[28] Being individual confessions of a trauma, the Lebanon films construct a narrative limited to one single subjective point of view, that of the victim.

These recent film texts thus do not suggest a point of negotiation between collective and personal history (as Anita Shapira contends regarding *Khirbet Khizeh*),[29] but rather aim to create an ultimate personal history in which the nation and the national are absent. The recurring dream in *Waltz with Bashir,* in which very young naked men, on the edge of puberty, are seen coming out of the sea, rifles hanging across their bony torsos, best illustrates this idea. They walk to the shore of an empty modern city. This city could be Tel Aviv or Beirut or any other Mediterranean city, which reflects the potential interchangeability of the situation. The three playful soldiers might have arrived this way in Beirut but they equally well might not. The message conveyed is that memory is arbitrary and nations and their politicians tend to appropriate it for their own aims. The animation aesthetic through which the memories of the narrator's friends are subjectively reconstructed in *Waltz with Bashir* becomes a form of narrative paralysis intended to postpone memory. The moment that the documentary footage is revealed, however, creates a moment of truth that retrospectively illuminates the whole of the imagined war scenes, as if to say, some of it was probably true, but the trauma created a veil that distorted the vision and removed the guilt.

In "History's Broken Wings: 'Narrative Paralysis' as Resistance to History in Amos Gitai's *Kedma*," Nurith Gertz and Gal Hermoni contend that "the (narrative) paralysis is tantamount to a post-traumatic rhetoric that marks the historical condition, on which the movie is created as post-traumatic."[30] When the linear, teleological narrative movement as the ideological apparatus of hegemony becomes perturbed or paralyzed, the result is subversion and opposition to the dominant narrative. Thus, they continue, this paralysis, attributable to the condition of post-traumatic stress disorder, as suggested by Freud, is, in a sense, the post-traumatic condition and should be read as one of historical-political resistance. This paralysis that can be found already in the bystander position of the earlier Israeli war films is at the heart of all three Lebanon films analyzed in the last section of this essay. All of them thus constitute a political attempt to deal with the trauma that the violent Israeli history has imposed on the Israeli soldier. As such it represents a post-national attitude according to which the individual soldier's sacrifice becomes meaningless.

Notes

1. Ella Shohat, *Israeli Cinema: East/West and the Politics of Representation* (Austin: University of Texas Press, 1989); Nurith Gertz, *Motion Fiction: Israeli Fiction in Film* (Sipur Me HaSratim: HaSiporet HaIsraelit VeIbudea LeKolnoa) (Tel Aviv: Open University Press, 1993).

2. The best-known film on this topic is Gilberto Tofano's *Siege* (1970), set after the Six-Day War and retracing the life of an Israeli widow (Gila Almagor) in the shadow of her dead husband, and the Israeli cult of bereavement in general. Another example is Moshe Mizrahi's *The House on Chelouche Street* (1971), whose plot at first sight deals with a fatherless Sephardic family in the old Tel Aviv area but in fact is entirely conditioned by the 1948 war threat. Thirty years later, the latent heroic presence of the national narrative would be ridiculed in Nir Bergman's *Broken Wings*, in which the father dies following a bee sting.

3. Shohat, *Israeli Cinema*, 59.

4. Miloh's cinematic adaptation frames the original plot with the visit of the dead hero's son to his grandfather in 1967, thus showing the relevance of Zionist prestate values to poststate ideology.

5. Judd Ne'eman, "The Death Mask of the Moderns: A Genealogy of the New Sensibility," *Israel Studies* 4 (1999): 100–126, at 30.

6. The best example would be Rafi Bukaee's *Avanti Popolo* (1986), which still today remains unique in the sense that it turns the battlefield of the Sinai desert into a "magic realism" playground in order to convey the film's humanism (Yael Munk and Judd Ne'eman, "'Avanti Popolo,' or the Battle Cry of the Fallen," in *Film and Politics in the Middle East and the Maghreb*, ed. Josef Gugler [Austin: University of Texas Press, forthcoming]).

7. Janet Burstein, "Yehuda 'Judd' Ne'eman," *Bomb Magazine* 95 (Spring 2006), http://www.bombsite.com/issues/95/articles/2807.

8. Nitzan Ben-Shaul, "Fellow Traveler: The Cinematic Political Consciousness of Judd Ne'eman," *Shofar: An Interdisciplinary Journal of Jewish Studies* 24, no. 1 (2005): 94–106, at 97.

9. In her book *Motion Fiction: Israeli Fiction in Film*, Gertz contends that none of the Israeli films of this period (1977–89), to which she refers as "the films of the Others," succeeded in providing an answer to the many Israeli conflicted situations.

10. S. Yizhar, *The Story of Khirbet Khizeh* (Sipur Hirbet Hizah) (Tel Aviv: Zmora-Bitan Publishers, 1989). Amos Gitai's *Kedma* (2002) relates to this same period but this time from the point of view of the immigrants who had just fled Europe after World War II and had been sent to the battlefields in Palestine.

11. Anita Shapira raises the possibility that the fictional village of Khirbet Khizeh may in fact be a reference to all the Arab villages that were emptied during the Israeli War of Independence ("'Hirbet Hizah': Between Remembrance and Forgetting," *Jewish Social Studies* 7, no. 1 [2000]: 1–62, at 8).

12. The low-angle shot used to glorify the protagonist was a major shooting technique in national cinema. Enabling the portrayal of the protagonist against the sky the shot created a kind of aura for those whom the film wanted to designate as heroes.

13. Hannan Hever, *Literature Written from Here* (Sifrut She Nichtevet Mekan) (Tel Aviv: Yedyot Hahronot; Hemed Books, 1999), 20.

14. Yizhar, *Story of Khirbet Khizeh*, 78.

15. See Tom Segev, *1967: Israel, the War, and the Year That Transformed the Middle East*, trans. Jessica Cohen (New York: Metropolitan Books, 2005).

16. Questioning the issue of collective memory, historian Anita Shapira offers a comprehensive account of the controversy over the literary text and its adaptation in her article "Hirbet Hizah."

17. As described, for instance, in the final scene of Miloh's *He Walked in the Fields*, in which the hero, Uri, is shown actively involved in the mining of a bridge in order to distract the British soldiers and enable the landing of illegal Jewish immigrants from the sea, an act that would lead to his death, which is to be read as a sacrifice for the nation.

18. Rafi Bukaee, "Shylock du Désert," *Cinéma Méditerranéen Montpellier—Actes des 10e Rencontres* (Montpellier: La Fédération des Œuvres Laïques de l' Hérault, 1988), 10–11. In this interview, Rafi Bukaee refers to his participation as a cameraman in the filming of Amos Gitai's documentary *Field Diary*.

19. Munk and Ne'eman, "'Avanti Popolo,' or the Battle Cry of the Fallen."

20. Yael Munk, *Exiled in Their Borders: Israeli Cinema between Two Intifadahs* (Tel Aviv: Open University Press, forthcoming) (in Hebrew).

21. Orly Lubin, "The Woman as Other in Israeli Cinema," in *Israeli Women's Studies*, ed. Esther Fuchs (New Brunswick, NJ: Rutgers University Press, 2005), 301–16, at 307.

22. A close reading of the film reveals a tight connection between its landscape and that of the

Lebanon War. According to Tamar El-Or, the mud that is shown all through the war sequence does not refer to the time of the Yom Kippur War, as no rain fell at that time, but rather to what is usually named "the Lebanese morass," metaphorically referring to Israel's growing involvement in the war against terrorist organizations in Lebanon (see Tamar El-Or, "Faces of Israeliness," *Theory and Criticism* [Teoria VeBikoret] no. 18 [Jerusalem: Van Leer Jerusalem Institute Press, 2001], 242–27 [Hebrew]).

23. Irma Klein, *Amos Gitai: Cinema, Politics, Aesthetic* (Amos Gitai: Kolnoa, Politica, Estetika) (Tel Aviv: HaKibbutz HaMehuhad Publishing House, 2003), 336.

24. Raz Yosef, "The National Closet: Gay Israel in 'Yossi and Jagger,'" *GLQ—A Journal of Lesbian and Gay Studies* 11, no. 2 (2005): 283–300, at 290.

25. Since its very first days, Israeli cinema hardly represented IDF women as protagonists. Mostly featuring as supporting characters intended to add an extra appeal to the war narrative, the representation of IDF women soldiers was limited, thus unconsciously emphasizing the irrelevance of women to the military. Directed by women, *Close to Home* successfully addresses this issue, leading to the demystification of the unisex image of the IDF as generally promoted in the world. Another Israeli film, though documentary, that courageously attacks this issue is Tamar Yarom's *To See If I'm Smiling* (2007), which deals with the trauma of those women who served in the occupied territories in combat units and had to face violence as part of their military mission.

26. *Beaufort* is based Ron Leshem's bestseller, *If There Is a Heaven* (Tel Aviv: Zmora-Bitan Publishers) (Hebrew).

27. Shmulik Duvdevani, "The Victim in the Tank Will Win," Ynet, October 16, 2009, www.ynet.co.il/articles/0,7340,L-3790700,00.html (Hebrew).

28. The few examples are the photos of Israeli leaders in the fort's bunker in *Beaufort* and the animated portraits of the then defense minister Ariel Sharon or journalist Ron Ben-Ishay. In both cases these historical portrayals intentionally blur their reference to reality.

29. Shapira, "Hirbet Hizah," 1–62.

30. Nurith Gertz and Gal Hermoni, "History's Broken Wings: 'Narrative Paralysis' as Resistance to History in Amos Gitai's Film *Kedma*," *Framework: The Journal of Cinema and Media* 49, no. 1 (2000): 134–43, at 134.

Chapter 17

A Woman's War

The Gulf War and Popular Women's Culture in Israel

Rachel S. Harris

In 1994 the film *Shirat Hasirena* (*Siren Song*), directed by Eytan Fox, sold more tickets in Israel than all the other Israeli films made that year—combined. The screenplay was an adaptation of the best-selling novel by the same title, and both were written by Irit Linor. In 1999 the film *Ha-Chaverim shel Yana* (*Yana's Friends*), directed by Arik Kaplun, won ten Israeli Academy awards and was a box office success in Israel and abroad. Critics have taken neither film seriously; instead, they were viewed as part of the rise of "chick lit" and "chick flicks" of the 1990s in Israel. Both the book and the films were romantic comedies set during the Gulf War and were part of a new wave in Israeli cinema to make "light, pleasant, social" films about contemporary Israeli life.[1] These "chick" genres have formulaic and archetypal structures, plotlines, characters, and even landscapes, yet scholars of women's literature identify essential differences in chick lit and the traditional romance, which in many ways they appear to emulate.

> One key differentiator between a romance novel and a chick-lit novel with romantic elements is that in a chick-lit novel the identity of the romantic hero isn't always immediately apparent. In a romance novel, if the heroine meets a handsome man in the first chapter, it's a good bet that he's the hero. If a chick-lit heroine meets a handsome man in the first chapter, he could be the hero. He could also turn out to be a jerk who breaks her heart, or he could become her gay best friend. On the other hand, Mr. Wrong can look like a viable option at least for a time.[2]

The medieval courtly romance had already given way to the gothic during the eighteenth century, and by the end of the twentieth century a clearly defined set of tropes that played in a satirical, ironic, and even burlesque fashion emerged in romantic women's fiction. These include the centrality of the female protagonist, a turbulent path toward true love, and an ultimate submission often represented by a ceremonial unification (marriage, exchange of property, kiss). The women's fiction and film of the Gulf War produced in Israel readily correspond to these conventional models, yet they also represent a regional difference that reflects local cultural and social variations. The use of the Gulf War is one such identifier. But not only does it represent a regional particularity, its use within this genre serves to provide an opportunity to create a feminized discourse of war, one that challenges traditional representations of militarization in Israel suggesting a serious and dramatic undertone to what appears an otherwise frivolous stylistic choice.

For many Israelis the culture of the Gulf War was represented in popular TV and particularly in comedy shows, such as *Zehu Zeh* and *Eretz Nehederet,* and in newspapers that were able to respond to the changing daily experience. Despite the richness of this material, this chapter is not concerned with immediate reactions during wartime. Instead, it explores the ways in which the war was encoded in popular culture over time. Perceived as unusual, particular images and icons, unique to this war, were selected and highlighted in its much later representation in literature and cinema. Particularly, this chapter explores the creation of a repertoire of iconic images, why it seems that they were selected (and what they mean for the perception of the war), and raises larger questions about subsequent reflections on future kinds of wars and their possible depictions in Israeli culture.

Jean Baudrillard's seminal article, "The Gulf War Did Not Take Place," argues that the remote and virtual nature of the Gulf War, the heightened period of expectation, and its distance from previously established military norms led the Gulf War to be a war unlike any other: a war that appeared not to have happened. Although speaking to a European audience, distant from where the war took place, this conception is equally true for Israel. Discouraged by America from retaliating for Iraqi attacks, and in the main removed in a traditional sense from the theater of war, it can be said with some certainty that for Israel there are many ways in which the Gulf War did not occur. It was the first war in which soldiers and tanks were not deployed, no supplies were sent, and the Israeli government did not provide military support or engage in other public manifestations of combat. "It was the first war in which the Israelis did not face a real enemy who could be fought face-to-face or tank-to-tank."[3] Despite rhetorical attempts by the Israeli leadership to "glorify the war and Israel's role in it" by drawing on "all the old narratives of previous wars," these attempts were "doomed to failure" given the gap between "the resolute bravery and heroism they praise[d] and the absence of any bravery and heroism in this war."[4] Israel did, however, for two months in the winter of 1991, experience violence through the shelling of Tel Aviv and its vicinity by inaccurate scud missiles. "The targets perceived by Western television viewers as imaginary were described in Israeli culture as poltergeists, whose invisible hands fired missiles."[5] Although these shells were launched, they were not fired on battlefields but on urban locations—and unlike depictions of Beirut whose images of urban war are part of the public consciousness today, most of the time Tel Aviv appeared relatively quiet, and its citizens maintained an appearance of social normality.[6] Thus we can accept an argument that posits the notion that the Gulf War was not like other military experiences in Israel's turbulent history, and this may explain the paucity of fictional material written on this war.

Israeli narratives on war have dominated the Hebrew literary tradition from a time before there was a state. Hebrew poets responded artistically to the pogroms in Europe, and the First World War.[7] Subsequently, a pattern of nationalist and military war narratives evolved through the poetry of the 1948 Generation and the epic 1940s and 1950s war novels. Vivid war imagery flourished in poetry and music following the Six-Day War (1967), and a burgeoning cinematic tradition that began with films of the 1948 war has depicted the Six-Day War (1967), Yom Kippur War (1973), and more recently has produced several internationally award-winning movies of the Lebanon War (1982). The intifadas have also engendered a cultural and artistic response, and as Adriana X. Jacobs shows, following the most recent violence in Gaza, an outpouring of poetry on the web revealed more material than could be published.[8] In fact the representation of war in every form of Israeli culture is central, widely recognized and canonical, as this volume has explored. Here and elsewhere, scholarship by Esther Fuchs and others demonstrates that war in general, as well as the Israeli military services and their representation, is dominated by men.[9] In turn these experiences and images construct the Israeli notion of masculinity, impacting every level of society. Within society, women are marginalized both in relation to the Israeli conceptualization of war and the actual military experience that is extended to their fictional representations. Women appear as wives, mothers, girlfriends, and helpmates, detached from the action. A scholarly discourse has arisen recently presenting the social and particularly domestic constructions of women's role during wartime, where they function in specific support roles such as "birthing the nation" and fighting the ideological war on the home front by providing resources, nurturing care, and protective home environments for the soldiers.[10] When not supportive of war, women are perceptually associated (or actually involved) with peace movements.[11] Despite the presence of women in the IDF, their association with CHEN (the women's corps), until its recent disbandment, has further institutionalized the perception of Israeli women soldiers as attractive objects: "comprised of two overlapping components. Neatness and sexuality—women serve a sexual need for the army."[12] Women are taught to use the army as a place to find husbands, and the hypersexual atmosphere whereby women are encouraged to be sexually available and are placed in subservient positions to male commanders models institutionalized sexual harassment.

Reluctance to deploy women to serve in combat has further resulted in few women having illustrious service records, serving in positions of leadership, and receiving the status and respect that men acquire for fulfilling these tasks. Fuchs has observed in reference to fiction about the War of Independence that there is a distrust of the "active army woman," which threatens the traditional Judeo-Christian endorsement of "woman's place in the home."[13] Her sexuality becomes a weapon; she is described with "sadomasochistic proclivities"; and there is "not only contempt for military women in power, but a vision of woman as an outsider who is incapable of comprehending even the most basic facts about the army."[14] In fact, "successful military women may compromise the traditional image of male fighters and defenders of women and children and may also undermine the ethos of male bonding."

> In a military context, woman is reduced to a sex object and sex to a mechanical activity intended to relive physiological tensions rather than to gratify emotional needs. Because one must not give in to normal human needs for love and intimacy, women and sex become objects of derision.[15]

Women are excluded from the experiences and narratives of war while their traditional roles as "nurturing and protective" in the position of "wives and mothers outside the army or as nurses and auxiliary soldiers within the army,"[16] are highlighted. "On the other hand, the constant threat of war and the continuous political instability create a strong need for security within the private sphere, a need which is often translated into a nostalgic vision of the patriarchal tradition."[17] In turn, the "military mobilization of men depends upon women playing the 'proper' roles of being feminine; that is, prone to capture and worth defending."[18]

Recent changes in Israeli culture and society have led to an increasing representation of women's experience of the areas previously considered the masculine aspects of war—most notably in films like *Close to Home* about women soldier's experience of serving, or through studies such as the work of Orna Sasson-Levy on women serving in the IDF. Employing the language of men's experience of war, women have begun to narrate their own counter experience of engaging in violence, being heroic, and *serving*. In contrast to the hyperfeminization of most IDF women, those who do serve in elite units, jobs, and in higher-ranked positions are prone to increased masculinity.

Orna Sasson-Levy notes that "women soldiers in masculine roles adopt various discursive and bodily identity practices characteristic of male combat soldiers, which signify both resistance and compliance with the military gender order. [. . .] At the same time, women's adoption of masculine identity practices can be interpreted not as subversion but as collaboration with the military androcentric norms thereby strengthening rather than challenging the military gender order."[19] Furthermore, "on some bases women soldiers are ordered to "conceal their femininity" and are forbidden to wear perfume, makeup, or jewelry. These orders reflect the military perception that women cannot command as women."[20] The dichotomy of the canonical tradition of establishing women's roles as traditional homemakers and sexual fodder, and its countercanons in which women engage in masculine roles in masculine ways, can clearly be identified in Hebrew literature as well.

In contrast to the rich and profuse depictions in literature and cinema of other wars in Israel, the soldiers' experiences, and even those of the Palestinians, Egyptians, and

Lebanese—thereby revealing an abiding interest in exploring a wide range of military affects, the Gulf War has been almost entirely neglected. That is, it has been neglected within a canon that described the masculinity of war, usually by men and about men, or offered a counternarrative of women in combat who also experienced this war, either by depicting women as hypermasculine or as victims trapped in the futility of men's wars, remote from the action and lacking meaningful agency.[21] The unusual nature of the Gulf War makes it different from all other military incursions or activities, and perhaps in turn, this has also led to its sparse treatment.[22]

If we consider that traditional battlefield tropes include sand, rocks, bunkers, uniformed soldiers, jeeps, barbed wire, tanks, food parcels from home, reserve call-up notices (*tzav shmoneh*), guns, bases, dry land and burning trees, the language and the imagery of the Gulf War is dramatically different and particular to this war alone. Baudrillard comments on this specificity:

> Two intense images, two or perhaps three scenes which all concern disfigured forms or costumes which correspond to the masquerade of this war: the CNN journalists with their gas masks in the Jerusalem studios; the drugged and beaten prisoners repenting on the screen of Iraqi TV; and perhaps that sea-bird covered in oil and pointing its blind eyes towards the Gulf Sky. [. . .] Not images of the field of battle, but images of masks, of blind or defeated faces, images of falsification. It is not war taking place over there but the disfiguration of the world.[23]

For Israelis, unlike traditional preparation and participation in battle, the Gulf War took place in people's homes, and the activities were instead domestic. They included preparing a specific room in the home, stocking up on groceries, and taking care of children in the face of bombing. It is precisely the very nature of preparing the domestic realm for war that highlighted the extent to which the private sphere, which had always served as the safe haven, was now threatened.

Dominant images of the Gulf War were those of the safe room with its household furnishings (beds, sofas, lamps, and tables); carrying at all times, and wearing during times of warning, a gas mask; having special incubator boxes for babies and domestic animals; and stocking up on supplies such as water, canned food, and other emergency items. *Yana's Friends* structures its plot line along the air raids so that the audience can follow the development of the relationships between two main characters from one air raid to the next. While the sirens and the accompanying panic create a visceral sense of urgency, the domestic environment and the evolving love affair provide the comic relief uncharacteristic of other war films.

The urban landscape associated with the Gulf War was dominated by windows with large Xs in tape—so that windows that broke would be less likely to shatter, thereby reducing potential injuries from shrapnel—and by windows that were covered with special plastic sheeting and masking tape. Pronounced were images of Tel Aviv's empty roads and readily available parking. Part of this major narrative of emptiness and desertion was the stay-or-flee discourse. Options included staying in the region but moving out of areas thought to be targets (while often continuing to work in Tel Aviv during the day); fleeing to other parts of the country, particularly to hotels in Jerusalem and Eilat, which added the sense of vacation to the experience; or to kibbutzim and the Galilee region, which suggested homecoming and protection by the land (part of Israel's historic narrative of existence); or leaving the country and going abroad, particularly to family in Europe and the United States.

Yana's Friends subverts the traditional narrative of available choices and coping mechanisms by focusing on a new Russian immigrant, a young woman who chose to come to Israel despite its political and economic instability. Without an alternative home to escape to or money to afford hotels elsewhere, she is obliged to transform the domestic environment of her shared rented Tel Aviv apartment into a safe haven—safe from the missiles, from her ex-husband, and from her Soviet past. Yana's perceptions of the Gulf War are contrasted to those of her sabra roommate, Eli, who went through basic Israeli military training and is portrayed in the film as an embodiment of Israeli masculinity. Handsome and sexy, Eli works as a videographer and on the side turns Yana into his personal voyeuristic project as his camera and his gaze follow her along the streets of Tel Aviv and around their apartment. Eli starts out as a classical male lead—his gaze controls our vision of Yana, and, functioning as a knight in shining armor, he rescues Yana from the financial troubles caused by her ex-husband. This sense is heightened during the early missile attacks when he runs into her room to ensure her safety, discovers she has no sealed space, and takes her to his own sealed bedroom; this then leads to their first sexual liaison. The next morning, however, Yana refuses Eli's proffered romantic entanglement, but the following missile attack leads to a repetition of the previous encounter. Eli comes to look forward to the shelling of Tel Aviv as it becomes entwined with his sexual relationship with Yana. Consequently, the sealed room becomes a physical and metaphorical space for Eli and Yana's nascent relationship.

The sealed rooms dominate the Gulf War cinematic imagery and discourse for multiple reasons. The intense fear of biological and chemical weapons was extremely pronounced at the beginning of the conflict, and individuals stayed in their apartments rather than using the unsealed communal bomb shelters, which were often unprepared to function in their designated role and instead generally served as the building's communal storage area. In turn, being in sealed rooms within private apartments heightened the sense of isolation and decreased the sense of communal participation, collective memory, and shared experience that had characterized previous Israeli wars. Instead, families were secluded together, while wearing gas masks, which were isolating and restricted interaction, heightening tension and creating psychologically stressful environments as frightened families were trapped together for long periods of time. Furthermore, stress was aggravated by sleep deprivation resulting from nightly attacks. Sportswear became an iconic image of the conflict as people slept fully clothed in case of late night emergencies. With work often slowing down and children without school, casual wear or "sweats" in bright colors became the clothing associated with the war, suggesting comfort rather than the battle fatigues (in khaki) and military boots evocative of other conflicts.

Precisely because of these domestic landscapes, removed from the expected imagery, the Gulf War appeared increasingly feminized.[24] But even more than the absence of weaponry, Baudrillard muses over the digitalization of the war. He argues that its presentation on television and in the media increased the sense of the wars' comportment as if it were a computer game or a movie. The firing was remote and nonspecific and the war is viewed in his mind through TV screens, but in Israel this voyeuristic portrayal can be expanded to consider citizens who stood on roofs to watch the rockets being fired at night or observed the action from the large apartment windows that offered a view of Tel Aviv that contrasted with the customary representations of war in mass media. Comparative to the later imagery from the urban destruction in Lebanon, the Gulf War's impact on Tel Aviv was seen as rather minor and mediated through the safety of a TV screen. Eli's lens in *Yana's Friends* echoes this voyeuristic experience.

In her study of the recent portrayals of Russian immigrant women within the politics of Israeli cinematic representations of gender and ethnicity, Olga Gershenson emphatically states that films such as *Yana's Friends* exemplify the postpolitical trend in contemporary Israeli cinema where the traditional focus on the collective experience shifts toward the private individual.[25] Both in *Siren Song* and *Yana's Friends,* the Gulf War is experienced as a private affair and not as a collective ideologically motivated effort. Furthermore, *Yana's Friends* actualizes the distancing and detachment from the military action not only through its focus on the feminine and the domestic but also through the engagement of such postmodern techniques as quotation and pastiche to enhance the genre ambiguity. As we observe the interactions between Yana and Eli in their apartment, we are also treated to the English-language news sounds and visuals of the Gulf War–related footage, on Eli's TV monitors. Supplemented by the authentic shots of Tel Aviv landscape produced by Eli's camera in a cinema verité mode, the news pastiche creates a quasi-documentary ambience of the film, reminiscent of "reality TV" that gradually emerges as a spectacle within a spectacle.

The camera's focus on interior spaces of Yana and Eli's Mandate-era Tel Aviv apartment separates them from the urban hustle and bustle of the streets below as well as from the threat of Iraqi missiles. Within this limited space two women—the new immigrant Yana and the old immigrant landlady Rosa—gain more and more agency as the story unfolds. At the time when Yana and Eli discover a cache of papers in the attic that reveal Rosa's only son was killed in the Six-Day War, Rosa herself discovers that Yitzhak, her long-lost lover from the time they both fought in the Second World War in Europe, is presently also a new immigrant in Israel. The memories of the Second World War and the Six-Day War—with their attendant imagery and ideological baggage—intrude on Yana and Eli's romance in the sealed room. While the Gulf War may be the war that didn't really happen, the other two wars mentioned in the film left a lasting impact on the Jewish psyche.

In relation to the depictions of domestic environments during the Gulf War, it is useful to consider Valerie Begley and Olga Gershenson's insights into the theory behind gendered construction of spaces. They point out,

> Like discourse, space is always political. Space can discipline by restricting access, and empower by giving presence. Spatial organization is a historical and cultural product of meshing and clashing discourses of the body, sexuality, and morality. Instead of being "neutral," our notions of space are informed by a set of gender, class, and race terms. Therefore, the everyday spaces of our homes, offices, streets, and cities not only reflect existing social relations and identities but also actively produce and re-produce them.[26]

Both in *Siren Song* and *Yana's Friends*, gendered space frames our perceptions of the Gulf War and negotiates the changing roles of male and female characters. Men's lack of a specific role within this war, and their opportunity to be heroic and masculine, is pronounced. Similarly, the lack of weapons as the universal phallic symbol highlights the visual focus on nonmilitary objects as well as nonmilitary subjects. Men are cast in the role of lovers and not warriors. Although confined to their urban living quarters, they work with women to build a safe environment. Within this context, the choice of romantic comedy is not accidental. Following Laura Mulvey, Gershenson states that romantic comedy is "a genre that often treats repressed social issues with aspects of melodrama, a genre that conventionally serves as a safety-valve for ideological contradictions."[27] Indeed, the traditional Israeli war narrative comes into conflict with the genre of chickflick, redirecting the paramount preoccupation with national survival toward the more generalized pursuit of happiness.

In *Yana's Friends*, the female protagonist is "absorbed" or assimilated into Israeli society through the strategy of a romantic relationship with the quintessential sabra. However, Gershenson points out,

> Intimacy between Yana and Eli takes place in the moments not only of Yana's personal fears and insecurities, but of highest national fears and insecurities—during the First Gulf War, underscoring [. . .] the ever-present possibility of national annihilation. Significantly, their intimacy takes place in a sealed room, during the missile attacks, accompanied by the sounds of sirens, as both she and Eli wear gas masks. The threat of war facilitates unity among the everyday disunity of Yana and Eli. Later, the gas masks become necessary equipment—prosthetics—on which their physical connection depends. The gas mask standardizes everyone's face (metaphorically united in the face of danger) and additionally renders everyone mute, eliminating linguistic gaps and muffling accents. Once the threat of war has passed, Eli's seduction of Yana succeeds only when missile attacks are simulated through his use of recorded sounds and images of past missile attacks.[28]

The Gulf War thus exists in the film on several different levels simultaneously: it is the actual historic-political context of the plot, it is the quasi-documentary reality TV quoted throughout the film, and it is also the simulacrum of the war, an integrated representation that overlays the characters' memories of the war experience.

The creative interplay between the collective Zionist mythology of the state and universal individuality of romantic chickflicks is a fundamental feature of the works under discussion, which thrive on the tension generated by the similarities and differences between these two life philosophies. By choosing to build narratives according to the chick-flick conventions of romantic comedy, the book and films under discussion enable an anticanon vector for contemporary Israeli culture. This choice becomes the message, and it functions as a method of distancing, thereby perpetuating the largely virtual existence of this military conflict. The hyperimagined Gulf War emerges from these two films as yet another incarnation of the simulacrum. As the distinction between what is real and what is imaginary (also what is authentic and what is derivative) becomes more blurred, the hyperimagined, televised political landscape of the Middle East can be conceptualized as a fictional terrain several times removed from anything even remotely conceived as "an original." Thus the films that deal with the transformation of gender roles within this domesticated military conflict contribute to the popular subject of the ways in which hyperreality can be viewed as a form of reality by proxy.

Both *Siren Song* and *Yana's Friends* use the background of the virtual Gulf War to foreground the stories of women, their love lives as well as their place in Israeli society. *Siren Song* is the story of Talila Katz, a thirty-two-year-old account manager for an advertising agency. She has a close relationship with her sister who is married to Amos and has two children, and to her divorced parents, with whom she speaks daily. The plot is a romantic quest to find love with Noah Ne'eman, the soy food engineer, after being heartbroken by Ofer Strasberg (a copywriter at his father's agency where she last worked and with whom she had a two-year relationship). A brief fling with Ronen Marco, the head of her current agency, ensues at the beginning, but otherwise much of the novel is about developing new friendships with her advertising colleagues at the firm, engaging in romantic escapades, and managing her own and others' fears and experiences of the war. The film strips away the role of the additional characters in Talila's life and their experience of war, leaving us with only the protagonist's saga. Her relationship to the war and her oblivion to the preparations around her are contrasted continuously with public broadcasts, discussions, and news programs on television screens and radio broadcasts that appear in almost every scene and to which all the other adults are fixated.

Yaron Peleg has described the novel as one that "legitimized the trashy or pulp romance in Hebrew letters for the first time." It was commended for depicting "real sex"—while other critics commended the lack of "the usual Jewish-Israeli existential anxieties like the Holocaust, the Arab-Israeli conflict, or religious or ethnic tensions. [. . .] 'a welcome rejection of the over politicization of life and art in Israel'"[29] The romance genre, which developed in the 1990s, offered a new frivolous vehicle for Israeli women writers responding to the despondent failed loves of the novels of the

1980s.[30] Characterized particularly by sexual liberation and romance, these novels often explored women's spaces such as Shifra Horn's *Four Mothers* and Dorit Rabinyan's *Persian Brides* and were, like *Shirat Hasirena,* hugely popular, such that for the first few years of the 1990s, the best-seller list in Israel was almost entirely dominated by women's fiction. For the first time since the 1950s a gap opened between the popular "low" fiction, and the more respectable "high" fiction of Yehudit Hendel, Yehudit Katzir, Orly Castel-Bloom, and others.

The protagonist's focus on romantic entanglements and her career, along with the representation of upper-middle-class, yuppy Tel Aviv lifestyles, have led to the suggestion that apart from "the Scud missiles that rain on Tel Aviv nightly, the Middle Eastern environment barely rears its inconvenient head." Instead, critics laud Talila Katz, the woman at the center of the novel. "The heroine's most admired trait is her stubborn and oblivious pursuit of True Love, irrespective of the primitive and anachronistic conflict that rages around her, for which she has little patience and even less regard. Part of the novel's charm at the time was its refusal to acknowledge or deal with the complex Middle East situation and its insistence on having fun like the rest of the civilized world."[31] The "low" romance genre of *Siren Song* departs from the conventional view of Middle Eastern politics and presents the war through hyperfeminine imagery, but it does not exist, as Peleg claims, without acknowledging the "anachronistic conflict." Rather, the experience of the war becomes central to the plot and shapes every aspect of the imagery, costume, plot, emotional motivations, and setting of the novel and film adaptation.

Talila Katz with her sexual freedom, financial independence, romantic quests, and about-town lifestyle, bears a remarkable resemblance to the fictional woman hero who gained prominence in Anglo-American culture during the 1990s. Comparisons have been drawn with Bridget Jones, and in turn between Bridget Jones, Ally McBeal, and later with Carrie Bradshaw.[32] The re-presentation of the central female protagonist during the 1990s and 2000s was taken seriously in feminist cultural discourse, such as responses to the appearance of Ally McBeal on the front of *Time* magazine with three pioneering feminists, Susan B. Anthony, Betty Friedan, and Gloria Steinem, and the question "Is Feminism Dead?"[33] Israeli feminism, however, has always had its own twist: if the near-constant state of war cannot be entirely ignored, it needed to be assimilated in such a way that would allow the female protagonist in film and fiction to live the lifestyle of her American and European peers by developing a number of coping mechanisms. Both *Siren Song* and *Yana's Friends* relate well to the model seen in the film *Cherry Season,* about the Lebanon War, a film that is exemplary of "the new, Israeli, postmodern, urban cinema of the 1990s, which was set in the modern city and tended to totally disregard Israeli wars, Israeli politics, and the Israeli setting—part of this cinema predates the Gulf War, but expresses trends that the latter war reinforced: fatigue with war, fatigue with politics, fatigue with national slogans, disinterest in Israeli history, and lack of confidence in the Israeli leadership."[34] Predicated on these very feelings of political fatigue, both works examine not only the immediate responses to the threat of Iraqi missile attacks within the larger context of the female protagonists' romantic lives, but also the mechanisms of distancing oneself from the actual military conflict and of mediating the experience of war through the visual aid of a TV screen or a panoramic window.

Talila Katz is beautiful, competent, professionally successful, independent, financially secure, and responsible. She is more than the passive object of the IDF CHEN soldier, and she is also a significantly stronger female character than any of her American or English counterparts. If Bridget Jones is indeed about "celebrating the self" and not "striving toward perfection through repentance and atonement," then this is what is shared with Linor's character.[35] Yet unlike Bridget, known for her notorious and comic failures, Talila is able to manage domestic affairs (she can cook, clean, shop successfully) and make decisions about her life.[36] Nor are we led to consider her competence to be a universal measure of the modern woman. Rather, Talila is contrasted with her sister and mother who cannot (and do not) cook, and with her friend, Shira.

> Alona didn't cook and she hardly knew how to turn on the microwave. Amos cooked because as a psychologist he couldn't be seen to be a chauvinist and the children just warmed things up because otherwise they wouldn't have been allowed to watch television.

Or from chapter 22:

> I rang Shira because she was my most needy friend. She never had any money, things always got broken in her home and there was always some guy who was making her feel depressed. . . . Shira's logic never had any sense to it. On the other hand she couldn't cook either. (121–22)

Thus while Shira's life is an emotional, professional, and economic disaster, Talila remains very much in control of her life: "I hardly drank and certainly didn't dance" at the New Year's Eve party (19), "I did know what it did to my bank account," and "Strasberg were paying me a disgustingly large salary anyway. Ronen Marco just offered me more and I agreed" (13); and she remains confident about her own talents, "Strasberg was the first office I approached as being good enough for my fabulous academic merits. Nor did I think it would be difficult to get a job there as, in my opinion, I believe it to be sufficiently respectable to be able to value my intellectual abilities" (14). Although the tone suggests a tongue-in-cheek attitude, in fact she exudes overwhelming confidence that reflects her general professional success, as is illustrated by her description of the hiring search at Strasberg. She turns the tables and outwits the head of the firm by forcing a competition to write a lonely-hearts ad between herself and Ofer the "best copywriter" (and son of the owner) at the company. While he receives fifty-two replies for his male ad and twenty for his female ad, "I received so many replies that they jammed the server," yet as she realizes she "could have been sorted on the boyfriend front for the next 200 years but instead I fell in love with Ofer" (15). By chapter 3, we have been told that she owns her own apartment, that she is very tall and very attractive, extremely competent professionally, making a great deal of money, and could, if she chose, have a slew of suitors—though, as we learn, her great failing is falling for emotionally unavailable, and clearly unworthy, beaux.

The title of the novel, *Siren Song,* plays on both the sound of the sirens that are a part of Israeli life and particularly wartime, and Greek legend. Talila can be seen as a mythic figure: she is good at "luring" men, yet she also refuses the call of the siren, the voice that commands her actions or locations. During the war she insists on driving after dark, will not seal a room, and goes to a bar late at night. Her rejection of others' self-imposed curfew symbolizes independence and is contrasted with the general lack of self-determination evident among her peers. Furthermore, she uses the predictability of other people's conformity to engage in acts of emotional rebellion. On meeting Noah's girlfriend in Jerusalem, moments before the girl intends to drive to see Noah in order to arrive before dark, Talila surreptitiously slashes the tires of her car—knowing that this will significantly impinge on the weekend the couple would otherwise have spent together. Talia is conscious of the impact of the war, stating that she cannot depend on it to get her out of trouble forever.

These moments of comic irony underpin the novel's construction, which is dominated by situational humor—a truth of the romantic comedy genre, but the hilarity is clever rather than sardonic, derisive, or slapstick. Although Talila is on a quest for love and marriage she is not neurotic, and the jokes in the book are not predictable or at her expense, unlike the general representation of heroines in the Anglo-American tradition of "chick lit," but are actually witty, often made by her, and we laugh with the protagonist and not at her. Unlike Bridget Jones, Talila never repents for drinking or smoking more than she should have or of spending money on clothes. She is always aware of her actions, and her barbed comments are aimed with precision. When she scripts conversations, before they take place, they invariably play out in exactly the manner in which she planned, and are entirely successful.

Talila offers an alternative cultural model in the 1990s. In a period in which Elizabeth Bennet, Jane Austen's illustrious heroine in *Pride and Prejudice,* becomes the archetypal romantic heroine, Linor offers a challenging alternative.[37] Drawing on a stronger earlier model of womanhood, she chooses Shakespeare's Katherine, from *The Taming of the Shrew,* rather than the more popular and commonly recycled Elizabeth. Linur's intertext is "Kiss Me Kate" in its 1953 MGM version of Cole Porter's 1948 musical adaptation of Shakespeare's play, woven into a modern setting starring Kathryn Grayson and Howard Keel. The shrew's lineage evokes a powerful, independent, self-reliant if spiteful heroine, unlike the well-intentioned and comparatively innocent Elizabeth Bennet, and hence a woman who will not only meet her equal who she can educate (and whose shy pride she can pierce) but who can best her. Consequently, Linor suggests the need for a hero who can outwit and subjugate her, a hypermasculinity that far exceeds the gentle loftiness of a Darcy.[38]

This hypermasculinity is indicative of Israeli society and particularly soldiers during wartime, yet the Gulf War—precisely because of its ambiguity—has far fewer obvious candidates for Talila's affection. Talila in refusing to assume the role of victim, the traditional role of woman during wartime, highlights the vicarious position of the previously anticipated Israeli social order. Yet Kate is aware of the social expectation of marriage (and is well aware of her sister's situation—a parallel that also appears in the novel), and Kate does finally find her Petrucio. Talila too is aware of the situation surrounding her—even though she refuses to participate in the social construction of the war.

> I knew that during the time I was sitting in front of Ronen Marco and wondering what I saw in him, thousands of people were buying tinned and frozen food. While I was making my mind up about my sock drawer people were trying to buy flight tickets abroad, while I was sitting in front of the television and singing: "I hate men," for the however many number of times people were facing the daily reality that didn't even occur to me. Why should I care whether rockets would be dropped here or not. I, despite my shitty mood, saw myself shaking the wreckages from my Ofer dream and carrying Noah in my arms into the sunset. Sticky tapes and tinned corn didn't fit with that line of thought.
>
> On the other hand, I had a mother for that.[39]

Despite maintaining a heightened femininity (she is constantly reapplying her lipstick, combing her hair, and considering her clothing), she functions extremely successfully in a man's world without becoming masculine. Yet the imagery of war is integrated into the discourse of her femininity. For example, she dresses up for Noah by wearing red lipstick and a short, backless dress and describes herself as "a nuclear submarine, an Iraqi cannon."

Furthermore, this blurring of traditional gender boundaries can be seen in the portrayal of the hypercompetent male characters. Despite the suggestion of misogyny in drawing parallels with *The Taming of the Shrew,* all of the men are revealed to be domestically capable, often more so than the female characters. They live in neat, clean houses. The level of interest in their furniture reflects the peculiarity of each man and his tastes, but they all manage their homes impressively. Ofer comments continually on the furniture in Talila's home, and is himself an extremely organized housekeeper. Yaron buys coffee cups and towels for Tzila, and there is discussion that he may appear with a writing table as he doesn't like the one she has.[40] Talila's boss, Ronen Marco, is particular about his wardrobe, his hair, and despite his many failures in other ways, he returns to find the offices unsealed and immediately sets about to have the situation remedied. All of the men cook, including Talila's father, her brother-in-law (Amos), both boyfriends (Ofer and Noah), and other sundry male characters such as Yaron.[41] Nor are men feminized by these experiences of domesticity—they are ridiculed only at a nuanced level of individual neuroses, such as Ofer's desire for hypercleanliness, or Noah's failure to tie his shoelaces.

Particularly noticeable is the depiction of male responses to the Gulf War. Like Eli whose masculinity is assured in *Yana's Friends,* Noah's is demonstrated through his service in *Milluim* (reserves) after their first date, and Amos is frequently described as a man who was a parachutist and an MP, thus their heroic masculine identity is preserved in its traditional form. Nevertheless, in the face of the Gulf War there is a sense of panic, fear, and often hysteria, even by male characters, and the public manifestations of these emotions are often preceded by a period of impotence, or a lack of sexual desire. Ronen flees to Amsterdam on the pretext of a conference; Amos moves his family at first to his father-in-law's home, then to a hotel in Jerusalem, then to a friend's apartment, and finally his wife moves to a kibbutz. Amos continues to work in Tel Aviv but will not stay in his own home and finally ends up staying with Talila. Ofer and Noah are responsible about wearing their gas masks. Yaron becomes hysterical and needs to be taken care of despite his otherwise macho behavior—so much so that Tzila manages to finally seduce him by offering him care and warmth. Although he briefly leaves her for Anat the secretary, Anat is even more hysterical and following another night of bombing, he returns to Tzila's emotional shelter. Thus the women are as heroic as the men—but they are not masculinized. Talila, who repeatedly refuses to take the threat of chemical warfare seriously and will not carry or wear her mask, does recognize the danger of the shells, and after breaking up with Noah, finally uses the building's bomb shelter when she is afraid (at this time she is the only one to do so). After the attack Noah phones, and Ofer visits, to make sure she is safe. Thus the men are also associated with protectiveness, and their behavior corresponds to the traditional male role of "white knight," also exhibited by Eli in *Yana's Friends.* Nor are these individual positions monolithic. At the close of the novel Noah also begins to experience ambivalence about fear of the war, and he finally stays in bed rather than bother to wear his mask or seal the room.

Drawing parallels, particularly noticeable in the first twenty-six chapters of the book, all references to love or romance are immediately preceded or followed by references to war. On a date with Noah, the only conversation that is not related to sex that Talila can find is her suggestion that "we can talk about the Gulf Crisis and discuss whether there will be a war and whether we'll be hit with missiles." Talila finds letters from Noah's ex-girlfriend in Boston who says it isn't a good idea for them to get back together, and "then the letter continued, with nothing less than some political thoughts about the Gulf Crisis" (49–50). Conversations by Talila's mother about the impending wedding of her ex-husband—and how to stop it—become intertwined with her attempts to prepare to deal with the impending war, such as buying up the "entire country's stock of duck tape" and other supplies. When his fiancée leaves the country, Talila's mother moves in with him rather than be alone during the war, thereby hoping to end the relationship and return to her husband.

Thus the anticipation, expectation, and concerns about love and romance are paralleled, compared, and essentially equated to the same emotional experiences of war.

Talila, in analyzing the discussion of her developing relationship with Ronen who takes her out to dinner and movies, continues to be sexually interested—if not adventurous, and is comfortable in her home, sleeping there every night—immediately transitions to war in her thoughts: "I tried to think about him positively, which wasn't difficult—he didn't cause me any harm, and actually I attached myself to him like a masking tape to a window. I wouldn't have used that imagery had it not been for my mother who increased the frequency of our telephone conversations and has relentlessly asked me to buy some tinned food and that maybe she should come and seal a room for me," and then she ponders on her mother's advice to leave the country and visit an uncle abroad.[42]

Talila's mother also reflects the ambivalence of the war experience. Although she invests a great deal of time at the beginning of the novel preparing for war, and moves in with her ex-husband out of fear during the war, she also criticizes his girlfriend Hana for leaving and admonishes her daughters about the flight of Israelis abroad: "Did you see all those cowards? How they are running away from the country?" though she herself had proposed their departure at an earlier date (39).

The novel's relentless rhythm of the war that is examined each day, and the reactions to the missile attacks each night, evokes a sense of the Gulf War experience for Tel Avivians. The anticipation in early January is replaced by the daily ennui of those who remain in Tel Aviv once the war starts and the nightly fears when the missiles rain down. Talila's observations of the city and its inhabitants have the quality of a flâneur evoking the particularity of Gulf War imagery. She observes the absence of cars within the city, her ability to park by the door of the supermarket, the rapid adoption of casual clothing that marks out the inhabitants, and even her own dramatic changes in appearance from the highly quaffed advertising executive to the proto-typical housewife in Noah's borrowed casual sweats and faded t-shirt, who cleans and cooks all day. Her abandonment of makeup and particularly lipstick reveals that even she is not entirely immune to the impact of the war on Tel Aviv. Yet her femininity is not compromised, but rather transformed from the vamp seductress to the domesticated maid. Furthermore, she has also assumed the traditionally masculine role of flaneur. Her constant commentary on the landscape and the reactions of others adds a further dimension of surveillance to the already hyperobserved experience of the Gulf War.

This vigilance is echoed in references to Talila's windows, which become a refrain, and reflect the voyeuristic aspects of the war Baudrillard articulated. But the novel also represents the progression of people's responses, so that by the end of the novel the windows in Talila's apartment have solid wooden blinds that block out the view and the light, and all of the neighbors that had abandoned Talila's building have returned and meet together to sit in the bomb shelter. It is particularly this last response that returns the war to some modicum of the normality established by other military experiences in Israel.

By the end of the novel it has become clear that eventually the war will end and less and less attention is given to fear and expectation, and instead the routinization of response is depicted. During the final days of the war, the loose ends of the narratives are tied up. In *Yana's Friends,* Yana's Russian husband returns only to be finally rejected by Yana, suggesting her empowerment, which had begun with her abortion, finding work, and ceasing to wear the gas mask when in the sealed room with Eli. The characters in the many subplots find happiness and justice is dispensed. In *Siren Song,* Noah leaves the Boston girlfriend, Talila finds new employment, Amos and Talila's sister reunite, Talila's mother moves out of her husband's home and tolerates his impending marriage to the returning fiancée. Finally the war and narratives of it are concluded at a public celebration of Purim. The already carnivalesque occasion serves in the role as public celebration for the end of war. The streets are bedecked with bunting and flags like an Independence Day celebration. The use of Purim in the romantic narratives evokes the medieval romantic ending of a public ceremony (traditionally a wedding). In *Yana's Friends* all of the characters stroll among the celebrations, while the central protagonists Yana and Eli walk hand in hand. In *Siren Song* Talila returns home through the celebratory crowds, having made her final decisions about her career, and finds Noah sitting on the top stair by her apartment waiting for her. The couples, having overcome all personal, social, and military obstacles, and realizing their true love for one another, come together at this celebration. This effect is magnified in the sudden appearance of fireworks when the two kiss at the end of the film.

Using the traditional structure of a romance, *Yana's Friends* and *Siren* Song use the heightened domestic tensions of the Gulf War as a plot device for these highly feminized stories. This chapter offered a sampling of the ways in which the unique experience of the Gulf War empowered women—who became the caretakers and held centralized positions during the war, without neutralizing their femininity. In turn, despite men losing their traditional position of military command and heroism, they too are offered a multiplicity of roles, which complicate the notion of gender but do not emasculate them. Although subsequent literature of the intifadas and wars in Gaza return to the established modes of war representation, the peculiar case of the Gulf War offered a unique opportunity to consider alternative roles of women in wartime. By examining the treatment of the Gulf War in *Siren Song* and *Yana's Friends,* it is possible to shed some new light on the feminization of the war in contemporary Israeli culture, on the tropes and discursive patterns associated with the war, the treatment of female empowerment through the act of war, and the marshaling of this event within a romantic narrative tradition. As the Israeli permutations of chickflicks come into conflict with the established literary and cinematic responses to wars, we witness the emergence of a new, more feminine attitude toward war, one that allows competing narrative experiences space within a previously closed discourse. These in turn may be indicative of directions that Israeli culture could take in response to the new kinds of warfare Baudrillard anticipated.

Notes

My thanks go to Anna P. Ronell for her helpful and instructive comments on this essay and the joy of our ongoing conversations about Israeli chick lit.

1. Interview with Eytan Fox as part of the additional material "Behind the Sirens" on the recent DVD release of the film.

2. Shanna Swendson, "The Original Chick-Lit Masterpiece," in *Flirting with Pride & Prejudice: Fresh Perspectives on the Original Chick-Lit Masterpiece*, ed. Jennifer Crusie with Glenn Yeffeth (Dallas: BenBella Books, 2005).

3. Nurith Gertz, "The Medium That Mistook Itself for War: Cherry Season in Comparison with Ricochets and Cup Final," *Israel Studies* 4, no. 1 (1999): 153–75, at 170.

4. Nurith Gertz, *Captives of a Dream: National Myths in Israeli Culture* (Tel Aviv: Am Oved, 1995) (Hebrew). Translated and revised as *Myths in Israeli Culture: Captives of a Dream*, Parker-Wiener Series on Jewish Studies (London: Vallentine Mitchell, 2000), 136, English edition. Chapter 8 deals specifically with the Gulf War.

5. Gertz, "The Medium That Mistook Itself for War," 170.

6. Gertz, *Captives of a Dream: National Myths in Israeli Culture*, 135–36.

7. See Chaim Nahman Bialik's *Be-Ir Ha-Hariga*, or Glenda Abramson's *Hebrew Writing of the First World War* (London: Vallentine Mitchell, 2008).

8. See Adriana X. Jacobs's chapter in this volume, "From IDF to .PDF: War Poetry in the Israeli Digital Age."

9. Orly Lubin, "The Woman as Other in Israeli Cinema," in *Israeli Women's Studies: A Reader*, ed. Esther Fuchs (New Brunswick, NJ: Rutgers University Press, 2005); Hannah Naveh, ed., *Gender and Israeli Society: Women's Time* (London: Vallentine Mitchell, 2003); Orit Rozin, "The Struggle over Austerity Policy: Israeli Housewives and the Government," *Israel* 1 (2002): 81–118 (Hebrew).

10. Sachlav Stoler-Liss, "'Mothers Birth the Nation': The Social Construction of Zionist Motherhood in Wartime in Israeli Parents' Manuals," *Nashim: A Journal of Jewish Women's Studies & Gender Issues* 6 (Fall 5764/2003): 104–18; Susan Sered, *What Makes Women Sick? Maternity, Modesty, and Militarism in Israeli Society* (Hanover, NH: Brandeis University Press; University Press of New England, 2000); Meira Weiss, *The Chosen Body: The Politics of the Body in Israeli Society* (Stanford, CA: Stanford University Press, 2002), and Weiss, "Mother, Sister, and Soldier: Recollections from the Gulf War," *Te'oriya U-bikoret* 3 (Winter 2005) (Hebrew): 235–46.

11. Yael S. Feldman, "From Essentialism to Constructivism?: The Gender of Peace and War—Gilman, Woolf, Freud," *Partial Answers: Journal of Literature and the History of Ideas* 2, no. 1 (2004): 113–45; Michael Feige, "Peace Now and the Legitimation Crisis of 'Civil Militarism,'" *Israel Studies* 3, no. 1 (1998): 85–111.

12. Sered, *What Makes Women Sick?*, see 76, 78, 80–81, and 86. "Women soldiers, neither mothers nor true warriors, are in a problematic liminal state. It seems to me that the intense concern with the neatness and sexuality of women soldiers is an expression of that liminality. The 'proper' sexuality of the neat and attractive 'chen' soldier signifies that she is on the appropriate path to suitable motherhood within the collective. The obsessive fear that women soldiers will be raped by the enemy is an expression of the deepest possible threat to patriarchy: that women's motherhood will slip out of the control of the men to whom it 'rightfully' belongs."

13. Esther Fuchs, *Israeli Mythogynies: Women in Contemporary Hebrew Fiction* (Albany: State University of New York Press, 1987), 28.

14. Ibid., 29.

15. Ibid.

16. Ibid., 30.

17. Ibid.

18. Sered, *What Makes Women Sick?*, 69.

19. Orna Sasson-Levy, "Gender Performance in a Changing Military," in Fuchs, *Israeli Women's Studies*, 266–67.

20. Ibid., 269.

21. See films such as *Lemon Tree, Close to Home,* and *Free Zone.*

22. Meira Weiss examines the unique role nurses played in the Gulf War. While others dove for cover, these women rushed to hospitals surrendering themselves to danger and inverting the traditional gender order hierarchy in times of war, where women seek shelter while men are at the battlefront. In Weiss, "Mother, Sister, and Soldier."

23. Jean Baudrillard, *The Gulf War Did Not Take Place,* trans. and intro. Paul Patton (Bloomington: Indiana University Press, 1995), 108. Originally published in French as *La Guerre du Golfe n'a as eu lieu* (Paris: Galilée, 1991). Also available in Steve Redhead, ed., *The Jean Baudrillard Reader* (Edinburgh: Edinburgh University Press, 2008).

24. This situation was exacerbated for men because of the gas masks, which were carried like women's handbags; facial hair had to be removed so that the masks fitted properly, further emphasizing acts of emasculation.

25. Olga Gershenson and Dale M. Hudson, "Absorbed by Love: Russian Immigrant Women in Israeli Film," *Journal of Modern Jewish Studies* 6, no. 3(2007): 301–15, at 304.

26. Valerie Begley and Olga Gershenson, "Volumes: New Insights into the Gendered Construction of Space/s," *Journal of International Women's Studies* 6, no. 2 (2005).

27. Gershenson and Hudson, "Absorbed by Love," 304.

28. Ibid., 309.

29. Yaron Peleg, *Israeli Culture between the Two Intifadas: A Brief Romance* (Austin: University of Texas Press, 2009), 88, 89.

30. Yael S. Feldman, "From the *Madwoman in the Attic* to *The Women's Room:* The American Roots of Israeli Feminism," *The Americanization of Israel,* a special issue of *Israel Studies* 5, no. 1 (2000): 266–86; Feldman, *No Room of Their Own: Gender and Nation in Israeli Women's Fiction* New York: Columbia University Press, 1999), chaps. 5, 6 (see notes for chaps. 5 and 6 and bibliography, 306–7).

31. Peleg, *Israeli Culture between the Two Intifadas,* 90.

32. Kelly A. Marsh, "Contextualizing Bridget Jones," *College Literature* 31, no. 1 (2004): 52–72; Alison A. Case, *Plotting Women: Gender and Narration in the Eighteenth-and Nineteenth-Century British Novel* (Charlottesville: University of Virginia Press, 1999); Justine Ashby, "Postfeminism in the British Frame," *Cinema Journal* 44, no. 2 (2005): 127–32.

33. *Time* magazine, June 25, 1998.

34. Gertz, "The Medium That Mistook Itself for War."

35. Marsh, "Contextualizing Bridget Jones."

36. Irit Linor, *Shirat HaSirena* (Tel Aviv: Zemura Betan, 1991) (Hebrew) (all translations my own).

37. *Bridget Jones' Diary* plays continually with this character. Bridget is obsessed with the six-part BBC adaptation of the novel starring Colin Firth. The hero of the diary is Mr. Darcy, a connection of which both the character and the audience is well aware—but this link became highly postmodernist when, in the film adaptation, Mr. Darcy was played by Colin Firth. In the sequel, this became considerably more complicated when Bridget, now working as a journalist, is supposed to interview the real "Colin Firth." This hyperrealist complexity, more suitable for a Paul Auster novel than the romantic-comedy genre, meant that the scene was cut from the film, but inserted as an extra for viewers in the DVD release. This "meta" postmodernist experience is echoed similarly in *Shirat HaSirena*. The musical intertext is a cinematic adaptation of a written text that disappears in the film adaptation of Linor's own novel.

38. This subplot line is excluded from the film and is substituted instead for a love of Israeli popular music of the '60s—representing a strong Zionist narrative.

39. Linor, *Shirat HaSirena*, 74.

40. Yaron's purchases are in response to the missile attacks and his need to stay with Tzlila (Talila's colleague) for comfort. Tzlila mentions to Talila that she hopes there will be another attack soon so that she gets the writing desk.

41. Noah is even a food engineer.

42. Linor, *Shirat HaSirena*, chap. 5.

Chapter 18

Beaufort the Book, *Beaufort* the Film

Israeli Militarism under Attack

Yaron Peleg

Ron Leshem's 2005 novel *Beaufort* (the Hebrew title is *Im yesh gan eden,* lit. if there is a heaven) is a gritty military action novel that follows closely an infantry combat unit in Lebanon on the eve of Israel's withdrawal from that country in 2000. When it was released, the book was a runaway success. A first novel by a prominent journalist, it reached cult status almost immediately, sold more than 130,000 copies, stayed on newspapers' best-seller lists for well over a year, and won prestigious literary awards. When a film based on the novel was released two years later, in 2007, it met with similar success.[1] In a country whose life revolves around national security and whose army is a true people's army, it is not surprising that works of art dealing with the IDF would be popular. The peculiar thing about the story's literary and cinematic success, however, was that it told a story of isolation, desperation, frustration, and ultimately of defeat. Stranger still are the different ways the novel and the film present these events and the lessons they take from them. In the novel, the soldiers are old-fashioned patriots, albeit with a twist. In the film, the soldiers fight for no cause and die for no reason. By comparing the novel and its adaption into film this essay examines this paradox and identifies two conflicting currents that coexist in contemporary Israeli society regarding the Israeli military specifically and military politics in general.

Leshem based the novel on real events, although not on personal experience. In a postscript, he relates how he got the idea for the novel after meeting an exhausted and disappointed IDF officer, who served for several harrowing years in southern Lebanon facing the Hezbollah, and, after the army's withdrawal from that country, was reassigned to police the Gaza Strip. Leshem's novel is one of the first serious works that deals with Israel's eighteen-year stay in Lebanon (1982–2000). The aftermath of Israel's first war in Lebanon and the media's engagement with it are interrelated in the novel as a comment on the changing perception and role of the IDF in Israeli society.

The novel begins rather grimly with a prologue titled "He Is Not," which tells of a macabre game soldiers in the book play among themselves, trying to imagine the kinds of things their fallen comrades will never get to see or experience anymore: "Yonatan is not going to take his little brother to the movies anymore, Yonatan is not going to listen to the new disk [by his favorite artist], he is not going to know how good it feels to see your mother beaming with pride on the day you enter university or college, he is not going to know if his sister gets married," and so on. Thus even before the novel starts, young men die. Sweet, kind, shy, loving, and passionate men, full of promise and life, cease to exist. They are no more, as the title of the prologue tells us. Simply and abruptly.

These dead men are quite ordinary. There is nothing special about them, which is what makes them so special and endearing and their memory so painful; loving brothers, enthusiastic soccer fans, devoted friends, affectionate sons, good students, dedicated family men, and especially great and loyal lovers; in other words—Everyman. And these dead "Everymen" have other ordinary young men as friends; friends who sob bitterly over their bullet-pierced bodies, who go crazy with sorrow over their loss, who bury them to the sound of music they then play over and over and over again for months after the funeral.

Indeed, friendship is one of the major themes that animates the intense novel and also one of its chief attractions. Friendship, or more precisely, the camaraderie of young male soldiers, has been a major theme in Israeli letters and cinema, especially since the 1948 War of Independence. The early poems of Haim Gouri (*Pirhei esh*, "Fire Flowers," 1949), and stories by S. Yizhar ("Shayara shel hatzot," "A Midnight Convoy," 1950), set the golden standard for the bonds that were forged between young men under the intense pressures of battle during the state's incipience; bonds that were then mythologized especially through popular songs (*pizmonim* such as "hare'ut," meaning "The [military] Friendship"). *Beaufort* continues that tradition and in some ways even surpasses it and sets higher standards for *re'ut*, or military friendship.[2]

Leshem creates the passionate *re'ut* in the novel not just through the kind of story he tells, but also through its structure, and its unique language. Paradoxically, much of the novel's force comes from the peculiarly apologetic rhetoric of the narrator, a brave but emasculated officer. After the lugubrious opening, the novel takes up the familiar shape of a (group) bildungsroman when it goes back to the beginning to tell the story of the army unit that mans the Beaufort fortress throughout the book. We meet them as unruly fresh recruits during basic training, learn to know each one of them as individuals and accompany them during their socialization into a band of fighters, a united group of soldiers who are willing to die for each other and for their country.

One of the strongest elements of the bildungsroman is the familial language and imagery used to describe the soldiers and their place within the military organization. "The kids [or children] were then doing navigation training," recounts Liraz, a.k.a. Erez, the unit's commanding officer, about his first meeting with his underlings (22). "My older brother, Guy," he continues, "told me once that being a commander means to love. You receive thirteen fragile soldiers, call them 'kids,' drag them in diapers through a long journey . . . praying throughout that nothing bad happens to them" (24). The novel abounds with such references. Later, when his paternal relations with his soldiers change into brotherly love, Erez assumes the role of the rebellious teenage son in his constant fights with the higher command over military initiatives. He admires the senior commanders, and looks up to them as father figures, especially the ones who took part in the initial battle to capture the stronghold eighteen years earlier. But like an enthusiastic kid who wants his father to always be strong, he is also angry with them for being soft, for holding him back, and for their intention to withdraw from the mountain and from Lebanon altogether.

The scintillating argot that pulses through the novel also adds to its distinction and popularity and marks the tremendous revolution that Hebrew has undergone since the 1940s, when the language became native in a real sense for the first time:[3]

> Zitlawi—what a character[4] that guy is, a straight-shooter, with a cigarette tucked behind his ear and phrases that always sound like a string of profanities, even when they are not (which is not often). He gave us a whole language, imported from all over the army. He was the first to know all the newest swear words. Not only dirty words. He himself coined and popularized choice words and phrases that spread like wildfire. Thanks to him, the IDF dictionary grew by several new volumes every month. (27)

Erez's introduction to one of his soldiers, who is later killed, is followed by about two pages of vibrant examples from Zitlawi's linguistic innovations taken directly from the immediate world of actual soldiers, who, like most young men, want to have fun: sleep, hang out with their friends, and most of all have sex and find love.[5] This kind of edgy, naturalistic language and the soldiers' ribald conversations are the very stuff by which the old, mythological *re'ut* is being updated in the novel and to which it owes its popularity, at least in part. And while their special language defines the fighting soldiers as a distinct group and increases their intimacy, it also invites readers to take part in it and become part of the "national fighting family," *hamishpacha halochemet,* as various parts of the Israeli populace is referred to at times.

Language is one of several other factors that ostensibly distinguishes the unruly Beaufort men from idealistic soldiers of previous wars. This is true especially of consensual wars like the War of Independence (1948), the Six-Day War (1963), and even of the Yom Kippur War (1973), which created, fixed, and glorified the image of the Israeli soldier as a national martyr. The soldiers in *Beaufort* are separated from their literary predecessors by their motivation for national service as well as by their ethnic background. They are neither members of voluntary, elite units, nor Ashkenazi. The majority of them come from what was once termed "the other Israel," that is, lower socioeconomic groups.[6] Some of them, like Zitlawi, even have criminal or quasi-criminal records. Their identification with the state's (Ashkenazi) hegemonic culture, therefore, appears at first not as strong as that of Yizhar's soldiers or even soldiers in more contemporary works like David Grossman's 1983 *Smile of the Lamb*, for instance.[7]

Actually, *Beaufort* records a significant sociocultural shift that is directly related to the different nature or messages of the novel and the film. There has been a significant change in the demographic makeup of the IDF with a rise in the number of non-Ashkenazim in combat units in the last few decades. In the years following independence these units were more heavily populated by labor-affiliated Ashkenazim, who also inspired the soldierly image that was later mythologized in poetry and prose.[8] The novel's cachet comes from its recognition of this shift and the precise way it registers it—linguistically too. Erez and his men may be rough and thuggish, their Hebrew substandard, and their thoughts revolve around sex and games rather than the lofty Zionist ideals of their literary forebears, but they are just as brave, if not braver. The meeting between the Mizrahi Erez and the Ashkenazi Ziv makes this quite obvious:

> I am not sure what it is I liked about Ziv; something about him drew me to him. Maybe it was the fact that he was so "the man" (תותח). . . . He started out in the air force, then finished first at an elite engineering unit. He looked great, athletic, but trim. And modest. And hyperactive, running around, bugging me to fight him all the time, giving me massages. Sounds stupid, I know, but until then, until I met Ziv, I didn't have Ashkenazi friends. And he used to look at me kindly, never made fun of me even when I talked crap, was never patronizing. (122)

Ziv is an explosives expert who arrives one day at the fort to diffuse a roadside bomb that a soldier discovered nearby. Cool, collected, wearing gel in his blond hair and sporting designer sunglasses, he is immediately doubted by the impulsive and hot-blooded Erez, the boy from the "hood."[9] Pretty soon, however, Erez learns to know him and to admire his resolution and his eagerness to share in the dirty work of fighting. But Ziv is a relic and an exception in a novel where most other Ashkenazi soldiers—the coded "elite unit" is used to denote ethnicity (סיירת מטכ"ל)— don't do kitchen duty, as Zitlawi puts it, since "they have catering" (126). Ziv is also one of the only Ashkenazim who is given a significant mention in the novel. For the most part, Mizrahim share the heaviest burden of protecting the nation, and although the novel never says so explicitly, literary circumstances give these Mizrahi soldiers patriotic preeminence.

The trouble is that Erez and his men have missed the chance to join the uncontroversial heroes of the past, to stand beside the hallowed youth in Natan Alterman's iconic poem, "The Silver Platter," the girded boy and girl, who in their battle-soiled gear, tired beyond measure, silently serve their nation its independence on their dead bodies.[10] Changes in the new millennium mean patriotism no longer enjoys the accord it once held. Indeed, *Beaufort* seems aware of the changing zeitgeist in the way it serves up patriotism with a twist more palatable for a post-Zionist or postnational age. The men who occupy the forbidding fortress serve their country with courage and distinction while pretending to do nothing of the kind. Outright pretense may be an overstatement. The key, again, is the way or style in which the patriotic sentiments are insinuated with disingenuous cynicism, a mock-heroic calculation, in a disenchanted age, to elevate the valor of the men. "Spitzer and Zitlawi took care of the silence," recounts Erez on the tense night Ziv arrives at the fort,

> on two old, scratched guitars, which were handed down after they were donated by some kibbutz in the eighties. Spitzer played and Zitlawi accompanied him on makeshift drums, and everyone got caught up in an old army song about future peace, when flowers shall sprout from gun barrels and pretty girls will be driving tanks. I noted an impressive familiarity with the song's exact words, down to the very last stanza, including the smallest syllable about the last battle in a field of fire, and something about foliage and flowers of gold, and all kinds of words which I was sure Zitlawi never even heard of. The sun of Gaza and Raffah seemed like the most relevant thing just then, when everyone banged on the tables in unison. (112)

The entire passage is an extended play on words taken from a well-known army song (פרחים בקנה), which talks about the peace that shall come after a last, difficult battle. The piece, like many other similar songs, became popular during the height of Israeli militarism following the 1967 war.[11] But in the post-Zionist age after the First Intifada in 1987, such songs, with their upbeat music and guileless performance, have come to symbolize patriotic naïveté, a farcical sign of a bygone era.[12] Erez cannot identify with the song outright, because its music and sentiments have become hokey. And so he removes himself from the scene and narrates it from an emotional distance. But his account demonstrates that both he and his men are enraptured by it and try hard to recapture some of the old spirit that inspired it. Aware of its nostalgic value, the men nevertheless cling to the song and declare themselves heirs to an illustrious military legacy, all the more so because it has become battered.

In the end, though, the spontaneous way the soldiers break into this particular song and the fervent way they perform it is an eloquent if desperate appeal to an old military patriotism whose time had passed. Deep down, the soldiers know they are fighting a losing battle. Their suicidal zeal is fed by this tension, by the realization that they may have arrived too late to receive full credit for their sacrifice. The country, it seems, deems their enthusiasm misplaced. As I hope to show by discussing the film *Beaufort,* the cultural forefront has moved away from these sentiments, which the novel articulates so well as it seeks to prop it up through alleged irony.

And yet within the peculiar dynamics of Israeli culture, the novel's authority as a patriotic work derives from the very doubts that are cast on the value of the men's sacrifices. The great debates that rocked Israel toward the end of the 1990s about the merit of occupying Lebanon elevate the soldiers' service because they add an unusual burden to their long list of difficulties. The menace of the battlefield is not mitigated by the comfort of a nation unanimous in its support for the troops. Hezbollah, the enemy without, is joined by dissenting voices within Israel, which seriously undermine the soldiers' resilience.[13] But, again, rather than buckle under these pressures, the soldiers band together, and as they continue to risk their lives, even as they doubt their grim tale of survival, they transform into modern Zionist heroes. Their hesitation, their soul searching, and their continued fight against tremendous odds burnish them as patriots in the great tradition of Hebrew literature.[14]

The film, *Beaufort,* on the other hand, is another matter altogether. In some obvious ways it is a straightforward adaptation of the novel on which the author, Leshem, worked together with the director, Joseph Cedar. At the same time, much of the difference between the two works comes from the choice to focus on the last part of the novel, on the few months immediately before the withdrawal from Lebanon and the fort. In almost all respects the film is a negative mirror image of the novel. If the novel brings together a group of fighting friends that represents the nation, and gives their bonds depth that makes their breakup wistful, the film shows a disintegrating group of haphazard individuals. If the novel intimately acquaints us with the soldiers' patriotic resolution to hold on against tremendous odds, the film only shows the corroding effect of their oppressive surroundings. And if the novel uses doubt constructively, as part of a psychoanalytical process of awareness and healing, doubt in the film becomes haunting, a dramatized element of existential horror that is ultimately debilitating.

Even if the focus on the novel's end is the biggest reason for the film's different character, it does not necessarily have to be so. Many disaster films—and *Beaufort* has clear elements of the genre—acquaint viewers with the assembled characters prior to the disaster and then as it unfolds. Moreover, in many such films, the disaster actually brings the victims together and melds them into a cohesive group, even if only for a short time. In *Beaufort* the opposite takes place. The disaster the soldiers face, the threat to their survival, is destabilizing. It undermines them as a group and wrenches them apart. If we consider the real as well as the symbolic nature of the external threat—the Arab extermination of Israel—and the role it plays in Israeli psyche and culture, the group's undoing becomes significant indeed.

Simplistically speaking, the external threat to Israel's existence, even when and if it was imagined, has always been one of the culture's most unifying elements. The very concept of friendship, or *re'ut* mentioned above, grew as part of the responses to such threats. It was forged between the fighting men on the battlefields of 1948 and from that point on, as I showed, was enshrined in poetry and prose, which sustained and perpetuated it. That in *Beaufort* this very element is destabilized and eventually annulled marks a significant change. While the book clearly names the various threats the group faces—from the Hezbollah to dissenting voices within Israel, like the Four Mothers' organization—the external forces that menace the group in the film remain disturbingly obscure. Evoking the tensions of a thriller or horror film by suggesting vague and shadowy external forces, the cinematic depiction uses the dissension to create apprehension in the soldiers.

As a film, *Beaufort* advances precisely that sense of ominous danger, an unknown and inexplicable menace that scares the characters, confuses them, and slowly chips away at their confidence and, as a corollary, at their trust in one another. The confinement to an underground bunker, the claustrophobic cinematography's close-ups, the ominous silence that makes up much of the soundtrack, as well as the eerie music lend the film a distinct ghostliness, a forbidding sense that is foreshadowed already in the credits. As the screen goes black, a gray rectangle appears in its center. It is the end of an underground concrete tunnel viewed from the inside looking out. The outside light at the end of it is blinding. Slowly, a bulky figure enters the frame of light from the outside. Wrapped in light and enveloped by fog (vapor? smoke?) the figure makes its way inside haltingly, almost mechanically, zombielike. Only when it has fully entered the tunnel and we see a soldier in full gear, does the figure assume a more human aspect: the soldier leans wearily against the wall, fatigued yet strangely apathetic. The camera then zooms out and the tunnel, with the soldier in it, becomes the second letter of the film's Hebrew name: **בופור**, Beaufort. Floating in the middle of a black screen to the sound of eerie music that denotes a great abyss—a low electronic hum punctuated by faint and resonant metallic clinks and a slow, underlying drumbeat—the glossy letters look like lonely spaceships, lost in an ocean of darkness.

The futuristic, space-travel aesthetics of the opening are very different from the rest of the gritty and earthbound film. But the opening imparts well the sense of loneliness that pervades the film, a sense of disconnection from anything and anyone familiar that becomes apparent already in the film's opening shot in which the Beaufort fortress looms silently and inexplicably for more than ten seconds as a lonely mountaintop, an isolated redoubt. Moreover, the lone soldier who enters the tunnel comes in from a vague outside, an opaque space that remains unknown, unchartered, and dangerous throughout the film, as the fog that enwraps the soldier signifies. Nor does the tunnel appear as a place of refuge. Open to the outside, it cannot prevent some of the ghoulish vapor from entering and infecting, as it eventually does, the entire bunker with a bilious air.

In the novel, much of the menace that comes from the outside is alleviated by the soldiers' camaraderie, the intimate connections they foster, and the sense of family they create. The small space they huddle in underground physically brings them together. In the film, the cramped quarters are handled very differently. Rather than foster intimacy, the bunker in the film stands in the way of it. The bunker's courtyard above ground is a deadly zone and there is little refuge underground. Winding and narrow, unable to accommodate more than one soldier at a time, the bunker's tunnels seem to extend for miles, meandering like a confusing labyrinth that puts distance between the soldiers and drives them farther and farther apart. Ziv learns this on the night of his arrival, when he loses his way below ground trying to find the others. Increasingly unnerved by the indistinguishable twists and turns of the desolate tunnels, he urgently hurries along them. As his anxiety rises, so does his pace, until at one point he falls down a set of stairs that lead nowhere, symbolizing more than just his own descent. The bunker, it seems, is neither a haven nor even a temporary respite in an alien land. It is a house haunted, visited by the ghosts of the soldiers who inhabit it.

These artistic and atmospheric elements, which lend the film a vague sense of discomfort and uneasiness, are augmented by scenes that spell out much more clearly fundamental doubts about patriotism of the kind the novel often puts on display. In a scene that inversely reflects the patriotic fervor of the soldiers who burst into an old army song in the novel (see above), we see Erez watching Ziv's father on TV one night, speaking about his son's death. In this arresting scene Ziv's father calmly confesses to the interviewer—on national TV—how he is to blame for his son's death. "Are you angry, are you blaming anyone for your son's death?" he is asked. "No," he says, "I only blame myself." The interviewer is puzzled. The father then explains that the army doesn't know his son, nor is it really responsible for him (!) "I am responsible for him," he says, "he is my son. I educated him, and apparently, I didn't bring him up properly." The interviewer's confusion is apparent. Aren't you proud of him, he asks, for volunteering in an elite unit and for serving his country? Isn't that what Israeli society considers the highest duty, the highest calling? In response, Ziv's father talks about the way he was raised, and the ways in which his parents instilled in him the sense of his precious value. He confesses sadly that he in turn failed to communicate this himself: to teach his children "to be afraid" (לפחד) for their lives.

Significantly absent from the novel, this scene is perhaps the best articulation of the differences between the two works, and it can be compared to the singing described earlier.[15] Set against the soldiers' enthusiastic chorus, against their nostalgic musical revival of a favorite "golden oldie" that harks back to the triumph of 1967, is the gloomy room where Erez watches TV alone and in silence, resentful of the father's words yet at the same time also receptive to their subversive message. These two moments cannot be more disparate in the way they contrast group with individual, unity with loneliness, harmony with silence, cooperation with resentment, and perhaps most significantly, nostalgia with a rude awakening. The meaning of the father's words clash with everything Erez believes in, with his entire military career, built on a passionate desire to serve his country and a willingness to die for it if called to do so.

But the words of the bereaved father go deeper and further than that. In some ways they amount to nothing less than a revolutionary negation of Zionism. To eliminate Jewish fear was one of Zionism's most vigorous calls—fear of violence to one's person as well as violence to Jews as a group. The elimination of Jewish fear was also one of Zionism's most spectacular successes, so much so, in fact, that its opposite, military bravado, became one of Israel's most distinguishing characteristics after 1948. It also became one of the country's most dangerous excesses, as both the novel and the film make clear in their own ways. In manner and in message the sad and quiet poise of the bereaved father sets him against the jingoist clamor of the novel but also against the uncertainty and doubt that pervade the film. His solution to both, to an IDF bloated from pride and drunk with power, and to its blunder in Lebanon as an expression of a hubris that leads to the anxiety and confusion of the soldiers in the film, is a call to bring back a measure of the old Jewish fear. This is not a post-Zionist call for a return to the Diaspora by any means. Ziv's father is neither a deconstructionist nor a defeatist. His is the voice of sanity, of common sense, long lost it seems, in the tribal wars of the Middle East.

In the end, then, both the novel and the film seem to be expressing similar sensibilities. The main difference between them is one of understanding and awareness. That the old ways of conducting war in the Middle East are over is clear from both the novel and the film. In some profound ways, despite their jingoism, Leshem's soldiers seem to realize that times have changed. Cedar's soldiers, on the other hand, appear unaware of it, and leave the task of recognition to viewers. Perhaps this is what lends Leshem's men their tragic quality. It is their patriotic virtue that ultimately makes them fail. Cedar's men, on the other hand, seem victimized by a nightmarish world they do not comprehend. It is quite possible that both works were popular, despite the different ways they present the same reality, because they evoked or tapped into two conflicting notions or forces that coexist in Israel today: vestiges of the *ancient* Zionist *regime* that is waging an increasingly losing war against the inexorable forces of history, and a maturation of a culture that is coming to grips with the limitations of its power. So while the novel passionately but tragically depicts a last, Bar-Kochbian battle that is doomed to fail, the film already perceives this failure and mourns it sadly but honestly.

Notes

In-text parenthetical page numbers refer to the book by Ron Leshem, *If There Is Heaven* (Lod: Zmora-Bitan, 2005). The film, *Beaufort*, directed by Joseph Cedar, produced by Moshe Edery and Leon Edery, was released in 2007.

1. The film sold 300,000 tickets, more than any other Israeli film that year, and garnered prestigious prizes in Israel and abroad. It won the Israeli "Oscar," the Ohr Prize, the Silver Bear Award for best director at the Berlin Film Festival, and was nominated for the Academy Awards' Oscar prize for best foreign film that year, the first Israeli film to make that list since 1984.

2. Male bonding in its Israeli context has been examined thoroughly by various scholars. See, for example, Miri Talmon-Bohm, *Blues latzabar ha'avud: Havurot venostalgia bakolno'a hayisre'eli* (Lost sabra blues: Nostalgia in Israeli cinema) (Tel Aviv: Open University, 2001); and Danny Kaplan, *The Men We Loved: Male Friendship and Nationalism in Israeli Culture* (New York: Berghahn Books, 2006).

3. That is, used for the first time in the modern era as a mother tongue by a significant segment of the Jewish population.

4. The original Hebrew is "*ars*," which loosely means a greaser, a tough street kid.

5. A brief comparison to another iconic military novel, S. Yizhar's 1958 *The Days of Ziklag* (*Yemey tziklag*) makes this clear. Yizhar's work about a band of soldiers who fight to capture and keep a hill in the Negev during the 1948 war is famous not only for its prodigious size but also for its thick and recherche Hebrew. But unlike Yizhar, who was one of the last authors who set out to expand Hebrew "artificially" in order to enrich a resurrected idiom, Leshem recreates an *extant* military vernacular whose dazzling richness and inventiveness is only partially captured in the

book. If Yizhar approached the question of language from above or from outside, by scanning the vast Hebrew library for written examples, Leshem did so by recording slang, by carefully reproducing spoken, everyday language. Both linguistic corpora—Yizhar's high Hebrew and Leshem's military jargon—can be obscure for the uninitiated reader. But slang enjoys a temporal advantage as well as a stronger connection to the living language.

6. This includes Russian and other Ashkenazi soldiers as well, who by virtue of being new immigrants do not belong to the veteran strata of Israeli society.

7. Even though Uri, the protagonist, fights against the occupational policies of the IDF and the Israeli government, he does so in the name of old and what he considers purer Zionist ideals that the pioneers set in the 1920s.

8. These trends are further complicated today by the rising numbers of religious soldiers in combat units whose religious affiliation supersedes ethnicity.

9. The book uses "neighborhood" (שכונה), which has the connotation of "hood" in the sense black Americans use it.

10. This well-known and often-quoted poem is widely available. For a bilingual version, see http://zionism-israel.com/hdoc/Silver_Platter.htm.

11. The 1967 triumph, which greatly contributed to the militarization of Israeli society, curiously inspired many peace songs like this one at the same time. The first two stanzas read: When a sleepy spring shall awake in paleness / the last battle shall abate on the fiery fields / and a glorious morning shall from the mountains / rise with a song. The sun shall stand still between Gaza and Raffah / a moon shall grow white over Hermon / gun barrels will sprout flowers and girls will drive tanks / and soldiers will come back home in great numbers.

12. For more on this, see my book, *Israeli Culture between Two Intifadas: A Brief Romance* (Austin: University of Texas Press, 2008).

13. See chapter 9 in the book, which introduces these issues.

14. S. Yizhar's *The Days of Tziklag* comes again to mind here.

15. A somewhat similar incident, that may have inspired this scene, occurs on page 215 in the novel. One day Erez finds hanging on the bulletin board in the bunker's dining room a newspaper clipping with a story about a soldier in an elite paratroopers' unit who hid behind a rock and refused to charge forward after his unit was badly hit in an attack by the Hezbollah. Erez is appalled to read how the soldier tells the interviewer that "I didn't want to die for nothing," and confessed that he was afraid. In the film, Erez's attentive silence while Ziv's father speaks stands in contrast to his angry reaction to the newspaper story in the novel: "That shameless shit admitted he was afraid," Erez thinks in the novel, "the thought that we shouldn't be here in Lebanon occurred to him in the middle of battle," he regards with disdain.

Chapter 19

Shifting Manhood

Masculinity and the Lebanon War in *Beaufort* and *Waltz with Bashir*

Philip Hollander

Joseph Cedar's *Beaufort* (2007) and Ari Folman's *Waltz with Bashir* (2008) countered a widespread trend in Israeli cinema by focusing upon the First Lebanon War. In the 1990s a largely postmodern, urban Israeli cinema developed that gathered strength in the new millennium.[1] Through employment of techniques drawn from world cinema, Israeli directors voiced a perceived increase in Israeli citizens' disengagement from wider society and increased focus upon their narrowly defined personal lives.

Yet despite growing individualism and the jettisoning of Zionist tenets formerly considered central to societal maintenance, Israeli Jewish society remains surprisingly cohesive. Cinematic portrayal of Jewish subgroups resistant to the new individualism initially expressed this regnant cohesion. These subgroups had rarely found sympathetic representation in earlier Israeli cinema due to demands placed on filmmakers, even those who rebelled against it, by an overarching Zionist metanarrative. The arrival of a largely postmodern urban cinema marginalized debates concerning the Zionist metanarrrative and enabled filmmakers to employ greater technical and stylistic sophistication to portray subgroups. Films that did this successfully include Amos Gitai's *Kaddosh* (1999) and Gidi Dar's *Ushpizin* (2004), which offer divergent perspectives on social cohesion among Israel's ultra-Orthodox Jews; Joseph Cedar's *Time of Favor* (2000) and *Campfire* (2004), which explore life in Israel's newly assertive and highly unified national religious community; Dover Kosashvili's *Late Marriage* (2001), and Ronit and Shlomi Elkabetz's *To Take a Wife* (2005), which voice the staying power of Israel's Georgian and Moroccan Jewish communities respectively.

Through exploration of militarism's role in preservation of societal unity, Cedar's and Folman's films point to a broader and more critical link between Israeli Jews that challenges claims of individualism's growing place in Israeli society. As sociologist

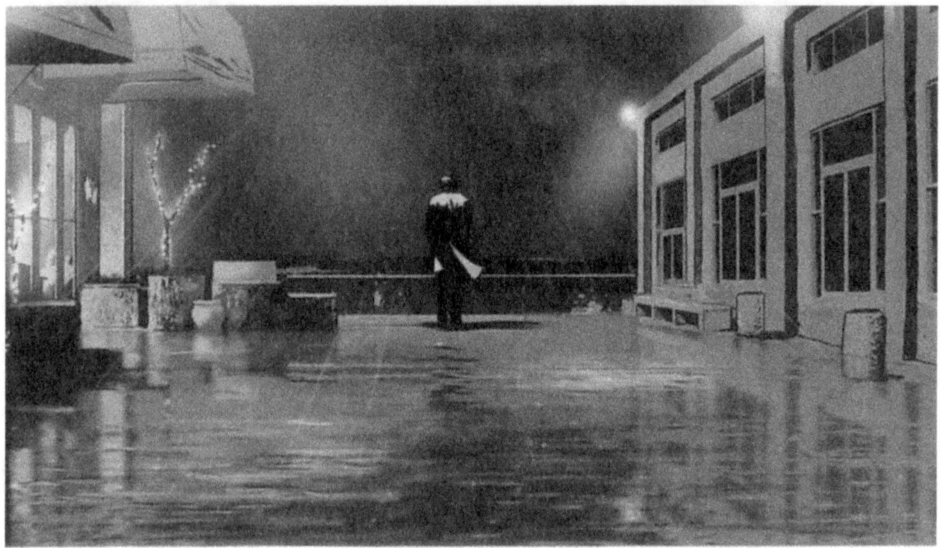

Waltz with Bashir (2008), directed by Ari Folman. Boaz Rein-Buskila shown here, with voiceover for this character by Mickey Leon.

Baruch Kimmerling explains, "all that remains of the original Israeliness of Israel [. . .] are its militaristic values, while the Jewishness that previously existed has been marginalized and counterbalanced."[2] Representations of urban life in films like *Year Zero* (2004), *Joy* (2005), and *Things behind the Sun* (2006) point to secular Israelis' marginalization of Jewishness in an increasingly globalized world characterized by alienation, social fragmentation, and consumer culture, but they fail to portray Israel's existent militaristic values that provide societal coherence. Organized around a "perceived need for institutional violence, requiring permanent preparation for both full scale war and occasional use of limited violence," these values "form a military-cultural complex" that "suffuses the structural and cultural state of mind of the collectivity."[3]

Despite its full and partial institutional and cultural expressions, militarism's main expression proves to be latent with many Israelis perceiving a universal civilian basis to their society and state. Nonetheless, the Israeli military proves central to the process of socialization in Israeli society in which can be found a production of its predominant form of masculinity.[4] As a result, understanding of Israel's social and political organization and power relations within it requires investigation of the ideological interplay of militarism, masculinity, and Israeliness.[5] Therefore it proves significant that *Beaufort* and *Waltz with Bashir,* two films that foreground the First Lebanon War and its Israeli male participants, reject the nation's idealization as a horizontal male brotherhood united by emotional bonds that prepare each member to die for its preservation, working instead to expose latent patterns of gender, power, and inequality characteristic of Israeli militarism.[6] Rather than assenting to or ignoring the hegemonic masculine norms inculcated to Israeli Jewish men during military service, both films address the detrimental reproduction of these norms as part of Israel's militaristically infused social

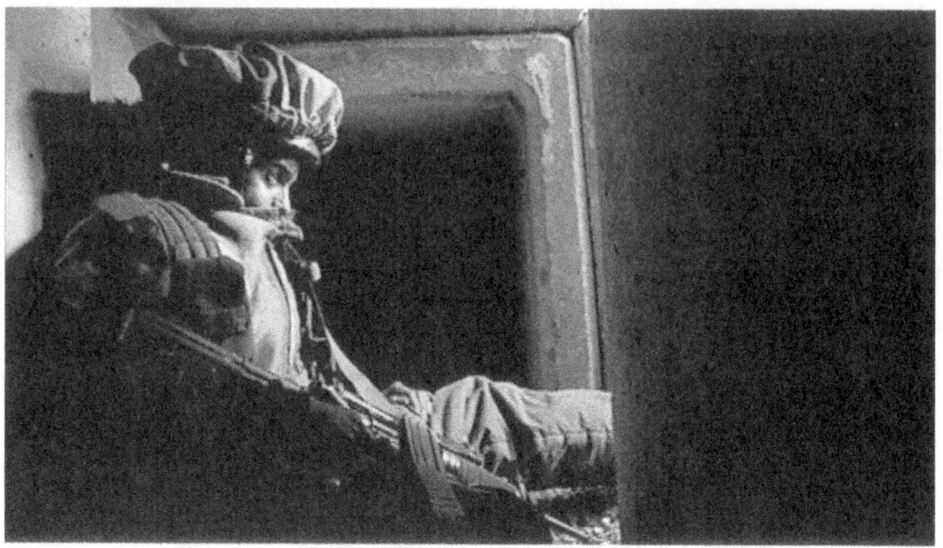

Beaufort (2007), directed by Josef Cedar.
The character is Sergeant Tomer Zitlaui played by Itay Turgeman.

organization.[7] By working to expand the masculine purview by stressing the importance of biological paternity and male nurturing, which have long been subordinated to more aggressive characteristics, and advancing the family as an important counterweight to the nation and its high tolerance for the collateral damage sustained advancing strategic aims, these films mount a meaningful challenge to the status quo. In different ways both films hope to advance possibilities for peace and societal betterment by alerting their viewers to the problematic model of masculinity used to underpin militarism's ongoing and deleterious role in Israeli social and cultural organization.

Although set during the Lebanon War and produced concurrently, the films portray different periods of Israeli involvement that account for the different bases they offer for their challenge to Israeli militarism and the form of masculinity it promotes. Therefore to better understand their convergences and divergences, as well as their messages, an overview of Israel's involvement in Lebanon and the major issues that warfare there has come to embody in the Israeli cultural imagination proves useful.

While Lebanon participated in the 1948 war, Israel considered it the least belligerent Arab country and the two states nearly signed a peace treaty. Yet following the PLO's rise in the late 1960s, its increasingly active factions made Lebanon an operational base following Jordan's expulsion of thousands of their fighters in 1971. Uncomfortable with an expanding Palestinian quasi-state in southern Lebanon promoting terrorism, the recently established Begin government ordered southern Lebanon's invasion in 1978. Israeli forces advanced to the Litani River and remained in Lebanon for three months in an effort to destroy PLO infrastructure and prevent terrorist incursions into Israel. The operation didn't obviate the Palestinian threat. Careful observers forecasted Israel's return.

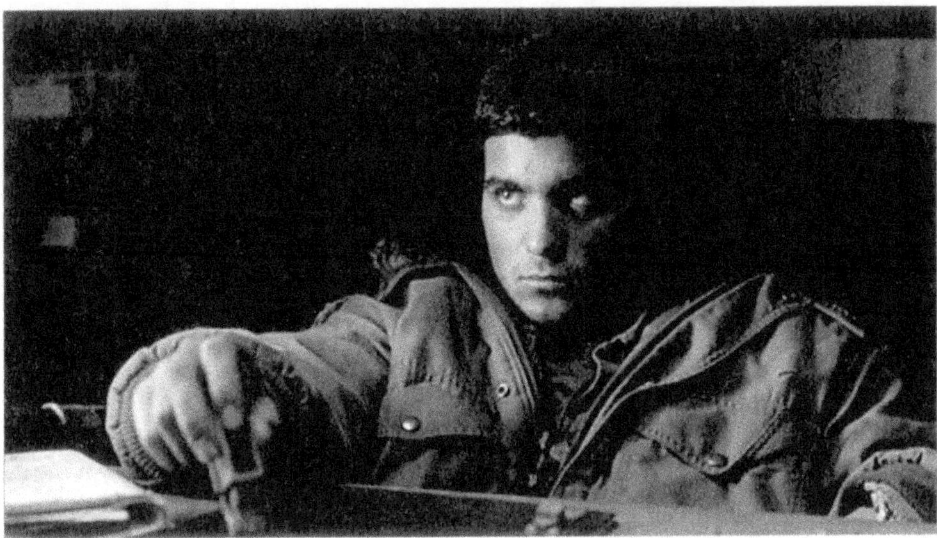

Beaufort (2007), directed by Josef Cedar. Liraz played by Oshri Cohen.

Defense Minister Ariel Sharon masterminded Israel's 1982 invasion, and, as Israeli historian Benny Morris has argued, his plan involved accomplishment of three separate aims.[8] Neutralization of the Palestinian threat in Lebanon again constituted the primary objective. The Israeli cabinet consented to incursion on this basis. Yet Sharon also wanted to exploit the ongoing Lebanese Civil War to improve Israel's strategic position. The civil war created a power vacuum in Lebanon, and Syria asserted itself there. Sharon viewed Syria as the primary threat to Israel following the Camp David Accords, and he looked to express Israel's Middle Eastern dominance through defeat and expulsion of Syrian forces in the Beka'a Valley. Neutralization of the Palestinians and expulsion of the Syrians would allow for promotion of a friendly Lebanese Christian regime ready to make peace with Israel.

Sharon's plan proved risky and didn't proceed smoothly, because Sharon needed to circumvent the desires of the Israeli cabinet that had only approved an operation to contain the Palestinian threat. Nonetheless, the expulsion of PLO fighters to alternative Middle Eastern locations, the destruction of Syria's air-defense system in the Beka'a Valley, and the installation of Israel's Christian ally, Bashir Gemayel, as president, made it appear that Sharon's gamble had quickly paid off. Yet Gemayel's assassination unleashed a chain of events that prevented Israeli assertion of eastern Mediterranean strategic dominance and establishment of a viable peace between Israel and Lebanon, while contributing to Hezbollah's replacement of the PLO as Israel's northern border threat.

Following Gemayel's death, his followers massacred hundreds of residents of Beirut's Palestinian refugee camps, Sabra and Shatila. Sharon, and Israel's complicity, provoked outrage in Israel as well as throughout the world and played a critical role in Israel's eventual withdrawal from Lebanon. Loss of public support, which only increased with mounting Israeli casualties at the hands of various Lebanese guerilla groups, eventually led to the unilateral withdrawal of Israeli forces to a small security zone in southern Lebanon, where it was believed they could protect Israel from threat. This withdrawal proceeded gradually and concluded in 1985. Hezbollah's increasing political and military power in southern Lebanon and its attainment of more advanced roadside bombs and missiles from Syria and Iran eventually led Israel to conclude that the security zone's maintenance no longer served its purposes. Its forces withdrew in May 2000.

With the Israeli military active in Lebanon for nearly twenty-five years, from Operation Litani to the Second Lebanon War, Lebanon constitutes a fertile experiential and imaginative realm for generations of Israeli soldiers sent there to fight, for their families, and for the whole Israeli population. Nonetheless, no consensus exists concerning the implications of this involvement enabling Israeli filmmakers to repeatedly mine its rich material for the artistic treatment of prominent issues. Earlier Israeli films point to three important themes treated through the prism of the Lebanon War. Eli Cohen's *Two Fingers from Sidon* (1986), produced soon after Israel's withdrawal to the security zone, points to the war's ability to assist directors in addressing issues related to Israel's place in the Middle East and its relations with its neighbors; Eran Riklis's *Cup Final* (1991), released just prior to the first direct Israeli-Palestinian peace talks, shows the war's suitability for inquiries into the Israeli-Palestinian conflict; Haim Bouzaglo's *Cherry Season* (1991) demonstrates how the media and arts can manipulate events like the Lebanon War to advance cultural and political norms.[9]

Cedar and Folman both start with the recognition of art's role in advancing cultural norms. Yet unlike Bouzaglo, who sees mass media tinged by manipulative use, Cedar and Folman engage its communicative potential, despite its dangers, to catalyze change. By exposing Israeli viewers to the constructed nature of their culture and its predominant masculine norms, they see a way of challenging a status quo grounded in a fatalistic belief in the Israeli-Palestinian conflict's irresolution and the impossibility of peace between Israel and its neighbors. Through selection of the three-month period leading up to the Sabra and Shatila massacres for filmic treatment, writer-director Folman, who served in Lebanon during that time, asserts his preference for the Israel-Palestine conflict as a tool for exposure of societal ills. Alternatively, by opting to portray a short period prior to Israel's withdrawal from the security zone, the younger writer-director Cedar, whose Lebanon War experience was limited to security zone service, affirms his conviction that reexamination of Israel's strategic position vis-à-vis its neighbors serves as the best way of illuminating societal deficiencies. Despite different approaches, however, both writer-directors work to shatter the illusory barrier between military and civilian life in Israel to reveal civil militarism's damaging effects.

Although Cedar calls for integration of civilian attitudes into military society and Folman strives to bring military realities to bear on civilian life, *Beaufort* and *Waltz with Bashir* both open with symbolic incursions challenging Israeli life's perceived bifurcation. This incursion proves uncanny in *Waltz with Bashir.* As Freud explained, familiar or homey things' sudden transformation produces a discomforting feeling of uncanniness.[10] Covered by a yellow-clouded sky and overrun by wild yellow-eyed dogs, as eerie extradiegetic music plays, Tel Aviv's engaging urban landscape undergoes a striking transformation in the film's opening scene. While the use of flash animation makes this transformation less immediate, vivid detail and the absence of cinematic elements to guide the viewer leave him/her as uncomfortable as the animated city dwellers witnessing the advance of a salivating and barking pack of dogs, past the Shalom and Azrieli Towers to one of Tel Aviv's famed Bauhaus structures, where they gather below the office window of a solitary figure who peers down at them. Having stopped traffic, trampled the reflected image of a parent and child, barked at a mother protectively sheltering her baby, knocked over café chairs, and forcefully shown its fangs, the pack's progress escalates the sense of threat. It seems ready to violently strike in a variation on Hitchcock's *The Birds* (1963). Yet the music fades and the animation seemingly tracks out from a close-up of the snarling dogs as the figure's voice-over narration bridges to the next scene, which offers a chic Tel Aviv Port bar communicating a more comfortable Israel.

The two scenes' divergent Tel Aviv's push the viewer to choose the more appropriate representation of reality. Sheltering its patrons from the driving rain outside, the bar's cozy and familiar confines negate the extant sense of threat. Intertitles identify the speaker as Boaz Rein-Buskilla. The viewer takes in his narrative together with his interlocutor, Folman's persona.[11] When Rein explains that the dogs demand his head from his firm's owners, one questions the first scene's believability and Rein's reliability. More so, when Rein identifies the scene as a recurring dream, the choice seems clear. The second scene of Tel Aviv constitutes the real Tel Aviv and the first scene of Tel Aviv proves to be Rein's private imaginings. Viewers identify with Folman when he attempts to throw off responsibility for his friend's strange dream and its connection to twenty-six dogs he killed at the outset of the Lebanon War. Yet Rein refuses to be pushed away. He tells Folman that he has used film as a form of psychotherapy and he looks to him for assistance.

Folman's decision to honor his friend's request underlies the film's creation. His speech patterns and vocabulary, his attire and gestures, and the behavioral code that leads him to meet his friend for a drink on a rainy late night, all point to Folman's maintenance of a healthy masculinity, but army service serves as an important, if not the primary, arena for expression of Israeli masculinity.[12] As Rein explains, his unit's members knew that he was incapable of killing a human. Consequently, his superiors ordered him to kill dogs when the unit entered into Lebanese villages to maintain the element of surprise. Rein's past weakness places his present masculinity in question and raises the possibility that his nightmare merely constitutes a new manifestation of earlier shortcomings. Folman served in Lebanon too. Yet neither nightmares nor flashbacks trouble him. Even when Rein brings up the Sabra and Shatila massacres, which occurred when Folman was stationed nearby, they evoke nothing for Folman, who explains, "it's not in my system." Nonetheless, as they embrace and part outside the bar, Folman tells Rein that he'll find a solution and things will be fine.

One is initially uncertain if Folman merely humors Rein. The image of Rein alone facing pelting rain and pounding white-capped waves makes it appear that Folman might leave him alone to inhabit his haunted Tel Aviv. Yet as a countershot frames Folman gazing on his friend, extradiegetic music starts and develops into a theme that will accompany a recurrent flashback that Folman will soon experience for the first time. Prior to the flashback, Folman stands facing the sea like Rein, and a yellow military flare illuminates the sky and evokes the yellow skies of Rein's dream. The first scene's uncanny Tel Aviv becomes shared property.

Folman's desire to remain friends with Rein and their shared masculine code lead him to delve into his recurring flashback and take on issues that challenge his masculine self-perception and the society that imposed its masculine standards upon him. As a result, the film chronicles Folman's process of individual self-discovery. Folman confronts repressed elements of the Israeli psyche condensed into the first scene's dogs that alter his understanding of Israeli society, as well as himself. Looking to have his Israeli viewers achieve a similar awareness and support an alternative masculinity he views as more in tune with Rein and Israel's future needs, the filmmaker turns to flash animation. By moving beyond the talking head or interview method for documentary film and embracing flash animation's ability to provide complex portrayals of its protagonists' subjective experience, *Waltz with Bashir* offers its viewers a captivatingly new view of Israeli society that maintains their interest as it offers an increasingly critical reexamination of Israeli society and proposes the alteration of its norms. Without flash animation and the defamiliarization that it produces, the film's challenge of extant masculine norms would be largely obviated.

While the familiar landscape of Tel Aviv provides an effective background for military life's penetration into Israel's seemingly civilian realm, most Israelis prove unfamiliar with conditions in the security zone prior to Israel's withdrawal. Consequently, viewers' grasp of how a new soldier's arrival at the eponymous Beaufort castle, a famed southern Lebanese outpost, embodies penetration of the civilian world into the military realm as *Beaufort* opens requires greater contextualization.[13]Intertitles introduce Beaufort as "a mythological symbol of heroism" dating back nine hundred years. Subsequently, a low-angle establishment shot of the mountaintop fortress reiterates the symbol's awe-inspiring nature, and a long shot of an erect Israeli flag waving above it voices Israeli possession of this symbol and what it embodies.

The next shot, which presents the poured concrete blocks and rocky surface of the base's upper level, belies the beauty the fort's name implies. Building on the tension between name and object, the camera centers on a lone soldier found in a guard station situated at the end of a walled trench. This image conveys confinement at odds with the initial shots' controlling power and heroism. The soldier soon ducks into a dark opening. A subsequent shot taken within a cramped, dark, and coffin-like space shows the soldier's tense preoccupied expression as he looks out into the light. This shot voices the dilemma Israeli soldiers face maintaining Beaufort's heroic code, for which the soldier serves as a synecdochic representative. They can inhabit the protective and stultifying darkness, with its death-like existence and possibility of premature death, or they can exit into the light and enjoy possibilities for a fuller life.

The vulnerability that accompanies emergence from protective darkness becomes evident following a cut to two racing soldiers advancing to an opening between two concrete barriers, a variation on the previous gateway image. At the left of a two shot squats Liraz, the base commander, and behind his right shoulder one finds his best friend and right-hand man, Oshri, the company sergeant. Their identical apparel and equipment and their sense of shared purpose as they earnestly advanced convey a sense of solidarity among the inhabitants of the fort's dark and protective spaces absent from the earlier sequence and hint at the male camaraderie that makes such a life tolerable. A reverse shot then presents a beautiful green field with a blue-skied ceiling contrasting sharply with the base's cement and gravel interior. When the two men run out into this Edenic space toward a helicopter that appears like a mechanized form of divine salvation, it momentarily appears that they are heading out to a better life. Yet the two men don't board. Instead they take two bags and return with a third soldier to the fort's safe interior spaces as mortar rounds fall around them and mar the previously Edenic field.

Ziv, the new arrival, whose wide eyes convey inexperience and shock upon arrival in a protected space, has been sent to liberate the base's soldiers, who have been trapped by an extant roadside bomb blocking the exit road, and the remainder of the film revolves around the sapper's ability to save the others. Oshri's ironic tone when he asks Ziv, "You came to save us?" expresses his doubt concerning Ziv's ability. Liraz, who most directly expresses the outpost's warrior code, believes Ziv's upper-class Ashkenazic leftist upbringing has made him soft. Consequently, when Ziv asks if such heavy mortar fire is common, Liraz takes him down a notch by jokingly responding, "it was calm until you showed up." This type of playful response, typical of Israeli military life, separates newcomers from veteran insiders, and Liraz and Oshri laugh at Ziv's expense. Sharing a sense of masculine bravado, the friends soon head out carefree into mortar fire in the wake of a frightened Ziv. In Liraz's mind, Ziv can't offer the base's soldiers anything and should steel himself to assume their standards.

When Ziv later states that bomb diffusion will prove dangerous and questions his mission, Liraz's antipathy for him and what he represents resurfaces. Liraz angrily jumps on him and portrays him as a coward. His hesitation, Liraz explains, will change nothing. At most somebody else will be sent to perform his assignment. Liraz views maintenance of the base and what it symbolizes as the unit's primary objective. Questioning of orders doesn't serve this mission. Free movement proves necessary for the base's proper resupply and for periodic granting of leave to its soldiers. The soldiers need periodic release from the base's strict masculine standards, but such deviation must occur far away so that civilian standards won't impinge upon the men's ability to protect themselves and their nation from unseen enemies.

Ziv will agree to disarm the roadside bomb, but maintenance of Beaufort and its standards doesn't interest him. He views disarmament as a first step in opening the base to alternative masculine standards derived from civilian society, which no longer unquestioningly accepts the military casualties that accompany a siege mentality. Ziv sees abandonment of the base's protective darkness for a more fulfilling, albeit vulnerable, existence and the quest for peace with Israel's neighbors as an appropriate future course. As Liraz's and Ziv's views compete for dominance in the besieged fort, which simultaneously represents Israeli society's self-perception, the soldiers' fate hangs in the balance. While Liraz's carefree trot through mortar fire voices the esprit de corps and the male camaraderie that buoy him, a cut to the solitary soldier featured at the film's outset sitting downcast in his dark grave-like space as incoming mortar shells envelop him in smoke and dust offers a more somber portrayal of military service and a vision more supportive of Ziv's suggested changes. Ziv's outlook will emerge victorious, but its successful path will prove surprising.

Both *Waltz with Bashir* and *Beaufort* advance their efforts to expose civil militarism through challenges to important facets of Israeli identity initially advanced by the first native-born Israeli Jewish generation.[14] *Waltz with Bashir*'s confrontation with earlier norms centers on rejection of foundation myths, but both films challenge Israeli memorial culture first instilled to preserve sabra norms.

Folman's recurring flashback most directly expresses *Waltz with Bashir*'s rejection of the Sabra generation's foundation myth. While Folman initially believes that it portrays events that occurred during the Sabra and Shatila massacres, he learns that these events didn't occur. Rather they serve as a compromise-formation sheltering him from knowledge of his role in the massacres, and analysis of his flashback reveals painful, but important, psychological issues the massacre raises.[15]

The character Elik in Moshe Shamir's 1951 novel *With His Own Hands* helped voice an important sabra foundation myth, and Folman's flashback challenges it.[16] The novel's opening line, "Elik was born from the sea," has been interpreted to stress the sabra's birth free of binding ties to Jewry's European and religious pasts. Consequently, he emerges a healthy Palestinian Hebrew male attuned to his environment and prepared to sanctify communal values through self-sacrifice.[17] Rather than emerging from the sea to a pleasurable childhood on Tel Aviv's beaches, Folman, his friend Carmi, and a third soldier awaken floating naked in the Mediterranean, stand facing Beirut's yellow flare-illuminated skyline, and walk to shore. As they proceed, Carmi's dog tag and the unidentified soldier's assault rifle become visible. In a symbolic overcoming of the sea's Diasporic "feminine" vulnerability, and an assertion of military power in Israel and beyond, they subsequently dress in military fatigues and ascend to the street. A reverse shot showing Folman approaching a store gate plastered with posters of Bashir Gemayel, which follows a shot of the armed men walking down the street, points to the pursuit of Sharon's plans as an advance toward masculine invincibility. Yet Folman turns and a sea of disturbed black-clad women engulfs him. His engulfment by these women, who evoke the wives, mothers, sisters, and daughters of those killed in Sabra and Shatila, symbolizes a return to the sea's "feminine" Diasporic vulnerability. The desire for masculine invincibility underlying the sabra myth is rejected once its human price becomes clear.

Building upon the flashback's implications, the film contests war and battlefield death's central role in Israeli masculinity's construction and presents an alternative vision grounded in awareness of masculinity's instability and complexity and the wider constellation of behaviors that define it. Cognizant of war cinema's role in maintenance of aggressive masculine norms, Folman creates a self-reflexive scene intended to challenge viewers' thinking about the representation and reality of war and masculinity. Francis Ford Coppola's *Apocalypse Now* (1979) shaped many Israeli soldiers' perception of war and proper masculine conduct during wartime, and, in a music-video-like scene recounting events of the war's first month, Folman samples material from it, such as the image of a soldier surfing in mortar fire. Yet his reference in the commentary to the scene as a comic homage points to Folman's ironic use of the earlier film, to point to its radical divergence from his experience. Rather than presenting masculine bravery and fearlessness, one is treated to friendly fire incidents and the erroneous targeting of civilians that question Israeli soldiers' judgment.

The somber tone Folman employs depicting his first day in Lebanon contrasts with the earlier scene's playful tone to best capture the human vulnerability and individual weakness war revealed to him. Ordered by a superior to "throw out" wounded and dead soldiers, Folman takes charge of a loaded armored personnel carrier (APC) and heads to the "great light" to dump its contents. In the advancing APC's depths, dead soldiers' emotionless faces and a wounded soldier's self-absorbed expression hint at the fine line separating Folman and his crew from a similar fate, and the fearful crew members shoot indiscriminately to maintain their distance. Earlier the dead and wounded numbered among the playful young men featured in the music video scene, but in their superior's eyes they've become disposable trash. While going toward the light constitutes a euphemism for dying people's approach to the afterlife, a deity toward which one advances as reward for sacrifice on the collective's behalf proves absent. Instead, at its destination, the APC and its crew proceed to a glimmering row of body-bag-covered stretchers and extend it.

To better explain young Israeli men's willingness to go to war despite the strong divergence between war's image and reality, the film exposes the importance of Israeli society's attribution of masculine vigor to battlefield dead. Folman's recent breakup with his girlfriend dominates his thoughts on a Beirut-bound helicopter flight. Voice-over narration expresses his thoughts and feelings at the time, while dreamlike images further portray his inner world. As he idealizes death and an end to breakup-induced suffering, soldiers carrying a flag-draped coffin walk past his youthful self. Folman's ex-girlfriend, Yael, soon tearfully follows behind the coffin, and, after evocation of the coffin's interment, tearfully crouches before his standardized military gravestone that replaces it. Not only would battlefield death put Folman out of his misery, it would also "prove" his embodiment of the Israeli heroic ideal and show him worthy of a woman's love. This fact underlies Yael's suffering following her ex-boyfriend's imagined death. Despite this sequence's fantastic nature, it points to Israeli society's manipulation of military fatalities and accompanying mourning rituals for youth mobilization.

In contrast, Roni Dayag's story points to the use of mourning rituals to stigmatize those who fail to live up to accepted Israeli standards of self-sacrifice. While the sight of Dayag's tank running over cars impeding its advance and driving through walls blocking its path communicates his crew's sense of masculine security and invincibility, a Palestinian ambush of his tank battalion tests it early in the invasion. Rather than returning fire when their commander is shot, the tank crew futilely tries to save him. After enemy fire sets their tank aflame, they, like other crews, flee for safety. Only Dayag finds cover. As the battalion's undamaged tanks retreat, he remains alone. Forced to choose between a futile attempt at masculine heroism or "feminine" survival, Dayag doesn't engage the enemy. Thoughts of his mother, their shared love, her reliance on him, and her intense grief if he were to die, lead Dayag to crawl into the nearby sea, reversing the prototypical movement from feminine vulnerability to masculine invincibility charted in Folman's flashback.

A military funeral following Dayag's swim to safety portrays his subsequent sense of stigmatization. While the family and soldiers upholding the self-sacrificial code encircle the deceased soldier's grave, Dayag stands excluded and alone in the distance. His battalion abandoned him. Yet he feels he abandoned it and his dead comrades by not dying with them. While he desires to commemorate these men, feelings of betrayal, shame, and failure make him feel inadequate and lead him to cut his painful ties with his comrades' families. As a shot of the mature Dayag occupying the same hilltop space outside of the cemetery communicates, these feelings don't dissipate. His efforts to distance himself fail too. His imagination continually returns him to his perceived betrayal, and he suffers from a sense of inadequacy.

Cognizant of such stigma and the restricted view of masculinity advanced by it, the film points to an extant tension between battlefield and biological elements within the Israeli masculine ideal. This tension, voiced in Folman's desire to prove his sexual attractiveness to his ex-girlfriend through war death, finds direct expression in Carmi Cna'an's life. While growing up, he was a chess champion and a talented math student. Imagining that other young men were "having sex like rabbits," he nonetheless suffered from low self-esteem. Consequently, he enlisted in an elite infantry unit to prove his masculinity and gain the opportunity to express his sexual virility.

While Carmi succeeds in his goal, his fantastic memory of his unit's amphibious landing in Lebanon stresses the absence of a tangible connection between battlefield valor and masculine sexual performance. In the memory, which interweaves voice-over narration with visual representation, Carmi heads north on a yacht he refers to as a "love boat." His fellow soldiers party, but Carmi becomes seasick and throws up, something that voices his perceived masculine shortcomings and lack of sexual preparedness. Yet as he lies in the boat's stern, a female giant swims toward him and boards the boat. Soon this beautiful naked figure picks him up, and, as she suckles him, jumps into the sea. Rather than drowning, Carmi keeps the fears and emotions symbolized by the sea in check as he floats along on the giant woman, who functions like a raft. As he lounges upon her in seeming postcoital bliss, the ship explodes and the message proves clear. While the warrior ethos brings Carmi sexual gratification, many soldiers upholding it die attempting to achieve the same result.

Building on this false linkage of military valor and sexual performance, Folman describes his first wartime leave when he recognized how this discrepancy could be exploited. When he was a child and the nation went to war, Folman was led to believe that the front constituted a masculine realm where men went to prove themselves, while the home front comprised a temporarily chaste feminine realm offering returning men sexual reward. Yet when Folman arrives home, his expectations go unrealized. His slow movement through the streets as those around him proceed at an accelerated pace voices the outdated nature of his belief. Teenage boys firing at video game targets in an arcade he passes might still dream of assuming his warrior role, but young women's distant stares point to a lack of interest in him and his military commitment. Life continues on without him, and a couple making out in public shows that Israeli women find nothing wrong with selecting mates from among noncombatants. Folman's ex-girlfriend Yael's solo dance in a discotheque drives this lesson painfully home.

While the outdated and bombastic rhetoric of Prime Minister Menachem Begin, who appears delivering a speech on a store's display televisions, encourages Folman's belief in the Israeli public's love and appreciation of the soldiers purportedly defending its northern border, the title lyrics to the postpunk band Public Image Limited's song "This Is Not a Love Song," which plays throughout the scene, more effectively communicates Israeli society's changed attitude toward its soldiers. The jarring replacement of Begin's image with those of the band members emphasizes the rapid societal changes that have occurred since Folman's childhood. The song's description of the sloughing off of social responsibility in pursuit of individual gain captures the rise in individualism that accompanied economic privatization during Likud rule. With this change, rhetoric exploits the advancement of personal and political aims that superseded earlier conceptions of the nation and the leadership's responsibility to the rank and file.

Begin embodies early state rhetoric and preaches the maintenance of outdated masculine standards, but the film points to Ariel Sharon and infantry commander Amos Yaron as conscious adherents of an amoral masculinity unconcerned with less powerful people's needs that comes to dominate Israeli society. In a breakfast montage, a plate with five eggs, a mammoth steak, and vegetables, fails to quell the insatiable desire that drives Sharon's amoral masculinity. Consequently, insatiable appetite, symbolized by his large knife, demands more extreme military measures to accomplish Sharon's territorial goals. In this Sharon contrasts sharply with an austere and increasingly squeamish Begin pictured preparing to take his pills after a single glass of tea. After achieving Begin's consent, Sharon tells Yaron, who eats off china on a villa balcony, to send his men in pursuit of Palestinian insurgents. One of Folman's comrades appears next. Cutlery falls from his plastic plate of canned meat and eggs as he defers his meal to obey Yaron's command and head into battle with his unit. They'll kill two RPG-wielding children and will be forced to deal with their actions' implications. While Sharon and Yaron show little concern for either these children or their charges, the incident traumatizes Folman. As a result, he represses it—a clear expression of his disgust with the amoral masculinity embodied by Sharon and Yaron, two men implicated for their involvement in the Sabra and Shatila massacres.

While Folman finds it difficult to face his morally questionable behavior during the Lebanon War, he eventually recalls his role illuminating the night skies for the murdering Phalangists during the massacres, as well as his presence at a guard booth just outside the camps when traumatized Palestinian women emerged to tell about what had happened. Rather than diminishing his persona's role in the massacres' immoral masculine expression, the director segues from flash animation to live archival footage taken by the first news cameramen to enter the camps and presents his viewers with the repressed reality that haunts Israeli society like the opening scene's snarling dogs. For Israel to truly become like the cozy sheltering environment voiced by the Tel Aviv Port bar, it must recognize the commonality of suffering faced by Jews and Palestinians. This commonality of suffering and recognition of shared weakness serves as a more effective path to peace and security than attempts to arrive at masculine invulnerability and the callousness of spirit it demands. Therefore the film rejects the masculine model Sharon embodies to point to other figures representing more positive attributes worthy of male emulation.

Folman's selection of interviewees for *Waltz with Bashir* points to characteristics that he viewed as preferable to military acumen and readiness for self-sacrifice as component parts of normative Israeli masculinity. While the film doesn't belittle the importance of the individual male's readiness to challenge the infinite, as expressed in Shmuel Frenkel's "Waltz with Bashir," where he twirls around while firing a machine gun to liberate his pinned-down unit, it compartmentalizes such action alongside Frenkel's competition in triathlons and survival sports. Such behavior suits individuals like Frenkel, but it doesn't elevate him above Rein and Dayag, who demonstrate moral conscience and independence of mind. Nonetheless Ron Ben-Yeshai and Ori Sivan assume a central position through their ability to voice positive attributes that the writer sees recognizably absent from standard representations of Israeli manhood. The film presents reporter Ben-Yeshai as a heroic figure due to his readiness to endanger himself to provide Israeli society with accurate information that will allow it to best govern itself and his sense of justice that leads him to be the first to step forward and challenge Sharon's tacit approval of the massacres. Meanwhile, Sivan, who is always portrayed caring for his large family, communicates tenderness and his ability to nurture Folman, as well as his children, points to what Folman sees as the necessary integration of seemingly feminine characteristics into the Israeli masculine norm.

While Folman promotes Sivan's nurturing tenderness in *Waltz with Bashir,* expression of similar tenderness in *Beaufort* underlies Liraz's feelings of enmity toward Ziv, who he views as a threat to the base's heroic ideal, but, when put to the test, Ziv shows himself capable of upholding this heroic ideal when he heads out to defuse the roadside bomb. In formation, the camouflaged soldiers who accompany Ziv proceed forward professionally, and, when they near the bomb, they follow standard protocol. After a soldier dresses Ziv in sapper gear with choreographed precision, Ziv advances and begins work. The soldiers' skillful efficiency entices the viewer to admire their abilities and accept the masculine norms Liraz asserts as necessary for their attainment. Yet when the bomb explodes and kills Ziv, the team fails to accomplish its mission. Consequently, Ziv's suddenly disembodied questioning of Beaufort's heroic ideal, and its cost, resurfaces.

While Israeli society works to silence those questioning its heroic ideal through elaborate military funerals meant to reinscribe its male youth with the outlook deemed most strategically conducive, *Beaufort* defers a military funeral's cathartic possibilities. Instead, following Ziv's death, it continues within the fort's confined space. The next scene opens with a tracking shot that follows Liraz to the dining hall, and, as he approaches, the Sabbath prayer *Lecha Dodi* can be heard. Out of respect for the religious tradition and the comfort that it offers in times of personal questioning, Liraz covers his head as he enters and sits down. The camera then pans and tracks in to a close-up of the medic, Koris, who failed to save Ziv. While Liraz stood paralyzed, he attempted mouth-to-mouth resuscitation. Secular like Liraz, he finds Liraz's use of the tradition to shelter himself from the implications of Ziv's death distasteful. Due to his tangible connection to death, Koris replaces Ziv as the primary questioner of the base's purposefulness. Consequently, he exits the dining hall in protest against the values Liraz promotes as base commander. Subsequently, Koris refuses the food and creature comforts given the soldiers following a military tractor's effortless opening of the entrance road that Ziv died attempting to reopen. Koris refuses to be distracted from the price of maintaining the base's heroic code that masks the soldiers' increasing role as faceless pawns in a broader strategic game.

Even as a government pressured to recognize that each Israeli soldier is someone's child orders preparation for abandonment of Beaufort and its heroic code, Liraz refuses to accept these orders' legitimacy. As Koris explained to Ziv, Liraz is thankful for having been given control of the fort and responsibility for enforcement of its masculine code. While Ziv speaks freely of his parents back home and Oshri tells about his girlfriend, Michelle, Liraz remains tightlipped about his civilian life. In actuality, he has little to remark about. He comes from a broken home. He likely would have been imprisoned for criminal behavior if the army had not presented him with an alternative. While mention is made of a girlfriend, it is clear that they have long since parted ways. The sense of shared purpose, solidarity, and comradeship that the fort's heroic code provides, shelters Liraz from his civilian life's barrenness, as well as Ziv's death's potential meaninglessness. He proves incapable of disengaging it even when on leave. More than belief in the base's masculine code's superiority, Liraz's fear of the vulnerabilities and weaknesses revealed in his civilian life push him to buck the order to remove inessential material from the base in preparation for a pullout. Consequently, like a contemporary Ahab, he gets into a fistfight with a soldier loading a truck. Removal of anything from the base amounts to acceptance of the masculine code's fallibility. Mounting casualties finally push Liraz to recognize the heroic code's limitations and the need for its rejection.

The events surrounding the death of Zitlawi, the solitary soldier pictured in the opening scene, prove pivotal to Liraz's transformation by making him aware of the limitations of his bonds to his fellow soldiers. As events unfold, one sees Zitlawi idling away the long boring hours of guard duty. While cooking on a hot plate, he uses his military radio to impersonate an Indian swami offering spiritual enlightenment through sex. When the imaginary paramour gives her consent, Zitlawi narrates the sexual act to the bemusement of his listeners, who appear in quick cuts. This lighthearted behavior expresses the men's sense of camaraderie that makes life palatable, but the guard booth's sudden explosion points to such solidarity's limitations. While the distance he maintained from Ziv helped preserve his faith in the base's heroic code, extinguishment of Zitlawi's burning guard booth and extraction of his fallen charge viscerally alert Liraz, who expresses his love for Zitlawi, to the heroic code's price. Before Liraz can process this experience, mortar fire hits Oshri and again challenges Liraz's bonds of affection. Unable to reach safety, Oshri calls to Liraz for help. Yet rather than rushing to save him, Liraz's fear of death momentarily trumps the heroic code he promotes. As he impotently watches, Koris, motivated by recognition of fundamental human weakness, drags Oshri to safety and medical care.

After Zitlawi and Oshri are airlifted out, soldiers scrub down the space where they received medical care, but their wounds' psychological effects can't be erased. Liraz encounters them when his eyes scan the room he shared with Oshri and take in his possessions. He begins to comprehend the absence left in death's wake. As he stands on the threshold of the base lounge, a television newscaster's announcement of Zitlawi's death drives this idea home. Still unwilling to confront irrepressible feelings of vulnerability and weakness, Liraz yearns for the momentary release offered by exacting vengeance upon those who have wounded and killed his friends. Yet his superiors refuse his request, preferring to maintain the base's heroic code in a strategically expedient way. Liraz agrees to use his leadership skills to achieve this, because it allows him to avoid leaving base to speak with Ziv's father or to visit Oshri, activities that threaten his masculine exterior.

Recognizing that a sense of equality and brotherhood underlie the fort's heroic code, Liraz works to bridge the psychological distance that separates him from his soldiers, but, despite initial success, he ceases to view the code as superior to the government's seemingly "feminine" retreat plan. Leaving his semiprivate room behind, Liraz bunks with the enlisted men and reassumes guard duty, even taking first watch at the station where Zitlawi was critically wounded to demonstrate that things can go on as before. Hoping to buoy the men, he then asks Shpitzer to play a song in Zitlawi's honor. The song's lyrics present a central flaw of Beaufort's warrior code. While the men can withstand physical suffering, they find it difficult to cope with the pain their suffering causes others. If they could suffer in isolation, the pain would be less burdensome. Yet while Liraz identifies with the lyrics and desires of such isolation, Koris's audible sobbing hints that the brotherhood the fort's men prize so highly means nothing since they can't communicate their inner emotions to their comrades. Taking

Koris's tears to heart, Liraz labors to develop his ties with the men serving under him. When Shpitzer arrives early to replace him on guard duty, Liraz expresses appreciation for his musical skill and his unique character. In so doing, he elevates Shpitzer above a mere pawn in a strategic game and breathes life into the concept of brotherhood. When a missile strike kills Shpitzer, however, his death does not occur in isolation. It profoundly affects Liraz, who questions the concept of brotherhood's use to promote Beaufort's heroic code.

When he sits alone in the lounge facing the television image of Ziv's father, Amos, Liraz's readiness to explore alternatives to the warrior code finds expression. Rather than seeing Ziv's military service as a sign of proper education, Amos views it and his son's death as indicative of miseducation. Together with other members of the *Arba Imahot* (Four Mothers) organization, Amos looks to reconfigure Israeli education, so that children will recognize their preciousness and hesitate before doing dangerous things, including elite army service. While Liraz would previously have rejected such a weak "feminine" attitude and turned the television off in disgust, he now perceives Amos's comments' applicability to his and Shpitzer's lives. What he had viewed as proper masculine conduct proves juvenile, something emphasized by his twirling of a toy truck as he listens to Amos.

The arrival of a truckload of land mines intended to destroy Beaufort and its outdated warrior code marks the shift in Liraz's outlook. While Liraz forcefully objected to evacuation of the fort and abandonment of its heroic ideal earlier, he now calmly calls his men to unload the means for Beaufort's destruction. Nonetheless, he still finds it difficult to imagine life without the warrior code, and he fears a renewed confrontation with his personal weaknesses. Yet when the sapper Meir helps him envision the Edenic possibilities following Beaufort's destruction, Liraz proves ready to abandon the siege mentality that has dominated his life to embrace the world regardless of self-exposure's inherent dangers. Consequently, the final order to destroy Beaufort and the heroic code that it has long embodied comes from Liraz. When he arrives back in Israel, Liraz lays down his helmet and his weapon, strips off his combat vest and winter gear, and breathes in deeply against a background of verdant green fields. Ziv's vision of a more fulfilling, albeit vulnerable, existence, grounded in a preference for the quest for peace with Israel's neighbors, rather than renewed military conflict, has become Liraz's vision as a result of what he learns in Lebanon.

Through selection of the First Lebanon War as the background for their films, Folman and Cedar countered a popular Israeli cinematic trend involving employment of advanced cinematic techniques to portray Israeli society's growing fragmentation and the difficulties faced by individuals attempting to influence it. Cognizant of the military's continuing role in unifying and shaping Israeli society, both directors employed the war and its male combatants to show the deleterious effects brought about by erection of an illusory barrier between civil and military societies. Rather than using the war to promote masculine standards grounded in a readiness to sacrifice everything for one's country, including one's life, the films promote alternative masculine forms grounded in the family's nurturing atmosphere that stress the pain of loss and the sanctity of human life, the lives of citizens and noncitizens alike. Through widespread adoption of such forms, the films gesture toward the possibility for eventual peace between Israel and the Palestinians, and between Israel and its neighbors. In their advance of the individual's ability to positively impact the future through careful analysis of the past and present, *Waltz with Bashir* and *Beaufort* combine aesthetic merit with an optimistic message largely absent from contemporary Israeli cinema. One can only hope that these films' aesthetics and message find broad audiences.

Notes

1. For a discussion of Lebanon War cinema against the background of this cinema see Nurith Gertz, "The Medium That Mistook Itself for War: *Cherry Season* in Comparison with *Ricochets* and *Cup Final*," *Israel Studies* 4, no. 1 (1999): 153–74. For overviews of Israeli cinema, see Ella Shohat, *Israeli Cinema: East/West and the Politics of Representation* (Austin: University of Texas Press, 1989); Nurith Gertz, *Sippur mehaseratim: Sipporet yisraelit ve'ibudeha lekolnoa'* (Tel Aviv: Open University, 1993), 13–60, 175–85; Yosefa Loshitzky, *Identity Politics and the Israeli Screen* (Austin: University of Texas Press, 2001).

2. Baruch Kimmerling, *The Invention and Decline of Israeliness: State, Society, and the Military* (Berkeley: University of California Press, 2001), 209.

3. Ibid., 209 and 213.

4. Danny Kaplan, *Brothers and Others in Arms: The Making of Love and War in Israeli Combat Units* (New York: Harrington Park Press, 2003), 113.

5. Edna Lomsky-Feder and Eyal Ben-Ari, introduction to *The Military and Militarism in Israeli Society*, ed. Edna Lomsky-Feder and Eyal Ben-Ari (Albany: State University of New York Press, 1999), 16; Sara Helman, "Militarism and the Construction of the Life-World of Israeli Males: The Case of the Reserve System," in *The Military and Militarism in Israeli Society*, ed. Edna Lomsky-Feder and Eyal Ben-Ari (Albany: State University of New York Press, 1999), 191–221.

6. For the classic study on nationalism, male brotherhood, and military sacrifice, see Benedict Anderson, *Imagined Communities* (New York: Verso, 1993). For a discussion of masculinity and nationalism's intersection in Israeli cinema, see Raz Yosef, *Beyond Flesh: Queer Masculinities and Nationalism in Israel Cinema* (New Brunswick, NJ: Rutgers University Press, 2004), 16–47. Important discussions of gender and sexuality's roles in Zionist culture's development include Michael Gluzman, *The Zionist Body: Nationalism, Gender, and Sexuality in Modern Hebrew Literature* (Tel Aviv: Hakibbutz Hameuchad, 2007); Mikhal Dekel, *The Universal Jew: Masculinity, Modernity, and the Zionist Moment* (Evanston: Northwestern University Press, 2010).

7. The term *hegemonic masculinity* was coined by theorist R. W. Connell. As Connell and James Messerschmidt explain, "hegemonic masculinity was distinguished from other masculinities, especially subordinated masculinities. Hegemonic masculinity was not assumed to be normal in the statistical sense; only a minority of men might enact it. But it was certainly normative. It embodied the currently most honored way of being a man, it required all other men to position themselves in relation to it, and it ideologically legitimated the global subordination of women to

men." R. W. Connell and James W. Messerschmidt, "Hegemonic Masculinity: Rethinking the Concept," *Gender and Society* 19, no. 6 (2005): 832.

8. For more on the 1982 Lebanon War, see Benny Morris, *Righteous Victims: A History of the Zionist-Arab Conflict, 1881–2001* (New York: Vintage Books, 2001), 494–560; Avi Shlaim, *The Iron Wall: Israel and the Arab World* (New York: Norton, 2001), 384–460; Martin Van Creveld, *The Sword and the Olive: A Critical History of the Israel Defense Force* (New York, Public Affairs, 2002), 285–306.

9. For more on these three films, see Gertz, "The Medium That Mistook Itself for War." For a critique of *Cup Final,* see Yehudah (Judd) Ne'eman, "A Good Arab Is a Film Arab," *Ma'ariv,* September 8, 1991; on *The Cherry Season,* see Yehudah (Judd) Ne'eman, "Soft Porn and Israeli War Films," *Ma'ariv,* July 26, 1991.

10. See Sigmund Freud, *Writings on Art and Literature* (Stanford, CA: Stanford University Press, 1997), 193–233.

11. Although labeled a documentary film, *Waltz with Bashir* is best classified as a fictional film integrating documentary footage and oral testimony. Rather than accurately portraying living figures, the film constructs personas for greater seamlessness. While Folman's persona will be referred to as Folman, important differences exist.

12. For more on Israeli male friendship tests see Danny Kaplan, *The Men We Loved: Male Friendship and Nationalism in Israeli Culture* (New York: Berghahn Books, 2006), 57–72.

13. The general public's ignorance of service conditions in the security zone led journalist Ron Leshem to investigate these conditions prior to the Israeli withdrawal. His interviews with Israeli soldiers serving there supplied him with material for his best-selling fictional work *If There Is a Heaven,* upon which *Beaufort* is based. The fictional text's ability to introduce readers to an unfamiliar world constitutes its strength. Differences between the works are too extensive to be treated in this essay.

14. For a full treatment of this generation and its role in the formation of Israeli identity, see Oz Almog, *The Sabra: The Creation of the New Jew,* trans. Haim Watzman (Berkeley: University of California Press, 2000). For more on the sabra's construction and deconstruction in Israeli cinema, see Nurith Gertz, "The Myth of Masculinity Reflected in Israeli Cinema," in *Modern Jewish Mythologies,* ed. Glenda Abramson (Cincinnati, OH: Hebrew Union College Press, 1999), 68–88.

15. A compromise-formation can be defined as a "form taken by the repressed memory so as to be admitted to consciousness when it returns in symptoms, in dreams and, more generally, in all products of the unconscious: in the process the repressed ideas are distorted by defense to the point of being unrecognizable." J. Laplance and J.-B. Pontalis, *The Language of Psycho-Analysis,* trans. Donald Nicholson-Smith (New York: Norton,1973), 76.

16. See Gershon Shaked, *Ha-sipporet ha-ivrit, 1880–1980,* vol. 4 (Jerusalem: Keter, 1993), 233–50.

17. See Moshe Shamir, *Bemo Yadav: Pirkei Elik* (Tel Aviv: Am Oved, 1975), 9.

CONTRIBUTORS

Editors

Rachel S. Harris is Assistant Professor of Israeli literature and culture at the University of Illinois at Urbana-Champaign in the Department of Comparative and World Literature and the Program in Jewish Culture and Society. Her essays have appeared in *Israel Studies*, *Journal of Modern Jewish Studies*, and *Journal of Jewish Identities (JOJI)*. She has guest edited a special issue of *Nashim* devoted to "The Jewish Woman and Her Body" (2012), and coedited a special issue of *JOJI* with Anna P. Ronell, "Russian-Jewish Diaspora Post-1970," *Journal of Jewish Identities* 4, no. 1 (2011). Her current book project is titled *An Ideological Death: Suicide in Israeli Literature*.

Ranen Omer-Sherman is Professor of English and Jewish studies at the University of Miami. His essays on Israeli and Jewish writers have appeared in the *Journal of Jewish Identities*, *Journal of Modern Jewish Studies*, *Journal of Modern Literature*, *MELUS*, *Michigan Quarterly Review*, *Modernism/Modernity*, *Prooftexts*, *Religion & Literature*, *Shofar*, and *Texas Studies in Literature and Language*. His books include *Diaspora and Zionism in Jewish American Literature: Lazarus, Syrkin, Reznikoff, Roth*; *Israel in Exile: Jewish Writing and the Desert*; and the coedited volume, *The Jewish Graphic Novel: Critical Approaches*.

Contributors

Glenda Abramson was born in Johannesburg, South Africa. She is Emeritus Professor of Hebrew and Jewish studies at the University of Oxford. Among her publications are *The Writing of Yehuda Amichai*, *Drama and Ideology in Modern Israel*, and *Hebrew Writing of the First World War*. She is editor of the *Journal of Modern Jewish Studies*.

Tal Ben Zvi is the Head of the School of Arts at Kibbutzim College of Education, Tel Aviv. Her doctoral thesis investigates representations of the Nakba in the Palestinian art of the 1970s and 1980s, as reflected in the work of artists who belong to the Palestinian minority in Israel. Aside from academic research, Tal Ben Zvi is an independent curator working on Israeli and Palestinian contemporary art. Her published catalogs include: *Abed Abdi, 50 Years of Creativity*, Umm el-Fahem Gallery (2010); *Men in the Sun*, Herzliya Museum of Contemporary Art (2009, with Hanna Farah-Kufer Bir'im); *Hagar—Contemporary Palestinian Art*, Jaffa: Hagar Association,

(2005); *Mother Tongue* (2004), in Yigal Nizri, ed., *Mother Tongue: A Present That Stirs in the Thickets of Its Arab Past,* Tel Aviv: Babel; *Self-Portrait: Palestinian Women's Arts,* Tel Aviv: Andalus (2001 with Yael Lerer); *New Middle East: Eleven Exhibitions, 1998–1999, at Heinrich Böll Foundation,* Tel Aviv, Jaffa: Hagar Association, (2000).

Galeet Dardashti earned her PhD in anthropology in 2009; her dissertation explored issues of cultural politics in the performance of contemporary Mizrahi and Arab music in Israel. Her recent publications include "'Sing Us a *Mawwal*': The Politics of Culture-Brokering Palestinian-Israelis in Israel," which appeared in *Min-Ad: Israel Studies in Musicology,* and "The Buena Vista Baghdad Club: Negotiating Local, National, and Global Representations of Jewish Iraqi Musicians in Israel," published in the book *Jewish Topographies: Visions of Space—Traditions of Place.* She currently teaches at both SUNY Purchase and the City College of New York (CUNY). She is also an active performer of traditional and original Middle Eastern and Arab Jewish music, both as the leader and vocalist for the all-female Mizrahi/Sephardi band, Divahn, and with her new multimedia musical project, *The Naming.*

Michael Feige is a sociologist and anthropologist and senior lecturer at the Ben-Gurion Research Institute, Ben-Gurion University of the Negev in Israel. His fields of interest are collective memory, social movements, the ideological settlers in the West Bank, and the national significance of Israeli archaeology. He is currently the coeditor of the journal *Hagar: Studies in Culture, Polity and Identities.* His 2009 book, *Settling in the Hearts: Jewish Fundamentalism in the Occupied Territories,* received the Shapiro Best Book Award from the Association of Israel Studies.

Esther Fuchs is the author of *Israeli Women's Studies: A Reader* and the forthcoming book *Israeli Feminist Scholarship.* She has published several books as well as numerous essays on gender and Holocaust studies, biblical studies, and Hebrew literature.

Shiri Goren is a Senior Lector in Modern Hebrew at Yale University. She specializes in Hebrew and Israeli literature and culture and Yiddish literature. Her current project, *The Home Front: Literary Engagement with Political Crises in Israel,* explores how terror affects real and imagined spaces in Israel of recent years. Goren is coeditor of the forthcoming volume *Choosing Yiddish: New Frontiers on Language and Culture,* which includes her essay on David Vogel. Her reviews have appeared in the *American Jewish Archives Journal* and *Modern Hebrew Literature,* and her articles have appeared in *AJS Perspectives,* among other venues.

Philip Hollander serves as an Assistant Professor of Israeli literature and culture at the University of Wisconsin–Madison. His current book project, titled "From Schlemiel to Sabra: Transforming Masculinity in Early Twentieth-Century Palestinian Hebrew Culture," explores early twentieth-century literature's role in the struggle to define and inculcate the gender and sexual norms considered best suited for the evolving Palestinian Jewish community's envisioned transformation into an autonomous national community.

Adriana X. Jacobs is currently an ACLS New Faculty Fellow at Yale University in the Department of Comparative Literature and the Program in Judaic Studies. Her areas of specialization include Modern Hebrew and Israeli poetry, translation studies, and comparative poetics. At present she is working on a book manuscript that examines how translation practices and politics have shaped Modern Hebrew and Israeli poetry. Her articles, reviews, and translations have appeared in several academic and literary publications, including *Prooftexts, Metamorphoses,* and *Zeek: A Jewish Journal of Thought and Culture.*

Danny Kaplan specializes in the anthropology of emotions through the prism of friendship and nationalism. He has conducted research on Israeli masculinity, militarism, media, and popular culture. He is the author of *Brothers and Others in Arms: The Making of Love and War in Israeli Combat Units* and *The Men We Loved: Male Friendship and Nationalism in Israeli Culture.* He heads the masculinity track in gender studies and teaches in the Departments of Sociology and Psychology at Bar Ilan University.

Philip Metres is the author of numerous books, including *abu ghraib arias* (poetry, 2011), *To See the Earth* (poetry, 2008), and *Behind the Lines: War Resistance Poetry on the American Homefront since 1941* (criticism, 2007). His work has appeared in *Best American Poetry* and *Inclined to Speak: Contemporary Arab American* Poetry and has garnered an NEA, a Watson Fellowship, two Ohio Arts Council grants, and the Cleveland Arts Prize. He teaches literature and creative writing at John Carroll University in Cleveland, Ohio.

Yael Munk is a senior faculty member in the Department of Literature, Language, and Arts at the Open University of Israel. She has published articles in Hebrew, English, and French on issues in Israeli cinema. Her book, *Exiled in Their Borders: Israeli Cinema between Two Intifadas,* will be published in Israel soon. Her research is concerned with colonialism criticism and postcolonial theory, the emergence of new and hybrid identities after the nation-state, postmodernism, women documentary filmmaking, and gender studies. This research for her essay was supported by the Open University of Israel's Research Fund.

Yaron Peleg is the Kennedy Leigh Lecturer in Modern Hebrew Studies at Cambridge University, where he teaches Hebrew literature and Israeli film and culture. He is the author of *Derech Gever* (Hebrew), *Orientalism and the Hebrew Imagination,* and *Israeli Culture between Two Intifadas: A Brief Romance.* He co-edited *Identities in Motion: An Israeli Cinema Reader.*

Esther Raizen is Associate Professor of Middle Eastern studies and Associate Dean for Research in the College of Liberal Arts at the University of Texas at Austin. She teaches modern and classical Hebrew language and literature and has been actively involved in the introduction of computer-assisted language instruction into the Hebrew language classroom and in the development of open source materials for Hebrew instruction. She is the editor of *No Rattling of Sabers: An Anthology of Israeli War Poetry.*

Noa Roei is a lecturer in literary studies and a research fellow at the Amsterdam School for Cultural Analysis at the University of Amsterdam, the Netherlands. Her research addresses representations of the military subject in contemporary Israeli art. Her published essays include "Framing Art as Action" in *Afterimage* and "A Treatise on Political Vision" in *Image and Narrative.* Aside from academic research, she has organized cultural events including the "Desert Generation in Amsterdam" exhibition and lecture series, and the "Fragments of Life" activist video film festival. Her research interests include critical theory, performance studies, art and activism, and the politics of contemporary Israeli art.

ADAM ROVNER serves as Assistant Professor of English and Jewish literature at the University of Denver. From 2007 through 2010, he was the Hebrew translations editor for *Zeek: A Jewish Journal of Thought and Culture.* His articles, essays, interviews, and translations have appeared in numerous academic and general interest publications. He is currently completing his book manuscript, *Promised Lands: The Untold Story of the Search for a Jewish Home,* an intellectual history of efforts to find territorial solutions to Jewish statelessness.

LIAV SADE-BECK earned her PhD from the Department of Behavioral Sciences at the Ben-Gurion University of the Negev. Her dissertation on Israeli mourning and memorial culture on the Internet was funded with support from the Hubert Burda Center for Innovative Communications and the Bereavement Fund at the Bob Shapell School of Social Work of the University of Tel Aviv, in cooperation with the Israeli Ministry of Defense. Her published essays include "Internet Ethnography—Online and Offline," which appeared in the *International Journal of Qualitative Methods,* and "Mourning and Memorial Culture on the Internet: The Israeli Case," which was published in *American Communication Journal.* She currently works for Tnufa (Hebrew for "momentum"), the Israeli government body responsible for supporting the Gaza Disengagement evacuees.

ILANA SZOBEL holds the Joseph H. and Belle R. Braun Chair as Assistant Professor of Hebrew literature in the Department of Near Eastern and Judaic Studies at Brandeis University. Her dissertation won the 2007 Association for Israel Studies Ben Halpern Award for Best Doctoral Dissertation in Israel Studies. Her scholarly interests include Modern Hebrew literature, Israel studies, feminist theory, psychoanalysis, and trauma studies. She is currently working on her book manuscript titled *Transparent Skin: Poetics of Estrangement, Politics of Trauma—The Work of Dahlia Ravikovitch.*

DAN URIAN is Professor in the Theater Department at Tel Aviv University. His research interests include sociology of the theater, drama in education, Israeli theater, and television drama. His books include *The Arab in Israeli Drama and Theater; The Judaic Nature of Israeli Theater: A Search for Identity; Theater in Society; The Ethnic Problem in the Israeli Theater;* as well as the coedited volume, *The Sociology of Theatre.*

INDEX

www.ingramcontent.com/pod-product-compliance
Lightning Source LLC
LaVergne TN
LVHW082157080826
844660LV00046B/1262

* 9 7 8 0 8 1 4 3 3 8 0 3 2 *